CINEMA SEwen

THE ADULTS ONLY GUIDE TO HISTORY'S SICKEST AND SEXIEST MOVIES!

EDITED BY
ROBIN BOUGIE

VOLUME

A FAB PRESS PUBLICATION

CINEMA SEWER VOL. 2

FIRST EDITION PUBLISHED BY FAB PRESS, MAY 2009

FAB PRESS LTD
2 FARLEIGH
RAMSDEN ROAD
GODALMING
SURREY
GU7 1QE
ENGLAND, UK
WWW.FABPRESS.COM

A CIP CATALOGUE RECORD FOR THIS BOOK IS AVAILABLE FROM THE BRITISH LIBRARY.

ISBN: 9781903254561

COVER ART BY THE ALWAYS AMAZING VINCE RAURUS. VISIT HIM AT:
WWW.VENIVIDIVINCE.COM

OTHER CONTRIBUTORS WITH WEBSITES YOU SHOULD CHECK OUT, YO:

REBECCA DART: R_DART.LIVEJOURNAL.COM
COLIN UPTON: CUPTON.LIVEJOURNAL.COM
HUGO: SERSUGG.LIVEJOURNAL.COM
ED VARULO: WWW.2DROOGIES.COM
JOSH SIMMONS: WWW.JOSHUAHALLSIMMONS.COM
JAN BRUUN: HTTP://HOME.ONLINE.NO/~JANBRUUN/
ED BRISSON: EDBRISSON.COM

EXTRA SPECIAL THANKS TO DAVE BERTRAND AND HARVEY FENTON!

DON'T FORGET TO VISIT:
WWW.CINEMASEWER.COM
AND MY DAILY ART BLOG:
BOUGIEMAN.LIVEJOURNAL.COM

THE BOUG

BEHIND THE SCENES AT:
CINEMA SEWER

BY: ROBIN JOEL BOUGIE 2008

WELCOME TO THE SECOND CINEMA SEWER BOOK! IT'S ABOUT 6PM ON A GRAY OVERCAST DAY HERE IN VANCOUVER. IT'S QUIET, BUT I CAN HEAR FAINT MUSIC IN THE BACKGROUND. MY LOVELY WIFE REBECCA IS IN THE OTHER ROOM, WORKING HAPPILY AND DILIGENTLY ON THE BACKGROUND DESIGNS FOR AN ANIMATED TV SERIES SHE

THE AUTHOR AND HIS KITTY

CREATED. A LOCAL STUDIO HAS JUST GREEN LIT THE SHOW TO GO INTO PREPRODUCTION. MY BELOVED ELDERLY CAT ORSON IS UNCHARACTERISTICALLY SCAMPERING AROUND THE APARTMENT LIKE A KITTEN. I THINK MAYBE REBECCA GAVE HIM SOME CATNIP.

THESE ARE TIMES FOR ME TO REMEMBER. I WRITE THIS INTRO AS A SNAPSHOT OF THIS MOMENT IN MY LIFE. HELL, JUST THE IDEA THAT I'M WRITING AN INTRO TO A BOOK IS FLABBERGASTING ON SOME LEVEL. FUCK, MAN ... I HAVE A BOOK? LIKE, FROM A PUBLISHER?? I'M NOT BRAGGING HERE, I ASSURE YOU -- I'M JUST SO THANKFUL. IT COULD ALL BE TAKEN AWAY IN A FLASH *SNAPS FINGERS* AND THEN I'D BE LEFT WITH NOTHING BUT WHAT YOU'RE READING NOW TO REMIND ME OF WHAT I HAD.

IT WASN'T ALWAYS GOOD. I'VE BEEN THROUGH MY TOUGH TIMES, LIKE SO MANY OF US HAVE. LIFE HAS **SO MUCH** SNOT TO LOB DOWN THE FRONT OF YOUR SHIRT, AND SOMETIMES IT IS GODDAMN FRUSTRATING WONDERING WHEN YOU'LL GET A BREAK FROM THE ASS RAPING. I FEEL LIKE I'VE PAID SOME DUES, BUT THAT THERE WILL BE MORE TO PAY. AND THAT IS OK. I'VE EATEN SHIT. I KNOW HOW TO SWALLOW. YOU CAN ONLY CHOKE SO LONG BEFORE YOU LOSE YOUR GAG REFLEX.

MOVIES PROVIDE A PRETTY GREAT ESCAPE FROM THE SHIT, AND WRITING AND DRAWING ABOUT THEM IS EVEN MORE REWARDING SINCE IT IS TAKING A PASSIVE JOY, AND TRANSFORMING IT INTO A CREATIVE ONE. THE RITUAL AND ACT OF CREATING CINEMA SEWER HAS BEEN FAR MORE REWARDING AND PROVIDED MORE JOLLIES FOR ME THAN IT WILL FOR EVEN ITS BIGGEST FANS. I SELFISHLY CREATED THIS THING PURELY FOR MYSELF -- TO MAKE MYSELF LAUGH, GET BONERS, SHARE MY OBSESSIONS, AND FEEL FULFILLED. IF IT DOES THE SAME FOR YOU, GREAT .... BUT IT'S ONLY GRAVY.

WHOOPS. LOOK AT THE TIME. IT IS TIME TO MAKE DINNER. I'M GONNA GO MAKE SPAGHETTI, AND WE'LL SPEND SOME MORE TIME TOGETHER TONIGHT.

OK, IT'S ABOUT 5AM NOW. I'M OFTEN UP UNTIL 7AM OR SO WORKING ON COMICS, WRITING ARTICLES FOR C.S., AND DOING FREELANCE WORK. THE TIME BETWEEN THEN AND MIDNIGHT IS WHEN I FEEL CALM, UNDISTURBED, AND CREATIVE. THE PHONE ISN'T RINGING, THE CITY IS QUIET, AND THE WIFE AND THE CAT

HUMP
HUMP

I FOUND THIS IN THE FILES. NOT SURE WHAT IT ORIGINALLY WAS DRAWN FOR, BUT IT DID END UP IN C.S. ISSUE #19.

ARE TUCKED INTO THEIR LITTLE BEDS.

I'VE HAD A FEW PEOPLE RECENTLY ASKING ME WHAT TOOLS I USE TO CREATE CINEMA SEWER, SO HERE IS A QUICK RUNDOWN OF MY PROCESS IN FOUR STEPS. MOST OTHER PEOPLE DO ALL THIS USING A DESKTOP PUBLISHING PROGRAM AND PHOTOSHOP, BUT TO GET THE HANDMADE AESTHETIC I WANT, THIS IS WHAT WORKS FOR ME:

1. I WRITE THE ARTICLES ON MY COMPUTER SO I CAN FACT CHECK, SPELL CHECK, AND HAVE A NICE, NEAT TEMPLATE TO WORK FROM. I TEND TO FORMULATE MY THOUGHTS PARAGRAPH BY PARAGRAPH, AND THEN EDIT THEM DOWN AND ARRANGE THEM IN AN ORDER THAT FLOWS AND SOUNDS GOOD WHEN I READ IT OUT LOUD. I PRINT THAT OUT, AND HEAD OVER TO THE ART DESK IN THE BEDROOM OF OUR SMALL CONDO.

2. I CUT A SHEET OF GENERIC PHOTOCOPY PAPER OUT TO THE EXACT DIMENSIONS OF WHAT THE FINISHED PRINTED PAGE WILL BE. I THEN RULE OUT MARGINS A HALF INCH FROM THE EDGE OF ALL 4 SIDES IN PENCIL, AND THEN DECIDE WHAT I'LL BE USING FOR ILLUSTRATIONS, AND IF I'M DRAWING THEM.

3. IF I'M DRAWING, I GET A SEPARATE SHEET OF PAPER, GRAB MY MECHANICAL 0.5 "DR. GRIP" PENCIL TO DRAW IT, AND THEN USE ONE, OR A COMBINATION OF THESE THREE PENS TO INK IT:

THE PENTEL POCKET BRUSH. IT'S REFILLABLE!

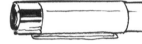

PIGMA MICRON PENS. I USE 01, 03, 05 + 08

STAEDTLER PIGMENT LINER. 0.3 AND 0.5

I USE A WHITEOUT PEN TO ERASE MISTAKES, AND THEN A SHARPIE ULTRA FINE POINT TO FIX THE ERROR, AS THAT IS THE ONLY KIND OF PEN I'VE EVER FOUND THAT WILL STAY FIRMLY PERMANENT ON TOP OF WHITEOUT AND WON'T SMUDGE.

4. I THEN CUT OUT MY ILLUSTRATION, AND GLUE STICK IT TO THE ORIGINAL PAGE WHERE I WANT IT TO GO. THE FLYING ELVES HELP ME DECIDE. I THEN DO MY LETTERING DIRECT-TO-INK (USING THE AFOREMENTIONED PENS) AROUND IT, AND TRY TO ENSURE THAT WHAT I'M WRITING LINES UP NEXT TO THE CORRESPONDING ILLO. I USED TO USE A RULER TO PENCIL OUT HUNDREDS OF GUIDELINES ON THE PAGE, BUT AFTER A FEW THOUSAND PAGES OF THIS SHIT IN THE LAST 11 YEARS, I CAN INK LETTERING FREEHAND NOW WITH ONLY A FEW HORIZONTAL PENCILLED LINES ON THE PAGE TO MAKE SURE THE TEXT ISN'T LOPSIDED.

ANYWAY, ENOUGH OF ALL THIS BORING TECHNICAL STUFF. WHAT YOU'RE ABOUT TO READ IS THE SECOND COLLECTION OF MY MAGAZINE CINEMA SEWER, AND THIS ONE COLLECTS ISSUES #13 THROUGH #16 (ORIGINALLY PUBLISHED 2003 TO 2005) PLUS **MOUNDS** OF BRAND SPANKIN' NEW CONTENT, REVISED N' UPDATED STUFF, AND ARTICLES THAT APPEARED IN NEW YORK'S SCREW MAGAZINE (R.I.P.) AND HOLLAND'S ZONE 5300 MAGAZINE -- WHICH NOT MANY OUTSIDE THAT COUNTRY HAVE SEEN.

IF YOU ENJOY THIS, BE SURE TO PICK UP VOL.1 AND MY ANNUAL 60 PAGE COMIC BOOK ANTHOLOGY SLEAZY SLICE, BUT EVEN IF YOU DON'T -- BE SURE TO LET ME KNOW WHAT YOU THOUGHT IN A CRITICAL AND CONCISE MANNER. FEEDBACK IS MY REAL PAYMENT.

ROBIN BOUGIE
EMAIL: MINDSEYE100@HOTMAIL.COM
WWW.CINEMASEWER.COM

JOIN ME ON THE NEXT PAGE, WON'T YOU? →

I GOT BORED TONIGHT AND DREW SOME CUDDLY LESBIANS WHILE I WAS WATCHING MUSIC VIDEOS AND FUNNY CAT CLIPS ON YE OLDE YOUTUBE. I LOVE THAT ONE WHERE THE HAIRLESS CAT IS TAKING A BATH!! HA HA HA HA!!

I ADMIT IT...
COLLEEN BRENNAN
CHANGED MY LIFE BOUGIE '03

I'M REALLY GLAD I HAPPENED UPON TALIESIN THE BARD. WITH A NAME LIKE THAT, YOU WOULD ASSUME THAT I WAS ABOUT TO BREATHLESSLY INFORM YOU ABOUT SOME ODDBALL DUNGEONS AND DRAGONS DEVOTEE WITH A PENCHANT FOR DRESSING UP IN PUBLIC AS A WIZARD. (PERHAPS I AM! I CAN'T CLAIM TO KNOW WHAT TALIESIN DOES IN HIS SPARE TIME) BUT THE REAL REASON YOU SHOULD STAND UP AND TAKE NOTICE OF ONE OF THE MOST OUTSTANDING GEEKS I'VE HAPPENED ACROSS IN YEARS, IS NOT FOR THE AMOUNT OF HIT POINTS HE CAN TAKE OFF YOUR CLERIC ELF LORD, BUT THE AMOUNT OF COCK HE CAN FUCKING RAM UP YOUR ASS.

THAT'S RIGHT BABY, TALIESIN IS A PORN STAR. WHA?! A COMIC CONVENTION-GOING, DOCTOR WHO-FANBOY WHO DOUBLES AS A COCK-FOR-HIRE?! **RIGHT ON!** THIS GUY GIVES THE REST OF US GEEKS A REASON TO LIVE. THERE IS **HOPE** MY OBSESSIVE AND SOCIALLY RETARDED FRIENDS! AND TALIESIN IS POINTING THE WAY! M'MAN IS A HERO FOR THE LITTLE GUY. WELL, MAYBE NOT. BUT HE SHOULD BE. THAT'S NOT TO SAY THAT HE DOESN'T HAVE LOTSA OTHER INTERESTS AND ACHIEVEMENTS TO SPEAK OF AS WELL. THIS JAUNTY BARD'S BIO FROM HIS OFFICIAL WEBSITE GOES A LITTLE SOMETHING LIKE THIS:

"THE MODERATELY MYTHIC TALIESIN THE BARD IS A POPULAR PART TIME PORN PERFORMER, PAGAN PUNDIT, PRACTICING POLYAMORIST, AND PROMINENT PROSEX PARTISAN, AS WELL AS BEING ADDICTED TO ATROCIOUS ALLITERATION. HE HAS STARRED IN NUMEROUS EROTIC EPICS INCLUDING: HUGE GRANT ON THE SUNSET STRIP, VIVA VANESSA, CANDY STRIPERS 2, LIVE SEX 2, ANAL HIGHWAY, COLOSSAL ORGY, EVERY NERD HAS A FANTASY, BREASTMAN'S KINKY POSITIONS, ORGY CAMERA #1, DIRTY DATING SERVICE #3, AND RETURN TO ALPHA BLUE. HE HAS ALSO WRITTEN AND DIRECTED SUCH FEATURES AS: OUR NAKED EYES, AMATEUR DREAMS: SAN DIEGO SEX FEST, AND THE POSITIVELY PAGAN SERIES. TAL IS A MASTER CLASS STORYTELLER. HIS XXX WEBSITE IS WWW.TALIESINTHEBARD.COM"

COLLEEN IN SCARED STIFF (1984)

I FIRST APPROACHED TAL BECAUSE OF HIS CLOSE PROXIMITY TO COLLEEN BRENNAN AND GEORGE PAYNE (WHAT WITH HIS CO-STARRING WITH THEM IN **CANDY STRIPERS 2** (1985), AND **RETURN TO ALPHA BLUE** (1984). I WAS IN THE MIDDLE OF RESEARCHING WHAT HAD HAPPENED TO COLLEEN AND GEORGE, WHO ARE DEAR TO MY SINFUL HEART NOT ONLY CUZ THEY USED TO RIP THE SHIT UP IN 1980'S ADULT FILMS, BUT BECAUSE THEY WERE ALSO THE STARS OF THE **VERY FIRST** PORN MOVIE I EVER LAID EYES ON: THE **INITIATION OF CYNTHIA** (1985).

I.O.C. IS MORE THAN JUST ANOTHER WANK TAPE TO ME. IT WAS AN AWAKENING. JUST SAYING THE TITLE DRAWS BACK SOME SERIOUS NOSTALGIA. I FIRST SAW THIS SHOT-ON-VIDEO MOVIE WHEN I WAS 15 AND HAD TRAVELED TO VISIT MY BROTHER WHO OWNED A HOUSE IN SASKATOON. HE WAS AT WORK, AND I HAPPENED TO PRESS PLAY ON THE VCR. ALL OF A SUDDEN THERE'S COLLEEN GETTING DOUBLE-STUFFED BY JOHN LESLIE AND JERRY BUTLER. MY MOUTH INSTANTLY WENT BONE-DRY, MY EYES ☆**DOINGED**☆ OPEN, AND MY SKULL CAVED IN -CAUSING MY BRAIN TO LIQUEFY AND BLAST OUT MY NOSE. THIS WAS A 90 MINUTE VIEW INTO AN ENTIRELY NEW WORLD. (GEORGE

TALIESIN THE BARD

PAYNE) HYPNOTIZES THE INNOCENT VANILLA-FLAVORED HOUSEWIFE (COLLEEN BRENNAN) AND COATS HER BOSOM WITH A BLAST FROM HIS HOT GLUE GUN BEFORE WHISKING HER AWAY TO HIS SKANKY DIMLY-LIT, S+M-THEMED SWINGERS CLUB - TO BE SLOWLY INITIATED INTO SWEATY JIZZUM-COATED DEPRAVITY.

LITTLE ROBIN WOULD NEVER BE THE SAME, I ASSURE YOU.

LAST YEAR I FINALLY TRACKED DOWN THE FILM ON VANCOUVER'S GRANVILLE STREET - IN ONE OF THE PORNO SHOPS THAT THE STREET IS KNOWN FOR. I ALMOST DIDN'T EVEN RECOGNIZE THE TAPE, SINCE I HAD NEVER SEEN THE PACKAGING, AND THE VIDEO COVER HAD AMBER LYNN IN A TYPICAL 80'S NEW WAVE HAIRDO AND STANCE (EVEN THOUGH SHE'D ONLY PLAYED IN A SMALL ROLE AS A CALL GIRL). WHEN I GOT THE TAPE HOME AND PLAYED IT, I WAS ASTONISHED THAT DESPITE 15 YEARS HAVING GONE BY, I HAD NEARLY EVERY LINE OF DIALOG AND ACTION COMMITTED TO MEMORY.

FUCK. PORN PRODUCERS SHOULD HAVE THEIR PERFORMERS RECITING GREAT NOVELS AND MATH EQUATIONS. TEENAGE BOYS ACROSS NORTH AMERICA WOULD INSTANTLY START ACING THEIR HOMEWORK!

BLAST MY ASS

"BUT I DON'T KNOW THESE M-MEN..." I SAID IN TIME WITH CYNTHIA. "OH, YOU WILL. YOU WILL " I COUNTERED ALONG WITH STEPHAN. FOR GOOD OR BAD, COLLEEN'S CUM SOAKED BILLY IDOL-ESQUE SNEER IN THE FINAL SCENE WAS FUCKING **BURNED** INTO MY PSYCHE.

AND THEN HERE'S TALIESIN, LIKE THE MODERN-DAY PAGAN SUPERHERO TO ALL THE LITTLE PORN NERDS THAT HE IS - COMING TO MY ONLINE RESCUE WITH AN ON SET BEHIND-THE-SCENES PHOTO OF HIMSELF AND COLLEEN FOUND IN A PILE OF HIS OFFICE CLUTTER, (IT DIDN'T REPRODUCE VERY WELL, SO I DIDN'T PRINT IT HERE) AND THESE WORDS FOR THIS ARTICLE:

"COLLEEN WAS MY FIRST FRIEND IN PORN. I HAD MET OTHERS BEFORE HER, BUT SHE AND I HIT IT OFF RATHER WELL WHEN WE FIRST MET. THAT WAS IN 1984 DURING THE PRODUCTION OF **VIVA VANESSA** (MY FIRST FILM), **VANESSA: MAID IN MANHATTAN**, AND (I THINK) **HOSTAGE GIRLS**, 3 MOVIES THAT WERE SHOT TOGETHER OVER A THREE WEEK PERIOD. SHOOTING TWO OR THREE MOVIES SIMULTANEOUSLY SAVES ON COSTS, AND WAS A COMMON PRACTICE IN PORN AT THE TIME."

INITIATION
of cynthia

18 YRS adults

STARRING **COLLEEN BRENNAN**
JOHN LESLIE   AMBER LYNN
JERRY BUTLER   KATHRYN MOORE
GEORGE PAYNE   SHARON CAIN

"THE FIRST SEX SCENE I EVER WATCHED BEING SHOT FEATURED DANIELLE AND GEORGE PAYNE. HENRI PACHARD WAS THE DIRECTOR. COLLEEN WAS ON THE SET THE SAME DAY. I WAS THERE TO OBSERVE AND WRITE ABOUT MY EXPERIENCE OF MAKING A PORN MOVIE FOR A SWINGERS MAGAZINE. SO, FOR THE FIRST FEW DAYS I PLAYED REPORTER, AND COLLEEN WAS VERY GENEROUS WITH HER TIME AND QUITE FORTHCOMING ABOUT THE BIZ AND HER CAREER. WE GOT TO BE FRIENDS. AFTER THAT I GOT MY FIRST TASTE OF WHAT IT WAS REALLY LIKE TO BE IN PORN IN A SCENE WITH VANESSA DEL RIO AND JERRY BUTLER."

"COL AND I NEVER HAD SEX (I'M SAD TO SAY) BUT WE WERE BOTH IN CANDY STRIPERS 2 IN 1985. THIS WAS AN EXCELLENT MOVIE. THE PLOT INVOLVED AN APHRODISIAC GAS ACCIDENTALLY BEING RELEASED IN A HOSPITAL. IF YOU'VE EVER WONDERED IF THE WOMEN IN PORN ACTUALLY ENJOY THE SEX OR NOT, WATCH COL'S SCENE WITH RON JEREMY. AT ONE POINT RON ATTEMPTS TO MOVE AWAY FROM COL AND INTO ANOTHER POSITION AND SHE CRIES OUT "DON'T STOP NOW!!" THAT LINE WAS NOT IN THE ORIGINAL SCRIPT. SHE REALLY WANTED RON TO KEEP GOING."

"COLLEEN HAD A MAINSTREAM ACTING CAREER AS WELL AS HER PORN WORK. SHE IS A TALENTED ACTRESS, AND APPEARED IN SOME OF THE BEST MOVIES AND BEST SEX SCENES EVER RECORDED. AT SOME POINT SHE AND I LOST TOUCH. I'M GLAD TO SEE SHE'S BEING FONDLY REMEMBERED IN THE PAGES OF THIS MAGAZINE."

SEX WITHOUT SHAME!

FROM RED GARTER (1986)

THE 1980s:
A DECADE OF EXCESS
(ESPECIALLY CAME WHEN IT TO **HAIR**)

FONDLY REMEMBERED INDEED. MATURE DURING HER XXX YEARS, AND (SOME SAY) SOMEWHAT AVERAGE LOOKING, COLLEEN WAS KNOWN FOR HER FIERY LIGHT RED HAIR, FRECKLES, SLIGHTLY PAUNCHY BODY, GENEROUS JUGGS, AND INSATIABLE LUSTY PERFORMANCES WHICH CONSTANTLY UPSTAGED HER USUALLY LESS-PASSIONATE CO-STARS.

COL WAS BETTER KNOWN FOR HER NON TRIPLE X ROLES, WHERE SHE WAS LISTED IN CREDIT ROLLS AS SHARON KELLY. SHE APPEARED IN CLASSIC SEXPLOITATION FILMS SUCH AS **ILSA: SHE WOLF OF THE $$** (1974), **SHAMPOO** (1975), **SUPERVIXENS** (1975), BEFORE TAKING A 7 YEAR BREAK AND RETURNING TO THE SPOTLIGHT AS BONEDOGGIN' COLLEEN BRENNAN IN MUCH LAUDED DICK STIFFENERS SUCH AS **CORRUPT DESIRES** (1983), **TRINITY BROWN** (1984), **TABOO 3** (1984), AND **STAR ANGEL** (1986) AMONG MANY OTHERS.

SHE HAD LITTLE PROBLEM GARNERING KUDOS FROM HER CONTEMPORARIES WITH MULTIPLE AWARDS AND LOTS OF RECOGNITION IN THE FORM OF PRESS AND A

COLLEEN IN: **DOWN AND DIRTY IN BEVERLY HILLS** (1986)

LITTLE KNOWN FACT:
COLLEEN WAS DISCOVERED DANCING AT THE "CLASSIC CAT TOPLESS CLUB" ON THE SUNSET STRIP, AND ASKED IF SHE'D LIKE TO STAR IN 1970'S "THE DIRTY MIND OF YOUNG SALLY". THE REST IS HISTORY!

BEST ACTRESS AWARD FOR **GOOD GIRL, BAD GIRL** (1984) FROM THE CRITICS' ADULT FILM AWARDS. TWO YEARS LATER SHE PICKED UP AN AWARD FOR **GETTING PERSONAL** (1986) AND ANOTHER NOD FOR **STAR ANGEL** (1986) FROM THE X-RATED CRITICS' ORGANIZATION.

WHILE COLLEEN WAS RECOGNISABLE WITHIN THE INDUSTRY AT THE TIME, SHE'S NEVER REALLY BEEN REMEMBERED AS ONE OF THE GREATS OF THE ERA, A DISTINCTION SHE DESERVES (SLAMS FIST ON TABLE). WHILE ALL OF THE OTHER MAJOR CRANK-YANKERS OF THE MID-80s SUCH AS GINGER LYNN, AMBER LYNN, TRACI LORDS, AND CHRISTY CANYON HAVE ALL RETAINED A DEDICATED CULT FOLLOWING AND A VISIBLE ONLINE FAN BASE, THERE SEEMS TO BE NONE FOR MY FAVORITE PASTY-WHITE 1980s REDHEAD.

HOLLYWOOD AND THE PORN INDUSTRY AREN'T SO UNRELATED WHEN IT COMES TO HOW THEY TREAT AGEING ACTRESSES. UNLIKE MEN, THEIR CAREERS BOTH START EARLIER AND END EARLIER, BUT THAT ISN'T TAKING INTO ACCOUNT THE GENRE OF "MILF PORN" OF WHICH COLLEEN IS CONSIDERED TO BE ONE OF THE FOUNDING MOTHERS.

IN CASE YOU'RE TOTALLY OUT OF THE LOOP, MILF MEANS "MOTHER I'D LIKE TO FUCK", AND BRENNAN (ALONG WITH KAY PARKER, ONA ZEE, AND GLORIA LEONARD) SPEARHEADED THE FETISH INTO THE MAINSTREAM BY HAVING A MATURE LOOK AND TAKING ON "MOM" ROLES -- OFTEN IN INCEST-THEMED TITLES. A PART-TIME PROSTITUTE DURING HER PORN YEARS, COLLEEN UNDOUBTEDLY HAD MOM-FETISH CLIENTS WHO WOULD HIRE HER TO TAKE THE ROLE OF THE NURTURING, LOVING, FELLATING MOMMY-FIGURE FOR AN EVENING. TODAY YOU WOULDN'T GET FAR IN PORN BY REFUSING TO DO ANAL OR LESBIAN SCENES, BUT COLLEEN DID JUST THAT IN THE 1980s ON THE STRENGTH OF HER ABILITY TO CONVINCINGLY PORTRAY AN AGEING HOUSEWIFE OR MOTHER CHARACTER.

GAWWD

MILF PORN REPRESENTS THE FASTEST GROWING AREA OF XXX, SAY LEADING DISTRIBUTORS AND RETAILERS, AND WAS EVEN RECENTLY INAUGURATED AS A CATEGORY AT THE AVN AWARDS -- THE OSCARS OF THE SKIN INDUSTRY. THE MASSIVE INTEREST IN FEMALE BODIES THAT ARE STARTING TO SAG AND WRINKLE IN THE WORLD OF EROTICA MAY VERY WELL BE AN EARLY LOOK AT THE NEXT IMPORTANT SHIFT IN WHAT SOCIETY DEEMS TO BE THE STANDARD OF BEAUTY. WHEN I SPOKE TO ONE OF THE STAFF MEMBERS OF ASKJOLENE.COM (ONE OF THE WEB'S MOST POPULAR PORN SEARCH ENGINES) HE TOLD ME HE WAS UTTERLY SHOCKED TO SEE THAT IN THE LAST 2 YEARS "MILF", "MOM" AND "MATURE", WERE **VERY** CLOSE TO OVERTAKING THE VARIOUS "TEEN" SEARCHES THAT HAVE LONG BEEN THE MOST POPULAR FETISH AMONGST ONLINE MASTURBATORS.

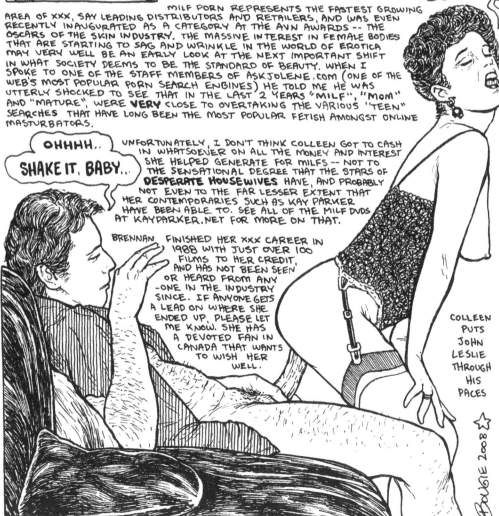

OHHHH..
SHAKE IT, BABY...

UNFORTUNATELY, I DON'T THINK COLLEEN GOT TO CASH IN WHATSOEVER ON ALL THE MONEY AND INTEREST SHE HELPED GENERATE FOR MILFS -- NOT TO THE SENSATIONAL DEGREE THAT THE STARS OF **DESPERATE HOUSEWIVES** HAVE, AND PROBABLY NOT EVEN TO THE FAR LESSER EXTENT THAT HER CONTEMPORARIES SUCH AS KAY PARKER HAVE BEEN ABLE TO. SEE ALL OF THE MILF DVDS AT KAYPARKER.NET FOR MORE ON THAT.

BRENNAN FINISHED HER XXX CAREER IN 1988 WITH JUST OVER 100 FILMS TO HER CREDIT, AND HAS NOT BEEN SEEN OR HEARD FROM ANY -ONE IN THE INDUSTRY SINCE. IF ANYONE GETS A LEAD ON WHERE SHE ENDED UP, PLEASE LET ME KNOW. SHE HAS A DEVOTED FAN IN CANADA THAT WANTS TO WISH HER WELL.

COLLEEN PUTS JOHN LESLIE THROUGH HIS PACES

BOUGIE 2008

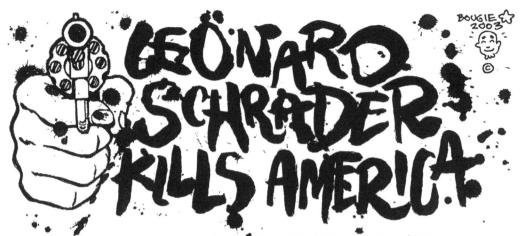

LEONARD SCHRADER KILLS AMERICA.

FIREARMS ARE ROOTED IN GLOOMY CHILDHOOD MEMORIES FOR LEONARD SCHRADER.

HIS FATHER'S BROTHER COMMITTED SUICIDE WHEN LEN WAS 8 YEARS OLD. FIVE YEARS LATER, THE SAME UNCLE'S ELDEST SON KILLED HIMSELF ON THE ANNIVERSARY OF HIS FATHER'S DEATH. FIVE MORE YEARS AFTER THAT, HIS SECOND SON COMMITTED SUICIDE ON THE SAME DAY. THE REMAINING SON WAS SAID TO HAVE LIVED IN CONSTANT FEAR OF TAKING HIS OWN LIFE AS WELL. LEONARD'S BRANCH OF THE FAMILY TREE WAS SOAKED IN BLOOD.

"THIS WAS WHAT WE GREW UP WITH," LEONARD TOLD AN INTERVIEWER IN 1994, "WE HAD TO KEEP THIS SECRET FROM EVERYBODY, THAT DAD'S ONLY RELATIVES WERE BLOWING THEIR BRAINS OUT."

LEONARD AND HIS LITTLE BROTHER PAUL LIVED IN REPRESSED, GOD-FEARING, MENTAL AND PHYSICAL AGONY THROUGHOUT THEIR YOUNG LIVES. THEIR PARENTS WERE STRICT DUTCH CALVINISTS AND WERE (FOR LACK OF A BETTER TERM) FUCKING BONKERS, HAPPILY BRINGING UP BABY ON A STEADY DIET OF GUILT AND FEAR.

"I GOT WHIPPED SIX, SEVEN DAYS A WEEK. JUST TO BE A NORMAL HUMAN BEING FOR 24 HOURS, BREATHING, EATING, GOING TO THE REST ROOM, HAVING A NORMAL LIFE, MEANT I WAS GOING TO BREAK 20 RULES A DAY. AND AT LEAST 3 OF THEM WERE WORTH A BEATING. I TOOK OFF MY SHIRT, MY FATHER LEANED ME OVER THE KITCHEN TABLE, TOOK THE EXTENSION CORD FROM HIS ELECTRIC SHAVER, AND WHIPPED MY BACK WITH THE PLUG SO I'D GET LITTLE PINPRICKS OF BLOOD, A NICE PATTERN OF DOTS UP AND DOWN MY BACK."

NOW THAT ISN'T TO SAY THERE WEREN'T GIDDY FUN-FILLED TIMES WHEN A GOOD OL' BELLY LAUGH COULD BE SHARED IN THE SCHRADER HOUSEHOLD - AS LEONARD REVEALED TO PETER BISKIND IN 1994: "WHAT SAVED ME WAS THAT MY MOTHER WAS HUMAN. MY FATHER WAS LIKE A MACHINE. MY MOTHER WHIPPED ME WITH A BROOM HANDLE IN THE KITCHEN. SOMETIMES SHE'D BREAK IT RIGHT OVER MY BACK. BUT IF YOU MADE MY MOTHER LAUGH, SHE COULDN'T GO ON. I WOULD SAVE JOKES JUST FOR THIS OCCASION." REAL SHITS N' GIGGLES.

THE TWO BOYS WERE FORBIDDEN TO WATCH MOVIES, TV, OR LISTEN TO POPULAR MUSIC. BUT... WELL, BOYS WILL BE BOYS, AND RULES ARE MADE TO BE BROKEN. "I WANTED TO SEE ONE MOVIE IN MY LIFE, AS AN ACT OF SIN," RECALLED LEONARD. "I WAS STANDING ON THE SIDEWALK, TRYING TO BOLSTER MY COURAGE. THEN FINALLY I BOUGHT THE TICKET, AND WENT IN. I'D BEEN TAUGHT THAT MOVIE THEATERS, THE BUILDINGS THEMSELVES, WERE DENS OF INIQUITY. I MADE A MINIMUM COMMITMENT, SAT DOWN IN THE LAST SEAT, END OF THE ROW, WHITE KNUCKLES. TERRIFIED. **TERRIFIED!**"

IT WAS 1959. LEN HAD WALKED INTO A THEATER THAT WAS SHOWING OTTO PREMINGER'S **ANATOMY OF A MURDER**, A CLASSIC COURTROOM DRAMA DEALING WITH THE MINUTIAE OF A MURDER/RAPE TRIAL.

"THE SCREEN PEELED BACK, AND IT WAS THE LAST JUDGE -MENT DAY. I SAW THE LORD GOD JEHOVAH, AND HOSTS OF ANGELS COMING DOWN, AND I WAS GONNA BURN IN HELL FOREVER - BECAUSE I WENT TO THE FUCKIN' MOVIES. I RAN OUTTA THE THEATER, 2 BLOCKS, 5 BLOCKS, UNTIL I CALMED DOWN, FURIOUS AT MYSELF."

CUT TO: 21 YEARS LATER.
LEONARD COMPILES, EDITS, AND WRITES NARRATION FOR THE FINEST MONDO-STYLE DOCUMENTARY EVER MADE ABOUT VIOLENT DEATH IN THE USA. THAT FILM WAS **THE KILLING OF AMERICA**, AND IT WAS MADE WITH MONEY RAISED IN JAPAN. HE SCOURED SEVERAL COUNTRIES, BUYING FOOTAGE FROM TV STATIONS AND "SECRET, HERMIT-LIKE COLLECTORS".

THE MATERIAL HE HAD SCRAPED FROM THE UNDERSIDE OF

L. SCHRADER - CIRCA 1980

WHATEVER BLOOD-ENCRUSTED TURD HE HAD
TURNED OVER WAS EXCLUSIVE AND TRULY
UNFORGETTABLE. FROM RACE RIOTS, TO
POLICE SHOOTINGS, TO INTERVIEWS WITH
NOTORIOUS SERIAL KILLERS, TO INSANE
RANDOM ACTS OF VIOLENCE ACCIDENTALLY
CAPTURED ON FILM, **THE KILLING OF
AMERICA** DELIVERED THE DISTURBING GOODS
WRAPPED IN A POWERFUL ANTI-GUN MESSAGE
WHICH WAS UNMATCHED IN THE YEARS PRIOR TO
2002'S **BOWLING FOR COLUMBINE**.

IN 1980 WHEN THE FILM WAS MADE, THERE
WAS AN ATTEMPTED MURDER IN THE U.S. EVERY
3 MINUTES, AND A MURDER VICTIM EVERY 20
MINUTES. "IN THE 80 YEARS OF THIS CENTURY,"
THE NARRATOR GRAVELY INTONES, "AMERICA
HAD MORE THAN A MILLION MURDERS, MORE
THAN ALL HER FATALITIES IN ALL HER WARS."
TO UNDERSCORE THE POINT, SLO-MO FOOTAGE
OF THE KENNEDY ASSASSINATION FILM BRINGS
THE STATISTICS A DEEP, HAUNTING RELEVANCY.
"BETWEEN 1900 AND 1963," LEONARD TOLD
THE UK'S FRIDAY REVIEW, "THE MURDER
RATE HAD HARDLY CHANGED AT ALL. BUT THE
RATE JUST SKYROCKETS AFTER THE
ASSASSINATION OF PRESIDENT KENNEDY!"

AS POWERFUL AS IT WAS, SCHRADER'S FILM
WASN'T GIVEN ANYTHING EVEN APPROACHING
A PROPER RELEASE. IN FACT, HIS KEEN AND
STUNNING MEDITATION ON AMERICAN VIOLENCE
IS VIRTUALLY UNKNOWN ON THIS CONTINENT,
EVEN AMONGST 'HARD CORE' GORE-JUNKIE
FILM GEEKS WHO SLAVISHLY RAVE AND DROOL
OVER THE FAR INFERIOR **FACES OF DEATH**.

THIS IS THE FILM ABOUT AMERICA THAT
AMERICANS WERE NEVER ALLOWED TO SEE.
IN FACT, IT WASN'T UNTIL 2001 - WHEN A
DVD VERSION WAS RELEASED - THAT AN UNCUT
VERSION WAS MADE AVAILABLE. THE CATCH?
IT'S A HARD-TO-FIND U.K. REGION 2 DISC, AND

THE OUT-OF-PRINT DUTCH VHS...

...AND THE U.K. REGION 2 DVD.

UNPLAYABLE ON MOST AMERICANS' DVD
PLAYERS. IN MANY WAYS, SCHRADER IS STILL
WAITING TO INTRODUCE AMERICA TO ITSELF.

IRONICALLY, THE U.K. WAS WHERE A YOUNG
MAN NAMED CHRIS BERTHOUD WAS ARRESTED
IN 1992 FOR ACCEPTING COPIES OF **THE KILLING
OF AMERICA** AND **GUINEA PIG: FLOWERS OF
FLESH AND BLOOD** FROM HIS MAILMAN. IN AN
INSANE MISCARRIAGE OF JUSTICE, HE WAS
ARRESTED, PROSECUTED, FINED $1200.00 US
AND WARNED BY A JUDGE THAT HE WAS LUCKY
TO HAVE AVOIDED JAIL TIME FOR HIS CRIME.
THE NEXT MORNING ONE NEWSPAPER
HEADLINE READ "DEATH CRAZE MAN'S SNUFF
MOVIE SHAME."

JUMP BACK TO 1974, WHEN LEONARD'S YOUNGER
SIBLING PAUL HAD ALREADY GONE ONTO FAME AS
THE SCREENWRITER OF MARTIN SCORSESE'S **TAXI
DRIVER**, AN UNMISTAKABLE LANDMARK EVENT IN
VIOLENT AMERICAN CINEMA. PAUL HAD WRITTEN
THE SCRIPT IN 10 DEPRESSION-FILLED DAYS WHILE
SPENDING HIS NIGHTS DRINKING SCOTCH WHILE
DRIVING AROUND IN AN OLD CHEVY NOVA AND
FEEDING QUARTERS INTO 8MM TRIPLE-X PEEP
SHOW BOOTHS. MOM AND DAD DISOWNED THE
BOYS. "FATHER AND I WILL MISS YOU IN
HEAVEN" READ A LETTER FROM HIS MOTHER,
WHICH CAME STUFFED WITH MULTIPLE CHURCH
SERMONS. LEONARD BOUGHT HIMSELF A BRASS
CROWN OF THORNS WHICH ACTUALLY DREW
BLOOD WHEN HE PUT IT ON HIS HEAD. HE KEPT
IT OUT IN THE OPEN - ON A TABLE NEXT TO
A .38 PISTOL.

THE TWO BROTHERS WERE DOING THEIR BEST TO
EXORCISE CHILDHOOD DEMONS ONTO AN

UNSUSPECTING PUBLIC, AND PAUL'S SCRIPT WOULD FULFILL THAT MANDATE IN SPADES AS **TAXI DRIVER** WOULD GO ON TO INSPIRE JOHN HINCKLEY TO TRY TO PUT A BULLET BETWEEN RONALD REAGAN'S EYES. OF COURSE, HE WOULD ONLY SUCCEED IN PARALYZING JAMES BRADY - WHO WOULD IN TURN WITH HIS WIFE PUT THE "BRADY BILL" (ONE OF THE MOST POWERFUL ANTI-GUN LAWS THE USA HAS EVER KNOWN) INTO EFFECT. ALL THIS FOR THE LOVE OF YOUNG JODIE FOSTER, WHOSE CHARACTER PAUL FLESHED OUT AFTER FINDING HIMSELF WITH AN UNDERAGE PROSTITUTE IN A HOTEL ROOM ON THE EVE OF GETTING THE **TAXI DRIVER** SCRIPT SOLD.

THE KILLING OF AMERICA WENT A LONG WAY TOWARDS SUMMING UP THIS STRANGE SENSE OF AMERICAN BIZARRO-TRAGEDY IN ITS JAW-DROPPING 90 MINUTES OF ARCHIVAL FOOTAGE. TED BUNDY, ED KEMPER, JACK RUBY, SIRHAN SIRHAN, AND LAWRENCE BITTAKER: THIS IS A NIGHTMARISH WORLD WHERE A DISGRUNTLED CUSTOMER TIES A SHOTGUN AROUND A TELLERS NECK WITH A COATHANGER, AND PARADES HIM DOWN POPULATED CITY STREETS WITH HIS FINGER ON THE TRIGGER FOR 3 FULL DAYS - TAUNTING THE HELPLESS POLICE AND REPORTERS. IT'S A DARK VIEWPOINT ON THE COUNTRY, AND IT'S NOT DONE SIMPLY FOR SHOCK VALUE AS WITH SO MANY OTHERS OF IT'S KIND. SCHRADER HAS SOME VERY PERSONAL TIES TO THE DUNG CLUSTER THIS FILM SCRAPES UP AND HURLS AT UNSUSPECTING VIEWERS:

"I WOULD BE SITTING ALONE IN SOME ROOM AT 3 O'CLOCK IN THE MORNING WITH A LOADED GUN, THINKING ABOUT BLOWING MY BRAINS OUT. IT WAS NOT 'I'M HAVING A BAD DAY, I WANT TO KILL MYSELF'; NO, THE DESIRE, THE NEED, FELT AS REAL AS A FUCKING TABLE. I WANT TO DO THIS, AND I NEVER WANT TO DO THIS. I'M THREE SECONDS AWAY FROM IT, AND I'M THREE MILLION YEARS AWAY FROM IT. I FELT THE FEVER OF THE TWO THINGS INSIDE ME FIGHTING. I WAS BREAKING OUT IN A SWEAT, MY TEMPERATURE WAS GOING UP FROM THE INTENSITY OF IT. SOMETIMES I WOULD JUST STARE AT THE WALL, TRYING TO QUIET THE HEAT DOWN, BUT SOMETIMES THE HEAT KEPT BUILDING, AND THAT'S WHEN I WAS LOOKING FOR THE GUN. TRIGGERED BY SOMETHING PHYSICAL, LIKE I COULDN'T SLEEP. I FOUND OUT THAT IF I STUCK THE BARREL IN MY MOUTH, LIKE SOME INFANT'S PACIFIER, I COULD FALL ASLEEP. IT WORKED FOR 2 OR 3 WEEKS, AND ALL OF A SUDDEN, IT DIDN'T WORK. I'D BEEN SUCKING ON AN EMPTY GUN. I KNEW IF I LOADED THE SONOFABITCH, I WAS GONNA SLEEP TONIGHT."

AS OF THIS WRITING, NEITHER LEONARD OR PAUL HAVE TAKEN THAT GIANT STEP TOWARDS THE BIG SLEEP, AND ARE STILL LIVING AND BREATHING QUITE SUCCESSFULLY, ALBEIT WITHOUT EACH OTHER'S COMPANY. (18 YEARS AGO IN 1985, THE TWO HAD A SERIOUS FALLING OUT WHILE WRITING AND DIRECTING THE FILM **MISHIMA**.) IN THE YEARS SINCE THEY'VE SEPARATED, PAUL HAS HAD A HAND IN WRITING **THE LAST TEMPTATION OF CHRIST** (1988), AND RECENTLY DIRECTED **AUTOFOCUS** (2002).

LEONARD WENT ON TO BE NOMINATED FOR AN ACADEMY AWARD FOR THE SCREENPLAY OF **THE KISS OF THE SPIDER WOMAN** (1985), AND NOW TEACHES SCREENWRITING AT CHAPMAN UNIVERSITY. NO WORD IF HE DOES IT WHILE WEARING HIS CROWN OF THORNS AND WAVING HIS .38 AT TARDY STUDENTS OR NOT.

I'LL KEEP YOU POSTED.   ☆ Robin Bougie 2003

☆ U P D A T E ☆

3 YEARS AFTER ISSUE 13 CAME OUT (IN WHICH THIS ARTICLE ABOUT LEONARD WAS PUBLISHED) I GOT AN EMAIL FROM HIM. HE'D BEEN SEARCHING FOR HIS NAME ON EBAY SO HE COULD BID ON FILM PRINTS, POSTERS, AND OTHER COLLECTIBLES FROM HIS OWN MOVIES, AND HE'D FOUND A DETAILED DESCRIPTION OF C.S #13 MENTIONING HIM BY NAME. I WAS THRILLED TO HEAR FROM HIM, AND OFFERED TO MAIL HIM THE MAGAZINE -- AN OFFER HE ENTHUSIASTICALLY TOOK ME UP ON. I WAITED FOR HIS RESPONSE TO READING IT, BUT ONE NEVER CAME. A MONTH LATER, I FOUND OUT WHY. LEONARD HAD PASSED AWAY ON NOVEMBER 2ND 2006 IN LOS ANGELES DUE TO HEART FAILURE. R.I.P. MR SCHRADER. I'M SORRY WE DIDN'T GET TO TALK MORE.
          ☆ R. BOUGIE 2008

THERE IS A PREVIOUSLY NAUGHTY NOTION THAT HAS BEEN COMING UP MORE AND MORE IN MOM N' POP MEDIA IN THE LAST FEW YEARS. I CALL IT: PUSSY VALUE. THE PUSSY AND ITS PERCEIVED VALUE TO ITS OWNER, AND THE PEOPLE WHO INTERACT WITH IT. THE MUCH-LAUDED TRAVELING ROAD SHOW "THE VAGINA MONOLOGUES" (A STAND-UP COMEDY, SPOKEN WORD INTERACTIVE EMPOWERMENT AND CELEBRATION PLAY FOR CUNT OWNERS) HAS PROBABLY GARNERED THE MOST PRESS, BUT DESPITE REPORTS TO THE CONTRARY, THIS VAGINAL-FLAVORED CAUSE CELEBRE IS A DEFINITE REACTION TO HEIGHTENED SOCIAL PUSSY VALUE, NOT AN INSTIGATOR OF IT.

LADIES AND GENTLEMEN, ARE YOU READY TO COME ALONG FOR THE RIDE? I SAY: "PORN IS TO BLAME!!!" AND I SAY IT WITH THE GUSTO OF A MAN WHO SHOULD KNOW. NOW JUST THINK ABOUT IT: WHAT HAS HAD THE LARGEST EFFECT ON THE PERCEPTION OF THE VAGINA IN NORTH AMERICA, IF NOT THE WORLD?

IT'S A STAGGERING THOUGHT ISN'T IT? THE CURRENT TOTAL OMNIPRESENCE OF SMUT IN OUR CULTURE HAS— AS A RESULT OF IT'S VERY EXISTENCE— MADE WOMEN'S SEXUALITY APPEAR MUCH MORE VALUABLE TO THEM THAN IT WOULD IN AN OTHERWISE LESS SEX-ORIENTED OR PORNOGRAPHY-FREE ENVIRONMENT. I MEAN, TRULY, YOU DON'T EVEN HAVE TO HAVE SEEN PORN FIRST HAND TO BE AWARE OF THE EFFECT IT HAS ON SOCIETY. I'M ALSO THINKING THIS HAS CAUSED AN ODD RELATIONSHIP BETWEEN FANTASY AND REALITY-BASED FEMALE SEXUAL RESPONSE. I'M NOT SAYING GIRLS NEVER KNEW THEY HAD "THE GOOD STUFF" BEFORE. I'M JUST POINTIN' OUT THAT THEY NEVER KNEW THEY COULD **FUCKING RULE** TIME AND SPACE WITH IT. IT'S A NEW SOCIETAL STATE OF MIND CULTIVATED AND BROUGHT ON BY OBSESSION.

ROBINS SOAP BOX

I DON'T THINK IT'S A COINCIDENCE THAT HARD-CORE PORN FILMS (WITH THE MONSTROUS EMERGENCE OF **DEEP THROAT** AS A CULTURAL PHENOMENON) AND FEMINISM CAME TO THE FOREFRONT OF AMERICAN CONSCIOUSNESS AT NEARLY THE SAME MOMENT IN HISTORY. I ALSO THINK IT'S AN OUTDATED GERIATRIC REACTION TO ASSUME THAT THE TWO ARE SOMEHOW INHERENTLY OPPOSED TO EACH OTHER.

I MEAN, WHO DOESN'T LOVE THE FACT THAT WE CAN LOOK BACK AT WHAT HAS TRANSPIRED IN THE WOMEN'S MOVEMENT AND REVEL IN THE IRONIC NOTION THAT IN THE LONG RUN, THE SINFUL XXX SLEAZE THAT STAUNCH RIGHT WING FEMI-NAZIS LIKE CATHARINE MACKINNON AND ANDREA DWORKIN FOUGHT AGAINST 20 YEARS AGO, SEEMS TO HAVE HAD A MUCH MORE POSITIVE EFFECT ON FEMALE SEXUAL PERCEPTION THAN THEY **EVER** DID?! THAT SHIT IS FUNNY, ESPECIALLY WHEN YOU TAKE INTO ACCOUNT THAT THESE DOUBLE-PLUS-UNGOOD ORWELLIAN THOUGHT-POLICE CONSIDERED THEMSELVES BENEVOLENT CRUSADERS FOR THE RIGHTS OF ALL WOMANKIND.

THE MAINSTREAMING OF PORN AND THE SEXUALIZING OF POP CULTURE HAS MADE FOR HUGE ADVANCEMENTS IN THE CONCEPT OF PUSSY VALUE, AND I ASSURE YOU, IT'S A THEORY DIRECTLY TIED TO THE BELIEF THAT KNOWLEDGE IS POWER. WOMEN ARE LEARNING. SISTAHS ARE SAVVY ABOUT WHAT KIND OF POWER THE FEMININE MYSTIQUE HOLDS OVER EVERY FACTION OF SOCIETY. YOU'D HAVE TO BE A RETARD NOT TO CLUE IN. AND YOU DON'T HAVE TO BE A SEX-POT OR A HOTTIE! GET RID OF YOUR SAD, OLD, ANTIQUATED HONEY-HOLE STEREOTYPES! THIS ISN'T ABOUT WOMEN BEING WEAK AND STUPID AND ONLY BEING ABLE TO ACHIEVE POWER THROUGH SEX. THIS ISN'T ABOUT BEING A "WHORE". THIS ISN'T ABOUT BEING A "VIRGIN". THIS IS A WHOLE NEW WORLD. DON'T YOU **DARE** CLOSE YOUR EYES.

EVEN IF ONE IS WILLING TO FORGET THE PORN INDUSTRY FOR A SECOND, (WHICH IS HARD, BECAUSE BY SOME ESTIMATIONS IT'S A BIGGER

PROFIT EARNER THAN HOLLYWOOD) IT'S STILL JUST THE TIP OF THE ICEBERG. OUTSIDE OF THAT IS THE FACT THAT FEMALE SEXUALITY IS USED - ALMOST EXCLUSIVELY - TO SELL MOUNDS OF CRAP TO US EVERY DAY, EVEN TO FEMALE CONSUMERS, OLD PEOPLE, AND CHILDREN. WE ALL HAVE URGES IN OUR AREAS. THOSE URGES ARE SIGNIFICANT TO THE ULTIMATE WARRIOR-STYLE BODYSLAM AND STRONGHOLD OF THE PUSSY DUE TO THE SOCIAL ACCEPTANCE OF SEXUAL IMAGERY, BUT THEY'RE ALSO RELATIVE TO A NUMBER OF OTHER CULTURAL FACTORS.

DIG IF YOU WILL - A PICTURE OF COUNTRIES WHERE PORN AND SEXUALITY IN FORMS OF POPULAR MEDIA IS STRICTLY VERBOTEN. THE THRESHOLD FOR WHAT IS DEEMED OBSCENE HEIGHTENS SIGNIFICANTLY. IN IRAN, WHERE WOMEN ARE FORCED TO WEAR THE FULL BODY CHADOR OUTSIDE OF THEIR HOMES, A PEEK AT A YOUNG LADY'S ANKLE PROVIDES BONERS RESERVED FOR A GIRL DOUBLE-FUCKED BY TWO BLACK STUDS IN NORTH AMERICA. UNDOUBTEDLY, ANTI-PORN ADVOCATES SEE THIS SCENARIO AS A POSITIVE, AND WOULD LIKELY TOSS IT BACK IN MY FACE AS PROOF THAT PORN CHEAPENS SEXUALITY BY DESENSITIZING ITS VIEWERS TO WHAT **SHOULD** AROUSE THEM IN THEIR DAY TO DAY LIVES. (WHATEVER THE HELL THAT IS.) IT'S LIKE MY BROTHER TOLD ME ONCE: "IF WOMEN WANT TO GO TOPLESS IN PUBLIC, THEN THEY SHOULD BE HELD TO TASK FOR ALL THE DRIVERS THEY KILL WHO SHOULD HAVE BEEN WATCHING THE ROAD INSTEAD."

IT'S ALL PART OF THE PERVERSE FANTASY THAT LESS FREEDOM MAKES PEOPLE BENEVOLENT AND DOCILE, AND THAT MORE FREEDOM MAKES THEM MISERABLE AND JADED. THIS INTOLERANT UTOPIAN SUBURBIA IS SAFE HAVEN FOR IGNORANT DUNG-GOBBLERS WHO SOMEHOW (EVEN WHEN PREVENTED BY LAW FROM CRIMINALIZING SEXUAL ACTIVITIES AND SEX ENTERTAINMENT WHICH ARE INTRINSICALLY HUMAN, CONSENSUAL, AND ABOVE ALL-PERSONAL) INFUSE A GENERAL CONTEMPT WITHIN SOCIETY AT LARGE FOR WHATEVER THEY HAVE CHOSEN TO CONDEMN. WELL, PITY THEM. THEIR DAY IS **OVER**. THEY DON'T WIELD THE POWER OF THE VAGINA. THEY'VE NEVER KNOWN HOW TO HARNESS ITS MYSTERIOUS ENERGY. IT'S NOTHING BUT A MUSHY, DILATED, BABY-CHUTE TO THEM. AND THEY ARE SCARED OF PUSSY, MY FRIENDS. THEY FEAR WHAT THEY DON'T UNDERSTAND. THAT'S NO WAY TO LIVE. **THAT'S NO WAY TO THINK.**

NOW, BEFORE YOU CONCERN YOURSELF WITH THE NOTION THAT I MAY BE GETTING OFF TOPIC, LET ME TIE THIS TOGETHER AND DROP THE OTHER SHOE. IT'S A SHORT RIDE AFTER ALL.

LET'S HAVE A MENTAL PARADE TO CELEBRATE THE FACT THAT THE AFOREMENTIONED INSULAR AND CONSERVATIVE MASSES HAVE LOST THEIR STRANGLEHOLD ON FEMALE SEXUALITY BEING PERCEIVED BY THE PEOPLE AS ONLY A METHOD OF ACHIEVING MOTHERHOOD. LET'S TAKE PART IN A MENTAL GANG RAPE AND ASS-FUCK THAT SICKENING NOTION BEFORE MASHING IT INTO OBLIVION. A WOMAN'S SEXUALITY IS INCREASINGLY MORE VALUABLE NOT ONLY TO SOCIETY, BUT TO WOMEN THEMSELVES. POWER TO THE PUSSY, LADIES. STEP RIGHT UP HERE TO THE EDGE AND ENJOY WHAT IT FEELS LIKE TO STUFF A BRICK UP REALITY'S ASS.

BUT WITH GREAT PUSSY COMES GREAT RESPONSIBILITY. YOU'RE JUST FOOLING YOURSELF IF YOU THINK THE GASTANK WAS FILLED UP BY THE VAGINA MONOLOGUES INSTEAD OF DEEP THROAT. THANK THE LEGACY OF THE MITCHELL BROTHERS, NOT JESSE HELMS. THINK OF LARRY FLYNT, NOT DOCTOR LAURA. HARDCORE, FUCK-ME-SUCK-ME, ASS-GRINDING ACTION HAS CULTIVATED THE NEW EDEN. LET IT GUIDE YOU THROUGH WHATEVER DARKNESS LAYS AHEAD UNDER THE DUBYA REGIME. LET IT LEAD YOU TO THE LIGHT. IT'S GOTTEN US THIS FAR; TRUST THE LUST.

IT'S A NEW CONSCIOUSNESS, AND PERHAPS IT'S TIME TO SEEK OUR LUBRICATED DESTINY. THE VAGINA IS A GAPING MAW, READY TO ENVELOPE EVERYTHING INTO THE SOFT FOLDS OF ITS DAMP, EARTHY SHELTER. IT'S THE ONLY CHOICE. THERE IS NO ESCAPE, NOR WOULD YOU EVEN KNOW HOW TO, SHOULD SUCH A THOUGHT EVEN DARE TO SNEAK PAST THE GUARDS - WHO WOULD SHOOT IT DOWN LIKE A DOG IF THEY EVER CAUGHT IT. DIRTY, DIRTY, DIRTY OUTSIDE PORNOGRAPHIC INFLUENCES HAVE SUPPLIED US WITH ALL WE'LL EVER NEED. THE SIN OF THE FLESH IS ALL THAT REMAINS. TAKE WHAT YOU WANT, GIRLS. OUR GUNS AREN'T LOADED. IT'S ALL YOURS, ALL OF IT. ENJOY, MY SISTERS. PORN IS THE DOOR. PORN IS THE LADDER. PORN IS YOUR SAVIOR.

-BOUGIE '03

ANYTHING GOES IN THE WORLD OF EXOTIC MODELS AND HOT-HANDED MEN!

CHECK IT OUT GIRLS! IT'S THE INFLATED SENSE OF PUSSY VALUE CHECKLIST!

☐ A GUY FRIEND TELLS YOU HE LOST HIS DICK IN A TRAGIC ACCIDENT, AND YOU INSTANTLY FEEL MORE COMFORTABLE AROUND HIM.

☐ YOU VIEW THE ACT OF SEX AS A "GIFT" THAT YOU BESTOW RESERVEDLY UPON CHOSEN PARTNERS.

☐ YOU THINK YOU ARE FOLLOWED BY RANDOM MALE STRANGERS ON THE STREET, BUT YOU AREN'T SURE.

BEWARE, THE BOUGIEMAN

HELLO, MY NAME IS COLIN UPTON AND TWO YEARS AGO I MOVED INTO THE SAME BUILDING AS CINEMA SEWER PUBLISHER, ROBIN BOUGIE. NOW, SOME OF YOU READERS MIGHT THINK THAT'S PRETTY COOL BUT BELIEVE ME IT'S BEEN A NIGHTMARE!

STRANGE THINGS HAPPEN HERE, UNEXPLAINED NOISES, SHRIEKS AND EVIL LAUGHTER ECHOES DOWN THE CONDO CORRIDORS AT NIGHT! TERRIFYING RENOVATIONS! OMINOUS THUDS, THE RATTLE OF CHAINS AND THE MEWING OF CATS THAT SOUND STRANGELY HUMAN. HORRIBLE STENCHES, LAUNDRY ROOM WALLS DRIPPING WITH A STICKY WHITE GOO OF UNIDENTIFIABLE ORIGIN... SPARE BODY PARTS IN THE DUMPSTER. ROBIN'S WIFE REBECCA IS ONLY HEARD, NEVER SEEN AND LEGEND HAS IT THAT A SILENT OGRE NAMED GIGANTOR LIVES IN THEIR BROOM CLOSET, READY TO CONSUME THE UNWARY... THERE'S A CONSTANT TRAFFIC OF ASPIRING PORN STARS, GEEK GOREHOUNDS, DEFROCKED NUNS, FAILED SERIAL KILLERS AND THE OTHERWISE MENTALLY DERANGED COME AND GO AT ALL HOURS OF THE DAY AND NIGHT...

THE NEIGHBOURS KNOW WHAT WILL HAPPEN TO THEM IF THEY COMPLAIN!

...AND YOU NEVER KNOW WHEN ROBIN WILL BE OUT THERE, WANDERING THE CORRIDORS WITH HIS TINTIN LOVE DOLL AND HIS HELLO KITTY RENDERING AXE, LOOKING FOR FUN.

COME PLAY WITH ME!

IF I'M LUCKY I CAN MAKE IT TO THE LAUNDRY ROOM UNMOLESTED.

I'M NOT.

HELLO COLIN.

!?!

REBECCA'S WORKING, WANNA WATCH A MOVIE WITH ME!

OH, NO THANK YOU REALLY, I GOTTA DO MY LAUNDRY...

AWW, C'MON! IT'S "SCHOOLGIRL VIRGIN MASSACRE" FROM JAPAN! IT'S GONNA BE AWESOME!

NO, PLEASE! I'M BEGGING YOU! I CAN'T WATCH ANYMORE FILTH!

YOU SILLY, IT'LL BE FUN!

NO!

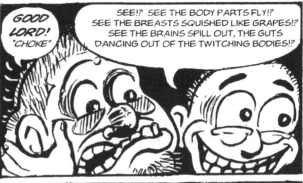

I AM A SOUL IN TORMENT, AWAITING IN DREAD FOR THE "NEXT TIME" THAT MY HUMANITY WILL BE PULVERIZED AND I AM REDUCED TO A QUIVERING MASS....

GROAN...

COLIN UPTON 04

ONE SENTENCE BOOK REVIEWS!

CINEMA SEWER? WHY ARE YOU SELLING THIS?

ATTACK OF THE B-MOVIE POSTERS ****
By Bruce Hershenson. 2000. $20.00 US
BRUCE - WHO HAS THE BIGGEST COLLECTION OF MOVIE POSTERS IN THE WORLD - PUTS OUT A COUPLE OF THESE SWEEEET FULL-COLOR SOFTCOVER COLLECTIONS EVERY YEAR, AND IN DOING SO, SHARES WITH THE REST OF US SOME OF THE MOST AMAZING POSTER ART EVER CREATED AT ONLY PENNIES ON THE DOLLAR OF WHAT IT WOULD HAVE COST US TO BUY THEM OURSELVES.

THE DEAD WALK **
By Andy Black. 2000. Noir publishing. $19.95 US
NOT A TERRIBLE EFFORT, BUT AT THE END OF THE DAY IT'S JUST AN AVERAGE ASSEMBLAGE ON ZOMBIE CINEMA THAT IS NOT EVEN CLOSE TO AS MUCH FUN TO READ AS THE MOVIES ARE TO WATCH.

THIS REMINDS ME A LOT OF THE FURRY FREAK BROTHERS.

INCREDIBLY STRANGE FILMS *** 1/2
Various Authors. 1986. RE-Search Publications. $19.95 US
THIS WELL LAID OUT COLLECTION OF ESSAYS AND INTERVIEWS WITH DUDES LIKE RUSS MEYER AND LARRY COHEN IS ONE OF THE BETTER KNOWN MODERN INDIE BOOKS ON CULT FILMS, AND IS DESERVING OF ITS STATUS.

JAPANESE MOVIE POSTERS *****
By Chuck Stephens. 2002. DH Publishing $19.95 US
THIS ASTONISHING FULL-COLOR COLLECTION OF CLASSIC JAPANESE YAKUZA, MONSTER, PORN, AND HORROR POSTERS IS A MOVIE NERD'S WET DREAM - AND ACTUALLY ALSO DOUBLES AS A CATALOG WHEN YOU REALIZE EVERY POSTER IN IT IS FOR SALE OVER AT WWW.DHP-ONLINE.COM

LAIN: AN OMNIPRESENCE IN THE WIRED *****
By Yoshitoshi Abe. 1998. AX Aeon. $93.95 US
HOLY FUCK... THIS OUTSTANDING JAPANESE IMPORT ART BOOK CELEBRATING THE ART AND DESIGN OF YOSHITOSHI ABE'S ANIMATED T.V. SERIES LAIN, IS THANKFULLY AS MIND-BLOWINGLY RICH AS ITS HEFTY PRICE TAG.

IS THIS FREE?
SORRY... NO
NEVERMIND THEN.

MENTAL HYGIENE: CLASSROOM FILMS 1945 TO 1970 ****1/2
By Ken Smith. 1999. Blast Books $24.95 US
FINALLY, A BOOK (AND A FABULOUS ONE AT THAT) OUTLINING THE AMAZING STORIES TO BE TOLD ABOUT CLASSROOM SCARE FILMS CONCERNING SEX, DRUGS, DATING, AND TRAFFIC SAFETY.

SEE NO EVIL: BANNED FILMS AND VIDEO CONTROVERSY *****
By David Kerekes and David Slater. 2000. Headpress. $25.95 US
THIS COMPREHENSIVE PAGE-TURNIN' HISTORY OF BANNED MOVIES IN THE U.K PUT TOGETHER BY THOSE BAD BOYS OVER AT HEADPRESS IS PROBABLY THE MOST ENTERTAINING BOOK CONCERNING CENSORSHIP OF FILMS EVER PENNED.

YOU'RE ROBIN BOUGIE?

CONTINUED ON NEXT PAGE

SHIT... I WISH I COULD DRAW LIKE DREW FRIEDMAN...

FROM: "TALES OF TIMES SQUARE"

THIS IS OK, BUT I KNEW THIS GUY IN HIGH SCHOOL WHO COULD DRAW WAY BETTER!
GREAT.

SLEAZOID EXPRESS *****
By Bill Landis and Michelle Clifford. 2002. Simon and Schuster.

WOW...THIS AMAZING AND HIGHLY RECOMMENDED WALK DOWN MEMORY LANE (CIRCA NEW YORK'S LATE 70s ERA TIMES SQUARE) IS DIVIDED INTO CHAPTERS SHOWING EACH INFAMOUS GRINDHOUSE THEATER OF 42ND ST - AND THE MOVIES THEY DISPLAYED. THE ONE FAULT? SOME OF THE FACTUAL INFO AINT SO FACTUAL.

SLIMETIME: A GUIDE TO SLEAZY MINDLESS MOVIES ****
By Steve Puchalski. 2002. Headpress. $24.95 US

STEVE, THE GUY BEHIND SHOCK CINEMA ZINE COLLECTS YEARS OF HIS SHARP (IF OCCASIONALLY PREDICTABLE) COMMENTS ON ALL THE WEIRD SHIT WORTH WRITING ABOUT FROM THE LAST 4 DECADES OF FILM, AND DOES IT WITH STYLE AND GRACE IN THIS HUGE 378 PAGE TOME. PRETTY MUCH A "MUST HAVE".

TALES OF TIME SQUARE *****
By Josh Allen Friedman (Brother of Drew) 1993. Feral House. $12.95

POSSIBLY THE BEST $12.95 U.S. I DRAINED THIS YEAR WAS ON THIS AMAZING, ZESTY, NOSE-TO-THE-PAVEMENT COLLECTION OF ESSAYS ABOUT THE CHARACTERS IN THE SLEAZIER CORNERS OF NEW YORK'S EARLY 80s/LATE 70s SEX INDUSTRY.

THAT'S BLAXPLOITATION *1/2
By Darius James. 1995. St. Martin's Griffin Publications. $14.95

THIS SHALLOW AND UNPROFESSIONAL COLLECTION OF 70s BLACK CINEMA REVIEWS IS HEAVY ON FUNKY SASS AND LIGHT ON CONTENT AND INSIGHT.

DROOL

VISA

HA HA HA
LOOK WHO FINALLY GOT HIZZELF A CREDIT CARD!
-MR. BOUGIEMAN!

BONGWATER BUTT BABES

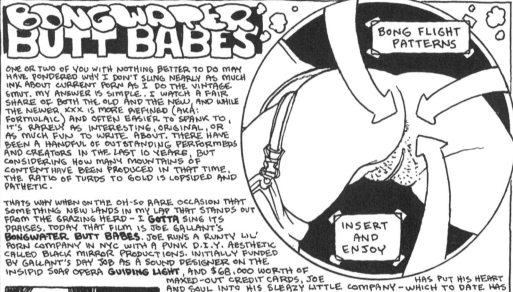

BONG FLIGHT PATTERNS

INSERT AND ENJOY

ONE OR TWO OF YOU WITH NOTHING BETTER TO DO MAY HAVE PONDERED WHY I DON'T SLING NEARLY AS MUCH INK ABOUT CURRENT PORN AS I DO THE VINTAGE SMUT. MY ANSWER IS SIMPLE. I WATCH A FAIR SHARE OF BOTH THE OLD AND THE NEW, AND WHILE THE NEWER XXX IS MORE REFINED (AKA: FORMULAIC) AND OFTEN EASIER TO SPANK TO, IT'S RARELY AS INTERESTING, ORIGINAL, OR AS MUCH FUN TO WRITE ABOUT. THERE HAVE BEEN A HANDFUL OF OUTSTANDING PERFORMERS AND CREATORS IN THE LAST 10 YEARS, BUT CONSIDERING HOW MANY MOUNTAINS OF CONTENT HAVE BEEN PRODUCED IN THAT TIME, THE RATIO OF TURDS TO GOLD IS LOPSIDED AND PATHETIC.

THATS WHY WHEN ON THE OH-SO RARE OCCASION THAT SOMETHING NEW LANDS IN MY LAP THAT STANDS OUT FROM THE GRAZING HERD - I **GOTTA** SING ITS PRAISES. TODAY THAT FILM IS JOE GALLANT'S **BONGWATER BUTT BABES**. JOE RUNS A RUNTY LIL' PORN COMPANY IN NYC WITH A PUNK D.I.Y. AESTHETIC CALLED BLACK MIRROR PRODUCTIONS. INITIALLY FUNDED BY GALLANT'S DAY JOB AS A SOUND DESIGNER ON THE INSIPID SOAP OPERA **GUIDING LIGHT**, AND $68,000 WORTH OF MAXED-OUT CREDIT CARDS, JOE AND SOUL INTO HIS SLEAZY LITTLE COMPANY - WHICH TO DATE HAS HAS PUT HIS HEART RELEASED A MERE 16 TITLES.

..DUUUDE...

PUFF PUFF PUFF

UNG

BUT PEEPS - TRUST ME. IT'S QUALITY, NOT QUANTITY. BLACK MIRROR REPRESENTS THE NEW GENERATION OF DEGENERATE NEW YORK SMUT-PEDDLERS, AND IF YOU'VE BEEN READING THIS MAGAZINE (OR OTHERS LIKE SLEAZOID EXPRESS AND SCOTT STINE'S FILTHY HABITS) FAITHFULLY, YOU KNOW HE HAS A GRAND LINEAGE OF SKANKY, SICK, LOW BUDGET NYC PORN TO LIVE UP TO. WITH BONGWATER BUTT BABES WHICH WAS FILMED IN A MERE 2 WEEKS, HE DOES JUST THAT.

FIRST OFF - AND PERHAPS MOST IMPORTANTLY - JOE HAS INVENTED A DILDO/BONG DESIGNED TO BE TUCKED INTO ANY GIVEN FEMALE PERFORMER'S WATER-PACKED POOPER, ON WHICH EVERYONE INVOLVED TAKES BIG TOKES OFF OF.

HOW FUCKING COOL IS **THAT**?! I COULD WATCH THAT ALL DAY - AND I'M NOT EVEN PARTICULARLY INTO DRUG CULTURE OR STONER VALUES.

"THE IDEA FOR 'BONGWATER' CAME TO ME IN A FLASH WHILE TALKING TO A FREAKY PORN FRIEND OF MINE ABOUT HIS TRYING TO EXPAND HIS BONG EXPERIMENTS," JOE ADMITTED TO ME VIA EMAIL, "IT'S PROBABLY BEEN MY MOST POPULAR TITLE SO FAR."

LUCY LUCY (STAR OF BLACK MIRROR'S **LUCY LUCY: SLUT GODDESS** AND HER GAL-PAL ERIKA COLE (PERHAPS BETTER KNOWN FOR HER COCK-SWALLOWING DEEPTHROATING DISPLAY IN 2001'S **GAGFACTOR 9**) HAVE A TOTAL STANDOUT SCENE, SEXILY DOMINATING, BUTT-BONGING, AND BLASTING SHITTY ENEMAS AT EACH OTHER - AND THE WALL OF THE OL' CRUSTY, COCKROACH-INFESTED CRACK MOTEL

THEY FILMED IN. WATCHING THESE TWO PSYCHO GIRLS FACES TOGETHER WHILE SIMULTANEOUSLY DEEP-SHORT OF MAGICAL, AND PROMPTED APPLAUSE FROM

THE GIRLS INVOLVED IN BLACK MIRROR TAPES ARE BUT THEN SHORT-HAIRED REDHEAD ALISHA ANGEL 2003'S **TEENS GONE BAD 2**) SHOWS UP IN THE BACK SCRUMPTIOUS IN HER "BAD KITTY" T-SHIRT, AND TO BREATHE. THAT CHANGES INTO CONFUSED HAVE TO SHIT", AND IS GOADED INTO GRUNTING I'M NOT INTO SCAT — BUT I LOVE BEING THROWN

"IT'S LIKE COOKIE DOUGH!" JOE GIGGLES, BEFORE THE STEAMING LOAF. A FEW SECONDS LATER, JOE HAPPILY COCK-REAMING HER FACE, PUSSY, AND IS ADORNED WITH FLIPPERS AND SNORKELING HER OWN BUM-DOOBAGE. THE SCENE ENDS AS BONGARRHEA ACROSS THE ROOM AND WALKS IN SOUNDS LIKE IT'S LOADED WITH PEOPLE TAKING IN A ROCK SHOW. YES - IT'S ALL HELLA NASTY, BUT THAT'S THE POINT!

"THIS IS A FEEL-GOOD FLICK SHOT ALL OVER MANHATTAN," CONFESSED JOE, "AN ODE TO SPRING, IN THE SPIRIT OF GODARD." WHEN I ASKED HIM IF THE ADDITION OF TURDS TO AN XXX VIDEO SEEMED TO HELP SALES, HE TOLD ME, "DOO-DOO JUST DON'T SEEM TO APPEAL TO EVERYONE, AND I'M NOT SURE WHY. A LOT OF MAINSTREAM VIEWERS TEND TO BE REFLEXIVELY DISMISSIVE OF IT... THOSE VIEWERS MAY ALSO HAVE ABSOLUTELY NO FAMILIARITY WITH SHIT AND PISS IN AN EROTIC SETTING, AND THAT'S A SHAME CUZ THERE'S NOTHING LIKE YOUR GIRLFRIEND SQUATTING OVER YOU WITH A FRESH MOUNTAIN STREAM FIRST THING IN THE MORNING."

ENTHUSIATICALLY AND VIOLENTLY SLAMMING THEIR THROATING A DOUBLE-ENDED DILDO IS NOTHIN' MY IMPROMPTU VIEWING PARTY.

REFRESHINGLY REAL AND AVERAGE LOOKING, (LAST SEEN GETTING A MESSY CREAMPIE IN ROOM OF SOME SCUMMY CLUB LOOKIN' ALL THE BOUGIEMAN MOMENTARILY FORGETS HOW REPULSION AS ALISHA SHEEPISHLY SAYS "I OUT A SEMI-SOLID LOG ONTO A PLATE FOR JOE. OFF GUARD, AND THIS DOES THE TRICK.

LIGHTING SOME INCENSE AND POKING IT INTO IS CLOTHES-PINNING HER NIPPLES BEFORE ASS. EVENTUALLY THE GOOD-NATURED ANGEL GOGGLES, (??) AND READY TO TOKE OFFA ALISHA BLASTS A VILE LOAD OF TO THE NEXT ROOM WHICH

ARE YOU JUST BLOWING SMOKE UP MY ASS?

"I'M TRYING TO GENERATE AWARENESS OF THE COMPANY AS CONTINUING IN THE BELOVED VEIN OF NYC'S GOLDEN AGE 70S SMUT, AND DOING IT IN A STRANGELY REPRESSED AND CONSERVATIVE MANHATTAN MINDSET, WHICH WAS DEEPLY IN PLACE LONG BEFORE 9/11!" JOE SAID, "NEW YORK WILL THROW OFF THE MCDISNEY/STARBUCKS MENTALITY AND GET BACK TO WHAT IT'S ALWAYS DONE BEST - LIVING !!"

GALLANT TELLS ME THERE IS A SEQUEL IN PRODUCTION, AS ARE A DVD RELEASE (WITH AUDIO COMMENTARY) AND GRAND PLANS TO MASS-MARKET THE BUTTBONG, "IT'S THE IDEAL COUPLE'S TOY FOR THOSE SEEKING FAR-OUT AND TRANSCENDENT MOMENTS." HE'S ALSO THREATENED TO COME AND VISIT US HERE IN VANCOUVER. "YOU HAVE THE BEST LOOKING HOOKERS IN THE WORLD THERE!"

BUTTBONG!

IT'S BOUGIE APPROVED !!!!

JOE ALSO GAVE ME SOME EXCLUSIVE BEHIND-THE-SCENES HIGHLIGHTS TO PASS ON TO CINEMA SEWER READERS:

"1) WE LIKED HOW IT LOOKED SO MUCH, THAT WE ENDED UP LEAVING LUCY LUCY'S RUNNY CASCADE OF SHITTY ENEMA WATER ON THE WALL IN THE CRACK HOTEL. LIKE A CAT MARKING HER TERRITORY.
2) ERIKA COLE ANNOUNCED THAT SHE SECRETLY LIKES TO STICK HER FINGER PERIODICALLY UP HER ASS AND SMELL IT THROUGHOUT THE DAY.
3) ALISHA ANGEL GOT PREGNANT SHORTLY AFTER I DID THAT SCENE WITH HER, AND MARRIED THE GUY. SHE'S EXPECTING ANY DAY NOW.
4) WE LEFT THE PLATE OF ALISHA'S SHIT AND INCENSE STICKS IN THE THEATER BY MISTAKE, AND I HAD TO GO BACK AND TAKE CARE OF IT THE NEXT DAY, LIKE CLEANING THE LITTER BOX.
5) THERE WAS A LOT MORE HEAVY BONDAGE/PISS/FUCKING BETWEEN LUCY AND ERIKA, BUT I HAD TO CUT IT FOR LEGALITY PURPOSES."

SNAP!

HA HA!

MAY I ALSO MENTION BEFORE WE MOVE ON THAT WHILE JOE HAD A COUPLE OF FINGERS UP ONE OF HIS COSTARS' RECTUMS, I NOTICED THAT WE BOTH HAVE THE SAME WRIST WATCH. IT'S THE LITTLE THINGS IN LIFE, ISN'T IT? HEH.. ANYWAY, YEAH... BONGWATER BUTT BABES, FUCKING **AMAZING**.

— BOUGIE 2003

TO MY GENERATION, THIS 1971 MOVIE WILL ALWAYS BE CONNECTED TO THE METALLICA "ONE" MUSIC VIDEO. TO THE EARLIER GENERATION, IT WAS AFFILIATED WITH THE DALTON TRUMBO BOOK. I HOPE THIS GENERATION DOESN'T FIND IT SYNONYMOUS WITH "THAT SHORT, CRAMPED, SHITTY REVIEW IN CINEMA SEWER."

Lee Caroll

The Cinema Sewer Interview

AFTER A CAREER THAT SPANNED 2 DECADES AND OVER 100 MOVIES, CLASSIC 80S PORN STAR LEE CAROLL (BIRTH NAME: LESLIE BARRISS) HUNG UP HER XXX SPURS IN 1995. WELL, MAYBE I SHOULDN'T REALLY CALL HER A PORN "STAR". LEE NEVER ACTUALLY HEADLINED OR STARRED IN ANYTHING, NOR DID THERE EXIST A LARGE FAN BASE FOR HER LIKE HER CO-STARS HAD. LEE WAS ALWAYS RELEGATED TO MINOR ROLES AND CAMEOS SINCE SHE WASN'T MUCH OF AN ACTRESS - NOR WAS SHE AS BEAUTIFUL
AS MANY OF HER FEMALE PEERS. IN FACT, LEE MAY HAVE BEEN ONE OF THE LEAST RESPECTED AND MOST DISSED WOMEN OF 80S SMUT - AT LEAST WHEN IT CAME TO PEOPLE WRITING ABOUT THE INDUSTRY. PORN REVIEWER DIVILLE ONCE WROTE "LEE CAROLL, I BELIEVE, IS INSANE. EACH TIME I SEE HER PERFORM" SHE STRIKES ME AS SOMEONE WHO FUCKS AS IF SHE'S BEEN INSTRUCTED BY HER NEIGHBORS DOG", AND PORN COLUMNIST D.B. GALE ONCE CALLED HER, "A SERIOUSLY UNATTRACTIVE WHORE".

RESPECT IS VERY HARD TO COME BY WHEN YOU'VE DARED TO AGE IN THE ADULT INDUSTRY - ESPECIALLY IF YOU'RE A WOMAN. ONE IMBECILE ON SOME INTERNET DISCUSSION GROUP EVEN SAID THAT, "LEE NOW LOOKS LIKE AN 80 YEAR OLD DRAG QUEEN. I WOULDN'T PAY TO STICK MY COCK IN HER." TRASH TALK LIKE THAT ABOUT PORN ACTRESSES JUST GETS ME DOWN SOMETIMES. THESE WOMEN ARE SOLELY JUDGED AND EVALUATED UPON THEIR APPEARANCE IN THE NUDE, AND I CAN UNDERSTAND THAT ON SOME LEVEL. BUT THE ENTERTAINMENT INDUSTRY (BOTH X-RATED AND OTHERWISE) JUST GOBBLES UP AND SPITS OUT SO MANY WOMEN LIKE LEE CAROLL. SHE BARES HERSELF TO US FOR DECADES FOR A MEAGER SUM, AND BY THE END OF HER RUN, ALL SHE GETS FOR HER TROUBLE IS A BUNCH OF NO-CLASS DIPSHITS SLAGGING HER BECAUSE HER TITS ARE DROOPY. GUESS WHAT MORONS? THAT'S WHAT HAPPENS WHEN BREASTS GET TO BE 40 OR 50+ YEARS OLD - **SO FUCK OFF** IF REALITY IS REALLY SO DISGUSTING TO YOU. YEAH, IT'S EASY TO FEEL SUPERIOR TO A NORMAL, AVERAGE LOOKING MIDDLE-AGED WOMAN WHEN YOU'RE SITTING THERE JERKING OFF TO CYBER PORN IN YOUR STINKY BVDS - YOU PIMPLY FACED PATHETIC LOSERS. GRRRR....

IN THE LAST FEW YEARS SHE WAS DOING VIDEOS, LEE WAS CONSTANTLY PUSHED INTO NON-SEX ROLES, A SURE SIGN OF A CUM-QUEEN'S CAREER BEING IN THE TOILET. DESPITE THIS, LEE IS FONDLY REMEMBERED BY MYSELF AND A FEW OTHERS AS A TOUGH SKINNED, FOUL MOUTHED, TAKE-NO-CRAP WOMAN WHO SLOGGED HER WAY THROUGH MOUNDS OF FUCK FILMS AND LIVED TO TELL THE TALE. AND THAT MY FRIENDS, REGARDLESS IF MISS CAROLL EVER APPEALED TO YOU OR NOT - DESERVES MAJOR PROPS. THE UNLOVED NEED A LITTLE LOVE TOO, SOMETIMES.

LEE WAS FINALLY HONORED IN 2003 AT THE AVN EXPO AWARDS SHOW WHEN SHE WAS ENTERED INTO THE PORN HALL OF FAME, AND WAS ALLOWED TO DIP HER "TWO GROTESQUELY MISSHAPEN TITS" (ACCORDING TO STEVE NELSON, AVN COLUMNIST) INTO WET CEMENT. LEE NOW MAKES HER LIVING AS AN ESCORT (AKA: HOOKER) AND ADVERTISES HER SEXUAL SERVICES ON THE NET. I WAS REALLY PLEASED TO GET THE CHANCE TO INTERVIEW THIS LITTLE KNOWN LEGEND VIA EMAIL:

HI LEE. THANKS FOR DOING THIS. HOW ARE THINGS?

They could always be better.

TRUE THAT. YOU STARTED IN PORN BACK IN 1980, IS THAT CORRECT? WHAT WAS IT LIKE IN THE ADULT INDUSTRY BACK THEN?

The same bullshit. But we made REAL movies that people really liked better. I think that's why so many people still remember myself and all the other legends. It was different then. Movies were made, not videos. People knew you and remembered your scenes. These days it's like the old loops.

LEE CAROLL - CIRCA 1983

I'M A HUGE FAN OF THE FILM **AMANDA BY NIGHT** FROM 1981, IN WHICH YOU WERE RAPED AT GUN POINT BY RON JEREMY. HAVE YOU SEEN THE FILM IN RECENT YEARS? IT'S A PRETTY FUCKING AMAZING BIT OF CLASSIC SMUT - AND IT STILL HOLDS UP TO THIS DAY.

I thought it was a super movie. I played a sweet massage girl. I sometimes wish I was really like that. A lot of fans remember that movie, especially my scene with Ron.

R. BOLLA WAS AMAZING IN THAT ONE AS WELL. AND VERONICA HART? WAGH..! DON'T GET ME

GOING. YOU ALSO GOT BUSY WITH THE LITTLE MAN... LOUIE "SHORT STUD" DEJESUS (WHO WAS OFTEN MISTAKEN FOR TATTOO FROM **FANTASY ISLAND**) IN A FREAKY LITTLE FILM CALLED **PERVERSIONS** FROM 1984. THAT GUY WAS AMAZING AS RALPHUS IN **BLOODSUCKING FREAKS**, AND I'VE HEARD HIM DESCRIBED AS "RON JEREMY AS A MIDGET WITH A BASKETBALL STOMACH". WHAT WAS HE LIKE TO WORK WITH? IS FUCKING A MIDGET AN ODD EXPERIENCE?

To be honest? Not really. A cock is a cock. Some are big, some are small, some thin, some fat. They all do the same thing: Fuck you.

I JUST THOUGHT IT MIGHT BE STRANGE. I READ THAT IN ONE OLD 8MM LOOP, DEJESUS HAD TO STAND ON A TABLE TO PORK SOME GIRL IN THE ASS, AND THEN ACCIDENTALLY FELL OFF. I DON'T KNOW IF THATS FUNNY - OR JUST SAD.

I didn't think it was strange. In those days I'd fuck anything.

DIRECTOR BILL MARGOLD ONCE CALLED YOU "THE MAE WEST OF X", AND "ONE OF THE MOST ECCENTRIC ADULT FILM SUPERSTARS OF ALL TIME". WHAT HAVE YOU DONE THAT WOULD MAKE PEOPLE CALL YOU "ECCENTRIC"?

I think it's because I am the way I am. A real person who tells it like it is.

TELLING IT LIKE IT IS, IS IN HIGH DEMAND. OR IF IT ISN'T - THEN IT **SHOULD** BE. ANYWAY, I SAW YOUR ESCORT SERVICE WEBSITE, AND IT LOOKS GREAT.

Thanks for the compliment.

YEAH, BUT THATS PRETTY AMAZING, GIVING YOUR FANS A CHANCE TO HUMP A LIVING LEGEND. DO YOU GET TO TRAVEL A LOT AS PART OF THAT? OR IS IT MOSTLY IN-HOUSE STUFF? DO DUDES HAVE INSANE REQUESTS, OR IS IT PRETTY MUNDANE FUCKY-SUCKY STUFF?

I travel a lot to all kinds of cities and I try to keep busy. And yes, there are many clients and people that will email me with off-the-wall stuff. I'll do it as long as it doesn't go against the grain.

WHAT'S YOUR DEFINITION OF "THE GRAIN"? EXCUSE MY NOSINESS, BUT WOULD YOU - FOR INSTANCE - PEE IN YOUR OWN MOUTH? OR UM... WHAT IF SOMEONE WANTED TO POUR VOMIT IN YOUR ASS AND HAVE YOU FART IT BACK IN THEIR FACE?

I'm not a taker; in that I'd only give, and not receive those lovely things you asked about to a sub.

LEE CAROLL - CIRCA 2003

"I AM THE WAY I AM."

I BEEN SEEIN' LEE FER TWO YEARS NOW! SHE'S TH' **DIRTIEST** WHORE I EVER BIN TOO!

PORN ACTRESS ANITA CANNIBAL ONCE SAID, "LEE CAROLL IS ONE OF THE ONLY WOMEN THAT COULD SAY 'LET ME SUCK YOUR DICK' AND MEN WOULD LIKE, RUN. THEY'RE ALL LIKE "HELL NO GIRL!" WHAT IS THAT ALL ABOUT? DID YOU DO SOMETHING TO PISS ANITA OFF? OR IS THAT SOME KIND OF WEIRD TERM OF ENDEARMENT THATS GONE OVER MY HEAD SINCE I'M NOT AN INDUSTRY GIRL?

I'm one VERY dirty talker, and the way I say things seem to scare people off. I'm very blunt and bold, and I don't care what I say or how I say it.

NOT TO BELABOR ANY SORT OF BAD OR ECCENTRIC REP YOU HAVE, BUT I TALKED TO A FELLAH ON AN ONLINE MESSAGE BOARD WHO SAW YOU STRIP AT A CLUB A FEW YEARS BACK, AND SAID THAT YOU LOOKED LIKE YOU 'COULD SLIT MY THROAT AND STEAL MY WALLET WITH ONE SWOOP'. I'VE NEVER SEEN YOUR LIVE SHOW, YOU MUST BE PRETTY DAMN AGGRESSIVE, LEE!

I am. Very. As far as real violence goes, I'm not into that. I can be really sweet when I want something. Besides, that guy must have been a fuckin' cheap wimp.

☆ **UPDATE:** NOT TOO LONG AFTER THIS INTERVIEW SAW PRINT, LEE SHUT DOWN HER ☆
☆ ESCORT SITE, AND MOVED TO VIRGINIA HOPING TO ESCAPE CREDITORS AFTER ☆
☆ RUNNING UP A $50,000 CREDIT CARD DEBT. SHE HAS NOT BEEN HEARD FROM SINCE. ☆

LEE CAROLL HIGHLIGHTS: PLAYING A NURSE IN A SEX THERAPY CLINIC IN **SKIN TIGHT** (1981). GETTING RAPED BY A COP PLAYED BY RON JEREMY IN **AMANDA BY NIGHT** (1981). TALKING SUPER NASTY (SHUT UP, CUNT FACE!) IN **KINKY COUPLES** (1990). BANGIN' LITTLE LOUIE DEJESUS IN **PERVERSIONS** (1984). PASSION PLAYING WITH ERIC EDWARDS IN **CHARLI** (1981). DOMINATING AND HUMILIATING HERSCHEL SAVAGE IN **8 TO 4** (1981).

"LEE CAROLL WAS HORRIBLE. SHE WAS OLD, SHE WAS DRUNK, AND SHE FUCKED LIKE A BOARD."
                                                    -TOM BYRON, PORN ACTOR AND DIRECTOR

"LEE CAROLL IS A NASTY, SKANKY-LOOKING PORN STARLET WHO MIGHT HAVE LOOKED LIKE TRAILER-PARK TRASH, BUT STILL GAVE ME HARD ONS DESPITE HER OVERALL APPEARANCE. SADLY THOUGH, HER IMPLANTS ON TOP OF HER ALREADY IMPRESSIVE NATURAL BREASTS MADE HER LOOK WORSE."
—UNCLE STEVIE (PORN CRITIC)

"I'VE ALWAYS WONDERED WHAT IT WOULD BE LIKE TO FUCK EITHER A WASHING MACHINE OR AN OCTOPUS AND I THINK I FOUND BOTH ANSWERS IN LEE CAROLL. I WORKED WITH HER IN SEXCALIBUR AND THE WOMAN DID NOT LET GO. IT'S LIKE TAKING ALL OF ARNOLD SCHWARZENEGGER AND SHOVING IT IN A PUSSY."
—BILL MARGOLD (WHO 'DISCOVERED' LEE IN 1980)

"I USED TO LET GUYS LICK MY CUNT WHEN I WAS ON STAGE. THAT TURNED ME ON SO FUCKING MUCH."
—LEE CAROLL, WHO HIT THE STRIPPER CIRCUIT IN '84

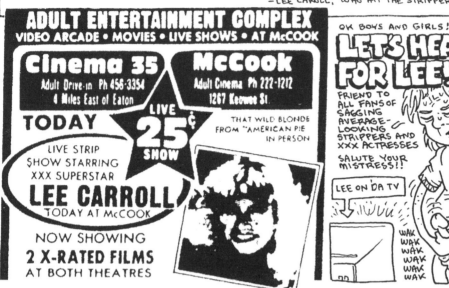

OK BOYS AND GIRLS!
LET'S HEAR IT FOR LEE!!
FRIEND TO ALL FANS OF SAGGING AVERAGE-LOOKING STRIPPERS AND XXX ACTRESSES
SALUTE YOUR MISTRESS!!
LEE ON DA TV
ACDC
WAK WAK WAK WAK WAK WAK
HONK
UNG

EXTRA BONUS!

HERE IS AN INTERVIEW THAT LEE DID WITH ADAM FILM WORLD MAGAZINE IN JUNE OF 1983.

ADAM: You have a New York City accent. Are you from there?

CAROLL: Yeah . . . I'm from the streets of New York. The big city.

ADAM: Is that why you're hip enough to fuck for money in porn films?

CAROLL: Of course *(laughs)*.

ADAM: Do you resent the sleazy public image that porn has?

CAROLL: No. I like sleaze. And what some people call sleaze is beginning to come into millions of American homes because of porn being on cable television. I know people are watching it. Porn is being watched. So our image is starting not to be sleazy anymore.

ADAM: You play the mature type in porn movies.

CAROLL: *(Cutting in)* Not really, I'm only thirty.

ADAM: You look older.

CAROLL: You really think so?

ADAM: Are you in porn films because there's a dollar bill on your clit?

CAROLL: I like getting paid for what I love to do, yes. But I'm not just into porn films for the money. I love to fuck, and to be able to get to fuck different people and get paid for it—to have people recognize that you are good at sex and get paid for it. It's the best of two worlds. Getting paid for what you love to do, and getting recognition too.

ADAM: Not to be facetious, but you would seem like the mature looking woman type that an X-rated producer would cast as turning out a young boy . . . giving him his first sex . . . Have you ever played that type of role?

CAROLL: No *(laughs)*. But I would love to play that type of role. I think it could be handled so romantically. You know, a lot of men like a young woman, particularly if they are older men. I feel women like to fantasize about young boys—breaking them into sex. Porn movies should be for women, as well as men. I think we should have scenes in porn films that are what women fantasize, like having sex with a young boy.

ADAM: Did you ever fuck a young boy in private life, since you have been a woman?

CAROLL: Yes. He was fifteen. It was so romantic. He was so sweet. There was only one problem. He shot his wad too quick. But he was really appreciative of getting my pussy. And he had a firm young body. I've done it several times since then with different "young boy" partners, and I have always loved the experience.

ADAM: Do you fuck a lot in your private life—or is that just your screen image?

CAROLL: I'm always fucking in my private life. I do a lot of orgying in my private life. I love to spend several days in bed, just having sex with my partner, only getting up to eat.

ADAM: A lot of porn actresses don't like fucking in the ass. Why?

CAROLL: It hurts! And it really hurts if the guy is too big or too rough.

ADAM: Do you like to fuck in the ass?

CAROLL: Not really. But if the guy I'm with *gets off* by fucking me in the ass, I will let him fuck me in the ass. Just put some grease on his ding-a-ling, that's all I ask. I am a woman, and I'm here to please.

ADAM: What if the dude put some cocaine on his dick, like the hustlers do?

CAROLL: That might be nice. -FIN-

SUICIDE CIRCLE

SION SONO HAS BEEN CREATING WEIRD, FORMALIST INDIE CINEMA EVER SINCE HE MADE THE UNCONVENTIONAL SHIFT FROM WRITING POETRY TO DIRECTING SOFTCORE GAY PORN. WHEN HE FINALLY BROUGHT HIS FANS **SUICIDE CIRCLE** (AKA SUICIDE CLUB) IN 2002, THE BESPECKLED JAPANESE AUTEUR HAD DESCENDED FURTHER INTO FREE FORM QUIRKINESS -- WITH A HEALTHY DOSE OF SOCIAL COMMENTARY FOR FLAVOR.

PERHAPS THE MOST FAMOUS ELEMENT OF THIS MEMORABLE MOVIE (BOTH WRITTEN AND DIRECTED BY SONO) IS THE OPENING SEQUENCE. THE AUDIENCE I WAS WITH AUDIBLY GASPED AS 54 CHEERY ASIAN SCHOOLGIRLS JOINED HANDS AND LEAPT IN FRONT OF A SPEEDING SUBWAY TRAIN. THESE CUTE GIRLS GETTING SPLATTERED INTO A SICKENING PASTE PROVIDES AN EARLY TASTE OF THE RESULTING SUICIDES TO APPEAR THROUGHOUT THE FILM.

THE WHEEL OF FLESH

AFTER THAT FRENETIC SUCKER PUNCH, SION GRABS THE LEASH AND YANKS THE AUDIENCE THROUGH A SERIES OF SEEMINGLY UNRELATED LOW-KEY SEQUENCES THAT SOMEHOW LEAD TO DISTURBING CLIMAXES -- MY FAVE BEING THE THE GROSS "WHEEL OF FLESH" HOUSED IN A WHITE BLOOD-CAKED GYM BAG. SONO TAKES THE TIME TO FILL THE VIEWER WITH THE SAME UNAVOIDABLE SENSE OF DREAD THAT HE INSTILS INTO HIS CHARACTERS, AND THERE ARE ENOUGH LYNCHIAN WAKING NIGHTMARES AND PLOT HOLES TO KEEP EVERYONE BOTH FRUSTRATED AND CONFUSED AT THE LACK OF COHESION.

IN SONO'S VERSION OF JAPAN, TEENS GO APE-SHIT FOR A POP GROUP CALLED DESERT (ALSO AMUSINGLY SPELLED "DESSERT", "DESART", AND "DESRET" THROUGHOUT THE FEEBLE SUBTITLE TRACK) WHO SEEM TO HAVE SECRET MESSAGES HIDDEN IN THEIR POSTERS, VIDEOS, AND LYRICS. COULD THEY BE THE CAUSE OF ALL OF THIS MADNESS, OR MAYBE IT'S THE VIOLENT GANG OF GLAM ROCKERS WHO LIVE IN A BOWLING ALLEY?

SION HIGHLIGHTS CONCERNS WITHIN A DISENCHANTED YOUTH-BASED SOCIETY, AND LEAVES US WITH AND ODD AND UNSETTLING THEORY THAT SUICIDE IS SOMEHOW INTIMATELY CONNECTED TO THE YOUNG. THE DIRECTOR HIMSELF MENTIONED IN AN INTERVIEW THAT HE SET OUT WITH SUICIDE CIRCLE TO EXPLORE THE PERCEPTION THAT MODERN DAY JAPANESE URBANITES HAD "LOST THE WILL TO LIVE".

ONE THING ABOUT THIS MOVIE IS CLEAR: THE PLOT WAS PURPOSEFULLY MADE CONFUSING SO AS TO KEEP THE VIEWER AS HELPLESS AS THE COPS TRYING TO SOLVE THE MYSTERY OF THE SUICIDES AND THE GROTESQUE WHEEL OF FLESH. ULTIMATELY THOUGH, IT'S LEFT UP TO THE INDIVIDUAL TO JUDGE IF SONO LOBBED TOO MANY QUESTIONS THAT REMAIN UNANSWERED (I DIDN'T EVEN MENTION THE INVOLVED TATTOO SUBPLOT) AND IF THEY FIND THEMSELVES HARD PRESSED TO DERIVE A SATISFYING CONCLUSION TO THE WHOLE THING.

— BOUGIE

YOU KNOW WHO WAS HOT?

MARISA MELL (BORN MARILES MOITZI). SHE WAS A GORGEOUS AUSTRIAN ACTRESS WHO MADE HER NAME AS A STAR OF 1960s ITALIAN B-PICTURES. SHE WAS BEST KNOWN FOR PLAYING EVA KANT IN "DANGER: DIABOLIK" (1968), AND STARRING ROLES IN "PERVERSION STORY" (1969) AND "SECRET AGENT SUPER DRAGON" (1966). SADLY, SHE DIED FROM THROAT CANCER IN 1992.

READER MAILBAG:

"YOU INTERVIEWED LEE CAROLL AND DIDN'T ASK HER ABOUT HER SUICIDE ATTEMPT?? INSTEAD YOU ASK HER IF SHE WOULD ALLOW SOMEONE TO VOMIT IN HER ASS SO SHE COULD FART IT BACK IN THEIR FACE?! WHAT ARE YOU, A RETARDED 9 YEAR OLD? TIME TO GROW UP. CINEMA SEWER COULD BE SO MUCH MORE IF YOU WOULD ONLY ALLOW IT."
— F.W. KIMBALL, OAKLAND

R.DART '03

SICK COMIC BOOKS I'D ♥ TO SEE AS MOVIES!

IT'S ALWAYS THE DAMN COMICS WE COULD CARE LESS ABOUT THAT PRODUCERS DECIDE TO CO-OPT AND MAKE INTO FILMS: MEN IN BLACK, THE MASK, SPAWN, CATWOMAN, BLADE... THE LIST IS LONG AND OVERWHELMING. WELL **FUCK THEM**, WE WANT SOME OF THAT OBSCURE WEIRD SHIT. THAT OVER-THE-TOP INSANITY WHERE YOU'VE GOTTA LEAVE THE KIDS WITH GRANDMA. I'M TALKIN' KICK-ASS, NON-P.C. EXPLOITATION CINEMA, PEOPLE, I'M TALKIN 'BOUT:

RAMBA

EROS COMICS (THE ADULT IMPRINT OF FANTAGRAPHICS BOOKS) PUBLISHES PRETTY MUCH EVERY ENGLISH LANGUAGE XXX COMIC BOOK WORTH ITS MUSTARD THESE DAYS, WITH MANY TITLES TRANSLATED FROM THE JAPANESE, FRENCH AND ITALIAN THEY WERE ORIGINALLY PUBLISHED IN. BUT OF ALL THESE HUNDREDS OF TITLES, THERE IS ONE THAT LASTED ABOUT A DOZEN ISSUES IN THE MID 90S, THAT MIXED CALLOUS VIOLENCE, BAD TASTE, AND HARDCORE FUCKING IN SUCH A DEPRAVED AND EXPLOITATIONAL WAY - ITS VILE STORY LINE WAS DESTINED TO STICK IN MY CRAW LIKE AN EXQUISITE WET DREAM. IN SHORT, IT'S A COMIC BOOK THAT WOULD MAKE FOR OUTLANDISH PORN-COMPOSED GRINDHOUSE CINEMA!

IN THE MID 80S, WRITER ROSSANO ROSSI AND ARTIST MARCO DELIZIA BEGAN WORK ON AN ADULT COMIC BOOK AND THEN SHOPPED IT TO A POPULAR SLEAZE PUBLISHER IN ROME CALLED BLUE PRESS. THAT SERIES WAS CALLED **RAMBA**, AND ONE CAN TOTALLY BE FORGIVEN IF PRONE TO AN EARLY DISMISSAL OF THE CONCEPT PURELY BECAUSE OF THE LAME REFERENCE TO THE STALLONE **RAMBO** SERIES. BUT DON'T BE TOO HASTY, THERE **IS** SOMETHING OF INTEREST HERE - ESPECIALLY IF YOU'RE A DROOLING PERVERT.

HERE'S THE LOWDOWN: RAMBA IS A FEMALE ASSASSIN-FOR-HIRE WITH THE UNINTENTIONALLY HUMOROUS WARDROBE OF AN 80S BON JOVI GROUPIE. SHE'S TEMPERAMENTAL, HAS AN ALARMING LACK OF REMORSE, AND TAKES EVERY CHANCE SHE CAN GET TO WORK SEX (OR AT LEAST SEX RELATED TORTURE OR HUMILIATION) INTO HER CHOSEN VICTIM'S LAST FEW MOMENTS. SHE'S TOTALLY IN CHARGE AS SHE RIDES AROUND ON HER BIG MOTORCYCLE, GUNS BLAZING, HANDING OUT PAIN AND SUFFERING TO ANYONE - AS LONG AS THE $$ IS GOOD, AND THE COCK IS **HARD**.

WHILE NORTH AMERICAN XXX ILLUSTRATORS GENERALLY SHY AWAY FROM MIXING DEATH AND SEX, ITALIAN ADULT COMICS (CALLED "FUMETTI") ARE RENOWNED FOR NOT SHYING AWAY FROM DISTURBING VIOLENT PORNOGRAPHIC IMAGERY, AND ARE OCCASIONALLY RENOUNCED AS MISOGYNISTIC BY THEIR DETRACTORS. **RAMBA** IS NO EXCEPTION, AND CAN EASILY BE VIEWED AS A WORTHY DESCENDANT TO THE BIG, BAD FUMETTI OF THE ROARING 1970S. ROSSI'S CREATION IS PACKED WITH VIOLENT DEATH, GRINDING ANAL PENETRATION, STICKY CUMSHOTS, BLOODY BULLET-RIDDLED CORPSES, GIANT 80S ROCKER HAIR, SLEAZY MAFIOSI, TENDER LESBIAN ENCOUNTERS, FELINE BEASTIALITY, DEFILED VIRGINS, MAGGOT-COVERED RAPE ZOMBIES, AND MOST AT THE FOREFRONT?

G.W.G. YES, IF YOU'RE INTO THE POPULAR GEEK FETISH OF NAKED OR SCANTILY-CLAD GIRLS WITH GUNS (BROUGHT INTO THE MAINSTREAM BY Q.T.'S **JACKIE BROWN**) YOU WILL NOT WANT TO PASS THIS BY. IT'S LIKE AN OFF-KILTER, SUB AUTOMATIC,

22

JESUS CHRIST! WHAT ARE YOU-- SOME KIND OF MUTANT?! THAT THING LOOKS LIKE A FOOTBALL WITH VEINS! DID YOU GROW UP ON A NUCLEAR TEST SITE OR WHAT--?!!

VERY FUNNY. YOU WANT IT, YOU TAKE IT, BITCH! I'M SICK OF BEING THE LAUGHINGSTOCK OF THIS FUCKIN' SHITHOLE!

JESUS! NOT BAD--! -- WHOA!! YOU GOT A HINGE ON THAT JAW OR SOMETHIN'?

cum-drenched version of Luc Besson's **LA FEMME NIKITA**.

So when Eros began to translate the series into English and put it out uncensored on the North American direct sales comics market, I was pleased and surprised to discover it. Early issues went into multiple printings, and a couple of years later, three soft cover book collections were released. The Seattle-based publishers weren't the first ones to take Rossi and Delizia's vile comic international though. **RAMBA** was serialized in a Euro comic anthology title from Sweden called "TOPAS" and was translated into Spanish in the early 90s as well.

Delizia's art is clean, gorgeously inked, and semi-realistic in style. If you've read any number of adult comics, you'll know that finding decent ink-studs is a chore in itself. He was replaced for the middle third of the English-translated issues (which make up about 1/4 of the Italian Ramba issues) by an artist named Valdambrini, who isn't nearly as talented - but employs a loose inking style that makes for an interesting counterpoint from Delizia. Mario Janni, with his slightly more cartoony version of Ramba also subbed in for an issue here and there.

Rossi's story lines are audacious and filthy, and don't let up for a moment. It's tightly plotted shit that somehow benefits from the fact that he never allows the characters to quietly reflect upon the insanity going on around them. Nearly every self-contained story has Ramba contacted by Ox, a lumbering go-to guy who dredges up work

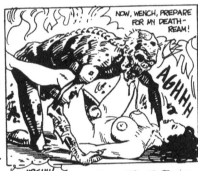

NOW, WENCH, PREPARE FOR MY DEATH-REAM!

AGHHH

(read: victims) so our heartless heroine can ice some assholes and put a few groceries in the pantry. At 20 grand a pop - and victims aplenty - one kinda wonders where all her money goes. She's like Mike Hammer, except instead of solving mysteries, she empties both her bladder and machine gun into the face of whomever she's been set upon - before softly masturbating herself with the corpse and then going home to get her juiced-up pussy licked clean by her cat.

That's not to say that this comic is redundant or boring. Things get spiced regularly with spy style espionage and back-stabbing, and there's even some bizarre witchcraft and hellish monsters that get unleashed between fuck sessions. I'm also a fan of the adventure where Ramba is appointed as an investigator in Antarctica and discovers a plot involving military-trained dolphins. Things go horribly awry when she's captured, forced to suck a "football with veins", then tied' up and raped in the asshole with a big icicle. But not to worry, she 'keeps her cool' (har har) and the bad guys end up riddled with enough bullets to arm a small army. Ramba kicks **much** ass.

URGHH! I FEEL YOUR INNARDS...

How fucking mean is this comic? Well, censors are always the best ones to ask those sort of questions. If they don't like it, it's probable that Cinema Sewer readers will. Shortly after its publication, Canada Customs - in Tariff item 9899.00.00 (Prohibited and admissible), named the 3 Ramba softcover graphic novels as "obscene" and "prohibited", and effectively banned the books.

I LOVE THIS JOB!! HA HA HA! ARGH!

RATATATATA

Hahaha!! "Banned" ha ha ha! That has to be the ultimate selling slogan of **all time**. Just tell people they can't have something, and they'll always want it! It is worth noting that Ramba's Tariff 9899.00.00 was also the one where Customs declared Pasolini's debauched epic **Salo - 120 days of Sodom** as finally being "admissible" after years on the

BANNED LIST - INSTANTLY MAKING IT SLIGHTLY LESS COOL TO CANADIANS EVERYWHERE.

PROSPECTIVE CASTING FOR THE RAMBA MOVIE:
RAMBA: MONICA BELLUCCI (IRREVERSIBLE)
OX: JAMES WESTMORELAND (DON'T ANSWER THE PHONE!)
VARIOUS VICTIMS AND BAD GUYS:
SID HAIG (SPIDER BABY)
PAUL REUBENS (PEE MUTHAFUCKIN' WEE, YO!)
ASHLEY BLUE (SEVEN THE HARD WAY)
MILA (MILA'S FUCK SLUTS)
YOKO NATSUKI (BEAUTIFUL TARGET)
VINCENT PASTORE (THE SOPRANOS)
SCORE AND SOUNDTRACK: TANGERINE DREAM (NEAR DARK)
DIRECTED BY: WILLIAM LUSTIG (MANIAC)

P.S. I SHOULD ALSO NOTE THAT THERE WAS A MOVIE IN THE LATE 80s IN ITALY THAT PLAYED IN PORN THEATERS CALLED **RAMBA: BEASTLY VENDETTA**, BUT IT WASN'T WHAT YOU MIGHT THINK. IT WAS SADLY JUST **GIRLS WHO DIG GIRLS B** - A BORING BARBARA DARE PORN VIDEO RETITLED TO TRY TO DRUM UP SOME INTEREST. TO ADD MORE CONFUSION: A NUDE UNDERAGE TRACI LORDS IS ON THE POSTER, AS ARE SOME HORNY LOOKING HORSES. NEITHER APPEAR IN THE VIDEO IN QUESTION.

LOOK FOR MORE "SICK COMICS I'D ♥ TO SEE AS MOVIES" INSTALLMENTS IN FORTHCOMING ISSUES OF CINEMA SEWER! ☆ THE BOUGIEMAN ─

BERT I. GORDON, VETERAN DIRECTOR OF HIS FAIR SHARE OF CAMPY 1950's MONSTER MOVIES TOOK ONE LAST MISGUIDED KICK AT THE OVERGROWN INSECT CAN WITH 1977's **EMPIRE OF THE ANTS**. OL' BERT (BLESS HIS HEART) TOOK HIS RETARDED DRIVE-IN BUG MOVIE VERY SERIOUSLY AND CAST JOAN COLLINS, THE PINNACLE OF HIGH SOCIAL GRACE AND CLASS IN HOLLYWOOD - AND A WOMAN WHOSE RESUME INCLUDES **THE BITCH**, **THE STUD**, AND **THE VIRGIN QUEEN**. (TAKE TIME TO PONDER THAT FACTOID WITH ME, WILL YOU?) BUT POOR JOAN IS TOTALLY IN OVER HER HEAD WHILE TRYING TO ACT ALONGSIDE GIANT ANT PUPPETS, AND ON THE VIDEO BOX ITSELF, IT STATES THAT THE MOVIE IS ONE "MISS COLLINS WOULD RATHER US FORGET!"

AFTER ESCAPING FROM A GIANT ANT ATTACK WHILE OUT IN THE MIDDLE OF NOWHERE, JOAN AND A LACKLUSTER GROUP OF ACTORS MAKE THEIR WAY TO THE NEAREST TOWN FOR HELP. OF COURSE, THE SHERIFF OF THE HAYSEED BURG IS AN ANT SLAVE. "ISN'T SHE BEAUTIFUL?" HE SAYS ABOUT THE QUEEN, "SHE'S FANTASTIC... WE MUST OBEY. WE HAVE NO CHOICE. SHE MAKES US DO IT." EVEN AFTER HE SPELLS IT OUT LIKE THAT IN PLAIN LANGUAGE, IT TAKES OUR LEAD CHARACTERS ANOTHER 40 MINUTES TO REALIZE EVERYONE IN TOWN IS UNDER THE GIANT ANTS' CONTROL! HI-FUCKIN'-LARIOUS!

SO YEAH, JUST LIKE YOU WERE HOPING, STATELY JOAN COLLINS TURNS INTO AN INSECT MIND-SLAVE. SHE BABBLES AND HUMS "TEDDY BEARS' PICNIC" WHILE THE ANTS BIND HER WRISTS AND EXPOSED TITS WITH STRANDS OF HARDENED SALIVA, AND THEN LAY EGGS IN HER ASS. HER PALE BUTT SWELLS, THEN VIOLENTLY EXPLODES AS SHE SHITS BUCKETS OF GRUBS AND LARVAE.

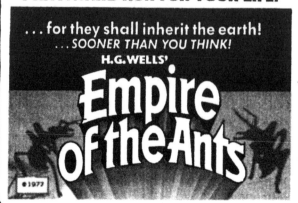

OK, I MADE UP THAT LAST PART. SORRY. BUT JOAN DOES BECOME AN ANT SLAVE WHILE THE REST OF THE CHARACTERS ESCAPE A GOOFY SUGAR-MAKING FACILITY THE ANTS SOMEHOW ORGANIZED. LUCKILY, THERE JUST HAPPENS TO BE A TANKER TRUCK CLEARLY MARKED 'FLAMMABLE' OUTSIDE THE BUILDING, AND ONE OF 'EM DOES...UM.. SOMETHING TO MAKE IT EXPLODE, ALTHOUGH IT SIMPLY LOOKS LIKE HE JUST STARTS UP THE ENGINE. SOMEHOW DOING THAT MAKES EVERYTHING NEARBY GO UP IN FLAMES, AND OUR GANG ESCAPES ON A BOAT.

FUCK, THIS SHIT IS **TERRIBLE** - BUT ALSO TOTALLY NUTTY AND FUN! CHECK OUT THE RECENT CHEAP MGM DVD! - ROBIN

THE SQUIRT-MASTER!

BY ROBIN BOUGIE '04

AXEL BRAUN WANTS THE WORLD TO SMELL HIS FINGERS

ITALIAN BORN AMERICAN CITIZEN AXEL BRAUN IS MAKING HIS PORN-GOD POPPA PROUD. THE SON OF CLASSIC PORN DIRECTOR LASSE BRAUN (WHO ALMOST SINGLE-HANDEDLY BROUGHT ON THE LEGALIZATION OF HARDCORE PORN IN EUROPE IN THE 1960S AND DIRECTED SOME GREAT 8MM LOOPS) IS ENTERING HIS OWN GLORY DAYS AND IS IN THE MIDST OF PROMOTING THIS TO ANYONE WHO WILL PAY ATTENTION. AFTER TAKING OVER AS THE GENERAL MANAGER OF POPULAR PORN COMPANY ELEGANT ANGEL, AND THE RECENT COMPLETION OF **CADILLAC HIGHWAY** FOR PRIVATE, THE DIRECTOR CELEBRATED HIS ACCOMPLISHMENTS BY ACCEPTING AN INVITATION TO GUEST ON TECH TV'S HIT LATE NIGHT SHOW "**UNSCREWED**":

"THE AUDIENCE WAS GREAT," BRAUN SAID, "WHEN I EXPLAINED THAT MY ONLY GIFT IS BEING ABLE TO MAKE WOMEN SQUIRT, I GOT A STANDING OVATION."

SQUIRT? FUCK, MORE LIKE HOSE DOWN INNOCENT BYSTANDERS, GUY. THIS FORMER ARMANI MODEL HAS HIS HANDS INSURED WITH LLOYD'S OF LONDON FOR $2 MILLION DOLLARS EACH - DUE HE SAYS, TO HIS AMAZING G-SPOT MASSAGING DIGITS.

"I KNOW THIS GUY IN ITALY WHO WORKS IN INSURANCE," BRAUN TOLD AN ONLINE INTERVIEWER, "AND HE HAD ME MAIL IN ALL THIS PAPERWORK, AND THEN A MONTH AND A HALF LATER THEY SEND ME A POLICY. $2 MILLION FOR EACH HAND. FOUR HUNDRED THOUSAND A FINGER!"

AXEL (WHO IS FLUENT IN 5 LANGUAGES) IS AN EXPERT WHEN IT COMES TO GETTING WOMEN TO GUSH, AND HE'S PUT HIS MONEY WHERE HIS MOUTH IS. THE INFAMOUS DR. SUSAN BLOCK (www.DRSUSANBLOCK.COM), A SEXOLOGIST WHO TESTED AXEL'S RESOLVE AND GIDDY BOASTS OF "I CAN MAKE **ANY** WOMAN EJACULATE." BY INVITING HIM FOR A 'HANDS ON/FINGERS IN' DEMO AT THE DR. SUSAN BLOCK INSTITUTE. ONLOOKERS WITNESSED AND FILMED AXEL SUCCESSFULLY OPENING THE VAGINAL FLOOD GATES ON NINE OUT OF TWELVE WOMEN WHO HE PROBED WITH HIS MUCH-PRACTICED TECHNIQUE. IT WAS THE FIRST TIME THAT AXEL HAD BUSTED OUT SOME SERIOUS G-SPOT SHIT IN A PROFESSIONAL MEDICAL CONTEXT.

BUT THERE IS NO SECRETIVE BULLSHIT ON THE AGENDA HERE. BRAUN'S OWN WEBSITE (www.AXELBRAUN.NET) GIVES AWAY HIS TRADE FEM-SPUNK SECRETS AND PROVIDES SOME REALLY NIFTY TIPS THAT, UPON READING, HAD ME FIDGETING TO EXPERIMENT. CHECK IT OUT, Y'ALL:

"AXEL BRAUN STARTED PERSONALLY RESEARCHING THE SUBJECT OF THE G-SPOT IN 1982, AND HAS SINCE PROVEN A NEW INTERESTING POINT: ALL WOMEN CAN EJACULATE! THE G-SPOT ORGASM, COMBINED WITH EJACULATION, IS MUCH LIKE THE MALE ORGASM, INCLUDING THE PHYSICAL FATIGUE. THE EJACULATE WILL COME OUT IN DIFFERENT FLOWS, AND ITS AMOUNT IS VERY INDIVIDUALLY DETERMINED. STIMULATING THE G-SPOT TO THE LEVEL WHERE IT WILL INDUCE FEMALE EJACULATION REQUIRES PATIENCE, TENDERNESS AND TECHNIQUE, BUT IT'S EASIER THAN YOU MIGHT THINK."

"THE G-SPOT LIES DIRECTLY BEHIND THE FRONT WALL OF THE VAGINA. THE SIZE AND EXACT LOCATION VARY. IMAGINE A SMALL CLOCK INSIDE THE VAGINA, WITH 12 O'CLOCK POINTED AT THE NAVEL. THE MAJORITY OF WOMEN WILL HAVE THE G-SPOT LOCATED BETWEEN 11 AND 1 O'CLOCK A FEW INCHES INSIDE THE VAGINA."

"START WITH STIMULATING THE VAGINA WITH TWO FINGERS AND SLOWLY WORK YOUR WAY TO THE POINT WHERE YOUR PARTNER WILL TELL YOU THAT SHE FEELS A PINCH. THAT'S THE G-SPOT! ONCE YOU'VE GOT IT, STIMULATE IT BY PRESSING ON IT AT REGULAR INTERVALS, HARDER AND HARDER, UNTIL YOU FEEL THE VAGINAL WALLS START CONTRACTING."

"NOW, LAY YOUR THUMB OVER THE CLITORIS AND SIMPLY SQUEEZE THE G-SPOT FROM BEHIND, MOVING YOUR FINGERS AS FAST AS YOU CAN. WHEN THE LIQUID STARTS TO SQUIRT OUT, **DON'T STOP!** THE ORGASM WILL BE VERY INTENSE, IT WILL ALSO REVOLVE. LET IT COME AGAIN ... AND AGAIN, RIGHT UP UNTIL SHE TELLS YOU TO STOP."

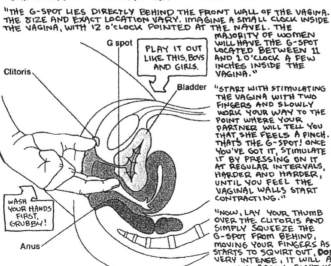

G spot

Clitoris

Bladder

Anus

PLAY IT OUT LIKE THIS, BOYS AND GIRLS.

WASH YOUR HANDS FIRST, GRUBBY!

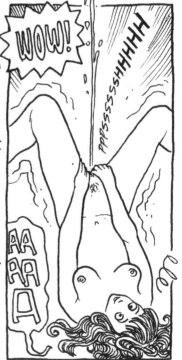

WOW!

PPRSSSSSSHHHHH

AAAAA

CONTINUED FROM PREVIOUS PAGE:

WHEN INDUSTRY GIANT "PRIVATE" SIGNED BRAUN TO A ONE MOVIE CONTRACT IN EARLY DEC. 2003, HE WAS ALREADY A MULTI-AVN AWARD NOMINATED DIRECTOR AND HAD **COMPULSION** UNDER HIS BELT. THIS IS A MOVIE SHOT ON 35MM THAT COST A MINT TO MAKE (COMPARED TO OTHER XXX FILMS) AND TOOK AN UNPRECEDENTED 6 MONTHS TO FILM.

IN 2004 BRAUN LEFT PRIVATE TO JOIN NEW SENSATIONS/ DIGITAL SIN, WHERE HIS OUTPUT WOULD GO ON TO WIN MULTIPLE AWARDS AT ADULT MOVIE AWARDS CEREMONIES THROUGHOUT THE WORLD.

ON CHRISTMAS DAY 2005, BRAUN MARRIED PORN STAR BELLADONNA'S SISTER. NO WORD YET HOW FAR HE'S GOTTEN HER TO SQUIRT.

SWITCHBLADE SISTERS (1975)

IF THERE EVER WAS A FILM THAT COULD BE CONSIDERED ESSENTIAL VIEWING FOR 1970S EXPLOITATION FANS, THIS WOULD HAVE TO BE IT. DIRECTOR JACK HILL SLAYS WITH THIS 1975 DRIVE-IN ASS-KICKIN' OPUS WHICH HAS ALL THE REQUISITE CHEESE AND THEN SOME: GIRL FIGHTS, GUN DUELS, SEX-STARVED REFORM SCHOOL GUARDS, A DRIVE-BY GANG RAPE, IN-SCHOOL PROSTITUTION, AND EVEN A VIOLENT AFRICAN AMERICAN-MAOIST REVOLUTION IN THE STREETS.

THE PLOT CHRONICLES THE TRIALS AND TRIBULATIONS OF THE DAGGER DEBS, AN ALL TEENAGE GIRL POSSE OF BAD-ASSES. WHEN THE SEXY NEW CHAIN-SWINGIN' CHICK ON THE BLOCK, LACE (ROBBIE LEE) JOINS THE GANG, SHE AROUSES THE JEALOUSY OF PATCH (MONICA GAYLE) AND THE GANGS LEADER MAGGIE (JOANNE NAIL) WHEN MAGGIES BOYFRIEND TAKES A LIKING TO HER. THE TREACHERY, INSANE DIALOG, COLORFUL ACTION, BALLSY BLOODSHED, AND TENDER TITTIES ON DISPLAY INVEST THIS GEM AS A TRULY REWARDING TRASH CINEMA EXPERIENCE.

AS A PERSONAL ASIDE, ONE OF THE BIT PLAYERS IN THE TOUGH-TALKIN' GANG IS THE CHUBBY-YET-ADORABLE DONUT – PLAYED BY LENNY BRUCE'S DAUGHTER, KITTY. IF THIS FILM HAS NOTHING ELSE GOING FOR IT, AT LEAST IT HAS HER – THE OBJECT OF A RATHER HEFTY SCHOOLBOY CRUSH ON MY PART. OH WHAT I WOULDN'T GIVE TO SLIDE THE COCKMEAT THROUGH THOSE SOFT MILKY-WHITE FLESH-PILLOWS... GUHHH... (ROBIN HIDES IN A CORNER + BEGINS FURIOUSLY BEATING HIS MEAT.) GET THE TARANTINO-APPROVED ROLLING THUNDER DVD, THE AUDIO COMMENTARY WITH JACK HILL AND QUENTIN IS PLENTY ENTERTAINING, YALL.

Mothers... lock up your sons
The **Switchblade Sisters** are coming!

Lace...
Maggie...
Patch...
Donut...
Bunny...

The wildest teen age girl gang that ever blasted the streets!

BALI BOOM BOOM (2004)

(WINNER OF THE C.S. #16 "NO CLASS AWARD")

UM... PORN STARRING VICTIMS OF THE BALI BOMBINGS? CAN YOU SAY "IN POOR FUCKING TASTE"? OCTOBER 12th 2004 MARKED THE TWO YEAR ANNIVER TERRORIST BOMBINGS THAT KILLED 202 INNOCENT WHAT SOMEONE WANTS TO THINK ABOUT AS THEY. ALLY, REALITY PORN PRODUCERS ASIA BOOTLEG ON THOSE DEATHS ('HILARIOUSLY' TITLED BALI ANNIVERSARY.

-SARY OF THE BALI NIGHTCLUB PEOPLE, WHICH IS - OF COURSE JUST BEAT THEIR MEAT. NOT SO COINCIDENT-RELEASED A TITLE WHICH CASHES IN BOOM BOOM) ON THAT SAME 2 YEAR

A FEW WEEKS LEADING UP TO THE TRAGIC EVENT, "MR. X PRODUCTIONS" HAD BEEN FILMING THE LOCAL GIRLS FROM "PADDY'S IRISH PUB" AND "THE SARI CLUB" LOCATED AT KUTA BEACH. UPON THEIR ARRIVAL BACK IN THE STATES, THEY REALIZED THE TWO CLUBS THEY HAD FILMED IN HAD BLOWN UP THANKS TO SOME TOURIST-HATING MILITANT TERRORISTS. BALI BOOM BOOM IS FULL OF X-RATED BAR SCENES, AND INCLUDES THE AFTERMATH OF THE HORRIFIC INCIDENT ALONG WITH SOME HOT "EXPLOSIVE" (SIGH) ACTION FROM RIMA, DONAH AND SARAH WHO LOST THEIR LIVES IN THE BLAST.

WHATS NEXT? "9-11 ASS SLUTS" ??? ONLY IN THE PORN INDUSTRY FOLKS...

BAD GEORGIA ROAD (1977)

YEEEEEHAW! TWO MOONSHINING RUM RUNNERS FIGHT OFF THE LAW, THE COMPETITION, AND EACH OTHER AS THEY HIT TOP SPEED WITH THEIR INTOXICATIN' LIQUID CARGO IN TOW. SULTRY CAROL LYNLEY PLAYS GOLDEN, A CRANKY, SEXUALLY UPTIGHT FASHION DESIGNER FROM THE BIG APPLE, AND GARY LOCKWOOD IS AN OUT-OF-CONTROL DRUNK HICK NAMED LEROY. TOGETHER, THEY'RE MAKIN' A DASH DOWN **BAD GEORGIA ROAD**.

THE CASTING IS PRETTY GREAT FOR SUCH A LOW BUDGET OBSCURITY. CAROL LYNLEY IS TODAY PERHAPS BEST REMEMBERED BY CULT FILM FANS FOR HER ROLE IN **THE POSEIDON ADVENTURE**. HER FAN BASE ENDURES FOR A REASON: BEAUTY, BRAINS, AND ACTING TALENT DON'T OFTEN COLLIDE IN A SWEET LITTLE PACKAGE LIKE THIS. GARY LOCKWOOD WILL ALWAYS BE REMEMBERED - IF FOR NOTHING ELSE - AS ASTRONAUT FRANK POOLE IN **2001: A SPACE ODYSSEY**.

THE MOONSHININ' OPERATION IS THE PLOT'S MAIN FOCUS, BUT THE FILM ALSO REVOLVES AROUND THE SEVERE CLASHING OF CULTURES AND SEXES - AS LIBERAL LYNLEY LOCKS HORNS WITH HER REDNECK CHAUVINIST COMPANION. EVENTUALLY LEROY HONORS HIS HILLBILLY HERITAGE, AND RAPES GOLDEN IN A POWERFUL SCENE WHICH, IN A NON-SOUTHERN DRIVE-IN STORY, WOULD HAVE BEEN WHERE THE FEMALE PROTAGONIST ENDURES THE VILE ABUSE, COLLECTS HERSELF, AND EXACTS REVENGE BY KILLING AND MUTILATING HER ATTACKER. BUT IN **BAD GEORGIA ROAD** THE FRIGID LASS IS "THAWED OUT" AND FALLS IN ♡ WITH HER RAPIST.

B.G.R. IS A REAL SLEEPER IN THE SENSE THAT IT SUCCEEDS ON ITS OWN MODEST LEVEL BEYOND REALISTIC EXPECTATIONS. FOR A ROOTIN', TOOTIN' NON-P.C. GOOD TIME, GRAB A SIX PACK OF LUCKY LAGER AND WATCH THIS AS A DOUBLE BILL WITH **SMOKEY AND THE BANDIT**. THE ONLY REAL LACKING ELEMENT IN BOTH FILMS IS A GENEROUS HELPING OF TITS AND ASS.

—BOUGIE '04

They're makin' time to the county line!

©1977 DIMENSION PICTURES INC.

BAD GEORGIA ROAD

MISTRESS OF MAYHEM

By Brian Johnson

Mistress Anne Murray, a butt-ugly, pug-faced, beached blonde, grossly obese dominatrix from Oklahoma, is one of, if not THE most brutal bitches to ever burnish a birch. Her infamous videos are legendary in the S&M underground, where even hardcore members of the lifestyle are shocked and sickened by her unbridled cruelty. She's done "mainstream" bondage videos, which are easily obtainable at almost anywhere but Blockbuster or WalMart, but it's her "under the counter" shows that, quite literally, have to be experienced to be believed. Most circulate throughout the underground as mere "clips", often without titles or credits, and for good reason-for they come as close to actual "snuff" films as their dubious legality allows.

Perhaps her most (in)famous video is the thoroughly sickening and truly bizarre cult favorite, "CHOCOLATE DELIGHT". No, it's not some Afro-centered fuck-fest, but rather a base exercise in coprophilia so disgusting and extreme, you'll abandon whatever hope you have left in humanity after viewing. Typical for hard underground S&M videos, CHOCOLATE DELIGHT is shot with no budget, no set, no plot, no "acting", but real screams, real pain and real action. What sets it apart from the norm is its unusual "victim" who is subject Mistress Anne's wrath - a feeble, seventy-plus year old man. Either possessing complete senility or a severe taste for the perverse, the sick old coot is seen in the opening scenes shackled naked in stocks as his wrinkled frame quivers in anticipation. Mistress Anne proceeds to fuck his flabby ass with a double dong, torture his cock and balls with a spiked glove, and generally sexually abuse him in a variety of agonizing techniques. Despite the advanced age of the "bottom", this is typical fare, and although his loud cries of serious pain are indeed hysterical, nothing presented thus far can adequately prepare one for what comes next...

The scene shifts abruptly to the massive Mistress sitting on the edge of a garish sofa, whilst the old duffer is on the floor, on his back, hands tied, face painted with the words "Toilet Slut" in red lipstick and a large funnel strapped to his head/mouth. Before you can say "fill 'er up", Mistress Anne squats over his joker-like mug and overflows the funnel with what seems like gallons of her "liquid gold" - Toilet Slut gulps and swallows as if a man dying of thirst, all the while being verbally abused and assaulted with the spiked glove of his tormentor. After a few minutes of piss-drinking, a bone-white dinner plate is produced. Mistress Anne leans over the couch, thrusts out her enormous buttocks and commands Toilet Slut to tongue her asshole. He obliges with glee and gusto. She moans and farts, he gags. Then he is ordered to place the plate under her cellulite covered ass while she grunts loudly, then squirts out the biggest, nastiest coil of turds a human being could possibly muster onto a dinner plate. She then spreads the still steaming feces onto crackers and feeds them to Toilet Slut, who chokes, gags, but seemingly loves his snack. "Do you remember the last time you ate my shit, slave?" Mistress Anne taunts him with her patented whine. "Yes, Mistress. It was the 4th of July, my birthday!" He eventually grows a half-soft boner and whimpers,"I'm so ashamed." And all the while, as unbelievable as it may seem, the sounds of

chickens clucking nonstop is heard throughout the entire video.

CHOCOLATE DELIGHT is one of the funniest, grossest and downright strange explorations of deviant and vile human sexuality ever filmed, and once seen, it'll burn its images deeply into your cranium and never be forgotten-no matter how much you wish it could be.

The twisted old goat has appeared with Mistress Anne in two other videos that I'm aware of (he's never credited, for obvious reasons), but reliable sources inform T.W.S.D.! fanzine that he is indeed, your Grandfather... on your Mother's side, both untitled, both unremarkable, but they do have their moments.

The lesser of the two features Mistress Anne putting the old man and an extremely tough female submissive through their paces. The obese female slave is mummified, caned, and electrically-shocked, but nary emits a whimper. Our old friend Toilet Slut, on the other hand, is a hoot. Mistress Anne attaches electrodes to his balls and makes him count-"1,2,3,4,5,6,OUCH!-1,2,3,4,OUCH!"

It's a scream to hear him yell at the top of his lungs and jump about a foot off the ground with each jolt, but not nearly as funny or perverse as the other video wherein he and a crippled retard are tortured by Mistress Anne and her hog-headed accomplice. The retard is eventually strapped to a table, sodomized with a large dildo and has his pubic hair

ripped out by the fistful by the wicked Doms. "I ben lookin' for two woman lik yew for ah muy wife", he explains (in seemingly total honesty) between loud screams of agony and pleasure. It's safe to say that this short, featuring the sexual torture of both a senile old man and a severely retarded cripple, is about as extreme as one can go in the "poor taste" dept., therefore is obviously well worth searching out.

But the coup de grace' for any Mistress Anne aficionado has to be her appearance in a video compilation of filth and degradation circulated by a N.W. U.S. motorcycle gang called "Seeing is Believing". This 6 hour (!) atrocity is an article in and of itself, but for our purposes here, we'll concern ourselves only with the Mistress Anne segment, which will undoubtedly strike mortal terror into the heart of any male of the species who is witness to it. In this notorious show, Mistress Anne Murray (and her assistant, a fat-ass known as "Deborah-Vation") puts a real hurtin' on a "normal" looking couple (both male and female). After much face-slapping, nipple-pinching, crotch biting, fist in the mouth gagging, ass-whipping and general abuse, the male slave is hung by his wrists from the ceiling, a leather hood is placed over his entire face... and a step-ladder with a hammer and a handful of nails is set beneath his nutsack.

With all the precision and skill of a drunken roofer, the mighty Mistress pounds about a half dozen nails straight through the

GET READY TO EAT MY SHIT YOU LITTLE PIG!

-YOU SICKEN ME!

BOUGIE '03

poor bastard's balls and into the ladder's top step. Then she takes several large needles and jams them hard through his cock-head. The pain inflicted was obviously excruciating, as he jumps violently and his muffled cries of "no more, no more" are heard from under the mask. The participants' excitement begins to build to a fever pitch as Mistress Anne prepares to remove one of the needles from his dick-head (as if they've done this before and know what is about to happen?!). As the needle is yanked from his cock, the blood squirts out like a high pressure water fountain. As the moans of pleasure and pain engulf the room, Mistress Anne rubs the blood into the faces and crotches of all involved, creating an orgiastic bloodbath so strange, so twisted and perverted, so horrifying, that one seriously begins to doubt one's own sanity. "Ohhh! It looks like he's coming blood!" Deborah-Vation breathes heavily... and, if you listen closely, you can almost hear Satan laughing in the background.

The last time I saw Mistress Anne was on one of the final episodes of the Phil

Donahue show (an obvious masochist himself, what with marrying the shrew-like Marlo Thomas) where she was a featured "Mommy" on a totally bizarre segment concerning the sexual kink/fetish "Infantilism" (wherein grown men act-out like babies: crying, dressing in baby clothes, playing with rattles, soiling their diapers, etc.) Has Mistress Anne gone soft on us, preferring powdering baby-men's bottoms over hammering their dicks to bloody pulps? Let's hope not, but regardless, she's already left her indelible bruise on America's corroded culture. In the not to distant future, as the human race as a whole becomes more asinine, more violent, less intelligent and fatter than ever, we as a species will come to recognize Mistress Anne as the cultural icon she most surely is. Like Betty Page, Marilyn Monroe or Princess Di, she will be worshipped and revered with cult-like devotion, placed on a pedestal few celebrities can even dream of achieving. Mistress Anne- she's fat, ugly, loud, self-absorbed, cruel and unusual - a perfect role-model and spokesperson for modern American junk.

CINEMA SEWER MOURNS THE PASSING OF BRIAN JOHNSON, CREATOR OF THE INFAMOUS B-MOVIE ZINE "THEY WON'T STAY DEAD". BRIAN DIED TRAGICALLY ON MARCH 21st 2002 OF CARBON MONOXIDE POISONING. THANKS SO MUCH TO ALAN FARE AND BRIAN'S WIDOW FOR ALLOWING C.S. TO REPRINT THE ABOVE ARTICLE WHICH ORIGINALLY SAW PRINT IN "FILM GEEK" #8. ♥ TO BRIAN. YOU WILL BE MISSED....

THE DEFIANCE OF GOOD (AKA DEFIANCE) 1974. DIR. BY ARMAND WESTON. 74 MIN.

VIRGINAL-LOOKING JEAN JENNINGS TURNS HEADS IN HER FIRST SCREEN APPEARANCE AS CATHY, THE INNOCENT AND WIDE-EYED DAUGHTER OF STRICT AND REPRESSED PARENTS WHO COMMIT HER TO A MENTAL HOSPITAL FOR SUCCUMBING TO PEER PRESSURE (!?!). MA AND POP THINK THEY MIGHT BE DOING CATHY A FAVOR, BUT RIGHT AFTER SHE'S BEEN ADMITTED, SHE'S TIED TO HER BED AND BUGGERED BY A TRIO OF FELLOW INMATES WHO ARE CLEARLY IN THE INFIRMARY FOR A REASON. AN INSENSITIVE DOCTOR IS OF NO HELP WHEN SHE SOBS AND COMPLAINS OF HER NIGHTMARISH ABUSE, SIGHING AND SIMPLY DRUGGING HER UP AND LEAVING HER TO THE ADVANCES OF HER SCARY CRO-MAGNON BUNKIES AND A BRUTISH MALE NURSE WHO GETS A PERVERSE THRILL FROM STICKING HIS FINGER IN HER BUM. THINGS LOOK BAAAAAD FOR POOR CATHY.

FINALLY SHE IS "RESCUED" BY THE HYPNOTIC DR. GABRIEL (PLAYED BY LAST HOUSE ON THE LEFT STAR FRED LINCOLN- BILLED AS "THE GROOVY DOCTOR") WHO GAINS CATHY'S TRUST BY PREACHING OF HIS WANT TO "FREE HER FROM SOCIETY'S WORN OUT CONCEPTS OF GOOD AND EVIL". SHE HAS LITTLE TO SAY IN THE MATTER WHEN THE ASYLUM SIMPLY HANDS HER OVER (WITHOUT EVEN BOTHERING TO NOTIFY HER PARENTS) TO OL' DOCTOR GROOVY WHO CALMLY TAKES HER TO HIS PRIVATE SANITARIUM FOR GIRLS. TURNS OUT THE DOC IS A GRADE-A PERVERT LOON TOON WITH A HEAVY FETISH FOR S+M AND WHIPS AND CHAINS. POOR, POOR CATHY. HER NIGHTMARE HAS ONLY BEGUN.

THIS IS PERHAPS THE FIRST, AND CERTAINLY ONE OF THE BEST HARD-CORE BONDAGE AND DISCIPLINE FEATURES EVER TO BE RELEASED IN THE US. RECENTLY ADULT VIDEO NEWS CITED THIS ABUSE-FILLED CLASSIC AS "ONE OF THE GREATEST CURRENTLY UNAVAILABLE ADULT TITLES." IT'S MARGINALLY DIFFERENT THAN ANY

ARMAND WESTON'S THE DEFIANCE OF GOOD

AN S+M CLASSIC UNEARTHED BY ROBIN BOUGIE

S+M THEMED FILM I'VE EVER SEEN- PROVIDING MUCH OF ITS TERROR FOR ITS LEAD VICTIM THROUGH NOT ONLY TORTUOUS BONDAGE SCENES, BUT DIRE AND GRUELING PSYCHOLOGICAL HEAD TRIPPIN'- WHICH IS OF COURSE FAR FREAKIER THAN YET ANOTHER CLICHED ASS WHIPPING OR SPANKING SCENE THAT JAM PACK TODAY'S TAME AND HOMOGENIZED B+D VIDEOS.

ADDING EVEN MORE INTEREST FOR PERVERTED COLLECTORS IS THE RUMOR THAT TEENAGE STAR JEAN JENNINGS WAS ACTUALLY 16 WHEN SHE MADE DEFIANCE. ALTHOUGH IF THAT IS INDEED THE CASE, I REALLY DON'T SEE WHY SHE WOULDN'T BE A HOUSEHOLD NAME AMONST THE PUD-PULLERS THE WAY TRACI LORDS IS. TRACI, OF COURSE, MADE HUNDREDS OF THOUSANDS OF PEOPLE WHO HAD BOUGHT VIDEOS AND MAGAZINES SHE APPEARED IN, INTO UNDERAGE PORN POSSESSORS WHEN IT WAS REVEALED IN MID-1986 THAT SHE HAD LIED ABOUT HER AGE AND HAD BEEN MAKING TRIPLE-X AS A MINOR FOR 2 YEARS.

ALPHA BLUE ARCHIVES IS THE ONLY COMPANY THAT SELLS AN UNCUT COPY OF THE MOVIE, AND THEY TOE THE PARTY LINE SO APTLY DESCRIBED BY ONE R.A.M.E. NEWSGROUP MEMBER WHO WROTE, "WE DON'T KNOW FOR SURE THAT SHE WAS UNDERAGE - NO ONE WAS THERE IN '73 CHECKING BIRTH CERTIFICATES. IF SHE DOESN'T LOOK UNDER -AGE, SHE ISN'T," WHICH IS FINE - BUT THE FACT IS, SHE DOES LOOK YOUNG, BECAUSE SHE'S PLAYING AN UNDERAGE GIRL. THAT WAS THE WHOLE POINT. JEAN WOULD GO ON TO MAKE 17 OTHER PORN FILMS (VIRGIN DREAMS, AUTOBIOGRAPHY OF A FLEA AND SHARON - AMONG OTHERS) BEFORE FALLING OFF THE FACE OF THE PLANET.

MY WIFE REBECCA SAYS:

PORN AGAIN?! ·SIGH·

HAHA!

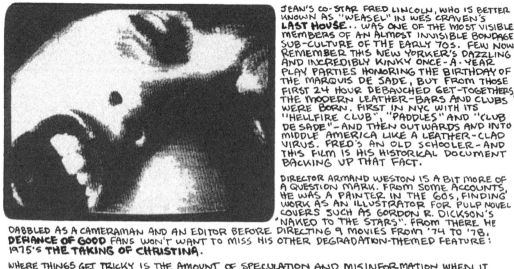

JEAN'S CO-STAR FRED LINCOLN, WHO IS BETTER KNOWN AS "WEASEL" IN WES CRAVEN'S **LAST HOUSE**.. WAS ONE OF THE MOST VISIBLE MEMBERS OF AN ALMOST INVISIBLE BONDAGE SUB-CULTURE OF THE EARLY 70S. FEW NOW REMEMBER THIS NEW YORKER'S DAZZLING AND INCREDIBLY KINKY ONCE-A-YEAR PLAY PARTIES HONORING THE BIRTHDAY OF THE MARQUIS DE SADE, BUT FROM THOSE FIRST 24 HOUR DEBAUCHED GET-TOGETHERS THE MODERN LEATHER-BARS AND CLUBS WERE BORN. FIRST IN NYC WITH ITS "HELLFIRE CLUB", "PADDLES" AND "CLUB DE SADE" - AND THEN OUTWARDS AND INTO MIDDLE AMERICA LIKE A LEATHER-CLAD VIRUS. FRED'S AN OLD SCHOOLER - AND THIS FILM IS HIS HISTORICAL DOCUMENT BACKING UP THAT FACT.

DIRECTOR ARMAND WESTON IS A BIT MORE OF A QUESTION MARK. FROM SOME ACCOUNTS, HE WAS A PAINTER IN THE 60S, FINDING WORK AS AN ILLUSTRATOR FOR PULP NOVEL COVERS SUCH AS GORDON R. DICKSON'S "NAKED TO THE STARS". FROM THERE HE DABBLED AS A CAMERAMAN AND AN EDITOR BEFORE DIRECTING 9 MOVIES FROM '74 TO '78. **DEFIANCE OF GOOD** FANS WON'T WANT TO MISS HIS OTHER DEGRADATION-THEMED FEATURE: 1975'S **THE TAKING OF CHRISTINA**.

WHERE THINGS GET TRICKY IS THE AMOUNT OF SPECULATION AND MISINFORMATION WHEN IT COMES TO THIS DIRECTOR. SOME THINK THAT HE WAS ACTUALLY A MAINSTREAM OR BETTER KNOWN PORN MOGUL WHO DIDN'T WANT TO GET TARRED AS A KINK-DIRECTOR. SOME SAY ANTHONY SPINELLI (**TALK DIRTY TO ME**) WAS INVOLVED IN THE WESTON MYTHOS. 60S B-MOVIE DIRECTOR DAVID FLEETWOOD (**THE SLIME PEOPLE**) HAS ALSO BEEN IMPLICATED, BUT PROBABLY ONLY BECAUSE OF HIS OUT-OF-CHARACTER RAPE PORNO, **A DIRTY WESTERN**, THAT CAME OUT AROUND THE SAME TIME AS **DEFIANCE**. EVEN MORE FRUSTRATING IS TRYING TO FIGURE OUT (PROVIDING HE WASN'T JUST A PEN NAME) WHEN ARMAND DIED. ALL THE SOURCES POINT TO DIFFERENT DATES, THE MOST POPULAR BEING MAY 26th 1988 AT THE TENDER AGE OF 56. ACCORDING TO LUKEFORD.COM, HE "DIED IN HIS SLEEP IN 1995". STILL ANOTHER NEWS ARTICLE FROM FEB. 2002 MENTIONS THAT HE HAD BEEN CONTACTED JUST BEFORE HE HAD DIED TO TAKE PART IN AN EVENING HONORING A FELLOW DIRECTOR - BUT HAD GRACIOUSLY DECLINED.

THE JANUARY 1983 ISSUE OF GENT MAGAZINE REVEALED THAT ANTHONY SPINELLI WAS IN FACT <u>SAM</u> WESTON, BROTHER OF CHARACTER ACTOR JACK WESTON -- BUT NOT RELATED AT ALL TO ARMAND.

WITH SOME WEIGHT BEHIND HIS WORDS (BEING AS HE WAS CLOSE FRIENDS AND EVEN WENT TO KINDERGARTEN WITH HIM) DIRECTOR CECIL HOWARD REVEALED RECENTLY THAT IT WAS WESTON WHO GOT HIM INTO PORN PRODUCTION, AND TOLD CINEMA SEWER CONTRIBUTOR DIMITRIOS OTIS THAT WESTON WAS BORN WITH THE NAME "ARMOND WESTON", AND THAT HE COULDN'T UNDERSTAND WHERE ALL THIS CONFUSION WAS COMING FROM.

SO, THE MYSTERY IS -- **THAT THERE IS NO MYSTERY**. HOW DO YOU THINK THE SCOOBY DOO KIDS WOULD LIKE THAT ONE? AT LEAST WESTON DIDN'T END UP BEING THE HOTEL MANAGER WEARING A WHITE BEDSHEET.

-BOUGIE

SWEET PUNKIN ·1975·

SOME OF C.J. LAING'S DETRACTORS (LIKE AL GOLDSTEIN FOR INSTANCE) COMPLAINED THAT THE CLASSIC PORN PERFORMER WAS A ROTTEN ACTRESS, BUT C.J. PROVED THROUGH HER ON-CAMERA DEEDS THAT SHE COULD DO ONE THING BETTER THAN ANYONE WHO CAME BEFORE OR AFTER HER MID-TO-LATE 70S TENURE IN ADULT ENTERTAINMENT: DEEP THROAT COCK.

MUCH HAS BEEN MADE OF LINDA LOVELACE'S ADMITTEDLY IMPRESSIVE SWORD SWALLOWING EFFORTS ON HARRY REEMS'S MINISTER OF PROCREATIVE AFFAIRS IN **DEEP THROAT**, BUT JUST IMAGINE IF SHE HAD TRIED THAT LITTLE MOVE WITH JOHN HOLMES'S CROTCH-INSANITY IN HER GULLET? LAING DID JUST THAT IN **SWEET PUNKIN**, TAKING ALL 13'1/2 INCHES RIGHT TO THE HILT. AND SHE DOUBLES UP THIS SUPERHUMAN FEAT BY ALSO DEEP THROATING TONY "THE HOOK" PEREZ, WHO WAS ONLY SLIGHTLY SHORTER, AND CONSISTENTLY HARDER THAN HOLMES'S COKED-OUT COCK EVER WAS. IN FACT, C.J. TAKES 'EM BOTH <u>AT THE SAME TIME</u>, ALONG WITH ANOTHER GUY IN A MIND-BOGGLING TRIPLE PENETRATION SCENE. ANYONE WHO THINKS OLD SKOOL SMUT ISN'T HARD ENOUGH SHOULD PEEP THIS SEEMINGLY INHUMAN GIRL EFFORTLESSLY TAKIN' MORE THAN A YARD OF FAT MONSTROUS COCKMEAT AT ONCE.

THE STORY PLACES LAING AS 'PUNKIN', A LUSCIOUS HILLBILLY PORN STARLET WHO LOSES HER JOB AND IS RESCUED FROM POVERTY BY AN ELDERLY MILLIONAIRE. BUT THE POOR OL' COOT HAS A FATAL HEART ATTACK WHILE HUMPING HIS INBRED BRIDE, PUTTING THE IGNORANT YOUNG WIDOW IN THE DRIVER'S SEAT WITH ALL THE MONEY SHE COULD EVER DREAM OF HAVING. SO WHAT DOES SHE DO WITH IT? FEED THE POOR? CLOTHE THE HOMELESS? NOPE. SHE TURNS THE STATELY MANSION INTO A SLEAZY FUCK-PIT OF CARNAL LUST. AND YOU GOTTA LOVE THE PACKAGING ON THE NEWLY RELEASED DVD EDITION WHICH STATES THAT C.J. "SEXUALLY PROVES THAT SHE IS BETTER THAN ALL OF THE SOCIETY HYPOCRITES PUT TOGETHER." THANK YOU LORD FOR CLASSIC FILTH LIKE THIS.

BY RADICAL TIM GOLUB '03

"LIKE, AWESOME!"

A NIGHT IN THE LIFE OF JIMMY REARDON (1988)

JIMMY REARDON (PLAYED BY RIVER PHOENIX IN A PERFORMANCE THAT MAKES ME GLAD HE'S DEAD) SPENDS THE ENTIRE MOVIE IN AGONY. OVER THIS, OVER THAT. HIS MAIN CONCERN IS HIS FRIGID GIRLFRIEND WHO WON'T LET HIM CROSS THE "MASON-DIXON LINE" INTO HER NETHER-REGIONS AND THEREBY OBVIOUSLY DOESN'T LOVE HIM. LIFE IS HARD FOR JIMMY, IT'S A GOOD THING HE HAS SOME SAFE HAVEN IN ONE GIRL'S BEDROOM, WHO GETS HIM TO **ROLEPLAY RAPE WITH HER**!!? YEAH, THE GIRL USUALLY GIVES HIM MONEY FOR HIS RAPIST SERVICES SINCE SHE'S RICH AND HE'S NOT.

JIMMY MEETS ONE OF HIS MOTHER'S FRIENDS, AND GIVES HER A RIDE HOME. SHE INVITES HIM INTO HER HOME, HE READS HER POETRY-THEREBY ACQUIRING THE RIGHT TO SLAM HIS CROTCH INTO HERS. EVENTUALLY JIMMY MAKES A SPECTACLE OF HIMSELF VAINLY ATTEMPTING TO USE HIS "DEEP" POETRY TO WIN HIS GIRLFRIEND BACK FROM THE RICH PREPPY STEREOTYPE SHE'S WITH, AND I WAS HOPING FOR A POETRY-OFF - LIKE LINES BACK AND FORTH BETWEEN THE TWO COMPETING GENTS - BUT NO DICE. THIS MOVIE NEVER GETS THE TINIEST BIT OF EMPATHY OUT OF ME. SHOULD I FEEL SAD FOR REARDON BECAUSE HE HAS THE BALLS TO DITCH HIS LIFE AND MOVE TO HAWAII, IF ONLY HE CAN FIND THE 75 BUCKS HE NEEDS? I JUST DON'T UNDERSTAND IT.

DREAM A LITTLE DREAM (1989)

EVER WONDER WHY COREY FELDMAN IS SUCH A POP CULTURE JOKE? HERE YOU GO. THIS FILM'S TOTAL IDIOCY SHOULD, BY ALL COUNTS, MAKE THIS THE MOST OBSCURE MOVIE ON A LIST WHERE IT'S ACTUALLY PROBABLY THE BEST KNOWN. AND YET - ON THE OTHER HAND, THE RANDOM NONSENSICAL NATURE OF THIS FILM ELEVATES IT TO THE PEAK OF UNINTENDED SUBTLE GENIUS. I FIND IT AMAZING THAT THROUGH EVERY STAGE OF THE FILMMAKING PROCESS, NO ONE EVER WONDERED WHAT THE HELL WAS GOING ON. THIS MOVIE IS BALLS-OUT INSANITY, BUT IS ALSO BITTERSWEET. I LOVE THAT IT EXISTS, WHILE ALSO WISHING I HAD NEVER SEEN IT.

THE STORY HINGES ON A SORT OF HALF-BODY SWITCHING PLOT, IN THAT SOME ABSOLUTELY NONSENSICAL RITUALISTIC/INTERPRETIVE DANCE BY AN OLD MAN REPLACES COREY'S TEENAGE PUNK ROCK PSYCHE WITH HIS OWN. AND WHAT A HILARIOUS MESS THAT SETS INTO MOTION.... BECAUSE OF COURSE, COREY FELDMAN IS **HARDCORE**! HIS BEST FRIEND IS A CRIPPLE NAMED "DINGER"! HIS OTHER BEST PAL IS A VIOLENT JOCK WITH ALL-TOO EASY ACCESS TO A GUN! AND WHILE CUTTING THROUGH PRIVATE PROPERTY ON THE WAY TO SCHOOL (AND THEREBY FLOUTING, FLOUTING I SAY, THE CONVENTIONS OF THE PERCY HOMEOWNERS' ACT OF 1924) HIS FRIENDS SING "WE'RE THE COOLEST GANG" OVER AND OVER AGAIN. I THOUGHT THAT IF YOU WERE COOL, YOU ALREADY KNEW IT, AND DON'T NEED TO CONSTANTLY ASSERT IT ALL THE TIME. HONESTLY.

NOW, I MUST SAY "BRAVO" TO MR. FELDMAN'S ACTING. AND BY BRAVO, I MEAN "YOU EAT ASS". WHEN DOES COREY FELDMAN REALLY GET INTO THE ROLE OF OLD MAN? IS IT WHEN HE'S ACTING LIKE COREY FELDMAN? OR HOW ABOUT WHEN HE'S DANCING AROUND LIKE MICHAEL JACKSON? THIS MOVIE HAS NO LOYALTY TO ITS OWN PLOT. MAYBE LIKE, THE SCREENWRITER AND THE DIRECTOR WERE DATING, AND SO THE FILM WAS LIKE, A LABOR OF LOVE? BUT THEN WHEN IT WAS GETTING MADE THE SCREENWRITER WAS CHEATING ON THE DIRECTOR SO HE SABOTAGED THEIR WORK OF ONCE BEAUTEOUS LOVE WITH COMPLETELY INEPT DIRECTORIAL CHOICES.

AWESOME!

GNARLY!

COREY? YOU EAT ASS.

RAD!

POP CULTURE JOKE

3 O'CLOCK HIGH (1987)

THE GORGEOUS SIMPLICITY OF THIS WAS WHAT WON ME OVER. AN ENTIRE PLOT BASED ON THE AVOIDANCE OF A FIGHT AT THREE O'CLOCK. THAT'S IT! THE ENTIRE FILM IS ALL ABOUT THE DIFFERENT WAYS OUR HERO JERRY GOES ABOUT TRYING TO AVOID GETTING HIS ASS KICKED. TOTALLY ROOLY. UNFORTUNATELY HOWEVER, JERRY - OR CASEY SIEMASZKO - IS TOTALLY A POOR MAN'S MATTHEW BRODERICK. HIS HAIRCUT IS JUST, JUST, INFURIATING, AND THERE WERE TIMES WHEN HIS DWEEBISHNESS WAS TOO MUCH FOR MY LOVE OF THE HIGH SCHOOL LOSER TO OVERCOME. LIKE HOW ABOUT HIS SALESMAN ROUTINE? "YOU KNOW WHEN YOU'RE DOING HOMEWORK IN BED...?" WHAT THE SHIT?

BUT THE KICKER THOUGH? NO LOVE STORY! IT'S LIKE

More fun than games!

JOY STICKS

JOY STICKS

THE ONLY TEEN MOVIE WITHOUT ONE. THEY EVEN SET IT UP SO BEAUTIFULLY WITH HIS BEST FRIEND AS A PRETTY, BUT SORT OF ALTERNATIVE/GEEKY GIRL THAT COULD TOTALLY HAVE HIT IT OFF WITH HIM. BUT THEY NEVER EVEN HINT AT THAT. MAYBE THOSE SCENES GOT CUT OUT. CRITERION? HELP US OUT HERE. THE CLOSEST THE LOVE ANGLE COMES OTHERWISE IS A GIRL IN A WHITE SWEATER, WHO HE BARELY EXCHANGES WORDS WITH.

INSTEAD OF LOVE, THE MOVIE INVESTS IN A MYRIAD OF SIMPLE DELIGHTS: MICROWAVING A SHIRT AND A POP TART AT THE SAME TIME; A "SUPERMOM" LICENSE PLATE; DIET COKE AND TOOTHPASTE; BARRY SONNENFELD'S WONDEROUS WORK AS A LIGHTING CONSULTANT; LISA SIMPSON IN A BIT PART; AND THAT'S ALL JUST IN THE FIRST 15 MINUTES?! AWESOME!! I JUST LOVE THE THRILLS AND EXCITEMENT THEY GET OUT OF SUCH A SIMPLE PLOT. AND WHEN JERRY PUKES OUT OF FEAR? MY GOD THAT WAS A NICE TOUCH. HOW CAN THIS MOVIE NOT BE GOOD? IT TEACHES YOU THAT VIOLENCE CAN IN FACT SOLVE PROBLEMS, TWO WORDS? **BRASS KNUCKLES.**

PRIVATE SCHOOL (1983)
WOW, YO. THE COMPLETELY NORMAL AND UNORIGINAL "GROWING PAINS" BEGINNING PREPARES YOU NOT AT ALL FOR THE BEAUTY OF THIS NUDITY-LADEN SEX-FEST. THE ANTAGONIST CHICK (IF YOU CAN CALL HER THAT) SERIOUSLY GOES TOPLESS 80% OF THE TIME SHE'S ON SCREEN. NOW **THIS** IS A MOVIE FOR TEENS. WHERE IS THE NUDITY IN TEEN MOVIES THESE DAYS, ANYWAYS? I DON'T KNOW WHAT HAPPENED, BUT I TOTALLY MISS THE EVER-NUDITY LOVIN' 80S WITH ALL ITS GRATUITOUSNESS.

ON TOP OF MILK-BAGS, THEY REWORK THE FORMULA FOR TEEN MOVIES ALTOGETHER. THE BIG DANCE/PROM SCENE IS FIVE MINUTES IN! THEN THERE'S PARENT-TEACHER DAY (WITH THE PEDOPHILIC FATHER), AND THAT'S NOT EVEN THE CLIMAX OF THE MOVIE. THERE ARE SO MANY PEAKS. LIKE SERIOUSLY, THIS BLOWS **PORKY'S** OUT OF THE FUCKING WATER. ABSOLUTELY EVERYONE INVOLVED IS OBSESSED WITH SEX. FROM THE RICH GIRL'S FATHER'S CHAUFFEUR, TO THE UGLY BEST FRIEND WITH THE STUPID HAT.

OH YES, I HIGHLY RECOMMEND THIS ONE, WITH ITS EXPLOITIVE GYMNASTICS ROUTINE, AND ITS TRIP TO THE SHOWER ROOM PACKED FULL OF PRETTY AND SHAPELY GIRLS. THIS MOVIE IS JUST SO HAPPILY GLEEFUL. THERE IS NOT A DROP OF MALICE IN THE ENTIRE MOVIE — JUST "LOOKIN' AT NAKED PEOPLE AND TALKIN' ABOUT SEX IS WHERE IT'S AT, DADDY-O" FUN. SERIOUSLY, FIND IT AND SEE IT. P.S. A FAT GUY FALLS OUT OF A SECOND STORY WINDOW NOT ONCE, BUT TWICE.

JOYSTICKS (1983)
ALL I KNOW IS THAT JOE DON BAKER IS ONE CAT **NOT** TO BE MESSED WITH. THE INFAMOUS "MITCHELL" STARS AS AN UNHAPPY FATHER TRYING TO SHUT DOWN A VIDEO ARCADE. AND BABY, THE ARCADE PORTRAYED HERE IS THE ULTIMATE MELTING POT OF TEEN CLIQUES. THEY'VE GOT PUNKS, HUNKS, SLUTS, VALLEY GIRLS, NERDS, AND ADULTS EVEN. IF I LEARNED ONLY ONE THING FROM THIS MOVIE, IT'S THAT VIDEO GAMES BUST DOWN SOCIAL WALLS. MAN, IF I HAD SEEN THIS ROMANTICIZED VIEW OF ARCADE CULTURE BACK IN MY FORMULATIVE YEARS, I WOULD PROBABLY NOT BE WRITING THIS REVIEW. I'D BE PLAYING A VIDEO GAME.

NOT ONLY IS EVERYONE WELCOME IN YON VIDEO PARLOUR, BUT IT'S ALSO A SEX-CRAZY CATHOUSE. SADLY, WE ONLY HAVE A COUPLE GIRLS DESIGNATED AS THE "NUDITY SUPPLIERS". WHAT THIS MEANS IS ALTHOUGH THERE ARE A FAIR AMOUNT OF BREASTS IN THE FILM, THEY ALL BELONG TO THE SAME 2 GIRLS. (ED. NOTE: OH MY GOD! THOSE GIRLS ARE MULTI-BREASTED FREAKS!?)

ONE THING THAT FREAKED ME OUT WERE THE HUGE CONTROLLERS THEY USED TO PLAY IN THE TOURNAMENTS. THESE WERE GIANT PHALLIC JOYSTICKS COMING OUT OF THE GROUND THAT THE TWO PLAYERS WOULD STRADDLE AND TOTALLY JERK AROUND IN AN EFFORT TO SCORE. POINTS THAT IS. IT'S SO DISTURBING; JUST THESE GIANT PENISES OPERATED BY PEOPLE WITH THE MOST INTENSE LOOK ON THEIR FACES. MY FAVORITE PART OF THOSE SCENES WAS WHEN THE "VIDIOT" (WHO PLAYS ON BEHALF OF THE EVIL JOE DON BAKER) STARTS GETTING ARROGANT ABOUT WINNING AND STARTS TO LICK THE BUTTONS TO PUSH THEM. I CAN STILL SEE THAT MENTAL PICTURE IN MY HEAD.

THE LAST AMERICAN VIRGIN (1982)
ANOTHER FILM FILLED TO THE BRIM WITH GOOD-TIME HAPPY THINGS.

A. THE MAIN VEHICLE IS A PINK STATION WAGON WITH A PINK FLAMINGO ON THE TOP.
B. PEOPLE SNORT SWEET N' LOW.
C. ACCIDENTAL ATTEMPTED MOTHER COPULATION
D. A LOCKER ROOM PENIS MEASURING COMPETITION; "WHOEVER'S GOT THE BIGGEST TOOL WINS THE POOL!" WHY WOULD THE PERSON SITTING AT THREE AND A HALF EVEN ENTER??

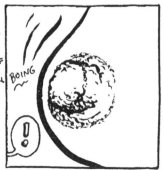

BOING

A CLOSE-UP OF A SCENE FROM **PRIVATE SCHOOL**

E. THE TRICKIEST AND CLEVEREST WAY EVER TO GIVE SOMEONE A RIDE. YOU LET THE AIR OUT OF HER SCOOTER'S TIRES, AND THEN WAIT UNTIL SHE CAN'T GET TO SCHOOL AND PULL UP LIKE A PRINCE CHARMING.

F. THE MOST HAPPENING PARTY **EVER**. TOTALLY 80s. I'VE NEVER BEEN TO A HOUSE PARTY WHERE PEOPLE DANCE. LET ME SAY NOW AND **FOREVER**: I WANT TO.

G. DRINKING AS A SOLUTION TO SADNESS.

H. BEST FRIENDS SEND THE DRUNKEN SOLUTION SEEKER ON HIS WAY IN HIS CAR. MAN - DRINKING AND DRIVING USED TO BE TOTALLY KOSHER.

I. STINKING DRUNK MAIN CHARACTER HITTING ON HIS PARENTS' ELDERLY DINNER GUESTS. "I THINK YOU NEED TO TAKE A COLD SHOWER GARY". "ONLY IF YOU JOIN ME BABY, CAUSE I KNOW WHAT YOU NEED!"

J. A GANG-BANG WITH A SPANISH CHICK.

K. STEALING THE PENIS CONTEST WINNER'S CAR AND DRIVING IT INTO THE OCEAN.

L. VIRGINITY LOSS TO AN IMPATIENT WHORE WITH STD'S.

M. THE ULTIMATE HUMP N' DUMP.

N. TEEN PREGNANCY.

O. AND THE ULTIMATE IN BAD TASTE: THE ABORTION CLINIC NUDITY. ALWAYS CALLED FOR. I WAS KICKING MY LITTLE FEET IN THE AIR AT THAT PART, I TELL YOU WHAT.

AND FINALLY, THIS MOVIE HAS THE MOST EXTREME AND NON-STOP ULTIMATE ENDING. THE MOST DEPRESSING AND QUICK ENDING TO A TEEN MOVIE I'VE EVER SEEN. SOOOOO CRESENT FRESH. IN FACT, I THINK THIS IS THE **ONLY** TEEN MOVIE TO END UNHAPPILY. KUDOS TO YOU LAST AMERICAN VIRGIN. NEEDLESS TO SAY, ONE OF MY DEFINITE FAVORITES.

STARTS FRI., JAN. 14th AT A SELECTED THEATRE NEAR YOU

NOT A LOVE STORY (1981)
EVER WONDERED ABOUT THE NATURE OF PORN AND HUMAN SEXUALITY FROM THE VIEWPOINT OF WOMEN WHO VIEW IT AS ONE OF THE MOST VILE EXPRESSIONS OF HUMAN LIFE? HOW ABOUT THE CONCEPT OF THE SUFFERING FEMALE GLORIOUSLY THRUSTING HERSELF INTO IMAGINED MARTYRDOM AND VICTIM-HOOD SIMPLY THROUGH THE ACT OF BARING HER NUDE FORM? SEEM KOOKY? WELL HAVE I GOT A MOVIE FOR YOU! **NOT A LOVE STORY** NOT ONLY PROBES AND PICKS AT THE MENTAL SCABS OF CENSORSHIP-BASED RADICAL FEMINISM, IT WAS ALSO PRODUCED AND DIRECTED BY ONE OF THEIR OWN EARTH-MOTHER-GRANOLA-CONSERVATISM-FLAVORED MEMBERS.

DIRECTOR BONNIE SHERR KLEIN OPENS HER CONTROVERSIAL 1981 DOCUMENTARY EXPLAINING HER REASONS FOR MAKING IT. THE IDEA STRUCK HER WHEN HER DAUGHTER, AN 8 YEAR OLD NAOMI KLEIN (THE NOW CELEBRATED AUTHOR OF THE ANTI-GLOBALIZATION BESTSELLER "**NO LOGO**") WAS GREETED BY "A ROW OF TITS AND ASS MAGAZINES" AT A LOCAL CONVENIENCE STORE. THE SCENE IS HOKILY RECONSTRUCTED, WITH BONNIE'S NARRATION GLIBLY INTONING "WHAT COULD SHE THINK OF HER OWN SELF AND OWN LITTLE BODY SURROUNDED BY THIS?" IN LATER YEARS, NAOMI'S MILITANT MOTHER HAS ADMITTED THAT THIS ENTIRE PREMISE WAS "A TREMENDOUS INVASION OF NAOMI'S PRIVACY", A FACT THAT A YOUNG NAOMI WAS QUICK TO RECOGNIZE. IT WAS HARD TO MISS: THE FILM MADE HER MOTHER BOTH A CAUSE CELEBRE WITH THE MAN-HATING ANTI-SEXUALITY ANDREA DWORKIN CROWD, AND AN INSTANT MORTAL ENEMY OF OUTSPOKEN PORN MONGERS LIKE LARRY FLYNT, WHO NAMED BONNIE "ASSHOLE OF THE MONTH" IN THE PAGES OF HIS MAGAZINE, HUSTLER.

FROM THERE THE DIRECTOR SHAMES AND HUMILIATES A STRIPPER NAMED LINDA LEE TRACEY INTO GIVING UP HER TRADE. TRACEY WHO IS ACTUALLY MORE OF A QUAINT BURLESQUE PERFORMER, IS AT FIRST DEFIANT AND STRONG - STATING THAT SHE DOESN'T FEEL THAT STRIPPING IS DEGRADING, AND THAT SHE FEELS PROUDLY AWARE OF HER SEXUALITY AND VIEWS HER GOOD-TIMEY ACT AS A PARODY OF EROTICISM. A STANCE THAT MAKES IT IMPOSSIBLE FOR HER TO

A TIDBIT CONCERNING **NOT A LOVE STORY**, FROM AN INTERVIEW WITH RON JEREMY. CONDUCTED BY CINEMA SEWER REPORTER AND SULTAN OF SIN: DIMITRIOS OTIS.

Dimitrios Otis - Would you describe yourself as a moral man?

Ron Jeremy - I like to think I am. I don't say I'm a big preacher. I don't think I walk around preaching this. But I think I have some rules and regulations I've gone by. I've chosen not to do any films which have any kind of coercion or anything strong against women. But what the Canada Film Board [sic - Jeremy is referring to the National Film Board] did and I thought was very disgusting - I'd love to have this on record - was a dirty, filthy stinking trick; and they did two things that I think were really heinous, in that NOT A LOVE STORY. These right wing conservatives, feminists - that's probably how they are, that made that movie called NOT A LOVE STORY, from Canada.

Number one: they used hard core to help sell the film while they're insulting it and knocking it. Who are they kidding? You think people don't see through that stupidity? Then they write how packed the theatre was when they played it. Yeah, people wanted to see hard-core, they're probably watching it with one hand. So they played it in parts of America, and I cracked up.

CONTINUED ON THE NEXT PAGE

CONTINUED FROM PREVIOUS PAGE....

I mean, how dare they use hard core in the movie when they are saying how disgusting and bad it is. They actually showed insertion with a girl named Patrice Trudeau doing a scene with a guy in a peep show booth. I said, "That's a hard core shot, I don't believe this."

They didn't put X's over it or bars or anything. They showed it. That's number one; it's the oldest and most hypocritical trick in the book - you insult something while you're making money off of it. They exploited this girl just as much as the porn people did, in fact more - the porn people paid her, the Canada Film Board did not. They just used old footage, calling it a documentary.

Number Two - the second thing that pissed me off, is that they always try to slant things their way, they kept showing S&M scenes of the man ball-gagging the woman, piercing the woman, nipple-clipping the woman. But anybody that knows anything about the world of S&M, and I don't cause I'm not in that world, or B&D — it's a whole separate part of a video store - knows there's JUST AS much if not more of the man being the slave and the lady being the dominatrix . She's putting her high heels in his back, he's wearing a ball gag, he's getting his nipples clipped. You ask any store owner - and I did - all over the US and Canada - and they'll say in the world of S&M and BD there's just as much - if not MORE - of the man being the victim or the subject or the bottom and the woman being the top. They even have companies in America that are run and owned by women, but that Canada Film Board had the audacity to just show the one side, to stress their viewpoint in a totally unfair, unbalanced attitude, and there's no way you cannot agree with me.

— THANKS TO SENORE OTIS

IDENTIFY WITH THE HARDCORE FEMINIST MOVEMENT WHICH HEAPS PITY UPON HER, AND FORCES HER INTO THE ROLE OF "VICTIM". BUT BEFORE THE CREDITS ROLL, KLEIN HAS PARADED HER IMPRESSIONABLE YOUNG "PROJECT" AROUND THE SLEAZIEST SECTIONS OF NEW YORK'S 42ND STREET, AND THROUGH COUNTLESS YELP-SESSIONS BY FEMI-NAZI SPEAKERS OF THE DAY LIKE DWORKIN, GRIFFIN AND LEDERER - AND FINALLY INTO A NUDE PHOTOGRAPHY SESSION. SOON AFTER, THE MODEL- NOW CONFUSED AND FEELING GUILTY FOR "DEBASING HERSELF", SUCCUMBS TO KLEIN'S NOTION THAT SHE'S ALLOWED HERSELF TO BE PATHETICALLY MOLDED AND SHAPED TO SATISFY MEN'S DESIRES FOR DOMINANCE. TRACEY BREAKS DOWN, ACCEPTS HER ROLE AS VICTIM, AND TEARFULLY SUBMITS TO KLEIN, ADMITTING THAT PORN IS ALL ABOUT "HEAVY POWER".

THE FILM DISPLAYS A SERIOUS LACK OF KNOWLEDGE OF THE HISTORY OF PORN, OR EVEN A BASIC UNDERSTANDING OF FILMS, PORNOGRAPHIC OR OTHERWISE, WITH IT'S OBVIOUSLY SLANTED EDITING. IRONICALLY, THIS INSUFFERABLY PREACHY FILM, NOW 23 YEARS OLD, HAS BECOME A VERY INTERESTING HISTORICAL DOCUMENT ITSELF, WITH FASCINATING FOOTAGE OF SLUMMY ADULT BOOKSTORES, PEEPSHOW BOOTHS, AND LONG-GONE THEATERS OF YESTERYEAR. THIS FOOTAGE, ALONG WITH THE EXAMPLES OF EXTREME PORN INTERSPERSED THROUGHOUT, WERE VERY "OUT THERE" AT THE TIME - CAUSING THE FILM TO BE BANNED FOR A TIME IN MANY MARKETS IN THE STATES, AND EVEN IN ONTARIO - THE BIRTH PLACE OF THE MOVIE. TODAY THE OFFENDING SCENES ARE FUCKING WICKED FROM A HISTORICAL STANDPOINT, BUT ARE ABOUT AS HARDCORE AND SHOCKING AS ANY GIVEN PIECE OF PORN-RELATED SPAM THAT MIGHT SHOW UP IN YOUR HOTMAIL ACCOUNT.

THERE IS AN EARNEST VIBE THAT BONNIE SHERR KLEIN AND HER FRIENDS WERE HONESTLY TRYING THEIR BEST TO GET A MALE-DOMINATED SOCIETY TO MAKE AMENDS FOR GENERATIONS OF FEMALE SECOND-CLASS CITIZENSHIP. THEY WERE HURTING, AND THEY WANTED SOMEONE TO PAY ATTENTION. BUT THIS FILM BEARS WITNESS TO THE FACT THAT THE SAD AND MISGUIDED STAUNCH CENSORSHIP TOWARDS SEXUALITY ITSELF IN THE EARLY YEARS OF ORGANIZED FEMALE EMPOWERMENT WAS CERTAINLY NOT THE ANSWER.

AND THE EFFECTS OF A FILM LIKE THIS ONE CAN BE QUITE POWERFUL. I REMEMBER READING THIS MINICOMIC BY LEANNE FRANSON IN 1993. HA! SO GOOD. ANOTHER ACCOUNT WAS THAT OF AUTHOR SONJA MILLS DETAILING HOW SHE WAS KICKED OUT OF A BELOVED LESBIAN WOMEN'S GROUP FOR DARING TO ADMIT THAT THE SEXUALLY EXPLICIT IMAGES IN THE DOCUMENTARY TURNED HER ON. THIS KIND OF THOUGHT-POLICING AND INTOLERANCE CERTAINLY BELIED THE "NEED TO UNDERSTAND" THAT DIRECTOR KLEIN PURPORTED TO HARVEST. NOWHERE WAS THERE ANY FORM OF CONTEXT SUPPLIED FOR THE FILMS CONTENT, AND NEITHER DOES THE MOVIE OFFER ANY SUBSTANTIAL OPPOSING VIEWS AS COUNTERPOINT.

THERE IS A SENSE THAT **NOT A LOVE STORY** WAS ORIGINALLY HERE TO "BLOW THE LID OFF" THE PORN INDUSTRY AND EXPOSE IT FOR THE EVIL EMPIRE IT'S PERCEIVED TO BE. INTERESTINGLY, ALL IT EXPOSES IS THE FACT THAT SOME PEOPLE TAKE

FROM LEANNE FRANSON'S *LILLIANE* #22 © 1993

A DISTURBING AMOUNT OF ISSUE WITH OTHER PEOPLE'S FREEDOM TO MAKE, SELL, AND CONSUME SEXUALLY EXPLICIT CONTENT.

THE FILM PRESENTS MEN (IRRESPECTIVE OF CLASS, AGE, OR PERSONALITY) AS WIELDING EQUAL POWER OVER WOMEN, WHO ARE PRESENTED AS INHERENTLY EASY TO MANIPULATE. IT ALSO IGNORES THE MEDIA'S ROLE IN SHAPING FEMALE DESIRES

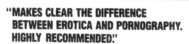

BOSTON REALLY LOVES "NOT A LOVE STORY"

NOT A LOVE STORY

a motion picture about
PORNOGRAPHY

AND BEHAVIOUR, AND NEVER BOTHERS TO SATISFACTORILY ANSWER THE BASIC QUESTION: WHAT IS PORNOGRAPHY? IT INSTEAD PRESENTS PORN AS A STATIC PHENOMENON THAT SHOULD BE DEFINED IRRESPECTIVE OF ANY PARTICULAR CONTEXT.

I THINK MOST SURPRISING TO PROPONENTS OF THE MOVIE WAS THE CONTENTIOUS AND UNEXPECTED EFFECT IT GENERATED WITHIN THE U.S. FEMINIST MOVEMENT ITSELF. WHILE THE NEW YORK-BASED WOMEN AGAINST PORNOGRAPHY (WAP) LAUDED THE MOVIE, VILLAGE VOICE CRITIC RUBY RICH DENOUNCED IT AS A "RELIGIOUS PARABLE" WHICH MERGES WITH RIGHT WING VIEWS ON SEXUAL REPRESSION. IN TURN, A GROUP OF FEMINISTS FROM NEW YORK, INCLUDING ROBIN MORGAN (WHO APPEARS IN THE FILM) WROTE A VENOMOUS RESPONSE TO RUBY RICH WHICH OBNOXIOUSLY QUESTIONED HER COMMITMENT TO THE WOMEN'S MOVEMENT BASED ON HER LACK OF SUPPORT FOR THE MOVIE.

"MAKES CLEAR THE DIFFERENCE BETWEEN EROTICA AND PORNOGRAPHY. HIGHLY RECOMMENDED."
—MS. MAGAZINE

NOT A LOVE STORY

a motion picture about
PORNOGRAPHY

Warning: If you are offended by graphic subject matter, we urge you not to see this film.

57TH PLAYHOUSE
Avenue of the Americas on 57th Street

IN 1987 BONNIE SHERR KLEIN'S LIFE WAS IRREVOCABLY CHANGED BY TWO SEVERE STROKES -- AFTER WHICH SHE WAS AFFLICTED BY "LOCKED-IN SYNDROME", A RARE NEUROLOGICAL DISORDER THAT LEAVES VICTIMS FULLY AWARE BUT UNABLE TO SPEAK OR MOVE. AFTER THREE YEARS OF THIS WAKING NIGHTMARE, SHE REHABILITATED ENOUGH TO REGAIN HER SPEECH AND LEARN TO BOOT AROUND ON A MOTORIZED SCOOTER SHE NAMED "GLADYS". SHERR KLEIN THEN EMERGED LIKE A PHOENIX FROM THE ASHES TO BECOME A PASSIONATE ACTIVIST FOR THE RIGHTS OF DISABLED PEOPLE. SHE ALSO MOVED TO VANCOUVER, WHERE I

SEE HER TOOTLING AROUND TOWN ON "GLADYS" -- ALTHOUGH I HAVE NEVER GROWN ENOUGH SCROTUM TO APPROACH HER ABOUT HER MOVIE. I'VE SEEN IT ENOUGH TIMES THOUGH, THAT I COULD PROBABLY QUOTE IT BACK TO HER.

LARRY FLYNT'S OVER THE TOP HUSTLER MAGAZINE COVER IMAGE THAT HAD ANTI-PORN FEMINISTS ACROSS THE CONTINENT CALLING FOR HIS HEAD IN THE EARLY 1980's.

NEVER MADE WIDELY AVAILABLE ON VIDEO OR DVD. THE ONLY WAY TO SEE THE MOVIE IS TO SCORE A BOOTLEG COPY, OR ORDER IT FROM THE STINGY-ASS NATIONAL FILM BOARD OF CANADA. IN ORDER TO GET THEM TO SELL YOU A $35 VHS COPY (THEIR SITE SAYS NOTHING ABOUT DVD??!) YOU 1.) MUST BE CANADIAN, 2.) MUST BE A TEACHER OR REPRESENTATIVE OF A SCHOOL.

—BOUGIE

"KLEIN'S PRETTY DEPRESSING VIEW IS THAT PORN IS NOT CULTURALLY DETERMINED, BUT BORN OF SOME 'INHERENTLY MALE' DRIVE TO HURT AND DEFILE. MOST DISTURBING OF ALL IS THAT KLEIN'S OWN CAMERA IS ITSELF OFTEN COMPULSIVELY AND RATHER UNPLEASANTLY VOYEURISTIC." - **TIME OUT FILM GUIDE**

"THE MOST INTERESTING INTERVIEW WAS WITH A WIFE AND HUSBAND WHO PERFORMED LIVE SEX ACTS TO EACH OTHER ON STAGE (SHE'S WHITE, HE'S BLACK). SHE ACTUALLY DEFENDS WHAT SHE'S DOING QUITE WELL, AND ACTUALLY HAD ME BELIEVING HER! IT'S HORRIFYING THAT SOME PEOPLE ENJOY THIS SORT OF ENTERTAINMENT."
—**WAYNE MALIN**, USA

"WHAT ABOUT THE LUSTFUL FEMALE GAZE? THE MOVIE DOESN'T GET INTO PORN THAT WOMEN MIGHT ENJOY, AND STEERS COMPLETELY CLEAR OF GAY MALE PORN AND S+M PORN WITH THE FEMALE AS DOMINATRIX -- TWO SUB GENRES OF EROTICA THAT BLOW KLEIN'S ARGUMENT OUT OF THE WATER."
—**ROB GONSALVES**, USA

THE SKELETAL UN-DEAD MAN THE HELM:

THE ATMOSPHERE OF AMANDO DE OSSORIO'S HORROR OF THE ZOMBIES...

BY:
SINISTER SAM McKINLAY
© 2004

paul NASCHY
emma COHEN
vic WINNER
helga LINE
cristina SURIANI

EL ESPANTO SURGE DE LA TUMBA

NASCHY'S "HORROR RISES FROM THE TOMB"

SKELETONS AND THE OCEAN HAVE ALWAYS HAD A STRONG CONNECTION. I RECENTLY PICKED UP THE COMPLETE SET OF REPRINTED 50s HORROR COMICS CALLED **TALES TOO TERRIBLE TO TELL**, AND ADORNING THE COVER OF ISSUE NINE WAS AN AMAZING COVER FROM THE HALLOWED DAYS OF PRE-CODE HORROR FEATURING A COUPLE OF SKELETONS - OR RATHER THE UNDEAD - ABOUT TO PICK UP A MAN WHO HAS BEEN STRANDED IN THE OCEAN. BEHIND THE SCENE LOOMS THE GALLEON THE SKELETONS DISEMBARKED FROM, ALSO COVERED IN A GHOSTLY SKELETAL CREW.

THIS STUNNING COVER BRINGS TO MY MIND THE JAPANESE HORROR CLASSIC **KYUKETSU DOKURO SEN** AKA "THE HUMAN SKELETON" (1968 DIR. BY HIROSHI MATSUNO) IN WHICH A MURDERED AND SUBSEQUENTLY SKELETAL CREW AND PASSENGERS ARE FREQUENTLY SHOWN CARTOONISHLY ABSTRACTED AND HANGING FROM THE BOAT TO THE WIDE-EYED ASTONISHMENT OF THE LIVE ACTORS. THE OTHER MAJOR FILM THAT COMES TO MIND IS AMANDO DE OSSORIO'S **HORROR OF THE ZOMBIES** AKA "THE GHOST GALLEON" (1974) WHICH FEATURES THE FAMOUS "BLIND DEAD", AND THEIR NEW DOMINION OVER THE OCEANS VIA A MENACING PARALLEL UNIVERSE/FOG AND A GHOST GALLEON.

SPAIN'S LEGACY TO 70s HORROR IS USUALLY OVERSHADOWED BY ALL THE ITALIAN GREATS OF THE GENRE STARTING FROM BAVA, FREDA, AND MARGHERITI'S GOTHIC FILMS THAT HELPED TO BUILD THE EXPORT INDUSTRY OF HORROR FILMS.

THE FACT IS THAT THE 70s WERE RUN BY THE GIALLO STRUCTURE AND THEME OF REALIST MYSTERY MURDER ACTS, EVENTUALLY DIRECTING THE ITALIAN HORROR BUSINESS INTO THE GOLDEN AGE OF GORE; THE EARLY 80s AND THE ZOMBIE SPLATTER PULLED ALONG BY NOW MODEST BUDGETS AND TALENTS SUCH AS LUCIO FULCI (FRESH FROM GIALLO MEDITATION HIMSELF).

SPANISH/ITALIAN CO-PRODUCTIONS SUCH AS TONINO VALERII'S **MY DEAR KILLER** (1972) WHICH BOASTED AMAZING CINEMATOGRAPHY, GEORGE HILTON AS THE LEAD, AND A VERY BARBARA STEELE-LIKE PATTY SHEPARD, WERE SOME OF THE BEST THRILLERS THE GENRE HAD TO OFFER IN THE 70s. "ATMOSPHERE" IS THE KEY WORD, AS THESE FILMS HAD A FIRM GRASP ON HOW TO MANIPULATE THE AUDIENCE'S REACTION BY MEANS OF A SPLENDID SPOOK SHOW SCENARIO. SPANISH HAUNTED HOUSE STYLE AND VISUALS HAVE ALWAYS HAD A VISCERAL UNDERLINING IN THE WORLD OF THE SPANISH HORROR FILM, ACHIEVING A STATUS UNLIKE EVEN ITALIAN HORROR FILMS POST-1970. DIRECTOR /WRITER/ACTOR PAUL NASCHY HAD MANY EXAMPLES - BUT ONE OF HIS FINEST ACHIEVEMENTS IS UNDOUBTEDLY HORROR RISES FROM THE TOMB (1972) DIRECTED BY THE GREAT CARLOS AURED - AND FEATURING SHOW-STOPPING HAUNTED AND CLAUSTROPHOBIC EVIL VIA VAMPIRISM, THE LIVING DEAD, DEAD SWAMPS, AND THE INESCAPABLE DARKNESS OF THE SURROUNDING LAKE AND THE LANDSCAPE.

BUT THE SPANISH DIRECTOR AT THE CENTER OF THE ATMOSPHERIC HORROR MOVEMENT IN HIS COUNTRY WAS AMANDO DE OSSORIO. OSSORIO HAD A GREAT PROLIFIC LINEAGE OF FILMS THAT RIVALED OR PARALLELED THE WORK OF JEAN ROLLIN IN REGARDS TO A PERVASIVE PERSONAL STYLE. FROM ONE OF HIS EARLIEST WORKS **FANGS OF THE LIVING DEAD** (1968) WHICH BOASTED A VAMPIRE PLOT LINE AND THE DARK COMPACT VISAGE OF A GOTHIC CASTLE, TO HIS LATER WORK **THE POSSESSED** (1974) WHICH FEATURED AN **EXORCIST**-STYLE STORYLINE EQUIPPED WITH DISTURBING AND EVEN DISTASTEFUL SEQUENCES COUPLED WITH THE MANDATORY SATANIC IMAGERY. OSSORIO EVEN HAD THE SPLATTER AND MASTERY OF THE MONSTER MOVIE COVERED, AS HIS **LORELEY'S GRASP** (1973) IS A FINE EXAMPLE OF

THE **CREATURE FROM THE BLACK LAGOON** AESTHETIC MIXED WITH GORE AND ANOTHER DARK LAKE (THE MONSTER'S HOME) THAT ACTS AS A DEPRESSING FOREGROUND TO THE ACTION AND THE STORY.

AMANDO DE OSSORIO'S MOST FAMOUS ACHIEVEMENTS IN THE WORLD OF THE HORROR FILM COLLECTOR ARE OBVIOUSLY HIS 'BLIND DEAD' FILMS. REVOLVING AROUND THE FRAMEWORK AND LEGEND OF THE NON-FICTIONAL TEMPLAR KNIGHTS THAT HAVE RETURNED AS THE ITALO-STYLE ZOMBIE UN-DEAD WITH THEIR EYES EATEN OUT BY BIRDS, (OR BURNED OUT, DEPENDING ON WHICH YOU PREFER) OSSORIO BUILT A MINI SPANISH EMPIRE AND SERIES AROUND THE LUMBERING AND SKELETAL HORSE-DRIVEN DEAD MEN. IN TOTAL, THERE ARE 4 FILMS IN THE SERIES (IF YOU DON'T COUNT JESUS FRANCO'S UNOFFICIAL X-RATED 1982 SEQUEL **MANSION OF THE LIVING DEAD**) THAT ARE ALL AMAZING AND WELL RESPECTED WITHIN THE ANNALS OF EUROTRASH FANDOM.

LIVING DEAD MEN—
Existing on the FLESH of
the YOUNG &
BEAUTIFUL!

HORROR OF THE ZOMBIES

starring MARIA PERSCHY • JACK TAYLOR
in EASTMAN COLOR

THE SERIES FEATURES THE INTRODUCTORY AND EXPLICIT **TOMBS OF THE BLIND DEAD** (1971) WHICH INCLUDES THE YOU-BECOME-A-ZOMBIE-IF-BITTEN-BY-ONE RULE, **RETURN OF THE BLIND DEAD** (1973) A MORE ACTION PACKED RIDE THAN THE FIRST, YET LACKS IN SOME OF THE DEVELOPMENTAL ISSUES, **HORROR OF THE ZOMBIES** (1974), AND THE EYE-BLEEDING **NIGHT OF THE SEAGULLS** WHICH WAS SOAKED IN SEASIDE IMAGERY IMPALED UPON EXAMPLES OF CREATURE WORSHIP AND TOWN PAGAN RITUAL.

MY FAVORITE FILM IN THE "FRANCHISE" AND THE MOST ELUSIVE TO FIND UNCUT (EVEN MORE SO THAN THE RARE PRINT OF THE PRE-ANCHOR BAY **TOMBS OF THE BLIND DEAD** THAT INCLUDED THE TRAIN MASSACRE) IS **HORROR OF THE ZOMBIES**. FOR THE LONGEST TIME, A COPY WAS FLOATING AROUND FROM "WORLD'S WORST VIDEOS" THAT WAS MISSING SOME KEY GORE SCENES, BUT HAS ALL THE STUNNING HAUNTED ATMOSPHERE OF THE GHOST GALLEON INTACT.

THE PLOT FOLLOWS SOME BIKINI MODELS WHO GET RAMMED HARD BY THE GALLEON DURING A PUBLICITY STUNT IN A POWER BOAT — HENCE THEIR DECIDING TO BOARD THE OLD SHIP TO DISCOVER THE BONE-CHILLING FACT THAT THE BLIND DEAD ARE LIVING ABOARD THE VESSEL IN COFFINS — JUST WAITING FOR NUBILE
VICTIMS. THE GALLEON'S INTERIOR AND EXTERIOR ARE THE ULTIMATE EXAMPLES OF A CINEMATIC GHOST SHIP, WITH OLD ROTTED, DANK, AND DECREPIT WOODWORK A SEARCH PARTY IS RUSTLED UP BY A CARING FRIEND, AND THE BRAINS BEHIND THE PUBLICITY STUNT (SPANISH HORROR MAINSTAYS JACK TAYLOR AND MARIA PERSCHY) ADD TO THE FUN AS THEY ALSO FIND THE ENVELOPING FOG AND GALLEON THAT LURKS WITHIN. THE GORE SCENES FOLLOW, AND THE PRIMARY CUT SCENE BECOMES VISIBLE (THE DISMEMBERING OF ONE OF THE SCREAMING GIRLS) AND THE BLIND DEAD ARE SEEMINGLY PUT TO DEATH AS THE VERITABLE TREASURE IS STOLEN AND THE COFFINS ARE TOSSED IN THE SEA.

IN SOME CIRCLES, **HORROR OF THE ZOMBIES** IS REGARDED AS THE WEAKEST IN THE SERIES, BUT I CONSIDER THESE OBJECTIONS TO THE FILM AS PURELY DUE TO THE LACK OF SMOOTHNESS AND PLOT DEVELOPMENT/FX, WITHOUT TAKING INTO ACCOUNT THE COMPETENT RING

INTERFILME P.C. (LISBOA).   TECHNICOLOR   70 m/m

OF ATMOSPHERE AND PURE CREATIVE ABSTRACTION THAT THE FILM ACHIEVES. YES, THE FOOTAGE OF THE MODEL BOAT ON THE WATER FORCES THE VIEWER TO SUSPEND SOME DISBELIEF, BUT THIS MOVIE IS STILL REPRESENTATIVE OF A PERFECT AMALGAMATION OF SPANISH HORROR STYLING FROM THE 70S, EXECUTED MASTERFULLY BY ONE OF THE LEADING CREATIVE AND DIRECTORIAL GENRE FORCES OF THE TIME. IT'S A CONDENSED CELLULOID ANOMALY THAT SUBJECTS THE VIEWER TO A BLEED OF ALL THE ITALO-GOTHIC STYLIZATIONS COUPLED WITH THE 'VAST' HISTORY OF THE DECREPIT EARLY 70S SPANISH HORROR.

☆☆☆ C.S. WRITER "SINISTER SAM" IS BETTER KNOWN IN NOISE MUSIC CIRCLES AS "THE RITA", AND HAS BUILT A SOLID REP IN THE HARSH NOISE GENRE WITH TOURS THROUGHOUT NORTH AMERICA AND JAPAN. —ED.

YET ANOTHER VICTIM OF THE BLIND DEAD IN OSSORIO'S "HORROR OF THE ZOMBIES".

Kit Kat EXPERIMENT #17

2003. AKA: "EXPERMENT AUSGELIEFERT SEIN 17"

GOOD CHRIST... THIS IS ONE INTENSE PORN MOVIE, AND HAS ONLY STRENGTHENED MY OPINION THAT ANYONE WHO HAS TOLD ME HOW SICK THEY THINK NORTH AMERICAN PORN HOUNDS ARE (SUCH AS JIM POWERS, MAX HARDCORE AND KHAN TUSION), HAVE NO FUCKING CLUE WHAT HAS BEEN COMING OUT OF GERMANY THESE DAYS.

"KIT KAT: EXPERIMENT 17" IS A SINGLE VIDEOTAPED SCENE THAT TAKES PLACE IN BERLIN'S INFAMOUS KIT KAT FETISH SEX CLUB, AND LASTS FOR NEARLY 2 HOURS. IT FEATURES A HERD OF GUYS AND ONE FRIENDLY LOOKING SHORT HAIRED BLONDE FRAÜLINE WHO, WHILE SUBMISSIVE AND CONSENTING, GETS ABUSED BEYOND IMAGINATION. I'M NOT GOING TO WASTE OUR TIME BY JUSTIFYIN OR CONDEMNING VICTIM FLAVORED GENDER POLITICS IN PORN, OR EXPOUND ON THE RIGHT OR WRONGS OF EXTREME DEBASEMENT AND HUMILIATION BASED XXX. JUST FEEL FREE TO APPLY YOUR OWN VALUES TO THIS BLOW BY BLOW SYNOPSIS.

THE "FUN" STARTS WITH OUR NAKED GERMAN PORN SLUT RIDING INTO THE OPULENT CLUB ON A SILVER 'RAZOR' SCOOTER BEFORE BEING CHASED AND HAULED DOWN LIKE WILD GAME BY A GROUP OF MEN IN SUITS, WHO THEN PLACE HER IN A WOODEN BONDAGE STOCKADE ON HER BACK, AND TAKE TURNS PISSING IN HER FACE AND OPEN MOUTH. THESE AREN'T GENTLEMEN, AND AFTER ABOUT 20 MINUTES OF THIS, THEY LET HER OUT AND SHE BLOWS A FEW OF THEM WHILE TAKING EVEN MORE PISS DOWN THE GULLET. IT'S QUIRKY, BUT THIS TIMID NERDY-LOOKING GIRL SEEMS TO GENUINELY ENJOY THE FLAVOR OF PEE, ONLY SEEMING DISTRESSED WHEN ONE OF THE COCKS POWERS ITS GOLDEN SPRAY UP HER NOSE, CAUSING HER TO COUGH AND GASP WILDLY FOR AIR.

THEY MOVE HER ON HER BACK TO A LONG WEIRD LOOKING LOUNGE CHAIR, AND 5 GLOOMY LOOKING EUROSTUDS PISS HARD IN HER FACE AT THE SAME TIME! KEEP IN MIND THE POOR GIRL HAS TAKEN BLADDER AFTER BLADDER OF WIZZ DOWN HER THROAT, AND HER GUT BAG HAS SWOLLEN TO UNCOMFORTABLE PROPORTIONS WITH THE AMOUNT OF LIQUID SHE'S INJESTED. IN RESPONSE, THE MEN TWIST AND WRENCH HER LEGS AND BACK OVER HER HEAD AND ORDER HER TO UNLOAD. SHE GROANS AND RELIEVES HERSELF ALL OVER HER OWN FACE WHILE 2 MORE GUYS RAIN YET ANOTHER GOLDEN SHOWER DOWN ON HER.

≡FFSSSHHH≡

AT THIS POINT YOU REALLY BEGIN TO FEEL FOR HER BECAUSE..... HOLY FUCK... IT'S FISTING TIME! THE GUYS TAKE TURNS ROUGHLY FISTING HER PUSSY USING A PUNCHING MOTION AND POWER THAT I DIDN'T THINK WAS POSSIBLE TO RECEIVE IN ONE'S GROIN WITHOUT SEVERE PHYSICAL TRAUMA — BUT SOMEHOW THIS AMAZING HUMP-MONKEY IS STRETCHED ENOUGH TO DO IT WITHOUT PASSING OUT. AT ONE POINT A FIST IS RAMMED **ALL** THE WAY UP INSIDE HER WHILE AT THE SAME TIME A RIDING CROP IS USED TO SMACK HER EXPOSED SWOLLEN BUTTHOLE!

AFTER THE MOANING GIRL'S ANUS AND VAGINA ARE VIOLATED BY MULTIPLE DIGITS, SHE'S EVENTUALLY ALLOWED TO SIT UP AND DRAIN SOME MORE OF HER RECYCLED PISS,

THIS PJRNZ IZ CRAY ZEEE

-- THIS TIME INTO THE MOUTH OF A SUBMISSIVE GUY WHO HAD BEEN HANGING AROUND WAITING FOR A WARM DRINK.

BUT THIS SEXUAL NIGHTMARE CAUGHT ON TAPE IS FAR FROM OVER. NOW IT'S BACK TO THAT UNCOMFORTABLE LOOKING STOCKADE (WHICH IS A WORD OF GERMANIC ORIGIN, I'LL HAVE YOU KNOW), THIS TIME ON HER KNEES. OUR STAR IS THEN PAINFULLY SPANKED WITH RIDING CROPS WHILE 5 MEN PISS IN AND ON HER, ANOTHER FINE GENTLEMAN STUFFS HIS WANG DOWN HER THROAT (MAKING HER GAG VIOLENTLY) JUST BEFORE THE STATELY SQUIRE BEHIND HER FIST FUCKS HER PUSSY SO HARD, HE ACTUALLY **LIFTS** HER BODY A COUPLE OF FEET OFF THE GROUND. AGAIN, THIS IS SOMETHING I PREVIOUSLY DID NOT KNOW WAS POSSIBLE WITHOUT DOING SOME DAMAGE TO THE FISTEE, BUT THIS CHICA IS A DAMN PRO! WHILE THIS IS GOING ON, THE SADISTIC CAMERAMAN GETS A CLOSE UP ON HER FACE AS HE JABS HIS HAND INTO HER DROOLING PIE HOLE OVER AND OVER, EVENTUALLY CAUSING HER TO PUKE UP HER YELLOW BUBBLING TUMMY CONTENTS.

HER CALM AND SILENT TORMENTORS LET HER OUT OF THE STOCKADE, FORCIBLY BEND HER OVER A TABLE, AND USE AN AGONIZINGLY HUGE INFLATABLE BUTTPLUG ON HER TUSH UNTIL SHE LOOKS NEAR HER BREAKING POINT. THEN IT'S DOWN ON ALL FOURS SO THE WHOLE GANG CAN TAKE TURNS ROUGHLY SODOMIZING HER. THE ANUS IN QUESTION IS OBVIOUSLY INFLAMED AND CAUSING HER A FAIR AMOUNT OF GRIEF, BUT I'LL BE DAMNED IF SHE ISN'T ENJOYING BEING A RECIPIENT OF THIS SADISM AND BRUTALLY PUNISHING PARADE OF WONDERS.

BRAAAPP
HONNK

KITKAT EXPERIMENT #17 "SWALLOWING FARTS"

A REPRIEVE (OF SORTS) COMES WHEN FIVE GUYS TAKE UP POSITIONS IN A LINE -- ON THEIR BACKS AND WITH THEIR LEGS THROWN UP IN THE AIR. BLONDIE THEN DILIGENTLY DROPS TO HER KNEES WHILE THEY EXPOSE THEIR PUCKERED POOPERS, AND GOES FROM SPHINCTER TO SPHINCTER PROBING AND DIGGING INTO THOSE BUNGPITS WHILE THEY **FART ON HER TONGUE!!** THE LIL' TROOPER BARELY REACTS TO THE POOCHED POOHOLES SPITTING BOWEL GAS INTO HER MOUTH, OBVIOUSLY QUITE ACCUSTOMED TO BEING RELEGATED TO THIS SORT OF DEHUMANIZING AND DEPRAVED SEX PLAY.

THE EVENTS OF THE LAST TWO HOURS ARE NOW WEARING ON HER AS THE MEN START SHOVING THEIR PORK SWORDS IN HER FACE AGAIN. DEEP THROATING IS NOW CAUSING HER TO SPIT UP, WHICH SHE APOLOGIZES FOR IN TRUE SUBMISSIVE STYLE. A FEW JIZZUM BLASTS ARE SHOT ON HER TONGUE BEFORE SHE'S GIVEN A TOOTHBRUSH AND BRUSHES HER TEETH USING THE BALL-BATTER AS TOOTHPASTE. FINALLY, 3 DUDES PISS IN HER OPEN MOUTH AT THE SAME TIME -- AND THIS IS THE FINAL HURRAH FOR THE POOR WOMAN AS SHE HURLS A VILE MIX OF SPERM, PISS (SOOO MUCH PISS) AND STOMACH CONTENTS I CAN'T IDENTIFY. GOOD LORD.

"I'M DEFINITELY GOING TO HELL FOR THIS ONE, GUYS -- SO BUY IT WHILE YOU CAN!!" WAS THE WORD FROM MIKE AT THE DVD MAIL ORDER SERVICE I GOT THIS FROM. MIKE HAS 100 DIFFERENT DVDS OF SICKENING AND JAWDROPPINGLY VILE RECENT GERMAN PORN THAT GLEEFULLY SKULLFUCKS HIS CUSTOMER'S BRAINS -- INCLUDING THE AMAZING AND SOMEWHAT INFAMOUS **BETTY EXTREME** FROM THOSE PERVERTS AT "GGG".

—BOUGIE

THE REACTION FROM READERS ABOUT THIS REVIEW WAS VARIED AND PLENTIFUL -- WITH MORE COMPLAINTS REGISTERED ABOUT IT THAN ANYTHING I'D PRINTED BEFORE. ONE SUCH CORRESPONDENCE FOLLOWS:

READER MAIL INTERVIEW: DEBATING
"KIT KAT EXPERIMENT #17"
(A conversation with John Curzon)

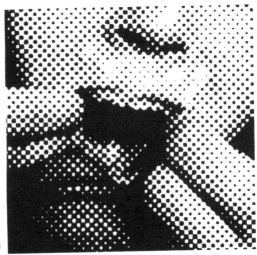

John Curzon: Hey Bougie man. It bothers me that the first time I'm writing to you after being a fan for quite a long time is a message with a beef rather than one of praise. Praise is definitely something you are overdue for, I've been reading Cinema Sewer since issue 8 and have completely loved it up until #16 and your article on the Kit Kat Experiment #17.

Honestly Robin, I read CS a lot and my tolerance for fucked up shit is high, but this article crossed a line. I felt ill after reading about all the terrible things done to that poor chicka. It's not the first (or probably that last) time you've written about freaky sex, but the difference between KKE and say, Bodil (He's referring to the article on Bodil Joensen in CS #13 - Ed) is that Bodil wasn't being hurt and humiliated in such a insanely brutal way.

You said yourself that you didn't think that some of the shit in KKE could be done without serious damage to the woman, and I wouldn't be surprised if there was damage done. But Bodil was fucking animals for her own pleasure and I have serious doubts that the girl from KKE was enjoying what was being done to her. I won't presume to know enough about the porn industry to say that I know what the conditions were that she was forced into "starring" and I do acknowledge that all porn has an element of exploitation going through it but this movie was just so BRUTAL in what it does.

ROBIN BOUGIE: UNFORTUNATELY, YOU ARE PRESUMING. UNTIL YOU SEE THE VIDEO FOR YOURSELF, I'M AFRAID THAT YOU WOULD BE IN BETTER SHAPE TAKING MY WORD FOR THE FACT THAT THE GIRL IN THIS TAPE WAS NOT FORCED AGAINST HER WILL. I KNOW IT'S NOT REALLY FAIR TO YOU SINCE MY DESCRIPTIONS OF THE TAPE PULLED NO PUNCHES AND TRIED TO PLAY IT OUT FOR MAXIMUM DESCRIPTIVE AND EMOTIONAL EFFECT, BUT I'M AFRAID I HAVE TO TAKE SOME ISSUE WITH YOUR ASSUMPTION THAT SIMPLY BECAUSE THE GENDER OF THE "VICTIM" IN THE TAPE WAS FEMALE, THAT SHE WAS AUTOMATICALLY COERCED OR NOT ENJOYING THE SEVERE TREATMENT BEING UNLEASHED UPON HER. IT'S AN ODD FORM OF SEXISM TO ASSUME THAT WOMEN ARE NOT ALLOWED TO ACTIVELY TAKE PART IN SUBMISSION AND HUMILIATION-THEMED FETISHISM — THAT THIS SOMEHOW EQUALS ACTUAL ABUSE.

I'VE SEEN TAPES WHERE SOME GUY IS LAYING ON THE GROUND AND HAVING HIS NUTS PAINFULLY SQUASHED WHILE SOME WOMAN ANGRILY SHOVES HER PUSSY IN HIS FACE — AND THESE GUYS SCREAM OUT IN BLISSFUL AGONY. THESE MEN ARE MASOCHISTS, AND DESPITE THE FACT THAT

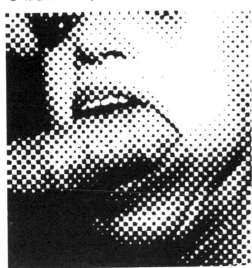

THESE "VICTIMS" ARE BEING ABUSED AND DEGRADED, OUR AUTOMATIC ASSUMPTION IS THAT THEY ARE PERVERTED SEX FREAKS. WE DO NOT FEEL PITY OUTSIDE OF THE OBVIOUS "I'M GLAD THOSE AREN'T MY BALLS BEING HAMMERED!" LEG-CROSSING OR A QUESTIONING OF HOW FUCKIN' MESSED UP YOU WOULD HAVE TO BE TO GET ENJOYMENT OF SUCH A THING. SO IF I WROTE A SYNOPSIS OF THAT TAPE, YOU WOULD NEVER WRITE TO ME AND SAY "HOW COULD YOU CONDONE THE ABUSE OF THAT POOR MAN??" BECAUSE YOU WOULD ACCEPT AND ASSUME HE WAS JUST A PERVERT THAT GOT OFF ON THAT KIND OF THING. PEOPLE RARELY GIVE WOMEN THAT SAME ALLOWANCE. SUDDENLY WHEN IT'S A WOMAN IN AN IDENTICAL ROLE WE MAKE ALL THESE ASSUMPTIONS, BECAUSE DESPITE WHAT WE LIKE TO THINK ABOUT OURSELVES, WE AS A SOCIETY STILL THINK OF WOMEN AS BEING MENTALLY AND PHYSICALLY INFERIOR, EASY TO MANIPULATE, AND NOT IN CONTROL. NIGGA PLEASE! FUCK THAT SEXIST SHIT!!

JC: I'm sorry man, but we can debate whether she was the victim or not but my assumption was anything but sexist. First of all, it's KKE!!! This video is a brutally misogynistic pornography. created to serve as masturbatory fodder for sadists. It is in itself sexist, so it's kind of contradiction that my concern for the actress would be sexist. And I would argue that in the case of a male masochist there is a lesser likelihood that he would be exploited, if only for the fact you hardly see men looking "exploited" in a porno.

RB: READING BACK OVER MY DESCRIPTION IN THE REVIEW, I FEEL THAT I'VE MADE IT OBVIOUS THAT THE GIRL IN THIS TAPE IS A TRIED AND TRUE SUBMISSIVE THAT GETS OFF ON SEXUAL HUMILIATION. SHE'S ALSO VERY EXPERIENCED AT WHAT SHE DOES, AS EVIDENCED BY THE FACT THAT SHE'S ABLE TO PERFORM JAW-DROPPING NEAR SUPERHUMAN ACTS OF PENETRATION, URINE INGESTION AND WHATNOT. THIS GIRL GETS A WET NASTY FART ON HER TONGUE AND SHE DOESN'T REACT OUTSIDE OF SMILING. THIS IS A PRO. SHE'S "IN THE LIFESTYLE", AS THEY SAY.

I DON'T MEAN TO COME DOWN HARD ON YOU, BUT THIS REALLY IS ONE OF MY PET PEEVES: GUYS WHO THINK THEY ARE DOING THE RIGHT THING COMING TO THE DEFENCE AND SEE THEMSELVES AS PROTECTING THE HONOR OF 'POOR DEFENCELESS WOMEN', AND WHO SAY THEY BELIEVE IN EQUALITY OF THE SEXES, BUT THEY DON'T THINK ABOUT WHAT THAT REALLY MEANS. I'M GONNA RANT A LITTLE HERE, SO HOLD ON TO YOUR HAT:

I VERY MUCH BELIEVE IN TOTAL EQUALITY, AND I HAVE THE UTMOST RESPECT FOR WOMEN — AND I WON'T LIE TO YOU MAN, IT MAKES ME A LITTLE ANGRY WHEN I GET MAIL FROM READERS (ALMOST ALWAYS MEN DESPITE THE FACT

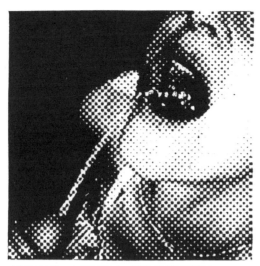

THAT CINEMA SEWER HAS A VERY LARGE FEMALE READERSHIP) WHINING AND COMPLAINING THAT I'VE REVIEWED SOME FILM THAT THEY THINK IS SEXIST OR CONDONES THE ABUSE OF WOMEN. I WOULD NEVER PROMOTE A FILM WHERE A WOMAN WAS BEING ACTUALLY RAPED. I FIND THAT PEOPLE WHO CAN'T ACCEPT THAT THERE ARE WOMEN OUT THERE THAT LOVE KINKY SEX - THEY ARE THE ONES WHO DON'T RESPECT WOMEN, NOT THE PERFORMERS IN THE KINKY VIDEO. WOMEN ARE NOT PRECIOUS STONES, THEY ARE HUMAN TOO. THEY SHIT, FART, THEY HAVE FETISHES AND DISTASTEFUL URGES JUST LIKE MEN DO. A HUMAN BEING IS A HUMAN BEING NO MATTER WHAT KIND OF WEIRD VARIATION OF CONSENSUAL ADULT SEX THEY HAVE. I DON'T MIND DEBATING THIS STUFF WITH YOU BUT I DON'T HAVE MUCH PATIENCE FOR HYPOCRISY.

JC: I believe that you have the right to publish reviews of whatever you want (and I EXPECT you to do it!), I believe that movies like this exist and that I can't just sweep them under the rug so it's not the exposure of KKE's existence that bothers me... really I think my huge problem with you is the fact that you blatantly advertise for this movie directly below your review. That's low Robin. Really fucking low man. The guy that you got this video from even said that "he's going to hell for this one". Now I'm not going to try and preach at you from a religious angle because I know that will fall on deaf ears, so any terminology that I use is more to make a point and describe intangible morality rather then condemn you on Christian terms, ok? Don't you think it was really irresponsible to make this video available to a wider audience?

RB: YES, I SUPPOSE I WOULD IF I ACTUALLY FELT THAT SOMEONE WAS BEING HARMED IN THE MAKING OF IT.

JC: I think that a video like this shouldn't be taken lightly, and so after a harrowing read full of some gut-wrenching descriptions you suddenly turn all bright and happy and say that this guy has lots of other movies to gleefully skullfuck me! Oh and I have to hurry to get it because it might not be for sale forever? Shit, well no time for introspection and thought about whether I should watch this or not.

Come on man, these movies are heavy shit. Even though I don't agree, if you want to make this stuff available to those who want it the least you could have done is used a little more neutral language, or put the ad someplace else in the mag... it may not be your responsibility of how people react to it but it is your responsibility to be wise about how you want to introduce people to smut like this.

RB: IS IT REALLY? IS IT MY RESPONSIBILITY TO MAKE SURE PEOPLE DON'T GET THEIR HANDS ON THIS GARBAGE? I'M SUDDENLY THE POLICEMAN TO MAKE SURE EVERYONE IS SAFE AND PLAYING NICE? DUDE, THAT IS THE EXACT

OPPOSITE OF WHAT I'M DOING WITH CS. WE'RE ALL GROWNUPS HERE. I GIVE MY READERS CREDIT. THEY AREN'T CHILDREN. I TRY TO WRITE IN A MODERN PSEUDO-CARNIVAL BARKER STYLE THAT IS SIMILAR TO THE CONTENT OF THE FILMS I'M WRITING ABOUT. I PLAY UP THE ASPECTS OF TRASH THAT INTEREST ME - AND THAT HAPPENS TO BE THE DIRTY, RAUNCHY, NASTY PARTS. I DON'T WANT OR NEED TO AGREE OR SHARE ALL THE OPINIONS AND KINKS EXPRESSED IN THESE FILMS TO ENJOY THEM. I'M NOT ABOUT BEING OVERLY CONCERNED WITH BEING SUBDUED, LITERARY OR EXERCISING "GOOD TASTE" (WHATEVER THE HELL THAT IS). I HAVE A LOT OF FUN WATCHING AND WRITING ABOUT THESE MOVIES, AND I WANT THAT TO COME OUT ON THE PAGE.

I'M NOT THERE TO TELL PEOPLE HOW TO FEEL ABOUT THIS STUFF, ALTHOUGH I CERTAINLY RESERVE THAT RIGHT AND OCCASIONALLY EXERCISE IT. I TACKLE A LOT OF WILD MATERIAL IN CS — VIOLENT, SEXUAL, RACIAL AND OTHERWISE. IF YOU WANT TO TRACK IT DOWN AND WATCH IT AND MAKE UP YOUR OWN MIND ABOUT WHAT IT IS, THEN BY ALL MEANS DO SO. THANK GOODNESS WE LIVE IN A PLACE WHERE WE CAN SOMETIMES DO THAT IF WE SMUGGLE PROPERLY.

JC: Well, After I read this article I went to the CS message boards and saw that there were enthusiastic people wanting to get ahold of this video. My problem became one of morality now; I don't think that something like this should be supported and profited on at all. This woman was abused horribly and to make money off of human suffering like that is an example in the absolute worst side of humanity. And I do not think that you did the right thing by making it such an easy video to aquire, first because you are exposing more people to something that on some moral plane is just bad for your soul (or karma, or whatever word you want to use) and second that you make it easier for someone to profit off the exploitation of this poor woman. And I remember that you said something along the lines of "you better get this quick before its gone" making it even more desirable. The reason I'm sending this email so long after I got the magazine was because I wanted time to reflect on it and make sure I knew what I felt about it before I just blasted out a knee jerk reaction. And while I didn't like the article and it does nothing for me and my sexuality I agree that you can write about whatever you want.

RB: YOUR OPEN MIND ABOUT FETISHES THAT ARE NOT UP YOUR PERSONAL ALLEY SHOULD ALLOW YOU TO TAKE ON THE IDEA THAT SOME WOMEN ARE AS MESSED UP AND PERVERTED AS SOME MEN ARE. IT'S TOUGH TO EVEN TRY TO TALK INTELLIGENTLY ABOUT CONTENT LIKE THIS, SINCE IT'S SO FUCKING MESSED UP, AND BASED IN DEGRADATION AND SEVERE POWER ISSUES. THE EASY WAY OUT IS TO GO INTO AN EMOTIONAL STATE AND IGNORE THE CORE AND

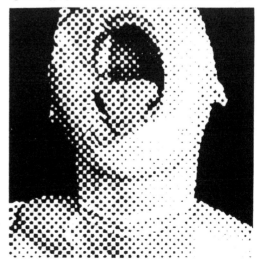

CONTINUED FROM PREVIOUS PAGE -

FOCUS ON 'SURFACE'. I'M NOT INTERESTED IN THAT.

JC: But I did lose a lot of respect for you in the way that you immediately start to shill for the seller of video, helping some worthless human waste profit off the brutal suffering of another human. Stuff like KKE stays underground and hard to find for a reason, I think that it is made for people with a sexual nature extreme enough to want to see that kind of pornography. But now I worry that once again human sexuality is going to be further desensitized by some assholes hanging out with their friends saying "Look what they do to this slut! hyuck hyuck".

RB: NEITHER THE MAKERS OF THIS TAPE, NOR IT'S STARS, NOR I HAVE ANY CONTROL OVER HOW PEOPLE REACT TO PORN OR USE IT. THEY WILL BRING THEIR OWN VALUES AND PLACE THEM UPON WHAT THEY SEE, JUST AS YOU HAVE -- ALTHOUGH I STRONGLY SUGGEST YOU ACTUALLY SEE THE TAPE IN QUESTION BEFORE YOU DECIDE THAT I'M A BAD PERSON FOR SIMPLY WRITING ABOUT IT.

JC: Well I got kind of knee jerky at the end there but hopefully it doesn't distract you from my main points. I feel bad that after loving your mag for such a long time that my first contact with you is over something like this. I used to think of you more as a creepy uncle who might try to grab a niece's ass at Thanksgiving dinner, but now you are something more... sinister. Less of a wide-eyed pervert and more of the kind of guy I worry that my girlfriend will run into on a dark night.

RB: OH BROTHER, YOU HAD ME RIGHT UP UNTIL THAT AND THEN YOU LOST ME. I LOVE REBECCA WAY TOO MUCH TO EVER BE GRABBING ANYONE ELSE'S ASS, MUCH LESS BE BOTHERING YOUR GIRLFRIEND, SHEESH...

CINEMA SEWER'S 20 FAVOURITE CANADIAN FILMS

IT'S TRUE THAT I WOULD NEVER BE CONFUSED AS A PATRIOT, BUT I DO REALLY LIKE LIVING IN THE GREAT WHITE NORTH, AND IT'S HIGH TIME THAT C.S. GAVE SOME PROPS TO THE NORTHERN LIGHTS OF CANADIAN FILM MAKING. CHECK IT....

1. VIDEODROME (1983) YES! YES! YES!
2. NOT A LOVE STORY (1981)
3. LAST NIGHT (1998)
4. ILSA: SHE WOLF OF THE SS (1975)
5. EXISTENZ (1997)
6. DEF CON 4 (1985)
7. A MARRIED COUPLE (1969)
8. CLASS OF 1984 (1982)
9. SCANNERS (1981)
10. THE WRONG GUY (1997)
11. ROCK AND RULE (1983)
12. DERANGED (1974)
13. TRIPLETS OF BELLEVILLE (2003)
14. THE DEVIL AT YOUR HEELS (1981)
15. VISITING HOURS (1982)
16. DEATH WEEKEND (1976)
17. RABID (1977)
18. ILSA: TIGRESS OF SIBERIA (1977)
19. VINYL (2000)
20. CAGED TERROR (1973)

HAH?

I'VE GOT MY MITTENS ON!!

PRISONER OF PARADISE

BRIT TRASH FILM REVIEWER JUSTIN BOMBA ONCE LOVINGLY CALLED IT "ILSA VS. JOHN HOLMES ON GILLIGAN'S ISLAND", BUT THIS BOB CHINN/GAIL PALMER PRODUCTION WAS FILMED ON LOCATION IN HAWAII, AND IS BETTER KNOWN AS **PRISONER OF PARADISE**.

SUPERDONG JOHN HOLMES PORTRAYS A SHIPWRECKED WW2 SAILOR WHO BOUNDS TO THE RESCUE OF TWO AMERICAN NURSES HELD CAPTIVE BY A TWISTED WAGNER-LOVIN' NAZI AND HIS THREE EVIL/HORNY FRAULEIN ASSISTANTS -- ONE OF WHICH IS PLAYED BY BLONDE BOMBSHELL SEKA.

THE "WADD" IS NOTICEABLY FLACCID IN MORE THAN ONE XXX SEX SCENE, AND AT ONE POINT (OFF CAMERA) THE COCAINE-FUELED JUNKIE ALLEGEDLY PUNCHED CO-DIRECTOR GAIL PALMER. ONLY A DAY LATER, HOLMES WOULD BRAWL WITH SEKA'S IDIOT HUSBAND, A NOTORIOUS SUITCASE PIMP WHO WAS KNOWN FOR MAKING EVERYONE ON A SET UNCOMFORTABLE WITH REALLY OBNOXIOUS DEMANDS AND RULES ABOUT WHAT HIS PROPERTY COULD, OR COULD NOT DO. BOB CHINN HOWEVER HAD A LOVELY TIME WITH JOHN. "IT WAS ONE OF THE BEST TIMES IN BOTH OF OUR LIVES," HE TOLD J. SUGAR.

QUOTES OF NOTE:
"DON'T CUM IN ME YOU AMERICAN SWINE!" - SEKA
"STOP YOU KRAUT BITCH, OR I'LL BLOW YOUR HEAD OFF!" - JOHN HOLMES

GAIL PALMER'S

Prisoner of Paradise

AN X RATED WAR MOVIE

STARRING
JOHN C. HOLMES
AND SEKA

RELEASED BY
CARIBBEAN FILMS N.V.   RATED X

THE HOTTEST THING ON WHEELS

THE CINEMATIC ROLLER DERBY PHENOMENON OF 1972

ONE OF THE COOLEST THINGS ABOUT THE HISTORY OF AMERICAN TRASH CINEMA IS TAKING INTO ACCOUNT THAT THE VARIOUS SUBGENRES IN THE DRIVE-IN EXPLOITATION PANTHEON EACH HAD THEIR OWN LITTLE TIME TO SHINE AND THEN WERE FORGOTTEN BY ALL BUT THE NERDIEST OF FILM ENTHUSIASTS. THE WOMEN IN PRISON GENRE ENJOYED A LIFE SPAN OF ABOUT 18 YEARS. MONDO MOVIES STOOD THE TEST OF TIME FOR 15 YEARS, BIKER MOVIES HAD A HEY-DAY OF ABOUT 10, BEACH PARTY FLICKS WERE AVAILABLE FOR 9 SUMMERS, BLAXPLOITATION PEAKED AFTER ABOUT 8 YEARS, AND THE PRE-HARDCORE PORN WHITECOATERS WERE ONLY AROUND FOR ROUGHLY 4 YEARS.

BUT VERY FEW KNOW THAT ROLLER DERBY CINEMA HAD A MEAGER RUN OF ABOUT 6 MONTHS IN 1972.

TO MOST POP CULTURE AFICIONADOS, ROLLER DERBY CROSSED ONTO THEIR RADAR IN THE EARLY 70s, BUT THE SPORT WAS ACTUALLY BORN IN CHICAGO DURING THE DEPRESSION, AND IN 1949 THE NATIONAL ROLLER DERBY LEAGUE WAS FORMED. IN THE 1960s MOST OF THE ORIGINAL OLD-TIMERS BEGAN TO LEAVE AS NEW SKATERS FOUND THEIR WAY TO THE GAME. CHARLIE O'CONNELL AND JOANIE WESTON WERE IMMENSELY POPULAR AND BECAME THE FOUNDATION OF THE NEXT ROLLIN' GENERATIONAL ONSLAUGHT OF A SPORT THAT WELCOMED AND INSTILLED A SENSE OF GENDER UNITY - AS MEN AND WOMEN SKATED TOGETHER ON THE SAME BANKED SPEEDWAY.

THIS NEW LOOK SPORT WAS YOUNG AND VIRGINAL, WITH SKATERS' AGES STARTING AT 15 YEARS OLD AND MAXING OUT AT JUST 26. IN 1961 THE SPORT WENT NATIONWIDE UNDER THE TITLE OF "ROLLERGAMES" WITH EVENTS BEING SKATED ALL OVER THE COUNTRY WITH TEAMS ADOPTING VARIOUS CITIES AS THEIR HOME BASE. THOUSANDS OF FANS LINED UP TO SEE THE PIONEERS WHO SKATED IN THE CHICAGO AREA, THE JOLTERS IN CINCINNATI, THE CHIEFS IN NEW YORK, THE L.A. T-BIRDS, AND THE MOST FAMOUS AND MOST SUCCESSFUL TEAM IN THE HISTORY OF THE SPORT, THE BAY BOMBERS WHO THRIVED IN SAN FRANCISCO AND OAKLAND IN THEIR FAMILIAR BROWN AND ORANGE UNIFORMS.

SOMEONE, SOMEWHERE, NEEDED TO DOCUMENT THIS COMPLETELY AMERICAN PHENOMENON. THAT SOMEONE TURNED OUT TO BE A YOUNG DOCUMENTARIAN NAMED ROBERT KAYLOR. **DERBY**, RELEASED THROUGH CINERAMA RELEASING IN 1971, AND FINALLY FINDING AN AUDIENCE IN 1972, IS AN OBSCURE CURIOSITY THAT PARTLY SERVES AS A FASCINATING LOOK AT THE WORLD OF 1970s PROFESSIONAL ROLLER DERBY, AND ALSO SEEMS TO BE A MISGUIDED ATTEMPT AT CINEMA VERITÉ. IN THE FILM'S FAVOR, IT THANKFULLY FEATURES SOME EXCITING AND AMAZINGLY VIOLENT ON-TRACK ACTION AS IT FOLLOWS THE BONE-CRUNCHING EXPLOITS OF THE BAY BOMBERS, BUT MUCH OF THE FILM IS FRUSTRATINGLY TRAINED ON A YOUNG FACTORY WORKER FROM DAYTON, OHIO WHO HAS NOTHING TO DO WITH THE SPORT OUTSIDE HIS FANTASY OF ONE DAY BEING A PART OF IT.

MIKE SNELL IS A SMARMY 23 YEAR OLD LADIES' MAN WHO NEVER TAKES OFF HIS SUNGLASSES - EVEN WHILE OPERATING HEAVY MACHINERY ON AN ASSEMBLY LINE WHERE HE WORKS. MIKE LIVES WITH HIS GAP-TOOTHED "OL' LADY", THEIR TWO SCREECHING 5 YEAR OLDS, AND A FREELOADING TEENAGE BROTHER NAMED BUTCH WHO SITS AROUND READING PLAYBOY. MIKE WANTS TO JOIN THE NEW ROLLER-GAMES LEAGUE, AND KAYLOR'S 16MM FILM FOLLOWS HIM AROUND AS HE TELLS HIS FRIENDS AND FAMILY ABOUT HIS PLANS FOR A NEW CAREER. UNFORTUNATELY, THE WHOLE THING STOPS THERE - NEVER FOLLOWING MIKE TO SEE IF HE CUTS THE MUSTARD AT THE 6 WEEK TRAINING CAMP HE TELLS EVERYONE HE'S SIGNED UP FOR. INSTEAD WE GET TEDIOUS FOOTAGE OF SNELL APPLYING FOR A LOAN SO HE CAN BUY A MOTORCYCLE, MIKE HANGIN' WITH HIS BEST BUDDY (WHO HAS A DODGE CHARGER AND A POSTER OF A SWASTIKA IN HIS ROOM), AND AN ARGUMENT ABOUT "HORN HONKING" BETWEEN HIS WIFE AND ONE OF HIS MANY MISTRESSES. IT'S AS IF KAYLOR RAN OUT OF MONEY AND WAS FORCED TO FINISH HIS DOCUMENTARY WITH FILM SCRAPS FROM THE EDITING ROOM FLOOR.

SO WHILE **DERBY** LEFT TRUE FANS WANTING MORE, THE LEAGUE ITSELF ROLLED RIGHT ALONG. THE SEX APPEAL OF TIGHT BODIED YOUNG WOMEN AND MEN, COMBINED WITH THE AGONIZING AND DOWNRIGHT DESTRUCTIVE VIOLENCE ERUPTING FROM BOTH GENDERS WAS UNRIVALED IN ANY OTHER SPORT, AND PROVIDED ROMAN ARENA-STYLE THRILLS FOR FANS - WHO SCREAMED FOR BLOOD FROM THE SPEED DEMONS TRAVELING AROUND AND AROUND ONLY A FEW FEET IN FRONT OF THEM. THE TIME NOW SEEMED RIGHT FOR HOLLYWOOD TO STEP IN.

WHEN NEWS BROKE THAT MGM WAS PROMOTING A BIG SUMMER MOVIE FOR THE SUMMER OF 1972 STARRING SMOKIN' HEART THROB RAQUEL WELCH, THE TRADE PAPERS

FARRAH FAWCETT GOES UNDERCOVER IN THE **CHARLIE'S ANGELS** EPISODE "ANGELS ON WHEELS"

A LOCKER ROOM LOOK
AT THE TOUGHEST BROADS
IN THE WORLD!

UNHOLY ROLLERS

R RESTRICTED
Under 17 Requires Accompanying
Parent or Adult Guardian

STARRING
CLAUDIA JENNINGS
PLAYBOY MAGAZINES
"PLAYMATE OF THE YEAR"

COLOR by DE LUXE®
A ROGER CORMAN PRODUCTION
An AMERICAN INTERNATIONAL Release

LOUIS QUINN · BETTY ANNE REES · ROBERTA COLLINS

PRODUCED BY
JOHN PRIZER and JACK BOHRER · VERNON ZIMMERMAN · HOWARD R. COHEN · VERNON ZIMMERMAN and HOWARD R. COHEN
DIRECTED BY   SCREENPLAY BY   BASED UPON A STORY BY

© 1972 American International Pictures, Inc.

HOPPED ALL OVER IT. EVERYONE WAS EXCITED TO SEE WHAT FIRST-TIME DIRECTOR JERROLD FREEDMAN WAS GOING TO PULL OUT OF HIS HAT WITH **KANSAS CITY BOMBER**.

TO START THINGS OFF, K.C. CARR (WELCH) IS CHALLENGED BY BIG BERTHA BOGLIANI (PATTI "MOO MOO" CAVIN) TO A ONE-ON-ONE DUEL WHERE THE LOSER HAS TO LEAVE KANSAS CITY AND NEVER RETURN. "EVERYTHING GOES," SAYS THE REF, AND K.C. IS SOUNDLY BEATEN TO A PASTY PULP IN THE ENSUING SLUGFEST.

SHE FINDS HERSELF QUICKLY TRADED OFF TO THE PORTLAND LOGGERS, WHO ARE OWNED BY AMBITIOUS BURT HENRY (KEVIN McCARTHY). HERE K.C. STRUGGLES TO FEND OFF LONELINESS, KEEP HER BOSS HAPPY, AND GET ALONG WITH HER TEAM-MATES WHO TAKE AN INSTANT DISLIKE TO HER -- ESPECIALLY OL' DRUNKEN JACKIE BURDETTE (HELENA KALLIANIOTES) WHO REGARDS K.C. AS A POTENTIAL USURPER TO HER ROLE OF TEAM LEADER. THE MAJORITY OF THE MOVIE TAKES PLACE IN PORTLAND, BUT THE CHOICE FOR THE TITLE WAS THE RIGHT ONE. I CAN'T PICTURE MOVIEGOERS PLUNKING DOWN CASH FOR TIX TO A ROLLER DERBY MOVIE CALLED "PORTLAND LOGGER".

K.C. IS TRAPPED AND ANGRY, AND THE TRADE TAKES HER AWAY FROM HER TWO FATHERLESS KIDS -- WALT (STEPHEN MANLEY) AND RITA (A 9 YEAR OLD JODIE FOSTER!). THE TWO RUGRATS ARE RAISED BY THEIR EQUALLY PISSED OFF GRANNY, AND ABOUT THE ONLY FRIEND K.C. HAS IS HORRIBLE HANK HOPKINS, AN AGEING PLAYER WHOM SHE FALLS INTO

RAQUEL VS. BELLY DANCER IN "KANSAS CITY BOMBER"

Anyone who saw "Five Easy Pieces" will instantly recognize Raquel Welch's tormented roller skating rival in Metro-Goldwyn-Mayer's "Kansas City Bomber." Helena Kallianiotes made a powerful movie debut as the tough Alaska bound hitchhiker whose major concern was the ecological rape of America.

In "Kansas City Bomber," the Greek-born actress co-stars as a veteran Roller Games queen whose position is challenged by the team's new skater, played by Raquel. With concave cheeks topped by high, prominent cheekbones, swirls of coal black hair and the look of an overdue volcano, Helen's dramatic ability stems from the school of hard knocks rather than some chic acting class.

She remembers, "We came from Greece when I was 10. We didn't have much. Our fortune was to be in America. One day at a Greek picnic, I did an impromptu belly dance and people threw pennies. I thought, 'Hey, this is a far-out way to make money.' So I began teaching myself belly dancing."

As the "Kansas City Bomber," Raquel Welch skates the "grudge race of the century" against her fierce rival, played by Helena Kallianiotes (l.). The MGM action-drama features banked track thrills set against backstage conflict.

BED WITH. HORRIBLE HANK, AS ADVERTISED, ISN'T MUCH TO LOOK AT, SO IT IS AN ODD PAIRING.

THIS IS A CHARACTER DRAMA WRITTEN BY BARRY SANDLER (WHOSE ORIGINAL DRAFT WAS WRITTEN FOR A UNIVERSITY THESIS) AND ABOUNDS IN THE GRITTY, SMOKEY ATMOSPHERE OF THE ARENAS WHERE THE SPORT WAS PLAYED. THESE WERE RUN-DOWN INDOOR STADIUMS WHERE FANS AND PLAYERS ALIKE SMOKED MARLBOROS AND GUZZLED PABST BLUE RIBBON. BUILDINGS THAT HOUSED A DYING SPORT, WHERE THE STANDS NEVER SEEM TO HAVE MORE THAN A COUPLE HUNDRED PEOPLE IN THEM, ALTHOUGH THEIR BLOODLUST IS AUTHENTIC AND PRIMAL.

THE ENDING SURE IS OPEN-ENDED. I WAS LEFT WANTING TO KNOW WHAT HAPPENED NEXT. WHAT ABOUT K.C.'S KIDS? WHAT BECAME OF JACKIE?? MAYBE THIS WAS INTENDED TO BE THE FIRST PART OF A TRILOGY OR SOMETHING. ALSO, THE WORDS "ROLLER DERBY" DON'T ACTUALLY APPEAR IN THE MOVIE AT ALL. INSTEAD IT'S REFERRED TO AS "THE ROLLER GAME", A PHRASE THAT HAS THE STINK OF LITIGIOUSNESS ALL OVER IT.

THERE ARE QUITE A FEW BELOVED SKATERS FROM THE SPORT'S PAST PLAYING THEMSELVES IN THE FILM, INCLUDING "LITTLE RICHARD" BROWN, LEON JACKSON, AND RALPHIE VALLADARES. BROWN DOES A COMPLETELY INSANE MOVE WITH A TRASH CAN, AND

THE HOTTEST THING ON WHEELS

MGM Presents

RAQUEL WELCH IN

KANSAS CITY BOMBER

PG   METROCOLOR   MGM

I TOTALLY MADE THIS FACE ——> THE AMAZING JUDY ARNOLD IS IN THERE TOO, WHICH IS GOOD BECAUSE DESPITE HAVING A SENSATIONAL PAIR OF TITS AND AN ASS THAT EVERY TEENAGE BOY IN AMERICA WANTED TO INSERT HIS KNOB INTO, RAQUEL DIDN'T HAVE MUCH IN THE WAY OF DERBY SKILLS. ARNOLD, A FAMOUS ROLLER DERBY STAR IN THE 1960s AND 70s (WHO ROSE TO STARDOM PLAYING WITH THE PHILADELPHIA WARRIORS) DID RAQUEL'S STUNTS FOR HER -- WITH WELCHS DETRACTORS POINTING OUT THAT SHE SHOULD HAVE DONE HER ACTING FOR HER AS WELL.

IT WASN'T FOR A LACK OF EFFORT. PREVIOUS TO FILMING, RAQUEL REPORTED TO AN OVAL TRACK BUILT FOR HER ON A HOLLYWOOD BACK LOT, WHERE SHE SKATED 5 HOURS A DAY FOR 3 MONTHS. HER TUTOR WAS FAMOUS SKATER PAUL RUPERT WHO TAUGHT HER THE BASICS OF STRIDING ON THE BANKED TRACK AND ON HOW TO TAKE FALLS (FALL BACKWARDS -- IF YOU FALL FORWARDS YOU COULD BREAK YOUR WRIST) OF COURSE, IN ONE OF THE INSTANCES WHERE RAQUEL'S FACE WAS NEEDED IN THE SHOT, SHE FELL AND BROKE HER WRIST, HOLDING UP SHOOTING FOR 6 WEEKS. STUDIO HEADS WERE FURIOUS, AS THEY HAD ALREADY SUNK A LOT OF MONEY INTO THE PROJECT.

THE HOTTEST THING ON WHEELS

MGM Presents

RAQUEL WELCH IN

Kansas City Bomber

Also Starring KEVIN McCARTHY · Screenplay by THOMAS RICKMAN and CALVIN CLEMENTS · Story by BARRY SANDLER · Music · DON ELLIS · Executive Producers JULES LEVY and ARTHUR GARDNER · Produced by MARTY ELFAND · Directed by JERROLD FREEDMAN · METROCOLOR

PG PARENTAL GUIDANCE SUGGESTED
Some material may not be suitable for pre-teenagers   MGM

THE CURIOUS THING ABOUT RAQUEL (FOR THOSE OF YOU TOO YOUNG TO REMEMBER) WAS HER UNUSUAL STANDING IN THE MAINSTREAM STUDIO SYSTEM. SHE WAS CERTAINLY A STAR AND A PERSONALITY, YET VERY FEW PEOPLE EVER WENT TO HER MOVIES. SHE WAS LIKE ZSA ZSA GABOR BEFORE HER, AND PARIS HILTON AFTER. SHE WAS FAMOUS FOR BEING FAMOUS, AND WHEN HER ROLLER DERBY ALSO TANKED AT THE BOX OFFICE, WELCH DIVORCED HUSBAND/MANAGER PATRICK CURTIS AND RETURNED TO EUROPE.

"WHEN I WAS A KID, I SAW KANSAS CITY BOMBER, AND I REMEMBER THINKING HOW BEAUTIFUL AND STRONG RAQUEL WELCH'S CHARACTER WAS. SO I WENT HOME AND I DRESSED UP MY BARBIE LIKE HER CHARACTER. I BORROWED ONE OF MY BROTHER'S LITTLE TOY PLASTIC FOOTBALL HELMETS AND I MADE BARBIE A KANSAS CITY BOMBER OUTFIT"
      -- TWIN PEAKS AND BOXING HELENA STAR, SHERILYN FENN

SHE'S THE KANSAS CITY BOMBER
LET HER ROLL, LET HER ROLL
LET HER FLY THROUGH THE FURY OF THE RACE
THE CRY OF THE CROWD IS THE KEEPER OF HER SOUL
YOU CAN SEE IT BY THE RAGE UPON HER FACE
      -- LYRICS FROM "KANSAS CITY BOMBER", A SINGLE 60s FOLK SINGER PHIL OCHS WROTE FOR THE FILM, BUT WAS THEN DUMPED OFF THE SOUNDTRACK BY MGM.

B-MOVIE KING ROGER CORMAN KNEW THAT MGM HAD BIG PLANS FOR AUGUST. HE KNEW THAT SOME EXECS AND TRADE PAPERS WERE PREDICTING THAT THIS ROLLER DERBY MOVIE EVERYONE WAS TALKING ABOUT WAS GONNA BE ONE OF THE BIGGEST HITS OF 1972. AS HE WAS KNOWN TO DO, CORMAN HASTILY PUT TOGETHER A CAST AND CREW TO TRY AND CASH IN ON ALL THE HYPE BEING PREPARED FOR RAQUEL, AND BEAT THE BIG HOLLYWOOD STUDIO TO THE PUNCH.

THAT MOVIE WAS UNHOLY ROLLERS.

CLAUDIA JENNINGS

MIMI CHESTERSON SOUNDS LIKE A PORN STARLET'S NAME IF I'VE EVER HEARD ONE, BUT ASTONISHINGLY IT WAS THE LOVELY CLAUDIA JENNINGS'S BIRTH HANDLE. A STRAIGHT-A STUDENT IN HIGH SCHOOL, MIMI DISAPPOINTED HER PARENTS WITH THE RASH ANNOUNCEMENT THAT SHE WAS DROPPING HER ACADEMIC LIFE TO BECOME AN ACTRESS AND A MODEL.

SHE FOUND HERSELF A DUMPY APARTMENT AND BEGAN THE TYPICAL FRUSTRATING LIFE OF ANY ASPIRING PERFORMER. HER FIRST BREAK WAS A RECEPTIONIST JOB AT THE OFFICES OF PLAYBOY MAGAZINE TO MAKE ENDS MEET. NOT SURPRISINGLY, THE SMOKIN' HOT YOUNG LADY WOULD EVENTUALLY BE ASKED TO PARTICIPATE IN FRONT OF THE CAMERA NUDE FOR A PHOTO SHOOT. IN THE NOVEMBER 1969 ISSUE, THE CENTERFOLD PLAYMATE "CLAUDIA JENNINGS" IS NONE OTHER THAN OUR MIMI -- NOW RENAMED FOR THE SAKE OF HER YOUNG SISTERS. DESPITE HER SMALL CHEST, THIS FANTASTIC LOOKING GREEN-EYED REDHEAD WOULD BECOME ONE OF THE MOST POPULAR PLAYMATES THE MAGAZINE HAD IN THE SEVENTIES.

SOME MINOR ROLES ON TELEVISION WOULD SOON FOLLOW, AND EVEN AN OFF-BROADWAY SHOW IN NEW YORK WAS ON THE CARDS. CLAUDIA THEN DECIDED IT WAS TIME THAT A REPUTED AGENT WOULD REPRESENT HER, AND BEFORE LONG SHE HAD LANDED A SPOT IN **UNHOLY ROLLERS** -- UNABASHEDLY TRASHY DRIVE-IN EXPLOITATION CINEMA, AND HER FIRST LEAD ROLE. SHE WAS THRILLED. THE DREAM WAS COMING TRUE.

SHE HAD A LOT TO BE HAPPY ABOUT. CLAUDIA SHINES AS A TOUGH-AS-SHIT, SELF-DESTRUCTIVE, BALL-HAMMERING BABE WHO CLAWS HER WAY UP AND DOWN THE ROLLER DERBY RACKET. IT'S NOT A FLAWLESS MOVIE, BUT IT IS WONDERFUL IN THAT IT NEVER ALLOWS ITSELF TO CLIMB OUT OF THE GUTTER FOR EVEN A SINGLE FRAME. JENNINGS IS FUN TO WATCH IN HER ROLE AS A BRASSY BITCH -- EVEN THOUGH SHE IS MEANT TO COME OFF TOUGH AND REBELLIOUS, AND INSTEAD SEEMS SELFISH AND IMMATURE. EITHER IS FINE!

THE ACTION IS FAST PACED AND DYNAMIC, AND I LOVED THE HANDHELD SHOTS ACHIEVED BY ROLLER SKATING CAMERAMEN. WHEN CLAUDIA'S CHARACTER KAREN CRASHES AND BURNS FROM LETTING FAME AND EXCESS GO TO HER HEAD, IT SEEMS MORE LIKE AN AFTERTHOUGHT THAN A GRAND FINALE. STILL, THESE SORT OF GRITTY NON-ENDINGS ARE WHAT MAKE 70s U.S. CINEMA SO COOL, SO I'M QUITE CONTENT TO RECOMMEND THE FILM.

AS PAUL BRENNER WROTE IN HIS DEAD-ON NOV. 1972 NEW YORK TIMES REVIEW OF THE FILM: "KAREN BECOMES A HIT WITH THE ROLLER DERBY FANS. BUT SOON, HER DESIRE FOR VICTORY BECOMES AN OBSESSION AND SHE ENDS UP LOSING NOT ONLY HER COOL, BUT MOST OF HER CLOTHES AS WELL."

IN 1978, SOME 5 YEARS AFTER UNHOLY ROLLERS, CLAUDIA WENT TO CANADA TO STAR IN DAVID CRONENBERG'S LITTLE KNOWN DRAG RACING MOVIE **FAST COMPANY**. THE CONSISTENTLY SLEEPY-LOOKING ACTRESS WAS SUFFERING FROM SERIOUS COCAINE ADDICTION BY THIS POINT, BUT REMAINED CERTAIN SHE WOULD BE CHOSEN TO REPLACE KATE JACKSON ON CHARLIES ANGELS.

THE ROLE WENT INSTEAD TO LITTLE-KNOWN ACTRESS SHELLEY HACK. CLAUDIA TOLD FRIENDS SHE WAS DEVASTATED, AND WAS BESIDE HERSELF WITH DEPRESSION WHEN SHE RETURNED TO L.A. FROM CRONENBERG'S SHOOT. SHORTLY THEREAFTER ON OCTOBER 3, 1979, JENNING FELL ASLEEP BEHIND THE WHEEL WHILE DRIVING ALONG TOPANGA CANYON BOULEVARD. HER VW CONVERTIBLE WAS BLINDSIDED BY A VAN, AND CLAUDIA WOULD SADLY DIE IN THE ARMS OF A MEDIC WHO WAS TRYING TO FREE HER FROM THE MANGLED WRECKAGE. SHE WAS ONLY 29 YEARS OLD.

ROLLER DERBY'S GLADIATORIAL POPULARITY PEAKED IN 1972, AND KANSAS CITY BOMBER AND UNHOLY ROLLERS WERE RIGHT THERE TO RIDE THE CREST OF THE WAVE -- AND THEN GET SWEPT RIGHT UNDER IT. IT WAS ONLY ONE YEAR, ONE TINY BLAZE OF ROLLING GLORY, BUT ENOUGH TO GIVE THIS SHORT-LIVED SUBGENRE ITS SPOT IN MOVIE HISTORY.

SOME REPORTS CLAIM MGM WON THE 1972 CINEMATIC DERBY SWEEPSTAKES, AND

CORMAN'S FILM GOT FARTED UPON. OTHER MORE RELIABLE DOCUMENTS ON THE SUBJECT REPORT THAT THE UNDERDOG AMERICAN INTERNATIONAL PICTURES DESTROYED THE BIG MGM HOLLYWOOD EFFORT, WITH ONLY A FRACTION OF THE BUDGET. BELIEVE WHOEVER YOU WISH, BUT KNOWING ROGER CORMAN'S TRACK RECORD OF "NEVER MAKING A MOVIE THAT LOST MONEY", I'M INCLINED TO BET ON THE LATTER.

BUT FOR THE ROLLERGAMES LEAGUE, THE THEATRICAL SWEEPSTAKES BEING DUKED OUT BETWEEN THE TWO INDUSTRY PLAYERS WAS ABOUT AS IMPORTANT AS THE AMOUNT OF CORN IN A LOG OF SHIT. IN 1973, MERELY ONE YEAR AFTER RAQUEL WELCH AND CLAUDIA JENNINGS HAD BROUGHT THE SPORT TO THE COVERS OF LIFE MAGAZINE AND DRIVE-IN THEATRES ACROSS THE COUNTRY, THE ENTIRE CIRCUIT WAS SHUT DOWN. MOST INDUSTRY INSIDERS POINTED TO RISING GAS PRICES AS BEING TO BLAME FOR KILLING OFF ALL THE PROFITS MADE BY THE CONSTANTLY TRAVELING TEAMS, BUT IT'S ALSO BEEN SAID THAT THE SPORT HAD SIMPLY RUN ITS COURSE WITH FICKLE FANS.

THE MAINSTREAM TOOK ANOTHER COCKEYED PEEK AT THE SPORT WITH THE 1975 RELEASE OF NORMAN JEWISON'S **ROLLERBALL**. THIS LARGE BUDGET ACTION FILM STARRED JAMES CAAN AS AN ATHLETE COMPETING IN A BLEAK FUTURISTIC VERSION OF THE SPORT THAT WAS ALSO PART FOOTBALL AND PART MOTOCROSS. IT WAS THE MOST SUCCESSFUL OF ALL THE ROLLER DERBY THEMED FILMS OF THE ERA, BUT DIE-HARD FANS RIGHTFULLY DON'T CONSIDER IT TO BE PART OF THE GENRE WHAT WITH ITS FUTURISTIC PERVERSIONS OF THE SPORT'S RULES AND CONCEPTS.

WHEN THE 13th EPISODE OF **CHARLIE'S ANGELS** ENTITLED "ANGELS ON WHEELS" AIRED ON DECEMBER 22, 1976, AND FEATURED A QUIRKY PLOT THAT SAW FICTIONAL TORNADO ROLLER DERBY STAR KAREN JASON DYING IN AN ON-TRACK "ACCIDENT" DURING A MATCH, THE SPORT WAS AGAIN BROUGHT INTO THE LIVING ROOMS OF AMERICA. KAREN'S CONCERNED SISTER THEN HIRED THE ANGELS TO INVESTIGATE, WHILE FARRAH FAWCETT WENT UNDERCOVER AS "BARBARA JASON" AND EASILY WON A SPOT ON THE SUSPICIOUS SQUAD.

IT TURNS OUT THAT BETTY, ONE OF KAREN'S TORNADO TEAM-MATES IS UP TO NO GOOD, AND PLANS TO KILL MISS FARRAH AS WELL -- WITH THE HELP OF HER EVIL BOYFRIEND. THE PLAN ALMOST WORKS TOO, BUT THE FURIOUS FAWCETT GETS HER REVENGE ON BETTY, AND THE ANGELS TEAM UP WITH POLICE TO ARREST HER AS WELL AS THE TEAM'S COACH FOR PLANNING THE DEATHS OF HIS PLAYERS.

COLLABORATION WITH DORKY EPISODIC TV LIKE CHARLIE'S ANGELS SEEMED TO REPRESENT ONE FINAL KICK IN THE GOODIE BAG FOR THE SPORT, BUT THAT WASN'T THE END OF THE STORY. ON APRIL 24, 1977, ANN CALVELLO, LYDIA CLAY, AND THE REST OF ROLLERGAMES' BELOVED WHEELED VIXENS ROSE LIKE A PHOENIX FROM THE ASHES. THE FIRST TELEVISION BROADCAST OF THE NEW INTERNATIONAL ROLLER SKATING LEAGUE (AKA THE I.R.S.L.) BROUGHT IN RESPECTABLE RATINGS WHEN AIRED. FORMER FANS RETURNED, AND THE EXCITING NEW LEAGUE LASTED ANOTHER 10 FULL YEARS -- ALL THE WAY UNTIL DEC. 12, 1987, WHEN THE LAST BOUT WAS SKATED IN MADISON SQUARE GARDEN IN NEW YORK. AGAIN, FINANCIAL PROBLEMS WERE THE CAUSE OF DEMISE, NOT TO MENTION INVOLVEMENT WITH SHADY PARTNERS WHO SUDDENLY BACKED OUT. IT WAS AN UNDIGNIFIED END, AND A LOT OF FANS WERE UPSET.

A YEAR BEFORE THE SPORT WAS KILLED OFF YET AGAIN, ANOTHER FILM WAS PRODUCED ON THE SUBJECT. **ROLLER DERBY MANIA** (1986) WAS THE 1980s EQUIVALENT OF ROBERT KAYLORS PREVIOUSLY MENTIONED DOCO. IT DEPICTS A REAL LIFE SPORTING ATTRACTION, WITHOUT THE SIDESHOW ANTICS OF THE WRESTLING PROGRAMS THAT DERBY CULTURE SO OFTEN GOT DUMPED IN WITH. HERE WE HAVE THE STORY OF LEO SELTZER, THE ORIGINATOR OF THE SPORT. LEO WAS A DIRTY-NOSED FACTORY WORKER WHO IN THE EARLY 40s QUIT HIS JOB AND BEGAN HIS ODDBALL VENTURE WITH A HANDFUL OF SKATERS. BEFORE SELTZER WAS DONE, HE'D CRAFTED A MULTIMILLION DOLLAR ENTERTAINMENT OUT OF NOTHING. WE'RE ALSO INTRODUCED TO CELEBRITIES WHO WERE FANS AND FREQUENTED THE HIGH-BANKED

CLAUDIA JENNINGS FROM PLAYMATE TO ROLLER QUEEN

Making the segue from her recent triumph as Playboy Magazine's "Playmate of the Year," to roller-games star in American International's "Unholy Rollers," has been no mean feat for the beautiful, exciting Claudia Jennings.

Claudia does not depend on beauty alone to carry her to the top. Her quick mind encompasses a wide knowledge of world affairs, politics and current events. All of which creates a great demand for her appearance as a guest on many popular talk shows.

Already a veteran of many television dramatic roles and commercials, plus various stage portrayals, her ambition is to continuously secure roles which will show her great diversification as an actress and not type her on beauty alone. It was because of this ability to diversify that the transition from the sophisticated world of Playboy to the sweaty, screaming, rough-and-tumble world of the roller skating arena was comparatively easy for curvaceous Claudia.

Roller Game of the Week

on KTLA,
Los Angeles,
Sunday,
Feb. 13,
8-10 pm.

TRACKS. HUMPHREY BOGART, LAUREN BACALL, JACK BENNY, FARRAH FAWCETT AND RAQUEL WELCH ARE ALL EXPOSED AS ROLLER-FANATICS.

WHICH BRINGS US UP TO TODAY. WHEN I ORIGINALLY SUMMED THIS UP WHEN IT SAW PRINT IN CINEMA SEWER #15 BACK IN EARLY 2004, I DID SO LIKE THIS:

"THE FUTURE OF THE SPORT, AND THE CINEMA THAT IT INSPIRES SEEMS AWFULLY DARK. DIEHARD SKATERS FROM BACK IN THE DAY DO EXIST, AND HAVE TRIED TO REVIVE ROLLER DERBY SPORTS. THE LAST SUCH STAB AT A COMEBACK PIQUED TV VIEWER INTEREST FOR A COUPLE MONTHS IN THE EARLY 90s WHEN A FUTURISTIC ROLLER GAMES (PACKAGED FOR CABLE NETWORKS WITH THE FAR MORE POPULAR **AMERICAN GLADIATORS**) CAME ALONG. BUT BY THAT TIME, THE FOUR-WHEELED SKATERS LOOKED AS HIP AS YOUR GRANDMA TRYING TO DANCE LIKE MC HAMMER -- WHAT WITH IN-LINE SKATES NOW BEING ALL THE RAGE. THUSLY PASSED THE LAST WHIFF OF LIFE IN THIS GRAND COMPETITION, WHICH IS NOW REGARDED AS LAUGHABLY FRINGE, IF IT'S REMEMBERED AT ALL."

THANKFULLY, I COULDN'T HAVE BEEN MORE WRONG. WITHIN MERE MONTHS OF THIS ARTICLE SEEING PRINT, ROLLER DERBY SEEMED TO BE POPPING UP EVERYWHERE. ANOTHER YEAR AFTER THAT, A HOME-GROWN RESURGENCE OF YOUNG WOMEN IN EVERY MAJOR CITY IN BOTH THE U.S. AND CANADA WERE HAVING REGULAR BOUTS WITH PAID ATTENDANCE GROWING BY THE MONTH. A LOCAL VANCOUVER LEAGUE POPPED UP (SHOUT OUTS TO THE RAD LADIEZ IN TERMINAL CITY ROLLERGIRLS! WOOT!) AND BEFORE I KNEW IT, I WAS OVERHEARING PEOPLE TALKING ABOUT THE SPORT IN COFFEE SHOPS AND BARS. NOWADAYS, THE FUTURE LOOKS INCREDIBLY BRIGHT WITH ROLLERDERBY REALITY SHOWS, 2 MORE MOVIES RUMORED TO BE IN THE WORKS, AND PEOPLE WALKIN' AROUND WEARING DERBY GEAR. IT SEEMS LIKE ONLY A MATTER OF TIME BEFORE A NATIONAL PRO LEAGUE AND TV BROADCASTING ARE PART OF THE EQUATION AGAIN. WE'LL SEE.

UNLIKE WRESTLING, NOTHING IS SCRIPTED AND THE ACTION IS ALL VERY REAL IN THIS NEW ERA. THE WOMEN WHO JAM AND BLOCK TAKE THEIR SPORT VERY SERIOUSLY -- AND THE FANS GET INTO IT THE SAME WAY THEY DID BACK IN THE 1970s. WHAT OTHER ATHLETIC SPECTACLE FEATURES FURIOUS FEMALES TRAVELING AT HIGH RATES OF SPEED AND BASHING INTO ONE ANOTHER?

ONLY IN ROLLER DERBY, MY FRIENDS.

— BOUGIE '08

SADOMANIA (1981)

A COUPLE OF INNOCENT NEWLYWEDS ACCIDENTALLY TRESPASS ON THE PROPERTY OF ELEGANT TRANSEXUAL EUROSEX FILM STAR AJITA WILSON, WHO PLAYS THE EVIL WARDEN OF A WOMEN'S PRISON WHERE THE LADIES ARE ALL HALF NAKED, TREATED LIKE SLAVES, AND FORCED INTO PROSTITUTION.

THIS FUCKING AMAZING JESS FRANCO MOVIE COMES WITH THE HIGHEST CINEMA SEWER RECOMMENDATION, ON ACCOUNT OF ITS SCENES DEPICTING: A GIRL GETTING RAPED BY A DOG, FORCED LESBIANISM, AND AN INCREDIBLE, SADISTIC FULLY NUDE GLADIATOR BATTLE TO THE **DEATH**!!

THE UNUSUAL AJITA WILSON WAS HUGELY POPULAR IN GREECE AND TURKEY, BUT HER STAR WANED BY THE MID 80s, AND SHE SADLY PERISHED DUE TO A CEREBRAL HAEMORRHAGE CAUSED BY A CAR CRASH. :(

GET THIS. INVITE OVER SOME FRIENDS. DRINK SOME BEERS.

El campo del amor de los excesos diabólicos

S

SADOMANIA
(El 🔥 infierno de la pasión)

REMEMBERING GRAY

INDEPENDENT-INTERNATIONAL PICTURES CORP. PRODUCED AND DISTRIBUTED MANY TOP GROSSING FILMS FOR THE NORTH AMERICAN DRIVE-IN THEATRE MARKET. IN THE EARLY 70s, THE COMPANY WAS ONE OF THE INDUSTRY LEADERS IN THE CREATION OF SUCCESSFUL, LOW BUDGET EXPLOITATION, BLAXPLOITATION, AND HORROR -- AND YET WAS ONLY A SMALL OPERATION OWNED AND OPERATED BY DIRECTOR AL ADAMSON AND PRODUCER/DIRECTOR SAM SHERMAN.

SADLY, ADAMSON WOULD BE SLAUGHTERED BY LIVE-IN CONTRACTOR FRED FULFORD IN 1995, AND HIS BODY FOUND BURIED UNDER HIS FRESHLY LAID CEMENT AND TILE BATHROOM FLOOR. SAM SHERMAN ON THE OTHER HAND, IS STILL MAKING MOVIES, AND GRABBED A COUPLE HEADLINES IN 2002 WHEN HE BOUGHT THE OLDEST KNOWN PHOTO OF A U.F.O. (FROM 1870!) ON EBAY FOR $365.00.

SAM AND AL HAD THE MIDAS TOUCH FOR CREATING EXCITING TRASH, AND WOULD EVEN BORROW LARGE PORTIONS OF AN EXISTING FILM, WRITE A "PARALLEL STORY" SCRIPT, SHOOT NEW FOOTAGE, AND EDIT IT ALL INTO THE ORIGINAL. BEFORE YOU KNEW IT, I.I.P. HAD A BRAND NEW DRIVE-IN FEATURE WHICH WOULD ALMOST ALWAYS HAVE WONDERFULLY LURID POSTER ART BY A FELLAH NAMED DWIGHT GRAYDON MORROW.

BETTER KNOWN TO COMIC BOOK FANS AS GRAY MORROW, THIS MOSTLY FORGOTTEN BUT TREMENDOUSLY TALENTED ARTIST DIED IN HIS PENNSYLVANIA HOME OF A SELF INFLICTED GUNSHOT WOUND TO THE HEAD ON NOV. 6th, 2001. THE 67 YEAR OLD ARTIST LEFT A SUICIDE NOTE.

MORROW'S AGENT TOLD THE MEDIA THAT GRAY HAD BEEN DESPONDENT OVER OUT OF CONTROL DEBT AND PAINFUL HEALTH PROBLEMS THAT SHOWED NO SIGNS OF LETTING UP. THIS WAS A SHOCK, SINCE HE'D KEPT ALL OF THIS A SECRET FROM ALL BUT HIS NEAREST AND DEAREST. NONE OF

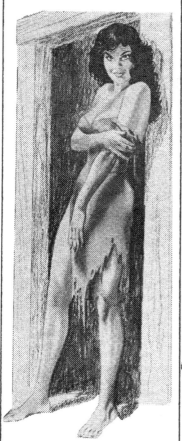

HIS FANS KNEW HE'D BEEN SUFFERING FROM PARKINSON'S DISEASE, AND THAT THE FINAL TRAGIC STRAW WAS THAT MORROW HAD RECENTLY LOST CONTROL OF HIS DRAWING HAND AND HAD TO QUIT THE TARZAN STRIP HE'D BEEN DRAWING FOR THE PREVIOUS 18 YEARS.

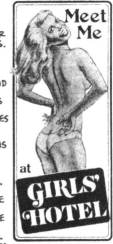

Meet the Naughty Young Girls who do their best work AT NIGHT—

TEENAGE MODELS

Starring JOHN VICKERY • THELMA HOUSTON • DIANE SOMMERFIELD
GILBERT DeRUSH • SID MELTON • DICK MILLER
with WILLIE BOBO and RAE SPERLING as "Chick"
Produced, Written & Directed by David Neil Gottlieb   in METROCOLOR
an [I.I.P] INDEPENDENT-INTERNATIONAL RELEASE   [R] RESTRICTED
copyright MCMLXXII INDEPENDENT-INTERNATIONAL PICTURES CORP

SAM SHERMAN AND AL ADAMSON WERE VERY IMPRESSED WITH GRAY AND HIS SEXY, EYE CATCHING ADVERTISING CAMPAIGNS THAT WERE MAKING MANY OF THEIR B-MOVIES INTO MASSIVE GRINDHOUSE HITS. ONE PROMOTIONAL STUNT WAS WHEN **FIVE BLOODY GRAVES** (1970) PLAYED NEW YORK AT THE CINERAMA PENTHOUSE. A DRAW WAS HELD THAT PROMISED: "FREE TO THE LUCKY WINNERS -- ONE FROZEN CORPSE!". THESE CONFUSED INDIVIDUALS WERE GIVEN A VOUCHER THAT THEY COULD REEDEM AT A LOCAL GROCERY STORE.... FOR A FROZEN CHICKEN.

GRAY MORROW'S CAREER OUTSIDE MAKING MAD CASH FOR I.I.P. WAS AN IMPRESSIVE ONE. HE WAS INTRODUCED TO CRACKED MAGAZINE BY ANGELO TORRES IN 1958, AND WENT ON FROM THERE TO DRAW FOR ATLAS COMICS, MARVEL, DC, DARK HORSE, ARCHIE, AND WARREN HORROR MAGAZINES SUCH AS "CREEPY" AND "EERIE". ON TOP OF HIS MOVIE POSTER AND COMICS OUTPUT, GRAY MADE A NAME FOR HIMSELF DOING MANY COVER PAINTINGS FOR DIGESTS AND PAPERBACKS IN THE PULP SCIENCE FICTION GENRE. IF THAT WASN'T ENOUGH, HE ALSO HAD AN IMPRESSIVE CAREER IN ANIMATION, WITH THE FONDLY REMEMBERED 1960s **SPIDER-MAN** SERIES TO HIS CREDIT.

I.I.P. DIDN'T LET THE FACT THAT THEIR PERFORMERS WERE IN THEIR MID-TO-LATE 20s STOP THEM FROM USING THE WORD "TEENAGER" TO BRING IN THE MONEY.

Young, Soft & Lovely —

Nothing is too Wild for them!

Teenagers for Sale

Color by DeLuxe   In PANAVISION   [R] RESTRICTED
an [I.I.P] INDEPENDENT-INTERNATIONAL release

GRAY WAS NOMINATED FOR THE HUGO AWARD FOR BEST PROFESSIONAL ARTIST IN 1966, 1967, AND 1968. HE IS SURVIVED BY HIS WIFE PATRICIA AND HIS DAUGHTER JULIET. I'M SAD I NEVER GOT TO MEET THE MAN AND TELL HIM HOW MUCH OF AN IMPACT HIS WORK HAD ON ME.

- - - - - - -

"GRAY'S BROOKLYN PAD IN THE 60s WAS A POP CULTURE MUSEUM SHOWCASING A GALLERY OF COMIC ART AND FANTASY ILLUSTRATION BY THE TOP OF THE LINE, ALL NEATLY FRAMED AND HUNG IN EVERY HALLWAY AND ROOM. THE EFFECT WAS IMPRESSIVE AND PERFECTLY SUITED THE MAN AT ITS CENTER -- TALL, HANDSOME, WITH NEATLY-TRIMMED VAN DYKE BEARD REMINISCENT OF VINCENT PRICE'S. GRAY WAS AN ENCYCLOPEDIA OF CINEMATIC KNOWLEDGE. LEONARD MALTIN, ROBERT OSBORNE AND RICHARD SCHICKEL CONSOLIDATED INTO A

2 TOUGH DUDES
put their thing together—

Super Cool & Wild!!

HE'S GOT WHAT EVERY WOMAN WANTS!

plus

MEAN MOTHER.

STUD BROWN

HE PACKS THE BIGGEST ROD IN TOWN!

COLOR by DeLuxe

R

INDEPENDENT-INTERN

ONE OF THE BEST BIKER MOVIES OF ALL TIME: SATAN'S SADISTS (1969)

MORROW ILLUSTRATES ANGELS' WILD WOMEN (1972)

Go Downtown and Meet Them~

They're always ready for ACTION!

MAIN STREET WOMEN

Color by DeLuxe

R RESTRICTED

an **IGI** INDEPENDENT·INTERNATIONAL release

SINGLE PERSONA. WHO ELSE COULD RATTLE OFF THE FILMS OF SKELTON KNAGGS WITHOUT A MOMENT'S HESITATION? OVER THE YEARS I COULD ALWAYS COUNT ON HIM TO BLOW ME RIGHT OFF THE STAGE WITH HIS UNBEATABLE REPOSITORY OF CELLULOID HISTORY."

     -- FRIEND AND FELLOW COMICS LEGEND, JIM STERANKO (FROM "GRAY MORROW: VISIONARY" BY MARK WHEATLEY)

☆ ☆ ☆ **GRAY MORROW'S POSTER ART CREDITS** ☆ ☆ ☆

FROM THE POSTER ART FOR:
GAME SHOW MODELS (1977)

ALL THE COLORS OF THE DARK (1972)
ANGELS' WILD WOMEN (1972)
BLACK HEAT (AKA GIRLS' HOTEL.1976)
BLAZING STEWARDESSES (1975)
THE BOOBY HATCH (AKA DIRTY BOOK STORE.1976)
BRAIN OF BLOOD (1972)
CINDERELLA 2000 (1972)
DRACULA VS. FRANKENSTEIN (1971)
DYNAMITE BROTHERS (AKA STUD BROWN.1974)
EVILS OF THE NIGHT (1985)
FIVE BLOODY GRAVES (1970)
GAME SHOW MODELS (AKA TEENAGE MODELS.1977)
HELL'S BLOODY DEVILS (1970)
I SPIT ON YOUR CORPSE (AKA GIRLS FOR RENT.1974)

LADY FRANKENSTEIN (1971)
LOVING COUSINS (1974)
MAIN STREET WOMEN (1977)
MEAN MOTHER (1974)
NIGHT OF THE HOWLING BEAST (1975)
NURSE SHERRI (1977)
NURSES FOR SALE (1971)
SATAN'S SADISTS (1969)
SPACE MISSION TO THE LOST PLANET (1970)
TEAM-MATES (AKA YOUTH GANGS.1978)
TEENAGERS FOR SALE (1970)
UNCLE TOM'S CABIN (AKA WHITE TRASH WOMAN. 1976)
ALSO LOOK FOR THE SUPER COPS (1974)
COMIC BOOK ADAPTATION MORROW DID.

VIBRATIONS

JOE SARNO WROTE AND DIRECTED APPROXIMATELY 75 FEATURE FILMS, AND WAS ONE OF THE MOST DISTINCTIVE AUTEURS TO EMERGE FROM THE 60s SEXPLOITATION SCENE. HIS BREAKTHROUGH MOVIE **INGA** (1968) WAS ONE OF THE FIRST X-RATED FILMS RELEASED IN THE USA, AND THE ENTHRALLING **VIBRATIONS** FOLLOWED A FEW MONTHS LATER.

MANHATTAN FEATURES PROMINENTLY IN THIS TALE STARRING THE SEXUALLY FRUSTRATED BARBARA -- A PIXIE-HAIRED WOULD-BE WRITER WHO SUPPORTS HERSELF BY TYPING MANUSCRIPTS FREELANCE TO SUPPLEMENT HER MEAGRE POETRY SALES.

A DEEPLY TROUBLED YOUNG LADY, ADORABLE BARB HOPES HER NEW APARTMENT (NEAR CENTRAL PARK) WILL BE THE START OF A NEW LIFE, BUT NOT LONG BEFORE SHE MOVES IN, HER SEXUALLY OMNIVOROUS BUXOM YOUNGER SISTER

☆ CONTINUED ON NEXT PAGE

CONTINUED FROM PREVIOUS PAGE ☆

JULIA APPEARS AT HER DOOR. THAT NIGHT JULIA REVEALS SHE WANTS TO CONTINUE THE INCESTUAL LESBIANISM THEY EXPERIMENTED WITH WHEN THEY WERE GIRLS. BARBARA LOVES HER SIS, BUT SIMPLY CAN'T GO THERE AGAIN. HELL, SHE HAS TROUBLE JILLING OFF WITHOUT GUILT, NEVERMIND TONGUING THE SOFT FLOWER PETAL FOLDS OF HER SISTER'S GROIN GULLY. JULIA RELENTS, BUT MASTURBATES IN FRONT OF HER SIBLING ANYHOW.

THE NEXT DAY, A REBUKED JULIA FINDS OUT THAT BARBARA'S MYSTERIOUS NEXT DOOR NEIGHBOUR IS A BISEXUAL LIBERTINE WHO STAGES ORGIES, AND DECIDES TO TAKE PART. HERE SHE'S MADE PRIVY TO THE SHUDDERING THRILLS OF THE ULTRA-SIZED CUNT-SCOURING HANDHELD MASSAGER. THE FUCKING THING IS THE SIZED OF A CANNED HAM!

BARBARA MEANWHILE, FINDS HERSELF ATTRACTED TO PARK -- AN ASPIRING WRITER WHO HAS HIRED HER TO TYPE UP HIS SHIT. WILL SHE BE ABLE TO KEEP HER HORNY SISTER AT BAY WHILE GETTING A ROMANCE OFF THE GROUND? CAN THE PRUDE KEEP HER DUDE FROM THE RUDE STEW?!

—BOUGIE

FRIDAY THE 13TH (1980)

COMPOSER HARRY MANFREDINI HAS SAID THAT CONTRARY TO POPULAR BELIEF, THE FAMOUS "CHI CHI CHI, HA HA HA" IN THE FILM'S SCORE IS ACTUALLY "KI KI KI, MA MA MA". IT IS MEANT TO RESEMBLE JASON'S VOICE SAYING "KILL KILL KILL, MOM MOM MOM". MANFREDINI CREATED THE EFFECT BY SPEAKING THE SYLLABLES "KI" AND "MA" INTO A MICROPHONE RUNNING THROUGH A DELAY EFFECT.

IN THE SCENE WHERE BILL IS FOUND IMPALED TO A DOOR WITH ARROWS, HIS EYE TWITCHES CONTINUALLY, 'CAUSE THE EYE MAKEUP THAT SAVINI APPLIED WAS BURNING HIS EYE AND CAUSING HIM EXCRUCIATING PAIN.

THE MOVIE WAS FILMED AT CAMP NOBEBOSCO IN NEW JERSEY, WHICH IS STILL IN OPERATION TO THIS DAY. THEY EVEN HAVE A WALL OF FRIDAY THE 13th PARAPHERNALIA ON HAND TO HONOUR THE MOVIE AND TO FREAK OUT THE CAMPING KIDDIES.

—BOUGIE

SWEET SUGAR (1973) AKA "CAPTIVE WOMEN 3"

POOR SUGAR. ARRESTED FOR DRUG POSSESSION AND PROSTITUTION AND THEN UNCEREMONIOUSLY SENT FOR A 2 YEAR SENTENCE IN A CENTRAL AMERICAN SHITHOLE WHERE SHE SPENDS HER TIME CUTTIN' CANE, KICKIN' ASS, BATTLIN' RACIAL VIOLENCE, AND THWARTING THE SLY ADVANCES OF EVERY PRISON GUARD THAT GETS WITHIN SNIFFING DISTANCE OF HER SULTRY HORMONES.

PHYLLIS DAVIS AS 'SUGAR' - BEST KNOWN AS THE SECRETARY ON T.V.'s **VEGA$**, AND AS "CLEO MITCHELL" ON **MAGNUM P.I.** - HAS GOT TO BE ONE OF THE BEST LOOKING WOMEN IN U.S. EXPLOITATION FILM HISTORY. SHE'S TOTAL RUSS MEYER STYLE: ROBUST BUILD WITH A SOLID ASS AND HEFTY HOOTERS, AND AN EXOTIC OVER-SEXED PERSONALITY TOPPED WITH A SMART-ASS MOUTH AND KNOWING SMILE. IT'S NO WONDER THAT RUSS CAST HER AS 'SUSAN LAKE' IN THE ROGER EBERT SCRIPTED **BEYOND THE VALLEY OF THE DOLLS** (1970).

LIKE EVERY W.I.P. MOVIE, THERE'S A REALLY NASTY WARDEN CHARACTER - AND THIS ONE ISSUES THREATS FROM A BATHTUB AND SHOVES A BURNING HOT GUN IN

Bitter days...Sweet nights

Her machete isn't her only weapon

Their world...
a plantation

Their battleground...
a tropical inferno

Now Showing

SWEET SUGAR

··· PHYLLIS DAVIS as SUGAR · ELLA EDWARDS · TIMOTHY BROWN
PAMELA COLLINS · CLIFF OSMOND ··· METROCOLOR

POOR SUGAR'S PANTS, NOT TO MENTION A MAD DOCTOR WHO'S CONDUCTING VARIOUS EXPERIMENTS WITH THE GIRLS AS GUINEA PIGS. IN ONE ODDBALL SCENE (THAT BORROWS HEAVILY FROM **BARBARELLA**), THE TWISTED QUACK CREATES AN ORGASM MACHINE THAT HE HOOKS UP TO EACH OF THE WOMEN. WHEN OUR GAL SUGAR GETS THE HOOK UP, SHE WRITHES IN ECSTASY UNTIL IT BLOWS UP!

THIS IS ONE OF THE GREATEST WOMEN-IN-PRISON FILMS OF THE 70S. IT'S ROUGH AND TOUGH, BUT ALSO LIGHT AND FUN AT THE SAME TIME. FINGER CHOPPINGS, WILD EXPLOSIONS, STOMACH IMPALEMENT, KILLER KITTIES, VOODOO RITUALS, EASILY TORN PRISON OUTFITS, FEMMES WITH BLAZIN' MACHINE GUNS, AND PHYLLIS DAVIS STRUNG UP AND FLOGGED. NEED I SAY MORE!?

SWEET SUGAR WAS A DRIVE-IN HIT IN ITS DAY, BUT STARDOM AND A DECENT CAREER NEVER REALLY PANNED OUT FOR DAVIS, WHOSE ONLY OTHER STARRING ROLE WAS IN 1973'S **TERMINAL ISLAND** - ANOTHER WOMEN (AND MEN) IN PRISON FILM, EXCEPT THE JAIL CELL IS AN ISLAND WHERE CONVICTED MURDERERS ARE DUMPED AND LEFT TO FEND FOR THEMSELVES. PRIOR TO **TERMINAL ISLAND**'s THEATRICAL WIDE RELEASE, IT HAD A DISASTROUS DEBUT AT A WOMEN'S FILM FEST IN TORONTO, WHERE MOST OF THE OFFENDED WOMEN IN ATTENDANCE WALKED OUT, INCLUDING THE DIRECTOR - STEPHANIE ROTHMAN! HA HA HA!! I LOVE THAT ANECDOTE ...

Raw violence and hot rage explode behind bars!

NAKED CAGE (1986)

FEMME FATALE RITA (CHRISTINA WHITAKER) PICKS UP A DOOFUS NAMED WILLY (JOHN TERLESKY) AT A TRUCK STOP, GETS HIM TO SNORT COKE OFF HER NIPPLES, AND COMMIT A BANK ROBBERY WITH HER, GETTING HIS NAIVE GIRLFRIEND MICHELLE (SHARI SHATTUCK) INVOLVED AS WELL.

MICHELLE UNEXPECTEDLY FINDS HERSELF IN PRISON DUE TO RITA'S FALSE TESTIMONY AND STRUGGLES TO STAY OUT OF THE HANDS OF THE CORRUPT, S+M LOVIN' LESBIAN WARDEN (ANGEL TOMPKINS). IF THAT TWISTED DYKE WASN'T ENOUGH, THERE'S AN EVIL GUARD NAMED SMILEY.

"WHAT'S ALL THE FUSS ABOUT?" HE SAYS AFTER RAPING AND STRANGLING A BLACK INMATE, "SHE WAS JUST EVERYDAY COON-POON!"

THINGS GET EVEN WORSE WHEN RAGING RITA GETS TRANSFERRED TO THE PRISON AND VOWS REVENGE ON MICHELLE, WHO WAS CRUCIAL IN PREVENTING HER BANK-HEIST ESCAPE.

EVEN AMONGST WIP AFICIONADOS, THIS FLICK IS WILDLY UNDERRATED. IT'S ONE OF THE LAST GREAT CANNON FILMS SLEAZE-A-THONS, AND I GIVE DIRECTOR PAUL NICHOLAS CREDIT; FACED WITH THE DAUNTING CHORE OF TRYING TO OUTDO HIS PREVIOUS WIP CLASSIC **CHAINED HEAT** (1983), HE PULLED OUT ALL THE STOPS. PAUL PUT ALL OF THE RIGHT INGREDIENTS IN THIS AMAZING NUT GLUE STEW, BUT THERE ARE TWO THINGS IN PARTICULAR THAT MAKE IT SUCH A MUST-SEE, AND MAKE BOUGIE-BOY TITTER WITH GLEE:

① IT'S A TIME CAPSULE OF AMAZING 1980s FASHION. MAXIMUM MONUMENTAL PERMS AND SHORT SPIKY PUNK HAIR, OFF-THE-SHOULDER SWEATSHIRTS AND DAY-GLO SCRUNCHIES, LOOPY GEOMETRIC JEWELLERY, GLOWING NEON IN EVERY ROOM, LADIES WITH SHOULDER PADS, SATIN SHEETS, NARROW TIES, ETC ETC ETC, IT'S LIKE SOMEONE CROSSED **TUFF TURF** WITH **CAGED HEAT**! DADDY <u>LIKE</u>!

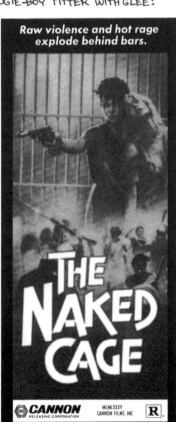

Raw violence and hot rage explode behind bars.

② CHRISTINA WHITAKER'S DELICIOUSLY SCARY OVER-THE-TOP PERFORMANCE. DON GUARISCO SAID IT BEST IN HIS NAKED CAGE WRITE UP ON HIS BLOG: "...SHE LOOKS LIKE A MEMBER OF THE GO-GO'S GONE BAD AS SHE SCHEMES AND SLASHES HER WAY ACROSS THE SCREEN IN A BLAZE OF NOSTRIL-FLARING FURY." IN MY MIND, WHITAKER JOINS THE PANTHEON OF SEMI-LEGENDARY W.I.P SUPERSTARS -- ALTHOUGH BESIDES FOR A STARRING ROLE IN **ASSAULT OF THE KILLER BIMBOS** IN 1988, AND A SHITTY DIRECT-TO-VIDEO SOFTCORE DONG SOFTENER CALLED **LOVE STREET** (1994), HER ACTING CAREER DRIED UP LIKE A WORM ON A HOT SIDEWALK. I'D LOVE TO EAT SOME NACHOS WITH HER TODAY AND FIND OUT WHAT SHE'S BEEN GETTING INTO.

RITA MENACES POOR MICHELLE

SOB

CITED BY SHE MAGAZINE AS THE SECOND GREATEST WOMEN IN PRISON MOVIE OF ALL TIME, THIS TITLE IS SADLY NOT AVAILABLE ON A REGION 1 DVD AS OF THIS WRITING, DESPITE PLEAS FROM MANY ONLINE FANS. AN UNCUT DISC WOULD BE GREATLY APPRECIATED, AS MY LONG OOP VHS TAPE VERSION IS EDITED (BOUGHT FOR $1.99 AT KINGSGATE MALL IN THE 'COUV! EASTSIIIIIDE, SNOW NIGGAZ!) AND MISSING RITA SLAMMING A KNIFE THROUGH THE TOP OF MICHELLE'S HAND, AS WELL AS ANOTHER SAD SISTER FORCED TO MUNCH GLASS BY A GNARLY BULLDYKE. WHAT IS THE HOLD UP, HERE? SOMEONE RELEASE A 2 DISC DELUXE SPECIAL EDITION OF THIS WITH AUDIO COMMENTARY BY CHRISTINA WHITAKER, ALREADY!

THE NAKED CAGE

CANNON
RELEASING CORPORATION

MCMLXXXV
CANNON FILMS, INC

R

PLEEEEEZE? I PROMISE I'LL KEEP MY ROOM CLEAN!

RICK SAVAGE'S STREETS OF N.Y.

OF ALL THE WORK I'VE DONE IN PORN OR BONDAGE VIDEOS, IT SEEMS LIKE I'VE RECEIVED THE MOST NOTORIETY FOR MY **STREETS OF NEW YORK** SERIES. HOW DID IT HAPPEN? WHY DID WE DO IT? WHERE DID THE IDEA COME FROM? HOW DID WE GET AWAY WITH HAVING FULL BLOWN, ALL-OUT HARDCORE SEX, OUTDOORS IN THE CITY OF NEW YORK?

IT WAS THE EARLY 90s. I HAD PROBABLY DIRECTED ABOUT 8 FEATURE PORN MOVIES AT THE TIME. **ANGELS WITH STICKY FACES, ANAL RESCUE 9-1-1, WHORE OF THE ROSES, BACKDOOR TO BROOKLYN, AWAKENING IN BLUE,** AND A FEW OTHERS. WE HAD SHOT 2 FEATURES OVER A 2 MONTH PERIOD - **THE MALTESE BIMBO,** AND **DIRTY.** I THOUGHT THESE WERE MY TWO BEST MOVIES (AS A DIRECTOR) TO DATE, BUT WE JUST COULDN'T FIND A BUYER. CABALLERO, ARROW, AND PLEASURE PRODUCTIONS HAD BOUGHT MOST OF MY MOVIES AT THAT POINT, BUT SUDDENLY THE MONEY WE HAD BEEN OFFERED FOR THESE 2 PIX WAS JUST

RICK AND CHINA LEE FROM STREETS OF NEW YORK PART 4.

"BREAK EVEN" MONEY. THERE WAS A TOTAL GLUT OF MOVIES COMING OUT. SO MANY PEOPLE WERE MAKING THESE LOW-BUDGET FEATURES, THE COMPANIES JUST WEREN'T PAYING MUCH FOR THEM. EVEN THOUGH WE HADN'T SOLD OUR LAST TWO VIDS, MY FINANCIAL BACKER (WHO WAS A TOTAL NOVICE IN THE ADULT WORLD) WAS HOT TO SHOOT THE NEXT MOVIE. I TOLD HIM, "NEVILLE, I APPRECIATE THE VOTE OF CONFIDENCE, BUT WE HAVEN'T SOLD THE LAST TWO. LET ME THINK ABOUT IT."

AT THAT TIME, THE TWO BIGGEST SELLERS ON THE ADULT MARKET WERE JOHN STAGLIANO'S **BUTTMAN** SERIES, AND **DIRTY DEBUTANTES.** GONZO (OR "REAL SEX") VIDEOS HAD BEEN BORN AND THE PUBLIC REALLY LIKED THEM. THE CONSUMER WAS TIRED OF STUPID PLOTS, AND I'LL POLITELY CALL IT "LESS THAN SPECTACULAR" DRAMATIC ACTING. MOST OF ALL, I THINK THEY WERE TIRED OF FAKE PORNO SEX. THE KIND WHERE THE ACTRESS MAKES NON-STOP PHONY FUCK SOUNDS AND USUALLY SAYS THE WORDS "OH YEAH" OVER AND OVER LIKE A BROKEN RECORD.

I ONCE DID A SEX SCENE WITH AN ACTRESS NAMED NATASHA SKYLER, AND SHE JUST KEPT SAYING "OH YEAH OH YEAH OH YEAH," AND I DON'T THINK SHE EVEN ONCE MADE EYE CONTACT WITH ME. SO, IN THE MIDDLE OF COCK-PISTONING NATASHA IN THE MISSIONARY POSITION, I ATTEMPTED TO MAKE "HUMAN CONTACT"... WHICH MIGHT SEEM LIKE A STRANGE THING TO SAY - SINCE MY PENIS WAS DEEP IN HER BODY AT THE TIME. ANYWAY, I STARTED ANSWERING HER "OH YEAHS" WITH MY OWN "OH YEAHS", ONLY MINE WERE POSED AS QUESTIONS. SHE WOULD SAY "OH YEAH!" AND I WOULD IMMEDIATELY FOLLOW IT WITH, "OH YEAH?". AFTER ABOUT 8 "OH YEAHS" ON EACH OF OUR PARTS, SHE FINALLY NOTICED THAT I WAS "TALKING" TO HER. SHE, QUITE CASUALLY, SLIPPED HER HAND BETWEEN HER TITS AND GAVE ME THE FINGER.

I'M NOT PUTTING DOWN OR CRITICIZING NATASHA SKYLER. SHE SEEMED LIKE QUITE A NICE HUMAN, BUT SHE DIDN'T WANT TO BE THERE WITH SOME GUY'S STIFF PRICK SLIDING IN AND OUT OF HER BODY. SHE JUST DIDN'T KNOW OF ANOTHER WAY THAT SHE COULD EARN THE 4, 5, 6, OR 7 HUNDRED DOLLARS A DAY THAT SHE WAS BEING PAID - SO SHE JUST GRINNED AND BARED IT, CLOSED HER EYES AND SAID "OH YEAH OH YEAH OH YEAH!"

I JUST GOT TO A POINT WHERE I WAS AT THE END OF MY ROPE WITH THE PHONY FUCK NOISES, AND JUDGING BY THE SALES NUMBERS THAT **DIRTY DEBS** AND **BUTTMAN** WERE PUTTING UP, I WASN'T THE ONLY GUY IN AMERICA THAT WANTED SOMETHING REAL. AS I BEGAN DIRECTING MY OWN MOVIES, I COULD NOW SPECIFY TO MY ACTRESSES, "IF YOU DON'T FEEL LIKE SAYING ANYTHING, DON'T. JUST BREATHE. ALLOW THE SEX TO HAPPEN."

ANOTHER APPROACH I HAD AS A DIRECTOR WAS THAT WE SHOULD NOT "STAGE" SEX IN VARIOUS POSITIONS FOR THE SAKE OF THE CAMERA, BUT RATHER, WE SHOULD DOCUMENT REAL SEX, THEN DO OUR BEST IN THE EDITING ROOM.

SO ANYWAY, I TOLD MY MONEY GUY, "LOOK, WE'RE GOING TO MAKE SOMETHING DIFFERENT. NOW, WHAT DO WE HAVE

THAT THE L.A. PORN SCENE DOESN'T HAVE? WE HAVE NEW YORK. WE HAVE NEW YORK FUCKING CITY. THIS PLACE IS NEVER GOING TO LOOK LIKE BEACHES AND HOT TUBS. HOLLYWOOD COMPANIES COME ALL THE WAY OVER HERE TO SHOOT MOVIES BECAUSE THERE IS NO CITY IN THE WORLD LIKE NEW YORK. YOU WANT THE URBAN SETTING? THIS IS THE ULTIMATE, AND THERE'S SO MUCH OF IT! YOU COULD SHOOT THOUSANDS OF SCENES HERE AND NEVER USE THE SAME BACKDROP TWICE."

MY INITIAL IDEA WAS THAT WE COULD SHOOT SOME FOREPLAY OUTDOORS. TRY AND GET SOME NUDITY, THEN RETREAT TO THE COMFORT OF A NICE BED IN NEVILLE'S APARTMENT TO FINISH THE SEX. BUT A STRANGE THING HAPPENED. I JUST STARTED TO REALIZE, "YA KNOW, THERE'S NOBODY AROUND. I GOT THIS GIRL BENT OVER A LOADING DOCK, A COUPLE OF MY FINGERS BURIED DEEP IN HER PINK WETNESS. WHO'S TO STOP ME FROM PULLING OUT MY PENIS AND GOING BALLS DEEP? FROM THAT POINT ON, WE TRIED TO GET SOME, IF NOT ALL OF THE HARDCORE SEX TO HAPPEN OUTDOORS.

I SUPPOSE THERE ARE SEVERAL FACTORS AS TO WHY **STREETS OF NEW YORK** WAS SUCH A BIG HIT. (AND NOT JUST IN THE STATES, "STREETS" WAS A WORLDWIDE SMASH. JOHN STAGLIANO CAME BACK FROM EUROPE AT ONE POINT AND TOLD ME THAT FOR THE FIRST TIME IN 3 YEARS, HIS **BUTTMAN** SERIES WAS NOT THE #1 SELLING ADULT VIDEO TITLE OF THE YEAR. STREETS OF N.Y. WAS NUMBER ONE.) TO EXPLAIN ITS POPULARITY, I GUESS WE COULD DELVE INTO THE PSYCHOLOGY OF THE EXCITEMENT FACTOR OF HAVING SEX OUTDOORS IN A PLACE WHERE YOU MIGHT GET CAUGHT. WE COULD TALK ABOUT THAT TABOO OF DOING SOMETHING IN A PLACE WHERE YOU AREN'T SUPPOSED TO BE DOING IT... BUT I ALWAYS JUST TRIED TO KEEP IT REAL.

I CAN'T GIVE THE CITY ENOUGH CREDIT. THE CITY WAS TO MY SEX SCENES AS THE RIGHT PICTURE FRAME IS TO A PAINTING. IF YOU'VE GOT A GOOD PICTURE, YOU'VE GOT TO PUT THE RIGHT FRAME AROUND IT. YOU TAKE A BEAUTIFUL FLOWER, AND YOU COULD LOOK AT IT WITH THE BACKDROP OF LOTS OF OTHER FLOWERS. OR MAYBE, YOU HOLD THE FLOWER UP AGAINST THE CONTRASTING BACKDROP OF BROKEN DOWN AUTOMOBILES, GRAFFITI ON BRICK WALLS, COBBLE STONE STREETS, OLD WAREHOUSES, FUNKY LOADING DOCKS AND GARBAGE. SUDDENLY, THE BEAUTY, THE FRAGILITY, THE VULNERABILITY OF THE FLOWER JUST JUMPS OUT AT YOU. I MEAN, HOW CAN YOU MISS THAT?

AS A DIRECTOR, I GUESS I'M MOST PROUD OF THE VIDEO, **DIRTY** - WHERE I HAD THE JOY AND CHALLENGE OF COHESIVELY KNITTING TOGETHER THE ENERGIES OF A CAST OF MOSTLY INEXPERIENCED ACTORS AND ACTRESSES TO MAKE A FINISHED PIECE OF WORK. AS A CREATOR OF HARDCORE ADULT VIDEO, I AM MOST PROUD OF **RICK SAVAGE'S STREETS OF NEW YORK**. I LOOK BACK ON SOME OF THESE IMAGES, SOME OF THOSE SCENES - AND I SCRATCH MY HEAD AND SAY, "HOW THE FUCK DID WE DO THAT?"

☆ RICK SAVAGE ©2003. VISIT www.RICKSAVAGE.com

A FEW TIDBITS YOU SHOULD KNOW ABOUT:

DIRTY HARRY

DON SIEGEL'S 1971 FILM STARRING CLINT EASTWOOD IS PROBABLY THE MOST INFLUENTIAL COP MOVIE MADE IN THE 1970s -- AND THERE WERE A LOT OF THEM.

THE LEAD ROLL WAS TURNED DOWN BY ROBERT MITCHUM, FRANK SINATRA, JOHN WAYNE, STEVE MCQUEEN, AND BURT LANCASTER.

WRITER/DIRECTOR JOHN MILIUS (CONAN, RED DAWN, APOCALYPSE NOW) CONTRIBUTED THE INFAMOUS LINE: "DO YOU FEEL LUCKY, PUNK?"

THE ORIGINAL TITLE WAS "DEAD RIGHT".

THE MOVIE WAS ORIGINALLY SET IN SEATTLE, BUT EASTWOOD AND SIEGEL VETOED THIS IDEA AND SAW TO IT THAT IT WAS SET IN SAN FRANCISCO.

A POLICE DEPARTMENT IN THE PHILIPPINES ALLEGEDLY WAS USING A PRINT OF THE FILM TO TRAIN YOUNG OFFICERS.

HARRY REFERS TO THE 44 MAGNUM AS THE "MOST POWERFUL HANDGUN IN THE WORLD", BUT THAT ACTUALLY ISN'T TRUE, NOR WAS IT THEN.

YE OL' BOUGIEMAN CHIN WAGS ABOUT SOME OF THE HIGHLIGHTS IN THE "STREETS OF N.Y." SERIES. BAM!

VOL. 2 (1994)
RICK TURNS BOFFING INTO SOME ODD X-GAMES STYLE SPORT AS HE ASS-POUNDS SOME POOR GERMAN GIRL NAMED MARLENA IN CENTRAL PARK IN THE MIDDLE OF A GODDAMN BLIZZARD! HE STAYS BUNDLED AND COZY WHILE SHE TREMBLES AND PRETTY MUCH TURNS BLUE BEFORE THE SCENE IS OVER, WHICH, IN THIS CASE IS WHEN THE CAMERA CONKS OUT DUE TO THE EXTREME CONDITIONS. WHO SAYS ROMANCE IS DEAD?

VOL. 4 (1995)
SAVAGE PICKS UP JENNIFER "CHINA" LEE AFTER WORK AT THE 'MEDICAL CENTER'. SHE SHEDS HER ADORABLE NURSES OUTFIT UNDER A SWUMMY OVERPASS AT BRUCKNER AND 3RD. RICK DIRECTS HER TO GRAB HER ANKLES AND THEN PENETRATES HER WITH HIS ANGRY LITTLE GENERAL. IT'S AN ALL-TIME CLASSIC "STREETS..." MOMENT WHEN RICK BLASTS HIS VANILLA FROSTING ONTO HER KISSER JUST AS A FAT STRANGER IN A GREEN T-SHIRT WALKS UP FROM OUT OF AN ALLEYWAY AND ASKS IF HE CAN HAVE SOME TOO.

VOL. 7 (1996)
JESSIE IS SLUMPED OVER, GIVING FRANK A MESSY BLOW JOB IN HIS CAR WHEN A SCARY HE-SHE STREET-WALKER APPROACHES THE VEHICLE, MAKING FOR ONE OF THE MORE INTERESTING MOMENTS I'VE EVER SEEN IN A MODERN STROKE TAPE. BEFORE LONG, SHE'S CURBSIDE-FINGERING HER OWN ASSHOLE. YOWZA! WHAT A GOIL!

VOL. 9 (1997)
ANNA'S TABOO FANTASY IS TO SCREW IN A GRAVEYARD, WHICH ADMITTEDLY ON PAPER SOUNDS REALLY F-IN HOT. BUT ONCE SHE STARTS GETTING A HOT BEEF INJECTION ON SOMEONE'S GRAVESTONE, IT'S NOTHING BUT DISRESPECTFUL AND UNCOMFORTABLE TO WATCH - WHICH NATURALLY MAKES IT A TOTAL HIGHLIGHT OF THE SERIES FOR ME.

12 VOLUMES CAME OUT BUT RICK JUMPED SHIP AFTER VOL. 4, LEAVING THE COMMAND IN NEVILLE CHAMBERS HANDS.

★ ★ ★ ★ ★ ★ ★ ★ ★ ★

READER ☆ MAIL:

"CAN I TELL YOU A SECRET? OK, IT'S NOT REALLY A SECRET, BUT IT IS PRETTY EMBARRASSING. I HAD A DREAM THE OTHER NIGHT THAT I GOT THE NEW C.S. AND YOU HAD DONE A FULLY (SEXY) ILLUSTRATED THING ALL ABOUT **MY** VA-JAY-JAY. HONESTLY!"

--CLARA S. CALGARY

PASTOR GAS: THE LEGEND OF THE FARTING TILTON

ONE OF THE INTERESTING THINGS ABOUT THE INTERNET IS THAT SOMEONE CAN BECOME A QUASI-CELEBRITY WITHOUT EVEN KNOWING IT. REMEMBER THAT GOOFY HOME VIDEO FOOTAGE A COUPLE YEARS AGO OF THAT FAT KID PRETENDING TO BE A JEDI KNIGHT? THAT GOT LINKED OUT TO EVERYONE AND THEIR DOG WITHIN ABOUT A WEEK OF FIRST APPEARING ONLINE AND BEFORE YOU KNEW IT - NATIONWIDE CABLE NEWS TELECASTS HAD STORIES DEVOTED TO THAT POOR STARWARS NERD DANCING AROUND HIS ROOM WITH HIS DORKY PLASTIC LIGHTSABER. HE HAD TO CHANGE SCHOOLS HE WAS SO HUMILIATED.

"FATHER!?"

"OHH YESSS, I SENSE YOUR PRESENCE..."

YES, THE SHORT HISTORY OF THE NET IS RICH WITH ODD VIDEO CLIPS BEING TRADED AND SHARED AMONGST HUNDREDS OF THOUSANDS OF PEOPLE - WHO THEN FILL FORUM POSTS AND BESTOW THE PRIMORDIAL 15 MINUTES OF FAME. BUT SURELY THE GREATEST OF THESE NUTTY CYBER-CELEBS MUST BE ROBERT TILTON, ALTHOUGH AS I WILL NOTE LATER, HIS VIDEO UNDERGROUND STREET CRED DATES BACK **FAR** FURTHER THAN THE WIDESPREAD USE OF THE INTERNET.

FOR THOSE OF YOU WONDERING, ROBERT TILTON IS AN ULTRA-SKETCHY AMERICAN TELEVANGELIST WHO PREACHES THE LORD'S WORD IN WILD, IRREVERENT, NONSENSICAL STYLE. AND HE DID SO UNHINDERED UNTIL SOMETIME IN EARLY 1985 WHEN A 4 MINUTE VIDEO CLIP FEATURING THE SPASTIC SNAKE-OIL SALESMAN WAS PASSED AROUND AMONGST FRIENDS AND WEIRD VIDEO TRADERS. ON THE TAPE IN QUESTION, TILTON LOOKS LOVINGLY INTO THE CAMERA AND PROVIDES HIS TRADEMARK LONG PAUSES, DEEP GRIMACES, SQUINTS, GRUNTS AND PRICELESS QUOTES. IT WAS OVER THIS QUIRKY TELECAST THAT SOMEONE - NO ONE IS QUITE SURE WHO - PUT SOME OF THE MOST BRILLIANT FLATULENT OVERDUBBING EVER CREATED.

"HONNKKK!"

"I **LOVE** TO GIVE THINGS AWAY."

YES, I KNOW IT SOUNDS IMMATURE AND STUPID, BUT THE FARTING TILTON TRANSCENDS ALL THAT, AND HAS TO BE ONE OF THE MOST FUCKING HILARIOUS THINGS I'VE EVER SEEN. I'VE WATCHED IT HUNDREDS OF TIMES, AND I'M NOT THE ONLY ONE. STILEPROJECT.COM, AN ONLINE MECCA FOR THOSE ENTHUSED BY THE LOW BROW AND TASTELESS SAID: "THE FARTING PREACHER IS PROBABLY ONE OF THE MOST COMPELLING SINGLE PIECES OF SATIRE IN HUMAN HISTORY."

THE FOOTAGE SPEAKS FOR ITSELF, BUT ONCE YOU KNOW THE HISTORY OF THE MAN STARRING IN IT, EVEN HEARTIER LAUGHS WILL BE BESTOWED UPON YE, BROTHERS AND SISTERS. BEHOLD:

IN THE MID 80S TO EARLY 90S, TELEVISION PASTOR ROBERT TILTON AND HIS WORLD OUTREACH CENTER CHURCH TRULY PERFECTED THE 30 MIN. GOD-HEAVY INFOMERCIAL, THOUGH NEVER CLAIMING TO STAND FOR ANY SPECIFIC FAITH. AT THEIR PEAK, TILTON'S PAID ADVERTISMENTS COULD BE SEEN IN ALL 263 U.S. AND CANADIAN TELEVISION MARKETS - AN INCREDIBLE ACHIEVEMENT! SCANDALS CAME AND WENT, BUT OL' REV. ROBERT SOMEHOW MANAGED TO AVOID THE SAME MEDIA SCRUTINY RESPONSIBLE FOR BRINGING DOWN JIM BAKKER, JIMMY SWAGGART, AND NUMEROUS OTHER EVANGELICAL LIARS AND CHEATS. HE TOOK THE $$$ AND RAN - ONLY TO COME BACK EVERY NIGHT AT AROUND 2AM AND TAKE THE $$$ AGAIN.

"YOU SEE..."

"FFTTT-BLAP!"

"I BELIEVE IN **BIG** MIRICLES."

APART FROM HIS ASS-BARKING, TILTON'S INDECIPHERABLE SPEAKING-IN-TONGUES IS IN A CLASS OF ITS OWN. YOU'LL FIND HIS ONLINE AUDIO CLIPS OF "MO LATA SHO BO-LO KA BEE BAA-TO" AND "OHH BEE-MA TO BAA GEE-BEE MA GO" AS CONFUSING AS THEY ARE AWESOME. BUT APART FROM HIS GRAYING POMPADOUR AND DORKY SHIT-EATING GRIN, WHAT REALLY SETS MR. TILTON APART FROM YOUR AVERAGE SCRIPTURE SPOUTER IS HIS ABUNDANT AND SHAMELESS ENTHUSIASM FOR COLLECTING VIEWERS' MONEY.

"YOU SEND ME THAT MONEY **RIGHT NOW** AND YOU **WILL** BE SAVED! THE LORD WILL PROVIDE! I SEE YOU NOW, OHHHHH YES I DO!" HOOTED A SQUINTING TILTON IN ONE EPISODE OF HIS TELECAST.

"BLOOOPP"

"HAL-EH-LOO-YA!"

"HA HA!"

THE ONLY THING CLOSE TO THE LEVEL OF INSANITY DISPLAYED BY THE CLASSIC WORLD OUTREACH INFOMERCIALS, WAS THEIR ASTOUNDING COLLECTION OF MARKETING MATERIALS - MOST OF WHICH HAVE SECURED THEIR RIGHTFUL PLACE IN HISTORY AS THE MOST UNUSUAL IN THE WORLD OF FAITH-BASED BRAND IDENTITY. IN THE EARLY 90S A SMALL BUT ACTIVE COLLECTORS' MARKET EVEN BECAME CENTERED AROUND THE "GIFTS", AS THEY WERE SNATCHED UP AND COVETED BY POP-CULTURE-OBSESSED TEENAGERS AND MAIL-ART ENTHUSIASTS WITH A TASTE FOR THE WEIRD AND IRONIC.

NO ONE HAD EVER SEEN ANYTHING QUITE LIKE WHAT ROBERT TILTON WOULD SEND TO THEIR HOUSE FOR FREE - ALL GIVEN OF COURSE, WITH THE HOPE THAT THE RECIPIENT WOULD FEEL AN OBLIGATION TO RECIPROCATE FINANCIALLY. THESE OVERSTUFFED ENVELOPES WERE SELF DESCRIBED AS "REDEMPTION PACKETS", BUT MOSTLY THEY CONSISTED OF A DOZEN BACK-TO-BACK PAGES OF TYPED AND SCRIBBLED NOTATIONS RESEMBLING NAPKIN DOODLINGS OF A TRAINED MONKEY. THEY ALSO CONTAINED "MAGIC PENNIES", RUBBER BANDS, SHORT BITS OF YARN, LITTLE METAL CROSSES, VEGETABLE SEEDS, PACKETS OF SALT, CARPET SAMPLES, AND EVEN TILTON'S LAWN CLIPPINGS IN PLASTIC BAGGIES THAT RESEMBLED BAGS OF POT. IT WAS LIKE GETTING A LETTER FROM A CRIMINALLY INSANE RETARD.

"RIGHT NOW... THIS **CLOTH** IS PLAIN FABRIC," ONE FOLD-OUT POSTER READ. A SWIFTLY SCRIBBLED RED ARROW SWEEPS AND WINDS BACK DOWN THE

FTTPPD

"HA HA HA! THE DAY OF MIRACLES HAS COME!"

BRAP

PAGE, POINTING TO A 2 INCH SQUARE OF NYLON-COTTON SCOTCH-TAPED TO THE PAPER. "BUT AFTER YOU SEND IT BACK WITH ONLY A $1000 VOW, IT WILL BE A MIRACLE CLOTH SATURATED WITH THE PRESENCE OF GOD!"

ASTONISHINGLY - AT ITS PEAK - TILTON'S MINISTRY PULLED IN AN ESTIMATED $80 MILLION PER YEAR, AND THE CHURCH DREW AS MANY AS 5,000 WORSHIPPERS TO A GRAND FIRE AND BRIMSTONE SUNDAY SERVICE WHERE TILTON WOULD PICK "STRANGERS" OUT OF THE AUDIENCE AND "HEAL" THEM USING "FAITH". IN EXCHANGE FOR "JUST A $1000 VOW", TILTON PROMISED MIRACULOUS BENEFITS TO BOTH HEALTH AND FINANCES. "IF JESUS CHRIST WERE ALIVE TODAY AND WALKING AROUND, HE WOULDN'T WANT HIS PEOPLE DRIVING VOLKSWAGENS AND LIVING IN APARTMENTS," HE SAID DURING ONE TELEVISED SERMON, "OHHH.... I KNOW HOW IT FEELS TO DRIVE DUMPY CARS, BURNING OIL, LEAKING OIL... -SOB-.... TRANSMISSIONS LEAKING OIL."

BUT GERMAN-MADE ECONOMY CARS WERE NOT TO BE THE MOST UPSETTING THING AHEAD FOR WORLD OUTREACH. THE TRINITY FOUNDATION, AN AGGRESSIVE TELEVANGELISM WATCHDOG GROUP TOOK NOTICE OF TILTON'S ANTICS (HOW COULD THEY **NOT**?) AND CONDUCTED TRASH SWEEPS OF THE DUMPSTERS BEHIND HIS MINISTRY H.Q. WHEN THEY TURNED OVER WHAT THEY FOUND TO ABC TELEVISION'S PRIMETIME LIVE, DIANE SAWYER STOMPED A MEDIA MUDHOLE IN TILTON'S ASS.

"BE-BA SO LA-KA FOO BA-BAY"

ON PRIMETIME LIVE'S TELECAST IN NOV. OF 1991, (WHICH INCLUDED AN INTERVIEW WITH A WOMAN WHO SPENT TWO DAYS OPENING MAIL FOR TILTON) IT WAS REVEALED THAT WORLD OUTREACH EMPLOYEES WERE INSTRUCTED TO REMOVE ANY CASH, CHEQUES, OR JEWELRY FROM RETURNED MAILERS, AND THROW THE THOUSANDS OF PRAYER REQUESTS IN THE SHIT-CAN. TO ADD INSULT TO NETWORK-AIDED INJURY, THE MINISTRY WAS THEN SUED SUCCESSFULLY BY A FORMER FOLLOWER (AND NOW JILTED SUCKER) NAMED VIVIAN ELLIOTT TO THE TUNE OF $1.5 MILLION. SOON AFTER THAT - CITING MASSIVE DAMAGE TO HIS CREDIBILITY BY THE PRIMETIME LIVE TELECAST, TILTON WENT OFF THE AIR. HIS WORD OF FAITH CHURCH WAS SOLD FOR $6.1 MILLION, WITH WHICH TILTON USED MOST OF TO SETTLE A MULTI-MILLION DOLLAR FRAUD LAWSUIT FILED BY HIS FIRST WIFE.

BEFORE TILTON COULD SAY "BE-BA SO LA-KA FOO BA-BAY", HE WAS MARRIED AGAIN - THIS TIME TO FORMER BEAUTY QUEEN LEIGH VALENTINE. BUT MISS VALENTINE QUICKLY DIVORCED HIM TWO YEARS LATER, CITING CONSTANT PHYSICAL ABUSE. ACCORDING TO LEIGH, (WHO BACKED UP HER STATEMENTS WITH PHOTOS OF HER UGLY BRUISES) ROBERT WOULD SLAM HER PRETTY FACE AGAINST WALLS, HURL TELEPHONES AND COFFEE MUGS AT HER HEAD, THROW HER DOWN STAIRS, DRINK HIMSELF INTO BLIND RAGES, (OFTEN DECLARING TO HER THAT HE WAS "THE POPE") AND WAKE UP IN THE MIDDLE OF THE NIGHT SCREAMING THAT "RATS WERE EATING HIS BRAIN".

"WHATS THAT?"

"MOKO-SHOKO LO TO DO BAA-DAA."

AND WHILE ALL THIS WAS HAPPENING, TILTON WAS **CONSTANTLY** FARTING.

NOT (AS FAR AS I KNOW) IN REAL LIFE, BUT IN THE VCRS AND COMPUTERS OF HUNDREDS OF THOUSANDS OF VIDEO TRADERS AND INTERNET NERDS. THE 4 MINUTE CLIP HAS BEEN CALLED "HEAVEN ONLY KNOWS", "THE FARTING TILTON", AND EVEN THE "JOYFUL NOISE" VIDEO, BUT THE NAME THAT SEEMS TO HAVE STUCK IS "PASTOR GAS". ANYONE WHO HAS SEEN IT WILL BE INSTANTLY AWESTRUCK BY THE FLAWLESS COMIC TIMING INVOLVED IN THE SOUND EDITING OF TILTON'S FARTS. MY FRIENDS, THIS IS ASS HUMOR OF THE HIGHEST CALIBER. EVEN BEN STILLER IS A FAN, AND HE HATES EVERYTHING.

BY 1988 COUNTLESS BOOTLEG COPIES WERE MAKING THEIR WAY ALL OVER THE WORLD. PEOPLE WERE MAKING VHS COPIES AND SENDING THEM TO THEIR FRIENDS, AND THIS UNDERGROUND NETWORK OF DISTRIBUTION RESULTED IN "THE FARTING TILTON" TURNING UP IN EUROPE, AUSTRALIA AND JAPAN. BY 1989, A NEW LESS SCRAMBLED-LOOKING VERSION WAS MAKING THE ROUNDS, COMPLETE WITH A NEW TITLE AT THE BEGINNING AND END THAT READ "HEAVEN ONLY KNOWS". AGAIN, COPIES OF THIS NEW VERSION PROLIFERATED LIKE WILDFIRE. I DISCOVERED IT MYSELF FOR THE FIRST TIME WHEN I GOT A TWO HOUR COMPILATION TAPE CALLED "RELIGIOUS QUACKS" IN THE MAIL FROM A TRADE PAL IN 1997. AROUND THAT TIME THE REVEREND'S

"I'M JUST WILD ENOUGH TO DO WHAT GOD SAID!!!"

FFRRIIP

"THANK YOU, JESUS."

FARTING FAME HIT ITS APEX WHEN AN EPISODE OF **THE DREW CAREY SHOW** DID A DIRECT HOMAGE TO IT - PLACING FAKE FARTS OVER TOP THE TITULAR STARS DIALOG. THE VIRGINAL TECHNOLOGY KNOWN AS THE INTERNET HAD SPREAD TILTON'S FARTS LIKE WILDFIRE, AND NOW EVEN MAINSTREAM AMERICA WAS IN ON THE JOKE.

WITH A SYNDICATED SITCOM NOD IN PLACE, THE STAGE WAS SET FOR SOMEONE TO CASH IN. A COMPANY OUT OF PORTLAND CLAIMED THAT THEY WERE THE ORIGINAL SOURCE OF THE CLIP, AND BEGAN TO SELL 4 MINUTE TAPES FOR $15 EACH. THIS SPREAD THE GAS EVEN FASTER, AND IN EARLY 1998, MARK AND BRIAN, THE HOSTS OF A NATIONALLY SYNDICATED RADIO SHOW GOT THEIR HANDS ON A COPY, REFERRED TO IT AS "THAT TAPE THATS GOING AROUND", AND GAVE IT 30 MINUTES OF FREE ADVERTISING ALONG WITH RESOUNDING APPROVAL. ROCK BAND SEBADOH BEGAN PROJECTING THE TILTON FART FOOTAGE ON A GIANT SCREEN BETWEEN ACTS, TWO SEPARATE METAL BANDS DID SONGS AND VIDEOS THAT TOOK TILTON TO TASK, AND RUMOR HAS IT THAT BERKELEY UNIVERSITY IN CALIFORNIA DEDICATED AN ENTIRE COURSE AROUND CULTURE JAMMING - WITH THE LOW-BROW GRACES OF "JOYFUL NOISE" BEING THE CENTERPIECE.

CONTINUED FROM PAGE 60

GEORGE RATLIFF (DIRECTOR OF **HELLHOUSE**) RECENTLY TOLD AN INTERVIEWER, "I THINK THERE SHOULD BE A DOCUMENTARY JUST TRACKING THE HISTORY OF THE FARTING TILTON VIDEO. I SAW A VERSION OF THAT IN LIKE, 1986. AND SINCE THEN I'VE PROBABLY SEEN 6 VERSIONS. THEY'VE BEEN EVOLVING. I WANT TO KNOW WHO'S BEEN PUTTING THEM OUT. THEY'RE CONSTANTLY BEING RECUT WITH NEW SOUND EFFECTS. IT'S TOO MUCH!"

RATLIFF WAS RIGHT. FANS OF PASTOR GAS BEGAN MAKING THEIR OWN VERSIONS, AND WERE POSTING THEM ONLINE OR ADDING THEM TO THE EXISTING SHORT AND SENDING IT ALONG TO THE NEXT PERSON. IT WAS BECOMING A WEIRD COMMUNAL ART PROJECT WITH NO ONE IN CHARGE. FANS ALSO BEGAN SELLING AND TRADING NEW COMPILATIONS, THE BEST KNOWN BEING A 2 HOUR TAPE CALLED "MONDO TILTON". THE WHOLE SUBCULTURE OF TILTON WAS NOW LIKE A FLATULENT GOD-FLAVORED VIDEO CULT, AND TRACKING ITS HISTORY BECAME ONE OF MY MINI-OBSESSIONS.

IN LATE 2000, A RUMOR BEGAN TO CIRCULATE THAT THE ORIGINAL FARTING TILTON HAD BEEN CREATED BY TWO DISGRUNTLED STAFFERS ON TILTON'S PAYROLL, AND THAT WHEN GOOD OL' BOB 'CAUGHT WIND' (SORRY, I COULDN'T RESIST!) OF WHAT THEY HAD CREATED, HE FIRED THEM. NOW HERE'S WHERE IT GETS SCARY: TURNS OUT THAT THE MYSTERIOUS PORTLAND COMPANY THAT SOLD THOUSANDS OF COPIES OF "PASTOR GAS", NORMALLY MAKES INFOMERCIALS.

UM.... 'INFOMERCIALS'? COULD IT BE THAT TILTON HIMSELF HAS FOUND A WAY TO PROFIT OFF THE HERDS LAUGHING AT HIS NOISY BUNGHOLE? NO ONE KNOWS FOR SURE, BUT TAKE THIS INTO ACCOUNT BEFORE YOU SHRUG OFF MY THEORY: TILTON NEVER **EVER** GAVE UP. HE'S BACK DOING TODAY WHAT HE'S ALWAYS DONE, AND IS AGAIN REACHING MILLIONS OF VIEWERS TOO YOUNG OR TOO SENILE TO REMEMBER THE PRIMETIME LIVE EXPOSE. HE'S FORMED MULTIPLE COMPANIES, BOUGHT A 50-FOOT YACHT, AND SCORED A CHUNK OF OCEAN FRONT PROPERTY IN MIAMI BEACH VALUED AT $1.3 MILLION. IT'S ROBERT TILTON WHO'S HAD THE LAST LAUGH.

ON THE EVE OF THE 20th ANNIVERSARY OF "PASTOR GAS", IT'S SAFE TO SAY THAT ROBERT'S PROBABLY SPEAKING IN TONGUES AND WILDLY FLATULATING TO EMPHASIZE HIS RAPTUROUS JOY AS WE SPEAK. IF WE'VE LEARNED ANYTHING FROM THIS MASTER OF "JOYFUL NOISE", IT'S TO PRAISE THE LORD AND TO BE-BA ME-FA FO-LO BEE DA-DAY!

☆ VISIT: WWW.WEIRDCRAP.COM/TILTON FOR A FIRST HAND LOOK AND LISTEN!

SCUMMY QUOTES FROM THE CINEMA SEWER:

"THERE ISN'T A WOMAN ALIVE THAT HASN'T FANTASIZED ABOUT GOING INTO A ROOM WITH A STRANGER AND SELLING HERSELF FOR MONEY"

--LOVELY LEE REMICK AS A REPORTER IN **HUSTLING**, FROM 1975.

DOUBLE TERROR...in 2 SHOCKING HITS!

SLAVES to their own STRANGE DESIRES!

THE YOUNG, THE EVIL AND THE SAVAGE COLOR

AND

IN THE WILD EYE

HE USED a CAMERA LIKE MOST MEN USE a WOMAN

AN AMERICAN INTERNATIONAL RELEASE IN COLORSCOPE

THE WILD EYE (aka L'OCCHIO SELVAGGIO) WAS THE FIRST DRAMATIC FILM FROM PAOLO CAVARA, WHO UNTIL THEN HAD BEEN THE CO-DIRECTOR OF THE TRASHY DOCUMENTARIES **MONDO CANE** (1962) AND **WOMEN OF THE WORLD** (1963) ALONGSIDE GUALTIERO JACOPETTI. TOGETHER WITH FRANCO PROSPERI, THE ITALIAN TRIO ORIGINATED THE ENTIRE MONDO TRASH-DOCO GENRE.

WITH THIS 1967 RELEASE, CAVARA SEEMED TO BE DAMNING BOTH THE FILMS HE HAD MADE PREVIOUSLY, AND HIMSELF. FROM WHAT I'VE READ ABOUT THIS EXTREMELY RARE FILM, **THE WILD EYE** TELLS THE STORY OF A REPORTER (NAMED - OF COURSE, PAOLO) TRAVELING THE WORLD AND DOING JUST ABOUT ANYTHING TO GET FOOTAGE FOR THE DOCUMENTARY HE'S WORKING ON.

PAOLO TAKES HIS CREW AROUND THE WORLD IN ORDER TO COMPLETE HIS MAD MISSION. FIRST IT'S INTO THE MIDDLE OF AN AFRICAN DESERT TO CHASE GAZELLES AROUND WITH JEEPS AND FILM IT. WHEN THEY RUN OUT OF GAS AND HAVE TO TREK BACK TO CIVILIZATION ON FOOT, THE OTHERS SUSPECT PAOLO OF FIXING THE SITUATION TO GET SOME GOOD FOOTAGE OF HIS CREW LOOKIN' BEDRAGGLED AND MISERABLE. OTHER QUESTIONABLE METHODS OF OBTAINING FOOTAGE INCLUDE PAOLO PAYING HIS CREW TO WHIP DRUG ADDICTS. THE FINAL STRAW FOR THE CAMERAMAN IS WHEN THE DIRECTOR PLEADS WITH SOME AMERICAN SOLDIERS TO EXECUTE A VIETCONG AGAINST A WHITE WALL TO PROVIDE A MORE ATTRACTIVE CONTRAST.

HE USED a CAMERA LIKE MOST MEN USE a WOMAN

IN THE WILD EYE

...sees things you wouldn't dare look at!

ITALIAN CINEMA HISTORIAN ALBERTO PEZZOTTA ONCE LAMENTED THE SCARCITY OF **THE WILD EYE** WHEN HE WROTE: "THE HOME VIDEO MARKET HAS RELEASED MANY FILMS BY OBSCURE ITALIAN DIRECTORS, BUT THERE ARE MANY GEMS YET TO BE DISCOVERED, LIKE PAOLO CAVARA'S **L'OCCHIO SELVAGGIO** (1967), WHICH SHOULD BE CONSIDERED THE MISSING LINK BETWEEN **PEEPING TOM** AND **CANNIBAL HOLOCAUST**."

PHILIPPE LEROY
DELIA BOCCARDO
COLORSCOPE
An AMERICAN INTERNATIONAL RELEASE

WHEN **L'OCCHIO SELVAGGIO** PREMIERED IN JULY 1967 IN THE KREMLIN PALACE OF CONGRESSES DURING THE 5th ANNUAL MOSCOW FILM FESTIVAL, THE AUDIENCE WAS REPORTEDLY SHOCKED WITH THE FANTASTIC SKILL OF CAVARA. THE SCREENING WAS A WILD SUCCESS WHEN THE LIGHTS CAME UP AND THE ENTIRE HOUSE ROSE AND APPLAUDED PAOLO WHO WAS PRESENT ALONG WITH SOME OF THE CAST MEMBERS. THE INCREDIBLE 35 MINUTE STANDING OVATION MADE IT EVIDENT THAT THE MOVIE SHOULD RIGHTLY CAPTURE THE BEST FILM AWARD FOR THE FEST. SEVERAL DAYS LATER THE WINNERS WERE ANNOUNCED, AND AMAZINGLY PAOLO'S MONDO EPIC GARNERED ZERO ATTENTION FROM THE JUDGES.

A USER OF THE IMDB CODE-NAMED "V-V-FIESTA" CLAIMED TO BE PRESENT AT A FILM CRITIC LECTURE IN A SMALL TOWN 150 KM FROM MOSCOW - WHICH TOOK PLACE ROUGHLY 6 MONTHS AFTER THE '67 MOSCOW FILM FEST. THE CRITIC REVEALED TO HIS AUDIENCE THAT THE FILM SELECTION COMMISSION RECEIVED **THE WILD EYE** FOR THE PROGRAM AT THE LAST MINUTE, AND WERE UNANIMOUSLY BLOWN AWAY - I'M TALKIN' ABOUT A SERIOUS CASE OF THE WHIM-WAMS. THE JURY ADMITTED AFTER THE FESTIVAL THAT THE FILM WOULD INDEED HAVE WON THE GRAND PRIZE - HAD THE CUBAN DELEGATION (THE USSR AND CUBA HAD VERY COMPLICATED RELATIONS AT THE TIME) NOT PROTESTED DUE TO THE WAY THE FILM DEPICTED THE EVENTS IN THE US-LED INVASION OF VIETNAM.

SADLY, THE FILM WAS EFFECTIVELY SQUASHED, AND PAOLO CAVARA WAS HEARD FROM VERY LITTLE SINCE. AS "V-V-FIESTA" WROTE, "THUS WE LOST A FANTASTIC DIRECTOR, BECAUSE IN CASE OF THIS VICTORY, HIS DESTINY MIGHT BE GLORIOUS."

- BOUGIE 04

THE WESTDALE 4
PHOENIX'S GREATEST GRINDHOUSE

by Shawn Johns

THE BIGGEST PROBLEM I HAD AFTER MOVING TO PHOENIX IN THE LATE 70S AFTER I HAD LEFT THE NEW YORK AREA WAS IN FINDING MOVIE HOUSES THAT WOULD SHOW THE KIND OF TRASH I WAS USED TO SEEING IN THE FILTH OF 42ND STREET. THE BIG STERILE MULTIPLEXES WOULD NEVER DARE SHOW ANY RISQUE FARE UNLESS IT HAD COME FROM A MAJOR STUDIO. OUT WEST MOST OF THE EXPLOITATION AND HORROR FILMS WERE SHOWN AT DRIVE-INS WHICH WAS OUT FOR ME SINCE I DIDN'T OWN A CAR. IT TOOK SOME SEARCHING - AND A LOT OF COURAGE - FOR ME TO FIND A GRINDHOUSE IN WHAT IS KNOWN AS THE ROUGHEST AREA OF PHOENIX.

THE WESTDALE 4 HAD IT ALL: SONNY CHIBA TRIPLE-BILLS, GORY HORROR AND BONE CRUSHING ACTION DOUBLE FEATURES, THE OCCASIONAL EXPLOITATION AND BLAXPLOITATION FLICK - AND MORE. WEEK AFTER WEEK, I WAS THE ONLY WHITE FACE SITTING IN THAT GRIMY FOUR-PLEX.

IN AN AREA THAT WAS EVERY BIT AS MEAN AND VIOLENT AS THE DEUCE, THE THEATER WAS LOCATED IN A SMALL SHOPPING CENTER SURROUNDED BY FOUR BLOCKS OF THRIFT STORES, A BLOOD BANK, HOUSING PROJECTS, 50 CENT HAMBURGER JOINTS - AND AT NIGHT? $3 AND $5 CRACKHEAD HOOKERS. ENGLISH IS THE SECOND LANGUAGE AROUND THAT BARRIO, AS IT'S MOSTLY A HISPANIC HOOD. OVER A DOZEN DIFFERENT GANGS WOULD HANG OUT IN THE AREA DAY AND NIGHT, MANY OF THEM GOING TO CHECK OUT THE KUNG-FU DOUBLE BILLS AT WESTDALE ON WEEKENDS WITH THEIR CHOLA GIRLFRIENDS. THATS NOT TO SAY THAT I DIDN'T OCCASIONALLY SEE SOME WHITE PEOPLE AROUND, BUT THEY ALMOST ALWAYS LOOKED LIKE THEY HAD JUST ESCAPED FROM JAIL.

SOMETIMES I WOULD GET STARES FROM SOME OF THE HOMEBOYS, LIKE "WHAT'S THIS GRINGO DOING DOWN HERE ?!", BUT I DIDN'T CARE. THIS GRINGO HAD FOUND HIS NEW GRINDHOUSE HOME AWAY FROM HOME. THE FIRST DOUBLE BILL I SAW THERE WAS IN THE LATE 70s- **PIRANHA** AND **NIGHT CHILD**. THIS WAS FOLLOWED A SHORT TIME LATER BY **TERROR** AND **THE LEGACY** TOGETHER ON A TWIN BILL.

THE PERIOD I WENT TO THE WESTDALE 4 THE MOST WAS FROM 1980 TO 1986. THATS WHEN I SAW SUCH WILD DOUBLE FEATURES AS **ZOMBIE** AND **THE TATTOO CONNECTION** (THERE WAS A MOSTLY BLACK CROWD THAT NIGHT, AND A RIOT ALMOST BROKE OUT BECAUSE SOME GUY WAS CAUGHT JACKING OFF IN THE MEN'S ROOM!) **DRIVE-IN MASSACRE** WAS TEAMED UP WITH **DRILLER KILLER**. ALSO MEMORABLE WAS **BODY SNATCHER FROM HELL** MATCHED UP WITH **BLOODY PIT OF HORROR**, AND **LAST HOUSE ON DEAD END ST.** PLAYING WITH THE **PEOPLE WHO OWN THE DARK**. SONNY CHIBA'S **DRAGON PRINCESS** UNSPOOLING WITH THE RARE DON EDMONDS EXPLOITATION FLICK **BARE KNUCKLES** WAS ALSO A TREAT.

NO OTHER INDOOR CINEMA IN PHOENIX WOULD DARE SHOW THIS KINDA STUFF. THE ONLY OTHER "WALK IN" THAT EVEN CAME CLOSE WAS THE TOWER PLAZA TWIN ON THE EAST SIDE.

THE WESTDALE WAS ALWAYS PACKED ON THE WEEKENDS, ESPECIALLY IF IT WAS PLAYING KUNG FU FILMS WHICH BROUGHT OUT AN EVEN ROUGHER CROWD THAN USUAL - ALTHOUGH STABBINGS AND SHOOTINGS WERE ALL TOO COMMON IN THE AREA. I REMEMBER WHEN THEY PAIRED THE LEON ISAAC ACTIONER **BODY**

Raw Force...
Invaders of the Jade Tombs.
UNTAMED AND UNLEASHED
TO KILL!

RAW FORCE
One Blow. The Deathblow! R16

CAMERON MITCHELL GEOFF BINNEY in RAW FORCE
starring JILLIAN KESSNER JOHN DRESDEN JENNIFER HOLMES
and HOPE HOLIDAY as Hazel Buck
Music by WALTER MURPHY Produced by FRANK JOHNSON
Executive Producers REBECCA BELLA and LAWRENCE WOOLNER
Written and Directed by EDWARD MURPHY An ANSOR INTERNATIONAL Picture
An ALFRED ZACHARIAS Presentation An AMERICAN PANORAMA Release
© 1981 AMERICAN PANORAMA

AND SOUL BACK TO BACK WITH **KID WITH THE GOLDEN ARM**, AND BLACKS IN THE AUDIENCE WERE ROOTING FOR LEON ISAAC, WHILE ALL THE MEXICANS WERE CHEERING ON THE CHICANO! I REALLY FELT LIKE I WAS BACK IN TIMES SQUARE THEN!

LEON ISAAC SEEMED TO BE POPULAR AT THE WESTDALE. ANOTHER TIME THEY SHOWED **PENITENTIARY 2** WITH **HORROR HOSPITAL**. ADMITTEDLY A VERY STRANGE COMBO, BUT THAT'S WHAT MADE GOING TO THE WESTDALE SO GREAT. EVERY SO OFTEN THEY'D RUN A TRIPLE BILL OF OLDER FILMS TOGETHER - FOR INSTANCE: **THE SHE BEAST**, **THE EMBALMER** AND **INVASION OF THE BLOOD FARMERS**. ANOTHER GREAT TRIO WAS **BRUCE LEE AND I**, **TEN FINGERS OF DEATH**, AND **STEEL EDGE OF REVENGE**.

SURE, THE THEATER ITSELF WAS A SCUMMY FLEA-PIT WITH HARD-AS-A-ROCK CHAIRS AND GUT-CHURNING CONCESSION STAND FOOD, NOT TO MENTION THE "FRIENDLY" PATRONS WHO'D LOVE TO FIND AN EXCUSE TO KILL YOU. BUT IF YOU WERE AS CRAZY ABOUT TRASHY MOVIES AS I WAS - AND STILL AM - THE WESTDALE 4 WAS THE ONLY PLACE IN TOWN. YOU JUST HAD TO LEARN NOT TO HANG AROUND ONCE THE THEATER HAD CLOSED.

YOU'LL SCREAM YOUR HEAD OFF!

BLOODSUCKING FREAKS R
IN COLOR • Filmed in GHOUL-O-VISION

FROM 1985 UNTIL THE MIDDLE OF '87, THE WESTDALE STARTED FEATURING KUNG-FU DOUBLE BILLS ALMOST EVERY WEEK. I SAW INCREDIBLY OBSCURE TITLES LIKE **BAD DOG FU**, **KUNG FU INFERNO**, **DRAGON ZOMBIES**, **BROTHERHOOD KILLERS OF KUNG FU**, **DON'T BLEED ON ME**, **BLACK HERCULES VS. THE YELLOW TIGER**, AND **DUNGEON OF THE NINJAS**.

THE CROWDS ALSO STARTED GETTING EVEN ROWDIER AROUND THIS TIME. MORE PEOPLE WERE BUYING DRUGS AROUND THERE THAN THEATER TICKETS. ATTENDANCE SLACKED OFF. PEOPLE WERE OBVIOUSLY AFRAID OF GETTING ATTACKED. IN THE LATE 80S, THE WESTDALE STARTED SWITCHING TO SPANISH MOVIES, AND TWO OF THE FOUR SCREENS WERE DEVOTED TO MEXICAN ACTION-THRILLERS IN THEIR ORIGINAL LANGUAGE. THEY STOPPED SHOWING ANY DECENT TRASHY DOUBLE BILLS BY THEN, ONLY PAIRING UP MAINSTREAM RELEASES ON THEIR THIRD OR FOURTH RUNS. THE PRICE OF A TICKET WENT DOWN TO A DOLLAR AT TIMES!

A LOT OF THESE CHANGES HAD TO DO WITH THE EXPLODING CRIME RATE, BUT THERE WERE ALSO THREE NEW VIDEO STORES WITH LOTS OF HORROR, ACTION AND KUNG-FU TITLES THAT OPENED WITHIN MERE BLOCKS OF THE WESTDALE, DRAWING THE TRASH-HOUNDS AWAY. MORE PEOPLE COULD AFFORD TO BUY VCR'S BY THEN, AND THE RENTAL STORES HAD "DOLLAR DAYS" TO BOOST MEMBERSHIP. BY 1992, THEY HAD CLOSED DOWN TWO OF THE FOUR SCREENS. THE REMAINING ONES SHOWED MAJOR RELEASES OR SPANISH FILMS, ALTHOUGH ADMITTEDLY, SOME OF THOSE LATINO FLICKS WOULD

CERTAINLY QUALIFY AS EXPLOITATION FARE.

SADLY, AS OF LATE SUMMER - EARLY FALL 1993, THE WESTDALE CLOSED DOWN FOREVER, LEAVING GRINDHOUSE FANS IN PHOENIX WITHOUT A THEATER TO FREQUENT. ALL THAT'S LEFT NOW IS SOME GANG GRAFFITI SCRAWLED ON THE BOARDED UP WINDOWS. SOMEWHAT FITTINGLY, BEFORE IT CLOSED, BRANDON LEE'S **RAPID FIRE** WAS THE LAST ENGLISH LANGUAGE PIC TO PLAY THERE, AND HAD A MARATHON RUN OF MORE THAN FIVE MONTHS NONSTOP!

AT LEAST THE WESTDALE 4 WENT OUT IN TRUE GRINDHOUSE STYLE. TO THE PEOPLE IN THAT RUN DOWN PHOENIX HOOD, IT WAS MORE THAN JUST ANOTHER THEATER. THE WESTDALE 4 WAS THERE FOR MORE THAN 20 YEARS AND PROVIDED THE BEST (OR WORST, DEPENDING ON YOUR POINT OF VIEW) IN MOVIE ENTERTAINMENT. I'M SURE I'M NOT THE ONLY ONE AROUND WITH FOND MEMORIES OF IT.

—SHAWN JOHNS

THE MEANEST CHIBA MOVIE YET!
CHIBA... IS BACK-
more deadly than any weapon!
SONNY CHIBA IS THE 'EXECUTIONER' R
IN COLOR
Distributed by TRANS CONTINENTAL FILM CORP.

EXCLUSIVE!

FREE KARATE LESSON COUPON TO THE FIRST 100 CUSTOMERS EVERY NIGHT.

REGISTER FOR DRAWING OF FREE COMPLETE KARATE COURSE - COMPLIMENTS OF:
KEMPO KARATE CHINESE School of Art Defense
27 E.SOUTHERN   420 N. 35TH AVE.

SILVER DOLLAR D.I.
7201 S. Central

WESTDALE
35th Ave & VanBuren

COOL WORLD

IN THE ORIGINAL SCRIPT FOR RALPH BAKSHI'S 1992 ANIMATED/LIVE ACTION CULT FILM, HOLLI WOULD WAS NAMED "DEBBY DALLAS". PORN STAR TRACI LORDS WAS CONSIDERED FOR THE ROLE, BUT LOST OUT TO THE BETTER KNOWN KIM BASINGER. BAKSHI'S PERSONAL CHOICE WAS DREW BARRYMORE.

AS A PUBLICITY STUNT, PARAMOUNT NAILED A HUGE CUT-OUT OF HOLLI WOULD ON THE HOLLYWOOD SIGN IN L.A.

★★★★★★★★★★★★★★
CARTER STEVENS
★★★★★★★★★★★★★★

Born Malcolm Worob, lifetime pornographer Carter Stevens created smut from both in front of the camera as well as behind it, and delivered top quality product throughout it all. From underground SM loops and features for RDF and Avon, theatrical features from the 1970s, to video-age S+M fetish fare, Stevens's presence in porn has been ubiquitous and legendary.

Some of his directorial highlights are:
LICKITY SPLIT (1974 w/ Linda Lovemore and Bree Anthony)
ROLLERBABIES (1976 w/ Susan McBain and Mary Stuart)
TEENAGE TWINS (1976 w/ Brooke and Taylor Young)
JAILBAIT (1976 w/ Tina Lynn and Sharon Mitchell)
PUNK ROCK (1977 w/ R. Bolla and Jean Sanders)
DOUBLE YOUR PLEASURE (1978 w/ Brooke and Taylor Young)
PLEASURE PALACE (1979 w/ Serena and Jamie Gillis)
WICKED SCHOOLGIRLS (1980 w/ Velvet Summers)
TWILITE PINK (1981 w/ Veronica Hart and Kandi Barbour)
BIZARRE STYLES (1981 w/ Vanessa Del Rio and Annie Sprinkle)
WHITE HOT (1984 w/ George Payne and Baby Doe)

In October 2007, Carter appeared on the www.avmaniacs.com message board. Intrigued by the conversation the various regulars of the classic porn forum of the board had been having with his porno peer from yesteryear (a gang-bang style interview with Shaun Costello that also saw print in Cinema Sewer #17), he decided to chime in and regale us with a few stories of his own. The first thing he did, however, was display a few bones of contention he'd had with what Costello had stated:

"Shaun seems to be ashamed of the time he spent in porn but I'm not. Sean's comments are an interesting mix of truths, half truths, and drug fuelled flights of fantasy. Shaun seems to remember being the first at a lot of things that he was merely a follower on. He did a lot of rip offs of both straight films and other porn films. His film THE LOVE BUS was a knock off of my film LICKITY SPLIT. He seems to remember discovering the "Young Twins" when my film TEENAGE TWINS the first time they ever worked on screen together. One of the sisters had done porn but I'm the one who found out she had a twin sister and managed to get them both on film for the first time."

"Shaun also had a lot of mean hurtful things to say about Sharon Mitchell. First off he states she started in films while she was

underage. Bullshit!. I met Sharon through a semi-ligit talent agent in South Jersey 3 DAYS after her 18th birthday. I "discovered" her and named her. Sharon is her real first name but the Mitchell comes from "Steve Mitchell", a name I used a lot when I acted in films. She was a bright articulate young lady who had the talent to make it as a legit actress but went off the deep end later on with heavy drugs".

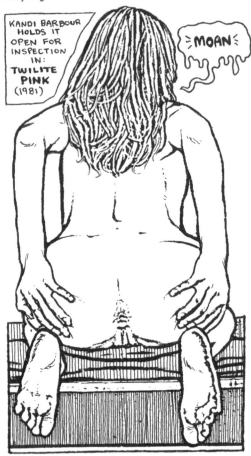

KANDI BARBOUR HOLDS IT OPEN FOR INSPECTION IN: TWILITE PINK (1981)

≥MOAN≤

The gauntlet was dropped. This was the real Carter Stevens, and the questions from board members (including myself) came fast and furious. The internet is far too temporary for my tastes, so here are some highlights from the online Carter Stevens forum dogpile printed on cold, hard paper:

Nick McBride: Did you rent your studio for the filming of Linda Lovelace having sex with dogs? Sounds unlikely to me, but that's what Sharon Mitchell says in the book "THE OTHER HOLLYWOOD".

Carter Stevens: I rented my studio out for a lot of people but I never worked with Linda Lovelace in features or loops. I had nothing to do with any of her films including the dog loops. I did rent out my studio for the shooting of the last 10 minutes of SNUFF and have been miscredited as having directed that footage which I did NOT do.

Thomas Wood: Speaking of the killing scene in SNUFF, what was your involvement with the Findlays?

Carter Stevens: I never knew Michael. He was killed before I met Roberta. I knew her when she was with Walter (sorry, forgotten his last name) who was her partner on a lot of films they did together. I worked for her several times as an actor on her own films but since we were both Camera "men", we never worked together on a crew for others.

Joshua Axelrad: You should know that the book Sleazoid Express cites you as the director of the "Snuff" sequence.

Carter Stevens: That damn rumour follows me everywhere. the simple fact is I owned a small studio that I rented out to the Producer (Alan Shackleton) so they could shoot the end sequence. The actual director was a gentleman named Simon Nuchtern. I helped move the lights around and provided props (I still have the little jig saw they cut her hand off with), the things a studio owner would do on a non-union shoot. I did NOT direct the sequence.

Joshua Axelrad: Well, keep in mind that the co-author of Sleazoid Express is Bill Landis, a notorious drug user who also acted in porn under the name "Bobby Spector".

AndyM: Maybe she wasn't telling the truth, but in "THE OTHER HOLLYWOOD", Sharon Mitchell claims that she was 17 when she made JOY, which she said was her first film, and that when the producers/directors found out, they stuck on the shelf until after she turned 18, and released it then. Jean Jennings was supposedly underage when she started, too, according to the same book. I guess Traci Lords and Alexandria Quinn were really the only two widely-publicised underage U.S. performers, and the only ones subject to a recall/boycott of their illegal product -- though I heard rumours about movies like WPINK being re-edited to cut out scenes of an actress who was supposedly underage at the time.

Carter Stevens: I don't want to argue with Sharon (after all it is her life), but I have the records to prove she was over 18. Maybe I'm wrong. Hell, it was a lot of years ago.

Chris Jefferys: Andy, I think you are referring to Ali Moore. I've heard that she may have been underaged in some of her videos, but my copy of WPINK has her scene fully intact. Don't know if it was re-edited later though.

Robin Bougie: Carter, not sure where you picked up that Shaun is ashamed of his time in porn, as I didn't get that at all from talking to him -- but a lot of things have been said on this message board, and I can't claim to have read it all. You worked with Long Jeanne Jeanne Silver in HOUSE OF SIN, what are your memories of working with her?

Carter Stevens: I loved Jeanne like a younger sister. She lived with me in my loft for almost a year (platonically only) and was sort of the house mother to all the girls I lived with and played with during that time. HOUSE OF SIN was special because she was always complaining to me that people only hired her because of her missing leg, and I put her in HOUSE OF SIN and shot around the fact that she had a missing leg. No where in that movie do you sense that she is anything but the beautiful sexy girl she was.

Robin Bougie: I'm a huge fan of TEENAGE TWINS and the Young Twins themselves, but there is so little out there in terms of info about them. Were they at all reluctant to sex each other up? Was this something they did when the camera was off? Or at home?

Carter Stevens: Shooting the twins was a real challenge. Sean got it right when he said they liked Quaaludes. In fact we all called them the Quaalude twins. Sexually they were rather unschooled. They did not fool around with each other off screen, it was strictly my idea to pair them up on

Teenage Twins

screen as I had never heard of it done in any movie before that. I do remember Eric Edwards coming up to me during shooting and telling me that he had a real problem. He had asked one of them to go out with him after the shoot and only after she had said "Yes" did he realise that he had asked out the wrong twin. When I found the male twins for Double Your Pleasure I had to fly down to Florida to get one of the female twins out of jail where she had been doing time for passing bad checks. In truth I think she had just gotten so stoned she had forgotten she had spent all her money and just kept writing checks long after the bank had closed the account.

Joshua Axelrad: Did TEENAGE TWINS cause you any legal hassles?

Carter Stevens: Not only did Teenage Twins NOT cause me any legal hassles it probably made more money than all my other films put together. It is far from my best work however. We had just put Rollerbabies in the can and were cutting it, (and that was the longest, most expensive, most complicated film I had done to date) and we were pretty burned out when Annie Sprinkle introduced me to one of the twins at another porn shoot we were all on. The twins had both been stewardesses for a couple of rinkydink southern airlines and had been laid off. (Actually I think they might have been fired because they were so flaky.) I met the sister and she said she might be interested. I called my distributor in Detroit and told him I needed money right away to make another film. He balked as I hadn't finished Rollerbabies yet but when I said I have a set of twins his wallet dropped open faster than his mouth. It was a real challenge making Twins as neither girl knew crap about sex. I remember Mary Stuart sitting in my kitchen with a dildo trying to teach the girls how to give head. And I swear I'm not kidding when I say up until then they thought the term "Blow Job" was literal. We cobbled together a script (yes my films had scripts) in no time and within 2 weeks we shot Teenage Twins. It was shot in one long 3 day weekend. We saved money by renting the camera equipment for a Friday and it didn't have to be returned till Monday morning all for one day's rental fee, so we shot most of our films in 3 day (pardon the expression) spurts. The kitchen and dining room shots were done in my real kitchen and dining room. the rest was shot in my studio on sets.

Joshua Axelrad: Carter, how did you find out about this site? Also, could you please provide some insight on your appearance in "INSIDE JENNIFER WELLES?"

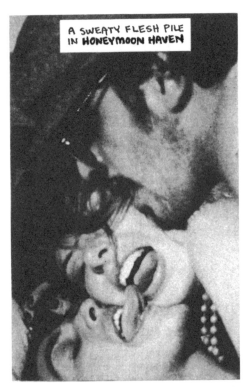

A SWEATY FLESH PILE IN HONEYMOON HAVEN

Carter Stevens: I discovered the site because I was bored and googled myself and saw my name pop up in Shaun Costello's comments. Actually it is funny how I got the part in INSIDE JENNIFER WELLES. I got a call from Joe Sarno's production manager that there was a part in the film that would be perfect for me so I called Joe right away and asked him about it. I knew Joe from years back when I had been a shift supervisor at Movielab, before I got into the creative end of the business. Joe immediately started to back-pedal and hem and haw about how he thought the part was already cast and quickly got me off the phone with a "I'll call you right back." I hung up and turned to my secretary and said "I think I just got the brush off". About 5 minutes later Joe called me back and fell all over himself apologizing. I explained that I produced and directed under the Carter Stevens name and acted under a lot of different names (mostly Steve Mitchell) and that I'd done over two dozen pornos. So he hired me on the spot and that's how I got "Inside" Jennifer Welles.

"HONEYMOON HAVEN"

STARRING
WADE NICHOLS
KAREN ST. JOY
RICHARD BOLLA
MARLENE WILLOUGHBY

A CARTER STEVENS FILM

RESTRICTED
limited admittance if under 18

Thomas Wood: I think Shaun mentioned that he never had a problem with the police but Roberta Findlay mentioned getting arrested. Did you ever have problems with the New York cops when shooting your films?

Carter Stevens: Oh boy, did I ever. Three days before the election in NYC, LICKITY SPLIT was the number one grossing film in the city and the police raided the theater and busted the manager for showing an "obscene" film. A day later they raided a theater in Queens where it was also showing and as luck would have it the distributor showed up just as the bust was going down and was arrested. They got his records and came after me several days later. They missed me thanks to an elevator starter in my building who warned me they were upstairs so I split back to my home in Jersey and called my lawyer. He arranged to have me surrender myself the following Friday, which I did at the Elizabeth St. Station in Chinatown. I was booked and charged with a felony, wholesale promotion of obscenity, and taken down to the Tombs where I was to be held for arraignment. As we were walking from the station to the tombs the Sgt. who was in charge said to me, "I saw your film, pretty good." I held up my handcuffed hands and asked "Then what the hell am I doing here?" He just shrugged and said "We all have a job to do. You do yours and I do mine." Small comfort. Since I was forewarned, I was clean shaven, and was wearing a very expensive 3 piece suit with my pockets jammed with candy so I wouldn't have to eat the famous baloney sandwich in the Tombs. Since I was turning myself in, the police had promised my lawyer that I would be released the same day but they hit a snag. Since I had never been arrested before my fingerprints weren't on file so they bounced back from Albany and had to be sent to the FBI to make sure I wasn't some killer on the lam. As the time ticked closer to the end of day court the arresting officer kept bouncing back and forth to keep me appraised of the situation. Of course with all the police attention my fellow convicts must have thought I was a high level mafia boss. Anyway, my lawyer had me replaced by my corporation in the indictment. The corporation pleaded guilty and paid a fine and I got back my fingerprints which hung on my office wall for many years thereafter. In the long run my legal fees and fines cost me more than I made on the damn film.

Ian Miller: I was wondering if you could tell me a little about the genesis of PUNK ROCK, which is a film I enjoy quite a bit, especially Bobby Astyr's performance. How did the Stilettos come to be in it?

Carter Stevens: In those days I hung out on the bottom floor of Max's Kansas City, and Punk was just starting to come into style. I was living with a girl named Honey who was a "punk", and she knew everybody in the New York punk rock scene. I'm an old folkie myself so punk was mostly noise to me, but one night I got a BJ from a BEAUTIFUL girl in the phone booth at Max's and asked her if she wanted to be in a movie. She was willing to be in a music scene but not in any sex. I won't mention her name here but she went on to become very big. She had a group then called the Stilettos and we worked them into the script for my next picture. However she left the group,

66

SHE WAS A TEENAGE RUNAWAY, KIDNAPPED
BY SEX SLAVERS... HE WAS THE PRIVATE EYE WHO HAD
TO FIND HER... IN THE SINISTER WORLD OF HARD
DRUGS, COLD BLOODED MURDER AND...

PUNK ROCK!

"The best of all possible worlds...sex, violence and hard punk rock! Absolutely the finest porn movie of the year...and I've seen 'em all!"
Jeff Goodman, FLICK Magazine

"Heads above 99 per cent of standard American porn...Go see it!"
NATIONAL SCREW
Al Goldstein's Magazine

A CARTER STEVENS FILM
STARRING WADE NICHOLS, RICHARD BOLLA
JEANIE SANDERS, NANCY DARE AND PAULA MORTON

and a girl named Elda (who was NOT a looker) took over the lead for the group. They were still interested in being in the film anyway. About 6 months after it came out punk music started to get big, and our distributor made me an offer to back an "R" rated version if I would cut out the sex and go back and shoot another hour of non-sex plot and music footage. We got permission from the owners of Max's to shoot upstairs and we wound up shooting 3 additional bands there. The film was released as PUNK

ROCK some places and ROCK FEVER in others and did NO business. If anyone is interested they can order a DVD of the "R" rated version directly from me.

[Editor's note: Carter may be too classy to mention her by name, but I'm not. The original lead singer of the Stilettos was Blondie herself; Debbie Harry!!]

Joshua Axelrad: Who were some of your favourite performers to direct?

67

THE HARDCORE SEX CHOPPED FROM CARTER'S **PUNK ROCK**, THE MOVIE WAS THEN MARKETED TO A DISCO LOVIN' PUBLIC AS A PSUEDO SEQUEL TO **SATURDAY NIGHT FEVER!** BECAUSE... PUNK AND DISCO ARE INTERCHANG-ABLE, RIGHT?

Carter Stevens: My favourite performers were for the most part the public's favourite performers. Jamie Gillis and Vanessa Del Rio top the list, but I used people like Eric Edwards and R. Bolla over and over because I used scripts and they would actually remember lines. As for the females, I discovered many new performers and loved working with them even if they had to be directed a lot. Of course many of them I partied with off screen and quite a few I even lived with on and off. Remember this was the era before AIDS and after the invention of the pill. Sex was clean and the air was dirty. My favourite performer of course was hands down Baby Doe. We were later married and have a son together.

Nick McBride: Did you direct Marc Stevens?

Carter Stevens: I used Marc Stevens in IN SARA'S EYES. It was not a good match. He was a pain in the ass. Although I knew him and ran into him a lot (he lived just down the hall from Annie Sprinkle) we never really got on together. I used to joke that he was only Mr. 10 1/2 if you measured from the knees up and I think he took it personally. He was really mostly gay and very heavily into drugs which is why he peaked so early in his career. We really didn't travel in the same groups.

Robin Bougie: I'm curious about what your experiences and memories of the anti-porn movement were -- both from the far left women's lib groups, and the far right Christian fundamentalists. The one thing they seemed to come together on was that they both hated images of sexuality.

Carter Stevens: The Christian fundamentalists came later for the most part, but the women's libber s, WOW did they ever hate us. I appeared on lots of shows with Andrea Dworkin (the most repulsive human being I ever met) and she hated me -- I mean HATED!! She was pathological. Normally she wouldn't even sit next to me on a TV set, like she was afraid I would reach out and touch her (fat chance! you couldn't pay me enough to touch her). I remember one radio show we did, it was Jamie Gillis and I, and she was the other guest. She wouldn't even sit in the same studio with us. But you have to remember that her claim was that all sex was rape! To her I was the anti-christ, even though I'm just a nice Jew boy from New Jersey.

Ian Jane: Rollerbabies is a personal favourite. As a rollerporn

enthusiast to the nth degree, I'd buy you a beer for this one if I could. Was roller porn just popular because roller skating was in at the time, and you were cashing in on a trend or was there more to it?

Carter Stevens: My loft in those days had 12 foot ceilings and our office space was cut up by 6' high partitions. So you could talk easily from office to office. This was just about the time ROLLERBALL had hit the theatres, and being big Sci-Fi geeks we had gone to see it. Now, whenever I interviewed potential actors and actresses I always asked them if they 1. had any special sexual talents we could use in a film (that's how I discovered Linda Lovemore and Veri Knotty) and 2. ask them if they had any special non sexual talents we could use in a film. Well, one afternoon a young lady answered me that she was a roller Derby skater and over the wall came Wesson Smith's loud voice, "IN THE FUTURE THERE WILL BE NO SEX BUT THERE WILL BE ROLLERBABIES!!" And thus the idea for Rollerbabies was born. Wesson Smith was in those days a young comic book writer, and went on to be a BIG

ROLLERBABES, AKA "ROLLERBABIES". 1976

comic book writer -- writing Wonder Woman and Superman for DC comics. We never saw the young lady again and had to go around NY asking every actor who would do XXX films if they could rollerskate.

Robin Bougie: Carter, what do you remember of Velvet Summers? Man, she was so cute...!

Carter Stevens: You mean "Little" Velvet Summers? That was the way we always listed her in the credits. I worked with Velvet on several films. Although she was in her mid twenties, she looked like she was 12. She was from Maine and lived with a biker. In fact she was a real biker chick.

VELVET SUMMERS

Swore like a truck driver, but she was game for most anything and was easy to work with. She was a small girl and liked high heels but everyone always put her in mary janes and pig tails for films just to make her look younger. The fact that she looked so young got lots of people in trouble. I was contacted once by a distributor who was busted for shipping a print of Wicked School girls over the canadian border. They hit him for kiddie porn but lucky for him I had copies of her ID and all her releases and paperwork on file. He beat the rap.

Robin Bougie: Aw man, I always assumed that Lil' Velvet must have gotten at least a few people into hot water with her very young looks, so that isn't too surprising. Some more stars that show up in your older films that I'd love to hear your two cents on are Kim Pope, Kandi Barbour (she of the weird lookin' nipples), and did you say that you discovered Veri Knotty??

Carter Stevens: Kim Pope was a lovely lady. Sweet, but she had parchment-like translucent skin. She had to use full body makeup in front of the lights or you could see every vein in her body. Only time that was a real pain in the ass was on the MOUNT OF VENUS set where her makeup kept wiping off on the cotton batting we were using for clouds. after a couple of hours the clouds were all pink.

Kandi Barbour was a space cadet. She lived with me in NY for a while and then lived with my production manager on the west coast while I was out there making Tinseltown. I once saw her call California from NYC just to find out what time it was in L.A. She had the most beautiful face in porn and did lots of non-porn modelling as well. She had a habit of never cashing checks until she needed the money so she might pull out a wrinkled 3 month old check for a couple of grand that she got for some commercial and have me cash it for her when she wanted cigarettes. Years later she gained lots of weight and lived over the Hubba-Hubba club in Honolulu. She danced topless there and ran around in a muumuu.

Yes, I discovered Veri, and gave her her name. Like I said, I always asked every new porn hopeful if they had any special sexual talents we could use in a film. Veri looked me straight in the eye and said brightly, "Yea, I can tie my cunt in a knot." Being quick on the uptake I think I said something like "HUH?" at which point she dropped her pants and showed me. I very quickly put her into

CAPTAIN LUST which I was production managing, and JAILBAIT which I was producing and directing. She quickly went on to become a star. I'm very sorry to report that Veri later got hooked on H and died from complications of her drug habit.

Joshua Axelrad: Have you worked on any non-porno material?

Carter Stevens: Of course. I worked on hundreds of non-pornos under my real name. For some reason I got a lot of work from Italian companies who came to the US to shoot on location. Don't know why, as I DON'T speak Italian. I worked a lot for Luigi Scattini who produced some films for Lina Wertmuller. One film I did for him as location mgr had a scene in it about the hero, Gerardo Amato, getting involved in a porno shoot in NY. As a joke I cast myself as the porno director. I don't think the film ever played in the US but I saw it in France. They dubbed my voice in by some guy with a deep basso profundo voice and I sat in the movie theater in France giggling to my self every time I opened my mouth in the film. The film was called BLUE NUDE (1977).

R.T. Gelling: Carter, did you know Tina and Jason Russell?

Carter Stevens: Jason was a rather (to be kind) plain looking guy with a badly pock-marked face. Tina was the most beautiful girl in the business at the time with long straight hair who gave probably the best blow job in the entire western world (deep throating isn't everything). She would only work with guys that Jason approved of, but the list was pages long so it wasn't a problem. I don't remember Jason ever getting a hard-on, but he got hired just for Tina. Poor Tina died of anorexia, and not alcoholism as I've read elsewhere. She was a poor sorry scarecrow the last time I saw her. What a waste.

TINA RUSSELL

James R: What was it like working with Lisa DeLeeuw?

Carter Stevens: I never worked with her, but one night with her stands out in my mind. We met at Barnard's (a popular bar with the porno crowd in those days) and I told her about a guy I knew who was an Oklahoma State Senator who was in love with her. We wound up running down Broadway together (this was in the days before cell phones) until we found a pay phone and we called the Senator long distance so she could chat with him. He offered to bring her down to Oklahoma and pay her a week's pay just to visit with him but I don't think she ever did it. I know for a fact at least one other porn star did take him up on his offer.

Nick McBride: Carter, I've always been curious as to how pornographers such as yourself found the girls willing to do porn in its early years, eg for loops. Shaun Costello suggested you cruised the streets for "young stuff" making it sound like you had a bunch of teenage runaways working for you. Did you just advertise for nude models? Did you have girls turn up expecting an acting or a modelling job who were surprised to learn they were expected to fuck some stranger on film? How many went through with it in these circumstances and how many backed out as fast as they could?

Carter Stevens: This was New York City in the late 70s and early 80s. Sexually it was the wild wild west. The easiest thing to find was new people. I advertised for "Adult" film actors in Show Business and Backstage two

newspapers that existed just for film and theater casting. I advertised in the Village Voice and even in the little free supermarket throw aways. I even advertised in the Columbia Spectator, the Columbia University newspaper (where I found my second lead for Sara's Eyes who was going for her masters degree in Languages). I didn't need to cruise the streets as they poured into my offices daily. We didn't need the casting couch as casual sex was the flavour of the day, and I had more sex than I could handle as it was. I did have a large loft with a lot of bedrooms and always had 3 or 4 ladies living with me at any one time -- which is probably why Shaun remembers my place the way he does. I only slept with about half the women I let live there otherwise I would have been dead by age 30 from exhaustion. Jean Silver called it "Carter's home for wayward women". All in all it was dirty work but somebody had to do it.

DR. PHIL ON PORN

DAAAMN, I **SO** WANTED TO WRITE "DR. PHIL **IN** PORN AS A HEADLINE JUST NOW. THAT WOULD JUST BE SO SATISFYING TO GET TO BREAK **THAT** STORY!

NO, INSTEAD I'LL BE USING THIS SPACE TO ALLOW THE GOOD DOCTOR TO DO HIS BEST TO HAVE YOU IMMORAL SINNERS SEE THE LIGHT. KEEP IN MIND THAT OPRAH'S RIGHT HAND MAN HERE WAS ABUSIVE TO HIS FIRST WIFE, HAD A LAWSUIT BROUGHT AGAINST HIM IN 2006 FOR MANIPULATING AND EDITING FOOTAGE OUT OF CONTEXT TO MAKE AN INNOCENT PERSON APPEAR TO BE A CRIMINAL, WAS SANCTIONED IN 1989 FOR AN INAPPROPRIATE RELATIONSHIP WITH A 19 YEAR OLD CLIENT, AND AS A RESULT IS NOT LICENSED TO PRACTICE PSYCHOLOGY, AND SETTLED A SUIT FOR $10.5 MILLION FOR SELLING USELESS WEIGHT-LOSS SUPPLEMENTS TO FATTIES WHO ONLY GOT FATTER.

HERE ARE HIS OPINIONS ON PORN:

"IT IS NOT OK BEHAVIOR. IT IS A PERVERSE AND RIDICULOUS INTRUSION INTO YOUR RELATIONSHIP. IT IS AN INSULT, IT IS DISLOYAL AND IT IS CHEATING."

"PORNOGRAPHY ISN'T REAL, IT'S A FANTASY. IT'S ALSO SOMEBODY'S DAUGHTER WHO HAS TAKEN A REALLY, REALLY WRONG TURN. SHE'S DEMEANING HERSELF, DEBASING HERSELF, HUMILIATING HERSELF AND SHE'S BEING EXPLOITED BY PEOPLE WHO ARE FUNDED BY YOU. IT'S A SICK, DEMENTED, TWISTED WORLD, AND IT'S NOT HEALTHY, NATURAL OR NORMAL."

"TELL YOUR PARTNER THAT VIEWING PORNOGRAPHY IS ABSOLUTELY, UNEQUIVOCALLY, UNACCEPTABLE IN YOUR RELATIONSHIP. DRAW A LINE: YOUR PARTNER NEEDS TO CHOOSE BETWEEN THE PORNOGRAPHY OR THE RELATIONSHIP."

YEE-HAW!
LETS GO GIT
SUM **HOOKERS!**

"YOU NEED TO ASK YOURSELF: WOULD YOU DO IT WITH YOUR PARTNER STANDING RIGHT THERE? DO YOU JUSTIFY THE BEHAVIOR BY SAYING 'IT'S HARMLESS', OR 'EVERYBODY DOES IT'?

MY FAVORITE RESPONSE TO THIS ON THE DR. PHIL MESSAGE BOARD WAS FROM 27 YEAR OLD KALINA WHO WAS IN A 10 YEAR RELATION-SHIP WITH A 'PORN ADDICT':

"HE SAYS IT'S NORMAL, AND THAT ALL GUYS DO IT. BLAH BLAH BLAH. I AM GOING TO LEAVE HIM 'CAUSE OF IT. I AM SAVING UP AND THEN I AM OUTTA HERE. I AM A PRETTY, SMART, KIND GIRL. I DON'T UNDERSTAND WHY HE DOES THIS AND I THINK IT'S SICK. I WENT OUTSIDE THE RELATIONSHIP, AND I DON'T REGRET IT. IT WAS AMAZING, I FELT WANTED, NEEDED, DESIRABLE, AND I HAVE FALLEN IN LOVE WITH THIS MAN."

YES, PORN IS IMMORAL AND SICK, BUT CHEATING IS TOTALLY **FINE**. FUCKING LOONS.

THE TARNISHED LEGEND OF JOHNNY WADD

JOHN HOLMES WAS NO ANGEL, BUT HE SURE HAD A MASSIVE PORK SWORD....
☆ BY: BOUGIE. 2003 ☆

NO MATTER HOW YOU FEEL ABOUT HIM, JOHN HOLMES IS A TRUE POP CULTURE ICON. AS AN ACTOR WHO WAS LEGENDARY BEYOND PROPORTION TO HIS THESPIAN SKILLS, HIS CAREER PENETRATED WORLDWIDE PSYCHE AND LEFT HIS SOGGY STAIN UPON IT FOR GENERATIONS TO COME.

IN THE WAKE OF JAMES COX'S **WONDERLAND**, WHICH ARRIVED IN LIMITED RELEASE LATE LAST YEAR TO GIVE A NEW STICKY SHOT OF SCUMMY COATING TO THE HOLMES LEGEND, I'D LIKE TO ADD MY TWO CENTS TO THE MIX, AND AT THE VERY LEAST, PERHAPS SPRINKLE SOME TRUTH ON THE SUGAR-COATED HYPE.

BORN JOHN CURTIS ESTES ON AUG. 8TH 1944 INTO AN ABUSIVE HOME IN RURAL OHIO, HOLMES BUMMED AROUND THE COUNTRY AND IN AND OUT OF MILITARY SERVICE UNTIL HE DROPPED ANCHOR IN LA. AND MARRIED HIS FIRST WIFE, A CONSERVATIVE HOMEMAKER.

UNDAUNTED BY DOMESTIC BLISS, THE JAUNTY YOUNG WADD PULLED HIMSELF UP BY HIS JOCKSTRAP AND PUT HIS BEST ORGAN FORWARD. JOHNNY WAS A MAN IN THE RIGHT PLACE, WITH THE RIGHT EQUIPMENT, AT THE RIGHT TIME. L.A. WAS THE PLACE TO BE IN 1969 (IF YOU WEREN'T IN NEW YORK) WHEN THE STAUNCH WALLS OF CENSORSHIP FELL JUST FAR ENOUGH TO ALLOW FOR A SLEAZY YOUNG BURGEONING PORN SUBCULTURE MADE UP OF 8MM LOOPS AND PEEPSHOW FILMS TO SLOWLY GROW TO A MINI FILM INDUSTRY. AND A MAN WITH A 13½ INCH DONG, WHO COULD SURPRISINGLY GET IT HARD (UNLIKE

HIS BLACK COUNTERPART LONG DONG SILVER) AND COULD EVEN CUM NEARLY ON CUE, WAS A PRIZED ASSET INDEED. BEFORE HE COULD SAY "OPEN WIDE!" JOHN WAS THE FUCKING KING, AND THE KING OF FUCKING.

BUT LET'S NOT PAINT GOLD ON A STATUE MOLDED FROM HORSE SHIT. DESPITE HIS "AW SHUCKS" PERSONA, MILDLY SARCASTIC, I'M-IN-ON-THE-JOKE ATTITUDE, AND MAMMOTH RAPID FIRE WEDDING TACKLE, HOLMES WAS HARDLY A STRAIGHT-SHOOTER. MORE LIKE A STOOL PIGEON, THIEF, WOMAN-BEATING PIMP, COMPULSIVE LIAR, JUNKIE, EGOMANIAC, AND ULTIMATELY A VICTIM TO HIS OWN LIFESTYLE OF 24-HOURS-A-DAY EXCESS.

TO QUOTE RODGER JACOBS, THE CO-WRITER AND CO-PRODUCER OF **WADD: THE LIFE AND TIMES OF JOHN C. HOLMES**, "JOHN HOLMES WAS THE EPITOME OF A SOCIOPATH, AND AN ANTISOCIAL PERSONALITY IN THE MOST BROAD AND EXTREME DEFINITION OF THE WORD. HE SAW OTHER PEOPLE AS THINGS TO BE MANIPULATED TO FURTHER HIS OWN NEEDS, NOTHING LESS, NOTHING MORE."

MIND YOU, RODGER COULD CERTAINLY BE ACCUSED (AND HAS BEEN) OF HAVING AN AGENDA AGAINST HOLMES AND PERHAPS PORN ITSELF WHEN HE ADMITTED IN 2000 THAT HE WAS "OBSESSED WITH DESTROYING" HOLMES, WHO HE BELIEVED TO BE "PURE FUCKING EVIL", AND EVERYTHING THAT IS "INHERENTLY EVIL ABOUT THE BUSINESS OF PORNOGRAPHY". I MEAN, THIS GUY USES THE WORD "EVIL" MORE OFTEN THAN DUBYA. THAT'S NOT GOOD.

BUT EVEN FRIENDS, FAMILY, AND FILMMAKERS WHO'VE TRIED TO PUT A POSITIVE SPIN ON HOLMES'S CAREER HAVE HAD TO CONCEDE

John Holmes

THAT CHUMMING AROUND WITH THIS WELL-HUNG HOMEBOY COULD BE A VERY TRYING AND FRUSTRATING EXPERIENCE. EVEN VANESSA DEL RIO RECALLS HIM AS BEING "RUDE", AND SHE DOESN'T HAVE A BAD WORD TO SAY ABOUT ANY OF HER OTHER OLD SKOOL COMPATRIOTS.

JOHN'S SECOND WIFE, LAURIE ROSE (AKA MISTY DAWN) KNOWN IN HER DAY AS "THE BUTTFUCKING QUEEN OF PORN" WEARILY INSISTS THAT JOHN HAD A HEART OF GOLD, SAYING "HE WAS GREAT TO ME.", EVEN AS OTHER, LESS BIASED PEOPLE IN THE KNOW RECOUNT HIS MANY ABUSIVE CRUELTIES TO HER AND THE OTHER WOMEN IN HIS LIFE.

WATCHING THE "LOST" INTERVIEWS AND OUTTAKES BETWEEN A 25 YEAR OLD JULIA ST. VINCENT AND HOLMES TO BE FOUND IN THE EXTRA FEATURES SECTION OF THE DVD RELEASE FOR JULIA'S VERY PRO-HOLMES DOCUMENTARY **EXHAUSTED** (1981) PROVES TO BE A 1ST HAND LOOK AT HOW EVASIVE AND SELFISH THE MAN COULD BE. DESPITE THE FACT THAT HE KNEW ROOKIE DOCUMENTARIAN JULIA WAS ROLLING PRECIOUS FILM SHE COULD SCARCELY AFFORD, A COKED-UP JOHNNY GOOFS AND NEVER ANSWERS A QUESTION WITH ANYTHING RESEMBLING A STRAIGHT OR EVEN COHERENT ANSWER. THIS WAS A TYPICAL GAME PLAYED BY A DUDE WHO - WHILE HE WAS TOWERING OVER THE PORN BIZ ITS MID 70S HEY-DAY - BELIEVED HE COULD DO NO WRONG.

P.T. ANDERSON KEPT THE HOLMES LEGEND ON PEOPLE'S LIPS IN 1997 WITH THE RELEASE OF **BOOGIE NIGHTS**, A FILM THAT IS AS MUCH AN ODE TO JULIA ST. VINCENT'S **EXHAUSTED**, AS IT IS TO THE MAN HIMSELF. WHEN

MEAN OL' JOHNNY WADD HAS A BIIIIIIIG GUN...

The Incredible John Holmes Super Pump Has Helped Thousands Of Men To Overcome The Problems And Insecurities Of A Penis That Is Too Small!

"AMBER WAVES" MAKES A TRIBUTE DOCUMENTARY TO P.T.'s HOLMES-ESQUE CHARACTER, "DIRK DIGGLER," HE SPOUTS ACTUAL HOLMES DIALOG FROM **EXHAUSTED** - INCLUDING THE SMUG BOAST OF "HE LETS ME BLOCK MY OWN SCENES" UTTERED BY HOLMES IN RELATION TO DIRECTOR BOB CHINN (THE INSPIRATION FOR "JACK HORNER" IN **BOOGIE NIGHTS**). A PAUSE FROM CHINN, AND THEN THE HILARIOUS: "NO I DON'T." JOHN COULDN'T EVEN STOP HIMSELF FROM FIBBING EVEN WHEN HE HAD NO CHANCE OF HOODWINKING ANYONE.

WHEN ANDERSON WAS ASKED BY ROUGH CUT MAGAZINE HOW IMPORTANT **EXHAUSTED** WAS IN THE PROCESS OF MAKING **BOOGIE NIGHTS**, HE ANSWERED, "CRITICAL. IT WAS SO CLEARLY MADE BY SOMEONE WHO WAS JUST BLIND TO WHAT JOHN HOLMES CLEARLY WAS. SHE TRIED TO MAKE THIS WONDERFUL PORTRAIT OF WHO HE WAS... SO HERE'S THIS NARRATION SAYING HOW HE'S A WONDERFUL GUY, AND IN THE BACKGROUND HE'S SLAPPING SOME WOMAN AROUND SAYING "SHUT UP BITCH!!""

BUT REGARDLESS OF HIS SHORTCOMINGS AS A MAN, JOHN'S FREAKISH 13 ½ INCH BEEFSTICK - AND THUSLY HIS FILMS - WERE NEVER ANYTHING LESS THAN ENTERTAINING. YOU SIMPLY HAVEN'T LIVED AS A PORN FAN UNTIL YOU'VE SEEN J.H. CRANK THAT BASEBALL BAT SIZED FLESH-TRUNCHEON UP THE ASSHOLE OF A GROANING CO-STAR. THRILL TO THE AMAZING MARILYN CHAMBERS TAKING THE WHOLE THING INTO HER BETTY CROCKER EASY BAKE OVEN IN BOTH **INSATIABLE** (1980), AND IN **UP 'N' COMING** (1983), WHERE SHE SCREAMS "MAKE IT HURT!" PERHAPS HOLMES'S BEST ANAL-WRECKING SCENE WAS WITH ANAL GODDESS CONNIE PETERSON IN **LITTLE FRENCH MAID** (1981), WHERE HE POUNDED HIS MONSTER SHLONG INTO CONNIE'S BUNG-HOLE WHILE PAUL THOMAS SIMULTANEOUSLY FILLED WHAT LITTLE ROOM WAS AVAILABLE IN HER ABUSED COOZE. AND A75'S **SWEET PUNKIN**? ONE WORD: **WOW**.

AS DETECTIVE "JOHNNY WADD", MR. HOLMES "CASED MORE CRACKS THAN HE CRACKED CASES" (SNORT) AND ALONG WITH BOB CHINN, CREATED THE MOLD THAT THE HOLMES LEGEND WOULD BE CAST WITH. NO ONE WOULD HAVE SAID IT AT THE TIME, BUT IN HINDSIGHT CHINN WAS TRULY AN UNHERALDED GENIUS WHO BROUGHT THE XXX INDUSTRY ONE OF THE

MOST ENTERTAINING AND (UNINTENTIONALLY) HILARIOUS CHARACTERS THAT THE ADULT INDUSTRY HAS EVER SEEN.

THE EXPLOITS OF THE WADD CHARACTER BEGAN IN 1970'S **THE DANISH CONNECTION**, AND CONTINUED FOR 11 FILMS. THESE 16mm MOVIES WERE FAR FROM CLASSY MAINSTREAM CINEMA, BUT LIKE MUCH OF THE PORN CONTENT FROM YON SWINGIN' 70s, THERE WAS AT THE VERY LEAST A PLOT AND AN EFFORT TO CREATE AN ACTUAL FILMGOING EXPERIENCE. **TELL THEM JOHNNY WADD IS HERE** WAS SHOT IN ONE DAY ON A BUDGET OF $750, AND WAS IN THE CINEMAS A MERE 7 DAYS LATER. THE END RESULT IS AN AWESOME BLEND OF THE SEXY AND THE OUTLANDISHLY STUPID.

HOLMES MADE BAGS OF COIN, EVEN IN A TIME WHEN FEMALE PERFORMERS MADE MEAGER AMOUNTS (COMPARED TO GIRLS TODAY), BUT STILL OUTGROSSED THE BOYS BY A HUGE MARGIN. HE BLEW ALMOST EVERY PENNY ON DRUGS, AND BECAME COMPLETELY UNDEPENDABLE AS A PERFORMER. THEN HE STARTED PIMPING OUT HIS 15 YEAR OLD GIRLFRIEND WHO LIVED IN HIS CAR. JOHN DIDN'T GIVE A FUCK, HE WAS FRANTICALLY SCHEMING TO SCORE HIS NEXT HIT.

INDUSTRY REPORTERS WERE INCREDULOUS. THEY COULDN'T OR WOULDN'T ACCEPT WHAT HAD HAPPENED TO THEIR KING. IN A DECEMBER 1981 ISSUE OF VELVET TALKS, TERRY BREWER WROTE, "IS JOHN HOLMES FINISHED AS AN X-RATED STAR? IT'S HARD FOR ME TO SAY, THAT'S BETWEEN JOHN AND HIS FANS. I'M NOT IN A POSITION TO CONFIRM

OR DENY THE RUMORS ABOUT DRUGS BEYOND REPORTING WHAT HOLMES HIMSELF HAS SAID. IT IS A FACT THAT HE DOESN'T LOOK HEALTHY, BUT THAT DOESN'T NECESSARILY MEAN HE'S KILLING HIMSELF WITH DOPE." TERRY WENT ON TO STATE THAT JOHN WAS PROBABLY JUST "FACING A MID-LIFE CRISIS".

BY THAT TIME THOUGH, THE BOTTOM HAD ALREADY DROPPED OUT ON HOLMES. FAME EVENTUALLY TOOK ITS TOLL AND LEFT JOHN SPIRALING THROUGH A LONG SLIDE OF COCAINE, QUAALUDES, VODKA, PETTY THEFT, AND A GROUP OF "FRIENDS" THAT COULD ONLY BE DESCRIBED AS A "BAD CROWD" PERHAPS, AS AN UNDERSTATEMENT. HIS PATHETIC DECLINE REACHED ITS CLIMAX WHEN HE RAN FROM BOTH THE POLICE AND THE MOB AFTER HIS ENTANGLEMENT WITH 4 GORY MURDERS ON WONDERLAND AVE. IN HOLLYWOOD ON JUNE 29th 1981, ONLY TO BE CAUGHT BY THE COPS AND TRIED FOR MURDER. HE WAS ACQUITTED OF ANY WRONGDOING DESPITE THE FACT THAT HE REFUSED TO DIVULGE WHAT HE KNEW ABOUT THE TORTURE AND MURDERS HE HAD WITNESSED FIRSTHAND.

JOHN ATTEMPTED TO CLEAN UP HIS ACT, BUT IT WAS FAR TOO LATE. HIS YEARS OF UNCHECKED ROMPING WITH OVER 14,000 WOMEN (AND A COUPLE HUNDRED GUYS) CAUGHT UP WITH HIM IN THE FORM OF THE DEADLY AIDS VIRUS. DESPITE THE FACT

THAT HE HAD BEEN DIAGNOSED WITH THE DISEASE IN 1985, JOHN (PREDICTABLY) LIED TO HIS OLD FRIEND BOB CHINN AND TOLD HIM THAT HE WAS SO SICKLY-LOOKING BECAUSE HE WAS DYING OF COLON CANCER. HOLMES DONNED THE GUN ONE LAST TIME IN **THE RETURN OF JOHNNY WADD**, AND SELFISHLY TOOK THE LIVES OF HIS CO-STARS IN HIS HANDS. NONE OF THE GIRLS HE FUCKED ON SET CONTRACTED THE DISEASE, BUT JOHN REPORTEDLY STATED THAT IT WASN'T NECESSARY TO TELL PEOPLE ABOUT HIS HIV STATUS BECAUSE EVERYONE IN PORN WOULD DIE - OR DESERVED TO FOR THEIR UNSPECIFIED BETRAYALS BEHIND HIS BACK.

BUT IT WAS JOHN HOLMES HIMSELF WHO WOULD EXPIRE IN MARCH OF 1988 IN SEPULVEDA, CA. HE WAS ONLY 43 YEARS OLD. HIS WIFE, THE "BUTTFUCK QUEEN", REFUSED TO LET ANY OF HIS FEW REMAINING FRIENDS VISIT HIM IN THE HOSPITAL OR ATTEND HIS FUNERAL.

THE MYTHOLOGY OF JOHN HOLMES

AS MENTIONED EARLIER, JOHN LOVED TO MAKE UP STORIES AND THEN TREAT THEM LIKE THEY WERE FACTS. MANY OF THESE OUTRAGEOUS MYTHS LONG OUTLIVED HOLMES HIMSELF. SUCH AS.....

* HOLMES LOST HIS VIRGINITY AT THE AGE OF 6 TO A SWEDISH NURSE NAMED FREIDA.
* AS A BOY, JOHN'S RICH AUNT PAID FOR "NUDE MODERN JAZZ BALLET CLASSES" FOR HIM.
* HE HAD TO ABANDON UNDERWEAR BECAUSE "I WAS GETTING ERECTIONS AND SNAPPING THE WAIST BAND 4 OR 5 TIMES A MONTH."
* JOHN MISTAKENLY KILLED TWO MEN BY FUCKING THEM IN THE ASS. HE WAS TRIED AND CONVICTED OF MANSLAUGHTER, AND SENTENCED TO ABSTAIN FROM FUCKING ANUSES.
* HOLMES HAD MULTIPLE DEGREES IN PHYSICAL THERAPY, MEDICINE, AND POLITICAL SCIENCE.

WONDERLAND (2003)

JAMES COX'S WONDERLAND FOCUSES ON CLASSIC PORN STAR JOHN HOLMES AND HIS UNCERTAIN DEGREE OF INVOLVEMENT IN A MULTIPLE MURDER ON WONDERLAND AVE IN L.A.'S LAUREL CANYON IN 1981. THE FILM BEGINS AFTER HOLMES'S CAREER IS WASHED UP, ENDED BY HIS DESCENT INTO DRUG ADDICTION, WHERE, TO SUPPORT HIS HABIT, HE BEFRIENDED A NUMBER OF DEALERS AND CRIMINALS. HE'S PAST HIS PORN STUD GLORY, AND IS NOW WILLING TO USE IT TO BETRAY ABSOLUTELY ANYBODY TO FEED HIS ADDICTION.

WONDERLAND VIEWS HOLMES, THE VICTIMS, AS WELL AS THEIR KILLERS, FROM A REMOVED STANCE. IT AVOIDS THE USUAL "ROMANCE OF REDEMPTION", AND DOESN'T SPIN THE PLOT INTO HAM-FISTED "TRAGIC HERO" TERRITORY. AS A CLASSIC PORN FAN WITH A GOOD AMOUNT OF PRIOR KNOWLEDGE OF THE MAN AND THE INCIDENT IN QUESTION, I FOUND THE MOVIE RESOLUTELY TRUE TO THE DISMAL TALE IT TELLS -- A RARE SITUATION FOR DRAMATIC BIOPICS WHICH ARE FAMOUS FOR ADDING FICTIONAL ELEMENTS FOR NO GOOD REASON. THIS IS NOT A MORALITY PLAY, AND HOLMES IS PRESENTED IN A FAR LESS ROMANTICIZED LIGHT THAN I EVEN EXPECTED.

IN THE FILM, WE HEAR TWO SIDES OF THE STORY, ONE FROM HOLMES HIMSELF, AND THE OTHER FROM A SURVIVOR (DYLAN McDERMOTT) OF THE SLAYINGS. BOTH, OF COURSE, PAINT COMPLETELY DIFFERENT PICTURES OF EACH OTHER, AS WELL AS OF THEIR ENEMY: WEALTHY DRUG LORD EDDIE NASH (THE INCREDIBLE ERIC BOGOSIAN). COX USES MULTIPLE VERSIONS OF THE CRIME AS A DEVICE, BUT IT'S NOT CENTRAL TO THE MEANING OF THE MOVIE, WHICH IS NICE FOR A CHANGE. ONE **RASHOMON** WAS PLENTY, THANKS.

VAL KILMER is John Holmes

KATE BOSWORTH

LISA KUDROW

JOSH LUCAS

DYLAN McDERMOTT

WONDERLAND

THE '80S UNPLUGGED
THE MURDERS UNVEILED
THE LEGEND UNZIPPED

IN CINEMAS JANUARY 29

LABELLED BY THE LAPD AS THE MOST GRUESOME CRIME SCENE SINCE THE TATE/LABIANCA SLAUGHTER, THE SORDID AND GORE-SOAKED WONDERLAND HOUSE WAS THE FIRST CRIME SCENE TO BE FILMED WITH A VIDEO CAMERA (BRAND NEW TECHNOLOGY!) BY POLICE, AS A WAY TO COLLECT VISUAL EVIDENCE. INCREDIBLY, THIS UNCENSORED CRIME SCENE VIDEO IS ACTUALLY AN EXTRA FEATURE ON THE DVD ITSELF. WATCHING IT, I COULDN'T DECIDE IF IT WAS IN TERRIBLE TASTE, OR IF IT WAS PERHAPS THE BEST SUPPLEMENTAL FEATURE I'D EVER SEEN. **MARRIED WITH CHILDREN**'S CHRISTINA APPLEGATE GREW UP A COUPLE BLOCKS FROM THE SITE OF THE MURDERS AND REMEMBERS SEEING THE BLOOD-SOAKED MATTRESSES ON THE STREET -- A POWERFUL MEMORY THAT LED TO HER AGREEING TO TAKE A SMALL ROLE.

I WAS THRILLED TO FIND OUT THAT THE FILMMAKERS TRACKED DOWN DAWN SCHILLER (HOLMES'S TEENAGE GIRLFRIEND), AND HIS WIFE SHARON. BOTH LADIES SERVED AS CONSULTANTS ON THE PICTURE, CHILLIN' ON THE SET AND SHARING THEIR INSIGHTS INTO HOLMES'S CHARACTER AND THE ERA. SEEING HER PAST RELIVED PROVED TO BE A VERY INTERESTING EXPERIENCE FOR SCHILLER, AND SHE STATED THAT SHE WAS REALLY IMPRESSED BY THE BONER-LOAD OF RESEARCH THE FILMMAKERS HAD DONE. "I REALLY FELT THAT IT WAS GOING TO BE AN HONEST PORTRAYAL, THAT THE TRUTH WAS GOING TO BE FINALLY TOLD."

ACTUALLY, I WAS INITIALLY CONCERNED WITH THE CHOICE TO CAST KILMER AS HOLMES (MATT DILLON WAS ORIGINALLY SLATED FOR THE ROLE BUT DROPPED OUT TO DIRECT **CITY OF GHOSTS**), BUT ONCE I SAW HOW DEAD-ON PERFECT AND IMPECCABLY VAL HAD GOTTEN JOHN'S PHYSICAL MANNERISMS AND PERSONALITY, I ALMOST FORGOT I WASN'T WATCHIN' THE 13 ½ INCH ORIGINAL PORTRAYING HIMSELF! I WOULD GO SO FAR AS TO SAY THAT VAL KILMER GIVES THE PERFORMANCE OF HIS CAREER -- AND I HOPE THAT ONE DAY HE WILL BE RECOGNIZED FOR WHAT HE DID HERE.

INTERESTINGLY, THE ACTOR WAS TOTALLY UNINTERESTED IN THE IDEA OF PLAYING HOLMES AT FIRST. IN FACT, DESPITE PLEAS FROM THE DIRECTOR AND HIS AGENT, KILMER LITERALLY REFUSED TO LOOK AT THE SCRIPT. EVENTUALLY HIS AGENT "TRICKED" HIM INTO READING IT BY ASKING HIM TO CONSIDER THE SMALLER, GRITTIER PART OF EDDIE NASH. ONCE KILMER CRACKED THE SPINE ON DAT MO-FO, IT WAS A DONE DEAL. HE CHANGED HIS MIND AND SIGNED ON FOR THE LEAD, AND ENDED UP GETTING SO INTO HIS RESEARCH FOR THE ROLE, HE EVEN SPENT THE NIGHT IN THE WONDERLAND AVE. CRIME SCENE DURING THE ANNIVERSARY OF THE HORRIFIC KILLINGS.

HARSHLY DISMISSED BY FILM CRITICS AND IGNORED COME OSCARTIME, I FIRMLY BELIEVE WONDERLAND IS ONE OF THE MOST UNDERRATED FILMS OF THIS DECADE. —BOUGIE

IT'S ALWAYS THE DAMN COMICS WE COULD CARE LESS ABOUT THAT PRODUCERS DECIDE TO CO-OPT AND MAKE INTO FILMS: MEN IN BLACK, THE MASK, SPAWN, CATWOMAN, BLADE... THE LIST IS LONG AND OVERWHELMING. WELL, **FUCK THEM**, WE WANT SOME OF THAT OBSCURE WEIRD SHIT. THAT OVER-THE-TOP INSANITY WHERE YOU'VE GOTTA LEAVE THE KIDS WITH GRANDMA. I'M TALKIN' KICK-ASS, NON-P.C. EXPLOITATION CINEMA. PEOPLE, I'M TALKIN' 'BOUT:

WHITE MAN'S BURDEN

CURSED WITH WHITE GUILT ABOUT HOW CAUCASIANS HAD FUCKED UP THE PLANET, JACK JACKSON (AKA JAXON) CREATED HIS MOST IN-YER-FACE COMIC, "WHITE MAN'S BURDEN" IN 1974 -- WHICH RAN IN THE GREAT "SLOW DEATH" #6. CHECK IT:

AN EXPLORATION OF RACIAL STEREOTYPES IN A POST-APOCALYPTIC WORLD (WHICH PREFIGURES ROBERT CRUMBS EXCELLENT "WHEN THE GODDAMN JEWS TAKE OVER AMERICA") JACKSON USES PEN AND INK TO GIVE FUCKIN' WHITEY WHAT HE DESERVES: ANNIHILATION AT THE HANDS OF ALL THE OTHER RACES.

"THE IMPLICATIONS OF THE LAST PANEL OF THE STORY LEAD ME TO SUSPECT THAT IN PART

> YOU ARE THE MOST ACCURSED RACE EVER TO PLAGUE THE EARTH! EVERYTHING YOU TOUCH TURNS TO SHIT! YOU ARE **DOOMED**, WHITEMAN!! DO YOU ACKNOWLEDGE YOUR GUILT??

> I DUNNO WHAT YOU'RE TALKING ABOUT... YOU'RE **NUTS**...

> AND SEE WHAT'S HAPPENED TO HIS WOMEN — HE'S TURNED THEM INTO FUNCTIONLESS, PAINTED MANNEQUINS — A TWISTED PARODY OF FEMININITY THAT FILLS THEM WITH **SELF**-CONTEMPT, AND DISGUST FOR THEIR MEN! YET, THEY CAN'T PULL THEMSELVES OUT OF IT BECAUSE THEY'VE PLAYED THE DUMMY SO LONG THEY'VE BEGUN TO **LIKE IT.**

JACKSON MAY HAVE BEEN DOING A PARODY OF WHITE SELF-LOATHING," WAS THE WORD FROM SELF-PUBLISHER AND COMIX HISTORIAN COLIN UPTON, "IN U.S. CAMPUSES IN THE 1960s, THERE WERE SERIOUS DISCUSSIONS ON WHETHER OR NOT WHITE BABIES SHOULD BE KILLED ON SIGHT, DISCUSSIONS DOMINATED BY WHITE COLLEGE STUDENTS."

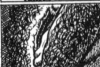

SORTA PATHETIC, AIN'T IT?

YEAH

UPTON CONTINUED, "YOUNG PEOPLE WERE CHALLENGING THE STEREOTYPICAL HEROIC VERSIONS OF AMERICA'S PAST, AND AFTER DOING THE RESEARCH -- REALISING THAT A LOT OF IT WAS NOT SO PRETTY. YOU HAD THE GENOCIDE OF THE FIRST NATIONS, THE LAND GRAB OF MEXICO BY TEXAS, AND THE OPPRESSION OF MINORITIES AND LABOR UNIONS BY THE LEGENDARY "HEROES", THE TEXAS RANGERS. TEXANS LIKE JACK JACKSON HAD THEIR SELF-IMAGE DESTROYED AND SOME WENT OVERBOARD THE OTHER WAY, DEPICTING WHITE MEN AS BEING UNIQUELY EVIL."

INDEED, THE TEXAS THAT JAXON GREW UP

MAYBE WHAT SHE NEEDS IS SOME *REAL* COCK FOR A CHANGE..

HUH? WOULDYA LIKE THAT?

WAGGLE PLOP   ZIP

IN WAS DEEPLY RACIST. IN FACT, HIS INSPIRATION TO DO COMICS CAME FROM A SCHOOL TEXTBOOK FILLED WITH RACIST IMAGERY. HE BEGAN BY PUBLISHING "GOD NOSE" IN 1964 IN AUSTIN (ARGUABLY THE FIRST UNDERGROUND COMIC **EVER**) THEN IN 1971 HE CO-FOUNDED RIP-OFF PRESS-- A PRINTING PRESS/PUBLISHING COMPANY. SO CONFIDENT OF THEIR SUCCESS, HE ISSUED A PUBLIC CHALLENGE TO MARVEL AND DC, WARNING THE BIG PUBLISHERS THAT THEIR ARTISTS AND WRITERS WOULD SOON BE ABANDONING THEIR "NEW YORK SWEATSHOPS" AND DEFECTING TO THE UNDERGROUND, WHERE THEIR WORK WOULD BE PUBLISHED "IN PRINT RUNS OF UPWARDS OF 100,000 COPIES", AND OWNED BY THE CREATORS THEMSELVES.

THAT UTOPIAN DREAM NEVER CAME TRUE IN JACK'S LIFETIME (NOR I DOUBT WILL IT IN MINE), BUT THE

AND SO THE THIRD WORLD COALITION LAUNCHES A MASSIVE ATTACK AGAINST THE FINAL STRONG-HOLD OF THE WHITES, AN ATTACK DESIGNED TO END THE SPECTRE OF WHITE SUPREMACY FOREVER.

YOU KNOW, ITS SORTA SAD, THINKING ABOUT THAT POOR, DUMB-SHIT REDNECK BACK THERE. I COULD ALMOST HAVE ADMIRED HIM, EVEN EMBRACED HIM AS A BROTHER. YET, TO THE END HE HELD US IN CONTEMPT, LIKE WE WERE SO MUCH DIRT..

YEAH.. I KNOW WHAT YOU MEAN— THE ONLY ONE OF THEM *WORTH* SAVING, BUT THE *VERY ONE* THAT HAD TO BE ELIMINATED. A MENACE TO SOCIETY, LIKE A RABID DOG!!

COMPANY DID FLOURISH IN HEAD SHOPS, AND JAXON FOUND THAT HIS NOSTALGIC REGARD FOR OLD E.C. COMICS WAS SHARED BY OTHER UNDER-GROUND ARTISTS LIKE RICHARD CORBEN, RAND HOLMES, GREG IRONS, AND DAVE SHERIDAN. TOGETHER THEY WOULD BE THE MAIN PLAYERS IN A COUPLE OF WEIRDLY BRILLIANT E.C. PARODY ANTHOLOGIES CALLED "SKULL COMICS", AND "SLOW DEATH".

AS MENTIONED, IT WAS IN "SLOW DEATH" #6 THAT JACKSON WOULD BUST OUT THE CULMINATION OF HIS BIZARRE AND UPSETTING SATIRICAL STRIPS WITH "WHITE MAN'S BURDEN", THE LAST COMIC HE DREW IN SAN FRANCISCO BEFORE MOVING BACK TO TEXAS.

IN IT, HE PUSHED UNDERGROUND COMIC POLITICAL SATIRE JUST ABOUT AS FAR AS ANYONE HAD; "IT WAS THE LAST COMIC STRIP I DID IN THAT SITUATION" HE SAID, "AND I REALIZED AT THE TIME THAT I WAS BECOMING REALLY CYNICAL AND DISILLUSIONED WITH ALL THE CRAP GOING ON AROUND ME."

THE COMIC BEGINS WITH "A COALITION OF THE BLACK, BROWN, AND YELLOW RACES" NEARING THE END OF THEIR BITTER WAR WITH "WHITEY"--HAVING CAPTURED THE LAST REMAINING SPECIMENS OF "THE NORDIC PEOPLES", AND CHAINED THEM TO A BUNKER WALL WHILE THEY DELIBERATE THE FATE OF THE SOLE SURVIVORS.

THE SOLDIERS SHOW THEIR CONTEMPT FOR THE WHITES, VERBALLY HUMILIATING AND TORTURING THE REMAINING "SNIVELLING, FAGGOTY LARD-ASSES".

VIVA LA RAZA!

POWER TO THE PEOPLE!

GUNG HO FAT CHOY!

THESE CAPTIVES ARE DEPICTED AS UGLY, SHALLOW, AND VILE. WHEN THE LONE MIDDLE-AGED HONKY FEMALE IS TAUNTED WITH THE PROMISE OF A GANG RAPE, SHE STATES HER DISGUST FOR THEM AS "PERVERTED LECHERS" EVEN WHILE SHE MOANS AND PULLS HER CUNT LIPS BACK, BEGGING THEM TO FORCE THEMSELVES ON HER. THEY ARE ONLY BEMUSED BY HER VULGAR DISPLAY.

AFTER GUNNING THEM DOWN WHERE THEY STAND ("ANIMALS! THEY MUST **ALL** BE TERMINATED!") THE VICTORIOUS COALITION FORCES PROWL THROUGH THE RUBBLE OF RUINED CITIES UNTIL THEY DISCOVER "THE SACRED PLACE OF THE OMNIPOTENT VOICE, WHERE THE WHITEMAN CLAIMS TO HAVE GOTTEN **THE WORD**!". HERE, GOD SPEAKS TO THEM, TELLS THEM THAT THEY ARE EACH MEMBERS OF THE CHOSEN MASTER RACE, AND THE WHOLE DEMENTED CYCLE OF MADNESS BEGINS ANEW.

NOT TOO SURPRISINGLY, THIS COMIC GOT JACK SOME DEATH THREATS FROM SOME HUMORLESS WHITE PEOPLE, SO AFTER GETTING THIS DERANGED (ALTHOUGH VERY THOUGHT-PROVOKING) TALE OUT OF HIS SYSTEM, HE DEVOTED THE REST OF HIS CAREER TO FAR LESS OFFENSIVE COMICS ABOUT AMERICAN HISTORY. HE GOT MARRIED, HAD A KID. SEEMINGLY HAPPY ENDING FOR OL' JAXON.

UNFORTUNATELY, HE WAS DIAGNOSED WITH TERMINAL PROSTATE CANCER IN EARLY 2006, AND SAT HIS SON DOWN TO TELL HIM HE MIGHT NOT BE AROUND MUCH LONGER. FOR THE PREVIOUS DECADE, HE'D BEEN FIGHTING A CRUEL BONE DISEASE THAT GNARLED UP HIS HANDS MAKING IT EXTREMELY PAINFUL TO DRAW.

LOOK! THAT MUST BE THEIR ORACLE, THE SACRED PLACE OF THE OMNIPOTENT VOICE, WHERE THE WHITEMAN CLAIMS TO HAVE GOTTEN *The Word*!

EVEN STILL, HE CONTINUED TO HONE HIS CRAFT. WITH THE IMPORTANT FATHER-SON HEART-TO-HEART OUT OF THE WAY, HE DROVE TO THE PLEASANT VALLEY CEMETERY IN STOCKDALE TEXAS -- THE CEMETERY WHERE HIS PARENTS WERE BURIED.

JACK KNELT ON THEIR GRAVE, PULLED OUT A GUN, AND SHOT HIMSELF. HE WAS 65.

IN A CURRENT ENVIRONMENT OF TOTALLY UNCONFRONTATIONAL AND **SAFE** MOVIEMAKING, I WOULD LOVE TO SEE A FILMMAKER ATTEMPT TO MAKE A THEATRICAL ADAPTATION OF JAXON'S "WHITE MAN'S BURDEN". IN AN INDUSTRY WHERE I AM TOLD CONSTANTLY IT HAS SUPPOSEDLY "ALL BEEN DONE", HERE IS A NARRATIVE THAT HAS NEVER SEEN AND THAT **NO ONE** HAS THE BRASS ONES TO DARE TAKE ON.

I'M OF THE OPINION THAT THIS ABILITY TO TAKE ON CONTENTIOUS, POLITICALLY INCORRECT MATERIAL THAT WILL **NEVER** TURN THE CREATOR A PROFIT IS WHY THE ART FORM OF COMICS IS INHERENTLY MORE EDGY AND ARTISTICALLY VITAL THAN A MEDIUM OF STAGNANT HOMOGENISATION AND GROUP-THINK, SUCH AS MODERN FILM.

-ROBIN BOUGIE '08

I AM A PORN REPORTER. AND MY BEAT IS: THE MEAT-BEAT!

OHHHHH. OHHHHH

YEAH

GROANN!
OH FUCK
OH FUCK
OH FUCK
OH FUCK
NNNG

UNH! GAH!!

HOLY!

WHAT THE SHIT IS GOING ON IN HERE?

CAN'T TALK... ...PORN... TOO... GOOOD!

MY TOP 30 FAVORITE CLASSIC PORN FILMS

AND BY CLASSIC - I MEAN SPECIFICALLY 1970 TO 1985 SHOT ON FILM THEATRICAL TRIPLE-X MOVIES. THIS IS THE BEST OF THE BEST, AND I'VE WADED THROUGH 100'S OF MOVIES TO BE ABLE TO COMPILE IT. MIND YOU, AT THE RATE THAT I'VE BEEN DISCOVERING FORGOTTEN CLASSICS, AT LEAST 10 OF THE FILMS ON THIS LIST WILL BE REPLACED SOON!

1. **The Taming of Rebecca** (1982) Dir. by Phil Prince
   Classic New York sleaze was never so nasty as it was here.
2. **Thriller - aka: They Call Her One Eye** (1974) Dir. by Bo Vibenius
   Astonishing. Comes R-rated and as an XXX. Get the XXX.
3. **The Defiance of Good** (1974) Dir. by Armand Weston
   Adorable Jean Jennings in the first (and best) S+M feature film.
4. **Midnight Heat** (1983) Dir. by Richard Mahler aka Roger Watkins
   Jamie Gillis stars as a hitman in a sexy hardboiled porn-noir.
5. **The Image** (1975) Dir. by Radley Metzger aka Henry Paris
   Metzger's top notch career was topped by this erotic ball-drainer.
6. **Sex Wish** (1976) Dir. by Tim McCoy
   The mean streets of NYC in all their glory. Zebedy Colt is loopy.
7. **Exhausted** (1981) Dir. by Julia St. Vincent
   This amazing documentary/love letter to John Holmes is a classic.
8. **The Taking of Christina** (1976) Dir. by Armand Weston
   SO good. Look for a short cameo by a young Tom Savini.
9. **Hot Summer in the City** (1976) Dir. by Gail Palmer
   Blaxploitation meets hardcore porn in a violent hostage drama.
10. **Pretty Peaches** (1978) Dir. by Alex DeRenzy
    Desiree Cousteau makes my penis want to stage a parade.
11. **Amanda By Night** (1981) Dir. by Robert McCallum
    The acting skills of Veronica Hart and Richard Bolla on full display.
12. **Teenage Fantasies** (1971) Dir. by Frank Spokeman
    Luscious cum-queen Rene Bond at her astonishing all-time best.
13. **Waterpower** (1977) Dir. by Gerard Damiano
    Jamie Gillis stars as the abusive and elusive enema bandit .
14. **Opening of Misty Beethoven** (1975) Dir. by Henry Paris
    Generally considered to be the finest film in hardcore history.
15. **Dr. Bizarro** (1983) Dir. by Phil Prince
    Convicted killer Phil Prince produces yet another deranged epic.
16. **Let My Puppets Come** (1976) Dir. by Gerard Damiano
    I defy you to jerk off to this oddball puppet porn comedy.
17. **Little Orphan Dusty** (1978) Dir. by Bob Chinn
    Rhonda Jo Petty fists her own pussy like the freak she is.
18. **Teenage Twins** (1976) Dir. by Carter Stevens
    Identical twin carpet-munching with Brooke and Taylor Young
19. **Naked Came the Stranger** (1975) Dir. by Henry Paris
    A lesser known, but no less brilliant offering from H. Paris.
20. **A Woman's Torment** (1977) Dir. by Roberta Findlay
    Tara Chung goes insane and camps out in a beach house.
21. **The Ecstasy Girls** (1979) Dir. by Robert McCallum
    This all-star cast headed up by Jamie Gillis is so great.
22. **Femmes De Sade** (1976) Dir. by Alex DeRenzy
    A giant rapist who sucks his own cock is abused at an orgy.
23. **Corruption** (1983) Dir. by Richard Mahler aka Roger Watkins
    The late Bobby Astyr at his demonic best in this morality tale.
24. **Deep Throat** (1972) Dir. by Gerard Damiano
    Historically speaking, the most important XXX film of all time.
25. **Cafe Flesh** (1982) Dir. by Rinse Dream
    Writer Jerry Stahl's quirky cult-porn-art film is a blast.
26. **Breaking It** (1984) Dir. by Svetlana
    You just can't have a top 30 porn list and leave out Traci Lords.
27. **Oriental Techniques of Pain and Pleasure** (1983) Dir. Phil Prince
    A crusty exploration of sexual deviancy by Avon productions.
28. **Babyface** (1977) Dir. by Alex DeRenzy
    Not very PC, but certainly boner-inducing. DeRenzy rules.
29. **Sweetcakes** (1976) Dir. by Howard Ziehm
    Another Young twins incestual sex smorgasbord for the eyes.
30. **Tales of the Bizarre** (1983) Dir. by Phil Prince
    Yet another hateful, creepy, sexual shit-scab by Phil Prince

CHLOE LOSES AGENT OVER BLOWJOB

CHLOE SEVIGNY (KIDS, GUMMO, BOYS DON'T CRY) HAS BEEN DROPPED BY THE WILLIAM MORRIS AGENCY BECAUSE OF HER HARDCORE 10 MINUTE ORAL SEX SCENE IN VINCENT GALLO'S CRITICALLY REVILED 2003 FILM BROWN BUNNY. PALS OF SEVIGNY SAID THE OSCAR-NOMINATED ACTRESS WAS ALREADY SEEN AS "INCREDIBLY DIFFICULT" BY THE STRAIT-LACED FIRM (WHICH SEEMS TO HAVE A BIG STICK UP ITS COLLECTIVE ASS), BUT THEN HER GLORIOUSLY GRATUITOUS SEX SCENE IN THE MOVIE ROGER EBERT CALLED "THE WORST FILM IN THE HISTORY OF THE CANNES FILM FESTIVAL", WAS THE FINAL STRAW.

SEVIGNY'S AGENCY REPS WERE ESPECIALLY ANGRY SINCE SHE TOOK THE RACY KNOB-GOBBLING ROLE WITHOUT CONSULTING THEM, AND THEN IGNORED THEIR ADVICE TO DROP OUT. "WILLIAM MORRIS NOW FEELS THAT HER CAREER IS TAINTED AND MAY NEVER RECOVER, ESPECIALLY AFTER RUMORS BEGAN CIRCULATING ABOUT THE EVEN MORE GRAPHIC OUT-TAKES THAT DIDN'T MAKE IT INTO THE ACTUAL FILM." A REP FOR THE HAUGHTY AGENCY CONFIRMED.

THE "MORE GRAPHIC OUT-TAKES" THEY REFER TO IS A SEMEN FACIAL FROM THE PECKER OF CO-STAR VINCENT GALLO. THE SCENE AS IT APPEARS IN THE FILM IS SANS ORGASM, BUT A JUICY FACE-PASTING (A FIRST FOR AN OSCAR NOMINATED ACTRESS) IS HEAVILY RUMORED TO HAVE BEEN LEFT ON THE CUTTING ROOM FLOOR.

SOME OF YOU MAY REMEMBER MY ARTICLE ABOUT THORA BIRCH'S PORN STAR PARENTS BACK IN ISSUE 12, EMBLAZONED WITH MY LENGTHY PENTHOUSE FORUM-STYLE BABBLINGS ABOUT MY DEEP-SEEDED CRAVING TO SEE MAINSTREAM ACTRESSES THORA BIRCH, CHRISTINA RICCI, ALYSON HANNIGAN... AND YES, CHLOE SEVIGNY DOING HARDCORE PORN.

HEH HEH... *DROOL* ONE DOWN, 3 TO GO! (ROBIN BEGINS TO FONDLE SELF IN ANTICIPATION, AND THEN GETS HIT IN THE HEAD WITH A SHOE BY HIS LOVELY WIFE REBECCA...)

78

FROM DAVID CRONENBERG, CREATOR OF 'SCANNERS'.

VIDEODROME
A TERRIFYING NEW WEAPON

**First it controls your mind
Then it destroys your body**

A STRUGGLING CABLE NETWORK CALLED CIVICTV IS FLOODED WITH SOFT-CORE PORN AND HARDCORE VIOLENCE, AND ITS OWNER MAX RENN (JAMES WOODS) IS ALWAYS OUT LOOKIN' TO PUSH THE ENVELOPE. HE'S FRUSTRATED WHEN HE CAN'T FIND WHAT HE'S LOOKING FOR, UNTIL HIS VIDEO PIRATE BUDDY PICKS UP A MOMENTARY SIGNAL THAT CHANGES EVERYTHING FOR MAX.

IT'S CALLED "VIDEODROME", AND WHILE JUST A BLIP ON THE SATELLITE FEED, MAX SEES ENOUGH TO GET OBSESSED WITH IT: A SINGLE ROOM OCCUPIED BY TWO MASKED SADISTS AND ONE SCREAMING WOMAN. NO PLOT, JUST SEXUALIZED TORTURE. I'LL LEAVE THE SYNOPSIS OFF THERE, AS TELLING YOU MORE ABOUT THE PLOT (WHICH GETS VERY WEIRD AND WONDERFUL, INDEED) WOULD JUST DIMINISH YOUR ENJOYMENT OF IT.

VIDEODROME IS GORY, UPSETTING, INSANE, AND CONSTANTLY FORCES YOU TO WONDER WHERE FANTASY AND REALITY BLUR, IN OTHER WORDS, AT WHAT POINT DOES WHAT WE SEE ON A MONITOR BEGIN DICTATING OUR REALITY? DESPITE BEING OVER 25 YEARS OLD, THIS QUESTION THAT DIRECTOR DAVID CRONENBERG DONKEY-PUNCHES US WITH IS EVEN MORE VALID TODAY THAN WHEN IT WAS FIRST QUERIED, AND ONE OF THE REASONS THIS REMAINS MY FAVORITE CANADIAN MOVIE, AND ONE OF MY TOP 5 HORROR FILMS OF ALL TIME.

INTERESTINGLY (FOR YOU MEGA-FANS LIKE ME), AN EPILOGUE WAS PLANNED IN WHICH MAX RENN, BIANCA O'BLIVION AND NICKI BRAND APPEAR ON THE SET OF VIDEODROME. BIANCA AND NICKI ARE SHOWN TO HAVE PULSATING, DRIBBLING VAGINAS GROWING OUT OF THEIR CHESTS, FROM WHICH EMERGE STRANGE, MUTATED SEX ORGANS. THE SCENE WAS SCRAPPED DUE TO COST, AND BECAUSE DEBBIE HARRY HAD STOMACH FLU, AND JAMES WOODS WAS VISITING RELATIVES.

WHAT THE HELL WAS HE THINKING?

Interview with Bo Arne Vibenius
(aka Alex Fridolinski aka Ron Silberman Jr.)
the director of THRILLER
aka "They Call Her One-Eye".

 by Jan Bruun

"THE ROUGHEST REVENGE MOVIE EVER MADE! THERE'S NEVER BEEN ANYTHING AS TOUGH AS THAT MOVIE."
— QUENTIN TARANTINO ON **THRILLER** TOTAL FILM MAGAZINE

B.A. VIBENIUS CIRCA. 2004

AS NEARLY EVERY FILM FAN KNOWS BY NOW, QUENTIN TARANTINO GOT DARRYL HANNAH'S MATCHING EYEPATCH AND CLOTHING FOR **KILL BILL** (2003/04) FROM THE SWEDISH 1970s FILM **THRILLER** OR **THEY CALL HER ONE EYE** AS IT IS SOMETIMES KNOWN.

IN EARLY 2004, CINEMATEKET IN OSLO NORWAY RAN A SERIES OF FILMS UNDER THE UMBRELLA OF "THE TARANTINO CONNECTION", SHOWING RARE MOVIES THAT HAD INFLUENCED THE FORMER VIDEO STORE CLERK. THEY MANAGED TO CONJURE UP A PROFESSIONAL QUALITY BETA TAPE OF THE RIDICULOUSLY OBSCURE ORIGINAL VERSION OF THRILLER — AND EVEN PERSUADED ITS DIRECTOR TO COME AND HANG OUT AND INTRODUCE THE FILM.

THRILLER IS THE HARROWING STORY OF A YOUNG GIRL WHO BECOMES MUTE AFTER BEING RAPED BY AN OLD MAN IN A PARK. WHEN SHE'S A YOUNG WOMAN SHE HITCHES A RIDE WITH A SMARMY GUY WHO TURNS OUT TO BE A PIMP — AND GETS HER HOOKED ON HEROIN BEFORE PIMPING OUT HER ASS. SHE TRIES TO RUN AWAY, BUT HE CATCHES HER AND GOUGES ONE OF HER EYES OUT. TO GET REVENGE, SHE SECRETLY GETS TRAINING IN MARTIAL ARTS, GUN SHOOTING AND DRIVING, AND THEN GOES ON A ROARING RAMPAGE OF REVENGE AGAINST THE PIMPS AND JOHNS WHO DEFILED HER.

CONT. ON NEXT PAGE

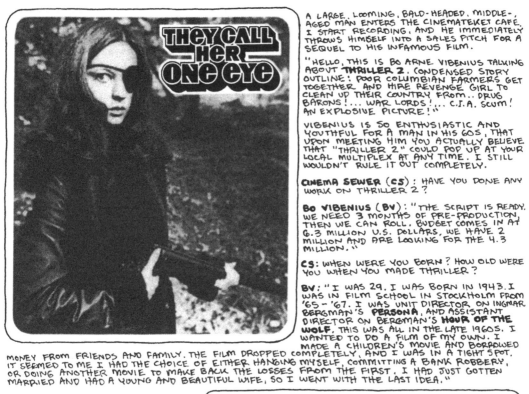

A LARGE, LOOMING, BALD-HEADED, MIDDLE-, AGED MAN ENTERS THE CINEMATEKET CAFE. I START RECORDING, AND HE IMMEDIATELY THROWS HIMSELF INTO A SALES PITCH FOR A SEQUEL TO HIS INFAMOUS FILM.

"HELLO, THIS IS BO ARNE VIBENIUS TALKING ABOUT **THRILLER 2**. CONDENSED STORY OUTLINE: POOR COLUMBIAN FARMERS GET TOGETHER AND HIRE REVENGE GIRL TO CLEAN UP THEIR COUNTRY FROM.. DRUG BARONS!... WAR LORDS!... C.I.A. SCUM! AN EXPLOSIVE PICTURE!"

VIBENIUS IS SO ENTHUSIASTIC AND YOUTHFUL FOR A MAN IN HIS 60S, THAT UPON MEETING HIM YOU ACTUALLY BELIEVE THAT "THRILLER 2" COULD POP UP AT YOUR LOCAL MULTIPLEX AT ANY TIME. I STILL WOULDN'T RULE IT OUT COMPLETELY.

CINEMA SEWER (CS): HAVE YOU DONE ANY WORK ON THRILLER 2?

BO VIBENIUS (BV): "THE SCRIPT IS READY. WE NEED 3 MONTHS OF PRE-PRODUCTION, THEN WE CAN ROLL. BUDGET COMES IN AT 6.3 MILLION U.S. DOLLARS, WE HAVE 2 MILLION AND ARE LOOKING FOR THE 4.3 MILLION."

CS: WHEN WERE YOU BORN? HOW OLD WERE YOU WHEN YOU MADE THRILLER?

BV: "I WAS 29. I WAS BORN IN 1943. I WAS IN FILM SCHOOL IN STOCKHOLM FROM '65 - '67. I WAS UNIT DIRECTOR ON INGMAR BERGMAN'S **PERSONA**, AND ASSISTANT DIRECTOR ON BERGMAN'S **HOUR OF THE WOLF**. THIS WAS ALL IN THE LATE 1960S. I WANTED TO DO A FILM OF MY OWN. I MADE A CHILDREN'S MOVIE AND BORROWED MONEY FROM FRIENDS AND FAMILY. THE FILM DROPPED COMPLETELY, AND I WAS IN A TIGHT SPOT. IT SEEMED TO ME I HAD THE CHOICE OF EITHER HANGING MYSELF, COMMITTING A BANK ROBBERY, OR DOING ANOTHER MOVIE TO MAKE BACK THE LOSSES FROM THE FIRST. I HAD JUST GOTTEN MARRIED AND HAD A YOUNG AND BEAUTIFUL WIFE, SO I WENT WITH THE LAST IDEA."

"I DECIDED TO MAKE THE MOST COMMERCIAL FILM EVER MADE, AND JUST TO PILE ON ANYTHING I COULD IN THE MOVIE. I DECIDED ON A REVENGE STORY WITH A GOOD LOOKING GIRL WHO GETS HURT, AND THEN EXECUTES A FORCEFUL REVENGE. IF WE COULD HAVE SOME GOOD MUSIC OR OTHER ADDED VALUES, THAT WOULD BE FINE. IN THE LATE 60S AND EARLY 70S THERE WAS A LIBERALIZATION OF PORN IN DENMARK AND SWEDEN, SO I THOUGHT IT WAS THE RIGHT TIME TO INCLUDE HARDCORE ELEMENTS IN A REGULAR FILM. BUT WE DIDN'T DO IT TO AROUSE THE AUDIENCE. THE SITUATIONS WHERE THE SEX OCCURS ARE DEGRADING. VERY EXPLICIT, THOUGH. IT WILL BE EXCITING TO SEE HOW THIS PLAYS TODAY. THE FILM HAS HARDLY BEEN SHOWN UNCUT AT ALL SINCE CANNES IN MAY 1973."

"IN CANNES, THIS AMERICAN CAME UP TO ME AFTER THE MOVIE AND CURSED A LOT AND WAS VERY VULGAR. BASICALLY WHAT HE SAID WAS: 'THAT WAS A FUCKING DISGUSTING MOVIE! WHEN IS THE NEXT SHOW?' THAT MAN TURNED OUT TO BE SAM ARKOFF OF AMERICAN INTERNATIONAL PICTURES. THEY BOUGHT RIGHTS TO THE FILM WORLDWIDE. THEN THE MORONS NOT ONLY REMOVED THE SEX SCENES, BUT COMPLETELY RE-CUT THE MOVIE INTO SOMETHING VERY DIFFERENT. THAT'S THE VERSION KNOWN AS **THEY CALL HER ONE EYE**. THAT VERSION WAS THE 17TH MOST SEEN MOVIE FOR A FEW WEEKS. IT WAS SHOWN IN 40 CINEMAS IN THE NEW YORK AREA ALONE."

CS: DID YOU GET ANY CASH OUT OF THIS?

BV: "YES! THEY PAID ME A GOOD SUM OF MONEY UPFRONT, AND I WAS ABLE TO CLEAR ALL MY DEBTS. BECAUSE I PAID MY DEBTS THEN, I HAVE NEVER HAD ANY PROBLEM OBTAINING CREDIT LATER ON."

CS: WHAT OTHER REACTIONS DID YOU GET IN CANNES?

BV: "IT WAS A GREAT SUCCESS. THERE WAS A BIDDING WAR TO GET THE FILM."

THE MOVIE THAT HAS NO LIMITS OF EVIL!
FIRST THEY TOOK HER SPEECH...
THEN HER SIGHT...
WHEN THEY WERE FINISHED SHE USED WHAT WAS LEFT OF HER FOR HER OWN FRIGHTENING KIND OF REVENGE!

CHRISTINA LINDBERG

Executive Producer BO A. VIBENIUS · Directed by ALEX FRIDOLINSKI · In Eastmancolor

A UNITED PRODUCERS Release

BV: "THE AUDIENCE APPLAUDED AND CHEERED. WE COULD ONLY AFFORD ONE SCREENING THOUGH. I HAVEN'T REALLY SEEN IT MYSELF FOR 25 YEARS. I WAS INVITED TO THE FANTASTIC FILM FESTIVAL IN LUND, SWEDEN A FEW YEARS AGO. THEY SHOWED AN OLD PRINT WHERE SOMEONE HAD STOLEN MOST OF THE SEX SCENES. CHRISTINA WAS THERE TOO."

CS: BEFORE CHRISTINA LINDBERG PLAYED THE MAIN CHARACTER IN THIS MOVIE, SHE HAD DONE SOME NUDIE FILMS...

BV: "YES, BUT NOT PORN. SHE DID FULL FRONTAL NUDITY IN SOFT SEX FILMS, SEX COMEDIES AND SUCH."

CS: WHAT WERE YOU THINKING WHEN YOU INCLUDED THE HARDCORE PORN?

BV: "WELL, I HOPED THAT IT WOULD BE SHOWN THE WAY IT WAS MADE. LOOKING BACK ON IT, IT'S A SHITTY FILM, BUT WITH INTERESTING ASPECTS TO IT. ESPECIALLY WHEN YOU THINK ABOUT HOW FAST IT WAS MADE. WE STARTED SHOOTING OCTOBER 6th 1972. WE HAD EVERYTHING FINISHED, EDITED AND ALL BY NEW YEAR'S EVE. QUITE FAST FOR A 35mm FEATURE FILM. AND WE BROUGHT IT IN FOR LESS THAN $60,000. ONLY NINE PEOPLE IN THE CREW. SO IF YOU'RE GONNA SAY ANYTHING ABOUT ME AS A FILMMAKER, I GUESS IT WOULD BE THAT I'M REALLY GOOD AT MAKING LOW BUDGET FILMS AND PUTTING THAT MONEY UP ON THE SCREEN. WHETHER YOU LIKE WHAT YOU SEE IS A DIFFERENT STORY."

CS: THESE HARDCORE SEX SCENES, WERE THEY FILMED LATER ON WITH OTHER ACTORS?

BV: "THERE WAS A COUPLE THAT WORKED IN LIVE SEX SHOWS. I ORDERED THE MATERIAL AND SOME DUDE DELIVERED IT. I DIDN'T DIRECT THOSE PARTS MYSELF."

☆ FOOTNOTE: I WAS AT A DISADVANTAGE WHILE TALKING TO VIBENIUS AS I DIDN'T GET TO SEE **THRILLER** UNTIL THE DAY AFTER. AND I HADN'T SEEN ANY OF HIS OTHER FILMS EITHER. LATER ON, WHEN I HAD MY CONNECTIONS IN THE TAPE TRADING CIRCUIT COUGH UP A COPY OF THE EVEN MORE HARD-TO-GET **BREAKING POINT**, I DISCOVERED AN EVEN GLOOMIER FILM ABOUT A RESERVED ACCOUNTANT WHO IS SECRETLY A SERIAL KILLER. DARK, DEPRESSING, VIOLENT, AND WITH HARDCORE FUCKING PERFORMED BY THE ACTUAL ACTORS IN THE FILM. SO IT TURNED OUT THAT I WAS TALKING TO A PORN DIRECTOR AFTER ALL. I TRIED TO CONTACT HIM VIA EMAIL AND ASK WHY HE HAD MADE ANOTHER VIOLENT TRIPLE X MOVIE AFTER ALL THE TROUBLE WITH **THRILLER**, BUT GOT NO REPLY. ☆

SCENE MAT 1-A
BEAUTY — Swedish actress Christina Lindberg, who was discovered when she was first photographed on a beach in 1968, stars in the adventure-thriller film, "They Call Her One Eye."

SCENE MAT 1-B
REPRISAL — Christina Lindberg, blinded in left eye by attacker, plans revenge in the action-filled thriller film, "They Call Her One Eye."

CS: WHAT DO YOU THINK ABOUT THE WAY TARANTINO HAS USED ELEMENTS FROM **THRILLER** IN **KILL BILL**?

BV: "I THINK IT'S COOL. I DIDN'T LIKE IT WHEN HE STOLE THE ENTIRE PLOT OF **RESERVOIR DOGS** FROM SOME ASIAN MOVIE, (ED; **CITY ON FIRE** IS THE FILM IN QUESTION) BUT NOWADAYS IT SEEMS HE'S A BIT MORE UPFRONT WITH HIS INFLUENCES. HE KNOWS THE FILM GEEKS WILL BE AT HIS THROAT AGAIN IF HE DOESN'T OWN UP TO EVERYTHING. BUT **KILL BILL** ISN'T REALLY A GOOD MOVIE. HE WORKS REALLY WELL WITH MUSIC, AND THERE ARE SOME STUNNING VISUALS. HE MIXES IN ANIMATION, AND HAS ALL THESE CUTE REFERENCES TO OTHER FILMS, BUT AFTER **THE MATRIX**, MOST FIGHT SCENES SEEM BORING BY COMPARISON."

CS: IS IT CORRECT THAT **THRILLER** WAS THE FIRST FILM BANNED IN SWEDEN?

BV: "NO. BUT I'M THE ONLY SWEDISH DIRECTOR WITH TWO FILMS THAT ARE TOTALLY BANNED. I MANAGED TO MAKE ANOTHER ONE CALLED **BREAKING POINT**. THEY'RE BOTH STILL BANNED."

CS: IS IT TRUE THAT A REAL CORPSE WAS USED IN **THRILLER** WHEN THE EYE IS GOUGED OUT?

BV: "I'LL ANSWER ANY QUESTION APART FROM THAT ONE. I'LL SAVE IT FOR MY AUTOBIOGRAPHY."

In Eastmancolor Ⓡ

THEY CALL HER ONE EYE
A CRUEL PICTURE

EYE PATCHES FOR GIRLS — THE NEWEST FAD!

You have seen the wide publicity enjoyed by the man in the Hathaway Shirt with the eye patch. Now, there is an eye patch for girls, too. Every girl will want one.

EYE PATCHES — Have your cashier, candy girls and usherettes wear eye patches (as actress Christina Lindberg does in "They Call Her One Eye") to call attention to the opening of the picture at your theatre. Start the campaign two weeks ahead of your play date.

SPECIAL SCREENING — Was Frigga justified in the manner she took out ruthless revenge on those who wronged her? Invite a panel of psychologists, teachers, priests, rabbis and police officials in your community to view the picture. Ask your local TV or radio station, or newspaper to assign a reporter to interview them as to their opinion.

CS: WAS IT STILL ONLY THE CUT VERSION THAT CAME OUT ON VIDEO IN THE 1980s?

BV: "YES, BUT NOW ALL THE RIGHTS HAVE REVERTED BACK TO ME. BUT THERE'S AN AMERICAN FIRM THAT HAS APPROPRIATED A LOT OF MATERIAL, AND ARE PLANNING A DVD EVEN THOUGH THEY DON'T HAVE THE RIGHTS."

CS: SYNAPSE?

BV: "THAT'S RIGHT. THERE WAS A BUSINESS IN NEW YORK CALLED CHROME ENTERTAINMENT, AND THEY BOUGHT THE RIGHTS. THEN THEY ALMOST WENT BANKRUPT AND SOLD THE RIGHTS TO SYNAPSE FOR A PITTANCE. SYNAPSE CLAIMS TO HAVE ACTED IN GOOD FAITH, BUT I'LL FIGHT THEM ON THIS. IT'S NOT JUST IMMATERIAL PROPERTY, BUT ALSO A COLLECTION OF PHYSICAL OBJECTS LIKE PHOTOS, POSTERS, ETC THAT THEY NEVER PAID FOR. THAT'S STOLEN GOODS AFTER 3 MONTHS. THEY'VE ALSO TRANSPORTED THIS ACROSS STATE LINES WHICH MAKES IT A FEDERAL CRIME."

CS: SO YOU WANT EVERYTHING BACK SO YOU CAN PUT OUT THE DVD YOURSELF?

BV: "YES. BUT ON THE OTHER HAND, I WOULD DO A DEAL WITH SYNAPSE AT ANY TIME IF THEY WOULD OFFER ME A REASONABLE PAYMENT."

CS: AMONGST VIDEO TRADERS THIS FILM IS COVETED, SO THERE'S CLEARLY A MARKET DEMAND FOR IT.

BV: "EVEN OLD POSTERS GO FOR $350, AND I'VE GIVEN ALL MINE AWAY!"

CS: ARE YOU FAMILIAR WITH OTHER NOTORIOUS 70s RAPE-REVENGE FLICKS LIKE **LAST HOUSE ON THE LEFT** AND **I SPIT ON YOUR GRAVE**?

BV: "NO, I NEVER SAW ANY OF THOSE."

CS: TELL ME ABOUT **BREAKING POINT**.

BV: "SEX AND VIOLENCE THERE TOO. IT'S AN EVEN SHITTIER FILM. I HAVE A SIX CHANNEL RECORDING OF THE MAIN THEME MUSIC BY ANTON KARAS. IT'S A WEIRD FILM. IT WILL BE PUT OUT ON VIDEOTAPE AS WELL, BUT I ONLY HAVE VIDEOTAPE TO SOURCE FROM."

CS: WHAT HAPPENED TO IT? DID IT EVER GET SEEN IN CINEMAS OR ON VIDEO?

BV: "NO, NOT MUCH. I PREMIERED IT IN A SEVERELY

VICTIM — Christina Lindberg seeks escape

CUT VERSION FOR A COUPLE DAYS TO GET MY GUARANTEED SUM OF MONEY FROM THE SWEDISH FILM INSTITUTE. TO GET THE MONEY, THE FILM HAS TO BE SHOWN SOMEWHERE. THE ORIGINAL NEGATIVE WAS STOLEN AND DISAPPEARED TO THE U.S."

CS: THERE ARE COPIES OF A FRENCH SECAM TAPE FLOATING AROUND...

BV: "IT DID ACTUALLY PLAY FOR 17 YEARS IN FRENCH CINEMAS, BUT I NEVER SAW ANY OF THAT MONEY. ONE AND A HALF MILLION FRANCS THEY OWED ME. IF I SHOULD GIVE ANY ADVICE IT'S THIS: NEVER PUT YOUR OWN MONEY INTO A FILM, AND TAKE THE MONEY AND RUN IF YOU GET ANY. YOU'LL NEVER SEE ANYTHING LATER ON. I WENT OVER TO THE AIP OFFICES TO LOOK OVER THEIR BOOKKEEPING ON **THEY CALL HER ONE EYE**. THEY FIX THEIR BOOKS TO ENSURE THAT FILMS NEVER GO SUBSTANTIALLY INTO THE BLACK SO THEY HAVE TO SHARE PROFITS. THEY CHARGED THEIR ENTIRE TRAVEL BUDGET FOR THE WHOLE COMPANY TO OUR FILM".

CS: A CLASSIC SCAM. WOULD YOU HAVE WANTED TO DIRECT MORE THAN THE FOUR FILMS THAT YOU'VE DONE?

AND THEN:

SYNAPSE FINALLY ANNOUNCED A STREET FOR THEIR THRILLER DVD: SEPT. 28th 2004. WHEN WE CONTACTED THEM AND TOLD THEM THAT VIBENIUS HAD TOLD US THAT HE PLANNED TO SUE THEM FOR THIS ACTION, WE GOT THIS REACTION FROM THEIR LAWYER:

"Synapse Films purchased all assets of Chrome Entertainment which included Chrome's rights to the movie Thriller a/k/a They Call Her One Eye. The assignment by Chrome of rights to the movie upon sale of all their assets is expressly allowed under the Distribution Agreement signed by Bo Vibenius. Synapse will assert all legal means to protect and defend its rights to this movie which were lawfully acquired from Chrome."

Charles A. Fiedler, Esq.
General Legal Counsel to Synapse Films

CONTINUED FROM PREVIOUS PAGE:

BV: "OF COURSE. BUT I'M PRACTICALLY BLACKLISTED IN SWEDEN. I CALL PEOPLE ASSHOLES, THEN THEY BECOME BOSSES IN THE SYSTEM THAT DOLES OUT THE MONEY FOR FILM PRODUCTION. I WAS GOING TO DO A SCI-FI FILM WITH EDDIE CONSTANTINE, WITH MUSIC BY LUNDSTEN, BUT COULDN'T GET THE MONEY TOGETHER. THEY SAID THAT NO ONE WANTED TO SEE SCI-FI. A HALF A YEAR LATER, **STAR WARS** CAME OUT. NOWADAYS, I'M MAINLY LOOKING FOR MONEY FOR **THRILLER 2**, AND OTHER PROJECTS. WE ARE NOW SEEKING FINANCING FOR TWO HIGH BUDGET FILMS WRITTEN BY AN AMERICAN SCREENWRITER, AND WE ARE PLANNING A SOAP SERIES FOR T.V. SO IF ANY OF YOU READERS OUT THERE HAVE A FEW MILLION THAT YOU'D LIKE TO INVEST..."

INTERVIEW BY JAN BRUUN
HOME.ONLINE.NO/~JANBRUUN

I'M **AWFULLY** EXCITED TO FIND THIS **VERY** RARE 70s AD MAT FOR THRILLER WITH A VERY **ODD** RETITLING!

LOOK!

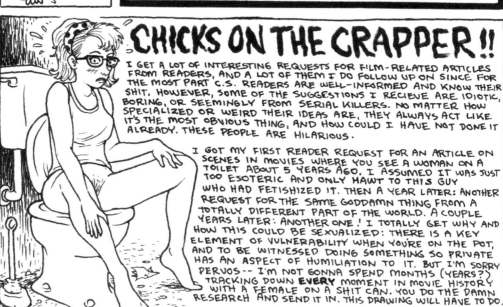

CHICKS ON THE CRAPPER!!

I GET A LOT OF INTERESTING REQUESTS FOR FILM-RELATED ARTICLES FROM READERS, AND A LOT OF THEM I DO FOLLOW UP ON SINCE FOR THE MOST PART C.S. READERS ARE WELL-INFORMED AND KNOW THEIR SHIT. HOWEVER, SOME OF THE SUGGESTIONS I RECIEVE ARE IDIOTIC, BORING, OR SEEMINGLY FROM SERIAL KILLERS. NO MATTER HOW SPECIALIZED OR WEIRD THEIR IDEAS ARE, THEY ALWAYS ACT LIKE IT'S THE MOST OBVIOUS THING, AND HOW COULD I HAVE NOT DONE IT ALREADY. THESE PEOPLE ARE HILARIOUS.

I GOT MY FIRST READER REQUEST FOR AN ARTICLE ON SCENES IN MOVIES WHERE YOU SEE A WOMAN ON A TOILET ABOUT 5 YEARS AGO. I ASSUMED IT WAS JUST TOO ESOTERIC AND ONLY HAWT TO THIS GUY WHO HAD FETISHIZED IT. THEN A YEAR LATER: ANOTHER REQUEST FOR THE SAME GODDAMN THING FROM A TOTALLY DIFFERENT PART OF THE WORLD. A COUPLE YEARS LATER: ANOTHER ONE! I TOTALLY GET WHY AND HOW THIS COULD BE SEXUALIZED: THERE IS A KEY ELEMENT OF VULNERABILITY WHEN YOU'RE ON THE POT, AND TO BE WITNESSED DOING SOMETHING SO PRIVATE HAS AN ASPECT OF HUMILIATION TO IT. BUT I'M SORRY PERVOS -- I'M NOT GONNA SPEND MONTHS (YEARS?) TRACKING DOWN **EVERY** MOMENT IN MOVIE HISTORY WITH A FEMALE ON A SHIT CAN. YOU DO THE DAMN RESEARCH AND SEND IT IN. THIS DRAWING WILL HAVE TO DO.

CINEMA SEWER INTERVIEW DAVID HESS

MY GOOD FRIEND BEANBAG THE CAT ASKED IF HE COULD WRITE THE INTRO TO THIS ARTICLE. TAKE IT AWAY, BEANBAG!

OH MY GOD. WHAT? WHAA**AAA**T? YOU...OK, YOU MUST KNOW ALL ABOUT DAVID HESS, RIGHT? OH MY GOD. YEAH. DON'T EVEN, DON'T EVEN, OK? IT'S NOT EVEN LIKE HE'S ALL NOT...OH, OK? MY GOD. OH-MY-GOD, OK? FOR SURE, YOU SAW **LAST HOUSE ON THE LEFT**, RIGHT? RIGHT? THE HOUSE ON THE LEFT? OK. WHAT? OK, THAT WAS SOOO**OOO** SCARY RIGHT? OH REALLY. OK? AND THAT'S NOT EVEN, LIKE... HE'S BEEN IN OTHER MOVIES, RIGHT? IT'S NOT LIKE-"OH I'VE ONLY BEEN IN THIS ONE, LIKE RIGHT? THIS ONE MOVIE?". RIGHT? NOT EVEN, NOT EEE**EEE**VEN. OK. BECAUSE IT'S NOT LIKE HE WASN'T A TOTAL FUCKING HARDASS IN **HITCH-HIKE** AND LIKE, **LAST HOUSE ON THE EDGE OF THE PARK**, RIGHT? OK, NO WAIT-OK? THAT WASN'T A LAST HOUSE, WAS IT? IT WAS JUST A HOUSE, RIGHT. RIGHT? OH MY GOD. OK... THAT'S LIKE NOT EVEN THE... UM.. OK. DAVID HESS RIGHT? WHAT? OF COURSE, OK? HE'S ALL "BLA**AAA**! I'M A FUCKING CRAZY PSYCHO, OK?" AND IT'S NOT EVEN LIKE... YOU JUST GET ALL, LIKE: "OK. THATS OK."

THIS INTERVIEW WAS CONDUCTED BY CINEMA SEWER BOY-REPORTER, AND CORRESPONDENT TO THE STARS - ED BRISSON. BEANBAG WANTED TO TAKE PART IN THIS PHONE INTERVIEW, BUT HE WAS LOCKED IN THE BATHROOM THROUGH IT'S DURATION. IT WAS FOR THE BEST.

CAN YOU TELL ME A LITTLE ABOUT HOW YOU MADE THE TRANSITION FROM MUSIC TO ACTING?

It wasn't much of a transition, I just fell into it to tell you the truth. I'd always been interested in acting. I had done some off-Broadway. I'd studied with Stella Adler. I was with the Actors' Playhouse for awhile. I took some classes from Sandy Meisner. They were some very major influences in the late fifties/early sixties in New York in picking up the Stanislavsky method and moving people along in terms of getting their internal feelings on the stage as opposed to getting out there and emoting. Last House came along and they originally wanted me to do the music on it. They'd heard about me, but they hadn't met me. And then my sister's boyfriend (Martin Kove) said, "Why don't you try out for one of the roles?"

The actors that they originally had decided that they didn't want to do the film at the last moment. Last House was originally supposed to be a porno, but the people that they had cast in the hardcore scenes decided that they didn't want to do it. So I walked in there and acted pretty crazy and they hired me. One of the first questions that they asked me was, "Would you do a porno scene?" and I said absolutely not. So on the basis of that, they changed their mind and made it a V for Violence.

LATER ON YOU WORKED WITH WES CRAVEN AGAIN ON A SHORT FILM THAT WAS SUPPOSED TO BE RELEASED AS PART OF AN ANTHOLOGY CALLED "TALES THAT WILL RIP YOUR HEART OUT"...

You know, Wes and I have gone back and forth over the years. We're both two strong personalities. When we're together and away from the film industry, we get along fine. But when it comes to making film together... and I don't know what his opinion on this is, I've never discussed it with him...I don't think that I fit into his idea of what he would want from an actor, or there haven't been roles that fit me. Which to me is bullshit anyway, if you're an actor you can do any role. Except, I guess if you're a man, it's hard to play a woman.

WAS THE FILM FINISHED?

I don't think that it was ever finished. That was my feeling. The guy who produced it was a very good friend of Wes's and he pushed him to move away from the softcore films that he was making into more mainstream films. Actually, I shouldn't say mainstream, I'd say guerrilla. Maybe now they'd be considered mainstream. Anyway, I don't think it was ever finished and I've never seen anything. Wes and I did one thing together and that was it. I played the devil. He was a cowboy.

AND YOU WORKED WITH HIM AGAIN IN SWAMP THING. THE RECENT DVD RELEASE OF THAT FILM WAS PULLED BECAUSE MGM ACCIDENTALLY RELEASED THE UNCUT VERSION ON A DISC THAT WAS SUPPOSED TO BE PG. DO YOU KNOW IF THERE ARE ANY PLANS FOR A RELEASE OF THE DISC?

Hmmm... I didn't know about that. I guess, based on that, and the success of Last House, they probably will. Last House, I don't know how many copies it sold, but it's available everyplace you could possibly go. Somebody told me that they found a copy at Wal-Mart! I've made Wal-Mart! I guess I've finally reached mainstream at this point in my life.

YOU WORKED WITH LEE MARVIN IN AVALANCHE EXPRESS. HOW WAS IT WORKING WITH HIM?

DAVID HESS...star of
LAST HOUSE ON THE LEFT is loose again...
DON'T GO IN THE PARK!

HOUSE ON THE EDGE OF THE PARK

Due to the shocking nature of this film no one under 17 will be admitted.

Starring David Hess • Annie Belle
Directed by Roger D. Franklin • Produced by Franco DiAnnunzio • Music by Riz Ortolani
A Bedford Entertainment / Trio Entertainment Release

There were a lot of people in my life who were instrumental in, more or less, carving out my acting career. I guess the person I grew up watching as a kid was John Garfield, who was a New York actor who was in a lot of Noir films. He was a boxer. My dad boxed in college. He was tough. He made some incredible Noir films. He just really struck a chord with me.

Lee became a really good friend in his later years. He was actually my son's godfather. When Gina and I got married, we had a Jewish ceremony and he was one of the guys who held the huppah. He was a really good friend. It wasn't so much what he said, it was what he did. He would stand on the set while I was doing a scene and he would give me a critique on it -what I could do, where I could take it. If he didn't say anything, then I knew I was doing the right thing. Robert Shaw was very similar too. I had two very good teachers on that set.

ON YOUR WEBSITE, YOU CLAIM THAT THE FILM YOU DIRECTED, "TO ALL A GOOD NIGHT", WAS RELEASED ON VIDEO AND WAS BARELY RECOGNIZABLE AS THE FILM YOU SHOT. HOW DID IT DIFFER?

BRISSON AND HESS HASH IT OUT...

As to whether or not that film was not the same as what I shot, that's a bit of a misnomer. The film was fine. The problem was that we didn't have enough footage to make the transitions that I wanted to.

GIVEN THE CHANCE, WOULD YOU DIRECT ANOTHER FILM?

Of course I'd direct another feature. It's a question of raising the money and probably having the right to script it myself. I mean, nobody is coming to me with a script to direct. Maybe they will now that my career seems to be a little regenerated.

YOU WORKED WITH FRANCO NERO ON 3 FILMS (21 HOURS AT MUNICH, HITCH HIKE, AND JONATHAN OF THE BEARS). WAS THERE EVER ANY ANIMOSITY BETWEEN THE TWO OF YOU? I KNOW THERE WAS THE PROBLEM IN HITCH-HIKE WHERE NERO ACTUALLY BROKE YOUR NOSE DURING A FIGHT SCENE...

Never. We both laughed at it. It's kind of become a folklore of film. I've always blamed the stunt guy. For me, you don't do a scene 19 times without someone making an error.

YOU WERE ALSO INJURED DURING LHOTL, SPRAINING YOUR ANKLE GOING DOWN A FIRE ESCAPE. DID THIS EFFECT YOUR ATTITUDE TOWARDS DOING ANY OF YOUR OWN STUNT WORK?

No. A sprained ankle wouldn't affect me much. I was captain of my rugby team playing for, what was then known as, the Eastern Rugby Union. I was playing at a pretty high level of rugby, so a sprained ankle wouldn't affect me very much.

THE SCORE THAT YOU CREATED FOR L.H.O.T.L WAS WRITTEN, IN YOUR OWN WORDS, "AS A COUNTER POINT TO THE ACTION." I'VE READ THAT YOU ARE ALSO DOING SOME SOUNDTRACK WORK FOR THE FILM "CABIN FEVER", CAN YOU ELABORATE A LITTLE ON HOW YOU APPROACH SOUNDTRACK WORK?

My essence is music. When I act, I'm acting to music. Obviously, when I'm scoring, I'm scoring to music. I've had two parallel careers that have come out of my song writing. Having said that, I've always felt that the most jarring way to write a film score...if you can, a lot of films won't afford you the opportunity...

but if you can, if it's available, it's very important that you counterpoint the scene. It expands the scene and it goes further into the nerve endings of the audience. So when ever I've had the chance, I've always counter pointed. I've scored other films and I've done the same thing. Then you ask yourself, what does counterpoint mean? Well it means that instead of writing boxed film music, you take some chances with the thematic material that you are using that may not sound like it fits there, but if it does, then you go with it.

Cabin Fever sounds like it's going to be a prominent release. [Cabin Fever director] Eli has been a fan of mine and the music from Last House since he can remember. He grew up on it. So when he had the opportunity to get in touch with me, he asked if I would rewrite some of the music from Last House, update it. Both of my kids are musicians and they do a great version of The Road Leads to Nowhere, so I said, why not let them do a version for the end credits. Eli thought it was a great idea. We went into the studio and recorded 2 songs for them, one that my oldest son Jessie wrote and a version of The Road Leads to Nowhere.

OVER THE LAST FEW YEARS IT SEEMS THAT THERE HAS BEEN A HUGE BOOM IN HORROR FILM PRODUCTION. A LOT OF THE PEOPLE WHO ARE MAKING THE FILMS NOW ARE CHILDREN OF THE VIDEO GENERATION. THEY GREW UP WITH THESE FILMS IN THEIR HOMES AND WATCHED THEM REPEATEDLY. DO YOU FIND THAT YOU ARE GETTING A LOT MORE CALLS NOW? IT SEEMS THAT MANY OF THESE FILMMAKERS ARE INTERESTED IN INVOLVING SOME OF THE ACTORS THEY GREW UP WITH IN THEIR FILMS.

You know it's amazing. Here I am 60 and yes, I've been getting dozens of calls and I can't tell you how many magazine interviews I've been doing. I used to sort of eschew that sort of stuff. Not that I was getting a lot of calls, but there was no contact between me and my audience, my fans, for years. I don't think that was the fault of either of us. That's just the way the business was set up. They weren't calling horror film stars. All of a sudden, two or three years ago that began to change and I began to change with it because I had the opportunity to go to conventions and found that there was an

audience out there that really likes me and appreciates what I've done. Moreover, I felt I owed it to them to meet with them; they paid a lot money to see these films.

I did a convention out here last year called Monsters Among Us and the people from Dominion Films came over and asked if I'd like to do a film with them. Over the past year, I've had more than half a dozen offers to do films and I'm probably going to do most of them. If I feel that the script and the people who are going to do the film aren't up to my standards, I'll turn the film down. Other than that, I look at everything.

IS THERE ANYTHING THAT YOU ARE WORKING ON NOW?

I'm going to LA to shoot a film for Dominion called The House in the Middle of Nowhere. People tease me because I do a lot of films with House in the title. (Laughs) Maybe they can come up with a new word for house. I'm also doing a film with Ulli Lommel about the Zodiac Killer. I'm playing the Cypher, the guy who was in contact with the killer, deciphering the messages that he sent out. It's a wonderful role and I'm really excited about it. That's supposed to begin in December.

Ruggero Deodato sent me a script and he wants me to do a film with him. And then Ulli and MGM are working on a deal to do a 3rd sequel to the Boogeyman series. I'll be playing a priest in that and Karen Black will be playing a nun. That should be fun. Udo Kier should also be playing a role in that too.

It was a student film. The guy who made that film was working in a video store in Mill Valley, which is were I was living at the time. I came in to the video store one day and he said, "I'm a student filmmaker, how would you like to do a film with me?" I said, "Well, OK. Can you tell me a little more about it?" We began to talk about it and he was very serious about it. He got a lot of help from the college and there were some people involved who had done some films before, so it wasn't totally amateur. At the time I wasn't doing anything and it seemed like the right time to give something back. There are very few ways that an actor can give back, unless you're wealthy and can give money to charity, but money isn't always the best route as far as I'm concerned. If you give your time and you can pass your knowledge onto someone else, that seems to me to be more important than just saying, "Here's a $1000, don't bug me anymore."

So, we shot Nutcracker in 10-15 days. I played a character named John Gard. It's sort of a convoluted story. There are two brothers and one is bad and one is good, but the bad brother turns out to be the good brother and the good brother turns out to be the bad brother. And there's a revenge issue involved. It was a neat student project that I feel really good about having been involved in. Now if you ask me if I think it's a good film... (laughs)... I don't think it's a particularly good film, but that's more a result of the constraint issue. He made it for practically no money at all on weekends. Everyone worked for free.

Oh yeah. It's not that I didn't like the films...it's like with the records that I wrote, for me it was always the creative process and I always felt that if you do what you like, then the money will come. You won't starve. Maybe you'll sleep on a couch for a month or something like that when you're out of cash. But you won't sleep out on the streets if you continue to follow your muse. I've always done that. It was never a question of monetary gains; it was always a question of doing the best job that I could within the best circumstances. So, I was always surprised when people would contact me and say, "You're this horror film legend." It would always surprise me and it still does. It's not me. I don't feel like a legendary person.

Are you asking me if we had sex together? Is that what this question is about?

That scene is absolutely real, but I would never answer the question as to whether or not we had sex together. That's a real personal question. You'd probably have to go to Corinne and ask her. But, it was as real as a sex scene could ever be, I can tell you that.

I don't even know who intimated that.

It depends on what Corinne wants. If she wants that to remain part of folklore, then I'm not even going to go there.

She would have protested if she didn't like the way...

Let's put it this way, Corinne and I still talk. We're really close friends. Literally, we love each other. She was wonderful because, during the part that leads up to the sex scene and in some of the other scenes, I had to pretty much bash her around. I'm not that kind of person. I don't mind bashing around someone on the rugby field, but I find it hard to hit a woman. Even if I'm getting paid for it and it's in a film and they know their role. I'm a pretty gentle person when it comes to that. I would never force an issue with any woman.

I would never...I wouldn't do it.

The rape scene in Last House, that was an emotional rape, because I set that up that way with Wes. She was scared to death of me. She wasn't faking her emotions. But if you look at the scene, it was filmed with clothes on.

For the most part, you don't think about penetration. If it happens, it happens. And I'm sure that it has happened on many sets.

I'll give you a hint - look at House on the Edge of the Park, OK?

I'll go no further than that. Call Annie Belle and ask her what happened.
—FIN

A Story Of Contemporary Family Witchcraft In California.

COLUMBIA PICTURES Presents

THE BROTHERHOOD OF SATAN

BROTHERHOOD OF SATAN (1971)

A FAMILY IS TRAPPED IN A DESERT TOWN BY A CULT OF SATANIC SENIOR-CITIZENS IN THIS UNDERRATED INSTALMENT IN THE UNOFFICIAL "CREEPY LITTLE TOWN HIDING A DARK SECRET" GENRE. SEEMS THE OL' DEVILS NEED 'X' AMOUNT OF TOTS TO COMPLETE A BODY SWITCHING RITUAL, AND THEIR BRAT (A YOUNG GERI "FAKE JAN BRADY" REISCHL!) IS PRIMO MATERIAL.

THE OCCULT SCENES ARE PRESENTED IN AN ODD MATTER-OF-FACT WAY AS TO MAKE THEM UNSETTLING AND EXTREMELY EFFECTIVE -- PARTICULARLY THE OPENING SEQUENCE INVOLVING AN ARMY TANK CRUSHING A CAR.

WHEN THE FILM WAS ORIGINALLY RELEASED (SHOWN AS A DOUBLE FEATURE WITH GEORGE LUCAS'S THX 1138) THEATREGOERS WERE HANDED AN UNUSUAL LOOKING PACKET OF "SATAN'S SOUL SEEDS" WHEN THEY PURCHASED THEIR TICKETS. EACH PAPER ENVELOPE (ILLUSTRATED WITH THE MOVIE'S LOGO) CONTAINED TWO SEEDS, WHICH WERE, ACCORDING TO THE CRYPTIC INSTRUCTIONS, SUPPOSED TO PROVIDE PROTECTION "FROM THE BLACK MAGIC OF THE BROTHERHOOD OF SATAN".

IT'S NOT KNOWN FOR CERTAIN IF ANYTHING (HELLISH OR OTHERWISE) EVER SPROUTED FROM THOSE SEEDS.

SATAN'S SOULS

·JAILHOUSE 41·

顕けさ破れた
鉄格子の中！
乾ききった女囚の
冷たい裏情に
一瞬よぎる恨みの殺意

FEMALE CONVICT SCORPION

(1972) DIRECTED BY SHUNYA ITO. JAPAN.

THE GOLDEN AGE OF SEXPLOITATION SAW A LUSCIOUS MASS OF WOMEN-IN-PRISON (AKA: W.I.P) CELLULOID IN WHICH THE FANTASY WORLD ONGOINGS OF BARE, BEAUTIFUL AND ANGRY SEX KITTENS BEHIND BARS PROVIDED A CONVENIENT BACKDROP IN WHICH TO CASCADE ACROSS DRIVE-IN SCREENS A SEAMY, CREAMY ASS-LOAD OF VICIOUS CATFIGHTS, LESBIANISM, COMMUNAL SHOWERING, AND NIGHTMARISH TORTURE SEQUENCES.

THIS WAS A GENRE THAT WOULD COME AND (SADLY) GO, BUT WOULD NEVER BE FORGOTTEN IN THE MANY COUNTRIES WHERE IT WAS CREATED AND EXPELLED UPON VERY APPRECIATIVE AUDIENCES. SOURCES AS DIVERSE AS ARGENTINA

(ATRAPADAS - 1984), HONG KONG (BAMBOO HOUSE OF DOLLS - 1974), CANADA (ILSA: SHE WOLF OF THE SS - 1974), ITALY (GESTAPO'S LAST ORGY - 1976), INDONESIA (WAR VICTIMS - 1983), SPAIN (ESCAPE FROM HELL - 1979), BRAZIL (AMAZON JAIL - 1982), AND THE USA (CAGED HEAT - 1974), SPEWED FORTH THE DEPRAVED SWILL OF THIS GENRE FOR A GOOD 10 YEARS OR MORE.

BUT DAMN... LEAVE IT TO THE PERFECTIONISTIC JAPANESE TO TAKE A SOMEWHAT STANDARD COOKIE CUTTER PLOT DEVICE AND HOIST IT TO THE NEXT LEVEL. DON'T GET ME WRONG... FILMS LIKE JACK HILL'S BIG BIRD CAGE (1972) AND GERARDO DE LEON'S WOMEN IN CAGES (1971) WERE MORE EXPLOITIVE AND CARTOONISH OVER THE TOP, BUT IT WAS SHUNYA ITO - DIRECTOR OF FEMALE CONVICT SCORPION: JAILHOUSE 41, WHO ALLOWED THE GENRE TO PROUDLY PUSH ONE OF IT'S OWN OUT OF A FLEA-BITTEN INBRED PACK, AND INTO LE' ARTHOUSE CINEMA (WITH A CAPITAL "C").

ADMITEDLY, F.C.S.J.41. HAS NEVER GOTTEN ITS DESERVED ATTENTION AMONGST THE HOITY-TOITY CINEPHILE CROWD, AND HAS MUCH OF ITS RUNTIME DEVOTED TO THE ESCAPE ATTEMPT IN THE OUTSIDE WORLD RATHER THAN THE HORRORS PERPETRATED UPON IMPRISONED FEMALE FLESH AND MINDS. BUT PAY NO MIND, THIS IS NOT ONLY ONE OF THE MOST WELL MADE W.I.P. FILMS, IT'S ALSO ONE OF MY FAVORITE FILMS OF ALL TIME - REGARDLESS OF GENRE.

I LOVE THIS MOVIE SO MUCH, IT MAKES ME WANT TO DANCE AROUND WITH MY DICK STUFFED IN SOME FRENCH BREAD.

IN FACT, TO SIMPLY LUMP THIS INTO THE W.I.P. ARENA AND BE DONE WITH IT, WOULD BE TO IGNORE ALL THE OTHER SPICEY AND SWEET FLAVORS COMMINGLING IN THIS RECIPE. YOU CAN STOKE OFF A REFERENCES AND NODS TO THE OCCULT, SPAGHETTI WESTERNS, FEMINISM, TRADITIONAL JAPANESE PERIOD DRAMAS, MUSICALS, BLOOD-SOAKED HOSTAGE POTBOILERS, AND MISOGYNISTIC B-MOVIES. EVEN WITH THE GENITAL MUTILATION AND FRENZIED MOB BEATING SCENES PUT ASIDE, THIS IS NOT YOUR TYPICAL JAPANESE EXPLOITATION FARE. PERHAPS THE MOST FASCINATING ASPECT HERE, IN THE FACE OF THE BRUTAL FILTH AND SLEAZE - IS THE CARE AND UTTER BRILLIANCE THAT ITO HAS DISPLAYED TO INTERTWINE ALL THESE STRINGS INTO A HALLUCINOGENIC TAPESTRY OF UNPARALLELED BEAUTY AND DIGNIFIED GRACE.

(EWW... DID I JUST WRITE "HALLUCINOGENIC TAPESTRY"?? WHAT THE FUCK?!)

I'VE BEEN AROUND THE BLOCK A COUPLE O' TIMES, AND RARELY HAVE I SEEN SUCH ASTONISHING USE OF COLOR, LIGHT AND CAMERAWORK IN THE EXPLOITATION FILM WORLD. IT'S JUST... JUST... BREATHTAKING. AND I HAVEN'T EVEN BEGUN TO SING THE PRAISES OF THE TITLE CHARACTER, THE VICIOUS ARCH-CRIMINAL PLAYED BY THE ENIGMATIC MEIKO KAJI, WHO HAS BEEN WRONGFULLY SENT TO THE BIG HOUSE BY A BETRAYING BOYFRIEND. KAJI BACKS UP HER AWE-INSPIRING CAMERA PRESENCE WITH ACTING THAT PUTS MY IRON-CLAD STOMACH IN KNOTS. ROGER CORMAN COULD ONLY HAVE DREAMT OF A LEAD ACTRESS THIS TALENTED FOR ONE OF HIS W.I.P MOVIES.

SCORPION: PLAYED BY MEIKO KAJI

JAILHOUSE 41 WAS THE 2ND INSTALLMENT OF A 6-PART SERIES, AND BY ALL ACCOUNTS WAS THE BEST OF THE LOT. THE SERIES BEGAN WITH 1972'S FEMALE CONVICT #701, CONTINUED WITH DEPARTMENT OF BEASTS (1973) NEW FEMALE CONVICT SCORPION (1976), AND FINISHED WITH SPECIAL CELLBLOCK X (1977). IN 1991 TOSHIHARU IKEDA, DIRECTOR OF THE ASIAN CULT FAVE EVIL DEAD TRAP RESURRECTED THE SERIES WITH DEATH THREAT, AND SUCCEEDED SOMEWHAT IN PAYING HOMAGE TO THE MYTHOLOGICAL FEELING OF THE ORIGINAL FILMS.

I WILL SAY NO MORE, BECAUSE TO SIMPLY RELATE PLOT POINTS OF FEMALE CONVICT SCORPION: JAILHOUSE 41 WOULD JUST NOT DO IT JUSTICE. AND I DON'T WANT TO BE RESPONSIBLE FOR ACCIDENTALLY SWAYING YOU AWAY FROM THE FILM. HUNT DOWN THE IMAGE ENTERTAINMENT 2002 DVD RELEASE. THE UNCUT 89 MINUTE TRANSFER LOOKS REALLY DECENT, AND COMES ALONG WITH THE FILM'S ORIGINAL JAPANESE TRAILER, AND A NICE GATEFOLD PACKAGE WITH MORE HISTORY AND INFO CONCERNING THIS AMAZING MOVIE.

4 THIRTY IN THE MORNING

PLEASE VISIT JOSH SIMMONS'S WEBSITE: JOSHUAHALLSIMMONS.COM

SHAW BROTHERS

THROW A 'HELLUVA' PUNCH

1973 IS THE YEAR OF THE SHAW 'HITS'

WINNING CONTESTANTS FOR
1973

SHAW BOX OFFICE IS SURE BOX OFFICE

SHAW BROTHERS DVD ROUNDUP

BACK IN THE LATE 60s, 70s, AND 80s, MANY OF THE MOST ENTERTAINING HONG KONG FILMS CAME OUT OF ONE STUDIO-SHAW BROTHERS. IN 2002, A REPUTABLE CHINESE DVD COMPANY - CELESTIAL - BEGAN TO RESTORE AND RELEASE A HUNDRED OR SO TITLES A YEAR FROM THE SHAW CATALOG, MANY PREVIOUSLY CONSIDERED LOST, AND MOST SEEING A HOME FORMAT RELEASE FOR THE VERY FIRST TIME. WITH THESE SPOTLESS LETTERBOXED PRINTS ARRIVING ON DVD IN LOCAL CHINESE DVD STORES AND WEBSITES LIKE WWW.POKERINDUSTRIES.COM AND WWW.HKFLIX.COM, THERE IS MORE REASON THAN EVER TO START DELVING INTO THE NEARLY FORGOTTEN HISTORY OF CHINESE EXPLOITATION, HORROR, AND MARTIAL ARTS MOVIES.

MY BIG PROBLEM WHEN SHOPPING FOR THE CELESTIAL/SHAW RELEASES, IS KNOWING WHAT'S WORTH BUYING - SINCE NO VIDEO STORE HAS THEM AVAILABLE TO RENT. THERE ISN'T REALLY ANYONE OUT THERE ONLINE OR IN PRINT WHO IS EVEN BOTHERING TO MAKE A TRUE EFFORT TO REVIEW THESE DISCS AND LET PEOPLE

KNOW WHICH ONES ARE BORING AND SUCKY, AND WHICH ONES ARE STELLAR. THE FEW NERDS THAT I'VE FOUND WHO ARE POSTING REVIEWS ON INTERNET MESSAGE BOARDS HAVE COMPLETELY QUESTIONABLE TASTE, AND I'VE NOTICED THAT THEY HAVE LITTLE TO NO INTEREST IN TRASHY, SLEAZY, BLOODY OR CAMPY ENTERTAINMENT - WHICH IS TOTALLY WHAT I STOKE OFF OF.

SO I'VE TAKEN IT UPON MYSELF TO BUY A SHITLOAD OF DISCS AND GIVE A SEMI-PERMANENT HOME TO A CELESTIAL/SHAW COLUMN, EXPOSING THE DUDS AND THE MUST-HAVES. THE REVIEWS WILL BE TINY SINCE THERE ARE A LOT OF MOVIES TO GET THROUGH, AND VERY LITTLE SPACE TO DO IT IN.

YOU'LL NEED AN ALL-REGIONS PLAYER BEFORE YOU START BUYING THESE, UNLESS YOU'RE BUYING THE BOOTLEG VERSIONS WHICH PLAY ON ANY PLAYER - BUT LACK ALL THE SPECIAL FEATURES. HOW DO YOU TELL THE REGION 3 VERSION FROM A BOOTLEG? THE BOOT WILL COST YOU FROM $5 TO $10, AND THE REAL DEAL GO FROM $15 TO $25.

5 OR 4 STARS IS A TOTAL MUST HAVE FOR ANY CINEMA SEWER FAN, WHILE 1 STAR REPRESENTS A TOTAL WASTE OF MONEY.

MORE FROM '74 SHAW IN '74

THE MASTER OF KUNG FU

THE BAMBOO HOUSE OF DOLLS

"THE KILLER SNAKES"

ALL MEN ARE BROTHERS

HEROES TWO

"THIS TIME I'LL MAKE YOU' RICH"

"NA CHA AND THE 7 DEVILS"

SHAO LIN MARTIAL ARTS

COMPLETED CO-PRODUCTIONS

Bamboo House of Dolls (1974) One of the most entertaining women-in-prison films ever made. Sleazy, sexy, and fun. The soundtrack is funky and really memorable. *****

Death Duel (1973) Beautiful swordplay epic shot on lush wooded sets. Total eye candy. *** 1/2

The Killer Snakes (1974) Dark and freaky version of WILLARD, but with snakes instead of rats, and plenty of nasty sex . ****

The Lizard (1972) This James Bond rip-off in a 1930s setting was considered lost for years. Too bad it didn't stay that way. Boring. I could barely keep my eyes open. *

The Teahouse (1974) Chen Kuan-tai is Cheng, an ass-kickin' crime fighter who cleans up th' hood with a Teahouse as a base of operations. *** 1/2

Big Brother Cheng (aka The Teahouse 2 1975) The story continues, and more criminal ass is kicked. I love the dynamic opening credits especially. ***

Intimate Confessions of a Chinese Courtesan (1972) Absolutely stunning rape revenge shocker set in a brothel in ancient China. Gorgeous cinematography. *****

Heroes Two (1973) By-the-numbers Kung-Fu that didn't do much for me. **

The Mighty Peking Man (1977) Tacky, goofy, and utterly fantastic giant ape movie starring Danny Lee and a white jungle girl. Cool miniature buildings get destroyed! **** 1/2

36th Chamber of Shaolin (aka Master Killer 1978) Who couldn't love this martial arts spectacular starring Gordon Liu from the KILL BILL movies? The training sequences are totally dope. *****

Human Skin Lanterns (1982) Quirky, magic-filled slasher movie set in ancient China. Sadly has some gore scenes cut from this print. Dammit. ***

The Merry Wife (1971) A teenage schoolgirl marries her 35 year old teacher. Plenty of swingin' 60s style shenanigans ensue as they try to keep it a secret. **1/2

The Bastard (1973) A young beggar in turn of the century China also happens to be a kung-fu prodigy. He befriends a cute beggar-girl and they have adventures. Pretty cool. ***

Twinkle Twinkle Little Star (1982) This insane and unusual sci-fi comedy has musical numbers, alien abductions, and a bizarre spoof of Star Wars! ***1/2

The Sexy Killer (1976) An awesome HK version of Jack Hill's "Coffy" (nearly a shot for shot remake) which totally holds its own. Chen Ping is a sexy killer indeed! *****

The Call Girls (1977) Based on the HK "Starlets-for-sale" prostitution scandal of the 70s, this just doesn't get sleazy enough. Starring Danny Lee. **

Women of Desire (1974) Tedious relationship-drama that doesn't live up to the sexy cover art, but there is a great violence packed finale. Snag it if it's cheap. **

Passing Flickers (1982) This non-fiction behind-the-scenes look at the saucy goings-on in and around Shaw Bros studios is too silly in its presentation to be highly recommended. **1/2

Police Force (1973) Fast forward through all the early precision formation marching scenes, and you'll find a really cool revenge-themed cop-sploitation drama. ****

Boxer from Shangtung (1972) Underrated martial arts film features a homeless kung-fu bum who becomes a rich gangster - Scarface-style! Very cool. ****1/2

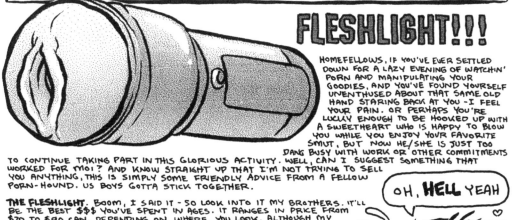

FLESHLIGHT!!!

HOMEFELLOWS, IF YOU'VE EVER SETTLED DOWN FOR A LAZY EVENING OF WATCHIN' PORN AND MANIPULATING YOUR GOODIES, AND YOU'VE FOUND YOURSELF UNENTHUSED ABOUT THAT SAME OLD HAND STARING BACK AT YOU - I FEEL YOUR PAIN. OR PERHAPS YOU'RE LUCKLY ENOUGH TO BE HOOKED UP WITH A SWEETHEART WHO IS HAPPY TO BLOW YOU WHILE YOU ENJOY YOUR FAVORITE SMUT, BUT NOW HE/SHE IS JUST TOO DANG BUSY WITH WORK OR OTHER COMMITMENTS TO CONTINUE TAKING PART IN THIS GLORIOUS ACTIVITY. WELL, CAN I SUGGEST SOMETHING THAT WORKED FOR MOI? AND KNOW STRAIGHT UP THAT I'M NOT TRYING TO SELL YOU ANYTHING, THIS IS SIMPLY SOME FRIENDLY ADVICE FROM A FELLOW PORN-HOUND. US BOYS GOTTA STICK TOGETHER.

THE FLESHLIGHT. BOOM, I SAID IT - SO LOOK INTO IT MY BROTHERS. IT'LL BE THE BEST $$$ YOU'VE SPENT IN AGES. IT RANGES IN PRICE FROM $70 TO $90 CAN, DEPENDING ON WHERE YOU LOOK, ALTHOUGH MY CHEAP ASS SPENT A YEAR WANDERING AROUND LOOKING FOR ONE ON SALE UNTIL I JUST STOPPED SCREWING THE POOCH AND TOOK THE PLUNGE ON ONE OF THE NEW ONES AVAILABLE ON EBAY. I HAD SOME PAYPAL CREDIT BURNING A HOLE IN MY HARD DRIVE, SO I FIGURED THE TIME WAS RIGHT TO BUY INTO THE FLESHLIGHT MYTHOS.

THE FLESHLIGHT MAY SEEM LIKE A SILLY NOTION, BUT THIS IS THE NEXT GENERATION OF POCKET PUSSY - THIS IS BIG NEWS! IT'S MADE OUT OF THE SAME SEMI-SOLID SOFT GOOEY LIFELIKE STUFF AS THE INFAMOUS REALDOLL, AND SHARES THE SAME ORGASMIC BENEFITS, EXCEPT IT'S 1/100th OF THE PRICE, AND IT COMES DISGUISED - NINJA STYLE - AS A BIG INDUSTRIAL SIZED FLASHLIGHT. (NO, IT DOESN'T LIGHT UP!)

WHEN MINE ARRIVED IN THE MAIL, I RAN HOME FROM THE POST OFFICE AND FUCKED THE SNOT OUT OF IT! IT'S NOT QUITE AS MINDBLOWING AS ALL THE HYPED-UP ADVERTISING SAYS (THEY CLAIM IT'S AS GOOD OR BETTER THAN REAL PUSSY), BUT IT'S CERTAINLY A HUGE UPGRADE FROM THE OL' HAND, OR ANY OTHER PSEUDO-PUSSY SEX TOY - HAVE NO DOUBT.

THE 'SKIN' IT'S COMPRISED OF IS SILKY SMOOTH, SMELLS LIKE VANILLA, AND YOU CAN WARM IT UP TO SKIN TEMPERATURE IN HOT WATER, OR GO NECROPHILE-STYLE. THE SENSATION IT BESTOWS ENVELOPES THE WAY

OH, **HELL** YEAH

A SOFT, WARM, INVITING PUSSY DOES - WHICH IS PRETTY MUCH THE BEST FEELING IN THE WORLD LAST TIME I CHECKED. THE ONE BUMMER (NOT COUNTING THE OBVIOUS FACT THAT IT'S NOT AN ANIMATE OBJECT OR A PERSON WHO YOU CAN SNUGGLE WITH AND SMOOTCH) IS THAT YOU HAVE TO ADD LUBE ABOUT EVERY 5 MINUTES BECAUSE THE NATURAL SUCTION OF THE THING STARTS TO CHAFE YOUR BEEF ONCE THE LUBE DISSIPATES, BUT I BET ONE COULD GET AROUND THAT BY USING A NON-WATER BASED LUBE, WHICH I HAVEN'T DONE YET. THE COOL THING ABOUT THIS IS, THE MORE LUBE YOU USE, THE LOOSER THE PUSSY FEELS. SO IF YOU WANT TO REPLICATE THAT 18 YEAR OLD PUSSY FEELING, OR THE SOMEWHAT LESS POPULAR 80 YEAR OLD CUNT - **THE POWER IS YOURS!! WOW!**

WHEN I FIRST GOT WITH THE FLESHLIGHT, I STARTED JUST BY JACKING MY COCK WITH IT LIKE I WOULD WITH MY HAND, BUT THE REALISTIC FEELING ON MY DICK ENVOKED SOMETHING PRIMAL AND MADE ME FEEL LIKE I SHOULD BE FUCKING IT, AND NOT IT FUCKING ME - SO I LAID ON MY SIDE AND HUMPED IT THAT WAY. AFTER A COUPLE WEEKS OF GETTING USED TO HOW IT FELT, I WENT BACK TO USING IT LIKE I HAD TO BEGIN WITH, AND GOT OFF REALLY EASILY. BEFORE YOU SAY "DID I REALLY NEED TO READ THIS?" TAKE INTO ACCOUNT THAT AFTER MASTURBATING THE SAME WAY FOR THE LAST 20 YEARS, I'M UNDERSTANDABLY A LITTLE THRILLED TO FINALLY HAVE A NEW TECHNIQUE OPTION. THIS IS A NEW ERA!

UPON BEING INTRODUCED TO MY NEW TOY, MY SWEETIE REBECCA WAS ALL LIKE, "AWWW! NO FAIR! DO THEY MAKE ONE FOR GIRLS TOO?" DUH... THEY HAVE BEEN FOR DECADES, IT'S CALLED A **DILDO.** SORRY GIRLS, BUT IT'S THE BOYS' TURN TO EXPERIENCE A SEX TOY THAT'LL REVOLUTIONIZE HOW WE REACH THE BIG 'O'.

SOCK IT TO ME BABY (1968)

SLEAZY LARRY HUNTER PLAYS RON BAKER, A FLABBY BOOZE-GUZZLIN' ALCOHOLIC WHO LIVES OFF HIS WIFE'S BANK ACCOUNT. HE'S ALSO OBSESSED WITH "THE YOUNG STUFF", AND HE DOESN'T MIND WHO KNOWS IT. "LOOK AT THAT BEAUTIFUL RUMP! THOSE PERFECTLY SHAPED BREASTS!" THINKS UNCLE RON WHILE SPASTICALLY OGLING HIS TEENAGE FUCKSLUT NIECE SUSAN WHO WRITHES NAKED ON HER BED. "SHE'S READY FOR SEX AND I'M READY TO GIVE IT TO HER..BUT I MUSTN'T! SHE'S ONLY A CHILD! WHAT SORT OF DEGENERATE AM I?"

UH, THE NORMAL GARDEN-VARIETY KIND? DIRECTOR LOU CAMPA MADE A FEW OTHER SEXPLOITATION MOVIES LIKE THIS ONE BEFORE HIS DESCENT INTO THE SEAMY WORLD OF MOB-FINANCED HARDCORE.
- BOUGIE '08

Short Eyes

SHORT EYES FOLLOWS THE ANIMALISTIC GOINGS-ON OF "THE TOMBS" (MANHATTAN'S INFAMOUS DETENTION CENTER/PRISON). THE INHABITANTS OF THIS HARDENED SOCIETY WITHIN A SOCIETY ARE THROWN INTO AN AGITATED MURMUR WITH THE ARRIVAL OF A CLEAN-CUT MIDDLE-CLASS YUPPIE (BRUCE DAVISON) WHO HAPPENS TO BE A "SHORT EYES" (PRISON LINGO FOR A CHILD MOLESTER). THE WHITE NEWBIE NERVOUSLY TRIES NOT TO ATTRACT THE ATTENTION OF THE PRIMARILY BLACK AND PUERTO RICAN UNDERPRIVILEGED AND BADASS MASSES, WHO FOR THE MOST PART DESPISE "WHITEY". WILL THE THRONGS OF FRUSTRATED AND ANGRY INMATES RIP SHORT EYES LIMB FROM BLOODY LIMB? OR SIMPLY HUMILIATE AND DEHUMANIZE THE CHILDFUCKER INTO A QUIVERING MASS OF JELL-O? NO DOUBT— THIS FILM IS ONE OF THE MOST REALISTIC, MEMORABLE, AND DOWNRIGHT FRIGHTENING PORTRAYALS OF PRISON LIFE EVER COMMITTED TO CELLULOID.

THE SCREENWRITER AND CO-STAR (PLAYING THE ROLE OF "GO-GO") WAS MIGUEL PINERO, WHO WROTE THE FILM IN AN INMATES' PLAYWRITING WORKSHOP WHILE INCARCERATED ON A LONG PRISON TERM FOR ARMED ROBBERY IN SING SING. THE PLAY EVENTUALLY FOUND ITS WAY TO BROADWAY, AND THEN TO THE BIG SCREEN, WHERE ACTORS ON SET FOUND THEMSELVES IN THE REAL 19th CENTURY MANHATTAN PRISON WHERE PINERO'S SCRIPT TOOK PLACE, PLAYING THEIR ROLES AMONGST ACTUAL CRIMINALS WHO PROVIDED THE FILM WITH A LITTLE LOCAL COLOR.

"SHORT EYES reaches a new level of intensity. A picture of hellfire and brimstone" —NEW YORK POST

"SHORT EYES gets us by the throat...the most emotionally accurate, frightening movie about American prisons ever made." —NEW YORK MAGAZINE

PINERO HIMSELF MISSED THE FILM'S NEW YORK PREMIERE WHEN HE WAS ARRESTED FOR ARMED ROBBERY — YET AGAIN. THE 40 GRAND HE RECEIVED FOR THE FILM WAS GONE IN A MATTER OF DAYS, AS HE GAVE IT ROBIN HOOD STYLE TO HIS MANY HOMELESS FRIENDS AND FORMER PRISON PALS IN NYC. MIGUEL REPORTEDLY LIVED ON THE STREET EVEN AFTER THE FILM WAS RELEASED TO CRITICAL ACCLAIM, USING A PHONE BOOTH ON THE LOWER EAST SIDE AS HIS OFFICE — OFTEN RELYING ON NEARBY JUNKIES AND VAGRANTS TO POSE AS RECEPTIONISTS. PINERO DIED TRAGICALLY YOUNG OF LIVER FAILURE DUE TO HIS MANY YEARS OF EXTREME DRUG AND ALCOHOL ABUSE IN 1988. A FILM WAS MADE ABOUT HIS LIFE IN 2001 CALLED **PINERO**.

LOOK FOR THE AWESOME CURTIS MAYFIELD PULLING DOUBLE DUTY AS AN ACTOR AND COMPOSER FOR **SHORT EYES**, PRIOR TO HIS HORRIFIC ON-STAGE ACCIDENT IN 1990 WHICH MADE HIM A QUADRIPLEGIC BEFORE HE DIED OF DIABETES IN 1999. 70S COUNTRY MUSIC FANS WILL ALSO BE HYPED TO SPOT FREDDY FENDER (SANG "WASTED DAYS AND WASTED NIGHTS") HERE THE SAME YEAR "THE LATIN COWBOY" WAS LANDING NOMINATIONS AT THE GRAMMYS. BOTH FREDDY AND CURTIS LEAD QUIRKY, BUT BEAUTIFUL SING-ALONGS IN ORDER TO PASS THE TIME A LITTLE EASIER.

ANOTHER AMAZING STORY IS THAT OF TITO GOYA, WHO IS A REAL STANDOUT AS "CUPCAKES"— THE CELLBLOCK'S MOST LUSTED-OVER PIECE OF ASS. TITO WAS PINERO'S OCCASIONAL LOVER, AND WAS ARRESTED A FEW YEARS LATER FOR A MURDER HE COMMITTED 8 MONTHS AFTER **SHORT EYES** WAS RELEASED. HE WAS EXECUTED ON DEC. 1ST 1985. KEEP YOUR EYES PEELED FOR LUIS GUZMAN (**BOOGIE NIGHTS, CARLITOS WAY**) MAKING HIS FIRST ON SCREEN APPEARANCE AS AN EXTRA. HE'D APPEAR YEARS LATER ON TV'S **OZ**, BRINGING THE CYCLE FULL CIRCLE.

MIGUEL PINERO'S SHORT EYES
Starring BRUCE DAVISON and JOSE PEREZ
Also starring NATHAN GEORGE, DON BLAKELY, SHAWN ELLIOTT, MIGUEL PINERO, TITO GOYA, JOSEPH CARBERRY and KENNETH STEWARD
Guest Stars CURTIS MAYFIELD and FREDDIE FENDER
Directed by Robert M. Young · Produced by Lewis Harris
Screenplay by Miguel Pinero · Executive Producer Marvin Stuart
Music Scored and Composed by Curtis Mayfield · Edited by Ed Beyer

She has the power to set objects afire with just one glance.

FIRESTARTER

Will she have the power...to survive?

FIRESTARTER (1984)

DREW MAKES STUFF BURN JUST BY LOOKING AT IT, AND CAN READ PEOPLE'S THOUGHTS. SHE'S A FIRESTARTER, TWISTED FIRESTARTER. SHE'S THE BITCH I HATED, FILTH-INFATUATED. SHE'S THE PAIN I TASTED — FELT INTOXICATED.

A LET DOWN, AND NOT REALLY THE SUM OF ITS PARTS, FIRESTARTER WAS ORIGINALLY TO BE DIRECTED BY JOHN CARPENTER — WHO WAS IN HIS FUCKING PRIME THEN. ACCORDING TO CARPENTER, UNIVERSAL EXECS REMOVED HIM FROM THE PROJECT IN THE WAKE OF THE BOX OFFICE FAILURE AND CRITICAL DRUBBING THEY RECEIVED FOR **THE THING** (1982). IT'S ALSO A BUMMER THAT JENNIFER CONNELLY LOST THE ROLE TO DREW BARRYMORE, WHO IS A FIRESTARTER, A TWISTED FIRESTARTER.

THE REASON IT FAILS IS THAT IT TRIES TO FAITHFULLY ADAPT STEPHEN KING'S BOOK AT THE EXPENSE OF PACING. IT'S A 500 PAGE BOOK SHOVED INTO A 2 HOUR MOVIE, AND THEY DIDN'T EVEN USE LUBE.

—RB

DON'T MUCK AROUND WITH A GREEN BERET'S MAMA!

He'll take his chopper and ram it down your throat!

CHROME AND HOT LEATHER

WES BISHOP and LEE FROST present "CHROME and HOT LEATHER" starring WILLIAM SMITH
TONY YOUNG · MICHAEL HAYNES · PETER BROWN · MARVIN GAYE
MICHAEL STEARNS introducing KATHY BAUMANN and LARRY BISHOP as Gabe
Produced by WES BISHOP · Photographed and Directed by LEE FROST [GP] COLOR A MOVIELAB
Screenplay by MICHAEL ALLEN HAYNES & DAVID NEIBEL and DON TAIT
Story by MICHAEL ALLEN HAYNES & DAVID NEIBEL · Music by PORTER JORDAN · An AMERICAN INTERNATIONAL Release

IT'S GREEN BERETS VS BIKERS, AND ONLY ONE WILL WIN! A CRUSTY BIKER GANG CALLED 'THE WIZARDS' TERRORIZES AND KILLS TWO INNOCENT AND ATTRACTIVE GIRLS - UNAWARE THAT ONE OF THE YOUNG LADIES WAS THE FIANCE OF AN ARMY SERGEANT. WHEN INFORMED, THE GREEN BERET AND HIS ARMY PALS PUT A PLAN INTO ACTION TO DO WHAT THE COPPERS CAN'T - CATCH THE BIKER SCUM WHO OFFED KATHY AND HELEN!

FIRST UP, THE ARMY BOYS BUY WIMPY LOOKING RED DIRT BIKES. THEN, AFTER A COMICAL TRAINING SEQUENCE (THAT SEEMS TO GO ON FOREVER AND HAS THEM AS NOVICES BECOMING MOTOCROSS EXPERTS IN WHAT SEEMS TO BE A COUPLE HOURS OF SPLASHING THROUGH SOME MUD) THE 4 VIGILANTES GO AFTER THE WIZARDS. THE RESULTING VIOLENCE IS STRICTLY 'G' RATED, AND HARDLY BEFITTING OF THE GENRE. WITH THE EXCEPTION OF SOME BIKER CHICKS GETTING SLAPPED SILLY BY THEIR MEN, THIS WOULD HAVE PROBABLY MADE IT TO TV IN THE 70s UNTOUCHED BY CENSORS - EVEN IF THE ORIGINAL AMERICAN INTERNATIONAL AD CAMPAIGN TRIED HARD TO SUGGEST OTHERWISE. BUT IT'S HARD TO BE TOO LET DOWN SINCE IT'S ALL SCORED WITH A COOL SOUNDTRACK BY AN UNCREDITED GROUP THAT SOUNDS LIKE GRAND FUNK RAILROAD.

NOT ONLY DID CULT CLASSIC CINEMA SEWER FAVE LEE FROST DIRECT THIS, BUT HE CAST PETER BROWN AND MOTOWN LEGEND MARVIN GAYE - IN ONE OF ONLY 2 FILMS HE EVER APPEARED IN.

RAW MEAT (1972) AKA "DEATH LINE"

THE LONDON SUBWAY IS THE LONGEST AND OLDEST UNDERGROUND RAIL SYSTEM IN THE WORLD (MEASURING 253 MILES ALTOGETHER), AND SOMETHING IN THEM IS KILLING PEOPLE. THE SOMETHING IN QUESTION IS A FIFTH-GENERATION SURVIVOR OF A TUNNEL CONSTRUCTION CREW WHO GOT TRAPPED IN A CAVE. THE SHAGGY MONSTROSITY LIVES ON SEWER RATS, AND

The Most Terrifying Journey You Will Ever Make... to the land of the HUNGRY DEAD!

RAW MEAT

THE OCCASIONAL SUBWAY EMPLOYEE HE HANGS ON HOOKS IN HIS DEN.

OVERALL I RECOMMEND THIS ALTHOUGH IT COULD USE ABOUT 15 MINUTES LESS TALKY-TALK AND 15 MORE MINUTES OF PEEPS LOST UNDERGROUND + SCARED. ALSO: WHO THE FUCK ARE THE ZOMBIE-TOGA GIRLS ON THE POSTER?? THEY AREN'T IN THIS.

EMANUELLE IN AMERICA (1977)

FAR FROM THE SOFT-FOCUS TENDER STORY OF SEXUAL LIBERATION THAT THE ORIGINAL JUST JAECKIN MOVIE WAS, **EMANUELLE IN AMERICA** IS A SICK, SCUM-COATED OFFERING FROM THE LATE JOE D'AMATO -- THE ITALIAN KING OF DEGENERATE HORROR-PORN.

EMANUELLE, THE FASHION MODEL PHOTOGRAPHER/INVESTIGATIVE JOURNALIST (PLAYED BY THE ELEGANT LAURA GEMSER) PRIES INTO THE ODD SEXUAL PECCADILLOES OF THE RICH AND FAMOUS, AND INFILTRATES AN ARMS SMUGGLER'S HAREM. NOTHING MUCH HAPPENS IN THE FIRST 40 MINUTES OF THE MOVIE (EXCEPT A BUNCH OF T+A), BUT HERE SHE COVERTLY CAPTURES PHOTOS OF THE WEALTHY ENJOYING THE CHARMS OF A HOST OF JAW-DROPPINGLY SEXAAAY

YOUNG WOMEN. NOTHING SEEMS TO BE TABOO TO THESE SAUCY MILLIONAIRES, AS EMANUELLE SOON DISCOVERS WHEN SHE SPIES ON A GIRL MASTURBATING A HORSE. NO, THE SCENE IS NOT CLEVERLY STAGED... D'AMATO ACTUALLY SHOT BEASTIALITY FOOTAGE FOR HIS FILM! **COOL!**

FROM THERE, THE JET-SETTING EBONY GODDESS TRAVELS TO VENICE WHERE SHE ATTENDS AN XXX ORGY SO EXPANSIVE, IT WOULD HAVE TICKLED OL' CALIGULA HIZSELF. AFTER SNAPPING SOME MORE PERVY PICS (WHAT PAPER DOES SHE WORK FOR, **SCREW**?) SHE HEADS OFF ON HER NEXT EROTIC ADVENTURE - A TRIP TO AN ISLAND WHERE WEALTHY WOMEN PAY TO ACT OUT THEIR SEXUAL FANTASIES WITH SOME HUNKY DUDE-CAKES. IT'S WHILE SNOOPIN' 'ROUND HERE THAT OL' MANNY STUMBLES ONTO SOMETHING INCREDIBLY DISTURBING. FAINT-HEARTED VIEWERS MIGHT WANT TO TURN OFF THE DVD ABOUT NOW.

IN ONE OF THE ROOMS, A COUPLE HAS SEX ON A BED WHILE AN 8MM PROJECTOR FLASHES DOWNRIGHT SCARY FOOTAGE OF MEN IN SOME FORM OF MILITARY UNIFORM SAVAGELY RAPING AND TORTURING FEMALE VICTIMS.

ONE WOMAN HAS HER BREASTS GROTESQUELY SAWED OFF WITH A MACHETE, WHILE ANOTHER IS IMPALED VAGINALLY ON A LARGE WOODEN SPIKE. GIANNETTO DE ROSSI'S MAKE UP FX ARE REMARKABLE, AND EVEN BY HARDCORE RAPE PORN STANDARDS -- THE FOOTAGE IS DISQUIETING. ADDING TO THE EFFECT, THE FILM IS GRAINY, HAS NO SOUND, AND IS SHOT WITH SUCH UNPLEASANT REALISM THAT MANY HAVE AND CONTINUE TO BELIEVE IT TO BE A GENUINE SNUFF FILM. THESE FEW MINUTES WOULD BE A HUGE INFLUENCE ON DAVID CRONENBERG, WHO WOULD GO ON TO DO A TONED DOWN VERSION OF THE SCENE FOR 1983's REMARKABLE **VIDEODROME.**

SHAKEN, EMANUELLE RETURNS TO NEW YORK AND TELLS HER EDITOR THAT SHE'S STUMBLED ONTO A SNUFF RING, AND WANTS TO LOOK INTO IT. FROM THERE SHE GETS HOOKED UP WITH A MYSTERIOUS GOVERNMENT OFFICIAL WHO SHOWS HER EVEN MORE FOOTAGE OF GIRLS BEING MUTILATED. EMANUELLE GETS PHOTOS OF THE SCREEN, AND HER INVESTIGATIONS EVENTUALLY LEAD TO A FIRST HAND VIEWING OF A SNUFF MOVIE BEING MADE, BUT THE PAPER REFUSES TO PUBLISH HER STORY. THE CONSPIRACY OF SILENCE CONTINUES BECAUSE THE PEOPLE BEHIND THIS UNDERGROUND MENACE ARE JUST **TOO** POWERFUL. GOOD IS RENDERED USELESS, AND EVIL RISES VICTORIOUS ONCE AGAIN. PHEW!

THE FILM ITSELF, TO BE HONEST, IS NOT VERY GOOD. THE STORY LINE IS CONVOLUTED, THREAD BARE, AND PLOT HOLES ARE PLENTIFUL. IT IS, HOWEVER, ONE OF THE MOST CONTROVERSIAL SEX AND GORE EPICS IN EXPLOITATION HISTORY, AND SHOULD ENTERTAIN ENOUGH TO MAKE YOU FORGIVE AND FORGET ANY SUCH FAILINGS. THIS WAS THE FIRST WIDELY RELEASED PRODUCTION TO DEFINE WHAT AN ACTUAL SNUFF PICTURE LOOKED LIKE. PRIOR TO THIS, THE URBAN LEGEND HAD NO VISUAL REPRESENTATION ASIDE FROM **PEEPING TOM** (1960) OR **SNUFF** (1976) TWO MOVIES THAT, WHILE GHASTLY IN CONCEPT, WEREN'T WIDELY SEEN AND DIDN'T REALLY DO MUCH TO VISUALLY DEFINE THE CONCEPT.

—BOUGIE

18 AND UP

BY WOBBINY BOBBINY BOUGIE!

ONLY THE TRULY OBLIVIOUS WOULDN'T FEAR AGEING IN THIS YOUTH-CRAZED SOCIETY WE RESIDE IN. WITH THE TIGHT, FRESH, TONED, TEENY-BOPPER EXAMPLES PUT FORWARD AS THE ULTIMATE 'IDEAL' BY EVERY FACTION OF THE WORLD AROUND US, ONLY A DELUDED WASTOID WOULD PUT ON A BRAVE FACE AND TRY TO CONVINCE HIM/HERSELF THAT YOUTH IS 'ONLY A STATE OF MIND'.

IT'S IMPOSSIBLE TO ESCAPE IT. YOUTH-OBSESSIVE POP CULTURE IS OMNIPRESENT IN NEARLY EVERY ASPECT OF NORTH AMERICAN ENTERTAINMENT. MAGAZINES, TV, MUSIC, ADVERTISING, AND FILM. THE ADULT ENTERTAINMENT INDUSTRY IS BY NO MEANS ABSENT FROM THAT LIST -- IN FACT, FROM MANY PEOPLE'S CONCERNED PESPECTIVE (EMANATING FROM BEHIND FURROWED BROWS AND GRITTED TEETH) IT IS THE FRONT RUNNER.

YOUNG, HOT, STICKY TEEN PUSSY IS THE MOST POPULAR SELLING FEATURE FOR ADULT FILMS AND VIDEOS, WITH ONLY THE LESBIAN, BIG-TIT, AND MILF FACTIONS COMING EVEN REMOTELY CLOSE IN TERMS OF OVERWHELMING POPULARITY. IN TODAY'S MAINSTREAM MARKET, EVERY MAJOR PORN COMPANY HAS A TEEN LINE, AND MANY OF THE INDUSTRY'S NUMEROUS PORN MOGULS DEAL IN THAT TIGHT, 18 YEAR OLD FLESH (OR MORE IMPORTANTLY, 18 YEAR OLD **LOOKING** FLESH) EXCLUSIVELY!

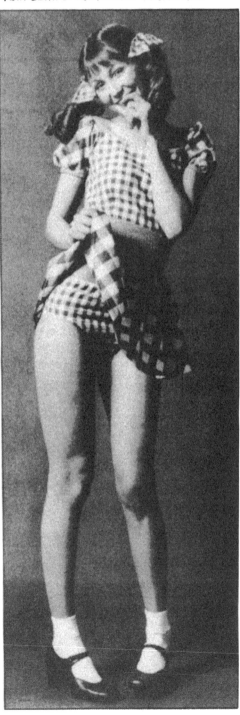

DESPITE THE PREDICTABLE OBJECTIONS OF THE MORAL MAJORITY, LEGAL YOUTH-THEMED PORN IS JUST ABOUT THE MOST NATURAL FORM OF EROTICA AVAILABLE TO MEN, ESPECIALLY WHEN YOU TAKE HUMAN CIVILIZATION'S HISTORY INTO ACCOUNT. THE REASONS FOR THE ATTRACTION ARE NUMEROUS, BUT IT SHOULD MOSTLY BE TAKEN INTO ACCOUNT THAT MOST MALES LOST THEIR VIRGINITY TO FELLOW TEENAGERS, AND HAVE A DEEPLY SET MEMORY OF THOSE FEMALES BEING THE ULTIMATE GOAL -- THE OBJECT OF DESIRE. DESIRE EQUATES TO FANTASY, AND FANTASY IS WHAT PORN IS ALL ABOUT.

I DARE SAY IT'S NEARLY IMPOSSIBLE TO ARGUE THEIR AESTHETIC APPEAL, AND EVEN SCIENCE IS ON THE SIDE OF THE TEEN-PORN FAN. THE PRIMAL BIOLOGICAL RESPONSE TO YOUTH IS OBVIOUS. THEY MAY NOT BE ALL THAT BRIGHT, BUT LIKE IT OR NOT IN TERMS OF FURTHERING THE SPECIES THE TEENAGER MAKES THE PERFECT MATE. THEY TEND TO BE HEALTHIER AND PRONE TO PRODUCING HEALTHY OFFSPRING, AS WELL AS EASIER TO IMPRESS AND WOO THANKS TO THEIR LACK OF EXPERIENCE.

I HAVE A HARD TIME UNDERSTANDING THE POSITION OF ANGRY CONSERVATIVES WHO CAN'T SEE THE DIFFERENCE BETWEEN A PAEDOPHILE AND SOMEONE WHO THINKS AN 18 YEAR OLD IS A PRIME CANDIDATE FOR A FUCK FILM. IT'S NOT UNNATURAL OR SHAMEFUL TO BE STIMULATED BY TEENS. IT'S THE RESULT OF OUR EVOLUTION. IT'S HARD-WIRED. TO DENY IT IS DISHONEST.

THERE ARE, OBVIOUSLY, OTHER CONTRADICTORY OPINIONS TO MINE EVEN WITHIN THE DEGENERATES IN THE ADULT INDUSTRY ITSELF. LONG-TIME PORN DIRECTOR HENRI PACHARD HAS OFTEN OUTLINED HIS ANTI-18, PRO-21 AGE-LIMIT THOUGHTS IN INTERVIEWS AND ESSAYS.

ADMITTEDLY, THE HEAVEN-SENT TEENAGE PRESENCE WASN'T ALWAYS THE POWERFUL, WALLET-SUCKING OVERLORD OVER THE XXX INDUSTRY THAT IT IS NOW. CERTAINLY THERE WERE ALWAYS EXAMPLES OF YOUTH-RELATED SMUT BEING PRODUCED, (SOME OF WHICH ARE THE BEST MOVIES CREATED IN THE EARLY YEARS OF HARDCORE), BUT THEY WERE JUST ANOTHER TOPIC IN THE PILE (ALONG WITH SWINGERS, ORIENTALS, NURSES, BLACK-ON-WHITE, RAPE, ORGIES, HIPPIES, THE OCCULT, ETC) THAT A

DIRECTOR MIGHT THINK TO ALIGN HIS FILM WITH AS A MARKETING GIMMICK.

IT'S GOTTA BE UNDERSTOOD BY THE NEXT GENERATION OF PORN ENTHUSIASTS THAT IT HAS ONLY BEEN

IN THE LAST 15 TO 20 YEARS THAT WE CAN LOOK BACK AND SAY THAT THIS ONE-TIME NICHE SUB-GENRE OF ADULT ENTERTAINMENT HAS BECOME THE #1 INSPIRATION TO PULL PUD. IT CAN'T POSSIBLY BE A COINCIDENCE THAT THE UNDERAGE-LOOKING PUBIC HAIR STYLE (AKA: **NONE**) CAME TO BE THE NORM AT PRECISELY THE SAME MOMENT IN PORN HISTORY, CAN IT ?

I FUCKING THINK NOT.

THE THING

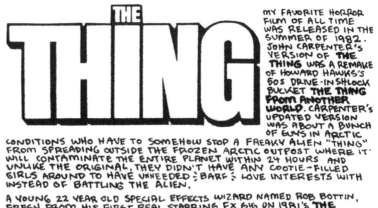

MY FAVORITE HORROR FILM OF ALL TIME WAS RELEASED IN THE SUMMER OF 1982. JOHN CARPENTER'S VERSION OF **THE THING** WAS A REMAKE OF HOWARD HAWKS'S 50S DRIVE-IN SHLOCK BUCKET **THE THING FROM ANOTHER WORLD**. CARPENTER'S UPDATED VERSION WAS ABOUT A BUNCH OF GUYS IN ARCTIC CONDITIONS WHO HAVE TO SOMEHOW STOP A FREAKY ALIEN "THING" FROM SPREADING OUTSIDE THE FROZEN ARCTIC OUTPOST WHERE IT WILL CONTAMINATE THE ENTIRE PLANET WITHIN 24 HOURS AND UNLIKE THE ORIGINAL, THEY DIDN'T HAVE ANY COOTIE-FILLED GIRLS AROUND TO HAVE UNNEEDED ; BARF ; LOVE INTERESTS WITH INSTEAD OF BATTLING THE ALIEN.

A YOUNG 22 YEAR OLD SPECIAL EFFECTS WIZARD NAMED ROB BOTTIN, FRESH FROM HIS FIRST REAL STARRING FX GIG ON 1981'S **THE HOWLING**, WAS BROUGHT IN TO CREATE SOME OF THE MOST INTENSE AND FUCKED-UP CREATURE-BASED GORE EFFECTS IN FILM MAKING HISTORY. BOTTIN LIVED, WORKED AND SLEPT ON THE SET - WORKING HIS CREW 7 DAYS A WEEK FOR OVER A YEAR. ONLY WHEN THE PROJECT WAS COMPLETED DID CARPENTER SEND THE FRAZZLED HEADCASE TO A HOSPITAL WHERE HE WAS DIAGNOSED WITH EXTREME EXHAUSTION.

BOTTIN AND A LOT OF OTHER PEOPLE WORKED LIKE RABID DOGS TO MAKE **THE THING** A MASTERWORK OF THE GENRE. THE STORY LINE HAS A FEW LOOPHOLES, BUT THE UNANSWERED QUESTIONS ARE WHAT MAKES THE FILM'S PREMISE SO EFFECTIVE. THEY ADD TO THE STORY'S SICKENING AMOUNTS OF NAIL-BITING, PARANOIA-PACKED CLAUSTROPHOBIA.

BUT ABOVE ALL IN MY MIND **THE THING** IS A PERFECT EXAMPLE OF WHY EVEN REVOLUTIONARY CUTTING EDGE COMPUTER EFFECTS TURN OFF SO MANY FANS OF EXCELLENT OLD SKOOL GORE, FANTASY, AND SCI-FI CINEMA. THIS FILM IS A CONSTANT REMINDER THAT WATCHING OTHER FILMS WITH EVEN EXCELLENT COMPUTER CGI EFFECTS, IS ABOUT AS THRILLING AS WATCHING YOUR NEPHEW PLAY HIS FAVORITE VIDEO GAMES.

WHEN YOU SEE ALL THE GOO, LATEX, PYROTECHNICS, AND PUPPET PARTS CONTROLLED BY A CREW OF ARTISTS AND TECHNICIANS, YOUR WILLING SUSPENSION OF DISBELIEF IS OBVIOUSLY WORKING. YOU **KNOW** IT'S FAKE, BUT WHAT MAKES IT SO MUCH MORE INTERESTING WHEN COMPARED TO A HIGHLY DETAILED CGI PIECE, IS THAT YOU'RE AWARE THAT IT IS AN **ACTUAL** OBJECT. I PICTURE JOHN CARPENTER AND HIS CREW STANDING THERE AND FILMING IT ON AN ACTUAL SET, AND WITH PROPS THAT ACTUALLY EXIST. IT'S LIKE A FORM OF IMAGINED TACTILITY, AND IT'S IMPORTANT.

THESE WERE ARTISTS AND CRAFTSMEN/WOMEN WHO BROUGHT THEIR OWN PERSONAL VISION AND THE SIGNATURE OF THEIR STYLE TO THE WORK THEY CREATED. YOU COULD WATCH A FILM AND SEE AN EFFECT AND SAY, "WAS THAT A STAN WINSTON !? WAS THAT A TOM SAVINI ?" THE ARTIST BROUGHT

☆ CONTINUED FROM PREVIOUS PAGE ☆

THEMSELVES INTO THEIR ART SO VIVIDLY. WITH A COMPUTER ANIMATED EFFECT THERE'S A COMMITTEE SITTING IN FRONT OF COMPUTERS, PUSHING BUTTONS OR MAYBE PUTTING A WHITE DOT COVERED CAT SUIT ON AN ACTOR. THE IMAGINED REALITY IS ALL YOU ARE LEFT WITH. THE TACTILITY AND SIGNATURE OF THE ARTIST IS GONE. THE EXPERIENCE IS SO FAR LESS RICH DESPITE THE SKILL OF THE TECH NERDS.

ONE OF THE REASONS GENERATIONS OF PEOPLE WERE SO ENTHRALLED WITH MOVIES LIKE **KING KONG**, **THE WIZARD OF OZ**, OR **THE THING** -- WAS BECAUSE THEY KNEW THAT SOMEWHERE THESE FANTASTIC PLACES, THINGS, AND CHARACTERS EXISTED. THERE WAS ACTUALLY A WONDERFUL MOMENT IN TIME WHERE THAT INCREDIBLE SPACE WAS REAL...IF ONLY FOR THE TIME IT TOOK TO FILM IT, AND MAYBE ONLY IN MINIATURE.

WITH A COMPUTER EFFECT, IT NEVER EXISTED AT ALL. EVER. IT WAS JUST CODE.

HOW FUCKING DEPRESSING IS THAT?
-BOUGIE · 2004 ·

JOHN RITTER'S TESTICLES

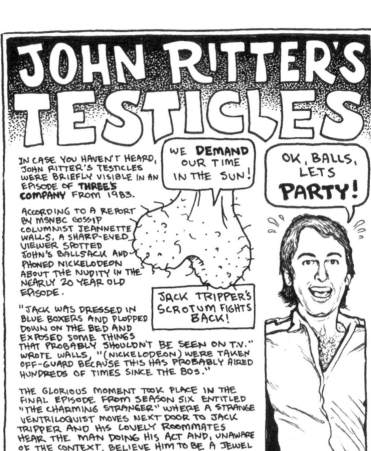

IN CASE YOU HAVEN'T HEARD, JOHN RITTER'S TESTICLES WERE BRIEFLY VISIBLE IN AN EPISODE OF **THREE'S COMPANY** FROM 1983.

WE **DEMAND** OUR TIME IN THE SUN!

OK, BALLS, LETS **PARTY!**

ACCORDING TO A REPORT BY MSNBC GOSSIP COLUMNIST JEANNETTE WALLS, A SHARP-EYED VIEWER SPOTTED JOHN'S BALLSACK AND PHONED NICKELODEON ABOUT THE NUDITY IN THE NEARLY 20 YEAR OLD EPISODE.

JACK TRIPPER'S SCROTUM FIGHTS BACK!

"JACK WAS DRESSED IN BLUE BOXERS AND PLOPPED DOWN ON THE BED AND EXPOSED SOME THINGS THAT PROBABLY SHOULDN'T BE SEEN ON T.V." WROTE WALLS, "(NICKELODEON) WERE TAKEN OFF-GUARD BECAUSE THIS HAS PROBABLY AIRED HUNDREDS OF TIMES SINCE THE 80s."

THE GLORIOUS MOMENT TOOK PLACE IN THE FINAL EPISODE FROM SEASON SIX ENTITLED "THE CHARMING STRANGER" WHERE A STRANGE VENTRILOQUIST MOVES NEXT DOOR TO JACK TRIPPER AND HIS LOVELY ROOMMATES HEAR THE MAN DOING HIS ACT AND, UNAWARE OF THE CONTEXT, BELIEVE HIM TO BE A JEWEL THIEF AND A MURDERER.

A REPRESENTATIVE FOR NICKELODEON WAS QUOTED AS CONFIRMING "YES, HIS SCROTUM FALLS OUT OF HIS SHORTS" AND WENT ON TO STATE THAT THE SCENE WOULD BE EDITED FROM FUTURE TELECASTS. ONE COULD ALSO ASSUME THAT THE NEW **THREE'S COMPANY** TV SERIES DVD IS ALSO EDITED - BUT I HAVEN'T CHECKED IT OUT YET TO CONFIRM.

IN ONE OF HIS LAST TALKSHOW APPEARANCES BEFORE HIS SAD UNTIMELY DEATH, RITTER WENT ON **LATE NIGHT WITH CONAN O'BRIEN** TO JOKE ABOUT THE EMBARRASSING TESTICULAR REVELATION.

"IT WAS A BRIEF SHOT, AND ONLY LASTED A SECOND. NO ONE BACK THEN NOTICED IT, AND WHEN IT WENT OUT OVER THE AIR, THERE WERE NO VHS RECORDERS OR DVD PLAYERS AROUND THAT COULD CATCH IT."

YOU **AND** YOUR BALLS WILL BE MISSED, JOHN.

REST IN PEACE

JAWS 3-D (1983)

MAN, I HAVE SUCH FOND MEMORIES OF WATCHIN' THIS ONE AS A KID. WITH IT'S 35 FOOT SHARK TAKING APART AN ENTIRE SEA WORLD THEME PARK, IT'S NOT AS GOOD AS THE ORIGINAL -- BUT I STILL LIKE TO WATCH IT OCCASIONALLY WITH SOME NACHOS AND CHEESE DIP. IT'S A LOT OF **FUN!**

DAVID BROWN AND RICHARD D. ZANUCK (PRODUCERS OF THE FIRST TWO FILMS) PITCHED THIS AS A SPOOF UNDER THE TITLE OF "NATIONAL LAMPOON'S JAWS 3, PEOPLE 0". JOE DANTE WAS ATTACHED AS DIRECTOR, AND THE MOVIE WAS TO OPEN WITH JAWS AUTHOR PETER BENCHLEY BEING EATEN IN HIS POOL BY A SHARK. THE SCRIPT ALSO INCLUDED A NAKED BO DEREK, ALIENS IN SHARK COSTUMES, AND A GALA SONG AND DANCE NUMBER.

CRAZY BUT TRUE! -BOUGIE

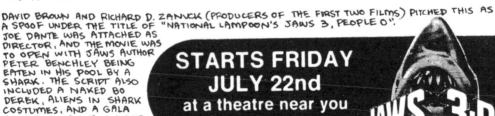

STARTS FRIDAY JULY 22nd at a theatre near you
subject to classification   Theatres Branch Ont

JAWS 3-D

CINEMA SEWER: MAYA APPRECIATION PAGE

DEAR BOUGIE:
WHILE VIEWING SOME OF YOUR PRODUCTION STILLS FOR YOUR BIBLICAL PORN EPIC "THE CUMMING OF JIZZUS", I WAS QUITE TAKEN WITH YOUR FEMALE STAR, MAYA. I LOOKED FOR HER ON THE INTERNET, AND AFTER SEEING A GOOD DEAL OF HER PERFORMANCES (MOSTLY KINKY STUFF LIKE FISTING). I'VE COME TO THE CONCLUSION THAT SHE IS THE HOTTEST GIRL I'VE EVER SEEN IN A PORN FILM. SHE HAS A RARE QUALITY. SOMETHING I'VE NEVER SEEN IN PORN. IF I WERE MAKING AN X-RATED MOVIE TODAY (WHICH I'M NOT) I WOULD BUILD THE WHOLE THING AROUND MAYA, AND LET HER DO HER THING. WHEREVER SHE GOES, I HOPE MAYA IS HAPPY, AND I MEANT WHAT I SAID ABOUT HER. IF YOU SEE HER AROUND, ASK HER IF SHE WANTS TO HAVE A BRIEF AFFAIR WITH A 100 YEAR OLD FORMER PORNOGRAPHER.

    —SHAUN COSTELLO

ANYONE WHO ISN'T FAMILIAR WITH SHAUN AND HIS EXCELLENT 1970s AND 80s CLASSIC XXX FILMOGRAPHY NEEDS TO GOOGLE THAT SHIT RIGHT NOW.

HIS DROOLING LETTER IS ONE OF A FEW THAT I'VE RECIEVED CONCERNING VIEWER OBSESSION WITH THIS MOSTLY UNKNOWN PORN PRINCESS. SADLY, MAYA DROPPED OUT OF PORN A YEAR OR SO AGO, AND AT LAST CONTACT, MENTIONED THAT SHE WAS STUDYING TO BECOME A VET. I MISS HER BEAUTY, GRACE, AS WELL AS HER ABILITY TO CASUALLY TAKE BASEBALL BATS UP HER AMAZING ANUS.

SPEAKING OF WHICH, THAT REMINDS ME OF MY FAVOURITE MEMORY OF HER. MAYA USED TO LIVE A BLOCK FROM ME BEFORE SHE LEFT VANCOUVER, AND ONE NIGHT SHE, MATT DADDY, CHELSEA CHAINSAW, AND I WERE GOOFIN' ON THE WINE AND PEACH COOLERS. AT ONE POINT I BEGAN GOOD NATUREDLY HARRASSING HER ABOUT HER ABILITIES AND HOW SHE COULD POSSIBLY TAKE ALL THOSE FISTS UP HER BUMHOLE ALL THE TIME AND NOT HAVE TO WEAR "DEPENDS" ADULT DIAPERS BY THE AGE OF TWENTY FIVE. HER CALM AND INSTANT RESPONSE TO MY JUVENILE TAUNTING?

> SUCH A DIRTY, DIRTY, GIRL ....

SHE WHIPPED DOWN HER JEANS AND PANTIES IN ONE MOTION, BENT OVER, STUCK HER ASS IN MY FACE, YANKED HER ASS CHEEKS AS WIDE OPEN AS THEY WOULD SPLIT, AND PROCEEDED TO GIVE ME A LONG, INTIMATE LOOK AT HER WONDEROUS POOPER.

I HAD TO CONCEED. IT LOOKED VERY TIGHT AND NORMAL. MY NOSE WAS ABOUT AN INCH AWAY FROM IT, SO I FEEL I CAN REPORT THIS FACT WITH SOME AUTHORITY. I CERTAINLY SUPPOSE THAT IT WAS THE QUICKEST WAY TO END ANY AND ALL ARGUMENTS OR RUMORS ABOUT THE CONDITION OF YOUR PUCKERED POOCH-HOLE!

ALL THE BEST TO YOU IN YOUR NEW CAREER, MAYA. YOUR FANS AND FRIENDS IN PORN WILL NOT SOON FORGET YOU.

    —ROBIN BOUGIE JAN. 2009

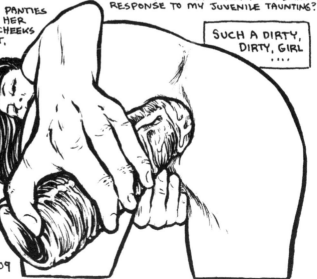

THE HAND THAT TIME FORGOT

BY: RICHARD BRANDT

"What kind of movie would a fertilizer salesman from El Paso, Texas make?"
-- Michael Weldon,
The Psychotronic Encyclopedia of Film
#

For many years, *Manos: The Hands of Fate* must have been the Holy Grail for aficionados of obscure, low-budget, really godawful cinema: seldom mentioned, hardly ever seen, exactly the kind of movie that, yes, a fertilizer salesman named Hal P. Warren would decide to make, one fine summer in 1966.

That all changed when the grandmeisters of *la cinema du fromage* at *Mystery Science Theater 3000* delved into the bottom of the barrel and found this epic lying in ambush. For those without access to Comedy Central or some other clue, *MST3K* (for short) is about two scientists who torture a space-bound employee and his robot pals by force-feeding them movies, into which they interject their own snide remarks and alternative dialogue. Bad movies. Really bad. Really, really, *really* bad.

As one of the scientists confided when *Manos* came up for its turn, "I think even we may have gone a little too far this time."

So, instant cult phenomenon. Even if 'admirers' is not quite the word, *Manos* has been embraced by legions of 'MSTies' and cult film fans who passionately argue its demerits over the Internet. Even Roger Ebert's forum on Compuserve isn't safe.

And yet, as we shall see, there very nearly wasn't a *Manos: The Hands of Fate* at all.

How to describe *Manos* fairly? I tell locals that it's about a couple who take a wrong turn on Scenic Drive (that being the one landmark in the film still recognizable after three decades) and wind up at a 'Lodge' managed by a cult leader, his wobbly-kneed sidekick, and his harem of lingerie-clad wives. Wow; a cult movie that's *really* a cult movie!

"So, Richard," my fellow film buff Craig tells me over the phone, "for the next Amigocon you should really round up some of the cast and have a reunion panel."

"Hmmm," I said, the gears in my brain starting to grind away implacably. Problem is, how to locate some of these folks thirty years after? Assuming they're not dead, who would have hung around after perpetrating something like *Manos* upon the townfolk?

Suddenly my dreams are haunted by the spectre of *Manos*. In my sleep I can see myself after grueling detective work uncovering a fugitive cast member; hey, that little girl who played the daughter must still be alive by now, eh? Only why hasn't she aged any by now.... *Aggggggh!* Time to wake up, eh?

To the rescue: my old pal Roy, who springs on me the revelation that two of his poker buddies had fessed up to being in the cast and crew. What's more, it turns out I had met both of these guys. Bob Guidry, the 'Director of Cinematography' as he insisted on being billed, had been doing public relations work while I was in the TV news business. Bernie Rosenblum (stunt coordinator and featured player, now a noted Southwestern photographer) I had met one night when Roy had been misinformed that a poker party was underway at his house.

So I begged and pleaded and cajoled for Roy to be our intermediary with these two legends of the cinema, and he brought back these terms: they'd come to a panel on *Manos* in return for free con memberships and dinner at La Hacienda Cafe.

Deal!

We ended up shifting the panel to late Sunday afternoon, as a big finale to wrap up the convention. Of course, throughout the weekend and especially as Sunday began to wane I kept a watchful eye out for Roy and his pals, to no avail. Finally, as we were knocking down some of the last items in the Sunday afternoon art auction, Roy breezed in with Bob and Bernie in tow. Craig and I sat them down, popped in a tape of the *MST3K* rendition of *Manos* for reference, and laid into "the *Manos* Guys ".

One of the first questions I asked was how they reacted to all the newfound public clamor for their work, what with *MST3K* picking it up and, I even hear rumors of a laserdisc edition.

"Well," said Bob, "we'd be extremely interested, because we're still owed a piece of the picture."

"Oh, really?"

"Yeah. Hal only raised $19,000 to rent the cameras and pay for the film and processing, and so he couldn't afford to actually pay any of us. So we were all working for a percentage of the profits. Like Mel Brooks in *The Producers*, I think he gave away several hundred percent of the picture...."

"So whatever possessed Hal to make something like *Manos* anyway?"

"Well, Hal met Stirling Silliphant [the Oscar-winning screenwriter of *In the Heat of the Night*] when he was scouting locations for *Route 66*, and the two of them got to be friends. Hal had a lot of conversations with Stirling about filmmaking, and became convinced he could make a movie himself."

So Hal wrote a screenplay -- a copy of which Bob whipped out of his satchel; Bernie produced the original shooting script, studded with Bob's camera-angle diagrams -- which he called *The Lodge of Sins*. (At some point during production, Hal decided to change the title to *Manos: The Hands of Fate*. Why? No man can say...Although as time wore on and tempers frayed, the crew began referring to the project as *Mangos: Cans of Fruit*.)

And then it was time to round up a crew and "A Cast of Local Stars!" as the poster would say.

"I was the grand old man of the bunch at thirty," Bob said.

"The rest of us were all in our twenties," said Bernie, "because if we'd been any older we couldn't have pulled it off. We were shooting the whole night through, then running home, showering and changing, and going to work."

"We all had day jobs," said Bob, "And it was a good thing!"

In fact, two of the cast, Stephanie Nielson and Joyce Molleur, lived in Las Cruces, about an hour's drive away. After Joyce broke her leg while performing a stunt early in the shoot, new parts were written for her and stunt-man-turned-actor Bernie, as a couple of kids who are perpetually hassled by the cops as they neck in their car. They start at dusk and are found still at it by dawn -- a moment which drew Bernie a rousing ovation from our audience -- but Bernie noted that the two of them were crammed into a convertible with her leg in a cast. "Not as fun as it looks," he concluded.

With Hal typecast as the hero 'Hal', the rest of the cast was largely recruited from the local community theater: Diane Mahree, as the damsel in distress; Tom Neyman, as the Master, who wears a black cape lined with red-embroidered fingers; and the tragic figure of John Reynolds, whose creepy Confederate-uniformed character of Torgo so endeared himself to *MST3K* that they incorporated him into their act.

"I heard a rumor on the `net," I said, "that John had committed suicide."

"That's no rumor," said Bob. "He killed himself about six months after the movie was finished. John was a troubled kid; he didn't really get along with his dad, who was an Air Force colonel, and he got into experimenting with LSD. It's a shame, because he was really a talented young actor."

Bob explained that John Reynolds had built himself the metallic rigging underneath his costume which produced his ungainly, knobby-kneed walk. One of the reasons he hates the *Mystery Science Theater* version, he said, is the silhouettes of the *MST* cast which block the bottom portion of the screen throughout the film. They obscure the few shots where you can see that Torgo actually does

have cloven-hoofed feet. The subtle explanation for Torgo's awkward gait: he's a satyr.

As for the Master's 'wives', they were recruited from a local modeling agency, Fran Simon's Mannequin Manor.

"And they gave poor Hal fits," said Bob.

"They kept doing little turns every time they walked. 'This is not a runway!' he would scream at them."

Bob then pulled out a script and read where the wives' attire was described as "flowing, white tight robes". Hal evidently had something sheer and diaphanous in mind, but Fran Simon wasn't having her girls parading around in some flimsy bit of nothing. So the wives' uniform onscreen is a translucent white nightgown over a girdle and a sports bra, with a red strip of cloth trailing from the back that we assume is supposed to represent a tail. Aside from the last, it's uncomfortably like watching your mother getting dressed. Not that the crew ever gave up hope, though:

"We kept asking ourselves, 'And when do we start shooting the European version?'"

So, armed with nineteen grand worth of equipment and film stock, Hal and his troupe headed for County Judge Colbert Coldwell's ranch in El Paso's lower valley (where the exteriors for *Manos* still stand), and commenced a grueling two-and-a-half-month shoot.

Some of the crew soon chafed under the prima-donnish hand of self-made auteur-and-star Warren.

"One day," Bob said, "just to show Hal up, I showed up on the set wearing a beret and a safari outfit and carrying a riding crop, and barking out orders like Erich von Stroheim."

Bob also got back by slipping in some decent camerawork against Hal's express orders.

"See that?" he says as we watch a shot of the setting sun reflected from a rear-view mirror onto Diane's face. "Art. Hal would hate it when I did that."

Certain technical limitations of a $19,000 budget also soon revealed themselves.

"We had a spring-wound 16-millimeter Bell & Howell," said Bob. "Now, the maximum wind of the Bell & Howell was 32 seconds, so that was the maximum length of any shot."

...which explains away one of the film's first mysteries: why a lengthy driving montage is patched together from a series of choppy takes.

Bob also explained away a scene in which two cops hear a gunshot, get out of their cars, take about three steps, look around and wave their flashlights, then without a word turn around, get back in their car and drive off.

"That's as far as our lights would illuminate," Bob said.

With limited lighting and a wide aperture, Bob had to apologize for the photography in some spots, which was, to put it politely, not quite in focus.

"At first," he said, "when we saw the dailies and I spotted any shots that were out of focus, we would do retakes. But as the film stock started to dwindle, Hal made it clear that our $19,000 worth would only go so far, so after a certain point we had to just leave the shots in."

The crew's motto became: "We'll Fix It in the Lab."

Bernie was especially disgruntled about the setup for his big stunt, when he goes rolling down a dangerously precipitous slope; it was shot from back of the crest of the hill, and so you can't see any of him as he goes rolling merrily away.

We asked if Bob had shot a cutaway of a rattlesnake that threatens our heroes.

"No," said Bernie, "that was a clip from a Disney nature film, I think."

"You can tell," said Bob. "You'll notice the snake was in focus."

So after a couple of months of ordeal in the desert, it was time for the grand premiere at the Capri Theater in downtown El Paso. Hal managed to attract a lot of local media attention. "Reputedly based on an old Mexican legend," quoted one reporter, "the tale has a surprise climax and people will not be admitted during the last 10 minutes of the program!"

Bob and Bernie and the rest of the cast and crew rented tuxedoes for the occasion; Hal outdid them and rented a searchlight to sweep the skies on opening night. He also rented one 1955 Cadillac limousine which would arrive at the door of the theater, unload a couple of the stars, then drive around the block to where the rest of the cast and crew were waiting, pick up two more, and make another run.

"We also shot the whole thing wild track" -- meaning no sound recorded on the set -- "then Hal, his wife, and Tom and Diane went to a sound studio in Dallas to do their voices. Everybody else in the film was dubbed in by two people."

"Wait a minute!" I said, incredulously. "You mean Torgo's voice was dubbed?!" -- the quavery quality of Torgo's voice being his most imitated trait -- and Bob confirmed this, yet another reason why John Reynolds's performance can't be properly appreciated.

The theater was packed to the balcony with local dignitaries, they recalled, and the suspense was unbearable; you had the trailers of coming attractions, a cartoon, a twenty-minute *True Life Nature Adventure* set in the Antarctic, and then finally, the feature.

"And then," said Bob, "as soon as Hal opened his mouth, you heard it from the balcony: a little..." and then he mimicked the small snorting sound of a suppressed guffaw.

"And as the film unreeled, and you heard more and more laughs and catcalls, I started to slide down further and further in my seat. All my life, I had lived for one thing: to see my name in the credits of a motion picture. Well, the credits for *Manos* aren't until the end of the picture, and I sneaked out before then."

Betty Pierce, the movie reviewer for the El Paso *Times*, was particularly taken with the climax, in which, she headlined, Torgo is "Massaged to Death", although she also claimed to see Torgo as the film's Existential Hero. (Torgo does in fact eventually rebel against the Master, a parallel no doubt to the relationship between Hal Warren and his crew.)

"For an amateur production," she went on, "the color came out very well, however, and perhaps by scrapping the soundtrack and running it with subtitles or dubbing it in Esperanto, it could be promoted as a foreign art film of some sort or other."

In spite of all this, Hal managed to find a distributor -- Emerson Releasing Corporation -- who gave the film its shadowy half-life of a theatrical run.

"You have to give Hal credit," Bob said, "if you have any idea, even in Hollywood, how difficult it is let alone to get a film made, but to get it finished, and get it through post-production, and then get it distributed...well what he did was something of a miracle."

On which note it was time to adjourn and escort the celebrities from the stage ("You two were glowing," Craig's lady friend said accusingly) and on to La Hacienda. Roy pulled out some replicas of the *Manos* poster art he had produced with his Mac, scanner and laserprinter so that we might get the local heroes' autographs ("Recognition at last!"). Outside the cafe, Bob and Bernie let us know that the adjacent road had actually been part of the driving-montage shoot, which prompted us all to pose for Craig's camera with a full moon overhead and genuine *Manos* scenery in the background.

"You know," I told them, reflecting on the genesis of this meeting, "this really is like a dream come true."

What about the rest of the *Manos* gang? One of the 'wives', Robin Redd, went on to a career as a genuine honest-to-God movie and TV actress. Tom 'The Master' Neyman dropped out of sight. The production's still photographer, a young Allied German soldier from Fort Bliss, discovered Susan Blakely on the campus of the University of Texas at El Paso, and went on to shoot for Vogue. Hal is long gone and his widow lives now in Colorado.

But Bob had one last word in defense of Hal's peculiar genius.

"Although I sneaked out of the premiere, I did go to the cast and crew party afterwards, at Bernie's parents' house. At one point Hal said to us, 'You know, maybe if we took it back and re-dubbed the dialogue, we could market it as a comedy.'"

"Well, look what happened," I said. "The son of a bitch was right!" ☼

ORIGINALLY PRINTED IN MIMOSA #18. 1996

MANY THANKS TO RICHARD BRANDT. YOU RULE!

DOGGY-POO

WHEN I FIRST HEARD OF DOGGY-POO I THOUGHT IT MUST BE A JOKE - COLIN UPTON 04

I CAN'T BELIEVE THAT I'M WATCHING A FILM ABOUT A DOG TURD!

BELIEVE IT OR NOT, "DOGGY-POO" IS A KOREAN ANIMATED FILM ABOUT THE SPIRITUAL JOURNEY (CERTAINLY IT'S NOT A PHYSICAL JOURNEY, AS "DOGGY-POO" THROUGH THE FILM DOESN'T BUDGE FROM WHERE HE IS SHAT) OF A BABY DOG TURD.

?

"DOGGY-POO" IS BASED ON A KOREAN CHILDREN'S BOOK CLASSIC, WHICH MUST'VE CAUSED SOME DIRTY WEE HANDS OVER THE YEARS...

MOMMY! CAN WE TAKE DOGGY-POO HOME WITH US?

"DOGGY-POO" IS SHAT OUT BY A POOCH ON THE SIDE OF THE ROAD. LONELY AND UNLOVED, "DOGGY-POO" SEARCHES FOR SOME MEANING TO HIS EXCREMENTAL EXISTENCE. WHY WOULD GOD ALLOW HIM TO SUFFER? WHY WAS HE... "BORN"? HE'S A WHINEY LITTLE SHIT... HA!

SOB

ANYWAY, "DOGGY-POO" ENCOUNTERS VARIOUS SOILS, FOLIAGE AND FOWLS WHO DISCUSS THE MEANING OF LIFE, EXISTENCE AND ACCEPTANCE OF ONE'S ROLE AND FATE.

THIS IMPROBABLE PLOT IS ACTUALLY A RATHER TOUCHING PARABLE THAT TEACHES A VALUABLE LESSON...

THAT ALL OF US, NO MATTER HOW LOWLY OR DESPISED, CAN BE OF SERVICE TO OTHERS...

SNIFF

...EVEN IF IT'S ONLY AS FERTILIZER.

I STILL CAN'T BELIEVE I'M WATCHING A FILM ABOUT A DOG DUMP!

P.S.-TECHNICALLY SPEAKING THE STOP-ACTION ANIMATION IS RATHER "HERKY-JERKY" AND OLD-FASHIONED BY TODAY'S STANDARDS. HOWEVER, THE SETS, LIGHTING AND STAGING ARE METICULOUSLY DONE RESULTING IN AN ATTRACTIVE LOOKING FILM...

"DOGGY-POO"
SOUTH KOREA 2003
DIRECTOR:
OH-SUNG-KWON

COLIN UPTON 04

103

WHAT IS WRONG WITH THE MOVIES?

I INTEND TO PROVE THAT THE COMMERCIAL MOVING PICTURE IS AN UNMITIGATED CURSE; THAT IT IS SO VILE IN ITS INFLUENCE THAT NO CHRISTIAN SHOULD EVER SET FOOT IN A MOVIE THEATER; THAT PARENTS SHOULD NOT ALLOW THEIR CHILDREN TO ATTEND ANY COMMERCIAL PICTURE SHOW. THE MOVIE IS THE FEEDER OF LUST, THE PERVERTER OF MORALS, THE TOOL OF GREED, THE SCHOOL OF CRIME, THE BETRAYER OF INNOCENCE. IT PICTURES MURDER AS ENTERTAINMENT, NAKEDNESS AND INDECENCY AS BEAUTY, DIVORCE AND REVELING AS PROPER AND LEGITIMATE. MOVIES DEBAUCH THE MINDS OF CHILDREN, INFLAME THE HEARTS OF SINNERS, AND HARDEN THE SOUL. THEY ARE A TRAP FOR THE YOUNG, A MOCKER OF GOD, A CURSE TO AMERICA!

I ONCE CONTENDED THAT THE MOVING PICTURE THEATER COULD BE A GREAT BLESSING TO MANKIND. I INSISTED THAT THE MOVIES DID ME NO HARM. BUT SADLY, I WAS FORCED TO CHANGE MY OPINION. I REMEMBER WALKING OUT OF A MOVIE THEATER IN SHAME, EMBARRASSED BY THE LEWDNESS OF A FILM THAT WAS SHOWN, WHERE I HAD TAKEN MY SISTER AND ANOTHER YOUNG WOMAN FRIEND. MY CONSCIENCE HURT ME. I WAS FORCED TO THE CONCLUSION, EVENTUALLY, THAT NO CHRISTIAN SHOULD ATTEND PICTURE SHOWS. THROUGH THE YEARS, THAT IMPRESSION HAS DEEPENED. I HAVE NOTICED THE EFFECT THAT MOVIES HAVE HAD ON THOSE WITH WHOM I HAVE COME IN CONTACT. THE PICTURE THEATERS ARE SO WHOLLY "SOLD OUT" TO SIN, THAT NO CHRISTIAN SHOULD EVER ATTEND ONE, AND IT IS DANGEROUS AND WICKED TO EVER ALLOW A CHILD TO ATTEND A PICTURE SHOW. I BEG YOU TO AVOID IT AS YOU WOULD AVOID THE PLAGUE!

THE MEN WHO MAKE THE PICTURES ARE GENERALLY IMMORAL MEN, LEWD MEN, LUSTFUL MEN. THE SAME THING IS TRUE OF THE WOMEN WHO APPEAR AS STARS AND LEADING CHARACTERS IN THE MOVING PICTURES. THEY ARE EMBRACED BY MANY MEN, FONDLED BY MANY MEN, WITH NO MAIDENLY MODESTY IN THE MATTER OF SEX. THE SUCCESSFUL ACTOR OR ACTRESS IS THE ONE WHO CAN ENJOY AND PARTICIPATE IN THE VERY FEELINGS AND THOUGHTS OF THE CHARACTERS THEY PORTRAY. THE RESULT IS A BREAKDOWN IN MORAL FIBRE, IN MODESTY IN RESTRAINT. LUST IS INCREASED. AFTER THINKING EVIL IN EVERY PICTURE, MOVIE PLAYERS ACT EVIL. MOVIE PEOPLE ARE NOTORIOUSLY IMMORAL.

WHY ALL THE SEX STORIES ON THE SCREEN? WHY THE BEDROOM SCENES? WHY IS IT THAT ALL THE ACTRESSES HAVE TO SHOW THEIR LEGS? WHY ALL THE SUGGESTIVE AND BAWDY LINES? WHY ARE THE LOVE TRIANGLES AND PROSTITUTES IDEALIZED IN THE MOTION PICTURES? THE REASON IS THIS — SUCH PICTURES WILL GET CROWDS, CROWDS OF THE LUSTFUL, CROWDS OF WHOM THEY MAY GET MONEY — THAT IS THE AIM OF THE PICTURE INDUSTRY. THE MOTIVE IS GREED, AND THAT MOTIVE PUTS THE MOVING-PICTURE INDUSTRY IN THE SAME CLASS AS THE SALOON KEEPERS, DOPE PEDDLERS, AND WHITE SLAVE TRAFFICKERS.

WE ARE TOLD THAT LOVE IS ONE OF THE GREAT THEMES OF THE MOVIES. BUT A LITTLE CONSIDERATION WILL SHOW THAT THIS "LOVE" IS NOT NORMAL, WHOLESOME AND GODLY LOVE LIKE THAT OF A MAN FOR HIS WIFE. RATHER, WHAT IS SHOWN IS SIMPLY PASSION, WITH NO RESERVE, NO RETICENCE, NO MODESTY, WITH NOTHING SACRED. THESE MOVIES HAVE MADE LOVE, WHICH ACCORDING TO THE BIBLE OUGHT TO BE LIKE THAT OF CHRIST FOR HIS CHURCH (EPH. 5:23-33) INTO ANIMALISM, INFLAMING SEX ORGANS, EXHIBITING SEX CHARMS, OPENLY ENJOYING SEX DESIRE AND FLAUNTING BEFORE THE WORLD. THE EXHIBITION OF THIS BEFORE THE EYES AND MINDS OF YOUNG PEOPLE IS A CURSE BEYOND HUMAN MEASUREMENT.

THIS OPEN, SHAMELESS, LICENTIOUS LOVE MAKING EXHIBITED BY THE MOVIES, WHICH INCLUDES LONG EMBRACES, IS WHOLLY UNWHOLESOME AND EVIL. THIS NECKING, THIS DISPLAY OF BODIES, THESE HOT KISSES, THESE SECRET MEETINGS ARE ALL SHOWN ON THE SCREENS AND ENJOYED BY MILLIONS OF AMERICAN PEOPLE OPENLY. THIS IS DISREPUTABLE, LICENTIOUS, AND EVIL! THERE WAS A TIME WHEN A MAN FELT HIMSELF FORTUNATE IF HE GOT A FLEETING KISS OR TWO BEFORE HIS SWEETHEART BECAME HIS BRIDE. IN THOSE DAYS, MEN CAME TO THEIR BRIDES WITH A LOVE THAT WAS HOLY AND LAID HANDS UPON THEM ONLY WITH REVERENCE AND HONOR. AND NOW, GOD

PITY US! HOW IS IT? YOUNG PEOPLE DANCE, SWIM (WITH FEW CLOTHES ON), AND TAKE ALL KINDS OF LIBERTIES WITH EACH OTHER'S BODIES. ARMS ABOUT ONE ANOTHER, FACE AGAINST FACE; IN PUBLIC PARKS, IN AUTOMOBILES, ON FRONT PORCHES. SUCH COUPLES KISS FREELY AND OPENLY, EVEN AT PUBLIC SOCIAL GATHERINGS!

EVERY CHILD THAT ATTENDS THE MOVIES REGULARLY IS SUBJECTED TO EXCITEMENT OF AN ABNORMAL AND EXTREME KIND, EXCITEMENT THAT AFFECTS THE NERVES – SOMETIMES FOR DAYS. THIS IS EXCITEMENT THAT AFFECTS SLEEP AND SCHOOL WORK. TO FILL MINDS OF GIRLS IN THEIR EARLY TEENS OR AT ANY AGE WITH THOUGHTS ONLY OF HUGS AND KISSES IS NO TRUE PORTRAYAL OF LOVE! I DO NOT WANT SEX DELINQUENCY TO APPEAR DESIRABLE, NAY, IRRESISTIBLE TO MY DAUGHTERS, NOR TO MY SELF, NOR ANYONE ELSE.

LISTEN TO THE TESTIMONY OF THIS FIFTEEN YEAR OLD COLORED GIRL:

"I FELL IN LOVE WITH GILBERT ROLAND. I WOULD IMAGINE I WAS THE LEADING LADY IN THE PICTURES HE PLAYED IN. I USED TO SIT AND DAYDREAM THAT ONE DAY I WOULD MARRY GILBERT ROLAND AND WE WOULD HAVE A LOVELY TIME UNTIL I WENT OUT WITH RAMON NOVARRO AND GILBERT WOULD CATCH ME KISSING RAMON."

THAT COLORED GIRL WOULD MAKE A SPLENDID MOVIE PICTURE ACTRESS! HOW WELL SHE LEARNED THE LESSON TAUGHT BY THE MOVIES. SUCH IMAGERY, SUCH DREAMS, SUCH DESIRES PUT IN THE HEART OF YOUNG PEOPLE WILL INFLUENCE POWERFULLY FOR EVIL.

WE CANNOT ALWAYS KNOW JUST WHAT SUBTLE INFLUENCE SATAN USES TO HARDEN A HEART AT A CRITICAL TIME, TO BREAK THE CONVICTION OF SIN, TO TRAP AND WAYLAY AND SIDETRACK ONE WHO HAS HEARD THE GOSPEL MESSAGE AND WITH WHOM THE SPIRIT OF GOD IS DEALING. BUT SURELY SATAN HAS IN MILLIONS OF CASES USED THE PICTURE SHOW TO DISTRACT THE MINDS AND HARDEN THE HEARTS OF THOSE WHO OTHERWISE MIGHT HAVE LISTENED TO GOD'S HOLY WORD.

ONLY AT THE JUDGMENT BAR OF GOD WILL MEN KNOW THE INCALCULABLE, ETERNAL, SPIRITUAL EVIL OF THE MOVIES! I AM NOT ALONE IN MY STAND AGAINST THE

B. R. K, Inc. Presents

LIVE Fast, Die Young

THE SIN-STEEPED STORY OF TODAY'S "BEAT" GENERATION!

MARY MURPHY · NORMA EBERHARDT
SHERIDAN COMERATE · MICHAEL CONNORS

Directed by PAUL HENREID Screenplay by ALLEN RIVKIN AND IE MELCHIOR ... HARRY ...
and RICHARD KAY Associate Producer EDWARD E BARISON A UNIVERSAL INTERNATIONAL PICTURE

SEE! **REVEALED FOR THE FIRST TIME!** ...intimate details of women's endless man-baiting..!

THE FEMALE Animal

Greek Maidens Enjoying Milk Bath

Roman Beauties Splashing In Marble Pools

An Exciting Exposure done with Adult Understanding

Finnish Girls Flogged in "Sauna" Bath

German Females in the Nudist Camp

and MUCH MORE!

MOVING PICTURE SHOW. THE BEST CHURCHES WILL NOT HAVE SUNDAY SCHOOL TEACHERS WHO ATTEND PICTURE SHOWS. THE GREAT MOODY CHURCH IN CHICAGO, ONE OF THE GREATEST IN ALL THE WORLD AND ONE OF THE MOST INFLUEN-TIAL, THE MOODY CHURCH, I SAY, REQUIRES EVERY ONE WHO APPLIES FOR MEMBERSHIP OPENLY TO RENOUNCE ATTENDANCE AT PICTURE SHOWS!

IN VIEW OF ALL OF THESE FACTS, FACTS CAREFULLY STUDIED, WISELY WEIGHED, AND MODERATELY BUT PLAINLY STATED – IN VIEW OF THESE FACTS, I SAY, WHAT SHALL WE DO ABOUT THE MOVIES? MAKING IT MORE DEFINITE, WHAT SHOULD YOU AT THIS MOMENT, READING THIS BOOK, DO ABOUT THE MOVIES?

PUT CHRIST FIRST TODAY AND QUIT THE MOVIES FOREVER!! I ASK YOU, DO YOU BELIEVE JESUS WOULD ATTEND THE PICTURE SHOWS IF HE WERE ALIVE TODAY? IF HE WOULD NOT ATTEND, YOU SHOULD NOT ATTEND. THINK HOW MUCH JESUS GAVE UP FOR YOU. HE PAID FOR YOUR SOUL SUCH A PRICE, THAT YOU SURELY CANNOT DENY HIM THIS!

HOW HAPPY YOUR FUTURE! HOW SAFE IS YOUR SOUL! ONE OF THESE DAYS EVERY MOVIE SCREEN WILL BE BURNED DOWN, EVERY MOVIE THEATER SHAVEN TO PIECES. YOU HAVE AN IMMORTAL SOUL THAT MUST SPEND ETERNITY IN HEAVEN OR HELL. WILL YOU TURN TO CHRIST TODAY AND SURRENDER TO HIM?

THE PRECEEDING PIECE WAS VIOLENTLY AND SINFULLY RIPPED FROM THE PAGES OF **WHAT IS WRONG WITH THE MOVIES?** A WILD AND SEARING 125 PAGE RANT AGAINST FILMS BY JOHN RICE - PUBLISHED WAAAAY BACK IN 1938 BY ZONDERVAN PUBLISHING HOUSE, GRAND RAPIDS MICHIGAN. RICE ALSO PUBLISHED A GUILT-BASED PAGE-TURNER CALLED **WHAT IS WRONG WITH THE DANCE.**

PUT CHRIST FIRST AND QUIT THE MOVIES FOREVER

ANGELS DIE HARD (1970)

USUALLY PORTRAYED AS THE VILLAINOUS OUTLAWS WHO ARE STONGLY ADVERSE TO FIGURES OF AUTHORITY, IN ANGELS DIE HARD, STINKY, DRUNKEN, RAPE-HAPPY BIKERS ARE THE HEROES RATHER THAN THE ANTAGONISTS. AUTHENTIC LOOKIN' BIKERS, HARLEYS, AND BARE TITTIES ARE THE HIGHLIGHTS OF THIS CAUSTIC WILLIAM SMITH VEHICLE.

SMITH AND HIS PARTNERS-IN-GRIME SEEK REVENGE ON AN INTOLERANT HICK TOWN WHERE ONE OF THEIR WHEELED BROTHERS WERE MURDERED. JUST TO SHOW US HOW MUCH HE'S MISSED BY THESE DUSTY HIGHWAY WARRIORS, THE FINAL TRIBUTE TO THE DEARLY DEPARTED IS A BLADDER-FULL OF PISS ONTO HIS GRAVE FROM EACH OF HIS BUDDIES.

DESPITE THE EFFORTS OF THE INTOLERANT SHERIFF'S PRETTY DAUGHTER TO QUELL THE VIOLENCE, ALL HELL BREAKS LOOSE AND A BLOODY BATTLE ENSUES. MEMORABLE SHIT INCLUDES A BIKER POETRY READING, AND A BIZARRE RAPE/SPAGHETTI - THROWING SEQUENCE. UNFORTUNATELY THERE IS LITTLE EFFORT TO EDIT OUT SLOW, MEANINGLESS TRANSITION AND FILLER FROM ITS 86 MINUTE RUNTIME.
                                                                                                    —BOUGIE

THEY LIVE HARD...THEY LOVE HARD...

"ANGELS DIE HARD!"

CHOPPER OUTLAWS!..
riding their hot
throbbing machines
to a brutal climax
of violence!

THEIR BATTLE CRY-
"KILL THE PIGS!"

IN COLOR

ORIGINAL SOUNDTRACK ALBUM NOW ON UNI RECORDS!

STARRING
TOM BAKER · WILLIAM SMITH

R

SPECIAL GUEST STAR
R.G. ARMSTRONG · WITH ALAN DeWITT · GARY LITTLEJOHN · RITA MURRAY · CARL STEPPLING · INTRODUCING **CONNIE NELSON**

EXECUTIVE PRODUCERS JANE SCHAFFER AND JAMES TANENBAUM · PRODUCED BY CHARLES BEACH DICKERSON · WRITTEN AND DIRECTED BY RICHARD COMPTON · A NEW WORLD PICTURES RELEASE

THIS FILM IS NOT YET RATED (2006)

AMERICANS ARE NOTORIOUS FOR BEING WEIRD ABOUT SEX AND NUDITY IN THEIR MOVIES. FILMMAKERS CAN HACK OFF LIMBS AND SHOOT BULLETS THROUGH HEADS AND ONLY GET AN R-RATING. SHOW SOME PUBES, HOWEVER, AND YOU'LL GET SLAPPED WITH AN NC-17. WHY ARE AMERICANS SO AFRAID TO ALLOW THE GENERAL POPULATION TO SEE A LITTLE SKIN IN A SEXUAL CONTEXT, BUT READY TO ACCEPT THOSE SAME BODIES BEING RIPPED APART? WHAT FUCKED-UP MESSAGE DOES THAT SEND -- THAT VIOLENCE IS MORE NATURAL THAN GETTING TURNED ON?

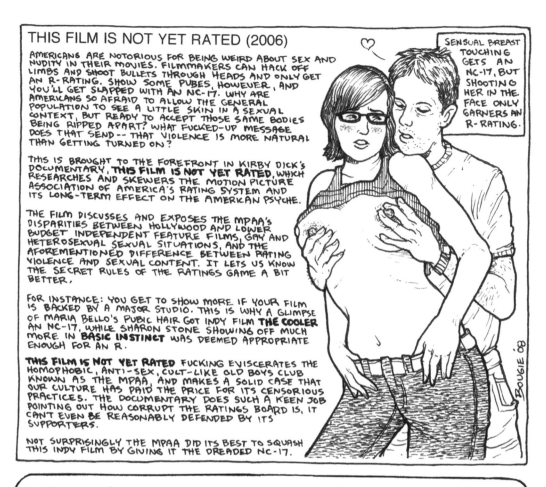

SENSUAL BREAST TOUCHING GETS AN NC-17, BUT SHOOTING HER IN THE FACE ONLY GARNERS AN R-RATING.

THIS IS BROUGHT TO THE FOREFRONT IN KIRBY DICK'S DOCUMENTARY, **THIS FILM IS NOT YET RATED**, WHICH RESEARCHES AND SKEWERS THE MOTION PICTURE ASSOCIATION OF AMERICA'S RATING SYSTEM AND ITS LONG-TERM EFFECT ON THE AMERICAN PSYCHE.

THE FILM DISCUSSES AND EXPOSES THE MPAA'S DISPARITIES BETWEEN HOLLYWOOD AND LOWER BUDGET INDEPENDENT FEATURE FILMS, GAY AND HETEROSEXUAL SEXUAL SITUATIONS, AND THE AFOREMENTIONED DIFFERENCE BETWEEN RATING VIOLENCE AND SEXUAL CONTENT. IT LETS US KNOW THE SECRET RULES OF THE RATINGS GAME A BIT BETTER.

FOR INSTANCE: YOU GET TO SHOW MORE IF YOUR FILM IS BACKED BY A MAJOR STUDIO. THIS IS WHY A GLIMPSE OF MARIA BELLO'S PUBIC HAIR GOT INDY FILM **THE COOLER** AN NC-17, WHILE SHARON STONE SHOWING OFF MUCH MORE IN **BASIC INSTINCT** WAS DEEMED APPROPRIATE ENOUGH FOR AN R.

THIS FILM IS NOT YET RATED FUCKING EVISCERATES THE HOMOPHOBIC, ANTI-SEX, CULT-LIKE OLD BOYS CLUB KNOWN AS THE MPAA, AND MAKES A SOLID CASE THAT OUR CULTURE HAS PAID THE PRICE FOR ITS CENSORIOUS PRACTICES. THE DOCUMENTARY DOES SUCH A KEEN JOB POINTING OUT HOW CORRUPT THE RATINGS BOARD IS, IT CAN'T EVEN BE REASONABLY DEFENDED BY ITS SUPPORTERS.

NOT SURPRISINGLY THE MPAA DID ITS BEST TO SQUASH THIS INDY FILM BY GIVING IT THE DREADED NC-17.

THE INCREDIBLE MELTING MAN (1977) 86 min

THIS THROWBACK TO SUCH "CLASSICS" AS **THE HIDEOUS SUN DEMON** AND **FIRST MAN INTO SPACE** FEATURES ALEX REBAR (YES, **THE** ALEX REBAR) AS ASTRONAUT STEVEN WEST, WHO STARTS TO GET SOGGY ON A MOLECULAR LEVEL AFTER HE AND HIS CO-SPACE GUYS VISIT THE SUNNY RINGS OF SATURN. THEY CRASH LAND ON EARTH (HUH?!) AND AFTER LEAPING FROM HIS HOSPITAL BED AND MUNCHING HALF OF HIS NURSE'S HEAD, WEST BEGINS WANDERING THE COUNTRYSIDE - BREATHLESSLY PURSUED BY THE HEROIC DR. TED NELSON AND HIS TRUSTY GEIGER COUNTER.

WEST (WHO HEARS WEIRD ASTRONAUT SOUNDS IN HIS NOGGIN) NEEDS "HUMAN CELLS" TO STAY ALIVE, SO HE SPENDS MUCH OF HIS FREE TIME DEVOURING ANYONE WHO HE HAPPENS TO STUMBLE ACROSS, INCLUDING A BORED FISHERMAN, AND TWO HORNY OLD FOLKS WHO DECIDE TO STEAL LEMONS AND PAY FOR THEIR CRIME -- IN **BLOOOOOD!!**

SEVENTIES T+A STARLET RAINBEAUX SMITH (REST IN PEACE, YOU BLONDE HAIRED BRAZEN LOVELY) SCAMPERS AROUND WITH HER LITTLE TITTIES HANGING OUT UNTIL SHE BACKS INTO A DEAD DUDE'S HAND, WHICH STILL MANAGES TO CLUTCH HALF-HEARTEDLY AT HER WELL-TURNED ANKLE. OH SHUT UP, YOUR CORPSE WOULD DO IT TOO. FUCKIN' RAINBEAUX SMITH, Y'ALL! I SHOULDN'T NEED TO SAY MORE THAN THAT.

CHARACTER MOTIVATIONS ARE EITHER MISSING OR CONFUSING, ACTING IS SECOND- OR THIRD- RATE, AND ALL OF THE NIGHT SCENES ARE SOMEHOW SHOT WITHOUT THE USE OF LIGHT. REGARDLESS, I FUCKING LOVED IT. IT MADE VERBALLY ABUSING MY TV WAY FUN.

FEATURES PLENTY OF SLOPPY, SQUISHY MAKEUP EFFECTS BY THE LEGENDARY RICK (**STAR WARS**) BAKER AND THE NOT SO LEGENDARY HARRY (**LASERBLAST**) WOOLMAN. PLUS: A CAMEO BY DIRECTOR JONATHAN DEMME (**CAGED HEAT, SILENCE OF THE LAMBS**). LOOK FOR A MST3K VERSION FROM THEIR 7TH SEASON. IT'S LOADED WITH DRIPPY-ASS LAFFS, BUT IT IS SADLY MISSING THE SCENE WITH THE LOVELY BOSOM OF RAINBEAUX.

OK, SO RENE BOND NEVER DONNED A LAME COSTUME THAT WAS A RIP OFF OF BATMAN'S, BUT SHE DID STAR IN SOME OF THE 70S' MOST ENTERTAINING AND FINEST XXX FILMS ALONG WITH HER BOYFRIEND RICK LUTZE. BE SURE TO CHECK OUT: **TEENAGE FANTASIES** (1971), **HONEY BUNS** (1975), **DO YOU WANNA BE LOVED?** (1977) AND ALMOST 300 OTHERS!

♡ PEACE OUT! ☮

INDUSTRIAL TELEVISION
CABLE FUCKING ACCESS UNDERGROUND TEEVEE

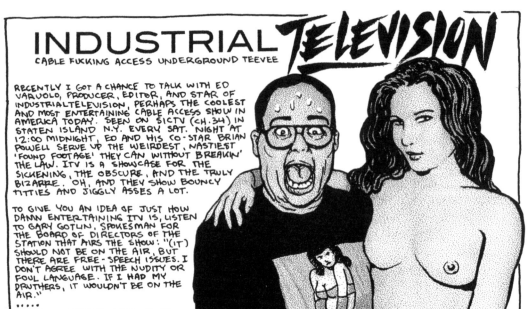

RECENTLY I GOT A CHANCE TO TALK WITH ED VARUOLO, PRODUCER, EDITOR, AND STAR OF INDUSTRIALTELEVISION, PERHAPS THE COOLEST AND MOST ENTERTAINING CABLE ACCESS SHOW IN AMERICA TODAY. SEEN ON SICTV (CH. 34) IN STATEN ISLAND N.Y. EVERY SAT. NIGHT AT 12:00 MIDNIGHT, ED AND HIS CO-STAR BRIAN POWELL SERVE UP THE WEIRDEST, NASTIEST 'FOUND FOOTAGE' THEY CAN WITHOUT BREAKIN' THE LAW. ITV IS A SHOWCASE FOR THE SICKENING, THE OBSCURE, AND THE TRULY BIZARRE. OH, AND THEY SHOW BOUNCY TITTIES AND JIGGLY ASSES A LOT.

TO GIVE YOU AN IDEA OF JUST HOW DAMN ENTERTAINING ITV IS, LISTEN TO GARY GOTLIN, SPOKESMAN FOR THE BOARD OF DIRECTORS OF THE STATION THAT AIRS THE SHOW: "(IT) SHOULD NOT BE ON THE AIR, BUT THERE ARE FREE-SPEECH ISSUES. I DON'T AGREE WITH THE NUDITY OR FOUL LANGUAGE. IF I HAD MY DRUTHERS, IT WOULDN'T BE ON THE AIR."
.....

OK, SO INDUSTRIALTELEVISION. PRETTY DAMN COOL. TELL ME ABOUT YOUR HUMBLE BEGINNINGS. YOU AND BRIAN HAVE BEEN AROUND FOR 8 SEASONS ON CABLE ACCESS, IS THAT RIGHT?

Brian and I knew each other from a band and then later doing special effects and makeup FX on "Combat Shock" ...we both had large video collections of obscure shit (lots of Beta format titles!)...we heard about (and saw) CTV (our local cable access channel) and constantly winced at the abysmal programing being foistered upon an unsuspecting public. "We could do better than this", said us. Having some film experience, we already had a leg up on other "producers" as far as lighting, sound, editing, etc. So in 1996, we decided to create the type of show that WE wanted to see.

ITV IS AN AMAZING MIX OF UNDERGROUND VIDEO ODDITIES, CLASSIC EDUCATIONAL FILMS, STRANGE COMMERCIALS, EXPLOITATION FILM TRAILERS, INSANE SEX-THEMED CRAP AND SO ON. HOW DO YOU GO ABOUT FINDING AND ARCHIVING THIS STUFF? IT'S ABSOLUTE GOLD!

Lately, (thankfully!) companies, indie producers, and fans have been sending stuff to us. But for the first 5-6 seasons we basically drew from our collections for content. We've been collecting tapes since 1982!

THAT CEREBRAL PALSY PORN FOOTAGE FROM EPISODE 145 OF ITV WAS FUCKING AMAZING. WHERE DID IT COME FROM? I KNOW A GUY WHO IS ON A PERSONAL QUEST FOR RETARD PORN, BY THE WAY.

Interesting story behind that, it was made in Canada with an arts grant! It was really hardcore! We could barely find 5 minutes of "R-rated" scenes for the segment. It was lent to me by a friend who works with film festivals. That's the only 'retard porn' I've ever seen.

ED (ABOVE) AND BRIAN BASK IN THE GLORY OF THEIR OBSCURITY WITH TWO LOVELY ADORING FANS

I HAVE THIS ONE VIDEO FROM THE 80s WHERE A GUY WHO IS OBVIOUSLY NOT A PORN ACTOR IS LYING THERE WHILE A GIRL IS TRYING TO RIDE HIS COCK, BUT THE KICKER IS THAT HE'S GOT THIS INSANE TUMOR OR GROWTH OR SOMETHING ON HIS WANG, AND SHE CAN'T FIT IT INTO HERSELF. HIS DICK IS ALMOST AS WIDE AS A LARGE BOTTLE OF COKE. THE SICK THING IS THAT THE TUMOR MOVES UP AND DOWN WITH HIS DICK-SKIN WHILE SHE JACKS IT.

That sounds absolutely disgusting and I am offended just reading about it! I want a copy.

HA HA! WHAT'S THE WEIRDEST THING YOU'VE PUT ON THE AIR? AND I'D LOVE TO KNOW WHAT YOUR PERSONAL FAVORITE SEGMENT YOU'VE PUT ON THE SHOW.

Hey, the retard porn thing comes close! Hard to nail down just one personal fave, but off the top of my head, clips of Budd Dwyer, Zena Fulsom, "Tard Spasm", Jap gore, VD/Highway Safety training films... one of which featured a real birth in the back seat of a police car!

UM... "TARD SPASM"? WHATS THAT? AND WHERE DID YOU FIND THAT FOOTAGE OF THAT PATHETIC GIRL SINGING (IF YOU CAN CALL IT THAT...) ABOUT HER FUCKING HAIRDRESSER? HILARIOUS...!

Tard Spasm is a great little piece from about 10 years ago, in which some local death metal band (I think in Florida) got a gig playing at a tard party, and one camera stays on the crowd "dancing"... I wet my pants the first time seeing this! The hairdresser clip came courtesy of TV Carnage. They're based in Canada, too. (Is there some sort of conspiracy here?) They issue DVDs of re-edited material culled from years of watching bad television. Just google "tard spasm" and "tv carnage" you'll find more info on them.

OH COOL,. THE "CARNAGE" GUYS. I GUESS I'VE JUST NEVER SEEN THAT VOLUME. I'VE GOTTA SAY, THE RUNNING "COMMENTARY" WHERE YOU TWO POP IN AND REACT TO WHAT WE'RE SEEING IS PRETTY HIT OR MISS. MOSTLY MISS. USUALLY YOU GUYS EITHER JUST STATE THE OBVIOUS OR JUST ACT KINDA OBNOXIOUS. IS THAT THE DESIRED EFFECT?

Yep, I guess that's where the MST3K/Beavis & Butthead influences come in. Funny you should say mostly miss, because we constantly get people coming up to us saying the inserts (visual commentary) of us where we pop in are one of the best things about iTv! We actually do it mostly to break up the monotony (especially on the long boring films) I guess we'll have to work on more "hits" and less "misses" in the inserts. Turning out a new 60 min. show every two weeks (with only 8 hours to edit it) does have its drawbacks, we never have enough time to do it right!

YOUR SHOW (ALONG WITH RICHARD METZGER'S RECENT **DISINFORMATION** DOCU-SERIES) REALLY REMIND ME OF A TELEVISED VERSION OF ADAM PARFREY'S "APOCALYPSE CULTURE" BOOKS. HAVE YOU PONDERED THE IDEA OF AN ITV 'BEST OF' DVD OR SOMETHING? THAT WOULD REALLY DO WELL, AND YOU NEED TO LEAVE A LEGACY!

You are correct, we are working on a "special edition" DVD, probably in the fall, along with a box set! Don't know how many we'll actually SELL, But it really comes down to promotion. We are now operating without any real backers nor major sponsors. Like I've said many times before, "I have no problem selling out and making a "PG" or even a disney version of industrialTELEVISION, just show me the goddamn money!...But until then I'm gonna put on the type of shit that I wanna fuckin' see!"

WELL, LET ME KNOW WHEN IT COMES OUT. IN THE MEANTIME EPISODES ARE AVAILABLE ON TAPE FROM 2-DROOGIES.COM FOR **FREE** WHEN YOU MAKE A DONATION VIA PAYPAL ON THEIR SITE! THANKS FOR YOUR TIME ED. KEEP UP THE GOOD WORK.

THE HILLSIDE STRANGLER (2004)

PLIES HIS TRADE AS A SECURITY GUARD AT A ROCHESTER N.Y. DEPARTMENT STORE, SHAKING DOWN YOUNG FEMALE SHOPLIFTERS IN HIS BACK OFFICE.

IN 1977 A YOUNG KEN BIANCHI (C. THOMAS HOWELL) PLIES HIS TRADE AS A SECURITY GUARD AT A ROCHESTER N.Y. DEPARTMENT STORE, SHAKING DOWN YOUNG FEMALE SHOPLIFTERS IN HIS BACK OFFICE. SICK OF HIS DEAD END EXISTENCE, HE MAKES HIS WAY TO SUNNY L.A. AND STAYS WITH HIS OLDER COUSIN ANGELO BUONO (NICHOLAS TURTURRO) WHO KEEPS A PITBULL AND FAVORS A SLEAZY HOLLYWOOD LIFESTYLE, INDULGING IN THE EXPLOITATION OF WAYWARD GIRLS, PORNO, AND STRIP CLUBS. KENNY SETTLES IN BUT HAS NO LUCK FINDING WORK, BEING TURNED DOWN FOR THE JOB HE ASPIRES TO THE MOST (BEING A COP) BURNS HIM ESPECIALLY.

FORTUNES CHANGE BRIEFY WHEN ANGELO SUGGESTS GETTING INTO THE "WHORE BUSINESS". BIANCHI LOVES THE SOUND OF THIS, AND IN NO TIME THE TWO GREASY MISOGYNISTS HAVE CORRALLED A LITTLE STABLE OF VICTIMIZED NAÏVE TEENAGE HUMP-SLUTS TO EXPLOIT. THEIR FIRST SEX SLAVE, AMBER, IS LURED INTO THEIR VILE CLUTCHES BY KEN'S CHARM, AND IS THEN TURNED OUT BY ANGELO'S HAIR RAISING CAPACITY FOR BRUTAL VIOLENCE AND MENTAL TORTURE. BUT AFTER BUYING AN EXCLUSIVE CHECKLIST OF CLIENTS FROM A SLINKY BLACK WHORE NAMED GABRIELLE, OUR BOYS ARE PAID A VISIT BY THE ORIGINAL OWNERS OF THE JOHN LIST; A RIVAL PIMP AND HIS THUGS WHO TAKE THE MONEY, GUNS AND GIVE THE RELIEVED HOES THEIR TICKET TO FREEDOM.

NOW WITH NO SOURCE OF INCOME AND SEEKING REVENGE, ANGELO AND KEN CRUISE AROUND LOOKING FOR POOR GABRIELLE. WHEN THEY PICK THE STREETWALKER UP ON SUNSET BLVD, KEN VIOLENTLY FUCKS AND STRANGLES HER TO DEATH IN THE BACK SEAT WHILE ANGELO DRIVES AND HOOTS HIS APPROVAL LIKE A DROOLING MANIAC. THEY UNCEREMONIOUSLY DUMP HER CORPSE AND EXCITEDLY CHECK THE PAPERS THE NEXT DAY, BUT THEIR NIGHT OF FUN DOESN'T EVEN RATE A MENTION. TURNED ON AND FASCINATED BY THE RELATIVE EASE AND LACK OF IMMEDIATE CONSEQUENCES FOR VICIOUSLY CROAKING A HOOKER, THE PAIR DEVELOP THEIR NEW MODUS OPERANDI: POSING AS PLAIN CLOTHES COPS

AND 'ARRESTING' HIGH HEELED 'CRIMINALS'. AMAZINGLY ENOUGH, MOST OF THIS IS A TRUE STORY, AND THE UNUSUAL RUSE OF BIANCHI AND BUONO IS SO DEPRAVED AND SNEAKY, IT LEADS THIS MOVIE NERD TO WONDER IF THEY WERE INSPIRED BY LEE FROST'S **A CLIMAX OF BLUE POWER** FROM 1974 (REVIEWED ELSEWHERE IN THIS VERY BOOK) WHERE AN IDENTICAL SCAM IS PERPETRATED ON THE PROSTITUTES OF LOS ANGELES.

THE CASE OF THE HILLSIDE SLAYINGS IS ONE OF THE MOST UNUSUAL AND GRUESOME IN THE ANNALS OF U.S. CRIME. WHILE MOST SERIAL KILLERS TEND TO WORK ALONE, THE TWISTED CRIMINAL CAREERS OF ANGELO AND KEN PROVED THAT PSYCHOTIC SADISM CAN RUN IN THE FAMILY. THEIR 15 VICTIMS (HOOKERS AND THEN EVENTUALLY OTHER FEMALES - FOUR OF WHICH WERE UNDERAGE, WITH ONE BEING ONLY 12) WHO WERE KIDNAPPED, RAPED, TORTURED, AND KILLED, PROVIDED THESE TWO EVIL S.O.B'S WITH A STEADY DIET OF FUCK-FLESH TO RAVAGE AND DISCARD. BIANCHI AND BUONO BECAME SO COMFORTABLE WITH SERIAL SEX MURDER IN SUCH A SHORT PERIOD OF TIME, THAT WITHIN TWO MONTHS THEY HAD PERFECTED IT TO A SCIENCE - THE ACT EVENTUALLY BESTOWING THEM WITH A SENSE OF THE BLASÉ RESERVED FOR JERKING OFF.

DIRECTOR CHUCK PARELLO (2000's **ED GEIN** AND **HENRY: PORTRAIT OF A SERIAL KILLER 2**) AND HIS CO-WRITER STEPHEN JOHNSTON SEEM TO THRILL AND REJOICE IN THE CRIMES OF THESE PSYCHOS, BRINGING A CALLOUS MATTER-OF-FACTNESS TO THE PROCEEDINGS. NO DOUBT ABOUT IT, THE VICTIMIZATION OF THE BIANCHI AND BUONO CASUALTIES IS UNAPOLOGETICALLY THE FOCAL POINT OF THIS FILM. PARELLO MENTIONED IN A RECENT INTERVIEW THAT IN MOST SERIAL KILLER MOVIES THE KILLER IS OFTEN LIKABLE, FUNNY, OR SEXY - SO HE WANTED TO RETURN THE VILLAIN BACK TO BEING NASTY, AND MAKE AUDIENCES "HATE" HIM.

AND YOU JUST MIGHT. THE KILLINGS ARE GRAPHIC AND GEARED TO TITILATE AND MAKE THE AUDIENCE FEEL SICKENED BY THEIR OWN REACTION TO THE ON-SCREEN MAYHEM. THE LIGHTING IS ALWAYS SUCH AS TO SHOW OFF THE STRIPPED WOMEN'S BREASTS AND ASSES AS THEY STRUGGLE, SOB AND SCREAM. THE INCENTIVE TO THE AUDIENCE IS TO "KEEP WATCHING, BECAUSE ANOTHER GRATUITOUS AND SLEAZY DISPLAY OF FLESH MIXED WITH BRUTAL VIOLENCE IS COMING RIGHT UP!". IT'S A DEGRANGED AND SLEAZY TALE TOLD IN A GRATUITOUS, NASTY, AND SHALLOW WAY. EXACTLY HOW A DERANGED AND SLEAZY STORY **SHOULD** BE TOLD, AND IT'S HOW IT USED TO BE DONE DURING THE BELOVED GRINDHOUSE ERA OF THE 1970s.

FORMER 80s TEEN HEART THROB C. THOMAS HOWELL EXCELS AS HE PLAYS AGAINST TYPE IN HIS ROLE AS BIANCHI, WHICH IS SURPRISING GIVEN THAT THERE IS VIRTUALLY NO DEPTH WRITTEN INTO HIS CHARACTER AND NO ATTEMPT TO SHED ANY LIGHT ON HIS MENTAL STATE OUTSIDE OF A FEW HACKNEYED CINEMATIC SIDE PLOTS DEALING WITH A PREGNANT GIRLFRIEND AND A PSYCHOLOGIST SCAM. I'M GLAD TO SAY THAT **THE HILLSIDE STRANGLER** IS (ALONG WITH **THE HITCHER** AND **THE OUTSIDERS**) ANOTHER FILMIC TESTIMONY TO THE VIRTUALLY UNKNOWN GREATNESS OF THIS ACTOR. NICHOLAS TURTURRO'S ROLE AS ANGELO BUONO IS SURPRISINGLY EFFECTIVE AND MOST VIEWERS WILL COME AWAY WITH A FEELING OF COMPLETE AND UTTER CONTEMPT FOR HIM.

PERHAPS AS THE FINEST TESTAMENT TO THE POWER OF THIS EFFORT FROM DIRECTOR PARELLO, I SHOULD POINT OUT AN ANGRY REVIEW BY A CRITIC FROM DALLAS WHO SAW THE FILM AT CANNES. LIKE A FURIOUS SUBURBAN HOUSEWIFE WITH KNEE-JERK REACTIONS TO SEVERE DEPICTIONS OF SEXUALITY AND VIOLENCE, SHE WALKED OUT 40 MINUTES INTO THE FILM SHE LATER CALLED "THE MOST DISGUSTING PILE OF GARBAGE EVER MADE". THIS REVIEW ALSO POINTED AN ACCUSING FINGER AT THE AUDIENCE (NOT INCLUDING HERSELF) SAYING " THE HILLSIDE STRANGLER'S AUDIENCE DEMOGRAPHIC WOULD BE THE LESSER INTELLIGENT SIDE OF MEN WHO HAVE COMMITTED VIOLENT SEX CRIMES. (THIS IS) A PRODUCTION OF THE LOWEST STANDARDS ON VIRTUALLY EVERY LEVEL. THE HILLSIDE STRANGLER IS ONE OF THOSE RARE PIECES OF CRAP THAT IS SO FUNDAMENTALLY REPUGNANT, THAT ANY AND ALL MEMBERS OF THE CAST AND CREW SHOULD FEEL A DEEP SHAME FOR BEING ANY PART OF THIS REVULTING PROJECT." AFTER READING THAT I WAS FUCKING HYPED TO SEE THE MOVIE!

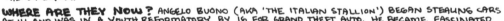

THE REAL KEN BIANCHI CIRCA 1979

THE HILLSIDE STRANGLER WAS RELEASED DIRECT-TO-DVD ON NOVEMBER 9th 2004 FROM TARTAN VIDEO USA. THE DISC IS WIDESCREEN, HAS A TRAILER, CAST INTERVIEWS, DELETED SCENES, AND AN AUDIO COMMENTARY BY THE DIRECTOR.

WHERE ARE THEY NOW? ANGELO BUONO (AKA 'THE ITALIAN STALLION') BEGAN STEALING CARS AT 14 AND WAS IN A YOUTH REFORMATORY BY 16 FOR GRAND THEFT AUTO. HE BECAME FASCINATED WITH HIS 'IDOL' SEX OFFENDER CARYL CHESSMAN, THE "RED LIGHT RAPIST" AND BEGAN TO EMULATE HIS VILE TECHNIQUES WHENEVER POSSIBLE, FREQUENTLY VIOLENTLY ABUSING HIS WIVES AND GIRL FRIENDS. IN 1977 ALONG WITH COUSIN BIANCHI HE BEGAN THE INFAMOUS "HILLSIDE SLAYINGS" IN L.A. ONE OF THEIR PROSPECTIVE VICTIMS WAS CATHARINE LORRE (DAUGHTER OF ACTOR PETER LORRE) WHO TESTIFIED THAT SHE'D BEEN APPROACHED BY 2 POLICEMEN, WHICH TIPPED THE AUTHORITIES OFF THAT THEY WERE DEALING WITH NOT ONE, BUT 2 KILLERS. BUONO WAS ARRESTED IN OCT. OF 1979 AND GOT 9 LIFE TERMS WITHOUT PAROLE. HE DIED OF NATURAL CAUSES IN PRISON IN 2002.

ANGELO BUONO

KEN BIANCHI'S MOTHER WAS A PROSTITUTE WHO GAVE HIM UP FOR ADOPTION AS AN INFANT. FROM 1971 TO 1973, 3 GIRLS WERE KILLED IN ROCHESTER THAT BECAME KNOWN AS THE 'ALPHABET MURDERS', AND MUCH LATER BIANCHI WAS FOUND TO BE RESPONSIBLE. IN 1977 HE MOVED TO L.A. WHERE HE AND HIS COUSIN TEAMED UP FOR A YEAR TO RAPE AND MURDER 15 PROSTITUTES AND MOTORISTS, DISPLAYING THE BODIES ON HILLSIDES NEAR FREEWAYS TO TAUNT POLICE. BIANCHI WAS FINALLY TIED TO THE SLAYINGS IN JUNE 1979 AND QUICKLY BETRAYED HIS COUSIN BY RATTING HIM OUT AS WELL. BIANCHI'S INITIAL DEFENCE FOR HIS ACTIONS WAS MULTIPLE PERSONALITY DISORDER (AN ALTER EGO NAMED STEVE), BUT WAS PROVEN TO BE AN OBVIOUS FAKER. KEN DROPPED THE CHARADE INSPIRED BY A

SELF PORTRAIT BY VERONICA COMPTON © 1995

IN THE LATE NINETIES SHE WROTE A BOOK CALLED "EATING THE ASHES."

VIEWING OF **SYBIL** ON THE EVE OF HIS PRETRIAL HEARING, AND WAS SENTENCED TO 9 LIFE TERMS WITHOUT PAROLE, IN WHAT WAS AT THE TIME THE LONGEST CRIMINAL TRIAL IN U.S. HISTORY.

IN JUNE 1980, KEN BEGAN CORRESPONDENCE WITH A 23 YEAR OLD WOMAN NAMED VERONICA COMPTON, WHO AGREED TO GO TO BELLINGHAM, STRANGLE A WOMAN THERE AND DEPOSIT BIANCHI'S SEMEN IN AND ON THE VICTIM TO MAKE THE POLICE AND MEDIA THINK THE REAL KILLER WAS STILL ON THE LOOSE. KEN SUCCESSFULLY SMUGGLED HIS SPOOGE TO THE SMITTEN VERONICA IN A RUBBER GLOVE MAILED TO HER IN A BOOK, AND ON OCTOBER 3rd 1980 SHE TOOK A YOUNG WOMAN TO HER MOTEL ROOM UNDER THE PRETENSE OF DOING SOME DRUGS TOGETHER. COMPTON THEN.... WELL... I DON'T WANNA GIVE AWAY THE ENDING TO THE MOVIE. CHECK OUT 2004'S **HILLSIDE STRANGLER** TO SEE HOW THIS TRUTH-IS-STRANGER-THAN-FICTION STORY ENDS.

— Robin Bougie

GAWD DAMN !!!

☆ JAPANESE SUKEBAN AND NAKED NUNS! ☆

KEEPING IN MIND THAT "SUKEBAN" TRANSLATES FROM JAPANESE AS "TEENAGE FEMALE DELINQUENT", AND THAT **SUKEBAN GUERRILLA** (1972) FEATURES SAID NUBILE RUFFIANS INITIATING EACH OTHER BY HOLDING ONE ANOTHER DOWN AND TATTOOING EACH OTHERS ENTIRE LEFT TIT, YOU SHOULD BE FULLY AWARE THAT ANY SERIOUS TRASH FAN WORTH THEIR MUSTARD WILL PROBABLY ADORE THIS FUNKY ASIAN TURD FROM START TO FINISH.

ANOTHER BOUGIE REVIEW

ART BY MR. MIKE MYHRE

A SHINJUKU-BASED MOTORCYCLE GANG OF SUKEBAN LED BY THE SEXY, PISSED-OFF SACHIKO RAMPAGES INTO KYOTO LOOKIN' FOR TROUBLE. WHILE SCAMMIN' MONEY FROM IGNORANT SIGHTSEERS BY UTILIZING THEIR VIOLENCE-FLAVORED SEXUAL CHARMS, THEY ARE CHALLENGED BY RIKA, LEADER OF A PROUD LOCAL GIRL GANG. AFTER A ONE-ON-ONE DUKE 'EM UP, RIKA CONCEDES DEFEAT TO SACHIKO IN HER OVERSIZED AVIATOR GLASSES - WHO THEN TAKES OVER THE MANAGEMENT OF THE KYOTO GANG WITH A VENGENCE. AND PEOPLE - THATS JUST THE FIRST 10 MINUTES!

AFTER THE GIRLS ENLIST A CUTE BALD TEEN MONK GIRL TO DON THE TATTOOED BREAST OF THE GANG AND SEDUCE THE PRIEST OF HER PARISH, THINGS GET REALLY CRAZY. PRETTY SOON SACHIKO (DESPITE HER TOUGH-AS-NAILS EXTERIOR) SURRENDERS TO LOVE AND FALLS FOR AN UP AND COMING BOXER, EXPRESSING HER INTEREST BY RAPING HIM. (HE RETURNS THE FAVOR BY PERVERSELY TAKING HER BY FORCE AS WELL) WILL THE DEFIANT BOXER BE ABLE TO HOLD HIS OWN AFTER SHE DRAGS HIM INTO HER VIOLENT GANGLAND WORLD? OHHH...IT'S SO GOOD!

"STOP BABBLING! DON'T TAKE US LIGHTLY 'CAUSE WE'RE CHICKS!"

UNDERAPPRECIATED DIRECTOR NORIFUMI SUZUKI IS IN FINE FORM HERE, AS HE WAS WHILE HELMING OTHER SLEAZY DICK-STIFFENERS SUCH AS **BEAUTIFUL GIRL HUNTER** (1979), **WET AND ROPE** (1979), AND THE ASTONISHINGLY GOOD GIRLS-SCHOOL NUNSPLOITATION BONDAGE BUNGHOLE BURNER **CONVENT OF THE SACRED BEAST** (1974), AN UNFORGETTABLE FILM HE MADE A MERE YEAR AFTER THIS GIRL-GANG OPUS SLAMMED INTO JAPANESE THEATERS.

AKA **SCHOOL OF THE HOLY BEAST**, THIS NASTY SLEAZEFEST HAS A WONDERFULLY SKEWED PERCEPTION OF CATHOLICISM (BORDERING ON OUTRIGHT DISDAIN) AS THE FILM CONSTANTLY WARPS AND PERVERTS RELIGIOUS CEREMONY AND JUXTAPOSES HOLY SYMBOLISM WITH DEBAUCHED SEX AND VIOLENCE. CALL IT SACRILEGIOUS IF YOU LIKE, BUT THE CINEMATOGRAPHY IN THIS ARTSY-LOOKING NUNSPLOITATION CLASSIC IS ABSOLUTELY GORGEOUS, AND HAS EVEN BEEN CALLED "POETIC" BY SOME.

THIS ONE HAS IT ALL: SELF FLAGELLATION, LESBIANISM, HUMILIATING TORTURE AND BONDAGE, CAT FIGHTS, RAMPANT NUDITY, BROTHERS DRESSED AS SISTERS, HORRIFIC INCESTUAL RAPE AND STICKY SEX. TO BEGIN WITH, BEAUTIFUL MAYA TAKIGAWA (YUMI TAKIGAWA) SPENDS HER FREE TIME DOING WHAT ANY YOUNG 18 YEAR OLD URBAN JAPANESE LASS WOULD. NAMELY: PLAYING ARCADE GAMES, HAVING CASUAL SEX,

DRINKING PURPLE MARTINI'S, AND UM... BELIEVE IT OR NOT - CHEERING HER BRAINS OUT AT A HOCKEY GAME. (?!)

ALL THIS SINFUL FUN SLIDES DOWN JUST HOURS BEFORE SHE ENTERS THE STRICTLY GOVERNED WORLD OF A JAPANESE CATHOLIC NUNNERY. HERE MAYA FINDS AN UNDERGROUND WORLD OF UNBELIEVABLE AND BIZARRE RITUALISTIC SUFFERING. THESE DAMN NUNS ARE SO REPRESSED AND HORNY THAT THEY'VE COME TO PERVERT EVERY HOLY ETHIC YOU COULD NAME - AND IT'S ALL SHAMELESSLY PARADED PAST THE VIEWER LIKE A WONDEROUS SELF-RIGHTEOUS PLAYGROUND OF CATHOLIC SIN, CRAMMED UP SEXPLOITATION STYLE!

BLASPHEMOUS CINEMA INVOLVING SUPPRESSED SEXUAL DESIRES IN A CONVENT IS ALMOST ALWAYS OF EUROPEAN ORIGIN, BUT THIS SMOKER FROM THE FAR EAST IS ONE OF THE BEST OF ITS GENRE.

THE OTHER STANDOUT FROM THE NORIFUMI SUZUKI FILMOGRAPHY CERTAINLY HAS TO BE **STAR OF DAVID: BEAUTY HUNTER** (1979). THIS MASTERWORK OF SLEAZE FEATURES SOME SERIOUS TABOO-BUSTING. AS ONE REVIEWER NOTED: "..A FILM WHERE INCEST IS THE NORM, BEASTIALITY IS A NOVEL CONCEPT, RAPE IS COMPLETELY COMMONPLACE, AND NECROPHILIA IS JUST ANOTHER WAY TO PASS SOME TIME."

TEENAGE KICKS AT THE CRESTVIEW DRIVE-IN Theatre

FONDLY REMEMBERED BY GEORGE CHACON '04

BACK IN THE LATE 70s ON FRIDAY AND SATURDAY NIGHTS, JUST BEFORE DUSK, MY BROTHER AND I USED TO GET ALL WOUND UP OVER WHAT MOVIES AND CHICKS FROM SCHOOL WE WERE GOING TO SEE THAT NIGHT AT THE OLD CRESTVIEW DRIVE-IN THEATER.

WE LIVED ABOUT A MILE AWAY FROM THE CRESTVIEW, AND WE'D RIDE OUR SKATEBOARDS THERE, DITCH 'EM IN THE HUGE BUSHES NEAR THE WEST WALL BY THE NUMBER 2 EXIT, AND EASILY CLEAR THE 8 FOOT WALL BY CLIMBING ONE OF THE MANY TREES ALONGSIDE IT. WE DID THIS WITH LITTLE REGARD OF GETTING CAUGHT, SINCE HALF THE PEOPLE WORKING AT THE CONCESSION STANDS AND THE PROJECTIONIST (OUR NEIGHBOR RICHARD) WERE GOOD FRIENDS OF OURS. IF WE SAW SOMEBODY BREAKIN' SPEAKERS OR JACKING CARS, WE'D RAT THEM OUT TO RICH OR WHICH EVER MANAGEMENT WAS ON HAND.

I WAS REALLY INTO HORROR MOVIES, WHILE MY BROTHER LIKED THE CHOP-SOCKY FLICKS. AND THAT PARTICULAR NIGHT THEY WERE PLAYING CHUCK NORRIS'S **GOOD GUYS WEAR BLACK** AND BRUCE LEE'S **CHINESE CONNECTION** ON SCREEN ONE, WHILE SCREEN TWO FEATURED **THE EXORCIST** AND **EXORCIST 2: THE HERETIC**. IT WAS A TOSS UP FOR WHICH SCREEN WE'D GO WITH. IT WAS KINDA COOL THAT YOU DIDN'T HAVE TO BE IN A CAR SITTING RIGHT NEXT TO A SPEAKER TO HEAR THE MOVIE, YOU COULD JUST CHILL BY THE SNACK BAR OR WALK AROUND LOOKING FOR FRIENDS CARS FROM SCHOOL, AND HEAR THE MOVIE JUST FINE. IF THE SNACK BAR WASN'T REALLY BUSY, WE WOULD TRY AND GET 'HOOK-UP'S' (FREE SODAS, POPCORN, CANDY, AND ICE CREAMS) FROM OUR BUDDIES WORKIN' THERE.

HOOK-UP'S!

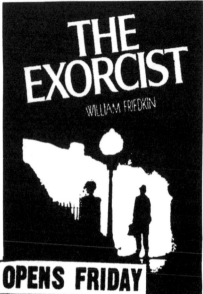

THE EXORCIST
WILLIAM FRIEDKIN

OPENS FRIDAY

THAT NIGHT WE WERE JUST KICKIN' BACK, TALKING, AND EYEBALLING ANY GIRL WHO SEEMED HALF WAY INTERESTED. MY BROTHER AND I ALWAYS PRETENDED TO BE OLDER THAN WE WERE, AND IF THE LADIES ASKED WE'D PROUDLY AND CONFIDENTLY LIE THAT WE WERE 18, HAD ROLLED UP WITH SOME FRIENDS WHO HAD PARKED CLOSER TO THE SCREEN, AND HAD ACCESS TO FREE SODAS. THAT NIGHT OUR SCHEME WORKED, AND TWO HALFWAY DECENT OLDER LOOKIN' LADIES INVITED US INTO THEIR CAR TO WATCH **THE EXORCIST** DOUBLE FEATURE.

I GOT WITH THE HEAVIER SET OF THE TWO, WHO MUST HAVE BEEN 25 OR SO, AND WHO HAD HERSELF A **BIG** ASS, AND AN EVEN **BIGGER** PAIR OF TITS. MY BROTHER

GOT WITH THE CUTE, SKINNY, FLAT-CHESTED CHICK IN THE BACK SEAT - WHO WAS PROBABLY 19 OR 20. EVERYTHING WAS REAL COOL WHEN THE PREVIEWS STARTED UP, WITH RICH PLAYING DISNEY'S **THE APPLE DUMPLING GANG** AND **JAWS** BACK TO BACK! WE BUSTED UP LAUGHING, AND EXPLAINED TO THE LADIES THAT RICH WAS CRAZY LIKE THAT, AND THAT MANAGEMENT WOULD BE CONSTANTLY TELLING HIM TO ONLY PLAY PREVIEWS FROM THE SAME GENRE. RICH WAS A FUCKING RIOT.

THE EXORCIST GOT SPOOLED ONTO THE PROJECTOR REEL AND OUR DATES GOT NERVOUS. "WE HEARD THAT THESE MOVIES ARE REALLY SCARY," THEY SAID. "WE'RE REALLY GLAD WE HAVE YOU GUYS HERE TO PROTECT US!". AND WITH THAT, WE GOT A LITTLE FIRST BASE ACTION - SOME HUGGIN' AND SMOOCHIN'... BUT WE COULD TELL THAT THE MOVIE WAS PUTTING THE LADIES OUT OF THE MOOD WHEN LITTLE REGAN WAS GETTING POSSESSED AND DOING EVIL SHIT. OUR "CLEVER"

"...SHE HAD HERSELF A **BIG** ASS, AND EVEN **BIGGER** PAIR OF TITS..."

COURSE OF ACTION TO CONTINUE GETTING PLAY WAS TO DISTRACT OUR DATES BY BUSTING OUT LAUGHING REALLY HARD WHENEVER SCARY SHIT APPEARED. SO THERE WE WERE - CRACKIN' UP AS LITTLE SATAN-GIRL IS PISSING ON THE FLOOR, MONKEY WRENCHING HER DOCTORS NUTS IN HER VICE-LIKE GRIP, VOMITING HER GREEN SNOT ROCKET INTO THE PRIEST'S OPEN MOUTH, STABBING HER COOTCH WITH A CRUCIFIX, AND BITCH-SLAPPIN' HER MOM CLEAR ACROSS THE ROOM!

IT DID SEEM TO HELP A LITTLE, BUT THE SHIT WAS JUST TOO SCARY AND WE DIDN'T REALLY GET ANYWHERE UNTIL **THE HERETIC** CAME ON. THAT LAME ASS BULLSHIT WAS LIKE SPANISH FLY AND PUT THEM BITCHES RIGHT IN THE MOOD! I USED **THE HERETIC** TO MY ADVANTAGE, GETTING TO KNOW EVERY INCH OF THOSE TWO LOVELY BIG BOOBIES. WHEN I WASN'T KISSIN' AND SQUEEZIN' THEM JUICY MELONS, I WAS ALL OVER THAT SWEET ASS. I PEEPED ON THE BACK SEAT TO SEE HOW THINGS WERE GOING, AND THEY WERE SUCKING FACE LIKE CRAZY. MY BRO WOULD LATER TELL ME THAT SHE JACKED HIM OFF WHILE HE FINGER BANGED HER, WITH STANK-FINGER TO PROVE IT.

THE MOVIE ENDED, AND THE GIRLS OFFERED TO HELP US FIND OUR FRIENDS ON THE BACKSIDE SCREEN WHO WE ALLEGEDLY HAD COME WITH. MY BROTHER AND I JUST LOOKED AT EACH OTHER AND SAID "NO, WE WERE JUST BULLSHIT'N. WE RODE HERE ON OUR SKATEBOARDS AND WE BETTER GET HOME BEFORE OUR DAD KICKS OUR UNDERAGE ASSES."

"...THEM BITCHES WENT CRAZY, SPITTIN' AND KICKIN'..."

MAN, THEM BITCHES WENT CRAZY, SPITTIN' AND KICKIN' US OUT OF THE CAR. WE REALLY THOUGHT THEY WERE GONNA TRY RUNNING OUR ASSES OVER. SO WE RAN SCREAMING TOWARDS THE TICKET OFFICE SO WE COULD HIDE.

RICH WAS LAUGHING SO HARD HE HAD TEARS IN HIS EYES WHEN WE TOLD HIM WHY WE HAD COME TEARING ACROSS THE LOT SCREAMING OUR HEADS OFF. ALTHOUGH THANKFULLY HE TOOK PITY ON US ENOUGH TO DRIVE US HOME AFTER WE PICKED UP OUR BOARDS.

MY BROTHER AND I ALWAYS TALK ABOUT THE GREAT TIMES WE HAD AT THE CRESTVIEW DRIVE-IN. GOOD TIMES AND WATCHIN' MOVIES. NOTHIN' BETTER.

FOXY BROWN (1974)

JACK HILL'S INCREDIBLE FOXY BROWN (STARRING PAM GRIER, WHO CHOSE TO WEAR HER OWN GROOVY CLOTHES IN THE ROLE!) TAKES THE IRRESISTABLE TRASHINESS OF HIS FILM **COFFY** (1973) EVEN FURTHER. CASE IN POINT: A NASTY SEQUENCE WHERE FOXY IS SHOT FULL OF NARCOTICS AND TAKEN TO A SECLUDED SHACK, BEATEN, RAPED AND OVERDOSED AGAIN - BEFORE SHE MAIMS ONE OF THE UGLY CLOWNS AND MERCILESSLY SETS THEM BOTH ON FIRE. THE MOVIE ALSO BOASTS A BRAWL IN A LESBO BAR, A GUY BEING HACKED UP BY SID HAIG'S PLANE PROPELLER AND THE INFAMOUS "PICKLE JAR" SCENE.

ACCORDING TO HILL, THIS WAS ORIGINALLY INTENDED TO BE A SEQUEL TO COFFY, AND THE WORKING TITLE WAS "BURN, COFFY, BURN!". AIP HOWEVER, DECIDED AT THE LAST SECOND IT DIDN'T WANT TO DO A SEQUEL -- EVEN THOUGH "COFFY" WAS A HUGE HIT FOR THEM.

IF YOU HAVEN'T SEEN THIS YET, YOU'RE REALLY MISSING OUT.

MITCHELL'S Sodom and Gomorrah

3 FILMS $2.75

ADULTS ONLY

IT WAS THE EARLY 1970s, A TIME WHEN HARDCORE FUCK MOVIES WERE STILL SOMETHING YOU EXPERIENCED IN A MOVIE THEATER SETTING.

WHILE AMERICA BATTLED WITH ITS OWN CODE OF MORAL DECENCY, A PAIR OF BROTHERS FROM ANTIOCH, CALIFORNIA REVOLUTIONIZED THE VIRGIN PORN INDUSTRY AND STRUCK FILTHY GOLD WITH AN INFAMOUS FILM CALLED:

"BEHIND the GREEN DOOR"

IT NOT ONLY LAUNCHED THE CAREER OF ADULT VETERAN MARILYN CHAMBERS, BUT ALSO MADE OVER 40 MILLION BUCKS.

ARTIE AND JIM MITCHELL WERE TOLD BY A JUDGE IN ONE OF THE MANY OBSCENITY COURT CASES REVOLVING AROUND THE SUCCESSFUL XXX FILM THAT THEIR MOVIE WOULD:

"...VIOLATE THE COMMUNITY STANDARDS OF SODOM AND GOMORRAH!"

BULLSHIT!

THE BROTHERS FELT THAT THE GAUNTLET HAD BEEN THROWN.

IN THE SUMMER OF 1974 THEY LEASED A HUGE RANCH IN THE HOT DESERT HILLS OF LIVERMORE CALIFORNIA, AND TRANSPORTED A "CAST OF THOUSANDS" TO WHAT THEY WOULD LATER CALL "A NIGHTMARE SHOOT" FOR A MOVIE THAT AUDACIOUSLY BORROWED ITS HARDCORE PORN PREMISE FROM THE BIBLE. THAT PORN FILM WAS CALLED "SODOM AND GOMORRAH: THE LAST SEVEN DAYS"

PRAISE HIM!

THINGS WERE ALREADY FALLING APART WHEN JIM AND ARTIE, STRESSED OUT ABOUT THE HUGE UNDER-TAKING, BECAME A "WEIRD TWO HEADED MONSTER" THAT COULDN'T AGREE ON ANYTHING, AND SEEMED TO BE TRYING TO SABOTAGE ONE ANOTHER CONSTANTLY.

GRAR!

RARG!

AMID THE CONFUSION, JIM'S WIFE ADRIENNE SHOCKED EVERYONE BY RUNNING OFF WITH ONE OF THE WELL-HUNG MALE STARS. 3 DAYS LATER THE FEMALE LEAD OF THE PICTURE DISAPPEARED AFTER GOING ON AN EXTENDED DRUG FUELED BENDER IN MEXICO.

ADRIENNE!

SPENDING ALMOST A MILLION SMACKERS ON THE 98 MIN. BIBLICAL HUMP EPIC, THE BAD BOY BROTHERS THOUGHT THEY'D HAVE A SURE FIRE HIT, BUT IT FLOPPED AT THE BOX OFFICE, AND THEN CRITICS CALLED IT:

"...BORING..."   "UNIMAGINATIVE"

"TOTALLY LIMP."

THE FAILURE PUT THE BROTHERS AT EACH OTHERS THROATS AGAIN.

FINALLY ON FEB. 27th 1991 JIM SHOT HIS BELLIGERENT AND VIOLENT COKE-HEAD SIBLING TO DEATH DURING AN ARGUMENT. JIM SERVED ONLY 3 YEARS IN PRISON FOR KILLING ARTIE.

IN 1993 A HILARIOUS COMEDY MOCKUMENTARY CALLED AND GOD SPOKE WAS RELEASED, AND WAS BASED LOOSLY ON THE MITCHELLS' MISGUIDED AND DOOMED ATTEMPT TO BRING THIS HOLY STORY TO PORN THEATERS. A LESS FUNNY STORY ABOUT THE BROTHERS LIFE CALLED RATED X, STARRING CHARLIE SHEEN AND EMILIO ESTEVEZ AS THE FEUDING MITCHELLS CAME OUT IN 2000.

THAT'S YER SLEAZY FILM HISTORY FER TODAY...

THE DIRT GANG (1972)

ONE OF AMERICAN INTERNATIONAL PICTURES EXPLOITATION DRIVE-IN SPECIALTIES WAS THE BIKER MOVIE, AND THIS WAS THE FINAL ONE THEY RELEASED. YES, **THE DIRT GANG** WAS THE END OF AN ERA, AND ONE OF THE LAST EXAMPLES OF A GENRE THAT HAD OUTLIVED ITS TIME.

THE TWIST ON THE FORMAT HERE HOWEVER, IS THAT THE BIKERS (RESPLENDENT IN THEIR CUT-OFF DENIM JACKETS) ARE MOTOCROSS GUYS. WHAT KINDA OUTLAW REBEL TOOTLES AROUND ON A YAMAHA?! REGARDLESS, I'M THRILLED TO REPORT THAT ALL THE NUDITY, VIOLENCE, AND DERANGED SCENARIOS FROM THE MORE SAVAGE ENTRIES TO THE GENRE STILL FLOP AROUND HERE IN WILD TESTICULATION -- EVEN IF NO ONE HAS A HARLEY.

they don't all use the little boys wash room

PAUL CARR IS "MONK", THE EYE PATCH-CLAD LEADER, WHO -- ALONG WITH HIS HOMEY "SNAKE", A CRAZY CHARLIE MANSON WANNABE, AND SOME GROOVY "HORNY MAMAS" (ONE OF WHICH IS THE FAT-TITTED USCHI DIGARD!) BURN RUBBER ACROSS THE DESERT, JUST HOPING TO FIND SOME HELPLESS TATER-TWATS TO MANHANDLE.

THE VICTIMS THEY DECIDE UPON TURN OUT TO BE A BUNCHA HOLLYWOOD SOFTIES, MAKING WHAT LOOKS TO BE THE SHITTIEST WESTERN EVER FILMED. AS A VIEWER, YOU'RE RELIEVED TO SEE THE DIRT GANG ROLL IN, ABUSE SOME NANCY-BOY ACTORS, PERFORM VARIOUS DISGUSTING DEEDS ON THE CREW, RAPEZ SUM WIMMINZ, START AN ORGY, AND GENERALLY CAUSE TOTAL DRUNKEN CHAOS.

THE DIRT GANG

ALL IN ALL, A PRETTY FUN MOVIE, AND ONE THAT WWW. SMITHEEAWARDS .COM NOMINATED FOR A LESS THAN COMPLI- -MENTARY ACCOLADE. THE DIRT GANG AD CAMPAIGN WAS CHOSEN FOR THE "WORST COVER COPY" AWARD, WITH THE JUDGES NOTING THAT "HE'LL GET A ... 250 LB DIRT BIKE RIGHT WHERE HE DOESN'T NEED IT" ONLY PROMPTS THE QUESTION "WHERE **WOULD** YOU NEED IT ??".

A GOOD QUESTION, AND ONE THAT I'M SURE DIRECTOR JERRY JAMESON WOULD HAVE LOVED TO HAVE ADDRESSED IN A SEQUEL.

EVERY DIRT TRAIL IS A ONE WAY, DEAD-END BATTLEFIELD AND A CHEAP, DUSTY BEDROOM...

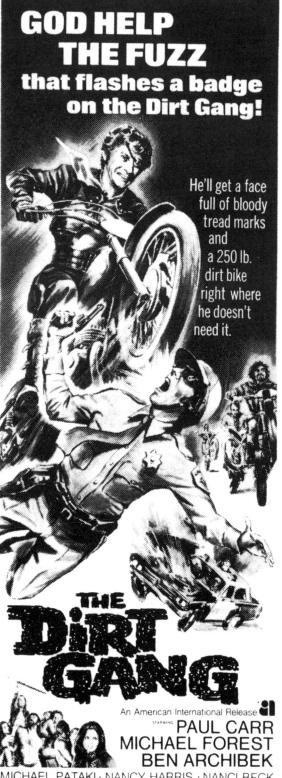

GOD HELP THE FUZZ
that flashes a badge on the Dirt Gang!

He'll get a face full of bloody tread marks and a 250 lb. dirt bike right where he doesn't need it.

THE DiRT GANG

An American International Release

STARRING

PAUL CARR
MICHAEL FOREST
BEN ARCHIBEK

MICHAEL PATAKI · NANCY HARRIS · NANCI BECK

Written by
WILLIAM MERCER and MICHAEL C. HEALY

Produced by
JOSEPH E. BISHOP

and ART JACOBS · Directed by JERRY JAMESON · COLOR by CFI · R

© 1972 American International Pictures, Inc.

CITY OF THE LIVING DEAD (1980) aka "The Gates of Hell"

CITY OF THE LIVING DEAD IS A GORE-SOAKED HORROR MOVIE THAT FINDS DIRECTOR LUCIO FULCI AT THE HEIGHT OF HIS POWERS. IT REALLY IS A VOMIT PUDDLE OF A CINEMATIC EXPERIENCE ABOUT A BUNCH OF UNFORTUNATE SOULS MIXED UP IN THE STRANGE GOINGS ON IN A LITTLE TOWN CALLED DUNWICH WHERE THE SUICIDE OF A PRIEST INEXPLICABLY OPENS THE GATEWAY TO HELL -- ALLOWING THE DEAD TO RISE FROM THEIR GRAVES AND FEED ON THE LIVING. I WONDER WHICH GATE OPENS AND WHAT GETS EATEN WHEN A PRIEST MOLESTS AN ALTAR BOY? Hmmm?

DUNWICH SEEMS NOT TO EXIST IN THE WORLD WE KNOW BUT IN SOME BUGGY, FOGGY HINTERLAND, A PLACE WHERE LOGIC HAS BROKEN DOWN AND THINGS SIMPLY HAPPEN WITH NO REFERENCE TO CAUSE AND EFFECT. A FANTASTIC CREEPY GOBLIN-ESQUE SOUNDTRACK BY FABIO FRIZZI COMPLETES THE EFFECT EXCELLENTLY.

DESPITE WHAT MANY HORROR FANS AND CRITICS MAY TELL YOU, IT'S NOT JUST THE BLOOD AND GUTS, BUT THE HAUNTING DREAMLIKE AMBIENCE THAT SEES THIS MOVIE THROUGH ITS MORE RIDICULOUS MOMENTS -- OF WHICH IT HAS ITS FAIR SHARE. THERE ARE PROBABLY A GREATER AMOUNT OF MAGGOTS AND WORMS IN THIS ONE FILM THAN ALL OF THE HORROR FILMS MADE IN NORTH AMERICA IN THE 1990s, AND THE REMARKABLE THING ABOUT THEM IS THAT THEY NOISILY FLY IN SWARMS. I WAS COMPLETELY UNAWARE THAT MAGGOTS COULD FLY OR MAKE ANY SOUND AT ALL, ACTUALLY. YOU KNOW, SINCE THEY LACK LUNGS AND WINGS.

BUT NEVER MIND THAT... THE GORE FX HERE ARE FUCKING LEGENDARY! MOST SHOCKING AND REVOLTING IS THE INFAMOUS "DEVIL'S SPEW" ENTRAIL BARFING SEQUENCE (ACTRESS DANIELA DORIA REALLY SHOULD HAVE BEEN PAID A WINDFALL SUM FOR WHAT THEY PUT HER THROUGH FOR THIS SCENE) THAT STILL MANAGES TO AMAZE EVEN JADED GOREHOUNDS. NOT ONLY THAT, BUT THEN WE'VE GOT PEOPLE SPONTANEOUSLY BLEEDING FROM THE EYES, BRAINS BEING RIPPED RIGHT OUTTA THE BACKS OF PEOPLE'S HEADS, NOT TO MENTION THE DRILLING OF JOHN MORGHEN'S FACE -- WHICH IS STILL ONE OF THE GREATEST CRINGE-INDUCING EFFECTS EVER CREATED FOR THE MOVIES.

THAT SCENE ALSO FURTHER PROVES THAT IN ITALIAN HORROR CINEMA, ANYONE IS FAIR GAME, ANYONE CAN FALL PREY TO A GORY DEMISE AT ANY TIME -- SO DON'T STEP OUT FOR A PEE BREAK. IN AN AMERICAN FILM OF THE SAME VARIETY, CLICHÉS (WHICH ARE ADHERED TO WITH A RELIGIOUS-STYLE FERVOUR) WOULD HAVE DICTATED THAT MORGHEN WOULD HAVE TO BE RESCUED OR DODGE THE DRILL AT THE LAST SECOND -- AND THEN STUCK AROUND TO SAY SOMETHING MEANINGFUL OR DO SOMETHING HEROIC IN THE FINAL ACT. NOT HERE MY FRIENDS. HERE THE BLOOD FLOWS IN RIVERS, BRAINS FLY, SKIN RIPS, SCREAMS RING OUT, AND A HEROIC ENDING IS LEFT ON THE CUTTING ROOM FLOOR.

VARIATIONS OF GERMAN ADVERTISING ART FOR "CITY OF THE LIVING DEAD"

IN FACT, THE INFAMOUS FINAL SCENE TO ONE OF THE MOST BAFFLINGLY ILLOGICAL HORROR FILMS I'VE SEEN IS WONDERFULLY FITTING, REGARDLESS OF THE MULTITUDE OF HOWLING COMPLAINTS ABOUT IT I'VE SPOTTED ONLINE. SUPPOSEDLY THE MOVIE'S DISJOINTED INEXPLICABLE ENDING IS THE RESULT OF A CANISTER OF FOOTAGE BEING DAMAGED OR LOST. WHAT YOU GET INSTEAD OF A RATIONAL WRAP-UP IS SOMETHING YOU REALLY HAVE TO SEE FOR YOURSELF TO (DIS)BELIEVE -- A FINALE THAT NEEDS A DOCTORAL DISSERTATION TO WRANGLE ITS PARADOXICAL MEANING.

BANNED IN VARIOUS COUNTRIES, THE MOVIE HAD AN ESPECIALLY ROUGH RAPING FROM THE VIOLENCE-SENSITIVE GERMAN CENSORS -- WHERE EACH RELEASE WAS BANNED OVER THE COURSE OF 20 YEARS. FIRST RELEASED THERE ON VHS WITH THE TITLE "EIN ZOMBIE HING AM GLOCKENSEIL" IN 1982, IT WAS PULLED -- AND A SECOND VIDEO WITH THE TITLE "EIN TOTER HING AM GLOCKENSEIL" WAS RELEASED WITH VARIOUS OBVIOUS CUTS. UNFORTUNATELY, IT WASN'T CENSORED ENOUGH, AND EVEN THAT VERSION WAS BANNED IN 1988. A FINAL VERSION WAS SUBMITTED -- HEAVILY CUT WITHOUT ANY REAL GORE LEFT AT ALL. AMAZINGLY, THIS THIRD VERSION WAS ALSO BANNED IN 2001.

—BOUGIE

☆ DOROTHY LeMAY ☆

BORN DOROTHY STATON ALDER IN 1954 AND RAISED IN DAYTON OHIO, DOROTHY LEMAY MARRIED RIGHT OUT OF HIGH SCHOOL AND MOVED WITH HER NEW HUSBAND TO SAN FRANCISCO IN 1976. WHILE WORKING AT A DESK JOB AT THE UNIVERSITY OF CALIFORNIA IN BERKELEY, SHE ANSWERED AN AD HAROLD ADLER PLACED THAT READ "MAKE MOVIES, MAKE $300 A DAY". AFTER SHE VENTURED IN, DISROBED SO HARRY COULD TAKE SOME POLAROIDS, ADLER'S AGENCY QUICKLY LINED HER UP AS A FARRAH FAWCETT LOOK--ALIKE IN A PRODUCTION CALLED **A FORMAL FAUCETT**. (TAGLINE: "SHE'S GOT ALL THE RIGHT PLUMBING!")

"HAROLD SET IT UP FOR ME TO MEET FRED LINCOLN, WHO WAS DOING THE FILM", LEMAY TOLD A PORN INDUSTRY REPORTER IN 1982. "IT WAS TRAUMATIC BECAUSE I DIDN'T KNOW WHAT WAS GOING ON. WE SHOT DURING A WEEKEND AND THE DAYS WERE ABOUT 20 HOURS LONG. I MADE $150 A DAY, FOR 2 DAYS. AT LEAST IT WAS BETTER THAN WORKING IN AN OFFICE THOUGH."

A RUDE AWAKENING WAS IN ORDER WHEN DOROTHY VENTURED DOWN TO HER LOCAL SMUT PALACE TO SEE HER BIG SCREEN DEBUT. SHE ENDED UP RUNNING OUT OF THE THEATER AFTER WITNESSING WHAT SHE LATER CALLED "A DISASTER", AND "GROSS". IT WASN'T THE GRAPHIC SEX THAT UPSET HER THOUGH. SHE HAD BEEN HORRIFIED THAT HER VOICE HAD BEEN DUBBED OVER WITH SOMEONE ELSE'S, AND THAT IT "DIDN'T MAKE SENSE".

FROM THERE SHE DID A FEW LOOPS FOR THE **SWEDISH EROTICA** LINE, AS WELL AS SOME GENERIC FUCKY-SUCKY FOR DIAMOND COLLECTION AND PLEASURE PRODUCTIONS. THEN LIVE SEX SHOWS FOR ALEX DERENZY AT THE PLAYPEN CLUB IN SAN FRANCISCO (BEFORE IT BECAME A GAY BAR), AS WELL AS AN INFAMOUS WEEK HAVING ANNETTE HAVEN CRAM ORANGE PLASTIC BALLS UP HER ASS ON STAGE AT THE MITCHELL BROS. THEATER. "I WAS SORE AS HELL AFTER THE SIXTH DAY OF THAT" LEMAY CONFIDED YEARS LATER. "I COULDN'T GO ON. ANNETTE TOOK THIS BIG DILDO AND STUCK IT IN ME, AND I SAID 'ANNETTE, YOU HAVE NO MERCY'."

KEEP GOIN' DOROTHY.. ..GREAT...

PLOSP SPLAP SHLURP

BOUGIE

SMALLER ROLES IN XXX FEATURE FILMS CAME ALONG: **BLONDE FIRE**, **FEMALE ATHLETES**, AND **SENSUAL ENCOUNTERS OF EVERY KIND**. BUT THE TRUDGE OF FUCKING ON CAMERA FOR A LIVING AND NOT HAVING ANYONE REALLY TAKE NOTE OR PAY YOU A DECENT WAGE GOT MIGHTY OLD REAL FAST FOR THIS PALE-SKINNED REDHEAD. AFTER SHOOTING WRAPPED ON **HIGH SCHOOL MEMORIES** (WHERE SHE PLAYED A NYMPHO CHEERLEADER) DOROTHY GAVE HER COOTCHIE A REST, STARTED DATING A GAFFER NAMED ERNIE SHE MET ON SET, AND GOT HERSELF A STRAIGHT BORING JOB AT ABC MESSENGER SERVICE IN HOLLYWOOD.

"I HAD MY FIRST LESBIAN AFFAIR BECAUSE I HATED ERNIE", SHE TOLD ADAM MAGAZINE.

TWO YEARS LATER, IN 1981, DOROTHY GOT A CALL FROM STEPHEN SAYADIAN (AKA RINSE DREAM) AND JERRY STAHL. THE TWO FRIENDS HAD TEAMED UP TO MAKE A PORN MOVIE WITH WHAT THEY HOPED WOULD BE A WEIRD ART-HOUSE PSYCHOLOGICAL TWIST, AND WHILE WATCHING **HIGH SCHOOL MEMORIES**, HAD DECIDED TO FIND AND CAST DOROTHY AS "MRS. VAN HOUTEN". THE FILM WAS TITLED **NIGHTDREAMS**, AND IT CATAPULTED LEMAY FROM SECOND BILL OBSCURITY TO PORN PRINCESS STARDOM.

"ANNETTE HAVEN TURNED IT DOWN. I WAS THE SECOND CHOICE", DOROTHY ADMITTED.

LEMAY WOULDN'T BE THE ONLY ONE LAUNCHED

LEMAY GETS FELT UP BY JULIET ANDERSON (AKA "AUNT PEG") IN 1982'S **VISTA VALLEY P.T.A.** IT'S QUITE A STEAMY SCENE! ROWR!

INTO THE SPOTLIGHT WITH **NIGHTDREAMS**. SAYADIAN WOULD GO ON TO MAKE 1982's **CAFE FLESH** (GENERALLY CONSIDERED TO BE THE LAST GREAT CLASSIC PORN FILM BEFORE THE VIDEO ERA), AND JERRY STAHL BECAME PERHAPS THE MOST SUCCESSFUL INDIVIDUAL SPAWNED BY THE 80s PORN SCENE. HE WOULD WRITE EPISODES OF **MOONLIGHTING**, **ALF**, AND THEN BECOME THE HEAD WRITER ON **CSI** -- WITH HIS TRANSGRESSIVE KINKY EPISODES GETTING THE HIGHEST RATINGS FOR (WHAT IS AS OF THIS WRITING) THE MOST WATCHED TELEVISION SHOW ON EARTH. HIS AUTOBIOGRAPHY **PERMANENT MIDNIGHT** WAS MADE INTO A DECENT MOVIE STARRING BEN STILLER.

DOROTHY LEMAY WOULDN'T FIND ANY SUCH LUCRATIVE SUCCESS AFTER **NIGHTDREAMS**, BUT SHE WAS ONE OF THE MOST (SEEMINGLY) HAPPY, HEALTHY, AND HORNY FEMALES OF HER ERA IN XXX. THE FOLLOWING ARE HIGHLIGHTS OF AN INTERVIEW SHE DID WITH JIM DAWSON OF "VELVET TALKS" MAGAZINE SOON AFTER THE WEIRDNESS THAT WAS **NIGHTDREAMS** CAPTURED THE INDUSTRY'S ATTENTION.

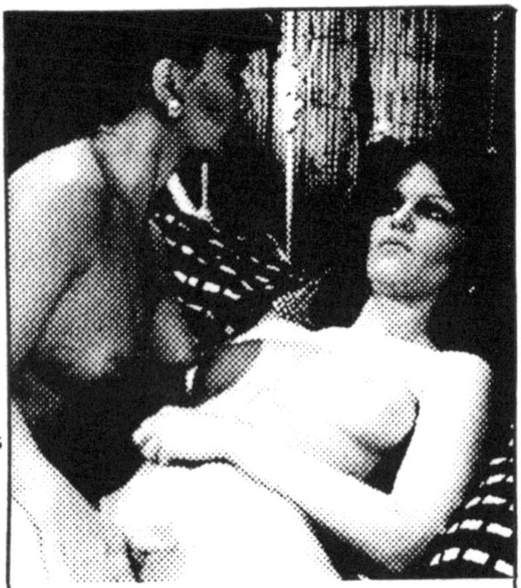

JD: DOROTHY, WHAT IS YOUR FAVOURITE KIND OF SEX?

LEMAY: MY FAVORITE POSITION IS DOGGY STYLE. I LOVE IT. [LOWERS VOICE] **LOVE IT**. AND I LIKE GETTING HEAD. PEOPLE TELL ME I ROLL MY EYES. THAT IS WHAT I'M KNOWN FOR, ROLLING MY EYES.

JD: LIKE WHEN YOU ROLL YOUR EYES INTO YOUR HEAD WHEN YOU SUCK ON A COCK?

LEMAY: YEAH! [LAUGHTER]

JD: HAVE YOU ALWAYS HAD AN ACTIVE SEX LIFE?

LEMAY: WELL, IN HIGH SCHOOL IT WAS TERRIBLE. I WAS SHY AND INNOCENT. I'M STILL INNOCENT, BUT I'M NOTHING LIKE I WAS THEN. I WENT WITH A GUY FOR FOUR YEARS AND I NEVER KNEW WHAT A CLIT WAS. MY BOYFRIEND WOULD ACCUSE ME OF MASTURBATING, AND I'D SAY: 'WHAT'S THAT?'. LATER I MARRIED A GUY AND MOVED OUT TO CALIFORNIA FROM DAYTON. SEX WAS OK BETWEEN US, BUT I NEVER CAME. WE GOT INTO A LOT OF KINKY SEX, WENT TO SEX MOVIES, MESSED AROUND IN PEEP SHOW BOOTHS, AND STUFF LIKE THAT, BUT I NEVER GOT OFF. THEN AFTER THREE YEARS OF MARRIAGE HE INITIATED AN ORGY, AND THIS GIRL WENT DOWN ON ME -- THE FIRST GIRL I'D EVER HAD SEX WITH. AND SHE MADE ME HAVE AN ORGASM! THAT REALLY TURNED MY HEAD AROUND. AFTER THAT I STARTED TELLING MY HUSBAND WHAT FELT GOOD.

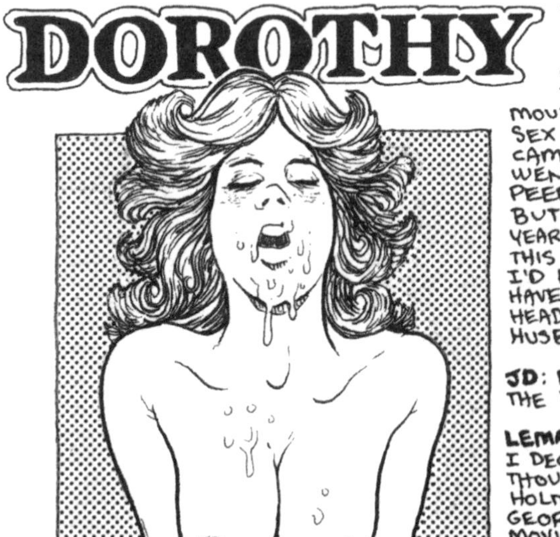

JD: **FORMAL FAUCETT** WAS YOUR FIRST FORAY INTO THE PORN BUSINESS?

LEMAY: YEAH, IT WASN'T UNTIL **CHOPSTIX** THAT I DECIDED THAT I REALLY LIKED MAKING FILMS THOUGH. AND **TROPIC OF DESIRE** WITH JOHN HOLMES -- I MADE THAT IN OCTOBER OF '78. GEORGINA SPELVIN WAS GREAT TO ME ON THAT MOVIE. I HAD ALWAYS JUST READ OVER MY LINES AND PRACTISED THEM MYSELF, BUT GEORGINA SAID 'LETS GO UPSTAIRS AND GO OVER THIS SCENE TOGETHER'. SHE TAUGHT ME TO PUT INFLECTIONS ON CERTAIN WORDS. WHEN THAT FILM CAME OUT, PEOPLE STARTED TELLING ME 'HEY, YOU CAN REALLY ACT!', BUT IT WAS SAM WESTON [DIRECTOR ANTHONY SPINELLI] THAT REALLY GOT ME INTO ACTING ON **VISTA VALLEY PTA**. BEFORE THAT, I HAD NEVER REALLY CARED. HE TOOK ME ASIDE AND TOLD ME 'YOU SHOULD SAY IT THIS WAY', AND I DID EXACTLY WHAT HE SAID AND IT TURNED OUT NICE.

JD: WHO ARE SOME OF THE PEOPLE WHO YOU'VE HAD DIFFICULTY WORKING WITH?

LEMAY: ONE GIRL I DIDN'T LIKE WORKING WITH IS

GEORGINA SPELVIN GETS HER DIGITS STICKY WITH LEMAY IN 1978's **TROPIC OF DESIRE**

DOROTHY

BOUGIE '08

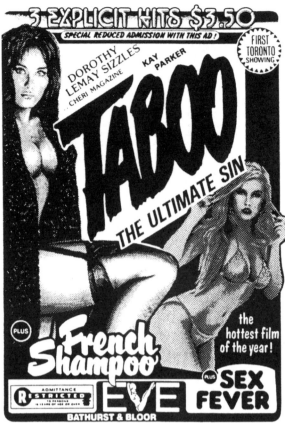
DESIREE COUSTEAU. SHE IS SO **COLD**. WHEN I'M DOING A SEX SCENE AND THE CAMERAS TURN OFF, I LIKE TO CONTINUE WHAT I'M DOING BECAUSE I'M ENJOYING MYSELF, AND I WANT TO KEEP THE FLOW GOING FOR THE NEXT SHOTS. I WAS WORKING WITH DESIREE ON... I THINK IT WAS FAUCETT... AND THE CAMERA MAN SAID CUT, AND I CONTINUED EATING HER PUSSY. SHE PUSHED ME AWAY! I SAID 'OK, IF THAT'S THE WAY THAT YOU WANT IT', BUT FOR THE REST OF THE SCENE I WAS DISTURBED BY THAT. I DON'T WORK THAT WAY. I THOUGHT IT WAS REALLY COLD OF HER TO DO THAT.

JD: ANYONE ELSE?

LEMAY: JESSE ADAMS WAS ALSO DIFFICULT. HE'S A TALL, BLONDE ACTOR I DID A LOOP WITH, AND HE'S REALLY BIG. I MEAN HIS COCK. WE'RE FUCKING AND I TOLD HIM 'YOU'RE HURTING ME', CAUSE HE WAS JUST RAMMING INSIDE ME. HE WOULDN'T LISTEN TO ME. SO FINALLY I MOVED AROUND IN ANOTHER POSITION JUST TO GET HIS COCK OUT OF ME, AND I STARTED GIVING HIM HEAD. AND HE SCREAMED AT ME. TOLD ME THAT I WASN'T DOING IT RIGHT. HE CRAMMED IT DOWN MY THROAT. I WAS GAGGING. HE GOT ME SO UPSET THAT I STARTED CRYING.

JD: RINSE DREAM SAID YOU HAD TROUBLE WITH THE BLACK ACTOR ON **NIGHTDREAMS**.

LEMAY: OH YEAH, THE CREAM OF WHEAT SCENE. [EDITORS NOTE: LEMAY HAS SEX WITH A GUY WEARING A MASSIVE BOX OF CREAM OF WHEAT.] I WASN'T TOO CRAZY ABOUT THAT SCENE AT FIRST BECAUSE I'D NEVER WORKED WITH A BLACK GUY BEFORE. IT WASN'T SOMETHING THAT I DIDN'T WANT TO DO, I HAD JUST NEVER MET ONE

IN THAT SITUATION. RINSE TOLD ME BEFORE WE SHOT IT THAT THIS GUY HAD NEVER HAD A BLOWJOB BEFORE. I SAID 'WELL, I'LL HAVE TO MEET HIM AND GET HIM RELAXED. WELL, WHEN I MET HIM, HE WAS TOTALLY BOMBED. THE SCENE ACTUALLY WENT VERY WELL, HE GOT IT UP AND EVERYTHING. BUT WHEN WE TRIED FOR THE CUMSHOT, IT DIDN'T HAPPEN. WE WORKED ON IT FOR ABOUT TWO HOURS THEN I TOLD HIM TO JUST FORGET IT.

JD: DO YOUR FOLKS BACK HOME KNOW WHAT YOU DO?

LEMAY: MY MOM DOESN'T. BUT I WAS IN THAT MOVIE **10** FOR ABOUT TEN SECONDS, IN THE SCENE WHERE DUDLEY MOORE WALKS THROUGH THE NUDE PARTY. MY BROTHER AND MY SISTER-IN-LAW AND HER FAMILY WENT TO SEE IT. THEY'RE BORN-AGAIN CHRISTIANS, AND THEY GOT UP AND WALKED OUT WHEN THEY SAW ME. I GOT THIS FRANTIC CALL AT 2 IN THE MORNING FROM DAYTON, AND MY BROTHER SAID 'WHAT HAVE YOU DONE?! IT'S A SIN!'. SO I CALLED MY MOM AND TOLD HER THAT I'D DONE IT OF MY OWN FREE WILL -- NOBODY FORCED ME TO DO IT -- AND THAT I WAS PAID WELL FOR DOING IT. AND SHE DIDN'T MIND AT ALL AS SOON AS SHE KNEW THAT I HADN'T BEEN FORCED. BUT I DON'T KNOW HOW SHE'D REACT TO MY PORNO FILMS. I'M SURE SHE'LL FIND OUT SOMEDAY. MY BROTHER KNOWS. ONE OF HIS FRIENDS SAW ONE OF MY LOOPS AND TOLD HIM, SO HE WENT TO THE PEEPSHOW TO SEE IT.

JD: HAS MAKING PORN FILMS CHANGED YOUR SEX LIFE?

LEMAY: OH YEAH NOW MORE THAN EVER I'M LETTING IT ALL OUT. I'M DOING ALL MY FANTASIES. I'VE ALWAYS HAD THE FANTASY OF FUCKING OUT IN THE OPEN, AND I FUCKED A GUY IN AN UNDERGROUND PARKING LOT. I ALSO GAVE HEAD TO A GUY IN AN AIRPLANE. I JUST REACHED

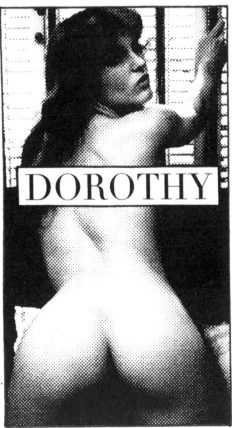

DOROTHY

121

OVER AND STARTED PLAYING WITH HIS COCK. I'D NEVER SEEN HIM BEFORE, AND I HAVEN'T SEEN HIM SINCE. I ALSO WANT TO STRAP ON A DILDO AND FUCK SOME GUY IN THE ASS, THE WAY LONI SANDERS FUCKS MY PUSSY IN **NIGHTDREAMS**. I WANT TO GET TIED UP SOME MORE TOO. I LIKE IT WHEN A GUY TIES ME UP AND BRINGS ME RIGHT TO THE POINT OF ORGASM

DESIREE COUSTEAU WAS A REAL **DICK HEAD** TO DOROTHY LEMAY

AND STOPS, OVER AND OVER. I **LOVE** IT! THIS GUY I'M FOOLING AROUND WITH RIGHT NOW HAS GOT A GOOD FETISH. THE OTHER DAY HE CAME ALL OVER MY FOOT, AND I CAME THE MOMENT HIS JISM SPURTED ON MY TOES -- I'D NEVER DONE **THAT** BEFORE. I'LL DO ANYTHING -- UNLESS IT'S IN FRONT OF A POLICE STATION.

◇ ◆ ◇ ◆ ◇ ◇

RETIRING IN 1985 AFTER AN 8 YEAR TENURE IN ADULT, TODAY DOROTHY IS BEST REMEMBERED FOR HER ROLE AS THE HORNY LITTLE SISTER SHERRY MCBRIDE IN THE INCEST-THEMED XXX CLASSICS **TABOO** (1980) AND **TABOO II** (1982).
　　　　　　　　　　　-BOUGIE

READER MAIL:

"I GOT TO GO TO SAN FRANCISCO FOR LITTLE OVER A WEEK IN AUGUST. IT WAS GREAT, JUST ME. MY FIRST NIGHT IN S.F. I HAD A REALLY CREEPY ENCOUNTER WITH THIS OLD ASIAN DUDE WHO BROKE INTO MY PORN BOOTH WHILE I WAS IN THERE MASTURBATING. HE JIMMIED THE DOOR OPEN WITH A CARD OR SOMETHING, THEN LOOKED AT ME AS I HAD MY DICK IN MY HAND. I THOUGHT HE WORKED THERE AND WAS GONNA ASK ME TO LEAVE! HAHA! HE GOT DOWN ON HIS KNEES AND OFFERED TO SUCK THE CUM OFF MY DICK AND HAND. EWWWW...! I SHOOED HIM OUT OF THE BOOTH, ZIPPED UP MY PANTS, AND JUST AS I WAS ABOUT READY TO LEAVE, I NOTICED THE PEEPHOLE GOING INTO THE BOOTH BESIDE MINE. THIS OTHER OLD PERVERT WATCHED EVERYTHING, AND I COULD HEAR HIM IN THERE WHEEZING AND BREATHING HEAVILY AS HE JACKED OFF IN THE BOOTH BESIDE ME.
FUCKING DISTURBING!"
　　　　　　-LONDON S. RED DEER, ALBERTA

THEY LOVES THAT FRESH MEAT! LONDON IS ONLY 19 YEARS OLD...

HELL UP IN HARLEM (1973)

THIS IS THE OFFICIAL SEQUEL TO LARRY COHEN'S **BLACK CAESAR**, WHICH CHARTED THE CAREER OF ITS TITULAR CHARACTER THROUGH HIS RISE TO DOMINANCE OVER HARLEM'S CRIMINAL UNDERWORLD, AND ENDING WITH HIS BLOODY DEATH. IF EVER A FILM COULD BE SAID TO HAVE **NOT** NEEDED A SEQUEL, BLACK CAESAR WAS IT.

ONLY ONE PROBLEM; IT WAS A HUGE HIT. SO LARRY WAS ENLISTED TO CONTINUE A STORY WITH NO LOGICAL MEANS OF CONTINUATION -- AND WORSE, HE HAD VERY LITTLE TIME IN WHICH TO DO IT. WHEN THE FIRST DAY OF HELL UP IN HARLEM'S SHOOTING SCHEDULE ARRIVED, THE SCRIPT WAS LITTLE MORE THAN A PLOT OUTLINE WITH A FEW KEY SCENES FLESHED OUT.

NOT SURPRISINGLY, COHEN ENDED UP WITH A TOTAL DUD. THE FILM IS ANAEMIC, AND HALF THE RUNNING TIME HAS NO APPARENT CONNECTION TO THE MAIN CHARACTERS' STORY ARCS. FAR TOO MANY SCENES WERE INCLUDED SOLELY BECAUSE COHEN HAPPENED TO HAVE FOUND A PRIME SHOOTING LOCATION AT A TIME WHEN HE STILL HAD ONLY THE VAGUEST IDEA WHAT HIS MOVIE WAS ABOUT.

AT LEAST IT HAD A COOL POSTER:

Black Godfather's Mad... and that's Real Bad!

Hell Up in Harlem

Samuel Z. Arkoff presents **FRED WILLIAMSON** in
"HELL UP IN HARLEM" A Larco Production
A Larry Cohen Film
Also Starring JULIUS W. HARRIS An American International Release
GLORIA HENDRY · MARGARET AVERY · D'URVILLE MARTIN
TONY KING · GERALD GORDON · BOBBY RAMSEN
Written, Produced and Directed by Larry Cohen
Musical Score by Fonce Mizell and Freddie Perren
Songs Performed by Edwin Starr · COLOR by Movielab
SOUND TRACK ALBUM AVAILABLE ON MOTOWN RECORDS AND TAPES
© 1973 American International Pictures, Inc.

HELL HOUSE (2001) Dir. George Ratliff

REBECCA AND I LINED UP FOR ALMOST 2 HOURS TO SEE THIS AT THE VANCOUVER INTERNATIONAL FILM FESTIVAL, AND WE **STILL** DIDN'T GET TICKETS. NEEDLESS TO SAY, IT WAS ONE OF THE BIG HITS OF THE FEST - AND FOR GOOD REASON. THIS VERY FUNNY AND SLIGHTLY SCARY DOCUMENTARY IS AN INSIGHTFUL LOOK AT AN EVANGELICAL CULT THAT USES A KIDS HALLOWEEN FUNHOUSE TO PREACH TO AND CONVERT NEW MEMBERS.

SPEAKING OF PREACHING... I WAS LISTENING TO THE DR. LAURA SCHLESSINGER RADIO TALK SHOW TODAY. HAVE YOU HEARD THIS? I REALLY LOVE IT. GETS ME ALL RILED UP. PEOPLE FROM ALL OVER NORTH AMERICA CALL IN (OVER 60,000 CALLERS A DAY!) AND ASK HER ADVICE ON THEIR VARIOUS DAILY QUANDARIES. THE "DOCTOR" THEN HAULS HER ASS ON UP TO HER IVORY TOWER OF MORAL SUPERIORITY, AND PROCEEDS TO BERATE AND NAG HER DEVOTED FLOCK LIKE THEY'RE 7 YEAR OLD RETARDS WITH SHIT-FILLED DIAPERS. ANYWAY, TODAY SHE WAS FERVENTLY BABBLING ABOUT HOW "SHACKING UP" AND "HAVING SEX OUT OF WEDLOCK" IS "THE MOST DISTURBING THING THERE IS".

UH... EVEN MORE DISTURBING THAN RUNNING OVER INFANTS WITH A TRACTOR? EVEN MORE DISTURBING THAN SLOWLY SLICING YOUR GENITALS WITH A RUSTY RAZOR? EVEN MORE DIS....

WELL ANYWAY, DR. LAURA IS A MORONIC HAG. HAVE YOU SEEN THIS HYPOCRITE'S UNALTERED NUDE PICTURES FLOATING AROUND? IT'S 100% FUN LISTENING TO HER ANGRILY RAIL AGAINST THE "IMMORAL" PEOPLE WHO MAKE/USE/SELL PORN WHILE YOU JACK OFF TO THE HOT PICTURES OF HER PALE BUT PERKY TITS AND HAIRY PUSSY. IT'S REALLY ONE OF THE SIMPLE (YET PURE) PLEASURES THAT LISTENERS OF HER SHOW ARE EVER LIKELY TO PARTAKE IN. SHIT, ESPECIALLY THAT SASSY ONE WITH HER LEGS SPREAD WIDE OPEN. GUHHHH....

MAN, WHEN THAT SHIT HIT THE FAN, I THOUGHT FOR SURE THAT LAURA WAS GONNA FINALLY DISAPPEAR UNDER SOME REMOTE RELIGIOUS ROCK SOMEWHERE. HER FIRST RATHER PATHETIC DEFENSE WAS TO DISHONESTLY CLAIM THE PHOTOS WERE FAKES. THEN, AFTER SHE QUICKLY LOST HER COURT CASE TO HAVE THEM SUPPRESSED, SHE GOT A FAT JUICY, PAINFUL LESSON IN HUMILITY WHEN SHE WENT ON THE AIR TO STATE THAT SHE FOUND THEM "EMBARRASSING". EVENTUALLY THE SOURCE WAS REVEALED TO BE VETERAN LOS ANGELES RADIO BROADCASTER BILL BALLANCE, A MAN WHO WAS PIVOTAL IN GETTING SCHLESSINGER HER START IN RADIO, AND TOOK THE PICS IN 1978 WHILE THE PAIR OF THEM WERE HAVING **AN AFFAIR** DURING HER FIRST MARRIAGE! OHHH.. **SWEET IRONY!** HOW I **ADORE** YE!

PERHAPS SACRAMENTO CA. JOURNALIST ANITA CREAMER PUT IT BEST: "SHE POSED IN PIGTAILS, HANDS ON HIPS. SHE SMILED BRIGHTLY FOR THE CAMERA, FLIRTING AND SAUCY AND DELIGHTED, NAKED AS THE DAY SHE WAS BORN. WE WOULDN'T BOTHER TO CARE IF SHE WEREN'T SUCH A SANCTIMONIOUS MEAN-SPIRITED, GOD AWFUL WITCH."

SHE'S NO DIFFERENT THAN RUSH LIMBAUGH, THAT FAT HATEFUL DOPE FIEND. WHAT THE HELL IS WITH THESE RIGHT WING RELIGIOUS NUTS? THEY JUDGE, CONDEMN, AND PREACH - AND THEN TAKE PART IN SINS JUST AS BAD OR WORSE THAN THOSE THEY WERE PISSING AND MOANING ABOUT IN THE FIRST PLACE. HOW ABOUT THE 237 PEDOPHILE PRIESTS IN BOSTON UP ON 45 MILLION DOLLARS WORTH OF RAPE AND MOLESTATION CHARGES? CHRIST, I REST MY CASE.

WAIT.... I DON'T WANNA REST MY CASE YET. I'M HAVING **WAAAAAY** TOO MUCH FUN RANTING! I REMEMBER ONE OF DR. LAURA'S CALLERS ASKING IF SHE SHOULD LET HER 9 YEAR OLD KID ATTEND A CO-ED SLEEPOVER PARTY. NOW, THIS PRUDISH SHIT-BAG RADIO HOST COULD HAVE SAID SOMETHING LIKE "THAT WOULD NOT BE PRACTICAL OR APPROPRIATE" OR SOME OTHER CONCERNED PARENTAL BULLSHIT, BUT INSTEAD THE INSANE HARPY FLEW OFF THE HANDLE AND ACCUSED THE PARENTS WHO WERE THROWING THE PARTY OF "LIVING OUT THEIR SEXUAL FANTASIES THROUGH THEIR CHILDREN". - SNORT- WHERE DOES SHE GET THIS STUFF?!

ANOTHER CLASSY MOMENT FROM A SHOW I HEARD LAST YEAR WAS WHEN SHE CLAIMED THAT SOCIETY CAN'T ALLOW GAY PEOPLE - OR AS SHE HORRIFICALLY CALLS THEM: "BIOLOGICAL ERRORS" - TO GET LEGALLY MARRIED BECAUSE "A LEGAL PRECEDENT WOULD BE SET" AND WE'D THEN HAVE TO "ALLOW PEOPLE WHO HAVE SEX WITH THEIR PARENTS TO GET MARRIED TO THEM". (??!?) THAT SHIT IS JUST CRAZY ENOUGH TO BE HILARIOUS. MIND YOU, HER HOMOPHOBIC COMMENTS WERE EVENTUALLY DETERMINED TO BE IN VIOLATION OF THE HUMAN RIGHTS PROVISION OF THE CANADIAN BROADCASTING CODE OF ETHICS, AND SHE THEN LOST THE MAJORITY OF HER STATIONS IN CANADA. LUCKILY C-FUN 1410 AM HERE IN VANCOUVER DIDN'T GET RID OF THE MENTALLY REPUGNANT COW.

THE IMPORTANT THING TO REMEMBER KIDS, IS THAT LAURA "SWEET ASS" SCHLESSINGER IS NEITHER A MEDICAL DOCTOR NOR ACCREDITED IN A DISCIPLINE ONE WOULD TRADITIONALLY LOOK TO FOR EXPERTISE IN MORAL, SOCIETAL, OR SPIRITUAL MATTERS. WHEN YOU GET ON THE HORN TO HER FOR ADVICE, YOU'RE ONLY TALKING TO A DISHONEST HYPOCRITICAL FUCKFACE WITH A RADIO SHOW. NOTHING MORE.

OH, AND **HELL HOUSE** IS ONE OF THE BETTER DOCUMENTARIES DEALING WITH EVANGELICAL CHRISTIAN FREAKS WHO SPEAK IN TONGUES, AND THE STRANGE ZEALOUS SUB-CULTURE THAT THEY FERVENTLY INHABIT. LOOK FOR THE HARD-TO-FIND PLEXIFILM DVD. IT'S LOADED WITH A TON OF EXTRA FEATURES, AND ONCE YOU GET IT YOU WON'T HAVE TO STAND AROUND FOR TWO HOURS HOPING THERE'LL BE ENOUGH SEATS IN YOUR HOUSE.

I SPREAD 4 THE LORD

"NO MAN WHO USES PORNOGRAPHY IS WORTHY OF FINDING A WIFE. IT'S A MORALLY BANKRUPT PRACTICE."

THAT'S RIGHT SCHLESSINGER... SPREAD 'EM, BABY!

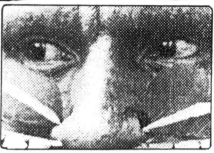

I STARTED COLLECTING CULT AND HORROR MOVIES ON TAPE IN THE LATE 80s - MOSTLY PIRATE COPIES FOR REASONS HAVING TO DO WITH BOTH COST AND AVAILABILITY. MOST OF THE FILMS I WANTED WERE BANNED IN MY NATIVE COUNTRY (NORWAY), BUT SOON I TRACKED DOWN **MONDO CANE** AND OTHER CREATIONS BY ITS DIRECTOR GUALTIERO JACOPETTI. BEFORE LONG I ALSO HAD LATER MONDO FILMS BY JACOPETTI'S COHORT ANTONIO CLIMATI AND OTHER ITALIANS LIKE MARIO MORRA, AND THE NOTORIOUS CASTIGLIONI BROTHERS RESPONSIBLE FOR **MONDO MAGIC** AND **SHOCKING AFRICA**. IN '97, I WAS IN NYC AND PICKED UP 3 MONDO TAPES FOR ONLY $3 EACH: **AFRICA: BLOOD AND GUTS**, **MONDO VIOLENCE** (AKA THIS VIOLENT WORLD) AND THE AFOREMENTIONED **MONDO MAGIC**.

FEW PEOPLE UNDER 50 HAVE EVEN SEEN THESE MOVIES IN A THEATER. IN THE LAST TWO YEARS I'VE MADE THE CINEMATEQUE IN OSLO DIG OUT THEIR OLD PRINTS OF **MONDO CANE** 1 AND 2 FROM THE VAULT (CONTAINING, AT LEAST IN PRINCIPLE - ONE PRINT OF EVERY FILM EVER SHOWN IN NORWEGIAN CINEMAS) AND SHOW THEM TO A WHOLE NEW GENERATION. THE FIRST SHOWING OF **MONDO CANE** WAS PRECEDED BY A MASSIVE MEDIA CAMPAIGN, SO A COUPLE HUNDRED PEOPLE SHOWED UP. I LECTURED ON THE MONDO GENRE AND SHOWED CLIPS FOR ABOUT 90 MINUTES BEFORE EVEN SHOWING THE MOVIE. BUT DESPITE THE BIG SCREEN IMAGE, THOSE 40 YEAR OLD WORN-OUT PRINTS WERE RATHER SAD COMPARED TO THE UTTER LUXURY OF AN AMAZING EIGHT DVD BOX SET FROM BLUE UNDERGROUND. YES, TECHNOPHILES REJOICE: ALL THE FILMS INCLUDED ARE COMPLETELY RESTORED FROM THE ORIGINAL NEGATIVES, SUDDENLY MAKING MY OLD VIDEO COPIES LOOK VERY FUZZY AND DATED.

SJOKKFILMEN FRA CANNES

MONDO CANE
ITALIENSK DOKUMENTAR-FILM
PROD. CINERITZ
CHNICOLOR

MONDO CANE (108 min.)

DESPITE WHAT YOU'VE HEARD, **MONDO CANE** WAS NOT THE FIRST OF ITS KIND. EDISON FILMED A HUMAN EXECUTION AND THE ELECTROCUTION OF AN ELEPHANT IN 1893, AND THE NOTORIOUS PROMOTER KROGER BABB PUSHED THE TRIBAL DOCUMENTARY **KARAMOJA** ON AMERICANS IN 1954. (HE LATER CAME BACK WITH THE RATHER INTENSE **KWAHERI** IN '64) NEVERTHELESS, THIS IS THE CLASSIC THAT MADE DOZENS OF LESSER TALENTS NAME THEIR MOVIES MONDO-SOMETHING TO CASH IN ON THIS FILM'S NOTIRIETY FOR A DECADE TO COME. HERE JACOPETTI AND PROSPERI (AND PAOLO CAVARA) ESTABLISHED THEIR TRADEMARK SARCASTIC NARRATION. LIVELY EDITING, AND HUMOROUS JUXTAPOSING OF IRONIC SCENES LIKE AMERICAN PET CEMETERIES WITH THE EATING OF DOGS IN KOREAN RESTAURANTS. THE FILM IS NO LONGER VERY SHOCKING, BUT IT'S STILL VISUALLY STUNNING AND NEVER BORING. TRANSLATED INTO ENGLISH AS "A DOG'S WORLD".

WOMEN OF THE WORLD (107 min.)

THIS FILM WAS RARELY SEEN SINCE ITS CINEMA RUN. IT'S A QUICKIE MOSTLY MADE UP OF LEFT OVERS FROM **MONDO CANE**. WE SEE WOMEN AROUND THE WORLD UNDERGOING VARIOUS FORMS OF TORTURE TO OBTAIN WHAT EVER HAPPENS TO BE CONSIDERED BEAUTY IN THEIR CORNER OF THE GLOBE. WE SEE WOMEN IN ISRAEL HAVING TO DO MILITARY SERVICE. (THERE ARE RUMORS THAT ONE OF THE LOVELY YOUNG ROUGHNECKS IS SEX ADVISER DOCTOR RUTH WESTHEIMER - AS SHE WAS IN THE ISRAELI WOMEN'S ELITE FORCES THE YEAR THIS WAS MADE.) AS THE BLURB GOES: "...THE FEMALE AS MOTHERS, MURDERERS, WARRIORS, AND WHORES." IT'S THE WEAKEST (AND MOST CASUALLY SEXIST) BUT IT'S STILL NICE TO BE ABLE TO FINALLY SEE IT. NARRATION BY PETER USTINOV.

MONDO CANE 2 (95 min.)

MORE OF THE SAME. SOME OF THE SCENES HERE WERE ALSO LEFT -OVERS FROM THE HUGELY POPULAR **MONDO CANE**. THEY VISIT A TRIBE WHERE IT'S CUSTOMARY FOR ALL THE GIRLS TO HAVE ONE KID BEFORE MARRYING, PROBABLY TO PROVE THEIR FERTILITY. KEEPING UP THE NASTY REMARKS, THE NARRATOR HAS TO GO AND REFER TO ONE OF THESE KIDS AS A "BASTARD". NICE ONE. INCLUDES THE INFAMOUS FAKE SCENE OF A MONK BURNING HIMSELF ALIVE, AND A HARROWING SPECTACLE FROM ITALY - WHERE DEVOUT CATHOLICS LICK THE STAIRS TO THE CHURCH UNTIL THEIR TONGUES BLEED.

AFRICA ADDIO - English Version (128 min.)
AFRICA ADDIO - Director's Cut (139 min.)

FROM THE OUTSET, J AND P MEANT TO MAKE ANOTHER EPISODIC, PARTLY LIGHT HEARTED DOCUMENTARY IN THEIR NOW FAMILIAR MONDO STYLE. THE END RESULT OF THEIR YEARS ON THE AFRICAN CONTINENT IS ONE OF THE MOST BRUTAL AND DEPRESSING FILMS YOU'RE EVER LIKELY TO SEE. MOST OF IT IS A NON-STOP INFERNO OF MINDLESS ANIMAL SLAUGHTER AND MERCILESS AFRICAN CIVIL WAR FOOTAGE.

I WAS ONLY FAMILIAR WITH THE UNAUTHORIZED "BLOOD AND GUTS" VERSION, WHICH CUT OUT 45 MINUTES, INCLUDING MOST OF THE HISTORICAL AND POLITICAL CONTEXT, LEAVING ONLY A

"IT'S A **DOGS** WORLD"

DART'04

CONFUSING GORE-FEST, NOW WE FINALLY GET TO SEE THE WHITE IMPERIALISTS ABANDONING AFRICA - LEAVING THE VARIOUS TRIBES TO FIGHT BETWEEN THEMSELVES. THE BACKGROUND AND NON-VIOLENT SCENES SHAPE THIS FROM A SCHOCKFEST INTO A REAL DOCUMENTARY, FULL OF UNIQUE FOOTAGE OF INCIDENTS WHERE JACOPETTI'S CREW WERE THE ONLY ONES PRESENT WITH CAMERAS. THE CRITICAL RESPONSE WAS SOMEWHAT SAVAGE ITSELF, WITH MANY PEOPLE CONSIDERING THE FILM TO BE OVERTLY RACIST. TOWARDS THE END THERE'S A LONG SCENE WITH WHITE MERCENARIES IN THE CONGO ROUTINELY EXECUTING BLACKS ON CAMERA THAT ARE SUPPOSEDLY GUILTY OF CRIMES. THE NARRATOR SAYS: "HE'LL NEVER FIGURE OUT WHY THE WHITES MAKE SUCH A FUSS TO FIND OUT WHO ATE THIS FELLOW'S LIVER... OR WHY THEY ARRESTED THOSE SOLDIERS WHO RAPED THOSE REBEL BITCHES IN THEIR CELLS." WHAT THE HELL?? THEY ALSO SEEMED TO BE MOSTLY CONCERNED WITH THE WHITE BOERS IN THE SECTION ON SOUTH AFRICA. THE FILMMAKERS ARE STILL PROUD OF THIS FILM AND CONSIDER IT TO BE AN IMPORTANT PIECE OF JOURNALISM. THEY WERE LATER ACCUSED OF ENCOURAGING THE VIOLENT EXECUTIONS SEEN IN THE FILM, AN ACCUSATION THEY BATTLED AGAINST AND WON OVER IN ITALIAN COURT.

ASIDE FROM THE LANGUAGE, THERE'S JUST MINOR DIFFERENCES BETWEEN THESE TWO CUTS. THERE'S SLIGHTLY MORE ANIMAL TORTURE IN THE ITALIAN DIRECTORS CUT.

"WOMEN OF THE WORLD"

★ FARGEFILM ★

Gualtiero Jacopetti's MONDE CANE
ble en verdens-suksess
NÅ KOMMER HANS
NYE SJOKKFILM
LA DONNA
NEL MONDO

GOODBYE UNCLE TOM:
THE MOST POLITICALLY INCORRECT FILM EVER?

GOODBYE UNCLE TOM - English Version (123 min.)
ADDIO ZIO TOM - Director's Cut (136 min.)

"UNCLE TOM" STANDS ON ITS OWN IN FILM HISTORY LIKE FEW MOVIES EVER MADE. SOMEHOW JACOPETTI AND PROSPERI THOUGHT IT WOULD BE A GOOD IDEA TO MAKE A FAKE MONDO FILM DEALING WITH AMERICAN SLAVE TRADE BACK IN THE 1800s. IN ORDER TO CREATE THIS DISTASTFUL AND UNFORGETTABLE FILM, J AND P WENT TO CHEVALIER'S HAITI AND LANDED CHEAP SETS AND EXTRAS FOR NEARLY 3 YEARS WITH THE QUIRKY DICTATOR'S BLESSING.

IN AN INTERESTING PSEUDO-DOCUMENTARY MOVE, THE TIME TRAVELLIN' JOURNALISTS ARE PRESENT BUT NOT SHOWN ON CAMERA - EXCEPT WHEN THEY ARRIVE IN A HELICOPTER (!). THIS FILM IS INSULTING, AND ON SO MANY LEVELS. FULL OF SNIDE AND CONDESCENDING DIALOG AND COMMENTARY - ALTHOUGH MOST OF IT IS JUST MEANT TO REFLECT THE ACTUAL ATTITUDES TOWARDS SLAVERY AT THE TIME. AS IT IS, THE FILMMAKERS NOW REGRET NOT INCLUDING SOME SORT OF DISCLAIMER WHEN THE FILM WAS RELEASED - TO MAKE CLEAR THAT THE RACIST ACTS AND OPINIONS EXPRESSED IN THE FILM WERE NOT THEIR OWN. EVEN IF YOU LOOK PAST THAT, JACOPETTI'S PEDOPHILIAC TENDENCIES SHINE THROUGH IN A SCENE WHERE NAKED YOUNG SLAVES OF BOTH SEXES ARE SOLD FOR $3000 EACH, AND IN SOME BEHIND-THE-SCENES SUPER-8 FOOTAGE THAT HAS JACOPETTI SWIMMING AND CAROUSING WITH A THRONG OF NEARLY NAKED PREPUBESCENT YOUNG HAITIANS.

IT'S TRUE THAT JACOPETTI'S POLITICAL SENSITIVITY WAS ALWAYS LIKE A BULL IN A CHINA STORE, AND BEING AN ITALIAN PRESENTING A VERY TOUCHY PART OF U.S. HISTORY DIDN'T HELP MATTERS MUCH EITHER. THIS FILM IS VIOLENT, EXPLOITATIONAL, AND OFFENSIVE NO MATTER WHICH VERSION YOU SEE, BUT THE LONG ITALIAN CUT IS THE "BEST", WITH ITS LONG PRESENT-DAY INTRO THAT HELPS A LITTLE TO PUT THINGS INTO PROSPECTIVE. A VERY NASTY ENDING WHERE BLACK MILITANTS BUTCHER AN ENTIRE WHITE FAMILY (INCLUDED IS A LITTLE BABY WHO IS SMASHED AGAINST A WALL) IS KEPT IN BOTH VERSIONS. APART FROM THAT, SCENES OFTEN SHOW UP IN A COMPLETELY DIFFERENT ORDER IN THE TWO CUTS - WHICH MAKES THESE TWO VERY DIFFERENT FILMS.

THIS ATROCITY CAUSED NEAR RIOTS AMONG BLACK CROWDS WHO CAME TO SEE THE FILM ON 42ND ST. IN NYC, AND COULDN'T BE SHOWN VERY MUCH IN THE US FOR THAT VERY REASON. WHEN YOU THINK ABOUT IT, THE DAY THIS MOVIE OPENED - WAS ALSO THE DAY JACOPETTI AND PROSPERI'S FILM CAREERS CAME TO A GRINDING HALT. AFTER THE CONTROVERSY OF **AFRICA ADDIO**, IT'S HARD TO GRASP HOW THEY EVER THOUGHT THIS INTENSE AND CONFRONTATIONAL FILM COULD EVER BE FAVORABLY RECEIVED.

THE GODFATHERS OF MONDO (90 min.) 2003

THE 8th DISC IS AN ALL NEW DOCUMENTARY ABOUT THIS GROUP OF MOVIES AND THE MEN WHO MADE THEM. WITH THE RARELY INTERVIEWED JACOPETTI AND PROSPERI, ALONG WITH COMPOSER RIZ ORTOLANI AND OTHERS. THIS IS A GREAT DOCUMENTARY, AND THOSE WITH LITTLE KNOWLEDGE OF THE MONDO GENRE WILL FIND IT REALLY FASCINATING AND QUITE INFORMATIVE.

EXTRAS:

ALL THE DISCS ARE JAM-PACKED WITH MANY FEATURES, EXCEPT THE ITALIAN VERSIONS AND THE **GODFATHERS**... DISC. GENERALLY THERE'S A VERY GENEROUS HELPING OF TRAILERS, (EVEN A VERY SCRATCHY COPY OF THE ULTRA RARE **AFRICA BLOOD AND GUTS** TRAILER!) POSTER AND PROMO ART, LOCATION STILLS AND LOBBY CARDS. **GOODBYE UNCLE TOM** ALSO HAS A WHOLE HOUR OF BEHIND-THE-SCENES 8MM FOOTAGE WITH COMMENTARY BY STILL PHOTOGRAPHER GIAMPAOLO LOMI, WHO SHOT IT.

BOUGIE '04

"MONDO-GO-GO" CONTINUED...

MONDO CANE HAS THE LITTLE LECTURE "THE UNOFFICIAL MONDO PHENOMENA" BY DAVID FLINT, AND OVERALL YOU'VE GOT DISCS FILLED WITH ALL KINDS OF RELEVANT MATERIAL AS BONUS FEATURES.

SURE, MONDOS ARE FREAKSHOWS. SURE, THEY'D LURE PEOPLE INTO THEATERS BY USING EVERY SET OF TITS THAT APPEAR IN THE MOVIE IN THE TRAILER AS WELL. SURE, THEY'D FAKE THE OCCASIONAL SCENE FOR DRAMATIC EFFECT... BUT TO MY MIND, THIS IS STILL THE MOST IMPORTANT PIECE OF FILM HISTORY TO BE RELEASED ON DVD THUS FAR. IF YOU'RE AT ALL INTERESTED IN THESE MOVIES AND YOU DON'T BOTHER TO GET THIS DVD BOX, YOU'RE JUST A FUCKIN' FOOL. LIST PRICE IS $150 U.S. BUT I GOT MINE FOR $94 AND SO CAN YOU IF YOU SHOP AROUND THE WEB. ONLY 10,000 NUMBERED COPIES WERE PUT ON THE MARKET, AND MOST COULD BE GONE BY NOW. THESE PEOPLE ALSO RELEASED A LONGER-THAN-EVER 100 MIN DVD EDITION OF D'AMATO'S BEASTIALITY PORN/SNUFF EPIC **EMANUELLE IN AMERICA**, SO YOU KNOW THEY MEAN BUSINESS.

WWW. BLUE-UNDERGROUND.COM

JAN BRUUN HAS BEEN WRITING FOR DOZENS OF PUBLICATIONS DURING THE LAST 20 YEARS. HIS WEBSITE IS AT:

HOME.ONLINE.NO/~JANBRUUN/

ZEBRA KILLER (1974 aka "Combat Cops")

NOT MANY REMEMBER THEM NOW, BUT THE ZEBRA MURDERS WERE A SERIES OF CONNECTED KILLINGS COMMITTED BY A BLACK SUPREMACIST SERIAL KILLER RING CALLED "THE DEATH ANGELS" WHICH TOOK PLACE IN SAN FRANCISCO FROM 1973 UNTIL 1974, AND WHICH LEFT AT LEAST 16 PEOPLE DEAD.

ACCORDING TO THE CULT'S BELIEFS, THE WHITE RACE WAS CREATED BY A KOOKY BLACK MAD SCIENTIST NAMED YAKUB WHO WANTED A RACE OF HONKEY INFERIORS TO RULE OVER. FURTHERMORE, THE DEATH ANGELS BELIEVED THEY COULD ACTUALLY EARN "POINTS" TOWARDS PARADISE IN THE AFTER-LIFE IF THEY KILLED AS MANY WHITES AS POSSIBLE BEFORE THEY KICKED THE BUCKET. EACH MEMBER WAS EXPECTED TO KILL AT LEAST (THEIR CHOICE:) 9 WHITE MEN, 5 WHITE WOMEN, OR 4 WHITE CHILDREN. I DON'T THINK ANY POINTS WERE AWARDED FOR WHITE DOGS.

DESPITE MULTIPLE PLOT HOLES, BAD ACTING AND VERY POOR PRODUCTION VALUES, A NUMBER OF KEEN SEQUENCES IN THE ZEBRA KILLER ARE INNOVATIVE AND ENTERTAINING. IT ALSO DESERVES SOME CINEMA SEWER KUDOS FOR BEING ONE OF THE **MOST** POLITICALLY INCORRECT RACESPLOITATION FILMS OF ALL TIME.

— BOUGIE

the **ZEBRA KILLER** HAS THE CITY IN PANIC

"NO BLACK MAN EVER KILLED LIKE THIS!!"

ARTHUR MARKS PRESENTS
the **ZEBRA KILLER**   COLOR
starring AUSTIN STOKER — JAMES PICKETT — HUGH SMITH
co-starring CHARLES KISSINGER — VALERIE ROGERS — TOM BROOKS — D'URVILE MARTIN AS "THE PIMP"
Screenplay by PHILIP HAZELTON   Produced by GORDON C. LANE & MIKE HENRY / Directed by WILLIAM CROFDER
A GENERAL FILM CORPORATION RELEASE   PG

FOUR OF THE APOCALYPSE (1975) Dir. by: Lucio Fulci

You know you're in for a treat when the write up on the back of a DVD starts with "Uncut. Uncensored. Unseen in over 25 years! The legendary blood-soaked western from the director of ZOMBIE and THE BEYOND." And it's a treat indeed.

The popularity of the spaghetti western was on the wane when films like A MAN CALLED BLADE and Fulci's FOUR OF THE APOCALYPSE were trotted out for an uninterested Italian audience, but each were important (not perfect) films in the genre's history.

The script is a rather interesting revenge story, but has a frustrating episodic feel which disrupts the flow of the narrative, and makes transitions between scenes and characters very rough-hewn and sloppy. On the plus side, Fulci devotes a fair amount of run-time to graphic brutality and even an odd cowboy-on-cowboy degradation scene involving booze. The film also looks gorgeous, thanks to the smooth cinematography of Sergio Salvati. The cast is also brilliant, with Fabio "Fabulous Testes" Testi in the lead, and nutzo Tomas Milian as the psychopath loner Chaco who kinda steals the show.

DART

"COME ON ARNOLD, TAKE OFF YOUR SHIRT !!"

DIFF'RENT STROKES: MY FAVORITE SICK-COM

A ROBIN BOUGIE JOINT

THE LOCATION WAS NEW YORK, AND THE CAST OF CHARACTERS FEATURED A WEALTHY WIDOWER NAMED PHILIP DRUMMOND (CONRAD BAIN) WHO LIVED IN A LUXURIOUS PENTHOUSE WITH HIS TEENAGE DAUGHTER KIMBERLY (DANA PLATO). DRUMMOND'S BLACK HOUSEKEEPER GREW SICK, AND UPON HER DEATHBED BEQUEATHED TO HER AFFLUENT BOSS HER TWO SONS, ARNOLD (GARY COLEMAN) AND WILLIS (TODD BRIDGES). THIS WAS THE GROUND BROKEN ON THE FIRST EPISODE OF DIFF'RENT STROKES - ENTITLED "MOVIN' IN", WHEN IT FIRST AIRED ON NOV. 3rd 1978. CRITICS HEAPED SHIT ALL OVER IT, WHILE HUGE AMOUNTS OF VIEWERS IGNORED THE CRITICS AND ATE THE SHOW UP.

THE SERIES, WHICH WAS ORIGINALLY TO BE NAMED "45 MINUTES FROM HARLEM", WAS IMMENSELY POPULAR, AND AT ITS PEAK HAD A STAGGERING 41 MILLION VIEWERS WHO WOULD TUNE IN WEEKLY TO HEAR PUDGY FACED ARNOLD SPOUT HIS CATCH PHRASE: "WHATCHOO TALKIN' 'BOUT, WILLIS?". (TRIVIA: WHEN IN SYNDICATION ON JAPANESE TV, THE LINE IS TRANSLATED FOR VIEWERS AS "JOKE ONLY ABOUT YOUR FACE.")

THE LAST EPISODE AIRED ON AUG. 30th 1986, BUT NOT BEFORE SERIOUSLY FUCKED-UP POOP SHOT DOWN THE CHUTE ON THIS BALSY-YET-INSIPID SERIES. MUCH HAS BEEN MADE OF ALL THE TRAGIC TABLOID WORTHY GOINGS-ON WITH THE FORMER CHILD STAR CAST AFTER THE SERIES WRAPPED, BUT LITTLE WAS SAID - THEN OR NOW - ABOUT WHAT A DRIVING FORCE FOR SAVAGERY AND PERVERSION THIS SITUATION COMEDY COULD OCCASIONALLY BE WHILE IT WAS IN THE MORALISTIC THROWS OF ENTERTAINING (AND PURPORTING TO TEACH) THE YOUTH OF AMERICA.

FIRST OFF, KEEP IN MIND THAT THIS WAS THE LATE 70s AND EARLY 80s. CHILDREN'S TV PROGRAMMING LIKE DIFF'RENT STROKES CERTAINLY WASN'T THE FIRST PLACE YOU'D THINK TO LOOK FOR THE JAW-DROPPING TOPICS ITS MIDDLE AGE WRITERS WERE BESTOWING UPON VIEWERS IN THE LATTER YEARS OF ITS 8 SEASON RUN. I'M GUESSING THEY MEANT WELL, BUT SOME OF THESE STORY LINES SEEM RIPPED FROM THE PAGES OF PULP NOVELS AND X-RATED GRINDHOUSE FILMS.

THAT'S NOT TO SAY THAT POOR MORALS AND DEBAUCHERY WERE ON DISPLAY IN **EVERY** 30 MINUTE EPISODE. MOST OF THE TIME THE DRUMMOND CLAN WAS IMMERSED IN THE USUAL BORING LIFE-LESSONS ABOUT HONESTY, GOOD MANNERS AND ALL THAT OTHER FAMILY VALUES HORSESHIT. BUT.... THEN THERE WAS:

JOKE ONLY ABOUT YOUR FACE, WILLIS!

ARNOLD AND DUDLEY FRAMING KAREEM ABDUL JABAR AS A CHILD-BEATER. (EPISODE 103) "BY TOMORROW, HE'LL JUST BE A TALL BLACK MEMORY!" POOR KAREEM!

KIMBERLY GETTING BULIMIA (EPISODE 181). "I WANT THE PERFECT BODY, AND I'LL DO ANYTHING TO GET IT. ~~ANYTHING~~ !!!" THRILL TO DANA PLATO'S OVER-THE-TOP EMOTING!

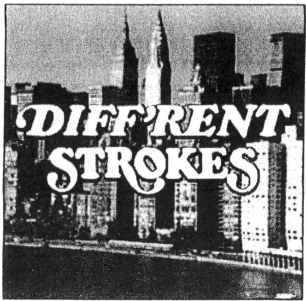
DIFF'RENT STROKES

WILLIS JOINING A GANG CALLED THE SCORPIONS, AND GETTING PUT IN JAIL. (EPISODE 50) "I'M VERY, VERY DISAPPOINTED IN YOU, WILLIS!" HARSH!

IN RECENT YEARS, I'VE NOTICED AN ODD TRICKLE-DOWN EFFECT ON THE PUBLIC'S PSYCHE CAUSED BY THE SHOW. I'VE READ INTERNET BOARD DISCUSSION POSTINGS WHERE PEOPLE SPEAK OF PSEUDO TRAUMATIC MEMORIES INVOLVING THINGS THEY WITNESSED ON THE SHOW AS KIDS. MANY HAVE A HARD TIME BELIEVING THE THINGS THEY SAW WEREN'T IMAGINED OR ALL PART OF SOME SURREAL CHILDHOOD NIGHTMARE INVOLVING TV PERSONALITIES.

KEEP CALM MY BABIES. THOSE THINGS REALLY HAPPENED. AND ON YOUR SACRED TRUSTWORTHY TV NO LESS. BUT IF WE TALK ABOUT IT, WE **CAN** LEARN TO HEAL.

THE MOST HARROWING OF THESE TELEVISED NIGHTMARES WAS A TWO PART STOMACH-TURNER CALLED "THE BICYCLE MAN" THAT AIRED IN FEB. 1983 DURING SEASON 5. IN IT, GORDON JUMP PLAYS A CHILD MOLESTER/BIKE SHOP OWNER NAMED HORTON WHO ENTICES ARNOLD AND HIS PAL DUDLEY TO MAKE PRIVATE VISITS TO HIS HOME SO HE CAN TRY AND GET THEM NAKED AND MACK ON 'EM.

PEOPLE... THE LATE GORDON JUMP WAS THE FUCKIN' MAYTAG REPAIR MAN! ONE OF THE MOST SEXLESS CHARACTERS IN TV HISTORY! WHAT IS THE MOST

WHAT A FESTIVE **JEST** IT IS TO BE MOLESTED !!

OUTSPOKEN MORMON IN SHOW BIZ DOING ON A TV PROGRAM SHOWING A COUPLE OF UNDERAGE BOYS HIS SHOE BOX FULL OF NAKED-KID POLAROIDS ?? ISN'T THAT KINDA LIKE BEING GANG RAPED BY THE CAST OF 'SESAME STREET OR SOMETHING?!

ANYWAY, AFTER THE PRECOCIOUS TYKES ARE LURED INTO HIS BIKESHOP/BACHELOR PAD UNDER THE FALSE PRETEXT OF EATING PIZZA AND CHOCOLATE SUNDAES, HORTON PULLS OUT A PORN MAG CALLED "CUTIE" FOR THE LADS TO OOGLE, CAUSING DUDLEY TO YELL "THESE LADIES ARE **NEKKID**!!" TO WHICH ARNOLD BREATHLESSLY EXCLAIMS "EXCEPT FOR THE LEATHER BOOTS!!"

AFTER THIS CRASH COURSE IN THE WONDERS OF PUSSY, HORTON GETS THE BOYS BOOZED UP ON WINE AND CONVINCES DUDLEY TO TAKE OFF HIS SHIRT AND CLIMB ON HIS FAT LUMPY BACK SO THEY CAN PLAY "KING OF THE JUNGLE". ARNOLD JOINS IN BY DONNING A SAFARI HAT AND SNAPPING PICTURES FOR HORTON'S COLLECTION. BEFORE LONG THEY MOVE ON TO A ROUSING GAME OF "TRAMPOLINE." MOST KIDS DON'T REMOVE THEIR SHIRTS AND JUMP UP AND DOWN ON AN OLD FAT MAN'S BED AFTER DOWNING A BOTTLE OF WINE - BUT I SUPPOSE NO ONE CAN ACCUSE GARY COLEMAN OR THE WISE CRACKIN' CHARACTER HE PLAYED ON DIFF'RENT STROKES OF BEING AVERAGE.

DURING ANOTHER VISIT, HORTON (WHO NOW WANTS THE KIDS TO CALL HIM "CURLY") TROTS OUT A SHOEBOX OF NAKED PHOTOS OF HIMSELF POSING WITH OTHER CHILDREN AND SOME X-RATED CARTOONS TO WATCH. NOW BEFORE I DESCRIBE ANYMORE, I SHOULD STOP THE CAR AND POINT SOMETHING OUT. THERE ARE JUST **TOO MANY** VALID REASONS WHY ARNOLD SHOULD HAVE BEEN TIPPED OFF TO HORTON'S LITTLE-BOY-CRAVING HORNDOGGERY. THE TWO MAJOR ONES BEING:

1. THE BOYS' CHARACTERS WERE 13. MAYBE AN 8 YEAR OLD WOULDN'T PICK UP ON A CREEPY OL' FAT MAYTAG MAN TRYING TO GET INTO HIS PANTS, BUT THESE TWO SHOULD HAVE HAD ALARM BELLS GOING OFF WHEN THE CARTOON MOUSE PORN GOT TROTTED OUT.

2. THE DUDLEY FACTOR: ARNOLD KNEW HE WAS THE ONLY BEING ON EARTH WHO COULD STAND TO BE AROUND DUDLEY LONGER THAN 5 MINUTES. IT WAS A TOTAL PITY FRIENDSHIP. ARNOLD WAS THROWING

8:00PM
Diff'rent Strokes
Join everybody's lovable 10-year-old, all his friends and some of his enemies in the fun and foolery!
Conrad Bain, Gary Coleman, Todd Bridges, Dana Plato, Charlotte Rae

ENEMIES AS A SELLING POINT ?!

THE DUD-MAN A BONE. HE SHOULD HAVE KNOWN SOMETHING WAS ROTTEN WHEN "CURLY" WAS DESPERATE TO NOT ONLY HAVE DUDS HANG OUT AN' CHILL, BUT TO DO SO SANS CLOTHING. UNFORGIVABLE.

FINALLY, ARNOLD GETS BORED AND **LEAVES** HIS POOR FRIEND TO THE ADVANCES OF THE DERANGED W.K.R.P. PERVERT, ONLY TO ARRIVE AT HOME AND CASUALLY TELL THE HOMESTEAD WHAT WAS GOING DOWN. CONRAD BAIN FLIPS AND GETS ON THE HORN TO THE FUZZ DOUBLE-QUICK. WHEN DRUMMOND, DUDLEY'S DAD, AND THE COPS ALL BUST IN, HORTON IS CAUGHT RED-HANDED WITH THE BOY IN THE BATHROOM PLAYING 'FLESHY PINK SUBMARINE' OR SOME SUCH SICK PEDO PAST TIME. (THAT SCENE IS BEHIND CLOSED DOORS...)

"HE GAVE ME A PILL. HE SAID IT WOULD MAKE ME FEEL GOOD" A GROGGY DRUNK AND STONED DUDLEY EXPLAINS TO HIS POPS.

AND HOLY **SHIT**...TO ADD INSULT TO SITCOM INJURY, DUDLEY'S DAD IS JUST ABOUT THE WORST FUCKING PROFESSIONAL ACTOR IN THE HISTORY OF TV. HIS FACE IS AN EMOTIONLESS BLANK SLATE AS HE CONFRONTS HIS SON ABOUT HIS ORDEAL. "IT'S NOT YOUR FAULT, SON." HE BLANDLY INTONES. DUDE MAY AS WELL HAVE BEEN READING HIS GROCERY LIST. HILARIOUS! IT'S LIKE SOME KINDA NIGHTMARE.

AS A COUPLE OF SIDE NOTES... THE BICYCLE MAN DEBACLE WAS REFERENCED ON AN EPISODE OF THE SATIRICAL ANIMATED SERIES **FAMILY GUY**. THE SCENE WITH ARNOLD AND DUDLEY CHILLIN' AT MR. HORTON'S PAD IS RECREATED JUST LONG ENOUGH TO SHOW "CURLY" BENDING OVER AND SAYING "ALL RIGHT, NOW I WANT YOU BOYS TO SCREAM REAL LOUD AT MY ASS."

AS USUAL, THERE ARE THE USUAL (PROBABLY UNTRUE) FANDOM RUMORS. ONE IS THAT THERE WAS A SCENE LEFT ON THE CUTTING ROOM FLOOR

I JUST **GOTTA** BE A MEMBER OF THE SCORPIONS, DAD!

WHERE HORTON WAS SNIFFING THE LITTLE BIKE SEATS ON HIS DISPLAY MODELS. APPARENTLY CONRAD BAIN WAS UPSET THAT THE SCENE WAS CUT, BECAUSE WITHOUT IT, THE BOY-FUCKER WAS LESS CREEPY AND EASIER FOR THE AUDIENCE TO PITY.

IF THAT WAS THE ONLY OUT-OF-CONTROL EPISODE TO SPEAK OF, THEN PERHAPS ONE COULD SIMPLY DEEM IT A DERANGED ANOMALY AND GIVE D.S. A CLEAN BILL OF HEALTH. BUT WHAT ABOUT EPISODE 179 ("SPEAK NO EVIL") IN WHICH A WHITE SUPREMACY GROUP COMES TO ARNOLD'S SCHOOL TO TALK ABOUT THE MASTER RACE TO STUDENTS? HE AND DUDLEY MAKE PLANS TO THROW ROTTEN FRUIT, ONLY TO BE STOPPED BY MR. DRUMMOND - WHO EXPLAINS TO ARNOLD THAT SINCE THEY LIVE IN THE USA AND LIVE BY THE RULES OF FREE SPEECH - RACISTS THEREBY HAVE THE RIGHT TO PREACH HATE IN JUNIOR HIGH SCHOOLS. (??)

OR BETTER STILL, HOW ABOUT EPISODES 138 AND 139 FROM JAN. 1984 ("THE HITCH-HIKERS") WHERE ARNOLD AND KIMBERLY THUMBED A RIDE WITH A WEIRD GRAPHIC DESIGNER FOR NASA? AFTER GETTING THEM HOME, HOG-TYING AND LOCKING A HORRIFIED ARNOLD IN A SIDE ROOM, THIS NEBBISH PSYCHO PUT THE MOVES ON THE FEMALE DRUMMOND HEIR - WHO WAS CLEARLY APPALLED BY HIS LUSTY ADVANCES. SOME SORT OF ALL-TIME-CREEPY-SITCOM-MOMENT AWARD SHOULD BE GIVEN OUT FOR THE FOLLOWING SCENE WHERE THIS MIDDLE AGED NERD-RAPIST DOES A SLOW DANCE WITH A SOFTLY SOBBING KIMBERLY TO "STRANGERS IN THE NIGHT", WHILE A HOGTIED ARNOLD HOWLS HIS DISAPPROVAL THROUGH HIS ELECTRICAL TAPE GAG.

ARNOLD DEFTLY ESCAPES WITH HIS LIFE BY SMASHING A WINDOW, BUT IS SO 'TRAUMATIZED' BY HIS ABUSIVE EXPERIENCE THAT HE HAS TO BE PUT UNDER HYPNOSIS TO REMEMBER HOW TO FIND THE APARTMENT WHERE POOR DANA PLATO IS STILL TRAPPED. THE SURREAL REARS ITS UGLY HEAD AS ARNOLD CRACKS LAUGH TRACK-ADDLED JOKES ABOUT EATING POPCORN AND DOGS, EVEN WHILE HIS PALE YUPPIE SISTER IS IN A RED-LIT DARKROOM MAKING DISTURBING LITTLE SEXY MOANS AND WHIMPERS AS THE DERANGED 'ROCKET MAN' TIGHTLY GRASPS HER WRISTS AND PUSHES HIS WEIGHT UPON HER. REMEMBER THAT TWISTED SITCOM SCENE IN **NATURAL BORN KILLERS**? LIKE THAT, ONLY NOT SATIRICAL.

ARNOLD TAKES A BREAK FROM BEING AN ASS-HAT ONLY LONG ENOUGH TO RECALL A LICENSE PLATE NUMBER. MERE MINUTES LATER THE COPS ARRIVE JUST IN TIME TO SAVE SOME HYSTERICAL TEENAGE VIRGINITY. GOD BLESS THE N.Y.P.D.! DURING THE SHOW'S OBLIGATORY WRAP UP, KIMBERLY AND ARNOLD - SHOWING ZERO NEGATIVE PSYCHOLOGICAL EFFECTS FROM THE DAY'S EARLIER EVENTS - CELEBRATE THE FUN THEY'VE HAD WITH A PARTY! WEEEEEEEEEEEEEEEE!!!! WHAT A FESTIVE JEST IT IS TO BE KIDNAPPED AND MOLESTED! PASS THE ICE CREAM!

THE FACTS OF LIFE (A D.S. SPIN-OFF SERIES ALSO FEATURING A YOUTHFUL CAST) MUST HAVE EMPLOYED A FEW OF THE SAME SADISTIC WRITERS. IN ONE EPISODE UNDERAGE TOOTIE DREAMS OF BECOMING A MODEL, AND TRIES HER DARNDEST TO FOLLOW THAT DREAM. BUT IT'S UP TO HOUSE-MOM MRS. GARRETT TO BUTT IN AFTER SHE'S MADE PRIVY TO HOW "PROVACATIVE" THE SHOOT WILL BE. WILL TOOTIE END UP ON THE COVER OF YOUNG BLACK TAIL?? TUNE IN AND SEE! OR HOW ABOUT ANOTHER EPISODE WHERE POOR TOOTIE IS ALMOST LURED INTO A SHAMEFUL LIFE OF PROSTITUTION WHILE ON A SIMPLE INNOCENT TRIP TO THE BIG CITY? WHOOP! TOOTIE WOULDA MADE A DAMN GOOD HO, Y'ALL!

THEY JUST DON'T MAKE SITCOMS LIKE THEY USED TO. PERHAPS THAT'S A GOOD THING. I GOT RID OF MY CABLE TV A FEW YEARS AGO IN FAVOR OF HAVING MORE TIME TO WORK ON CINEMA SEWER AND WATCH MOVIES. I'D HATE TO THINK I WAS MISSING FAMILY ENTERTAINMENT AS INSANE, SLEAZY, AND NIGHTMARISH AS GOOD OL' DIFF'RENT STROKES.

— ROBIN BOUGIE '03

She entered young and innocent, but came out the

Naked Rider ®

In Color

WOOO-WEEE! I LOVES ME A DONKEYCOCK SIZED DOSE OF SOUTHERN-FRIED CINEMA! IN THIS ONE, A FAT JACKASS NAMED "BIG JIM" OWNS EVERYTHING IN A SMALL RURAL TOWN, INCLUDING THE WOMEN! WHILE THE OTHER YOUNG BUCKS GO DUCK HUNTING, SWEATY OL' JIM BOFFS THEIR GALS, BUT BACK AT THE RANCH, HIS BORED YOUNG TROPHY WIFE MELODY IS IMPRISONED IN HER OWN HOME. SHE'S PAID A VISIT BY SNEAKY SAM, A HORSE (AND PUSSY) TRAINER WHO COAXES HER FROM HER GILDED CAGE AND DOWN TO THE STABLES -- IF YOU KNOW WHAT I MEAN.

THE TWO BECOME FAST PALS AND TORRID BOINKING-BUDDIES, BUT BEFORE YOU KNOW IT, BIG JIM COMES HOME AND RAGES OFF WHEN HE REALIZES THE MRS. STEPPED FOOT OUTTA THE HOUSE WITHOUT PERMISSION. ANGERED LIKE THE WILD INBRED REDNECK HE IS, HE STOMPS DOWN TO THE STABLES AND PUTS HIS COWERING BITCH IN HER PLACE, AND THEN GOES OUT HIMSELF FOR A MIDNIGHT MUFF MEETING WITH ONE O' THE LOCAL "COLORED GALS."

EVENTUALLY, AND MUCH TO MY RELIEF, MELODY GROWS A BRAIN AND DECIDES TO TRY AND RUN AWAY WITH STUDLY SAM, WHICH PREDICTABLY LEADS TO A BIGTIME COWSHIT-COVERED FISTICUFF BLOWOUT BETWEEN THE TWO HAIRY MANLY MEN. WILL IT END IN TEARS?!

THIS 1973 DRIVE-IN MOVIE WAS FINELY DIRECTED BY WILLIAM DIEHL JR, AND IS A SURPRISINGLY WELL TOLD LITTLE TALE WELL WORTH A LOOK NOW THAT IT'S OUT ON DVD FROM SOMETHING WEIRD VIDEO.

"I THINK WHAT CINEMA SEWER WILL BE PRAISED FOR BY MY BOYFRIEND, IS HOW FUCKING **HORNY** IT GETS ME! OFTEN AFTER I DID START READING YOUR BOOK, I'D END UP WITH HIS CUM ON MY TITS. SO, UM, THANX I GUESS.

YOUR FAN,"

T. SCOTT (CINEMA SEWER SUPERFAN)

GODMONSTER
☆ OF INDIAN FLATS ☆

I BET THE GEEKIER AND MORE KNOWLEDGEABLE MOVIE FANS AMONGST CINEMA SEWER'S READERS WOULD PICK THE CHEESIEST MONSTER EVER CREATED FOR A FILM AS THE ROLLED-UP-RUG THING FROM **THE CREEPING TERROR** (1964) OR THE RETARDED BIRD PUPPET FROM **THE GIANT CLAW** (1957). WELL, YOU COULD BE RIGHT, BUT ALLOW ME TO NOMINATE ANOTHER CONTESTANT FOR THE SWEEPSTAKES: THE 9 FOOT MUTATED SHEEP BETTER KNOWN AS **THE GODMONSTER OF INDIAN FLATS**. DID I SAY "A SHEEP"? WELL, THATS WHAT I'M TOLD. TO BE HONEST, HE LOOKS FAR MORE LIKE A GIANT SLOTH OR SNUFFALUFAGUS FROM SESAME STREET WITH THE MANGE. DIRECTOR FRED HOBBS PRODUCED, WROTE, DIRECTED, AND EVEN MADE THE COSTUME FOR THE GODMONSTER - AND MY GUESS IS THAT HE BOUGHT ALL THE MATERIALS HE'D NEED AT THE THRIFT STORE.

A RICH OIL-BARON LANDOWNER (PLAYED BY RUSS MEYER REGULAR STUART LANCASTER) WANTS TO KEEP HIS LITTLE NEVADA DESERT TOWN OF COMSTOCK FAITHFUL TO THE OLD WEST AS A MEANS OF KEEPING TOURISTS FLOODING THE AREA AND MAKING HIM A RICH(ER) MAN. LANCASTER INSURES HIS DICTATOR-LIKE POWER OVER THE TOWN WITH A GROUP OF GUNSLINGIN' THUGS HE CALLS "THE 601".

MEANWHILE, ACROSS TOWN IN DR. CLEMENS'S (E. KERRIGAN PRESCOTT) LAB, A FETUS CREATURE FOUND IN A SHEEP PEN IS STEADILY EVOLVING INTO A DORKY WOOL COAT-COVERED THING WITH AN OBVIOUS PAPIER MACHE HEAD AND A CURIOUS T-REX SHAPED BODY REPLETE WITH PERHAPS THE **BIGGEST** ASS ON ANY CREATURE IN MOVIE MONSTER HISTORY.

GRNK!

THE 'GODMONSTER' IS INADVERTENTLY SET FREE BY THE 601, AND MANAGES TO RUIN A LITTLE GIRLS PICNIC. LATER, A GAS STATION IS BLOWN UP DUE TO A PANIC-STRICKEN PUMP-JOCKEY WHO SCREAMS AT THE SIGHT OF THE GODMONSTER'S HUGE BUTTOCKS. THE CREATURE CONTINUES TO 'RUN' LOOSE, AND MANAGES TO DANCE WITH A HIPPY-CHICK, BEFORE PAUSING TO KILL SOME PEOPLE. HOW THIS ACTUALLY TRANSPIRES IS A MYSTERY, SINCE THE WADDLING MAMMAL SEEMS BARELY ABLE TO WALK, AND HAS LIMP APPENDAGES THAT SWAY FROM SIDE TO SIDE IN A VERY UNMENACING MANNER. HE ALSO BARFS YELLOW SMOKE WHEN FEELING UPSET.

EVENTUALLY THE SHEEP-TASTIC OGRE IS LASSOED BY A COWBOY POSSE ON HORSEBACK, AND BROUGHT FORTH BEFORE THE SIMPLE TOWNSFOLK IN A CAGE MOUNTED ON THE BACK OF A PICK-UP - WHICH IS THEN PROMPTLY PARKED IN THE TOWN DUMP WHERE EVERYONE GATHERS. EVIL OIL-BARON LANCASTER ANNOUNCES THAT HE WILL MAKE ALL THE TOURIST-BASED MOOLAH OFF OF "THE DAMAGED MONGOLOID BEAST". THE CROWD LIKES HIS IDEA AND RHUBARBS ITS APPROVAL. THEN SOMEONE YELLS "HE SOLD US ALL OUT! HE'S LYING!" AND THE PLEASED CROWD TURNS INEXPLICABLY VIOLENT AND NASTY IN A HEARTBEAT.

THE ENSUING RIOT IS PORTRAYED IN A WAY THAT CAN ONLY BE CALLED A MIXTURE OF THE MORONIC AND SURREAL. FIRST THERE ARE THE DUBBED-IN VOICES OF MONOTONE CHILDREN THAT REPEAT "LIES. LIES. LIES." OVER AND OVER. THEN PEOPLE START POINTING AT THE HELPLESS GODMONSTER IN ITS CAGE AND SCREAM "KILL IT!" BEFORE PICKING UP GARBAGE AND THROWING IT DOWN A CLIFF, ONLY TO RACE DOWN THE SAME HILL AT TOP SPEED THEMSELVES. I DON'T KNOW IF THATS HOW PEOPLE RIOT IN NEVADA, BUT IT SURE ISN'T HOW I WAS BROUGHT UP TO DO IT.

THE POOR FAT-ASSED GODMONSTER IS KILLED IN THE STUPID GARBAGE THROWING INCIDENT, AS ARE SEVERAL OLD WEST GUNFIGHTERS WHO APPEAR OUT OF NOWHERE. LANCASTER IS LEFT TO HIMSELF ON A PODIUM IN THE TRASH HEAP, AND MANIACALLY LAUGHS AND HOWLS "TIME IS THE ETERNAL JUDGE OF EVENTS!!" BEFORE THE CAMERA PANS AWAY TO SOME GRAZING SHEEP WITH OBVIOUS HUMAN VOICES THAT GO "BAA". A BRILLIANT END TO A BRILLIANT MOVIE. WEEEE-HEE-HEE!!!

NNN NNG!

IN 2001, THE GOOD FOLK AT SOMETHING WEIRD VIDEO TURNED THIS 1973 SHLOCK-CLASSIC LOOSE ON AN UNSUSPECTING PUBLIC WITH A MARVELOUS DVD SPECIAL EDITION WITH OVER 2 HOURS OF (MOSTLY UNRELATED) SPECIAL FEATURES - INCLUDING THE AMAZINGLY INEPT HIPPIE/BIGFOOT RAPE MOVIE "THE GEEK", WHICH WAS REVIEWED BACK IN CINEMA SEWER #11. YOU'LL ALSO THRILL TO THE CARNIVAL GEEK HORRORS IN THE 70 MINUTE 1964 FILM **PASSION IN THE SUN** (AKA "THE GIRL AND THE GEEK") YOU'VE GOTTA FIND THIS DVD. YOU WILL CHERISH IT AS YOU WOULD A TASTY HOT FUDGE SUNDAE.

PROVIDING YOU LIKE HOT FUDGE AND ARE NOT LACTOSE INTOLERANT.

— BOUGIE '03

GODMONSTER ART BY REBECCA DART '03

Best Endsongs (YET ANOTHER STUPID LIST...)

YOU KNOW WHAT I'M TALKIN' ABOUT. THOSE SONGS THAT START UP AS A STINGER DURING THE FINAL SCENE OF A MOVIE AND PLAY OUT OVER THE CREDITS. THE RIGHT SONG MAKES ALL THE DIFFERENCE. WHEN A FILM MAKER PLAYS THE GAME RIGHT, THAT SHIT SWELLS UP OUTTA NOWHERE AND PLASTERS FREAKY GOOSEBUMPS UP AND DOWN YOUR ARMS AND YOU'RE ALL LIKE "THEY JUST TOTALLY SAVED THE DAY WITH THAT SONG."

IT'S ALL ABOUT EDITING. THE WAY THE IMAGES AND MUSIC COMMINGLE TOGETHER. AND WHEN IT'S DONE WITH STYLE, IT'S MAGIC.

HERE'S MY PERSONAL TOP 10 EXAMPLES OF PRE-EXISTING SONGS THAT WERE WISELY MADE INTO AMAZING "ENDSONGS" (WARNING: SPOILERS TO FOLLOW)

1. HEAT (1995) - MOBY - "GOD MOVING OVER THE FACE OF THE WATERS" AFTER BLASTING A CAP IN HIS ASS, AL PACINO REACHES DOWN AND HOLDS ROBERT DENIRO'S HAND WHILE POOR ROBBIE RAPIDLY EXPIRES. MOBY IS CUED AND USED TO BRILLIANT EFFECT.

2. FIGHT CLUB (1999) - THE PIXIES - "WHERE IS MY MIND?" ED NORTON'S PLAN TO BLOW UP A VERY WORLD-TRADE-CENTER-ESQUE FINANCIAL HUB OF SKYSCRAPERS COMES TO IT'S 9-11 FRUITION JUST AS KIM DEAL COO'S HER FIRST ECHOED "HOOOOO" OF "WHERE IS MY MIND?". WOW. MORE LIKE, WHERE IS MY WALLET? THIS DVD IS A MUST-BUY.

3. LOST IN TRANSLATION (2003) - JESUS AND MARY CHAIN - "JUST LIKE HONEY". CRUNCHY OL' BILL MURRAY GIVES CUTE-AS-FUCK SCARLETT JOHANNSON A SMOOTCHIE AND A HUGLET BEFORE THE TWO GO THEIR SEPARATE WAYS. THE IMMENSE SPRAWLING ANTHILL SCENERY OF A GLORIOUSLY GREY TOKYO IS PAIRED WITH "JUST LIKE HONEY" AND THE WORLD WEEPS.

4. THE KILLING FIELDS (1984) JOHN LENNON - "IMAGINE". I DEFY YOU TO NOT FEEL YOUR HEART VIOLENTLY RIPPED FROM YOUR CHEST AS SYDNEY STEPS FROM THE TAXI TO GREET HIS LONG LOST FRIEND - DITH PRAN, JUST AS THE LENNON-ATOR PLUNKS THE FIRST FEW CHORDS ON HIS IVORY-WHITE STEINWAY.

5. RUNAWAY TRAIN (1985) ... OK, I CAN'T FIND THE CREDIT FOR WHO DID THIS MUSIC SINCE IT ISN'T LISTED IN THE CREDITS OR ANYWHERE ELSE. BUT THIS AMAZING CLASSICALLY ORCHESTRATED SECTION OF MUSIC PLAYS OUT PERFECTLY OVER JON VOIGHT RIDING ON TOP OF THAT TITULAR TRAIN CAREENING INTO OBLIVION. IT'S PROBABLY GERMAN OR SOMETHING.

6. HOT SUMMER IN THE CITY (1975) - THE LOVIN' SPOONFUL - "SUMMER IN THE CITY" TARANTINO ONCE CALLED THIS LITTLE KNOWN XXX BLAXPLOITATION/HOSTAGE FILM "THE GREATEST PORNO MOVIE EVER MADE". I'M BY NO MEANS A FAN OF THE LOVIN' SPOONFUL, BUT THEY ARE USED BRILLIANTLY AS BLONDE-STUMBLES OUT OF A RUNDOWN CABIN AFTER A NIGHT OF RUTHLESS RACE-ABUSE. DUDE, BEST ADULT CINEMA END SCENE. EVER.

HAIRED LISA BAKER TO FACE THE DAWN MOTIVATED SEXUAL

7. DOGTOWN AND Z-BOYS (2001) - DEVO - "GUT FEELING" IF ANY OF THE PREVIOUS CUES (SUCH AS ROD STEWART'S "MAGGIE MAY") OVER SLO-MO CLASSIC SKATEBOARDING FOOTAGE WEREN'T ENOUGH TO CONVINCE YOU THAT THIS DOCO IS FOR KEEPSIES, THEN DEVO GETTING PUMPED IN LIKE SOME ASS-CHERRY ON A BOFFO HOT FUDGE SUNDAE SHOULD SETTLE YOUR HASH. SETTLING HASH RULES.

8. DR. STRANGELOVE (1964) - VERA LYNN - "WE'LL MEET AGAIN". IF YOU'VE SEEN THE FILM LIKE YOU SHOULD HAVE, YOU KNOW HOW BOOTY-KICKIN' THIS IS. BOO-HOO-HOO-TEE KICK-IN.

9. ESCAPE 2000 (MST3K VERSION)(1984) - TOM SERVO - "LEAVE BRONX" THIS MASTERPIECE IS MADE UP OF THAT PLUCKY LIL' ROBOT, TOM SERVO SINGING "LEAVE BRONX!" WHILE WATCHING THE END OF THIS GOOFY ITALIAN RIP OFF OF **ESCAPE FROM NEW YORK**. WORTHY OF CULT STATUS.

10. JACKIE BROWN (1997) - BOBBY WOMACK - "ACROSS 110th STREET" Q.T. HAS OFTEN BEEN CALLED AN "ANNOYING GEEK", BUT HE HAD THE GOOD SENSE TO KNOW EXACTLY WHERE TO USE THE SELF-TITLED THEME FROM BARRY SHEAR'S 1972 BLAXPLOITATION EPIC, EVEN WHEN BARRY DIDN'T. THAT SHOULD COUNT FOR SOMETHING.

RUNNER UP: **MAGNOLIA** (1999) - AIMEE MANN - "SAVE ME"

—BOUGIE

I KNOW I ALREADY REVIEWED THIS BACK IN #6, BUT THAT REVIEW WAS FULL OF OMISSIONS AND ERRORS, AND .... I JUST WANTED ANOTHER CRACK AT IT.

WORDS LIKE 'NOTORIOUS', 'BRUTAL', AND 'DISGUSTING' ARE NEVER FAR FROM REVIEWERS' VOCAB ON THE RARE OCCASION ONE OF THEM DARES TO TRACK DOWN A VERY RARE COPY OF THIS U.S. 1972 EXERCISE IN SAVAGE RAPE AND XXX RATED PERVERSION. THIS WAS THE FIRST FILM FROM 'WARREN EVANS', A PORN DIRECTOR WITH MORE PSEUDONYMS THAN A NAZI WAR CRIMINAL. HE MADE THIS ONE AS 'HELMUTH RICHLER', AND HE WAS ALSO RESPONSIBLE FOR OTHER SEX-INSANITY IN THE FORM OF 1977'S **WATERPOWER** (AS SHAUN COSTELLO), AND **FIONA ON FIRE**. (1978 - AS KENNETH SCHWARTZ.)

A MUSTACHE-LESS HARRY REEMS IS THE RAPIST/VILLIAN CHARLEY, A HEADFUCKED MYSOGINISTIC VIETNAM VET WHO STALKS WOMEN AT RANDOM. HARRY GOT INTO THIS ROLE WITH SUCH REALISTIC GUSTO THAT HE EVEN MANAGED TO FREAK HIMSELF OUT! HE SWORE OFF "HEAVY ROLES", AND EVENTUALLY TURNED BORN AGAIN CHRISTIAN AND SOLD REAL ESTATE.

THE SCENE THAT GROSSES OUT MOST PEOPLE WHO SEE **FORCED ENTRY** IS THE RAPE OF LAURA CANNON'S CHARACTER. THIS WAS LAURA AT HER FINEST, AND SHE LATER BECAME THE FIRST HARDCORE ACTRESS TO POSE FOR PLAYBOY. HERE, SHE'S ATTACKED WHILE IN THE SHOWER AT HOME, TOSSED ON TO A BED WHERE SHE SHIVERS AND CURLS UP INTO THE FETAL POSITION. CHARLEY FORCES HER TO BLOW HIM AT GUN POINT, AND TELLS HER HE'S GOING TO FUCK HER ASSHOLE.

·THE FUN CONTINUES ON THE VERY NEXT PAGE, KIDS!·

HAHA!

IT'S FUCKIN' GOOSE BUMP A GO-GO!

(FORCED ENTRY - CONTINUED)

HER GASPING, COUGHING, WHIMPERING, SOBBING, AND REALISTIC LOOK OF NAUSEA WHILE REEMS HOLLERS "YOU'D BETTER START LIKING THAT, BITCH!" IS WHAT REALLY MAKES THIS HARD TO WATCH. IF PORN ACTRESSES COULD BE CONSIDERED AS CONTENDERS FOR ACADEMY AWARDS - THEN LAURA SHOULDA TAKEN ONE HOME FOR THIS SCENE, BECAUSE HER PERFORMANCE IS ASTONISHING.

THIS DEPRESSING MIX OF SEX AND VIOLENCE IS IMPORTANT NOT ONLY AS A PRIME EXAMPLE OF HOW EXTREME CLASSIC PORN COULD BE, BUT ALSO IMPORTANT IN THAT IT WAS SURPRISINGLY THE EARLIEST FILM TO DOCUMENT THE UNBALANCED STATE THAT MANY VIETNAM VETS RETURNED TO AMERICA WITH - PREDATING FILMS SUCH AS THE DEER HUNTER AND TAXI DRIVER BY A FEW YEARS. CHARLEY THE VET EVEN GETS AROUND TO RAPING HIMSELF SOME HIPPIE CHICKS BEFORE POPPING A BULLET THROUGH HIS SKULL IN THE FINAL REEL. HOWS THAT FOR BRINGING THE WAR HOME?

THE GRAINY DOCUMENTARY-STYLE RAPE SCENES ARE INTERSPERSED WITH ACTUAL WAR ATROCITY FOOTAGE, CREATING A CHILLING EFFECT THAT GOES A LONG WAY TOWARDS PUTTING THE VIEWER INTO THE HEAD OF A PSYCHOPATH. THAT'S CERTAINLY NOT THE MOOD DESIRED BY MOST PORNOGRAPHERS WHEN IT COMES TO THEIR PRODUCT.

AVN MAGAZINE EDITOR SUSIE EHRLICH LISTED THIS AS THE 6th GREATEST 'ROUGHIE' HARDCORE FILM EVER MADE. PREVIOUSLY AVAILABLE ON THE BOOTLEG MARKET AS PART OF THE ALPHA BLUE ARCHIVES AVON DYNASTY SET, FORCED ENTRY HAS BEEN MASTERED FROM THE ONLY KNOWN EXISTING FILM ELEMENTS WHICH SHOWED UP ON EBAY AND WERE SNAPPED UP BY THE FINE FOLKS AT "AFTER HOURS CINEMA" WHO THEN RELEASED A FANTASTIC DVD COMPLETE WITH NOTES BY DIRECTOR SHAUN COSTELLO! GET IT!
—BOUGIE

THE BOOK "NAKED CAME THE STRANGER" WAS A LITERARY HOAX PERPETRATED BY CONSERVATIVE MIKE McGRADY IN 1969 WHEN HE ASSEMBLED A NUMBER OF PROMINENT JOURNALISTS TO WRITE A DELIBERATELY TERRIBLE SEX NOVEL TO ILLUSTRATE THEIR OPINION THAT U.S. LITERARY CULTURE HAD BECOME VULGAR. THE BOOK WAS A HUGE HIT AND SPAWNED AN EXCELLENT PORN MOVIE BY RADLEY METZGER (AKA HENRY PARIS).

THE DVD RELEASE HAS AUDIO COMMENTARY BY HISTORIAN JIM HOLLIDAY.

DARBY LLOYD RAINS in
Naked Came The Stranger
COLOR   84 MINS.

Teenage Pajama Party (1977) aka New Wave Pajama Party

HOT STUFF!

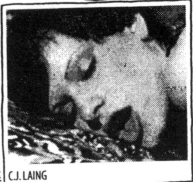

C.J. LAING

THIS IS THE 1ST FILM FROM DIRECTOR JIM CLARK WHO IS BETTER KNOWN TO PORN GEEKS AS THE DIRECTOR OF DEBBIE DOES DALLAS - WHICH HE MADE 3 MONTHS LATER. THANKS TO R.J. GALLENTINE FOR SENDING THIS IN FOR REVIEW, BUT SOMETHING WENT WRONG AND THIS COPY TURNED OUT BLACK AND WHITE. THE EFFECT UPON THE FILM IS ACTUALLY QUITE AMAZING AND FREAKY, GIVING THIS SLEAZY, SHOT IN N.Y.C 70'S RAINCOATER THE SHADOWED AESTHETIC OF A FRENCH ARTHOUSE FILM. THE EFFECT IS GORGEOUS, AND MAKES ME WISH THAT MORE (ANY?) OF THE CLASSIC SHOT-ON-FILM XXX OUTPUT OF THE 70S HAD BEEN FILMED IN BLACK AND WHITE.

THE PREMISE HERE FINDS 4 TEENAGE-LOOKING GIRLS ORGANIZING A PAJAMA PARTY AND THEN STAYING UP ALL NIGHT TO MAKE

DIRTY PRANK PHONE CALLS. THINGS REALLY START TO GET HOT N' HEAVY WHEN A LOCAL SWEATY PERVERT STARTS TO TALK NAUGHTY BACK TO THEM, AND BEFORE LONG THE SEXUAL TENSION LEADS THE GIGGLING GIRLS TO START MASTURBATING AND START MAKING OUT WITH ONE ANOTHER. REALITY AND PRIMAL FANTASY START TO BLUR WHEN EACH OF THE GIRLS BEGIN TO FANTASIZE THEMSELVES INTO SOME RATHER ODD AND UNUSUAL HUMP-BASED SITUATIONS.

TEENAGE PAJAMA PARTY IS ONE OF MY FAVORITE FILMS IN THE OEUVRE OF C.J. LAING. THIS ADORABLE SHORT-HAIRED CUM GOBBLING FUCKMONKEY WAS THE PROTOTYPE NEW YORK JEWISH ANAL SEX PRINCESS WHO BLAZED A TRAIL THROUGH SMUT FOR THOSE THAT FOLLOWED. C.J. MADE MANY MOVIES, BUT SINCE SHE OFTEN HAD FISTING AND VIOLENCE MIXED IN WITH HER SEX, MANY OF HER SCENES DIDN'T MAKE IT ON TO VIDEO AND WERE EDITED OUT. IN PARTICULAR, SOME OF HER NASTIER STANDOUT MOMENTS TO LOOK FOR ARE HER RAPE SCENES FROM SEX WISH (1976), THE TAKING OF CHRISTINA (1975), AND HER EYE-POPPING FISTING SEQUENCE FROM ANYONE BUT MY HUSBAND (1975).

C.J. GETS INTO SOME REALLY FUN STUFF HERE, TAKING PART IN A LESBO LICK-FEST WITH A YOUNG AND STUNNING SHARON MITCHELL, AND ALSO TURNS UP IN A HEATED INTERRACIAL 3 WAY WITH CANDY LOVE AND GILBERT PALMITIER BEFORE TAKING ON ANOTHER HUGE STUD WHO GIVES HER A GOOD HEAVY PORKING IN HER ANUS. FANS OF POPPED ANAL CHERRIES SHOULD ALSO NOTE THAT BARBI JAMES HAS HER ONE AND ONLY ANAL SEX SCENE ON DISPLAY HERE.

YEAH! P.J. PARTY!!

132

Early Porn Memories

by Edmund Varuolo

OH, HOW EASY IT IS THESE DAYS TO SIMPLY POP A VIDEOCASSETTE OR DVD INTO YOUR PLAYER, SIT BACK, RELAX, AND ENJOY A SEEMINGLY UN-ENDING PARADE OF LUSTFUL PERFORMERS WILLING TO DO JUST ABOUT EVERY SEX ACT FATHOMABLE. 30 YEARS AGO, THE ONLY WAY TO SEE PORN WAS TO GO TO A THEATER! YES, ONE WOULD HAVE TO THROW CAUTION TO THE WIND AND VENTURE INTO THE SEEDIEST PARTS OF TOWN, QUITE LITERALLY TAKING YOUR LIFE IN YOUR HANDS EACH TIME YOU DID.

"DON'T BE TOUCHIN' MY ASS MUTHA FUCKA! I'LL STICK MY FUCKIN' KNIFE IN YOUR GODDAMN CHEST, MUTHAFUCKA! YOU BE DEAD, MUTHA FUCKA!". YEP, THIS WAS THE KIND OF ADDITIONAL OFF-SCREEN DIALOG ONE WOULD BECOME ACCUSTOMED TO HEARING AT ANY NUMBER OF TIMES SQUARE GRINDHOUSES. ONE THEATER DOWN TOWN REGULARLY FEATURED MORE ACTION GOING ON BEHIND THE PROJECTION SCREEN THAN ON IT!

ALTHOUGH ALL THESE PLACES RAN STRAIGHT PORN, THE MALE

HOMOSEXUALS IN NYC WOULD HAUNT THESE JOINTS LIKE LIVING ZOMBIES. I CAME TO DREAD HAVING TO GO TO THE BATHROOM IN THESE DIVES. WHEN I COULD HOLD IT NO MORE, I'D RUN TO THE CAN ONLY TO BE GREETED BY A REGIMENT OF BOTTOM DWELLERS STANDING IN LINE ALL THE WAY UP THE STAIRS. THEY WERE NOT WAITING TO PEE, AS THEY ALL LET ME IN FRONT OF THEM TO GET TO THE URINAL! DOWN IN THE TOILET, I COULD FINALLY SEE WHAT THEY WERE ALL WAITING FOR. ONE STALL WITH A GLORY HOLE. THEY WERE ALL WAITING TO GET INTO THE STALL AND SUCK ANYTHING THAT CAME THROUGH THAT HOLE WITH ALL THE FERVOR THEY COULD MUSTER. NEEDLESS TO SAY, I HIGH-TAILED IT OUTTA THERE AND DID WHAT MANY OTHER SELF RESPECTING HETEROS HAD DONE BEFORE ME... I PISSED IN THE DECAYED HALL.

> *I high-tailed it outta there and did what many other self respecting heteros had done before me...I pissed in the decayed hall.*

THERE WERE SOME GOOD TIMES TOO... NO IT WASN'T ALL RUBBING ELBOWS WITH THE DEPTHS OF DEPRAVITY. ATTENDING A BONAFIDE PORN PREMIERE ON 48th ST, ANNIE SPRINKLE AND GEORGE PAYNE LIVE ON STAGE WITH THEIR OWN PA SYSTEM; WATCHING A LIVE S+M SHOW WHICH FEATURED A 7 MONTHS PREGNANT GIRL BEING WHIPPED AND ABUSED, LAUGHING AT THE OLD CODGERS THAT WOULD STARE OPENED-MOUTHED.... ...AHHH... THOSE WERE THE DAYS!

BEFORE THERE WERE LIVE SEX SHOWS, THERE WAS MONICA KENNEDY. SHE WAS AN EX-STRIPPER THAT WOULD LET ANY GUY GET UP THERE AND EAT HER OUT, LEAVING A TRAIL OF TISSUES ON THE STAGE AS SHE MOVED FROM ONE HORNY PATRON TO THE NEXT. FOR MONICA'S BIG FINALE, SHE'D BLOW 3 OR 4 LUCKY DUDES RIGHT ON STAGE - AND ALL THIS FOR JUST FIVE BUCKS!

TO VIEW THE MOST CURRENT CROP OF NUBILES WILLING TO BARE ALL FOR THE CAMERA, ONE HAD TO FREQUENT THE THEATERS THAT RAN ONLY 16 MM LOOPS. THESE FILMS ARE ALL BUT FORGOTTEN, BUT THEY WERE THE AMATEUR VIDEOS OF THEIR DAY, GIVING A FIRST CHANCE TO MANY AN ADULT STAR, ALTHOUGH MOST NEVER WENT BEYOND THEIR LOOP PERIOD.

PORNO IN DOLBY SENSURROUND? IT DID EXIST! ONE TITLE I REMEMBER WAS A EURO FLICK CALLED 'SOUND OF LOVE', WHICH CAPITALIZED ON THE EXPANDING SONIC BOMBARDMENT TECHNOLOGY... LOUD BREATHING AND SUCTION SOUNDS ASSAILED THE VIEWER FROM ALL DIRECTIONS! THERE WERE AT LEAST 2 OTHER FILMS PRODUCED IN THIS FORMAT, BUT I CANNOT RECALL THE TITLES.

IN X
RATED COLOR

**BAD
BUELAH**

A
FABULOUS
FLASH
OF THE
50's

**HIGH SCHOOL
FANTASIES**
DO YOU REMEMBER WHEN?
ADULTS ONLY

2nd
Smash
Week

**THE
WRATH
OF DECADE**

LASH CALL, BOYS!
SOUND & COLOR
FOR ADULTS
OVER 21 ONLY
EROS 1
CONT 9 AM TILL MIDNIGHT
732 8TH AVE 45th & 46th ST 581-4594

"UNHEARD OF! Farley Granger,
Kim Pope and Marc Stevens in
a lavish production...
unbelievably explicit!
...graphically
violent!
A DOUBLE
TURN-ON!"
— Weisman

PENETRATION
The ultimate ⓧ crime
Some women deserve it!
FARLEY   KIM
GRANGER · POPE
MARC   SYLVA
STEVENS · KOSCINA
WITH CAMEO APPEARANCES BY
HARRY REEMS & TINA RUSSELL

BACK IN THE EARLY 'ANYTHING GOES' DAYS OF
PORN, A FLICK NAMED **ANIMAL LOVER** DREW PACKED
HOUSES IN TIMES SQUARE. IT FEATURED DANISH
PLUMPETTE BODIL JOENSEN (SEE CINEMA
SEWER #13 - ED) AND VARIOUS FARM ANIMALS.
CROWDS COULD ONLY STARE IN UTTER DISBELIEF
AT WHAT WAS TRANSPIRING ON THE SCREEN.
REGARDLESS, I SAW FEW (IF ANY) WALK OUTS.
FOLLOWING A CRACKDOWN IN THE MID-70S,
ANIMAL AND UNDERAGE PORNOGRAPHY WERE
CLEARED OUT OF THE AREA, AND THAT WAS THAT
FOR **ANIMAL LOVER**. INTERESTINGLY, THE SAME
THEATER WENT ON TO RUN A DOUBLE BILL OF AN
EDITED-DOWN VERSION OF **DEEP THROAT / THE DEVIL
IN MISS JONES** FOR THE NEXT 7 OR 8 YEARS.

SEEING A MOVIE THAT WAS PLAYING ON 42ND ST
DEMANDED THAT THE PORNOPHILE BE VERY ALERT
TO WHAT WAS GOING ON AROUND THEM. THE
SMELL OF POT (AND LATER CRACK) WAFTING
THROUGH THE PLACE TO THE ACCOMPANIMENT OF
STRANGE SUCKING SOUNDS ORIGINATING FROM
THE BACK ROW OF SEATS. IT WAS ABANDON ALL
HOPE YE WHO ENTER HERE. EVERY TIME A
CLOSE-UP WOULD FILL THE 60-FOOT SCREEN, YOU
COULD COUNT ON HEARING STEAM-ESCAPING
SOUNDS FROM SOME POOR BASTARD CAUGHT IN
A MASTURBATORY FRENZY.

THE BEST THING ABOUT HAVING TO WATCH A FILM
ON THE "DEUCE" WAS THE CONCESSION STANDS
IN THOSE GRAND OLD THEATERS. NOT JUST
CANDY, MIND YOU, BUT WITH A FULLY STOCKED
SNACK BAR FEATURING SODA, HOT DOGS,
POPCORN, ETC... THE KIND OF STUFF YOU'D
FIND IN MAINSTREAM MOVIE HOUSES! CHRIST,
THEY EVEN HAD A "VISIT THE SNACK BAR"
CARTOON! SEEING A PORN FILM WAS AN EVENT!

SOON AFTER THE ADVENT OF VIDEO, MOST OF
THESE PLACES CLOSED, WITH THE REMAINDER
SWITCHING OVER TO THE LOWER QUALITY VIDEO
PROJECTION SYSTEM THAT SURVIVE TO THIS DAY
IN THE FEW PORN THEATERS THAT STILL EXIST.
SHIT, IT'S A HELL OF A LOT EASIER AND CHEAPER
TO STICK A TAPE IN AND PROJECT IT (RATHER
POORLY I MIGHT ADD...) THAN TO HAVE TO HIRE A
REAL PROJECTIONIST. SOME OF THESE THEATERS
KEPT THE OLD SCREENS UP, AND USED THEM
WITH THE VIDEO PROJECTORS, TRYING TO STRETCH
THE IMAGE TO FILL THE IMAGE AREA! THIS
RESULTED IN A STRANGE OBLONG-LIKE APPEARANCE
TO THE BODY PARTS DISPLAYED ON IT. IS IT ANY
WONDER THESE PLACES FOLDED?

ANYHOW, THE NEXT TIME YOU'RE ABOUT TO PLAY
THAT NEW TAPE OR DVD YOU'VE JUST PURCHASED,
WITH ALL THE GREAT LOOKIN' BABES, AMAZING
TECHNICAL QUALITY, OVER TWO HOURS LONG... IN
THE COMFORT AND RELATIVE SAFETY OF YOUR
OWN HOMES... TAKE A MOMENT TO REFLECT
ON THOSE WHO TOILED 30 YEARS AGO, TO GET
YOU WHERE YOU ARE NOW.
— ED VARUOLO

ALL THE DEVIL'S ANGELS
a.k.a. THE PSYCHIATRIST (1978)

TED ROTER WAS ONE NUTTY
BELGIAN CHEESE LOG. M'MAN
WAS A SEX INDUSTRY PIONEER
WHO GOT HIS START BY
CO-DIRECTING THE RAY DENNIS
STECKLER ATROCITY **LEMON
GROVE KIDS MEET THE
MONSTERS** IN 1965. HIS NEXT
ENDEAVOR, THE SOFTCORE DRAMA
NORMA (1970), ABOUT A WOMAN'S
SHATTERED SEX LIFE - HAD THE MEMORABLE
CAMPAIGN WHICH PROCLAIMED "NORMA...SHE'S
NOT QUITE NORMAL!"

NEITHER WAS TED.

IN THE MID 70S, ROTER CAME INTO HIS OWN
AS A HARDCORE DIRECTOR WHO OFTEN
STARRED IN HIS OWN FILMS. TED WAS VERY
COMPETENT AT WEARING BOTH HATS, AND
APTLY PROCLAIMED HIMSELF THE JOHN
CASSAVETES OF XXX. UNDER THE NOM-DE-
PLUME PETER BALAKOFF, HE CREATED AN ODD
AND UNIQUE SERIES OF L.A.-MADE HARDCORE
MOVIES RELEASED UNDER THE BANNER OF

ANOTHER
BOUGIE
REVIEW!

**'SEX SEA
HIJACKERS'**
these girls all go down at sea

Adults Only   In Color

NY PREMIERE
2 FIRST RUN HITS!

OK-YES
and
AIRLINE COCKPIT
PLUS Special Short

ALL
COLOR
SHOW
ADULTS
ONLY
CAPRI Cinema
8th Ave at 46th St. 581-4444
CONTINUOUS FROM 9 A.M. MIDNITE SHOWS DAILY

"A FUNKY,
FUNNY
.... FILM!"
Erotic Entertainment of the Highest Quality!
BEST FILM OF ITS KIND!"
— WEISMAN, STAG

WE'RE
COMPLETELY
UNINHIBITED!

**My Erotic
Fantasies**
Starring MARC STEVENS · BREE ANTHONY · ANNIE SPRINKLES
"BIG" SALLY STROKE and a BEVY OF BOUNTIFUL BEAUTIES!
AN EXTRAORDINARY ⓧ FILM   COLOR

134

BELLADONNA FILMS. MUCH LONGER IN LENGTH THAN THE AVERAGE 70 MIN. SKIN FLICK OF THE 70S. HIS OUTPUT WAS SOMETIMES MADDENING, SOMETIMES TASTEFUL, AND USUALLY WONDERFULLY UNCONVENTIONAL.

ALL THE DEVIL'S ANGELS IS ONE OF TED'S BETTER MOVIES, AND ONE OF THE FEW READILY AVAILABLE THANKS TO ALPHA BLUE ARCHIVES AND SOMETHING WEIRD VIDEO. THE PLOT IS DANGEROUSLY SCHIZO, WITH THE STORYLINE CONSTANTLY WEAVING AND LEAVING ME IN AN ENGROSSED STATE OF BEWILDERMENT. IT'S FRACTURED AND DREAMLIKE, NOT SO UNLIKE THE LEGENDARY 'CUT-UPS' CREATED BY WILLIAM BURROUGHS AND BRION GYSIN, AND JUST WHEN YOU THINK YOU'VE GOT IT FIGURED OUT, YOU SUDDENLY GET THE SENSE THAT THE COPY YOU'VE BEEN WATCHING HAS BEEN ACCIDENTALLY EDITED OUT OF SEQUENCE - AND YOUR MIND RACES TO TRY TO PUT THE PIECES BACK INTO PLACE.

ONE SECTION OF THE MOVIE HAS TED PLAYING A BELGIAN SHRINK WHO SPECIALIZES IN PATIENTS WHO BELIEVE THEMSELVES TO BE POSSESSED BY THE DEVIL. HE TRUNDLES AROUND, LECTURES AT SCHOOLS, AND RUNS HIS NUTHOUSE FILLED WITH PERVERTS, HORNY GIRLS AND NURSES. TED'S USUAL LEADING LADY, THE BLONDE SWEETIE GENA LEE, PLAYS JEAN - A NANCY DREW-ESQUE UNDERCOVER MYSTERY GIRL WHO INFILTRATES HIS FREAKY SCENE AND   CONSTANTLY SEEMS TO BE RETRACING HER CHARACTER ARC INSTEAD OF FORWARDING IT. THIS CONNECTS US TO THE OTHER DIRECTION THE MOVIE GOES, WHICH IS TO FOLLOW TED AS A HOODED SEX SHAMAN WHO GATHERS HIS FOLLOWERS TO FUCK AND SUCK ONE ANOTHER WHILE PRAYING TO THE DARK OVERLORD.

THE CASTING IS SURPRISINGLY GREAT - BUT NOT ALWAYS OF THE HIGHEST CALIBER WHEN IT COMES TO THE OL' THESPIANISM. TED HIMSELF IS FUCKING GREAT AND EASILY BELIEVABLE AS THE OLDER AND WISER PSYCHIATRIST, AND THE DOZEN OR SO GIRLS CAST ARE CUTE IN A PLAIN EVERYDAY MANNER, AND DON'T LOOK AT ALL LIKE GAUDY, JADED PORN STARS. IN FACT NEARLY ALL OF THEM HAD NEVER STEPPED IN FRONT OF A MOVIE CAMERA BEFORE OR SINCE.

IN TERMS OF HUMPY-PUMPY, THIS IS PACKED WITH SOMEWHAT HO-HUM UNINSPIRED COUPLING, AND YET TED EXECUTED THE FILMING OF IT WITH THE LYRICISM OF A EURO-SMUT ART WANKER. THERE IS ALSO A SLY LAYER OF KINK PRESENT, ESPECIALLY WHEN WE'RE INTRODUCED TO A FEMALE DOMINATED UNDERGROUND SOCIETY THAT TED SOMEHOW MANIPULATES FOR HIS OWN PLEASURE. IN FACT, THE 'GOOD DOCTOR' SEEMS TO CONSTANTLY HAVE SOME GLASSY-EYED, NEGLIGEE CLAD YOUNG PATIENT DOWN BETWEEN HIS LEGS GOBBLING HIS KNOB WHILE HE COOS "GOOOOD GIRL... GOOOD GIIIRL...". THESE SCENES AREN'T THE ONLY 'LITTLE GIRL GAMES' GOING ON. A BUNCH OF SNOTTY TEEN INMATES SNEAK INTO ONE BOY'S ROOM AND MAKE HIM KISS THEIR DIRTY BARE FEET. LATER WHILE WEARING LITTLE HOTPANTS - THEY TAUNT HIM (SUMMER CAMP STYLE) INTO FLASHING HIS PECKER FOR THEM.

TED ROTER IS A VASTLY OVERLOOKED AND NEARLY FORGOTTEN PORN AUTEUR WHO SADLY PASSED AWAY IN 2000 AT THE AGE OF 70 WHILE LIVING IN NEW YORK.

HEH
HEH
HEH
HEH

A CLIMAX OF BLUE POWER aka "The Impersonator" aka "Deviate in Blue" (1974)

THIS IS A ROUGH N' TOUGH ADULTS ONLY SHIT SCAB DIRECTED BY '60S AND '70S ROUGHIE-MEISTER LEE FROST - UNDER THE PSEUDONYM F.C. PERL. (SEE CINEMA SEWER #12 FOR MORE ON LEE)

A CRAZY SECURITY GUARD DRIVES AROUND HOLLYWOOD (SOME AMAZING STREET FOOTAGE OF THE SLEAZY SECTION OF THE BOULEVARD HERE) IN A FAKE POLICE CAR, PRETENDING TO BE A MEMBER OF THE LAPD SO HE CAN RUFF UP AND SEXUALLY HUMILIATE THE LOCAL PROSTITUTES. HE 'ARRESTS' THE GIRLS, DRIVES THEM OUT TO THE COUNTRY, AND THEN HAS THEM ROLL AROUND IN THE MUD LIKE PIGS BEFORE HE VIOLENTLY RAPES THEM. **NASTY**, NASTY STUFF....

BAWL!!

THIS DETESTABLE ANTI-HERO HAPPENS TO WITNESS A MURDER WHILE SPYING ON A YOUNG WOMAN WHO KILLS HER HUSBAND. HE RETURNS THE NEXT DAY IN HIS COP GEAR TO CAPTURE THE MURDERESS, BLACKMAIL HER INTO SUBMISSION, AND THEN HAVE HIS WAY WITH HER WHILE HOLDING HER AT GUNPOINT. AT ONE POINT THE SICKO EVEN DRESSES LIKE AN UGLY WOMAN, AND GIVES HER A FUCKING BUBBLE BATH! THIS IS ONE **WEIRD** MOVIE!

THIS DOMINATION-PACKED ASS-BLASTER WAS RELEASED THEATRICALLY IN 1975 BY PHOENIX INTERNATIONAL PICTURES, AND FEATURED ANGELA CARNON (AS LINDA HARRIS), RENE BOND, JASON CARNS (AKA WILLIAM QUINN), WES BISHOP, AND CAMEO APPEARANCES BY PRODUCER BOB CRESSE AND EURO SEX STAR USCHI DIGARD.

THE 25 BEST MOVIES ADAPTED FROM COMIC BOOKS!

BY: THE BOUGIEMATIC MAN ☆2009☆

I HAVE WATCHED A GREAT MANY MOVIES BASED UPON THE ART FORM OF SEQUENTIAL ART, AND HAVE BEEN READING COMIC BOOKS FERVENTLY SINCE I WAS IN GRADE SCHOOL. WHAT WITH HOLLYWOOD'S APPARENT LACK OF IDEAS AND RECENT HISTORY OF ADAPTING AND RECYCLING ANYTHING AND EVERYTHING THAT EVER SOLD MORE THAN A DOZEN COPIES OFF THE OLD "HEY KIDS, COMICS!" DISPLAY STAND, YOU'RE PROBABLY HUNGRY FOR ALTERNATIVES TO ALL OF THOSE SHITTY COMIC BOOK MOVIES.

YES, FOR EVERY WORTHWHILE EFFORT, THERE ARE A DOZEN **GHOST RIDER**s, **CATWOMAN**s, **HOWARD THE DUCK**s, AND **SUPERMAN IV: THE QUEST FOR PEACE**s. IT'S ENOUGH TO MAKE ONE REALLY WONDER IF IT IS EVEN POSSIBLE TO USE COMICS AS A DECENT SPRINGBOARD FOR QUALITY THEATRICAL CINEMA.

WELL, I'M HERE TO TELL YOU THAT IT IS, MY FRIENDS. IT IS.

25. PERSEPOLIS (2007. France)

ONE OF THE MOST IMPORTANT ANIMATED FILMS OF THE LAST FEW YEARS WAS BASED ON MARJANE SATRAPI'S AUTOBIOGRAPHICAL COMIC BOOK OF THE SAME NAME, AND FOLLOWS A YOUNG LADY AS SHE COMES OF AGE AGAINST THE BACKDROP OF THE IRANIAN REVOLUTION. THE FILM DREW SERIOUS COMPLAINTS FROM THE IRANIAN GOVERNMENT, AND WAS BANNED IN LEBANON -- PROOF THAT THEY DID THIS RIGHT.

24. MYSTERY MEN (1999. USA)

AN IMPRESSIVE COMEDIC CAST OF WILLIAM H. MACY, BEN STILLER, AND HANK AZARIA PLAYING A TRIO OF WACK SUPERHEROES WITH TOTALLY UNIMPRESSIVE POWERS WAS A FLIPPITY FLOP UPON ITS RELEASE, BUT HAS SINCE DEVELOPED A RESPECTABLE CULT FOLLOWING. LOOSELY BASED ON THE BELOVED INDY COMIC "FLAMING CARROT" BY THE TALENTED BOB BURDEN. FUNNY SHIT.

FROM "DRAGONHEAD". M. MOCHIZUKI

© 1977 Paramount Pictures Corporation

"BARBARELLA" QUEEN OF THE GALAXY

23. SIN CITY (2005. USA)

POSSIBLY THE MOST FAITHFUL ADAPTATION IN THE HISTORY OF COMIC-TO-MOVIE FILMS TO EVER COME OUT OF AMERICA. THE ONLY PROBLEM IS THE COMIC THE MOVIE WAS BASED ON WASN'T ANYTHING BUT SOME WEAK-ASS NOIR/POTBOILER EYECANDY. WATCH IT WHILE DRUNK.

22. DRAGON HEAD (2003. Japan)

ON A VERY RARE OCCASION, A MOVIE BASED ON A COMIC ACTUALLY MANAGES TO ADD TO A STORY BY BEING TRIMMED AND FIT INTO A SHORTER 2 HOUR THEATRICAL BLUEPRINT. THE ORIGINAL MINETARO MOCHIZUKI MANGA FOR THIS POST APOCALYPTIC DRAMA ABOUT TWO TEENS WANDERING A DESTROYED JAPAN IS A DRAWN OUT 10 BOOK SLOG THAT CONSTANTLY REITERATES AND COVERS THE SAME GROUND. JOJI IIDA'S LIVE ACTION VERSION IS MUCH MORE LEAN AND SUCCINCT IN ITS DEPRESSIVE MISERY.

21. WHEN THE WIND BLOWS (1986. UK)

(SEE THE REVIEW FOR "WHEN THE WIND BLOWS" ELSEWHERE IN THIS BOOK -- SPECIFICALLY IN THE CHAPTER ON POST APOCALYPTIC MOVIES)

20. IRON MAN (2008. USA)

JUST WHEN WE WERE BEGINNING TO WORRY THAT IT WAS IMPOSSIBLE TO MAKE A MARVEL COMIC SUPERHERO MOVIE THAT DIDN'T SUCK, ALONG COMES JON FAVREAU'S BIG BUDGET BARN-BURNER BASED ON THE LONG-RUNNING COMIC OF THE SAME NAME. HOW PERFECT WAS THE CASTING OF ROBERT DOWNEY JR. AS TONY STARK -- THE ALCOHOLIC BILLIONAIRE? THIS ALMOST MADE UP FOR THOSE GODDAMN X-MEN MOVIES.

IRON MAN

19. ICHI THE KILLER (2001. Japan)

TALENT-PACKED TAKASHI MIIKE ADAPTED THIS GORE-PACKED ZINGER FROM A CULT COMIC BY HIDEO YAMAMOTO, IN WHICH A WIMP TRANSFORMS HIMSELF INTO A BLOOD CAKED RABID DOG OF A MAN WHOSE POWER AND STRENGTH IS DERIVED FROM STRESSFUL MEMORIES OF HIS BOYHOOD HUMILIATIONS. AND TO ADD A SALTY TWIST? THE HERO SQUIRTS A LOAD EACH TIME HE KILLS. TRIVIA: YOU KNOW THE CLOSE-UP DURING THE INTRO SEQUENCE WHEN THE TITLE RAISES OUT OF A PUDDLE OF CUM? MIIKE REVEALED RECENTLY THAT THE JIZZ WE SEE IS REAL. EWWWWWW.

18. CASTLE OF CAGLIOSTRO (1979. Japan)

THE SECOND OF THE ANIMATED LUPIN III MOVIES, THIS WAS WRITTEN AND DIRECTED BY HAYAO MIYAZAKI AS HIS FIRST FEATURE A FULL 5 YEARS BEFORE HE'D FIND THE MUSTARD TO START UP THE LEGENDARY STUDIO GHIBLI. BASED UPON THE POPULAR COMICS BY MONKEY PUNCH, THIS QUICK-PACED ADVENTURE IS FAR AHEAD OF ITS TIME, AND FIRST MADE ITSELF KNOWN TO ME IN MY LOCAL VIDEO GAME ARCADE IN 1985 AS A "DRAGON'S LAIR" STYLE LASER DISC GAME CALLED 'CLIFF HANGER'. I WAS THRILLED, YEARS LATER, TO DISCOVER THAT IT WASN'T JUST A GAME, BUT A FULLY REALISED CAPER MOVIE WITH A SUAVE SPY SAVING A KIDNAPPED BRIDE AMIDST SOME OF THE MOST DELIRIOUS ACTION SEQUENCES EVER DEVISED.

AKIRA

17. BARBARELLA (1968 France/Italy)

THANK YOU JANE FONDA, FOR BRINGING TO LIFE JEAN-CLAUDE FOREST'S EROTIC HEROINE IN THIS CAMPY SCI-FI POP-ART ROMP. THE SET AND COSTUME DESIGNS ARE FUCKING UNBELIEVABLE, AND BARBARELLA'S WAY-OUT 40th CENTURY ACCOMPLISHMENTS CONSIST OF HER FUCKING VARIOUS ALIEN SPECIES. A SEXUAL TORTURE DEVICE CALLED THE "EXCESSIVE MACHINE" IS A HIGHLIGHT, AS IS JANE'S OPENING CREDIT ANTIGRAVITY STRIPTEASE. HOW WAS THIS RATED PG?! OF COURSE , A REMAKE IS IN THE WORKS AS I WRITE THIS. I   IMAGINE IT'LL LACK ALL THE CHARM OF THE ORIGINAL.

16. A HISTORY OF VIOLENCE (2005. USA)

GOOGLE "COMIC BOOK MOVIES" AND LOOK IN ON ALL THE INTERNET CHATTER THAT YOU LIKE, BUT I CAN TELL YOU NOW THAT YOUR AVERAGE MESSAGE BOARD MORON SIMPLY ISN'T AWARE THAT THIS CRONENBERG INSTANT-CLASSIC ABOUT A MILD-MANNERED MAN WHO BECOMES A LOCAL HERO THROUGH AN ACT OF VIOLENCE -- WAS BASED ON A GRAPHIC NOVEL. THEY'RE TOO BUSY DEBATING THE MERITS OF THE CGI EFFECTS IN THE **INCREDIBLE HULK** MOVIES, WHICH ARE FRANKLY ABOUT AS IMPRESSIVE AS THE GRAPHICS IN THE VIDEO GAMES MY NEPHEWS PLAY. TRIVIA: THIS WAS THE LAST WIDELY-RELEASED MOVIE TO COME OUT ON VHS.

15. AKIRA (1988. Japan.)

OPERATING AS THE BREATHTAKING INTRODUCTION TO MODERN JAPANESE ANIMATION FOR AN ENTIRE GENERATION OF POP-CULTURE NERDS, KATSUHIRO OTOMO'S LANDMARK FILM VERSION OF HIS OWN EARLY 80s MANGA SERIES OPENED EYES TO THE POSSIBILITIES OF WHAT ANIMATED MOVIES COULD BE. SET IN 2019's "NEO-TOKYO", THE MOVIE CAPTURES THE BASIC SETTINGS AND CHARACTERS FROM THE ORIGINAL 2182-PAGE EPIC, ALTHOUGH THE PLOT DIFFERS A LOT.

RICA (1973)

14. RICA and its sequels (1972, 1973, Japan)

IN THE 1970s TARO BONTEN (ONE OF THE MOST FAMOUS TATTOO ARTISTS IN JAPAN AT THE TIME) CREATED A COMIC BOOK SERIES ABOUT A LOVELY-BUT-DEADLY HALF-BREED HELLCAT NAMED RICA. BORN AS A RESULT

OF HER MOTHER BEING RAPED BY AN AMERICAN SOLDIER, MISS RICA TOOK ON THE YAKUZA AND A MYSTERIOUS MILLIONAIRE WITH EQUAL SAVAGERY, MAKING THE COMIC A BEST SELLER IN ASIA. TARO EFFORTLESSLY INFUSED HIS WORK WITH A DYNAMIC EXPLOITATION MOVIE STYLE THAT CAUGHT THE ATTENTION OF TOHO STUDIOS, WHO CREATED A GREAT 3-PART LIVE-ACTION MOVIE SERIES TO COMPETE WITH RIVAL TOEI'S BOFFO "PINKY VIOLENCE" FILMS.

PORCO ROSSO

13. TEKKONKINKREET (2006. Japan)

THIS COLORFUL ANIMATED FEATURE FROM THE ALWAYS IMPRESSIVE STUDIO 4°C WAS ADAPTED FROM "BLACK AND WHITE", A THREE-VOLUME MANGA SERIES BY TAIYO MATSUMOTO. TWO STREET URCHINS (A TOUGH BOY NAMED BLACK, AND AN INNOCENT GLEE-FILLED KID NAMED WHITE) END UP TAKING ON THE YAKUZA AND GET INTO WAY MORE TROUBLE THAN THEY KNOW WHAT TO DO WITH. VIOLENT, TOUCHING, AND EXQUISITELY RENDERED. THIS IS THE ANIME YOU BUST OUT FOR THAT CLOSE-MINDED PERSON WHO THINKS ALL ANIME IS GARBAGE.

12. PORCO ROSSO (1992. Japan)

TAKING ON A VERY BRIEF LIFE AS A FEW WATERCOLORED COMIC PAGES IN AN ANIMATION MAGAZINE, PORCO ROSSO BECAME ONE OF HAYAO MIYAZAKI'S LESSER APPRECIATED, BUT STILL TOTALLY WORTHWHILE FILMS. THIS WHIMSICAL YARN REVOLVES AROUND A 1930s-ERA SEAPLANE PILOT WHO IS CURSED WITH THE BODY OF AN ANTHROPOMORPHIC PIG. ACTING AS A BOUNTY HUNTER IN THE ADRIATIC SEA, HE CHASES AIR PIRATES FOR $$$ AND LONGS FOR ROMANCE. EVERY MOMENT OF THIS LOVINGLY PRODUCED MOVIE FEELS LIKE A VALENTINES DAY CARD TO THE HISTORY OF AVIATION.

11. ZERO WOMAN: RED HANDCUFFS (1974. Japan)

BASED ON THE STYLISH COMICS OF TORU SHINOHARA (WHO ALSO DID THE FEMALE CONVICT SCORPION MANGA), THIS PSYCHOSEXUAL THRILLER BY DIRECTOR YUKIO NODA IS FUDGE-PACKED WITH EXPLICIT VIOLENCE, RAPE, TORTURE, AND MURDER. ONE OF THE MORE NOTORIOUS PINK FILMS TO BE EJACULATED OUT OF THE JAPANESE FILM INDUSTRY, THE PERVERSE PLOT OF ZERO WOMAN FOLLOWS A GANG OF SAVAGE THUGS WHO KIDNAP THE DAUGHTER OF A BIG-TIME POLITICAL FIGURE. THE OFTEN-NAKED MIKI SUGIMOTO IS THE TITULAR ANUS-KICKER WHO IS HIRED TO LAY WASTE TO THE CRUEL KIDNAPPERS.

I LOVE THIS PLACE! I COME HERE ALL THE TIME!

IS THAT SO?

10. AMERICAN SPLENDOR (2003. USA)

WELCOME TO THE ESOTERIC LIFE OF HARVEY PEKAR, A CRANKY FILE CLERK FROM CLEVELAND WHOSE CULT FAVORITE SELF-PUBLISHED COMIX USED TO GET PIMPED ON LETTERMAN BACK IN THE DAY. PAUL GIAMATTI DOES A QUALITY JOB PORTRAYING PEKAR, AND EVEN MORE EERIE IS HOW DEAD-ON THE SUPPORTING CAST ARE AT CHANNELLING ROBERT CRUMB AND TOBY RADLOFF. AN EXCEPTIONAL MOVIE ABOUT ONE OF THE BEST AUTOBIOGRAPHICAL COMIC BOOKS EVER MADE.

9. LONE WOLF AND CUB (And its sequels. Japan. 1972/1973/1974)

SIMPLY PUT: THE GREATEST SAMURAI CINEMA EVER MADE BY SOMEONE NOT NAMED KUROSAWA OR KOBAYASHI. ADAPTED FROM THE MANGA BY KAZUO KOIKE AND GOSEKI KOJIMA, THIS ONGOING STORY OF A ONE-MAN WAR WAGED BY A SHOGUNATE EXECUTIONER AND HIS INFANT SON HAS INTRIGUE AND A LEGENDARY SLOWBURN MAGNIFICENCE TO IT. PLUS: A WOODEN BABY CART ARMED WITH KNIVES AND MANY SPLENDID AND EXAGGERATED HIGH-PRESSURED GEYSERS OF THE RED STUFF. FUCKING EPIC.

SO WHAT HAVE YOU GUYS BEEN UP TO?

NOTHING. WORSHIPING SATAN.

FROM "GHOST WORLD" BY: DAN CLOWES

8. GHOST WORLD (2001. USA)

TWO CYNICAL, UNSOCIAL TEENAGE GIRLS SPEND THEIR LAST AWKWARD SUMMER TOGETHER AFTER HIGH SCHOOL GRADUATION, AND INADVERTENTLY END UP INFILTRATING THE LIFE OF A 40-SOMETHING RECORD COLLECTOR. IT SEEMED UNLIKELY THAT TERRY ZWIGOFF COULD PROPERLY BRING THE DAN CLOWES GRAPHIC NOVEL TO THE BIG SCREEN WITHOUT LOSING SOMETHING SPECIAL ALONG THE WAY, WHICH MADE IT ALL THE MORE PLEASING WHEN IT TURNED OUT AS TERRIFIC AS IT DID. A NEW "CATCHER IN THE RYE" FOR A GENERATION OF IRONY-OBSESSED HIPSTERS.

7. LADY SNOWBLOOD (1973. Japan)

THE WILD TALE WITHIN THIS BREATHTAKING EXPLOITATION ARTHOUSE MOVIE STARRING MEIKO KAJI BEGINS WHEN A WOMAN NAMED SAYO LOSES HER HUSBAND AND THEIR SON TO A BAND OF CRIMINALS WHO ATTACK THE FAMILY. SAYO IS TAKEN INTO SLAVERY TO BE RAPED AND BEATEN, ALTHOUGH WHEN THE OPPORTUNITY ARISES, SHE STABS ONE OF HER TORMENTORS AND KILLS HIM -- WHICH RESULTS IN HER ARREST. UNABLE TO AVENGE THE DEATH OF HER FAMILY, SHE SEDUCES A GUARD IN ORDER TO CONCEIVE A BRAT, AND DIES IN CHILDBIRTH. VIGOROUSLY TRAINED FOR REVENGE HER WHOLE LIFE, HER DAUGHTER YUKI BECOMES A MERCILESS KILLING MACHINE, AND LEARNS HOW TO USE BOTH HER BLADE AND HER SEXUAL APPEAL AS WEAPONS. A MUST SEE.

6. OLDBOY (2003. S.Korea)

A MAN SPENDS TEN YEARS CONFINED IN A PRIVATE ROOM, AND HAS NO IDEA WHY. HIS ONLY FORM OF ENTERTAINMENT IS A TV SET AND HIS OWN DELIRIUM. SUDDENLY, ONE DAY HIS BIZARRE INCARCERATION COMES TO AN ABRUPT AND UNEXPLAINED END, AND HE'S FREE TO TRY AND RECLAIM WHAT IS LEFT OF HIS LIFE. THIS INTENSE, BARE-KNUCKLED URBAN THRILLER FROM KOREA WITH ITS MEGA-CRAZY TWIST ENDING FINDS ITS GENESIS IN A JAPANESE COMIC BOOK FROM GARON TSUCHIYA AND NOBUAKI MINEGISHI.

5. MINDGAME (2004. Japan)

DUE TO SOME VILE INJUSTICE I AM NOT AWARE OF, THIS RADICAL ANIMATED MOVIE HAS NOT YET FOUND A RELEASE ON ANY HOME FORMAT IN NORTH AMERICA, NOR WAS IT GIVEN MUCH OF A THEATRICAL RUN OUTSIDE OF A FEW FILM FESTIVAL SCREENINGS -- WHICH IS WHERE I WAS LUCKY ENOUGH TO CATCH IT. I DO INDEED DOUBT THAT MANY PEOPLE HAVE EVER SEEN ANYTHING LIKE THIS MIRACULOUS BUTTER-BLAST OF IMAGINATION THAT WASHES OVER YOU AND MELTS RIGHT INTO YOUR BRAIN LIKE A WAKING DREAM. I'D GO INTO THE PLOT HERE AND NOW, BUT I'D PREFER THAT YOU DID YOUR BEST TO HUNT THIS DOWN VIA WHATEVER NEFARIOUS MEANS YOU NEED EMPLOY, AND ALLOW IT TO UNLOAD RIGHT IN YOUR FACE. -- JUST LIKE IT DID TO ME. TRUST ME, IT IS WORTH THE HUNT.

4. RIKI-OH: THE STORY OF RICKY (1991. H.K.)

WOW. JUST: **WOW**. WORDS STRUGGLE TO DO IT JUSTICE, SO ONCE AGAIN, I'M NOT GOING TO BOTHER WITH A TRADITIONAL SYNOPSIS. THIS MARTIAL-ARTS/GORE/MEN-IN-PRISON ATROCITY IS SO REDONKULOUSLY OVER-THE-TOP AND DESPERATE TO ENTERTAIN AT ALL COSTS -- THAT YOUR EYES NEARLY BLEED AND THEN CATCH FIRE AS YOU STRUGGLE TO TAKE IN THE CINEMATIC INSANITY. THIS IS THE KIND OF MOVIE THAT STAPLES YOUR TITS TO THE COFFEE TABLE AND RESTS ITS TESTICLES ON THE BRIDGE OF YOUR NOSE. YOU KNOW YOU NEED THIS, RIGHT?

3. DANGER: DIABOLIK (1968. Italy)

DON'T TAKE MY WORD FOR IT, COMIC ART MASTER AND HISTORIAN STEPHEN BISSETTE (CREATOR OF THE DC CHARACTERS "THE SWAMP THING" AND "CONSTANTINE") TEACHES FILM APPRECIATION, AND HE FEELS THAT DANGER: DIABOLIK WAS "THE BEST ADAPTATION OF COMIC BOOK TO FEATURE FILM, BAR NONE." DIABOLIK IS A SUPERSPY CAT-BURGLER WHO HAS A TOTALLY CHOICE GADGET-PACKED UNDERGROUND LAIR, A SWEET SILVER SPORTS CAR, AND A FOXY BLONDE BITCH WHO LIKES TO ROLL AROUND NAKED IN A HUGE PILE OF HIS MONEY. BASED ON ONE OF THE LONGEST-RUNNING ITALIAN COMICS OF ALL TIME, WHICH WAS CREATED BY ANGELA AND LUCIANA GIUSSANI -- TWO COOL AND TALENTED SISTERS FROM MILAN.

HAYAO MIYAZAKI'S **NAUSICAÄ OF THE VALLEY OF THE WIND.**

2. FEMALE CONVICT SCORPION
(And its sequels. 1972/1973. Japan)

AKA: **FEMALE PRISONER 701: SCORPION.** ONE OF THE FINEST WOMEN-IN-PRISON FILMS EVER MADE, AND AMONG THE BEST EXPLOITATION MOVIES TO COME OUT OF ASIA. NOT TO OVERSTATE THINGS, BUT I'D GO SO FAR AS TO SAY THAT THIS QUADROLOGY STANDS AS MY FAVOURITE FILM SERIES OF ALL TIME. MEIKO KAJI ELECTRIFIES THE SCREEN AS THE STOIC "SCORPION", A WOMAN WHO IS BETRAYED BY HER GANGSTER BOYFRIEND AND SENT TO A TRULY NASTY AND CORRUPT PRISON TO SUFFER FOR HIS SINS. THIS TRAUMATISING EXPERIENCE AND HIS BETRAYAL HARDEN HER IN WAYS THAT MUST BE SEEN TO

BE BELIEVED. I CAN'T GET ENOUGH OF THIS.

AAAAND... DRUMROLL:

1. NAUSICAÄ OF THE VALLEY OF THE WIND (1984. Japan)

THE **CITIZEN KANE** OF MANGA IS LIFTED UP TO THE SCREEN WITH ALL OF ITS BEAUTY,
WONDER, AND FANTASTIC ENTERTAINMENT VALUE FULLY INTACT. ONE OF THE TRUE LANDMARKS
OF ANIMATION, 25 YEARS AFTER ITS THEATRICAL
RELEASE MIYAZAKI'S MASTERPIECE CONTINUES TO TAKE
MY BREATH AWAY EVERYTIME I SEE IT. IN 1982, A COMIC
ABOUT A KINDLY WARRIOR PRINCESS OF A FICTIONAL
VALLEY APPEARED AS A SERIAL IN "ANIMAGE" MAGAZINE
FROM TOKYO. THE SEQUENTIAL NARRATIVE SOON PROVED
SO POPULAR THAT PUBLIC DEMAND CRIED OUT FOR A FILM
VERSION -- SOMETHING MIYAZAKI TIRELESSLY TOILED ON
EVEN AS HE WAS STRUGGLING TO MEET DEADLINES FOR
THE EPIC COMIC BOOK VERSION. TREMENDOUS STUFF.

NOTE: I REALLY DID TRY TO SHOEHORN SOME OF THE
BETTER AMERICAN SUPERHERO STUFF (**WATCHMEN**,
THE ROCKETEER, **BATMAN BEGINS**, **THE DARK KNIGHT**,
SPIDERMAN 2, **SUPERMAN 1+2**) INTO THIS JUST SO IT
WOULDN'T SEEM LIKE I WAS EXCLUDING THEM ON PURPOSE DUE TO GENRE SNOBBERY OR
SOMETHING. DAMMIT, I TRIED -- BUT I JUST <u>COULDN'T</u> DUMP ANYTHING FROM THE LIST.
SORRY FANBOYS!

THE BLAIR WITCH PROJECT (1999)

IT'S VERY INTERESTING, THE WHOLE BLAIR WITCH
PHENOMENON.

I DON'T THINK I'VE EVER SEEN, IN MY LIFETIME,
A MOVIE THAT HAD **THAT** KIND OF VENOMOUS
BACKLASH TO IT'S POPULARITY. IT WAS SWEEPING,
OVERPOWERING, AND TOOK A MOVIE THAT CRITICS
AND THE GENERAL PUBLIC WERE GENUINELY
THRILLED ABOUT AT THE ONSET (IT IS TO THIS DAY
THE BIGGEST MONEY-MAKING INDEPENDENT
MOVIE ASIDE FROM **DEEP THROAT**, AND HAD THE
HIGHEST RATIO OF BOX OFFICE SALES TO
PRODUCTION COST IN AMERICAN FILMMAKING
HISTORY) AND MADE THE TITLE INTO A VIRTUAL
SWEARWORD. IN FACT, HEATHER DONAHUE
HAS STATED THAT THE TIDAL WAVE OF NEGATIVITY
HAS EVEN LED TO HER HAVING THREATENING ENCOUNTERS AND DIFFICULTY OBTAINING
EMPLOYMENT. NOT A LOT OF LEAD ACTRESSES FROM $248 MILLION DOLLAR BLOCKBUSTERS
HAVE THAT COMPLAINT.

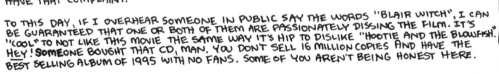

TO THIS DAY, IF I OVERHEAR SOMEONE IN PUBLIC SAY THE WORDS "BLAIR WITCH", I CAN
BE GUARANTEED THAT ONE OR BOTH OF THEM ARE PASSIONATELY DISSING THE FILM. IT'S
"COOL" TO NOT LIKE THIS MOVIE THE SAME WAY IT'S HIP TO DISLIKE "HOOTIE AND THE BLOWFISH."
HEY! **SOME**ONE BOUGHT THAT CD, MAN. YOU DON'T SELL 16 MILLION COPIES AND HAVE THE
BEST SELLING ALBUM OF 1995 WITH NO FANS. SOME OF YOU AREN'T BEING HONEST HERE.

I DON'T CARE HOW MUCH YOU HATED IT, THE BACKLASH AGAINST B.W.P. WAS 99% IN RESPONSE
TO THE HYPE ITSELF, NOT THE MOVIE. GOING BACK A LITTLE FURTHER IN POP CULTURE HISTORY,
IT'S LIKE HOW PEOPLE RESPONDED TO THE POPULARITY OF DISCO MUSIC. WHEN PEOPLE SAY THAT THEY
"HATE DISCO", USUALLY THEY ARE REFERRING TO THE FACT THAT THEY DON'T LIKE THAT IT BECAME
POPULAR. IF THE GENRE HADN'T BEEN HUGE, NO ONE WOULD HAVE CARED.

PEOPLE ARE SHEEP, AND THEY LIKE WHAT THEY'RE TOLD TO LIKE, AND HATE WHAT THEY'RE TOLD TO HATE.

The Most DEADLY WOMEN whoever stalked The EARTH...

WONDER WOMEN

PG
COLOR

WONDER WOMEN (1973)

STATIONED ON A PRIVATE ISLAND OFF THE
COAST OF MANILA, DR. NANCY KWAN SENDS
FIVE KILL-CRAZY KUNG-FU AMAZONS TO
SNATCH THE WORLD'S TOP ATHLETES FOR
USE IN SOME MAD SCIENTIST-STYLE
TRANSPLANT PROCEDURES.

I'VE BEEN WATCHING A LOT OF BALLS-OUT
FILIPINO ACTION MOVIES LATELY, BUT THIS
CELLULOID HAEMORRHOID MAY WELL BE
THE MOST ENTERTAINING OF THE BUNCH.

PAVING THE WAY FOR FOXY ACTRESSES LIKE
JOAN CHEN AND LUCY LIU, NANCY KWAN
WAS THE FIRST REAL ASIAN-AMERICAN
FILM STAR. UNFORTUNATELY HER RUN AS

☆ CONTINUED ON FOLLOWING PAGE

A LEADING LADY WAS VERY SHORT, AND BEFORE LONG SHE WAS APPEARING IN DRIVE-IN SWILL TO PAY THE RENT. ALSO OF NOTE: BEAUTIFUL 70s EXPLOITATION PRINCESS ROBERTA COLLINS, BUG-EYED FROG-BODY VIC DIAZ, AND SASSY SID HAIG AS A PENIS SALESMAN.

NEED ANOTHER REASON TO GET HYPED? WELL, WONDER WOMEN IS WRITTEN AND DIRECTED BY BY THE VASTLY UNDERRATED ROBERT VINCENT O'NEIL, WHO WROTE **VICE SQUAD** (1982) AND DIRECTED **ANGEL** (1984)-- UNARGUABLY TWO OF THE BEST PROSTITUTE-THEMED MOVIES OF THE 1980s. OH, AND WHO DID HE HAVE TO BLOW TO GET A PG-RATING FOR THIS INSANITY?

violences...cruautés...

LE CAMP DES FILLES PERDUES

SS Experiment Love Camp (1976)

AKA CAPTIVE WOMEN II: ORGIES OF THE DAMNED
AKA SS EXPERIMENT CAMP
DIRECTED BY SERGIO GARRONE. ITALY

GARRONE'S EUROTRASH ODE TO FASCISM AND SEXUAL TORTURE WAS BANNED IN BRITAN IN THE 1980s "VIDEO NASTY" WITCH HUNT, BUT CONSIDERING THE LEWD AND EYECATCHING POSTER AND ADVERTISING ART, I'M SAD TO REPORT THAT IT'S SOMEWHAT TAME - EVEN BY TODAY'S STANDARDS.

THATS NOT TO SAY THAT IT'S LIKE WATCHING SESAME STREET THOUGH. IT'S SET IN A SECRET CAMP IN NAZI GERMANY WHERE SS OFFICERS MATE WITH PRISONERS IN CRUEL SEXUAL EXPERIMENTS FOR "THE IMPROVEMENT OF THE RACE", AND THEY 'AINT TALKIN' 'BOUT THE INDY 500. THERE'S SOME NUDITY, SOFT CORE SEX, AND THE AFOREMENTIONED TORTURE - WITH THE TWO HIGHLIGHTS BEING:

1) THE POOR GIRL WHO IS PUT INTO A CONTROLLED WATER TANK, AND THEN HAS TO ENDURE BEING ALTERNATELY BOILED AND THEN FROZEN TO DEATH AS HER CRAZY KRAUT TORMENTERS TOY WITH THE TEMPEARATURE SETTINGS.
2) WHEN THE COMMANDANT ORDERS THE REMOVAL OF A HUNKY SOLDIER'S NUTS, PROVOKING A RESPONSE OF, "OK, YOU BASTARD...WHAT HAVE YOU DONE WITH MY BALLS?"

PRETTY SILLY, BUT THEN THIS ENTIRE GENRE IS TOTALLY LUDICROUS. IT'S LIKE THE PRODUCERS SAT AROUND AND THOUGHT, "HEY! YOU KNOW WHAT'D MAKE THE MOST HEINOUS EPISODE IN MODERN HUMAN HISTORY MORE FUN?! **TITS**!!"

THE TRUE ENTERTAINMENT BENEFITS OF **SS EXPERIMENT CAMP** COME THANKS TO ATROCIOUS DUBBING AND INSANE DIALOG. "WITH ALL THESE BEAUTIFUL WOMEN ARRIVING, LETS HOPE IT'S A SECRET MISSION OF A SEXUAL NATURE, HEH HEH.." IS UP THERE, BUT THE REAL JAW-DROPPER COMES WHEN A FEMALE PRISONER (WHO HAS BEEN REPEATEDLY RAPED BY A SADISTIC FEMALE DOCTOR) PLOPS MARMALADE ON HER DAILY BREAD AND OPENLY SIGHS: "I HAVEN'T HAD MARMALADE FOR AGES! IF THESE GUYS KEEP TREATING US LIKE THIS, THEY'VE GOT MY VOTE!"

NEW YORK RIPPER (1982)

DIRECTED BY LUCIO FULCI

A BLADE WIELDING PSYCHOPATH WHO TALKS LIKE DONALD DUCK (!?!) IS QUACKING UP A STORM IN NEW YORK CITY WHILE KILLING YOUNG BEAUTIFUL WOMEN. NYPD DETECTIVES PLAYED BY JACK HEDLEY AND PAOLO MALCO FOLLOW THE TRAIL OF BUTCHERY FROM THE DECKS OF THE STATEN ISLAND FERRY TO THE SLEAZY SEX SHOWS OF TIMES SQUARE.

IT'S AN 80s SLASHER MOVIE OF THE HIGHEST ORDER AND AT THE TOP OF ITS GENRE, BUT IT'S ALSO GOT GIALLO STYLINGS. ALL OF THE TRADEMARK RED HERRINGS ARE SYSTEMATICALLY EXCLUDED, INCLUDED, AND THEN OCCASIONALLY CHOPPED INTO BLOODY CHUNKS IN THIS VICIOUS FILM WHERE ONE ASTONISHING HIGHLIGHT IS A VERY GRAPHIC SCENE FEATURING A BROKEN BOTTLE BEING RAMMED INTO THE VAGINA OF **ANTHROPOPHAGUS** STAR ZORA KEROVA.

AND SHE'S FAR FROM THE ONLY VICTIM TO GET IT IN AN OVERTLY NASTY FASHION. **RIPPER** HAS MORE THAN ENOUGH SHOCK EFFECTS TO MAKE IT STICK IN ANYONE'S CRAW, AND SOME OF THESE SICKENING SCENES HAVE YET TO FIND AN EQUAL. WOMEN ARE GUTTED FROM GROIN TO STERNUM (SHOT AMAZINGLY FROM <u>INSIDE</u> THE TORSO!), AND ONE HAS HER NIPPLE AND EYEBALL SLOWLY BISECTED WITH A RAZOR BLADE. EWWW...

THE KILLING IMPLEMENTS ARE THE REAL STARS, AND GET THEIR OWN CLOSE-UPS. WHEN THEY FLY THROUGH THE AIR TOWARDS A VICTIM, THE SOUNDTRACK FUCKING CRANKS RIGHT UP AS THE SINISTER WEAPONS MAKE A "SWIIIISHH!!" BEFORE FINDING THEIR FLESHY TARGETS. THE DAMAGE IS EXTREME, AND FULCI ZOOMS IN AS THE BLOOD JETS OUT.

NEW YORK RIPPER HAS STIRRED MUCH DISCUSSION OVER THE YEARS, AND HAS FOUND ITSELF BANNED ABOVE ALL IN PLACES LIKE THE UK AND GERMANY WHERE STRICT VIOLENCE-IN-ENTERTAINMENT POLICIES RESIDE. THE VIOLENCE AND DEATH IN THIS FILM IS STARK AND **BRUTAL**, ULTIMATELY

«de slachter van New York»

THE NEW YORK RIPPER

Jack Hedley   Almanta Keller
Howard Ross   Andrew Painter

een film van Lucio Fulci

EASTMANCOLOR TECHNISCOPE®   CONCORDE FILM

PROMPTING MULTITUDES OF KNEE-JERK CRITICS AND REVIEWERS TO LABEL IT AS "MISOGYNIST CRAP", "MADE FOR WEIRDOS WHO GET OFF ON WATCHING WOMEN GETTING TORTURED", AND "THE MOST EVIL FORM OF FILMMAKING." WHILE NOT TOTALLY UNTRUE, THIS SORT OF REACTION IS SHORTSIGHTED AND BETRAYS THEIR FRAGILE VANILLA SUBURBAN SENSIBILITIES. FULCI WAS A MASTER AT THE VIOLENT-GORE GENRE, AND OFTEN GLEEFULLY PUSHED THE ENVELOPE IN TERMS OF BAD TASTE. IT JUST SO HAPPENS THAT IN THIS PARTICULAR FILM, THE KILLER FULCI FEATURED IS A MISOGYNIST AND CHOSE TO MURDER WOMEN. IF A FILM FEATURES A CHARACTER WHO IS RACIST, DOES THAT AUTOMATICALLY MAKE IT A RACIST MOVIE? I'D LIKE TO THINK NOT.

THE ACTING IS GREAT, THE DONALD DUCK VOICE HILARIOUS, AND THIS IS FULCI AT HIS SICKEST. THE FINALE HAS A WONDERFUL TWIST WHICH YOU'LL NEVER EXPECT, BUT IF YOU BUY OR RENT THE ANCHOR BAY DVD - DON'T LOOK AT THE BACK COVER IF YOU'RE INTERESTED IN FIGURING OUT WHO THE KILLER IS ON YOUR OWN. YOU'VE BEEN WARNED: SUPER-SPOILER.

THIS MOVIE IS **VILE!**

ROBIN'S A WHINY LITTLE SELF-PUBLISHIN' BITCH

BOUGIE '03

A-ANYBODY WANT A FREE COPY OF MY MAGAZINE? IT TOOK ALL OF M-MY TIME AND MONEY TO MAKE.

HELLO?

HEY FAGGOT! I MIGHT TAKE ONE OF THOSE TO WIPE MY ASS WITH...

!OH! T-THANK YOU!

...BUT YOU GOTTA MAKE IT WORTH MY WHILE, BITCH.

:WHIMPER:

JAB FUCK JAB

HA HA HA!

OH GOD! I'VE GOT SO MANY MORE -SOB- COPIES TO GET RID OF!

IT'LL BE A RELIEF WHEN THEY JUST PISS IN MY FACE.

walking down 42nd street ☆ BY SHAWN "OLD MAN" JOHNS ☆

TO ME AS A TEENAGER, NEW YORK'S INFAMOUS 42ND STREET WAS THE GREATEST PLACE ON EARTH. IT CONTAINED EVERYTHING YOU'D NEVER SEE IN MAINSTREAM AMERICA, AND FOR THE BRAVE OF HEART IT'D PROVIDE THRILLS NO CIRCUS OR CARNIVAL COULD EVER HOPE TO SHOW YOU.

I'D USUALLY WALK OVER INTO TIMES SQUARE FROM THE GRAND CENTRAL TERMINAL AFTER TAKING A 45 MINUTE TRAIN RIDE IN FROM WESTCHESTER CO. MIXED IN WITH A SEA OF HOMELESS VAGRANTS, HOOKERS, PIMPS, MENTAL CASES MUMBLING TO THEMSELVES, CONMEN TRYING EVERY KIND OF HUSTLE KNOWN TO MAN, STREET GANGS, OLD NASTY PEDOPHILES TRYING TO PICK UP YOUNG BOYS, AND OTHER ASSORTED PSYCHOS, THERE WERE THOSE BRIGHT, GLARING NEON SIGNS OF THE DEUCE MOVIE HOUSES. THESE GRAND THEATERS WOULD ENTICE THE PUBLIC IN WITH ALL MANNER OF LURID DELIGHTS. DOUBLE AND TRIPLE BILLS OF GORY HORROR, KUNG-FU, VIOLENT PORN, AND ACTION FILMS LINED UP THE STREET IN EVERY ONE OF THE 10 OR SO THEATERS OPEN, THEIR HUGE MARQUEES DISPLAYING THE MOST VIOLENT SCENES

FROM EACH FILM.

THE DEUCE

Ilsa Harem Keeper of the Oil Sheiks/Wanda the Wicked Warden: The last movie I saw on 42nd Street, there was a stabbing in the middle of the theater. When the fight broke out, everyone screamed and crouched by the seats until the cops came. We stayed there until they took the troublemakers away, then got back in our seats and watched the end of the show.

MOST OF THE FILMS SHOWING WOULDN'T SEE THE LIGHT OF DAY IN ANY SUBURBAN THEATER AND SOME WOULD ONLY PLAY 42ND FOR A WEEK OR LESS, THEN BE GONE FOREVER. FILMS LIKE **CRY RAPE, NAZI LOVE CAMP 27, SLAVES IN CAGES, MEAN MOTHER, TORTURE DUNGEON, MY FRIENDS NEED KILLING**, AND

THE KILLER WORE GLOVES. EVEN WITH TODAY'S MASSIVE AMOUNTS OF TITLES RELEASED ON VHS AND DVD, MANY STRANGE LITTLE FILMS THAT PLAYED THE DEUCE HAVE YET TO SHOW UP ANYWHERE ELSE.

AT THE AGE OF 14, ONE OF MY GREATEST THRILLS WAS GOING TO SEE **ILSA: SHE WOLF OF THE SS** AT ITS "WORLD PREMIERE" AT THE APOLLO 42ND. EVEN THE NORMALLY ROWDY TIMES SQUARE AUDIENCE WAS SHOCKED TO SILENCE AT MANY OF THE FILM'S EXTREMELY BLOODY TORTURE SCENES. IT WAS TRULY AN EXPERIENCE I'D NEVER FORGET. I'LL ALSO NEVER FORGET THE ANGRY CROWDS OF YOUNG BLACKS LINING UP TO SEE THE

N.Y. PREMIERE OF **NIGGER LOVER** PLAYING WITH **THE HOT BOX** AT THE LYRIC THEATER. AT A SHOWING OF **LORD SHANGO** AND **A KNIFE FOR THE LADIES** AT THE HARRIS, SOMEONE SNATCHED A PURSE UP ON THE BALCONY AND TOOK OFF INTO THE STREET — LEAVING THE POOR WOMAN SCREAMING FOR HELP. BEFORE LONG MEMBERS OF THE JADED AUDIENCE WERE YELLING AT HER TO "SHUT UP!". THE FUNNIEST MOMENT OCCURRED AT THE NEW AMSTERDAM ONE NIGHT DURING **THE RUNAWAYS**, WHEN SOME GUY LET OUT A TREMENDOUSLY LOUD FART SENDING THE CROWD

INTO HYSTERICS! IT WAS SLEAZY-FUNNY MOMENTS LIKE THESE THAT MADE MOVIEGOING ON 42ND ST. SO ENJOYABLE.

BETWEEN THE YEARS OF 1974 TO 1977, I TRIED TO MAKE WEEKLY TRIPS INTO TIMES SQUARE TO GO SEE ALL SORTS OF BIZARRE FILMS. NOT TOO MANY WOULD VENTURE INTO THE FREEZING WINTER COLD TO TAKE IN **SHRIEK OF THE MUTILATED** AND **MOON CHILD**, BUT I WOULD WITHOUT THINKING TWICE! MY DEVOTION TO THIS SLEAZY WORLD BECAME AN OBSESSION. I'D BECOME DETERMINED TO SEE EVERY OBSCURE VIOLENT CULT FILM EVER MADE — AND AT THE TIME, THE ONLY WAY TO SEE THEM WAS ON TIMES SQUARE. SOMETIMES I HAD TO GET MY COURAGE UP WITH A BOTTLE OF SANGRIA MIXED WITH APPEDRINES TO GET MY NERVE UP — AND THE OL' ADRENALINE FLOWING, JUST SO I COULD BE IN THE RIGHT STATE TO ENTER THAT BIZARRE WORLD.

NOW, VIRTUALLY ALL OF TIMES SQUARE AS I KNEW IT HAS BEEN DESTROYED, AND ALL THE GREAT MOVIEHOUSES CLOSED IN ORDER TO "CLEAN UP THE AREA" AND MAKE IT PALATABLE TO ALL THE MINDLESS ZOMBIE-LIKE SOULESS MASSES THAT WORSHIP THEIR GOD DISNEY AND THE N.I.M.B.Y. WAY OF LIFE.

BUT MY MEMORIES OF 42ND STREET ARE ALWAYS FRESH AND KEPT ALIVE BY MY WRITINGS AND BY WATCHING SLEAZY GORE FLICKS ON MY VCR. MY HAT IS OFF TO ALL THE GREAT 42ND STREET THEATERS LIKE THE HARRIS, LYRIC, SELWYN, APOLLO, NEW AMSTERDAM, LIBERTY, ANCO, CINE 42 TWINS, AND TIMES SQUARE... BECAUSE WITHOUT THEM MY TEEN YEARS WOULD HAVE BEEN MUCH EMPTIER.

REST · IN · PEACE

ROBIN, WHAT ARE YOU WORKING ON?
EBAY DVD'S

UM... YOU'RE BUYING MORE?
MUST HAVE MORE
YES

DON'T YOU ALREADY HAVE 80 DISCS YOU HAVEN'T EVEN LOOKED AT YET?

ROBIN?

SWEET BABY JESUS, HELP ME!!!

CANNIBAL FEROX

NEXT TO **CANNIBAL HOLOCAUST** (1980) THIS 1981 UMBERTO LENZI EFFORT IS GENERALLY CONSIDERED BY EUROTRASH FANATICS AS THE MOST UPSETTING AND MOST INFAMOUS OF THE LEGENDARY ITALIAN CANNIBAL-THEMED HORROR MOVIES. I'D CERTAINLY CITE IT AS ONE OF MY ALL-TIME GORE-HORROR FAVES, WHAT WITH ITS AMAZING MACHETE-CASTRATION AND HARROWING BREAST/HOOK IMPALEMENT SCENES. THIS IS <u>NOT</u> A MOVIE FOR THE MEEK.

RETITLED "THE WOMAN FROM DEEP RIVER" IN AUSTRALIA TO CASH IN ONE OF LENZI'S PREVIOUS CANNIBAL FILMS (**THE MAN FROM DEEP RIVER** 1972), THE MOVIE CONTAINS SEVERAL ON-SCREEN ACTUAL ANIMAL KILLINGS. THOUGH HIS EVIL CHARACTER MESSILY MASSACRES AN ANIMAL IN THE MOVIE, ACTOR JOHN MORGHEN STRONGLY OBJECTED AND REFUSED TO PARTICIPATE (A DOUBLE HAD TO BE USED). DIRECTOR UMBERTO LENZI TRIED TO CONVINCE HIM TO DO THE KILLING BY TELLING HIM, "DENIRO WOULD DO IT", TO WHICH MORGHEN RESPONDED: "DENIRO WOULD KICK YOUR ASS ALL THE WAY BACK TO ROME!".

SALO: 120 DAYS OF SODOM (1975)

SHORTLY AFTER CRITERION RELEASED SALO IN 1997, THE DVD WAS PULLED FROM CIRCULATION AND BECAME THE MOST SOUGHT-AFTER DISC IN THE FORMAT'S HISTORY. DESPITE HAVING THE WORST TRANSFER AND POOREST SUBTITLES OF ANY CRITERION OFFERING, PRICES GOT RIDICULOUSLY HIGH IN ONLINE AUCTIONS. IN 2008, IT WAS FINALLY GIVEN A PROPER DOUBLE-DISC RERELEASE.

BANNED IN SEVERAL COUNTRIES (BECAUSE OF ITS GRAPHIC PORTRAYALS OF RAPE, HUMILIATION, TORTURE AND MURDER) DIRECTOR PIER PAOLO PASOLINI BASED HIS CONTROVERCIAL MOVIE ON THE NOVEL BY THE MARQUIS DE SADE, AND SET IT IN THE FASCIST PERIOD OF THE LAST DAYS OF MUSSOLINI'S REGIME IN ITALY. IT WOULD BE PASOLINI'S LAST FILM, THOUGH. HE WAS MURDERED SHORTLY BEFORE ITS THEATRICAL RELEASE.

DESPITE THE SEVERE CONTENT, I FIND THE MOVIE SOMEWHAT STALE, AND HAVE BEEN KNOWN TO FALL ASLEEP WATCHING IT.

145

CAGED TERROR (1973)

GOLDEN APPLES OF THE SUN

FILMED IN MONTEBELLO QUEBEC AND RELEASED IN CANADA ON JUNE 6th 1973 (ALTHOUGH FILMING WRAPPED IN NOVEMBER 1971) THIS "HORROR" MOVIE BY BARRIE ANGUS McLEAN HAD A BUDGET OF $130 THOUSAND DOLLARS, AND A WORKING TITLE (**GOLDEN APPLES OF THE SUN**) POMPOUSLY LIFTED FROM THE YEATS POEM "THE SONG OF WANDERING AENGUS".

FORGOTTEN OR TOTALLY UNHEARD OF EVEN TO MOST CANADIANS, CAGED TERROR IS A STRANGE CREATURE. PART PRETENTIOUS LOAD OF POO, PART GENUINELY ATMOSPHERIC EXPLOITATION MOVIE, THIS IS THE ONLY GENRE FEATURE I KNOW THAT WOULD HAVE ONE CHARACTER SPOUT OFF: "YEAH, WELL, YOU PROBABLY THINK THE SONG OF SOLOMAN WAS AN ALLEGORY FOR CHRIST'S LOVE OF THE CHURCH..."

NEARLY AN HOUR OF THIS MOVIE CAPTURES NOTHING MORE THAN A MAN AND A WOMAN WALKING THROUGH THE WOODS AND BABBLING PSEUDO-INTELLECTUAL GOBBLEDEGOOK. ALMOST EVERY LINE OF DIALOGUE DELIVERED HERE IS UPROARIOUSLY AND UNINTENTIONALLY FUNNY ("I FEEL THAT LIFE IS MADE UP OF AS MANY TINY COMPARTMENTS AS THIS POMEGRANATE ... BUT IS IT AS BEAUTIFUL?") THE PRETENSION IS CRIPPLING.

IF IT SOUNDS LIKE I HATED THIS MOVIE THEN I'M GIVING THE WRONG IMPRESSION. IN FACT, I WAS REALLY ENTERTAINED BY JUST HOW FAR BARRIE McLEAN WOULD TAKE THIS CONCEPT AND MILK IT. THE DUDE (PERCY HARKNESS) THINKS HE'S THE OUTDOORS JAMES JOYCE, AND CAN IDENTIFY WHAT BIRD A SPECIFIC FEATHER CAME FROM BECAUSE HIS DAD TOOK HIM FISHING ONCE. THE CHICK (ELIZABETH SUZUKI) IS A PONTIFICATING FLOWER CHILD WHO REALLY HAS NO FUCKING CLUE, SO NO MATTER WHAT BULLSHIT PERCY WAXES POETIC ABOUT, SHE THINKS HE'S ABSORBING AND BRILLIANT.

TOGETHER THEY WALK, AND THEY TALK, AND THEY WALK SOME MORE. THEN MORE TALKING. WAS THERE EVEN A SCRIPT, OR DID THEY JUST LET TWO COLLEGE STUDENTS TRY TO IMPRESS EACH OTHER FOR AN HOUR AND THEN SERVE IT UP UNEDITED? "GOLDEN APPLES..." SEEMS TO REALLY, **REALLY** WANT TO BE SOMETHING IMPORTANT, AND WORKS TO ATTAIN THIS BY REACHING IN DESPERATION FOR ELEMENTS OF INGMAR BERGMAN. THE WAYS IN WHICH IT FAILS IN THIS QUEST ARE ACTUALLY FAR MORE ENTERTAINING THAN IF IT HAD SUCCEEDED.

AFTER BROWBEATING HIS NUBILE ASIAN-AMERICAN GAL-PAL WITH QUASI-PHILOSOPHICAL DOUCHEBAGGERY FOR THE BETTER PART OF AN AFTERNOON, THIS YOUNG URBAN PROFESSIONAL SPOTS A CABIN IN THE WOODS. IT'S A...

... WHAT THE SHIT? SOMETHING HAPPENS! HOLY CRAP! LOOK OVER THERE! IT'S A COUPLE OF VIETNAM VETS! THEY DO SCARY THINGS LIKE SING FOLK MUSIC, AND ONE OF THEM IS NAMED "TROUBADOUR"!

SOME GUNS ARE FIRED, SOME FEELINGS ARE HURT, PERCY GETS TIED UP, ELIZABETH GETS FELT UP, AND IT ALL CULMINATES IN SOME BIZARRE PSYCHOLOGICAL TORTURE TAKING PLACE IN A FUCKING CHICKEN COOP! **COOL!** THE DYNAMICS OF THIS SCENE ARE TOTALLY DIFFERENT THAN IF IT HAD EVEN REMOTELY MATCHED THE PREVIOUS 2 ACTS. THE JUXTAPOSITION WORKS, AND SOMEHOW, SOMEWAY -- ALL THE PRIOR SMOKE GETTING BLOWN UP OUR ASSES BECOMES WORTHWHILE. WHAT WAS INTENDED AS AN INTELLECTUAL CIVICS LESSON BECOMES A CRASH COURSE IN VIEWING DISCOMFORT AND CANADIANA WEIRDNESS THAT CINEMA SEWER READERS WILL LOVE TO HATE -- OR MAYBE EVEN LOVE TO LOVE. RECOMMENDED.

THE AMAZING BARRIE McLEAN PRODUCED 42 FILMS FOR THE NATIONAL FILM BOARD OF CANADA, AND FIRST STARTED AS A MUSIC EDITOR AND ASSISTANT CAMERA OPERATOR. IN 1961 HE LEFT THE FILM BOARD FOR AN EXCEPTIONALLY VARIED CAREER, BUT IN 1990 29 YEARS AFTER LEAVING THE BOARD, McLEAN RETURNED AS EXECUTIVE PRODUCER OF THE NFB's FAMED ANIMATION STUDIO. BARRIE McLEAN DIED SUDDENLY IN APRIL 1998.

-BOUGIE '08

IN **ON THE RIGHT TRACK** GARY COLEMAN PLAYS A HOMELESS SHOESHINE BOY WHO KNOWS HOW TO PREDICT THE WINNERS AT THE HORSE RACES, AND LIVES IN A LOCKER IN CHICAGO'S UNION STATION. HE'S BELOVED BY ALL THE WORKERS IN THE STATION, ESPECIALLY BY THE PIZZA GUY AND THE CUTE CASHIER GIRL IN THE ARCADE. HOLY SHIT, WAS THIS **STUPID.**

JOY (1975 AKA "I WANT MORE") OPENS WITH A GROUP OF HIGH SCHOOLERS, AMONG THEM A VERY YOUNG CINEMA SEWER FAVE SHARON MITCHELL WHO PLAYS THE TITLE ROLE. JOY IS A TIGHT LITTLE PRUDE WHO REFUSES TO PUT OUT FOR HER BOYFRIEND, HOPING TO REMAIN A VIRGIN UNTIL MARRIAGE -- BUT IS INSTEAD RAPED BY TWO MEXICANS. YOU KNOW HOW IT GOES.

BEING RAPED IS PRESENTED AS A WONDERFUL EYE-OPENER FOR JOY, THE INTRODUCTION TO AN OBSESSION THAT WILL MAKE HER A CUM-CRAZY NYMPHO. AS A RESULT SHE BEGINS RANDOMLY FUCKING MEN ACROSS NEW YORK, CREATING A MALE "RAPE" EPIDEMIC AS SHE WANDERS THE STREETS AS A SLUTTY SEX VIGILANTE, MOLESTING THRILLED MEN RIGHT WHERE THEY STAND. OF NOTE IS HER CREEPY BACK-ALLEY STALKING OF RICHARD (**CANNIBAL HOLOCAUST**) BOLLA, AND FORCING HERSELF ON A BOOKWORM IN A SUBWAY CAR. THE POLITICALLY INCORRECT AND BRAZENLY ANARCHISTIC POLITICS WITH WHICH THIS MOVIE IS FILLED, ARE FURTHERED BY THE PORTRAYAL OF THE NYC POLICE FORCE AS THE ONLY ONES AGAINST WHAT JOY IS DOING. TO EVERYONE ELSE, SHE'S A HERO.

LT. HANDCOCK (JACK TEAGUE) HAS HIS HAND ON HIS COCK WHEN WE FIRST MEET HIM, AND HE LAUNCHES A MASSIVE SEARCH FOR THE CUM-FUELED TEENAGER. HE PUTS A BLACK COP WITH A BIG FAT DONG ON THE JOB. HIS NAME IS BARNS AND HE TAKES HIS JOB SERIOUSLY. ("I'LL PUT THAT CUNT IN HER PLACE!") WHEN HE FINALLY CATCHES UP TO THE YOUNG WOMAN, HE DRAGS HER INTO A FILTHY STAIRWELL, BRUTALLY RAPES HER, BLOWS HIS LOAD ON HER FACE, THEN PLACES HER UNDER ARREST. AMAZINGLY, THIS GRIM SUBJECT MATTER IS PRESENTED AS SEVERE IN A MOVIE WHERE ALL THE OTHER SEX IS PLAYED FOR LAUGHS.

A MOVIE LIKE **JOY** WOULD HAVE FEMINISTS RIOTING IN THE STREETS IF IT WERE RELEASED IN THEATRES TODAY, ALTHOUGH IT DOES A GOOD JOB OF APING **DEATH WISH** (1974) AND DRAWS A VALID PARALLEL BETWEEN SEXUAL FRUSTRATION AND VIOLENCE. THE DEEDS OF JOY ARE PRESENTED AS FUNCTIONING AS A PUBLIC SERVICE, WITH A NUMBER OF MONTAGES SHOWN OF PEOPLE HAPPILY CUDDLING AND KISSING IN THE CITY AS A RESULT OF JOY'S LEGEND GROWING AND THEIR NEW-FOUND DESIRE TO LOVE TOTAL STRANGERS THEY MEET IN PUBLIC.

AFTER BEING CAUGHT AND ARRESTED, JOY IS TIED TO A GURNEY AND INTERROGATED BY HANDCOCK. "YOU'RE A DANGEROUS CRIMINAL!" HE TELLS HER WHILE HE WAVES HIS PISTOL IN HER FACE. SHE RESPONDS BY FELLATING THE HANDGUN, AND BEGGING TO BE FUCKED IN THE PUSSY WITH IT. HE AGREES TO DO SO, AND THEN FEEDS THE AMOROUS TEEN SOME DICK. HE LETS HER GO IF SHE PROMISES TO LEAVE TOWN AND NEVER COME BACK, SO SHE HOPS ON THE NEXT PLANE -- BUT NOT BEFORE PARTAKING IN A GRAND FINALE 5 PERSON GANG BANG ON A URINE-CAKED FLOOR OF AN AIRPORT MENS ROOM. THE SCENE IS FILTHY AND **VERY** HOT.

JOY *joy* XXX STARRING Sharon Mitchell Richard Bolla Melinda Marlowe

JOY SET A STANDARD FOR HIGH QUALITY CINEMATOGRAPHY IN XXX, AND WAS PROMOTED AS A BREAKTHROUGH THAT COULD LIFT THE UNRESPECTED ADULT FILM INDUSTRY TO CONVENTIONAL FILMMAKING STANDARDS. THE MOVIE IS SOMETIMES CREDITED TO **MANIAC** AND **VIGILANTE** DIRECTOR BILL LUSTIG (WHO WENT ON TO START THE AWESOME "BLUE UNDERGROUND" DVD LABEL) BUT THE ACTUAL CREDIT WAS "HARLEY MANSFIELD", WHO MANY CLAIM WAS CHUCK VINCENT. APPARENTLY, VINCENT THOUGHT THE RAPE-PACKED FILM WAS TOO VIOLENT TO PUT HIS REAL NAME ON.

STILL, THERE ARE DIFFERING OPINIONS. MOVIE ENTHUSIAST WADE PARKER STATED THAT "LUSTIG WAS INVOLVED IN SOME WAY WITH **JOY**. HE REMEMBERS SHOOTING IT, AND CONFIRMED THAT MITCHELL WAS ONLY 17 WHEN IT WAS SHOT. PRODUCERS HAD TO WAIT UNTIL SHE TURNED 18 BEFORE THEY RELEASED IT."

BUT I CALL BULLSHIT. IN AN INTERVIEW I READ WITH LUSTIG, HE DENIED MAKING **JOY**, BUT COPPED TO 2 OTHER PORN FILMS FROM THE ERA -- **HOT HONEY**, AND **VIOLATION OF CLAUDIA**. IT'S ALSO WORTH NOTING THAT THE NEW YORK LOCATION WHERE JERRY BUTLER KISSES VERONICA HART IN CHUCK VINCENT'S **ROOMMATES** IS USED IN **JOY** NUMEROUS TIMES, AND THE FILM WAS CUT TOGETHER BY CHUCK'S USUAL EDITOR.

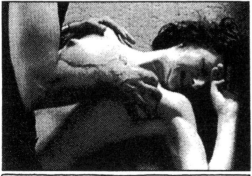

A COP NAMED BARNS BRUTALLY RAPES JOY.

RADICAL TIM GOLUB'S TEENBEAT — HA!! HA HA! HA HA! — THAT IS SO AWESOME!!!!!!

PREPARING THE PEOPLE FOR 100% TEEN CINEMA MELTDOWN

THE LEGEND OF BILLIE JEAN (1985)

BILLIE JEAN, PLAYED BY NONE OTHER THAN SUPERGIRL (HELEN SLATER), AND HER BROTHER BINX, PLAYED BY NONE OTHER THAN KUFFS (CHRISTIAN SLATER - AND NO - THEY AREN'T SIBLINGS IN REAL LIFE) ARE JUST OUT FOR SOME GOOD OLE DOWN HOME TEXAS FUN. IT'S SUMMER, AND THEY HEAD TO YON WATERIN' HOLE. BUT TODAY IS THE DAY THE LOCAL BULLIES (INCLUDING A CREEPY ONE WHO CONSTANTLY TAKES PICTURES OF THE LOVELY MISS JEAN) DECIDE TO REALLY TORMENT THEM. BINX AND BILLIE TAKE OFF ON BINX'S SCOOTER (WHICH HE LOVES MORE THAN ANYTHING ON EARTH) AND THE GANG - LED BY "HUBIE" - CHASES THEM IN A CONVERTIBLE. SO WHAT DO BILLIE JEAN AND BINX DO? THEY STOP FOR A MILKSHAKE. HEY...IT'S HOT IN TEXAS. WHY THE HELL NOT? ANYWAYS, EVENTUALLY THE SCOOTER GETS TRASHED, SO BILLIE JEAN TRIES TO GET THE REPAIR MONEY FROM HUBIE'S DAD, PLAYED BY RICHARD BRADFORD. UNFORTUNATELY, HE'S NOT WILLING TO HAND IT OVER WITHOUT SOME VAGINAL ENVELOPING. THINGS ESCALATE, AND BINX COMES IN AND SHOOTS HIM. THE KIDS FLEE, AND OUR MOVIE IS REALLY OFF AND RUNNING.

THE CAST - FOR THE MOST PART - IS REALLY GREAT. BUT PERHAPS THE BEST PERFORMANCE IS BY HELEN SLATER'S HAIR STYLIST. BILLIE JEAN'S HAIR, AND THE SUBSEQUENT MIMICKING CUTS THAT ALL THE YOUNG GIRLS THAT ADMIRE HER REBELLION GET, IS LIKE TOTAL POST APOCALYPTIC WASTELAND NEW WAVE. SHIT, MAN! CAN YOU IMAGINE LIVING IN A WORLD LIKE THIS? THE POST-FUTURISTIC HAIRSTYLES COUPLED WITH THE CONVENIENCES AND CONTRACEPTIVES OF OUR MODERN WORLD? SOUNDS LIKE HEAVEN TO ME.

HELEN SLATER AS BILLIE JEAN

BOUGIE

THERE'S A LOT OF HELLA COOL SHIT IN THIS MOVIE. I LOVED THE ABANDONED MINI GOLF COURSE LOCATION, BUT IT DID MAKE ME AWFULLY JEALOUS. I WISH I HAD A CASTLE I COULD GO HIDE IN, OR MAYBE EVEN MAKE OUT IN. A FRIEND OF MINE NAMED SARAH USED TO LIVE UP IN PARKSVILLE WHERE THAT HUGE FUCKIN' MINI GOLF COURSE IS. SHE USED TO DATE THE OWNER'S SON. I'LL LET YOU CONNECT THE DOTS. WHOO-HOO! OR HOW ABOUT THE RICH KID'S WATERSLIDE CONNECTING UP TO HIS BEDROOM WINDOW? IMAGINE GETTING UP IN THE MORNING? YOU'D JUST HAVE TO DRAG YOURSELF TO YOUR WINDOW AND LET THE FUN BEGIN.

REBECCA DART'S VERSION OF RADICAL TIM GOLUB

"I WISH I HAD A CASTLE I COULD GO HIDE IN, OR MAYBE EVEN MAKE OUT IN..."

TISSUE IN NOSE!

AND HOW OFTEN IS ONE ALLOWED TO BEAR WITNESS TO SUCH A COHESIVE REBELLIOUS YOUTH UNDERGROUND? EVERYWHERE THIS ADORABLE LITTLE FUGITIVE GOES, KIDS HELP HER AND ARE KIND TO HER. NO ONE IS RATTIN' OR FRONTIN'. IT JUST FELT AS IF ALL THESE KIDS WERE IN IT TOGETHER. THIS BECAME RATHER SURREAL IN ONE STRANGE SCENE WHERE BILLIE WANDERS INTO SOME INDUSTRIAL BASEMENT AREA WHERE ALL THESE STRANGE KIDS ARE JUST HANGIN' OUT — AND WITHIN SECONDS - ARE ALL CHEERING FOR HER.

BUT IT'S NOT ALL SMILES AND LOLLIPOPS. LET ME TRANSCRIBE MY NOTEBOOK REGARDING THE DISCOVERY OF LISA SIMPSON'S VOICE IN A CO-STARRING ROLE: "YEARDLEY SMITH NOOOOOO!". "YEARDLEY SMITH'S MOTHER HITS HER. GOOD." "FUCK YOU YEARDLEY SMITH." BROTHERS AND SISTERS, I'M NOT A CRUEL MAN. IT'S JUST HARD TO STOMACH YEARDLEY COMPLETELY BEREFT OF DIGNITY DUE TO HER POOR AND ANNOYING PERFORMANCE, ESPECIALLY SINCE I'VE FALLEN IN LOVE WITH LISA SIMPSON MORE THAN A COUPLE TIMES IN MY HORMONALLY CONFUSED PAST.

MY SECOND PROBLEM IS THE ABSOLUTE FUCKING HEAVY-HANDED NATURE THE MOVIE GOES INTO WHILE TURNING BILLIE JEAN INTO AN ALLEGORY FOR JOAN OF ARC. ONE CHARACTER EVEN GOES SO FAR AS TO SAY "YOU'RE SAINT JOAN!" GIVE ME A BREEEEEAAAKYK. I'M PRETTY SURE I COULD HAVE FIGURED IT OUT FROM THE BIG SYMBOLICAL BONFIRE SCENE AT THE END.

ALSO: METHINKS BILLIE JEAN AND BINX'S RELATIONSHIP IS A LITTLE TOO INTENSE FOR SIBLINGS. IN ONE SCENE WHERE CHRISTIAN SLATER'S BINX IS TALKING ABOUT VERMONT (VERMONT, VERMONT, ALWAYS VERMONT) HE MENTIONS SNOWBALLS, AND FOR A BRIEF SECOND AN IMAGE OF HELEN SLATER SNOWBALLING SOME OF CHRISTIAN'S TASTY LOVE JUICE FLASHED INTO MY HEAD. IT'S JUST REALLY HURT THE FILM MUCH - AND I'M STILL FULLY DOWN WITH THE B.J.

CLASS OF 1984 (1982)

IT'S A CRAZY WORLD WE'RE LIVING IN, AND THE NEAR-FUTURE WORLD OF **CLASS OF 1984** PREDICTED THAT IT WOULD ONLY GET CRAZIER. THIS IS A WONDERFUL MOVIE ABOUT A GROUP OF PUNKS (THE KIND OF PUNKS WHO MAKE BEING A PUNK COOL - ASIDE FROM ALL THE SWASTIKAS) CLASHING WITH THE NEW BAND TEACHER WHO REFUSES TO LOOK THE OTHER WAY. ESCALATION IS THE ORDER OF THE DAY HERE, SET AMID A BACKDROP OF YOUTHFUL HIJINKS, TEEN PROSTITUTION, VIOLENT ASSAULT, AND DRUGS DRUGS DRUGS. WHAT ELSE CAN I SAY?

CLASS OF 1984

CRAZEE PUNK ACTION!!

IT'S GOT IT ALL, MICHAEL J. FOX AS A BANDSTAND NERD WHO GETS THE SHIT BEATEN OUT OF HIM IS A HIGHLIGHT. OR HOW ABOUT THE RAPE OF A TEACHER'S PREGNANT WIFE? THIS IS ONE HARDCORE HIGHSCHOOL! ALTHOUGH THERE IS NO NUDITY OR PROLONGED VIOLENCE INVOLVED, THE POTENTIAL FOR BONECHILLIN' BLEAKNESS WAS **SO** MUCH GREATER. WHAT ABOUT A MISCARRIAGE? YOU KNOW, WITH BLOOD ALL OVER EVERYWHERE? AND THEN THE GANG COULD HAVE TAUNTED THE UPPITY MUSIC TEACHER WITH THE REMAINS OF HIS UNBORN KID SCOOPED INTO A DONUT BOX. A MISSED OPPORTUNITY FOR CINEMATIC BRUTALITY GEARED TOWARDS ANGERING AND HORRIFYING AN AUDIENCE. OH WELL.

I'M STILL TOTALLY IMPRESSED THAT THIS MOVIE IS FROM 1982, BECAUSE IT TOTALLY PREDICTED THE STATE OF THE NATION'S HIGHSCHOOLS. HOWEVER, THE RULING GROUP IS DEPICTED AS PUNK RAWKERS, AND IN REALITY TURNED OUT TO BE HIP HOPPERS. AH WELL, CLOSE ENOUGH. NEXT TIME YER GONNA WATCH ANYTHING LIKE **DANGEROUS MINDS**, **BLACKBOARD JUNGLE**, **HIGHER EDUCATION** ETC, YOU MUST STOP, BACK AWAY, THINK ABOUT WHAT YOU'RE DOING, AND WATCH THIS MOVIE INSTEAD. WITH THE POSSIBLE EXCEPTION OF **THE SUBSTITUTE** 1 THROUGH 3, I DON'T THINK THERE IS A BETTER VIOLENT HIGH SCHOOL MOVIE OUT THERE. IT'LL TRULY BE ONE OF THE BEST MOVIES YOU'VE SEEN IN A LONG TIME. SERIOUSLY. I KNOW THE SHIT YOU WATCH.

RADKAL TIM GOLUB - JAN. '04

ELECTRO SEX '75 (1970)

LET IT BE KNOWN THAT NOT ALL PORN CLASSICS ARE ACTUALLY 'CLASSIC'. SOME OF THEM, DESPITE BEING HISTORICALLY SIGNIFICANT - ARE ACTUALLY PRETTY FUCKING BORING. MIKE HENDERSON'S 16MM QUICKIE **ELECTRO SEX '75** WAS THE FIRST ADVERTISED PORN FEATURE IN MAJOR NEW YORK PAPERS, (APPEARING ON LABOR DAY 1970) ALSO MAKING IT THE FIRST IN NORTH AMERICA AS WELL. THIS WAS A NOT-SO-GALA OPENING JUST BEFORE THE PORN-CHIC PHENOMENON KNOW AS **DEEP THROAT** MADE XXX HIP. **ELECTRO SEX '75** ALSO BARELY MISSED BEING THE FIRST TRIPLE-X WITH A NARRATIVE, BY ONLY A FEW WEEKS - AN HONOR THAT GOES TO BILL OSCO'S **MONA**.

CHERI ROSTAND (WHO STARRED IN **AMERICAN SEXUAL REVOLUTION**, 1971), AND JILL SWEETE (FROM 1973'S **SEX IN THE BAG**) APPEAR AS SEX-ROBOTS WHO COVER UP THEIR TERRIBLE ACTING WITH PURPOSEFULLY STIFF PERFORMANCES. IT'S ALSO BEEN NOTED THAT THEY LOOK COMPLETLY STONED.

AFTER BEING INVENTED BY A DUDE NAMED PAUL (WHO LOOKS HARD-PRESSED TO EVEN FIGURE OUT HOW TO MAKE TOAST, MUCH LESS INVENT A CYBERNETIC 'REAL DOLL') THE TWO ROBO-SLUTS PUT ON A MECHANICAL SEXHIBITION EXPLORING EACH OTHER'S NUDE NOOKS AND CRANNIES. SOON PAUL AND A FRIEND WHOM HE'S SET ON IMPRESSING, ARE COMMANDING THE SEX-BOTS TO "MAKE LOVE", AND ARE PLEASED WHEN THE MACHINES (WHOSE ROBOTIC TITTIES SPORT TAN LINES?!) JUMP THEIR OBVIOUSLY DESPERATE BONES.

THE REST OF THE RUNNING TIME TEST DRIVING THERE IS LITTLE STORY TO SPEAK OF AS THE BOYS PLAY OUT "I WAS CREATED FOR YOUR PLEASURE. COME, LET THEIR HUMANOID SEX SLAVES, WHO DEADPAN LINES LIKE ME TAKE YOU INTO MY MOUTH." LATER, THEY COMPARE NOTES: "THEY CAN'T GET PREGNANT! THIS MAY JUST WIPE OUT REAL WOMEN ALTOGETHER!"

AFTER A TOTAL SNOOZE-FEST YAWNER OF AN ORGY, THE GUYS' LIMP WIENERS HAVE HAD ENOUGH. "STOP!" PAUL COMMANDS EMPATICALLY. BUT LIKE IN **METROPOLIS**, THE OVERWORKED ROBOT SLAVES REVOLT AS THE 'OFF' BUTTONS BEHIND THEIR EARS STOP WORKING FOR NO GOOD REASON! "WE WANT YOU ALWAYS.." THE ANDROID WHORES MOAN AND CHANT AS THEY FUCK THE SCREAMING BASTARDS TO DEATH.

TRUST ME, IT SOUNDS **WAY** BETTER ON PAPER THAN IT REALLY IS.

CINEMASEWER
MARQUEE INSANITY

HOORAY! FINALLY GOT SOME MORE DORKY FUCKED-UP MARQUEE PICS SENT IN. THANKS TO SEAN MACLAGGAN FOR MAILIN' THESE IN FOR US TO TITTER OVER. SORRY ABOUT THE SHITTY QUALITY OF THE COPIES, BUT WHAT CAN YOU DO? HAVE YOU GOT PICTURES OF INSANE FILM SIGNAGE? **SEND!!**

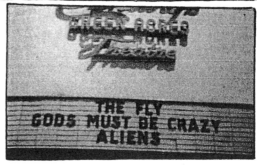

★★★★★★★

TIM + ROBIN IN "OOPSY DAISY"

HA HA HA!

WHILE SHOPPING FOR 70s EXPLOITATION + 80s TEEN MOVIES, OUR HEROES WITNESS A TROUBLING SIGHT!

BOYS? HELP OUT AN OL' VIDEO GEEK DOWN ON HIS LUCK??

COUGH

GOSH!

SHUCKS, OL' TIMER! WE'LL DO ANYTHING WE CAN TO HELP!

BOYS... IT'S A SAD TALE I WEAVE. MY AMAZINGLY COOL COLLECTION OF RARE VHS IS WORTH NOTHING NOW THAT DVD IS IN ALL THE STORES! I'M LOST AND SO ALONE.

RARE VHS!!? KICK HIS ASS AND STEAL HIS COLLECTION!!

YAY!

POUND KICK BEAT

YARG YOU BASTARDS!

I'VE BEEN STAYING UP REEEALY LATE IN THE LAST FEW MONTHS, TRYING TO WADE THROUGH THE 100'S OF UNWATCHED FILMS I HAVE. IT'S A LITTLE DISTURBING.

PONG

WINTER HEAT (aka Snowbound) 1975. 70min

FOUR CRUSTY CRIMINAL LOSERS BREAK INTO THE SNOW-COVERED RURAL CABIN OF THREE LOVELY CITY GALS AND RAISE HELL WHILE THEY HAVE THEIR WAY WITH THEM. THESE FANTASTICALLY DEMENTED SCUMBAGS, CONSISTING OF 3 GUYS AND THEIR MAIN SQUEEZE "AGNES" (HELEN MADIGAN - BETTER KNOWN FOR HER ROLE IN **NAKED CAME THE STRANGER**) ARE LED BY JAMIE "WORLD'S BIGGEST PERVERT" GILLIS, AND THEY BRING NEW MEANING TO THE TERM 'LOWLIFE'.

JOEY (RAY CARTER), BENJI (MICKEY HUMM), AND STEVIE (GILLIS) ARE ONE OF THE SEEDIEST PACKS OF BELEAGUERED BEATNIKS TO EVER SET FOOT IN A XXX FILM, AND TO MAKE MATTERS ALL THAT MUCH MORE EXCITING, THE 3 INNOCENT VICTIMS - JENNY (JENNY LANE) CLAIR (LISA YOUNG AKA JUDY WATT), AND GAIL (AN UNCREDITED BREE ANTHONY) ARE FRESH-FACED VACATIONING CUTIES WITH TENDER UNTOUCHED-LOOKING BODIES. SO BE PREPARED FOR THEIR VIOLATION, DEGRADATION, AND OVERALL "TOUCHING" AT THE HANDS OF GILLIS AND HIS PARTY CREW TO BE UNNERVING AND MEMORABLE.

THERE IS PLENTY OF ENTERTAINMENT HERE FOR THE PERVERSE AMONGST YOU. JENNY'S INCONSOLABLE WHIMPERING WHILE SHE SUCKS COCK AGAINST HER WILL IS NASTY ENOUGH, BUT THE TORTURED BEATNIK DIALOG TO SPOUT OUT OF THE PIE HOLES OF THIS GANG PROBABLY MAKES HER WISH THEY HAD STUFFED COCKS IN HER EARS AS WELL.

"THE PROBLEMS OF TODAY, THEY'RE GIVING EVERYBODY IN THE 'WORLD THE BLUES," BENJI LAMENTS. "I NEED TO GET RIGHT TONIGHT. I BEEN WRONG TOO LONG." CONCLUDES JOEY - BOTH GOOFS OBVIOUSLY IN LOVE WITH THE SOUND OF THEIR OWN VOICES.

DISTRIBUTOR ALPHA BLUE ARCHIVES APTLY DESCRIBES THIS 16 MM FILM AS "AN AMBIENT ROUGHIE WHICH STRIKES A RELAXED GROOVE THROUGH ITS INSULATED SETTING AND OCCASIONAL DISCO MUSIC INTERLUDES." BUT THE REAL TITTY TWISTER HERE IS GILLIS'S INCREDIBLE 'OATMEAL HUMILIATION' SCENE THAT STANDS OUT IN THE ANNALS OF RAPE PORN HISTORY FOR ITS ORIGINALITY. I DON'T WANNA GIVE IT AWAY, BUT SUFFICE TO SAY THE SEEDY WAY WITH WHICH OATMEAL IS UTILIZED HERE WILL HAVE YOU QUESTIONING ALL YOUR BREAKFAST CHOICES INTO THE FORESEEABLE FUTURE.

DIRECTED BY CLAUDE GODDARD WHOSE ONLY OTHER DIRECTORIAL CREDIT WAS TO HELM **BARBIE'S FANTASIES** (ALSO WITH GILLIS IN A STARRING ROLE) A YEAR EARLIER.

WINTER HEAT

Starring
SUE ROWAN
HELEN MADIGAN
LISA YOUNG
JAMIE GILLIS
BOB TUCKER

Explicit Action to Make You Blush!

They were stranded in a cabin when they discovered a burning lust for each other!

Produced and Directed by CLAUDE GODDARD

COLOR By TECHNICOLOR

ADULTS ONLY   XXX RATED

You've got to see it...to believe it!!!

"The Love God?"

BY: MIKE SULLIVAN ©2004

WHEN ONE THINKS OF DON KNOTTS, THERE'S A VERY GOOD CHANCE THAT PORN DOESN'T COME TO MIND. YET WHEN PORN AND MR. KNOTTS **DID** COLLIDE, THE RESULTS WERE NOTHING SHORT OF MIND BOGGLINGLY BRILLIANT. THINK ABOUT IT. WHAT PORNO MOVIE MADE WITHIN THE LAST 30 YEARS WOULDN'T HAVE BEEN IMPROVED IF DON KNOTTS HAD MADE AN APPEARANCE?

NOW - BEFORE YOU GOUGE YOUR EYES OUT WITH A FORK, KNOW THAT I'M NOT SUGGESTING THAT KNOTTS SHOULD ACTUALLY PARTICIPATE IN ANY OF THE HARDCORE SHENANIGANS. JUST HAVE HIM IN A NON SEX RELATED ROLE WHERE THE GUY CAN SPASTICALLY BEAT A COSTAR WITH AN IMMENSE DILDO. I'M SURE MANY OF YOU WOULD SAY THAT ADULT CINEMA HAS NO ROOM FOR MR. LIMPETT, AND THAT THE LAST THING PEOPLE WANT TO SEE WHEN THEY'RE MASTURBATING IS AN ELDERLY MAN IN A JAUNTY SCARF. ALTHOUGH I REALLY CAN'T VOUCH FOR THE LAST

STATEMENT, I CAN TELL YOU THAT THE ADULT INDUSTRY HAS MORE THAN ENOUGH ROOM FOR KNOTTS. IN FACT, IF YOU DON'T BELIEVE ME I'D LIKE TO POINT OUT A LITTLE FILM CALLED **THE LOVE GOD?** AS PROOF TO MY THEORY.

"WHAT IS THE LOVE GOD?", YOU MAY ASK. "THE LOVE GOD?" IS AN UNFLINCHING COMEDY THAT DARES TO ASK THE QUESTION, "WHAT IF HUGH HEFNER WAS A JITTERY, 30 YEAR OLD VIRGIN WHO SIMPLY STUMBLED INTO HIS FAME AND FORTUNE?"

THE FILM OPENS ON AN OBSCENITY TRIAL INVOLVING A PORNO RAG THAT IS NEITHER OBSCENE NOR TECHNICALLY EVEN PORN. (THEN AGAIN, MAYBE I'M JUST TOO JADED TO FATHOM THE EXTREME PERVERSITY BEHIND BARE BREASTS AND ARTICLES ON UNWANTED PREGNANCIES.) THE MAGAZINE'S PUBLISHER, OSBORN TREMAINE IS FOUND GUILTY AND HAS HIS FOURTH CLASS MAILING PRIVILEGES REVOKED. JUST AS OSBORN KISSES HIS VAGUELY DIRTY MAGAZINE GOODBYE, HE NOTICES THAT THE LONG RUNNING BIRD WATCHERS MAGAZINE "THE PEACOCK", IS CLOSING ITS DOORS. SEEING AN OPPORTUNITY TO GAIN BACK HIS MAILING PRIVILEGES, OSBORN CONS THE PEACOCK'S OWNER - ABNER PEACOCK (KNOTTS) INTO TAKING HIM ON AS A PARTNER. BUT BEFORE ABNER CATCHES ON TO OSBORN'S SCHEME, HE'S SHIPPED OFF TO SOUTH AMERICA IN SEARCH OF AN ULTRA RARE POSSIBLY PRE-FABRICATED BIRD - AND INSTEAD RUNS INTO JIM BEGG, AKA "CRAYOLA HAT" FROM **CATALINA CAPER.**

SOON THE FEDS DRAG ABNER BACK TO THE U.S. WHERE HE'S PUT ON TRIAL AND MADE OUT TO BE A "FILTHY DEGENERATE SEX FIEND" BY BOTH THE PROSECUTION AND THE DEFENSE. INEXPLICABLY, AMERICA FALLS IN LOVE WITH THIS UNLIKELY SEX SYMBOL, BUT JUST AS THE PEACOCK SELLS 40 MILLION COPIES, A SMALL TOWN PRIEST THREATENS TO DESTROY THE MAGAZINE BY REVEALING ABNER'S BIG SECRET.

DON'T LET THE FILM'S TOOTHLESS SATIRE, FLAT MADE-FOR-TV CINEMATOGRAPHY AND ONE JOKE PREMISE FOOL YOU. "THE LOVE GOD?" IS ONE DISTURBINGLY ODD FLICK FILLED WITH THE KIND OF IMAGERY ONE RARELY SEES OUTSIDE OF A FEVER DREAM. (CROWDS OF WOMEN WHO FLY INTO LUST FUELED FRENZIES AT THE MERE SIGHT OF DON KNOTTS!?) ADMITTEDLY, THERE ISN'T MUCH BEYOND THIS HOKEY "BARNEY FIFE GETS LAID" CONCEPT, BUT IT PROVIDES THE FILM WITH SOME OF ITS MOST JARRING MOMENTS. ONCE YOU SEE A LINGERIE-CLAD ANNE FRANCIS SEDUCE THE FUTURE RALPH FURLEY, YOU'LL NEVER FORGET IT NO MATTER HOW MANY TIMES YOU BASH YOUR HEAD OFF THE COFFEE TABLE.

> THE WORLD'S MOST ROMANTIC MALE?

Don Knotts "The Love God?"

A UNIVERSAL PICTURE   TECHNICOLOR® Ⓜ

"THE LOVE GOD?" IS NOT JUST ENDLESS SCENES DEPICTING THE EFFECTS OF KNOTT'S IRRESISTABLE MAN MUSK ON THE AVERAGE WOMAN, THERE'S ALSO MOMENTS OF CHEERFUL CREEPINESS TOO. IT'S NOT JUST BIZARRE THAT A "FAMILY FILM" SUCH AS THIS CONTAINS SUICIDE GAGS OR EVEN CASUAL MISOGYNY, IT'S JUST THAT THESE DARK CONCEPTS ARE PRESENTED IN SUCH A CAREFREE, LIGHTHEARTED MANNER. AT ONE POINT ABNER KNOCKS OUT HIS MOUSY FIANCEE - AND INSTEAD OF BEING ANGERED BY THE ATTACK, SHE APPEARS TO BE TURNED ON. IT'S MOMENTS LIKE THESE THAT MAKE THE FILM SUCH A WRONGHEADED GEM, AND IT'S EASY TO SEE WHY DAN CLOWES WANTED TO INCORPORATE CLIPS FROM IT INTO HIS BIG SCREEN ADAPTATION OF HIS COMIC BOOK **GHOST WORLD.**

ALTHOUGH OVERLOOKED AND FORGOTTEN BY MOST PEOPLE, "THE LOVE GOD?" SHOWCASES KNOTTS AT HIS FINEST. WHETHER SCREECHING HIS BIRD CALLS IN A CHURCH, OR PARADING ABOUT IN HIDEOUS MOD STYLE OUTFITS WHICH MAKE HIM RESEMBLE SID AND MARTY KROFFT'S IDEA OF A PIMP, KNOTTS HAS AN ANTSY GEEK-LIKE INTENSITY THAT CAN'T BE DUPLICATED. IT'S A SHAME THAT THE GUY NEVER CROSSED OVER INTO DRAMA BECAUSE HE DEFINITELY COULD'VE BECOME AN EFFECTIVE CHARACTER ACTOR.

WATCHING "THE LOVE GOD?" IS LIKE WATCHING A **FACES OF DEATH** INSTALLMENT HOSTED BY MR. ROGERS. IT'S A LOVEABLY SUBVERSIVE YET THOROUGHLY UNNERVING MIND FUCK THAT HAS ME EAGERLY ANTICIPATING AN AGED DON KNOTTS APPEARANCE AS A CANTANKEROUS PLUMBER IN THE UPCOMING **BONGWATER BUTT BABES** SEQUEL.

ADDENDUM: EFFORTS WERE MADE TO CONTACT MR. KNOTTS AND QUIZ HIM ON THE POSSIBILITY OF A GUEST SPOT IN SAID BONGWATER BUTT BABES SEQUEL. SADLY, DON PASSED AWAY ON FEB. 24th, 2006 IN LOS ANGELES.

Knotts: THE MAN, THE LEGEND

BORN JULY 21ST, 1924 IN MORGANTOWN WEST VIRGINIA FIRST SHOW BIZ JOB: VENTRILOQUIST MOST FAMOUS FOR HIS T.V. ROLES ON **THE ANDY GRIFFITH SHOW** (1959) AND **THREE'S COMPANY** (1979) HAS A SON AND A DAUGHTER FROM 2 MARRIAGES. WROTE HIS AUTOBIOGRAPHY IN 1999.

In the first chapter of his 1999 book "Apocalypse Movies", Kim Newman writes "The more complicated a civilization becomes, the more fun it is to imagine the whole works going up in flames."

THATS ME... SURVIVIN' AFTER DOOMSDAY...

Not enough of the general public (or film critics for that matter) understand or appreciate the wondrous appeal of the post apocalyptic film genre. But Newman holds his own when explaining the thrill and utter joy of putting your feet up and watching the world as we know it - come to a disastrous end.

"I think the appeal is getting rid of all the boring people in the world," he writes. "There's an aesthetic pleasure in ruins and a Peter Pan like joy to playing pirates. There's the selfish fact that we all envy posterity. When we die, we miss the end of the story and that can be infuriating."

So what makes a post apocalyptic film? (From here on referred to as a **P.A.** film) Well, first up - the "post" part denotes that the film depicts what happens to the world **after** whatever horrific event turns it upside down. So, for instance, **Dr. Strangelove** wouldn't count since it all takes place prior to Armageddon. The second word refers to the harbinger of doom itself, and the rad part is that it's always changing since cinematic apocalypses tend to go in and out of fashion. The most

SCIENCE FICTION THEATRE presents THE LAST MAN ON EARTH!

NADINE, WILL YOU HAVE SEX WITH ME? UGH! NOT IF YOU WERE THE LAST MAN ON EARTH, ROY! OH NO! THE WORLD HAS ENDED!!

HO-HO! LOOKS LIKE I'M THE LAST MAN ON EARTH! YOUR BLUFF IS CALLED!!

NADINE! Y-YOU'RE FUCKING A MONKEY! YES-AND YOU'D BEST DO THE SAME ROY-- I KEEP MY WORD!

IRONIC!

popular and pure "big one" is nuclear war, but there are also plenty of films that employ pollution and other forms of eco-doom, fascist tyranny, disease, asteroids, and even concepts as odd as a religion-based judgment day, zombies, and dragons. Whatever. If the non-event of Y2K has taught us anything, it's that if something seems scary in even the most abstract way, you can probably imagine a scenario where societal breakdown occurs because of it.

There are plenty of mainstream P.A. films that 99% of you either know or have seen - so you don't need to read about them here. **Waterworld**, **The Postman**, **Akira**, the **Matrix** trilogy, and the many **Planet of the Apes** films to name but a few. I'm going to concentrate more on the obscure or underrated productions in the genre's history, although I've also bypassed the geek-cherished **Escape from New York**, **1990: The Bronx Warriors**, and its sequel **Escape from the Bronx** since none of them are actually P.A. movies. (Despite what most people think) Rather than movies that take place in a run-down Big Apple of the future. Ok, lets do this:

THE AFTERMATH (1980. Dir: Steve Barkett)
Two astronauts return to earth only to find that it is lightly toasted by nuclear war. L.A. has been taken over by Cutter (Sid Haig! Yes!) and his vicious army of outlaw bikers who number, um, a dozen strong? These hombres are straight out of the 70's with flared bell bottoms n' shit. Despite severe budget restraints, Aftermath is somewhat savage and brutal, complete with exploding heads, people getting knifed in the eyes, and little kids getting killed. So while Cutter is busy raping and pillaging, the astronauts hook up with the only normal people left, one of which is Andy Kaufman's widow Lynne Margulies. You know, the one who was played rather ineptly by Courtney Love in **Man on the Moon**. She's very cute here in the only starring role of her short acting career. The FX (awesome looking models of a destroyed L.A.) were by the soon-to-be-respected Skotak Bros. who are three time academy award winners for **Aliens**, **The Abyss**, and **T2**.

I'LL BE SAFE IN MY SHELTER--- I CAN STAY DOWN HERE FOREVER IF NEED BE --- THE BOMBS CAN'T GET ME HERE!

AFTER THE FALL OF NEW YORK (1983)
This Italian post-nuke action picture by Sergio Martino opens on some eyepoppingly cool miniatures of New York meant to represent the destroyed city. The plot here is nearly identical to **Escape from New York**, except that the search is for the last living fertile woman, instead of a mission to save the U.S. President. It's been 15 years since the big boom, and while no children have been born, word has it that a lovely young lady resides amongst some survivors in the Big Apple. The city's inhabitants are dead or mutated from radiation, and only our hero, Parsifal (a name not nearly as cool as 'Snake Plissken', but oh well) manages to find her and tries to race her back to a lab where she can be forced to breed until her young body is used up and worn out. This movie just exudes violent entertainment value and Italian shoestring budget kick-assery. I ♡ Matthew Wilder's review that states that the film "may be the only grindhouse ripoff of a famous movie that out-invents the original by a power of one hundred" and that boasts "more visual ideas and

FREE FORM MOVEMENT THAN ANY GRINDHOUSE MOVIE OF THE PERIOD". STRONG WORDS, BUT NOT ENTIRELY UNTRUE.

ANAL FUTURE (1997 RATED XXX)
WELL SHIT, SO MUCH FOR THE OZONE LAYER. IT'S LONG GONE AND VARIOUS OTHER DISASTERS HAVE RENDERED THE PLANET IMPOTENT. MILLIONS HAVE PAINFULLY PERISHED AND MANKIND FACES EXTINCTION. DOESN'T THAT MEGA SEXY CONCEPT JUST MAKE YOU WANNA DROP YOUR SHORTS AND PLAY WITH YOURSELF?!? Mmm... GENOCIDE, THATS **HOT**. THE GOVERNMENT HAS CREATED A TASK FORCE, THE FBI (FEDERAL BUREAU OF INSEMINATION) TO FORCE MEN TO IMPREGNATE WOMEN. SADLY, MOST OF THAT IS INTRODUCED LAMELY IN TEXT DURING THE OPENING CREDITS, THE ONLY TRACES OF A PLOT TO FOLLOW CONSISTS OF SCRAPING SPUNK OFF GOO-COVERED LADIES AND PUTTING IT UNDER SOME CHEAP-ASS PROP THAT'S SUPPOSED TO RESEMBLE A MICROSCOPE. FBI MEMBERS SHARON MITCHELL AND MAXINE INTERROGATE MAILMAN TED WILSON FOR HIS SPERM; SAKI VISITS A MONK WITH THE SAME OBJECTIVE (EVEN THOUGH HE CURIOUSLY TRIES TO IMPREGNATE HER WOMB THROUGH HER BUTTHOLE), AND MELANIE MOORE AND CAL JAMMER WASTE PRECIOUS SPERM ON A LEISURE FUCK AND GET IN TROUBLE WITH THE HUMP-COPS. THE EXTRA LOUD MUSIC MAKES IT SOMETIMES IMPOSSIBLE TO HEAR THE DIALOG, AND WHEN THE SEX IS AS TYPICAL AND BORING AS IT IS HERE, THAT'S ALL YOU'VE GOT LEFT FOR ENTERTAINMENT VALUE.

THE BLOOD OF HEROES (1989)
PEOPLE ARE OFTEN SURPRISED TO LEARN THAT THIS UNDERRATED P.A. FILM IS ONE OF MY FAVORITE 80s MOVIES, BUT IT'S HARD FOR ME TO IGNORE THAT DIRECTOR DAVID PEOPLES TOOK A RELATIVELY SIMPLE P.A. THEME AND TURNED IT INTO A HEARTFELT SCI-FI ACTION ROAD MOVIE CENTERED AROUND A VIOLENT FUTURISTIC SPORT. IT HAS A COOL CAST (RUTGER HAUER, JOAN CHEN, DELROY LINDO, AND VINCENT D'ONOFRIO), A SCRIPT BY THE GUY WHO CO-WROTE **BLADE RUNNER** AND EXCELLENT DIRECTION AND BLOOD-SOAKED CINEMATOGRA-PHY THAT IS REMINISCENT OF THE BEST WORK OF PAUL VERHOEVEN. THIS IS A DESTROYED WORLD WHERE "JUGGING" KEEPS WHAT LITTLE IS LEFT OF SOCIETY FROM SLIPPING INTO OBLIVION. JUGGING IS A HORRIFIC CO-ED BLOODSPORT THAT IS A CROSS BETWEEN FOOTBALL, RUGBY AND HOMICIDE. EVERY TINY VILLAGE HAS A TEAM, AND

YOU PLAY THIS SHIT WITH A DOG SKULL. HOW FUCKING COOL IS THAT?! I'M SURPRISED MORE MOVIE NERDS DON'T SING THIS FILM'S PRAISES. AFTER BEING OUT OF PRINT ON VHS AND LASERDISC FOR MORE THAN A DECADE, BLOOD OF HEROES IS NOW AVAILABLE ON A CHEAP SHITTY DVD. IF ONLY CRITERION WOULD TAKE A PEEK AT THIS.

A BOY AND HIS DOG (1975)
A QUIRKY SATIRICAL CLASSIC BASED ON A NOVELLA BY HARLAN ELLISON WHICH ON OCCASION HAS BEEN CITED AS BEING OVERTLY MISOGYNISTIC. A YOUNG DON JOHNSON (**MIAMI VICE**) COMMUNICATES TELEPATHICALLY WITH HIS DOG AS THEY SCAVENGE THE WASTELANDS FOR THE ONLY TWO THINGS THAT

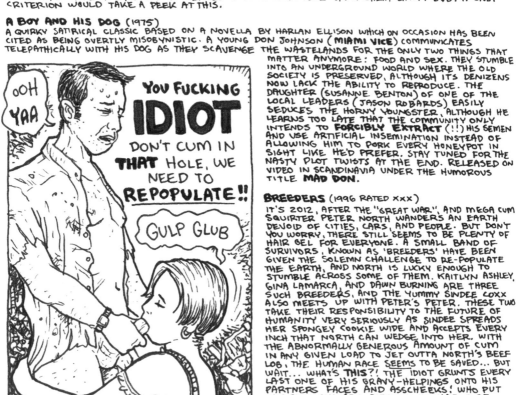

MATTER ANYMORE: FOOD AND SEX. THEY STUMBLE INTO AN UNDERGROUND WORLD WHERE THE OLD SOCIETY IS PRESERVED, ALTHOUGH ITS DENIZENS NOW LACK THE ABILITY TO REPRODUCE. THE DAUGHTER (SUSANNE BENTON) OF ONE OF THE LOCAL LEADERS (JASON ROBARDS) EASILY SEDUCES THE HORNY YOUNGSTER, ALTHOUGH HE LEARNS TOO LATE THAT THE COMMUNITY ONLY INTENDS TO **FORCIBLY EXTRACT** (!!) HIS SEMEN AND USE ARTIFICIAL INSEMINATION INSTEAD OF ALLOWING HIM TO PORK EVERY HONEYPOT IN SIGHT LIKE HE'D PREFER. STAY TUNED FOR THE NASTY PLOT TWISTS AT THE END. RELEASED ON VIDEO IN SCANDINAVIA UNDER THE HUMOROUS TITLE **MAD DON**.

BREEDERS (1996 RATED XXX)
IT'S 2012, AFTER THE "GREAT WAR", AND MEGA CUM SQUIRTER PETER NORTH WANDERS AN EARTH DEVOID OF CITIES, CARS, AND PEOPLE. BUT DON'T YOU WORRY, THERE STILL SEEMS TO BE PLENTY OF HAIR GEL FOR EVERYONE. A SMALL BAND OF SURVIVORS, KNOWN AS 'BREEDERS' HAVE BEEN GIVEN THE SOLEMN CHALLENGE TO RE-POPULATE THE EARTH, AND NORTH IS LUCKY ENOUGH TO STUMBLE ACROSS SOME OF THEM. KAITLYN ASHLEY, GINA LAMARCA, AND DAWN BURNING ARE THREE SUCH BREEDERS, AND THE YUMMY SINDEE COXX ALSO MEETS UP WITH PETER'S PETER. THESE TWO TAKE THEIR RESPONSIBILITY TO THE FUTURE OF HUMANITY VERY SERIOUSLY AS SINDEE SPREADS HER SPONGEY COOKIE WIDE AND ACCEPTS EVERY INCH THAT NORTH CAN WEDGE INTO HER. WITH THE ABNORMALLY GENEROUS AMOUNT OF CUM IN ANY GIVEN LOAD TO JET OUTTA NORTH'S BEEF LOG, THE HUMAN RACE SEEMS TO BE SAVED... BUT WAIT... WHAT'S **THIS**?! THE IDIOT GRUNTS EVERY LAST ONE OF HIS GRAVY-HELPINGS ONTO HIS PARTNERS FACES AND ASSCHEEKS! WHO PUT THIS MONOSYLLABIC DIPSTICK IN CHARGE OF REPOPULATING THE PLANET?!? **WE'RE DOOMED!!**

CINDY luv

TODAY I WANNA TALK ABOUT MY FAVORITE MOVIES.

THEY ALL BELONG TO ONE GENRE: THE POST APOCALYPTIC MOVIE!

THIS IS ME IN MY VERY FIRST ROLE. I PLAYED 'SURVIVOR #4' IN "ASSPOCALYPSE!"

FUCK ME YOU HERMA- PHRODITIC POODLE DICK!!

A LOT OF PEOPLE DON'T REALIZE THAT I'M AN **AWE**SOME ACTRESS. BUT SHIT, CHECK OUT THIS SCENE FROM "**ATOMIC CUM MONKEY**"

SERIOUSLY ROCK, WHAT EVER SHALL WE... UM... **DO?** SNIFF

LOOK AT THAT COMPOSURE! AND HE WAS IN MY ASS!!

..AND COULD STREEP OR JULIA ROBERTS KICK IT WITH **THIS** KIND OF DIALOG!?

MMPHG-LUB-BUB RIBBGLH-HUBBLE !!

BUT SERIOUSLY ...AFTER 37 APOCALYPSE- THEMED FILMS...

...AND OVER 20 ZOMBIE DP's HOW COULD I **NOT** LOVE IT!?

THE CRITICS SAY: "**CINDY LUV**, HOW DO YOU TAKE A CONCEPT AS BLEAK AS A NUCLEAR WASTELAND, AND MAKE IT SO **FUCKIN' HOTTT**?"

...IT'S SIMPLE...

I THINK OF THE END OF THE WORLD AS THE **MOTHER** OF ALL CLIMAXES!

© ROBIN BOUGIE AND MIKE MYHRE · 2005

YUP... THE END OF THE WORLD CAN BE PRETTY DAMN **SEXY**!

TAKE IT FROM **ME!**

CAFE FLESH (1982, XXX)
THE TIME... FIVE YEARS AFTER NUCLEAR WAR. THE SURVIVORS? POST NUKE THRILL FREAKS ABLE TO FEEL EVERYTHING BUT PLEASURE. THE SURVIVORS OF THIS SHITTY NEW WORLD BREAK DOWN TO THOSE WHO CAN, AND THOSE WHO CAN'T. 99% ARE SEX NEGATIVES, "EROTIC CASUALTIES", WHO WANT TO MAKE LOVE, BUT THE MERE TOUCH OF ANOTHER PERSON MAKES THEM VIOLENTLY ILL. THE LUCKY ONE PERCENT ARE SEX POSITIVES WHOSE LIBIDOS HAVE ESCAPED UNSCATHED. AFTER THE NUCLEAR KISS, THE POSITIVES REMAIN TO FUCK AND PERFORM FOR THE SWEATY VOYEURISTIC NEGATIVES WHO SIT AROUND IN CAFE FLESH AND WATCH WITH ANGER IN THEIR EYES. RINSE DREAM'S XXX CLASSIC IS WIDELY CONSIDERED TO BE THE LAST GREAT 35MM THEATRICAL PORN FEATURE MADE BEFORE THE INDUSTRY WENT NEARLY VIDEO EXCLUSIVE. WRITTEN BY JERRY STAHL (WHO WAS IMMORTALIZED IN **PERMANENT MIDNIGHT**) AND FOLLOWED BY THE INFERIOR **CAFE FLESH 2** AND **3**.

CITY LIMITS (1985)
AMID THE HOPELESSNESS OF A P.A. WASTELAND (WHICH LOOKS **FAR** TOO GREEN AND HEALTHY), BIKER GANGS RULE THE URBAN TURF. FOR NO VALID REASON, A YOUNG MAN (**CHRISTINE**'S JOHN STOCKWELL) LEAVES THE HOMESTEAD AND SETS OUT TO JOIN A GANG CALLED THE CLIPPERS. IN THE PROCESS THE GANG THWARTS A FACELESS CORPORATION AND ITS EVIL DRUG LORD (JAMES EARL JONES). VARIETY MAGAZINE SAID: "...EXTRAORDINARY VISUALS...... THE ACTION SCENES ARE WELL-EXECUTED AND

THERE'S A VIBRANT SCORE..." THIS
REVIEW IS ASTONISHING AND REEKS OF
PAYOLA, CONSIDERING THAT THIS
CINEMATIC TRAVESTY MAY BE THE MOST
BORING MOVIE ON THIS LIST. EVEN THE
MST3K VERSION WAS TOUGH TO SIT
THROUGH. LOOK FOR TOMMY CHONG'S
DAUGHTER, RAE-DAWN, AND **SEX IN
THE CITY**'S KIM CATTRALL IN A CO-
STARRING ROLE.

THE DAY AFTER (1983 MADE FOR TV)
THIS ORGY OF TELEVISED DESTRUCTION WAS ONE OF THE MOST MEMORABLE TV EXPERIENCES OF MY
CHILDHOOD, AND FOR MANY NORTH AMERICANS, THE TRUE HORRIFIC RAMIFICATIONS OF THE COLD
WAR WERE FINALLY EXPOSED TO THEM WITH THIS - VIA THE ONE SOURCE THAT THE MAJORITY OF
THEM TRUST UNQUESTIONINGLY: THEIR TVS. AS A 10 YEAR OLD, I GOT PRETTY SCARED WATCHING
'THE DAY AFTER', AND ALMOST STARTED CRYING A FEW TIMES. I HAD NIGHTMARES FOR DAYS, AND
I ENDED UP READING A LOT ABOUT NUCLEAR WAR AND REAGAN'S 'STAR WARS' SOON AFTER THAT,
TOPICS MY STUNTED LITTLE BRAIN HAD GIVEN VERY LITTLE THOUGHT TO PREVIOUSLY. THE STORY
DEPICTS THE LIVES OF A DOZEN AVERAGE AMERICANS BEFORE, DURING, AND AFTER THE BOMBS
FALL. EVEN THOUGH IT PULLS PUNCHES AND HAS STEVE GUTTENBERG AS A MAIN CHARACTER, MUCH
OF THIS MOVIE WILL GIVE YOU THE WHIM-WAMS EVEN TODAY. NOW AVAILABLE ON DVD.

THE LAST
DEFENSE.
THE LAST
HOPE.
THE BATTLE FOR
THE FUTURE OF
THE WORLD
HAS BEGUN.

DEF-CON 4
Defense Condition 4

DEF CON 4 (1985)
MY PICK FOR THE BEST CANADIAN-MADE P.A. FILM OF ALL
TIME! THE REVIEW IN T.V. GUIDE READ AS: "DEF-CON4 IS A
BLEAK VISION OF WHAT A NUCLEAR NIGHTMARE COULD
BRING, REDUCING HUMANITY TO ITS MOST PRIMITIVE
AND SADISTIC INSTINCTS", AND I AGREE WHOLEHEARTEDLY.
TIM CHOATE, KATE LYNCH, AND JOHN WALSCH ARE THREE
ASTRONAUTS ORBITING ABOVE EARTH IN A PLASTIC AND
CARDBOARD-LOOKIN' SPACESHIP. THEIR MONITOR
SUDDENLY GOES BLANK AND THEY PEEP HUGE FLASHES
OF LIGHT EMANATING FROM THE GLOBE. THESE THREE
HAVE WITNESSED THE MAJORITY OF HUMAN LIFE BEING
QUICKLY AND UNCEREMONIOUSLY SNUFFED OUT (GOOD
FUCKING RIDDANCE...) WHEN THEIR CAPSULE BEGINS ITS
AUTOMATIC DESCENT AND ENDS UP ON A BEACH IN
ONTARIO, THE ASTRONAUTS ENCOUNTER THEIR FIRST
GROUP OF SURVIVORS WHO KILL WALSCH AND
CANNIBALIZE HIS CORPSE. IT GETS WEIRDER AND MORE
DISTURBING FROM THERE, BUT STILL HAS SOME TIME FOR SOME ODDLY PLACED COMEDY. THE ONLY
REAL DETRACTION IS ITS ULTRA LOW BUDGET - WHICH CERTAINLY DOES SHOW. THE ANCHOR BAY DVD
IS RECOMMENDED, AS IS TERIYAKI CHICKEN - WHICH IS VERY TASTY TO EAT.

ENDGAME (1983)
ENDGAME WAS JOE D'AMATO'S SECOND P.A. FILM OF '83, FOLLOWING ON THE HEELS OF AN EARLIER EFFORT
CALLED **2020 TEXAS GLADIATORS**. A TELEPATHIC MUTANT NAMED LILITH (LAURA GEMSER) RECRUITS A
POST-WORLD WAR II TV GAME SHOW WARRIOR TO LEAD HER BAND OF MUTANTS IN A CARAVAN OUT OF
THE CITY. THE GROUP'S ADVENTURES IN THE WASTELANDS ARE QUITE ENTERTAINING, BEGINNING WITH
A GOOFY BATTLE SEQUENCE WITH A HUGE FORCE OF SADISTIC BLIND CULTISTS WITH A VAST ARRAY
OF UNUSUAL WEAPONS. LOOK FOR ALL THE FUN EURO-EXPLOITATION TRASH YOU MIGHT EXPECT
INCLUDING BIG NASTY EXPLOSIONS, BARE TITTIES, A SET MADE OF NOTHING BUT DIRT, THE HARSH
"RUNNING MAN" STYLE GLADIATOR GAME WHERE THE CONTESTANTS WANDER AROUND THE CITY AND
KILL EACH OTHER ON LIVE TELEVISION, AND A SCENE WHERE THE TELEPATH MAKES A BIG ROCK
FLOAT WHILE THE WIRE HOLDING THE STYROFOAM BOULDER IS EASILY SPOTTED BY THE AUDIENCE.

GAS-S-S-S (1970)
A DEADLY GAS KILLS EVERYONE OVER THE AGE OF 25, AND THE WORLD DEVOLVES INTO A ZANY KNEE
SLAPPIN' STRUGGLE FOR POWER. OUR HEROES ARE A BAND OF PEACE-LOVIN' HIPPIES WHO GO
CROSS COUNTRY LOOKING FOR UTOPIA, AND MANAGE TO SPEND MOST OF THEIR TIME MAKING
WITTY QUIPS AND SARDONIC TIPS OF THE HAT. IT'S A FREE-LOVE TIME CAPSULE
DIRECTED AND PRODUCED BY ROGER CORMAN, BUT IT'S ALL A BIT MUCH WHEN
ONE TAKES INTO ACCOUNT HOW ANNOYING IT IS TO HAVE TO WATCH A
TEDIOUS MOVIE THAT THINKS IT'S WAY MORE FUNNY THAN IT ACTUALLY
IS. THE SEGMENT THAT IS UNDOUBTEDLY AWESOME IS WHEN THE
HIPPIES ARE CAPTURED BY A SMALL-TOWN HIGH SCHOOL FOOTBALL
SQUAD THAT HAS NOW EVOLVED INTO A ROVING BAND OF DUNE-
BUGGY-DRIVING UNIFORMED
FASCISTS WHO SPEND THEIR TIME
TRAINING - NOT HOW TO SACK A
QUARTERBACK - BUT HOW TO PROPERLY
RAPE AND PILLAGE.

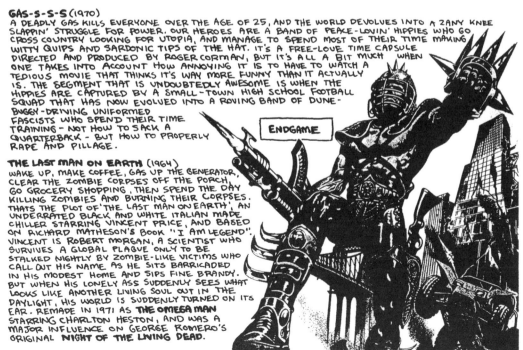

ENDGAME

THE LAST MAN ON EARTH (1964)
WAKE UP, MAKE COFFEE, GAS UP THE GENERATOR,
CLEAR THE ZOMBIE CORPSES OFF THE PORCH,
GO GROCERY SHOPPING, THEN SPEND THE DAY
KILLING ZOMBIES AND BURNING THEIR CORPSES.
THAT'S THE PLOT OF 'THE LAST MAN ON EARTH', AN
UNDERRATED BLACK AND WHITE ITALIAN MADE
CHILLER STARRING VINCENT PRICE, AND BASED
ON RICHARD MATHESON'S BOOK "I AM LEGEND".
VINCENT IS ROBERT MORGAN, A SCIENTIST WHO
SURVIVES A GLOBAL PLAGUE ONLY TO BE
STALKED NIGHTLY BY ZOMBIE-LIKE VICTIMS WHO
CALL OUT HIS NAME AS HE SITS BARRICADED
IN HIS MODEST HOME AND SIPS FINE BRANDY.
BUT WHEN HIS LONELY ASS SUDDENLY SEES WHAT
LOOKS LIKE ANOTHER LIVING SOUL OUT IN THE
DAYLIGHT, HIS WORLD IS SUDDENLY TURNED ON ITS
EAR. REMADE IN 1971 AS **THE OMEGA MAN**
STARRING CHARLTON HESTON, AND WAS A
MAJOR INFLUENCE ON GEORGE ROMERO'S
ORIGINAL **NIGHT OF THE LIVING DEAD**.

HUMAN ANIMALS (1982)

THANKS TO SINISTER SAM FOR TAPING ME THIS RARE SPANISH ART-FILM ODDITY BY DIRECTOR ELIGIO HERRERO THAT INVOLVES 2 MEN, A WOMAN, AND A DOG AS THE LAST LIVING MAMMALS ON EARTH. THE WORLD ENDS AND THINGS QUICKLY GO SOUR AS THE TWO DUDES GET PRIMAL OVER WHO GETS TO BE THE DOMINANT MALE AND FUCK THE POOR GIRL ANYWHERE AND ANY TIME THE PACK LEADER FEELS LIKE - ALTHOUGH SHE'S FAR MORE INTERESTED IN HUMPING THEIR K-9 FRIEND. THE FILM EMPLOYS A VERY ODD SOUNDTRACK, AND HAS NO DIALOG OUTSIDE OF A LOT OF GRUNTING, GROANING, AND BARKING. THE YOUNG LADY (CAROLE KIRKHAM - FROM NASCHY'S **LATIDOS DE PANICO**) SPENDS MOST OF THIS RUNNING AROUND HALF NAKED AFTER SHE USES HER CUTE DRESS AS A BANDAGE FOLLOWING A CRAB "ATTACK". NOW DON'T GET ME WRONG, THESE AREN'T GIANT MUTATED CRABS... JUST A HALF DOZEN INNOCENT LITTLE CRUSTACEANS THAT FOR SOME REASON MAKE THE WOMAN GO APESHIT. PERHAPS THE BEST PERFORMANCE IS TURNED IN BY LARRY THE POOCH, WHO ALSO PHYSICALLY IMPRESSES AS HE PORKS HIS LOVELY CO-STAR IN THE MISSIONARY POSITION! JOE BOB BRIGGS REPORTED THAT SOMEONE IN HIS NECK OF THE WOODS TOLD HIM THAT THE LOCAL RADIO STATIONS WERE REFUSING TO PLAY THE 'HUMAN ANIMALS' RADIO COMMERCIALS BECAUSE THEY SOUNDED LIKE A LIVE GANG RAPE!

IN THE YEAR 2889 (1967, TV)

LARRY BUCHANAN'S REMAKE OF **THE DAY THE WORLD ENDED** DEPICTS A DEVASTATING NUCLEAR HOLOCAUST THAT LEAVES TWO GROUPS OF SURVIVORS: 7 BICKERING HUMANS AND A GAGGLE OF TELEPATHIC CANNIBAL MUTANTS. THE FORMER FIND THEMSELVES STALKED BY THE LATTER DURING THIS FEEBLE 80 MINUTE UNAUTHORIZED REMAKE OF ROGER CORMAN'S ORIGINAL BORING MUTATED FILM. THE THREAT OF IRRADIATED RAIN, HUMANS AND ANIMALS, AND MAN'S CRUEL INHUMANITY FAIL TO RAISE AN OUNCE OF HORROR OR SUSPENSE, BUT THEY DO GET BIG LAUGHS IN THIS CRAPPY MADE-FOR-TV MOVIE. THE DAY-FOR-NIGHT FOOTAGE + SOUND EDITING ARE ESPECIALLY BAD.

LAND OF DOOM (1986)

THIS IS ONE OF THOSE VHS BOXES - LOOKIN' ALL KICKASS AND AMAZING - THAT I USED TO SEE SITTING IN THE LOCAL VIDEOSTORE WHEN I WAS A LITTLE RUGRAT WITHOUT A VCR. THE COVER ART WAS A STUNNER, AND THAT'S WHY I'M DEEPLY SADDENED TO NOTE THAT AFTER I FINALLY REDISCOVERED IT LAST WEEK FOR $2 AT THE FLEA MARKET - I HAVE LITTLE GOOD TO SAY ABOUT THE FILM ITSELF. I MEAN, MY EXPECTATIONS MIGHT HAVE BEEN UNDESERVEDLY HIGH, BUT THIS IS STILL PRETTY RANCID. THE RAVAGED FUTURE IS MADE UP OF SCATTERED HUMAN SETTLEMENTS IN AN ARID LAND, TERRORIZED BY RUTHLESS RAIDERS. SAID RAIDERS SEEM TO BE DEDICATED TO A 'SCORCHED EARTH POLICY', AND ONLY A HUNKY GIMP AND HIS HOT FEMALE COMPANION (WHO IS SADDLED WITH RAPE TRAUMA WHICH MAKES HER SUSPICIOUS OF ALL MALES) ARE BALLSY ENOUGH TO STAND UP AGAINST THE RAIDERS, CANNIBALS, AND JAWAS THAT THREATEN THE LAND. OK, I JUST REREAD WHAT I WROTE, AND THIS MOVIE SUDDENLY SOUNDS AMAZING! BEST LINE OF DIALOG? "YOU CAN'T CHANGE THE WORLD BY KILLING EVERY BODY!". SOMEONE PLEASE PASS THAT NUGGET OF OBVIOUSNESS ON TO GEORGE BUSH JR....

THE LAST WARRIOR (2000 AKA 'THE LAST PATROL')

A MASSIVE EARTHQUAKE SINKS L.A., THE EARTH IS KNOCKED OFF ITS AXIS, AND THE PACIFIC NORTHWEST FALLS INTO TOTAL CHAOS AS THE FEW REMAINING SURVIVORS ARRIVE AT AN ARMY BASE IN THE DESERT. MASSIVE FUCKING PLOT HOLES, A SELF-CONGRATULATORY AND MENTALLY INCOMPETENT SCRIPT, WOODEN ACTING, AND AWKWARD PACING PACKED TOGETHER IN A DIRECT-TO-VIDEO PACKAGE THAT'S JUST BAD ENOUGH TO BE... BAD. STARRING DOLPH LUNDGREN, NEED I SAY MORE?

MAD WARRIOR (1984)

MALSAM LIVES IN A BIG SILVER MUSHROOM IN "DEATH VALLEY", AND HAS HALF HIS FACE COVERED BY A METAL MASK, DR. DOOM STYLE. HE GOES CRAZY DURING THE FULL MOON AND HIS FACE MELTS. REYA IS SEARCHING FOR HER FATHER ZEUS, A DORKY SCIENTIST WHO LOOKS ABOUT TWO YEARS OLDER THAN SHE IS.

:GROAN:

APOLOGIES TO GARY ROBERTS

THESE TWO HAVE **NOTHING** TO DO WITH P.A. MOVIES, I JUST FELT LIKE DRAWING SOME CUTE LESBIANS.

156

REX DOES HIS BIT AS THE HERO OF THE FILM, RUNNING AROUND LIKE A BARBARIAN ON CRACK WHO HAPPENS TO WHIP OUT A BLUE LIGHTSABRE AND USE IT TO FUCK ENEMIES UP. THRILL TO THE MOST HILARIOUSLY OVER CHOREOGRAPHED FIGHT SCENES EVER FILMED, SHITLOADS OF NEEDLESS SLO-MO, AND A SOUNDTRACK THAT ENDLESSLY LOOPS. BEST LINE OF DIALOG? "YOU'RE CRAZY. CRAZY LIKE A MAD WARRIOR." CREATED IN THE PHILIPPINES, WHERE THE WORD "DOOD!" APPEARS TO MEAN "KILL!".

NEON CITY (1991)
STRANGERS OF VARIOUS RACES, SEXES, PROFESSIONS, AND SOCIAL CLASSES COME TOGETHER AND LEARN IMPORTANT LIFE LESSONS FROM ONE ANOTHER WHILE ON A ROAD TRIP THROUGH A SNOWY P.A. WASTELAND HAUNTED ENVIRONMENT. ON THE WAY THEY ARE MENACED BY 'SKINS' MARAUDERS WHO LOOK LIKE A BUNCH OF KISS ARMY REJECTS. YES, IT SUCKS JUST AS HARD AS YOU THINK IT MIGHT, ALTHOUGH I WAS ODDLY ENTERTAINED. FILMED IN UTAH, AND STARRING A VERY CRUNCHY MICHAEL IRONSIDE, AND FORMER PRINCE PROTÉGÉ VANITY - WHO ACCORDING TO THE IMDB, WAS ORIGINALLY GIVEN THE STAGE NAME OF "VAGINA" BY THE PURPLE-LOVIN' WIENER FROM MINNEAPOLIS.

NIGHT OF THE COMET (1984)
TWO TEENAGE SISTERS WAKE UP ONE MORNING TO FIND THAT EVERYONE ELSE IN L.A. HAS BEEN TURNED INTO RED DUST BY THE LETHAL RAYS EMITTED FROM HALLEY'S COMET. THEY DIDN'T REALLY LIKE THEIR PARENTS ANYWAY, SO IT'S NO BIG WHOOP. THESE BIG-HAIRED VALLEY GIRLS KARATE CHOP THEIR WAY THROUGH FLESH EATING ZOMBIES, TAKE OVER THE AIR WAVES AT A LOCAL RADIO STATION, AND, OF COURSE, FIND TIME TO GO ON A SHOPPING SPREE AT THE MALL WHILE "GIRLS JUST WANNA HAVE FUN" BLARES. AN 80s TEEN MOVIE UNLIKE ANY OTHER.

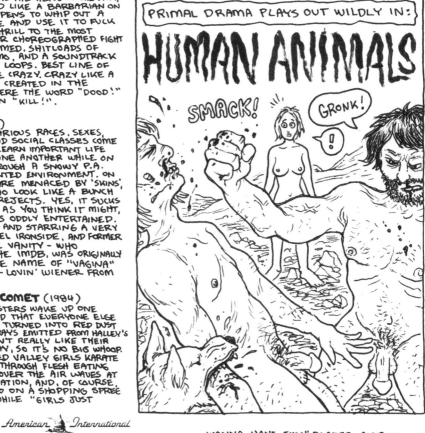

PRIMAL DRAMA PLAYS OUT WILDLY IN: HUMAN ANIMALS

SMACK! GRONK!

American International

The Last Man on Earth

NO BLADE OF GRASS (1970)
AS THE FILM BEGINS, A NARRATOR EXPLAINS THAT BY THE LATE 70s POLLUTION LEVELS AROUND THE PLANET WERE TOTALLY OUT OF CONTROL, WITH THE RESULT BEING A LANDSCAPE WITH A CONTAMINATED SUPPLY OF FOOD, AIR, AND WATER, LEADING TO A TOTAL COLLAPSE OF SOCIAL ORDER. LONDON IS ON THE VERGE OF BEING QUARANTINED, AND THERE ARE RUMORS THAT THE POPULATION WILL BE EXTERMINATED TO SAVE DWINDLING SUPPLIES. A HANDFUL OF PEOPLE HEAD OUT INTO THE COUNTRYSIDE - WHICH IS TOTALLY INHOSPITABLE AND ALMOST IMPOSSIBLE TO SURVIVE IN. THE AUDIENCE IS KEPT ON EDGE AS THEY ENCOUNTER RAPISTS, LOOTERS, KILLERS, AND OTHER SCUZZBALLS. BY ALL MEANS, KEEP AN EYE OUT FOR THIS RARE MOVIE, BECAUSE DIRECTOR CORNEL WILDE'S FILM IS SURELY ONE OF THE MOST UNSUNG AND OUTSTANDING ACHIEVEMENTS OF THE P.A. MOVIE GENRE.

ON THE BEACH (1959)
AN AMERICAN MILITARY SUBMARINE CREW FINDS THEMSELVES THE SURVIVORS OF A NUCLEAR CONFLICT, AND MAKE THEIR WAY TO AUSTRALIA IN AN EFFORT TO ESCAPE THE INEXORABLY EXPANDING AREA OF FALLOUT WHICH IS GRADUALLY WIPING OUT ALL FORMS OF LIFE. ONCE THEY ARRIVE IN THE LAND DOWN UNDER THE FILM SUDDENLY TAKES ON A TOTALLY UNFAMILIAR TONE TO P.A. FILM FANATICS. THERE ARE NO HEROKS, NO MUTANTS, NO HYSTERICS, NO SCENES OF WAR AND DESTRUCTION. IT'S JUST A MELANCHOLY GROUP OF PEOPLE GOING TO WORK, HAVING CASUAL GET TOGETHERS, DRUNKEN CONVERSATIONS ABOUT MORTALITY, AND LOVE TRIANGLES AS THEY WAIT FOR ONCOMING DEATH. WEIRDLY ENOUGH, THIS DOESN'T SUCK - BUT THAT'S MAINLY DUE TO AN AMAZING CAST CONSISTING OF GREGORY PECK, AVA GARDNER, FRED ASTAIRE AND GOOD OLD ANTHONY PERKINS. REMADE IN 2000.

IN **EXTERMINATORS OF THE YEAR 3000** A GUY NAMED ALIEN GETS A BIG THRILL OUT OF DRIVING HIS AWESOME CUSTOM BEATER NAMED "THE EXTERMINATOR".

HE ALSO FIGHTS WITH HIS GIRLFRIEND A LOT. HER NAME IS TRASH. SERIOUSLY.

DID I MENTION HE HAS A SWEET RIDE?

EXTERMINATORS OF THE YEAR 3000 (1983)

IN A NIGHTMARISH FUTURE, WHERE THE SEAS HAVE DRIED UP MAKING THE EARTH INTO A SANDY DESERT, WATER HAS BECOME A PRECIOUS COMMODITY. ARMED WITH A MAP, ONE GROUP OF PEACEFUL SURVIVORS SEARCH FOR A SUPPOSED WATER SUPPLY, UNTIL A GANG OF VILE BANDITS RAPE, PILLAGE AND KILL THEM AS THEY SCAVENGE FOR WATER OF THEIR OWN. ONLY A YOUNG BOY (AND HIS PET HAMSTER) SURVIVE THE SLAUGHTER TO TREK ON ALONE, SOON CONTRACTING THE SERVICES OF AN IMMORAL SLEAZE BAG NAMED ALIEN (?!?), WHO ALONG WITH HIS TRICKED OUT JALOPY ("THE EXTERMINATOR") AND HIS TOUGH GIRLFRIEND ("TRASH") TRIES TO HELP FIND THE TREASURE OF H2O. IT'S PRETTY INTERESTING HOW WELL THE PAVEMENT, CARS AND CLOTHES FROM 1983 HAVE HELD UP OVER A THOUSAND YEARS UP INTO THE YEAR 3000 -- BUT DON'T GET TOO DISTRACTED BY THE MANY PLOT AND LOGISTIC INCONSISTENCIES, OR YOU'LL MISS OUT ON ENJOYING A REALLY FUN AND ENTERTAINING ITALIAN P.A. MOVIE. BODY COUNT: 26, BARE BREASTS: 0, EXPLOSIONS: 43.

STRYKER (1983)

THE FIRST P.A. MOVIE BY A DIRECTOR THAT WOMEN-IN-PRISON FILM FANS WILL KNOW ALL TOO WELL -- THE AWESOME CIRIO H. SANTIAGO! HE'S MY PERSONAL PICK FOR TOP DIRECTOR IN THE GENRE BECAUSE OF HIS IMPRESSIVE FILMOGRAPHY: **WHEELS OF FIRE, DUNE WARRIORS, RAIDERS OF THE SUN,** AND **EQUALIZER 2000.** EVEN SO, STRYKER REALLY DOES REMAIN ONE OF HIS BEST EFFORTS. PACKED WITH RAD CHASE SCENES, A RED NECKERCHIEF GUY NAMED BANDIT, JAWA-STYLE MIDGETS, SHEEPSKIN FLASKS, A BLEAK DESERT WASTELAND, A BALD BAD GUY WITH A HOOK FOR A HAND, A **MAD MAX**-STYLE TRUCK-CHASE BATTLE, HARROWING RAPES, A MAN PEEING ON ANOTHER MAN'S FACE, TANKS, WARRIOR CHICKS WITH SHORT SHORTS, AND A TITLE THAT ALWAYS MAKES ME THINK OF THE "STRIKE HER!" GAG IN **AIRPLANE.** ABSOLUTELY ESSENTIAL FOR YOUR P.A. COLLECTION.

RAIDERS OF THE SUN (1992)

CIRIO SANTIAGO'S WEAKEST P.A. MOVIE, ALTHOUGH I HAVEN'T SEEN **EQUALIZER 2000** YET. IT IS STILL BETTER THAN MANY MOVIES IN THE GENRE, BUT COMPARED TO HIS EARLIER EFFORTS, IT LACKS ENERGY, SOUL, AND JUST FEELS LIKE IT'S JUST GOING THROUGH THE MOTIONS AT THIS POINT. MOSTLY IT'S JUST FRUSTRATING AND SAD TO SEE A LOT OF FOOTAGE AND LOCATIONS REUSED FROM HIS EARLIER P.A. MOVIES, HERE CUT TOGETHER TO MAKE ENDLESS FIGHTS AND BATTLE SCENES THAT FEEL MORE LIKE GROWN MEN PLAYING A LITTLE KIDS GAME OF "ARMY" THAN ANYTHING. IF YOU'VE NEVER SEEN A SANTIAGO P.A. MOVIE YOU'LL PROBABLY BE HAPPIER THAN A PIG IN POOP WITH THIS, BUT THOSE OF US THAT HAVE SEEN HIS TRUE GLORY WON'T BE NEARLY AS IMPRESSED.

HANDS OF STEEL (1986) AKA "ATOMIC CYBORG"

I WAS TOLD THIS IS A POST APOCALYPTIC MOVIE, BUT I DO BELIEVE IT IS MORE OF A DYSTOPIAN FUTURE THAT IS REPRESENTED. EITHER WAY, IT WAS A FUCKIN' HOOT, SO I PRESENT MY REVIEW HERE ANYWHO. IN THE NEAR FUTURE (ONE THAT LOOKS EXACTLY LIKE 1986, EXCEPT WITH MORE "THERE IS NO FUTURE!" POSTERS HANGING EVERYWHERE) THERE ISN'T MUCH TO DO EXCEPT ARM WRESTLE ALL DAY. AFTER DEFEATING GEORGE EASTMAN (WHO IS VERY UNCONVINCINGLY TRYING TO PLAY A MEXICAN) A NEW YORKER PASSING THROUGH A SMALL ARIZONA TOWN IS TAKEN OUT INTO THE DESERT, SUSPENDED IN MID AIR FROM HIS FEET, CALLED "A PIECE OF RAT TURD" (WHICH IS KINDA ROUGH,...HE'S NOT EVEN A **WHOLE**

I THINK THIS EXTRA IS LOST

H-HELLO? HELL-OOO?

THIS IS THE KIND OF MOVIE WHERE NUNS CUT THEIR OWN THROATS.

I REGRET NOTHING!

IN 2 SECONDS CATCH DOG'S CYCLE SLUT IS GONNA GET SHOT IN THE HEAD.

AWWWWWW!!!
ISN'T CATCH DOG JUST THE SADDEST WIDDLE WASTELAND WENEGADE EVER?

RAT TURD? JUST A PIECE OF ONE?) AND LEFT TO DIE IN THE BAKING SUN. HE RETURNS FROM HIS DESERT BEATING UNHARMED, AND TOTALLY CHALLENGES THE LOCAL ARM WRESTLING CHAMP TO A MATCH WHERE THE LOSER'S HAND IS FORCED INTO THE MOUTH OF A POISONOUS SNAKE. HARDCORE! IF YOU THINK THAT IS WICKED COOL, WAIT UNTIL YOU NOTICE THAT THE NASTY TRUCKER BAR THEY WRESTLE IN HAS A GARFIELD POSTER PROUDLY DISPLAYED ON THE DOOR, OR UNTIL FUCKING JOHN SAXON SHOWS UP WITH A HUGE LASER CANNON ON HIS SHOULDER! YES!! ONE OF THE STUNTMEN/ACTORS WAS KILLED DURING ONE OF THE MANY HELICOPTER STUNTS IN THIS SERGIO MARTINO BUTT-BURPER, AND THEY DIDN'T EVEN HONOR HIM WITH AN AKNOWLEDGE- -MENT OR A DEDICATION IN THE CREDITS. THAT IS THE HARSH WORLD OF ITALIAN CINEMA, RIGHT THERE.

2020 TEXAS GLADIATORS (1982)
FIVE METROSEXUALS FORM A POSSE OF POST- -NUKE DO-GOODERS, AND RIGHT VARIOUS WRONGS IN THEIR UNIFORM OF JEANS, BOOTS, BANDOLIERS OF AMMO, PERMED HAIR, AND MATCHING NECKLACES. THESE SHIRTLESS WONDERS ARE NISUS, CATCH DOG, JAB, RED WOLFE (THE TOKEN ASIAN GUY) AND HALAKRON. I KNOW, RITE? SOUNDS LIKE A SHITTY EARLY 90s IMAGE COMIC BY ROB LIEFELD! THE BOYS TRACK DOWN A BRUTAL PACK OF ZOMBIES WHO ARE SLAUGHTERING AND MAULING EVERYONE THEY CAN IN A MONASTERY. CURIOUSLY OUR "HEROES" WAIT PATIENTLY A FEW FEET AWAY WHILE THE CREATURES RAPE A NUN, ANOTHER NUN CUTS HER OWN THROAT WITH A SHARD OF GLASS, AND A PRIEST IS LITERALLY CRUCIFIED! WHAT THE FUCK ARE THEY WAITING FOR?! FINALLY AFTER IT SEEMS ALL THE VICTIMS ARE DEAD, THEY **SPRING** INTO ACTION! A LOVELY AND TERRIFIED YOUNG GIRL IS DISCOVERED BY CATCH DOG, WHO TRIES TO FORCIBLY PUSH HIS ERECT PENIS INTO HER VAGINAL OPENING BEFORE BEING PULLED OFF HER BY THE OTHER IDENTICALLY DRESSED HIMBOS. THEY BANISH HIM FROM THEIR GROUP OF SUPERFRIENDS, AND HE SKULKS OFF AND FORMS AN EVIL BIKER GANG THEY SPEND THE REST OF THE FILM FIGHTING. WHAT ARE YOU WAITING FOR? THIS IS ONE OF THE FIRST ITALIAN P.A. MOVIES! FIND IT!

WARLORDS OF THE 21ST CENTURY (1982)
(AKA BATTLETRUCK)
OH WOW. SERIOUSLY, WOW. FANS OF **THE WARRIORS, XANADU,** AND **MEGAFORCE** (LIKE ME FOR INSTANCE) WILL BE EXCITED TO SEE MICHAEL BECK IN ANOTHER STARRING ROLE, BUT THE KICKAZZ "BATTLETRUCK" IS THE STAR OF THIS MOVIE -- THAT IS FO' SHO'. THIS BLACK BIG-RIG BEAST IS A MENACING ENTITY. EVERY TIME IT APPEARED ON SCREEN I GOT EXCITED. OWNED BY COLONEL STRAKER (THE VILLAINOUS LEADER OF A BAND OF THUGS) THE BATTLETRUCK IS USED FOR MUCHO EVIL AS IT MENACES THE PEACE-LOVING, DEMOCRACY-UPHOLDING NEW ZEALAND COMMUNITY OF CLEARWATER. WHERE ELSE ARE YOU GONNA SEE CLIFF CLAVEN FROM CHEERS AS A GENIUS WHO BUILDS ARMOURED DUNE BUGGIES AND GETS HIS HAND TURNED INTO BEEF JERKY? PLENTY OF EXCELLENT ACTING, A PLOT THAT ISN'T A **ROAD WARRIOR** CLONE, GUITAR SOLOS, INCREDIBLE AERIAL CINEMATOGRAPHY, AND A FINAL EXPLOSIVE CONFRONTATION (BIKE VS. BATTLE TRUCK) THAT IS ONE FOR THE AGES. HIGHLY RECOMMENDED.

WORLD GONE WILD (1988)
I **LOVE** THE MAGAZINE AD THAT MEDIA DISTRIBUTION MADE TO MARKET THIS ENTERTAINING P.A. FILM, SO I'LL JUST QUOTE THAT AS MY REVIEW: "CAN BRUCE DERN SAVE MANKIND FROM ADAM ANT? AFTER THE COLOSSAL NUCLEAR WIPEOUT, WHO INHERITS THE EARTH? ADAM ANT'S CRAZED BAND OF CHARLES MANSON WORSHIPPERS, OR HIPPIE-MAGICIAN BRUCE DERN'S FLOWER

IN **WHEELS OF FIRE**, A MAN NAMED TRACE DRIVES HIS CAR AROUND A LOT.

> HE MEANS TO SAY I FREQUENTLY DRIVE, NOT "PARKING LOT!"

HIS LIL' SISTER SPENDS THE WHOLE FILM GETTING RAPED AND SEXUALLY SUBJUGATED BY STINKY WARRIORS.

> OY VEY...

> RAPING, ALWAYS WITH THE RAPING.

I TOTALLY WANT A FLAME THROWER.

> HELLOO DETROIT, ARE YOU READY **TO ROCK?!!**

...AND A TRIKE! A FUCKING TRIKE WITH A BAZOOKA GUY ON THE BACK!

CHILDREN, WHO FOLLOW THE GREAT TEACHINGS OF EMILY POST? FINDING OUT IS ALL THE FUN IN THIS SCI-FI ADVENTURE, WITH ACTION THAT MAKES MAD MAX LOOK LIKE A TEA PARTY. AT YOUR VIDEO STORE NOW."

WHEELS OF FIRE (1984)

ONE OF MY ALL-TIME FAVES! THIS IS A RIVETING MUSCLE CAR MEGA-MOVIE TAKING PLACE IN A BARREN DUSTBOWL POPULATED BY MURDEROUS BRIGANDS AND RADIOACTIVE MUTANTS. THERE IS ALSO A LOT OF FOOTBALL PADDING, WHICH IS NEVER A BAD THING FOR MOVIES OF THIS SORT. WHEELS OF FIRE FOLLOWS "TRACE", A ROAD WARRIOR CLONE WHOSE PERSONA IS TIGHTLY WRAPPED UP IN HIS EARLY 1970s FORD MUSTANG WITH SPIKES WELDED TO THE GRILL AND A JET ENGINE STRAPPED TO THE BACK. TRACE HAS A SISTER (FORMER PLAYBOY PLAYMATE LYNDA WIESMEIER) WITH NICE BIG SOFT FLOPPY TITS, WHO GETS KIDNAPPED BY THE BAD GUYS AND TIED NAKED TO THE HOOD OF ONE OF THEIR CARS. AFTER THE GOONS TAKE TURNS BANGING HER FOR DAYS ON END, SHE BEGS THEM FOR FOOD--PROMPTING THE MEMORABLE LINE: "LIKE SHIT, BITCH! WHY DON'T YOU GO FUCK A DOG? MAYBE HE'LL LET YOU HAVE A BONE! HAW HAW HAW!". TRACE, AMAZINGLY ENOUGH, GETS SO WRAPPED UP WITH OTHER CASUAL ADVENTURES THAT COME UP, THAT HE ACTUALLY SEEMS TO FORGET HE WANTED TO RESCUE HER.

OTHER REASONS TO LOVE THIS MOVIE: FLAME THROWERS, A TOUGH GIRL NAMED STINGER WHO HAS ONE OF THE BEST 80s FEATHERED MULLETS EVER, ROCK QUARRIES, A CUTE PSYCHIC CHICK, A COOL CASTLE LOCATION, THAT SAME BEARDED FILIPINO MIDGET THAT IS IN ALL OF CIRIO SANTIAGO'S MOVIES, AND A FUCKING ROCKET--SHIP! HELL YEAH, YOU NEED THIS. UNAVAIL. ON DVD AS OF THIS WRITING, BUT BOOTLEGS ON DVD-R OF THE OOP VHS DO FLOAT AROUND OUT THERE IN THE RIGHT CIRCLES.

THE QUIET EARTH (1985)

THE CAUSE OF APOCALYPSE IN THIS NEW ZEALAND MOVIE IS SOME KINDA ACCIDENTAL ENERGY FEEDBACK EXPLOSION THING, AND THE ONLY PEOPLE WHO ARE LEFT ALIVE ARE THOSE WHO WERE CURRENTLY IN A STATE OF DYING WHEN IT HAPPENED. SO, IF YOU WERE, FOR INSTANCE, POPPING PILLS AND IN THE MIDDLE OF AN OUT-OF-BODY MOVEMENT WHEN THE END HIT--YOU SURVIVED! SWEET DEAL! THE FIRST HALF IS AN INTERESTING STUDY OF A MAN SLOWLY GOING BONKERS DUE TO OPPRESSIVE SOLITUDE, WITH THE FILM EVENTUALLY FOCUSING ON HIM, A PRETTY GIRL, AND A BLACK GUY. WE GET TO SEE LOTS OF GOOD LOOTING, CROSS-DRESSING, ANTI-AMERICAN-ISM, SOME DECENT SEXUAL AND RACIAL TENSION, AND

> BAM!! SAPPHIC SALAD TOSSING!!

> MMMNUM

> DON'T MIND ME...JUST DRAWING MORE LESBIANS..

> EAT IT, BITCH!

STRYKER

WHINING ABOUT BEING "CONDEMNED TO LIVE". BOOO-HOOO. BASED ON A NOVEL BY CRAIG HARRISON, THE SCRIPT WAS CO-WRITTEN BY ONE OF THE THREE STARS OF THE MOVIE, BRUNO LAWRENCE. MOSTLY UNKNOWN OUTSIDE OF NEW ZEALAND, BRUNO SEEMS TO HAVE BEEN IN EVERY OTHER KIWI PRODUCTION IN THE 80s, AND DIED OF LUNG CANCER IN 1995.

TANK GIRL (1995)

TALENTED COMIC BOOK ARTIST JAMIE HEWLETT CREATED TANK GIRL IN 1988. THIS EXCITING, ORIGINAL CHARACTER EMBODIED ANTIAUTHORITARIAN ANARCHISM (JUST BEFORE THE WHOLE RIOT GRRL THING CAME INTO FASHION) AND BECAME AN INDIE FAVE AMONGST SEX-POSITIVE FEMINISTS, PRIDE-PARADE MARCHING LESBIANS, AND COMIC BOOK NERD-VIRGINS ALIKE. IN 1995, THE CULT COMIC WAS ADAPTED FOR THE BIG SCREEN, AND SHRILL LORI PETTY SNAGGED THE TITLE ROLE FROM 3 OF THE SPICE GIRLS WHO AUDITIONED. A YOUNG NAOMI WATTS PLAYS AN ADORABLE SHY NERD, ICE-T PLAYS A MUTATED KANGAROO, AND THERE ARE SONG AND DANCE NUMBERS. ONE NEWSPAPER CRITIC PUT IT BEST: "ENORMOUS ENERGY WENT INTO THIS MOVIE. I COULD NOT, HOWEVER, CARE ABOUT IT FOR MORE THAN A MOMENT AT A TIME, AND AFTER AWHILE ITS MANIC ENERGY WORE ME DOWN". THIS SILLY, SPAZZY MOVIE NEVER CLAIMS TO BE ANYTHING OTHER THAN WHAT IT IS, BUT FOR US P.A. FANS, IT DOESN'T HAVE MUCH TO OFFER ASIDE FROM FALSE HOPE IF YOU HAVEN'T SEEN IT YET. STICK TO THE COMIC.

ROLLERBLADE (1986)

IN A FUTURISTIC SOCIETY, REBELS CLASHING WITH A FASCIST STATE ARE AIDED BY ROLLER SKATING WARRIOR NUNS WHO GET NAKED A LOT. THE BAD GUY HAS A FREDDY KRUEGER-ESQUE PUPPET FOR A HAND, AND A PLAN TO USE A JET-POWERED SKATEBOARD TO LAUNCH HIMSELF ACROSS A HUGE CHASM. PEOPLE GET TOSSED INTO SHOPPING CARTS AND, INCOMPREHENSIBLY, ARE UNABLE TO GET THEMSELVES OUT. IF THERE HAD BEEN A BUDGET (IT COST $5000 AND MADE A MILLION DOLLARS ON VIDEO) I GUESS THESE VERY EMBARRASSING SHOPPING CART CHASES WOULD HAVE BEEN CAR CHASE SCENES. HILARIOUS, SURREAL THRIFT STORE-BUDGET INCOHERANCE THAT SOMEHOW SPAWNED FOUR FUCKING SEQUELS!

NEW NAME IS "SKUNX"

WE WILL SURVIVE! ♡

NEW NAME IS "DILL PICKLEZ"

☆ REBECCA + ROBIN 2016 ☆

RAVAGERS (1979)

BEING THE SLOBBERING AFICIONADO OF THIS GENRE THAT I AM, I WAS QUITE PUMPED TO FINALLY SEE THIS EXTREMELY RARE, FORGOTTEN AND ELUSIVE GENRE ENTRY. I DIDN'T KNOW MUCH ABOUT IT, EXCEPT THAT IT WAS GIVEN A REALLY INADEQUATE RELEASE BY COLUMBIA, AND RECEIVED EXTREMELY NEGATIVE REVIEWS BY THE HANDFUL OF CRITICS WHO BOTHERED TO SEE IT DURING ITS SHORT THEATRICAL RUN. THE SET UP IS PRETTY BASIC: IN A POST-APOCALYPTIC WORLD DIVIDED BETWEEN TWO GROUPS CALLED THE FLOCKERS AND THE RAVAGERS, A

EL PLANETA DE LOS BUITRES
(RAVAGERS)

RICHARD HARRIS · ERNEST BORGNINE · ANN TURKEL Y ART CARNEY

SURVIVOR (WHO DISLIKES VIOLENCE) AND HIS "PLEASURE GIRL" TRY TO FIND THEIR WAY TO A RUMORED SAFE HAVEN CALLED THE LAND OF GENESIS. ALL HOPE HAS BEEN LOST, FOOD IS SCARCE, AND THE VICIOUS RAVAGERS LOOT AND KILL WITH NO MERCY. THE MOVIE HAS A NOTABLE CAST, BUT A STRONG OPENING AND EXCITING FINISH ARE BADLY MARRED BY WHAT IS PERHAPS THE MOST BORING, PLODDING, TALKY SECOND ACT IN POST APOCALYPSE CINEMA HISTORY. IT'S ALSO RATED PG, AND A RAW, VIOLENT, FEROCIOUS R-RATED TONE IS WHAT THIS MOVIE REALLY NEEDED. TRIVIA: GILDA TEXTER (THE CUTE, PERKY, NAKED BLONDE GIRL ON THE MOTORCYCLE IN *VANISHING POINT*) DESIGNED ALL OF THE RATTY COSTUMES.

REIGN OF FIRE (2002)
CONSIDERING THE GENRE ISN'T VERY POPULAR WITH MAINSTREAM AUDIENCES ANYMORE, I WAS REALLY PLEASED TO SEE A HOLLYWOOD-MADE P.A. FILM SHOW UP IN THEATERS IN 2002, AND ESPECIALLY TO SEE ONE WITH SUCH AN INVENTIVE WAY FOR HUMANITY TO BE NEARLY WIPED OFF THE FACE OF THE PLANET - AN ONSLAUGHT OF KILLER DRAGONS! YOWZA! IN 2020 CHRISTIAN BALE (**AMERICAN PSYCHO**) IS THE LEADER OF A SMALL BAND OF DRAGON PLAGUE SURVIVORS WHO SHIVER IN THE DUNGEON OF A BRITISH CASTLE JUST WAITIN' FOR THE DRAGONS TO DIE OF STARVATION. A WAR-MAD AMERICAN (MATTHEW McCONAUGHEY) AND HIS TEAM OF MILITARY-TRAINED BUM-KICKERS ROLL UP IN SOME TANKS AND A HELICOPTER AND OFFER TO HELP THE COWERING PEEPS - BUT ONLY IF THEY TAKE PART IN THE EXTREME TACTICS TO DESTROY THE FIRE-BREATHING BEASTS. THERE ARE SOME REALLY FUCKING MORONIC LEAPS OF LOGIC (SKYDIVING OUT OF A HELICOPTER TO BATTLE DRAGONS !??) BUT OVERALL I WAS REALLY SATISFIED WITH THIS NEW TWIST.

SHE (1983)
ONE OF THE MOST BIZARRE AND HILARIOUS FILMS OF THIS GENRE, SHE COMES ON LIKE AN ASS-MOUNTED FIRECRACKER AND KEEPS ON ROCKIN' OUT CRAZY SHIT TILL THE BREAK O' DAWN. THIS **IS** THE APOCALYPTIC FUTURE: MUMMIES WITH SUN GLASSES AND POWER TOOLS, SAMURAIS, A FRANKENSTEIN MONSTER WHOSE HEAD EXPLODES, ORGIASTIC WEREWOLVES, A PSYCHIC COMMUNIST, NAZI FOOTBALL PLAYER BIKERS THAT CALL THEMSELVES 'NORKS' AND LIVE IN 'NORKVILLE', A BONDAGE FETISH CULT, SOME FREAK THAT WEARS A BALLERINA DRESS AND A GASMASK, A BIZARRE SOUNDTRACK BY MOTÖRHEAD, AND A WARRIOR GODDESS NAMED "SHE" PLAYED BY SANDAHL (**CONAN**) BERGMAN. SAINTS DELIVER US.

STEEL DAWN (1987)
SO HELP ME, I DID **NOT** WANT TO LIKE THIS. IT STARS PATRICK SWAYZE FER FUCK'S SAKE! BUT YOU GOTTA GIVE PROPS WHERE THEY ARE DUE, AND THIS IS BY FAR THE MOST ENTERTAINING SWAYZE FILM I'VE EVER SEEN. IT PLAYS LIKE A WESTERN (SPECIFICALLY **SHANE**) AS PATRICK PLAYS A GREASED UP NOMAD WHO WANDERS THROUGH THE DESERT BEFORE HAPPENING UPON A GROUP OF FARMERS WHO ARE BEING TERRORIZED BY A MURDEROUS GANG THAT'S AFTER THE WATER THEY CONTROL. I'VE SEEN THIS ON PLENTY OF "WORST FILM OF ALL TIME" LISTS, AND WHILE IT'S FAR FROM **CITIZEN KANE**, IT'S NOT FAIR TO HAVE SINGLED THIS OUT WHEN SO MANY OTHER P.A. MOVIES ARE FAR MORE IDIOTIC. **STEEL DAWN** IS TIGHTLY PLOTTED, DECENTLY ACTED, AND IT EMPLOYS INTERESTING ASPECTS SPECIFIC TO THE GENRE. RAMPANT NUDITY WOULD HAVE BEEN A WELCOME ADDITION THOUGH, ESPECIALLY WHEN ALL THOSE CAVE GIRLS SHOWED UP.

STEEL FRONTIER (1994)
THIS SHIT-KICKER OPENS STRONG WITH SOME AWESOME GORE (LEGS GETTING CUT OFF) AND GENERALLY FLATLINES FROM THEREON. WHEN MEGA-STUD 'YUMA' HOLLARS "ANGEL!!" HIS MOTORCYCLE SHOOTS PEOPLE, AND EVEN THOUGH HE STANDS AROUND PICKING HIS NOSE WHILE THE YOUNG WOMEN OF THE TOWN "NEW HOPE" ARE RAPED AND MOLESTED BY A GANG OF GOOFS, WE ARE STILL MEANT TO THINK THAT HE'S AN HONORABLE HERO AND A MAN OF PEACE. AND WHY DO ALL THE TOWN'S INHABITANTS WEAR FRESH NEW GARMENTS WHEN IT'S "BEEN 18 YEARS SINCE THE WORLD BURNED"?? MAYBE THEY SHOULD HAVE NAMED THE TOWN "NEW CLOTHES" INSTEAD. NOT GREAT, BUT BETTER THAN MOST OF THE DIRECT-TO-VIDEO WAVE OF P.A. FILMS IN THE 1990s.

SURVIVOR (1987)
A SOUTH AFRICAN/USA CO-PRODUCTION THAT DEFIED MY LOW EXPECTATIONS IN A BIG WAY. CHIP MAYER PLAYS AN ASTRONAUT WHO SPLATS BACK ON EARTH ONLY TO DISCOVER HE JUST MISSED OUT ON WWIII. HE WANDERS AROUND JUST LIKE ANY OF US WOULD - AND ALMOST GETS HIS BEFUDDLED ASS WASTED IN A MYRIAD OF WAYS - BEFORE MEETING AND FALLING FOR A SCARY GIRL WHO LIVES ON A BEACHED AND GUTTED RUSTY TANKER SHIP. THIS SURPRISINGLY REALISTIC AND UNDERRATED LITTLE TREASURE COULD HAVE BEEN ONE OF MY TOP 3 FAVORITE P.A. OF THE 80s IF NOT FOR THE REDUNDANT NARRATION, WHICH EXISTS ONLY TO ALLOW US TO HEAR THE CHARACTERS THOUGHTS OUT LOUD. WE ARE TOLD WHAT WE CAN CLEARLY SEE ON SCREEN FOR OURSELVES, AND IT DUMBS THE WHOLE MOVIE DOWN AND STINKS OF STUDIO MEDDLING. WHEN THE STUPID NARRATION KICKS IN, USE THE MUTE BUTTON. IT'LL GO FROM A 3 STAR TO A 5 STAR MOVIE INSTANTLY.

TIME OF THE WOLF (2003 AKA 'LE TEMPS DU LOUP')
NOW THIS IS SOME BLEAK-ASS FRENCH/GERMAN SCHNITZEL. BUT WHAT ELSE WOULD YOU EXPECT FROM MICHAEL HANEKE, THE DIRECTOR OF THE DOWNBEAT AND MENTALLY DRAINING SERIAL KILLER MOVIE **FUNNY GAMES**? ANNE (ISABELLE HUPPERT) AND HER CHILDREN (PLAYED BY LUCAS BISCOMBE AND ANAÏS DEMOUSTIER) TAKE SHELTER IN A RAILWAY STATION WITH SOME OTHER FRAZZLED REFUGEES, ALL BLINDLY HOPING THAT A TRAIN MAY SOON COME ALONG AND CARRY THEM TO SAFETY. SOME UNSPECIFIED DISASTER HAS RESULTED IN SEVERE SHORTAGES OF FOOD AND WATER, AND DESPITE THE FACT THAT HANEKE'S FRENCH COUNTRYSIDE LOOKS PERFECTLY NORMAL, THE AMBIGUITY RAISES THE FILM FROM WHAT MIGHT HAVE BEEN MERELY TOPICAL (AN ANTI-WAR DIATRIBE) TO A MUCH MORE TRAGIC EXAMINATION OF THE DETERIORATION OF CIVILIZATION. IT'S AS FUCKING BLEAK AS IT IS THOUGHTFUL, AND A MUST-SEE FOR PEOPLE WHO LIKE TO CRY AND FEEL SAD. YOU KNOW WHO YOU ARE.

WHERE THE FUTURE COLLIDES WITH THE PAST.

JOE LARA

STEEL FRONTIER

BO SVENSON • STACIE FOSTER • BRION JAMES

VIRTUALIA 1 - CYBER SEX (2001 XXX)
WELCOME TO THE YEAR 2118. THE EARTH HAS BEEN ALMOST COMPLETELY DESTROYED BY NUCLEAR WAR,
HUMAN LIFE ITSELF IS UNDER SERIOUS THREAT, SINCE MANY OF THE MALE SURVIVORS HAVE BEEN
RENDERED IMPOTENT BY THE RADIATION. 'VIRTUALIA' OFFERS HUMANS THE CHANCE TO ENJOY
JIZZY ADVENTURES THANKS TO HER DIGITAL NETWORK. ALTHOUGH THIS MYSTERIOUS CREATURE
KNOWS NOTHING ABOUT HER HISTORY AND HARSH FLASHBACKS WHICH CAUSE HER TO
SUFFER. THIS IS A BIGGER BUDGET PORN FILM, EMPLOYING DECENT STUDIO LOCATIONS, AND WITH
OUTDOOR SCENES SHOT IN SPAIN (INCLUDING THE REMNANTS OF AN ABANDONED ANCIENT CITY
AND SOME DESERT FOOTAGE). BUT IT'S ULTIMATELY SO FUCKING LIMP THAT YOU'LL WISH THAT YOU
HAD EITHER SETTLED ON EITHER A REALLY HOT PORN FILM OR A DECENT P.A. MOVIE, AND NOT
TRIED IN VAIN TO GET BOTH AT THE SAME TIME.

VIRUS (1980)
KINJI FUKASAKU'S ENTERTAINING ODE TO THE END OF
LIFE ON EARTH IS ONE OF MY ALL TIME FAVORITE
P.A. FILMS TO EVER COME OUT OF ASIA AND ALSO
ONE OF THE HARDEST TO FIND UNCUT. THERE ARE
VERSIONS ON DVD AVAILABLE IN NORTH AMERICA THAT
RUN A FULL HOUR SHORTER THAN THE EPIC 156 MIN
MASTERPIECE THAT IS AVAILABLE IN JAPAN ON A
BIG MULTIPLE DISC SPECIAL EDITION - WHICH IS THE
ONLY WAY THIS MOVIE SHOULD BE SEEN. BETTER
KNOWN FOR FILMS LIKE 2000'S **BATTLE ROYALE** -
AND HIS VARIOUS AMAZING YAKUZA MOVIES OF THE
1970S, FUKASAKU'S **VIRUS** IS A STARTLING LOOK AT
HOW SOME APOCALYPTIC WORLDWIDE SHIT WENT
DOWN VIA A KILLER VIRUS, AND THEN WHAT BECAME OF THE PLANET'S FEW ARTIC-BOUND BEINGS.
THE MASSIVE CAST IS GREAT ACCROSS THE BOARD, AND FUKASAKU'S DIRECTION IS FLAWLESS.

VIRUS
Directed by Kinji Fukasaku
Starring Chuck Conners, Glenn Ford,
Olivia Hussey, George Kennedy,
Masao Kusakari, Henry Silva,
Bo Svenson, Robert Vaughn

WARRIOR OF THE LOST WORLD (1983)
IN ONE OF THE STRANGER ORIGIN STORIES IN MODERN FILM
HISTORY, DIRECTOR DAVID WORTH WAS BLINDLY HIRED,
SHIPPED TO ITALY, AND TOLD TO START SHOOTING A FILM
WITH NO SCRIPT AND ONLY AN AIRBRUSHED MOVIE
POSTER AS A GUIDE. WHAT HE DELIVERED HAD ALL THE
ODDS STACKED AGAINST IT BEING OF ANY SORT OF
QUALITY, AND IT CERTAINLY DIDN'T OVERCOME THOSE ODDS
TO ANY GREAT DEGREE. CAN YOU IMAGINE BEING THE
POSTER ARTIST FOR THIS MOVIE?! YOU'D HAVE FELT LIKE
A FUCKING GOD. ANY LITTLE DETAIL YOU DECIDED TO ADD AS
BACKGROUND WOULD HAVE TO BE CREATED, FLESHED OUT,
AND GIVEN A BACKSTORY TO EXPLAIN IT'S SIGNIFICANCE.
YOU WOULD **GO MAD WITH POWER!!!** AS IT IS, ROBERT
GINTY (STAR OF THE **EXTERMINATOR** MOVIES) RIDES AROUND ON
A SUPER-CYCLE TRYING TO KNOCK MEGALOMANIACAL DONALD
PLEASENCE AND HIS GOOMBAH HENCHMAN FRED WILLIAMSON
DOWN A PEG BY BLOWING THEIR TOTALITARIAN SHIT UP. MST3K
DID A PRETTY FUNNY EPISODE FEATURING THIS MOVIE.

WARRIORS OF THE WASTELAND (1983 AKA: 'THE NEW BARBARIANS')
THIS IS SOOOO MUCH FUN! SCORPION DRIVES AROUND IN A
MUSCLE CAR WITH A BIG GAUDY PLEXI-GLASS BUBBLE ON THE
ROOF, VACUUM CLEANER HOSES HANGIN' OFF THE HOOD, AND A
REVEL PLASTIC SKULL MODEL KIT ROPED TO THE GRILL. HE'S
LIKE A THRIFT STORE MAD
MAD! HA HA! HIS ARCH
NEMESES ARE THE TEMPLARS,
A GROUP OF KINKY HOMO BOYS
WHO DRIVE AROUND IN CARS
THAT MAKE ANNOYING BUZZY
SOUNDS AND SHOOT MACHINE GUNS THAT EMIT BUCK ROGERS STYLE
LAZER BEAMS! THE JUMP-SUITED GAY BOYS ARE LED BY GEORGE
EASTMAN WHO YELLS THINGS LIKE "WE HAVE BEEN CHOSEN TO MAKE
OTHERS PAY FOR THE CRIME OF BEING ALIVE!" AND "THE WORLD IS
DEAD! IT RAPED ITSELF!". BUT IT'S POOR SCORPION WHO GETS
RAPED WHEN HE'S CAPTURED, BENT OVER, AND "INITIATED" BY
THE POST NUKE FAIRY-FASCISTS. DID I MENTION THE EXPLODING
HEADS?! LOTS OF EXPLODING HEADS, PEOPLE. **GET THIS MOVIE.**

> Don't worry, ducks.
> There can't be anything
> wrong with you.
> I expect it's just the
> after-effects of
> The Bomb

WHEN THE WIND BLOWS (1986)
JESUS CRISPIES, I'M NEVER SURE IF I SHOULD LAUGH OR CRY AFTER
SEEING THIS ANIMATED FILM BASED ON THE COMIC BY BRITISH CARTOONIST RAYMOND BRIGGS. THE
STORY PERFECTLY CARICATURES AN ELDERLY COUPLE LIVING IN SMALL TOWN ENGLAND, A SWEET OLD
PAIR WHO ARE DETERMINED TO KEEP THAT BRITISH STIFF UPPER LIP WITH NO CLUE ABOUT THE
SAVAGE EFFECTS OF THE NUCLEAR BOMBS WHICH HAVE JUST RECENTLY LANDED IN NEARBY URBAN
CENTERS. EVERYONE ELSE HAS EVACUATED, BUT LEFT BEHIND ARE THESE NAIVE INNOCENT
GRANDPARENTS WHO SLOWLY AND PAINFULLY DIE RIGHT BEFORE YOUR EYES. THE FACT THAT IT'S
ANIMATED IN A VERY CARTOONY STYLE, AND TAKES PLACE MOSTLY IN REAL TIME MAKES IT ALL THE
MORE DISTURBING. GET THIS CARTOON FOR THE NEXT LITTLE RUGRAT YOU HAVE TO BABYSIT, AND
WATCH HIM/HER PULL A PILLOWCASE OVER THEIR HEAD AND BLOW THEIR BRAINS OUT. YES,
THATS GOOD WHOLESOME ENTERTAINMENT.
—BOUGIE '05

BAD BAD GANG (1971) DIR. BY JON DONNE
THE BAD BAD GANG ARE THE COBRAS, A GROWLING HERD OF LSD
TAKIN', TOMAHAWK CARRYIN', FAT ASSED, HAIRY FREAKS ON BIG
CHOPPERS THAT HAVE A WATERBED IN THEIR SECRET CAVE
HIDEOUT, AND DIG ON THE ACT OF HASSLING & RAPING LUSCIOUS
SEX KITTEN RENE BOND WHILE HER REAL LIFE MEATHEAD
BOYFRIEND RIC LUTZE LOOKS ON. THIS SWEATY RETRO ROCKET
FROM THE PORNO CRYPT IS ONE OF THE EARLIEST HARDCORE
FEATURES AND REMINDS US THAT BACK IN THE EARLY 70S, RAPE
WAS SIMPLY A WAY OF BREAKING DOWN A WOMAN'S NATURAL
RESISTANCE TO SEX. (!!?) THE PLOT IS CONFUSED AND TOUGH
TO FOLLOW, THE PRINT IS TOTALLY SCRATCHED TO SHIT, BUT AS
THE PACKAGING SAYS: "AUDIENCES WEANED ON TODAY'S BLAND
BORING ADULT FILMS WILL BLOW A BOWEL OVER THIS SHOCK
PACKED, SEX-SOAKED RELIC FROM THE GOLDEN AGE OF PORN."

ASIAN RETITLING

SURE, IT'S EASY TO GIGGLE AT OUR CULTURAL DIFFERENCES, BUT I THINK IT'S PRETTY CLEAR THAT FILM DISTRIBUTORS IN ASIA ENHANCE, INVIGORATE, AND GLORIOUSLY REINVENT HOLLYWOOD TRIPE WITH EYE-CATCHING NEW NAMES. AND THANK GOODNESS THEY DO, BECAUSE SOME OF THIS CLICHÉ, UNEXCEPTIONAL SHIT NEEDS ANY AND ALL EXCITEMENT INJECTED INTO IT THAT IT CAN GET.

WHEN **THE CABLE GUY** WAS RELEASED IN HONG KONG, IT WAS RETITLED "TRUMP CARD SPECIALIST", AND **LIAR LIAR** BECAME "TRUMP CARD BIG LIAR". THESE ODD TITLES MAKE FAR MORE SENSE WHEN YOU KNOW THAT "TRUMP CARD" IS THE EAST ASIAN MOVIEGOERS NICKNAME FOR JIM CARREY. THIS CAN BE TRACED BACK TO THE SUCCESSFUL **ACE VENTURA** SERIES -- WITH "ACE" BEING TRANSLATED AS "TRUMP CARD".

BUT DIG ON THIS: THAT LOGIC VEERED **WAY** OFF TRACK WHEN THE FIRST **AUSTIN POWERS** MOVIE CAME OUT AND WAS NAMED "TRUMP CARD BIG SPY". IT, OF COURSE, STARRED MIKE MYERS RATHER THAN JIM CARREY, BUT DISTRIBUTORS APPARENTLY THOUGHT THAT THE FACT THAT IT WAS A COMPLETELY DIFFERENT HUMAN BEING WAS FAR TOO SUBTLE A DIFFERENCE TO WORRY ABOUT. WIGGLY WHITE GUYS ARE WIGGLY WHITE GUYS, RIGHT? THINK OF IT AS A SMALL TOKEN OF REVENGE FOR DECADES OF "JAPANESE, VIETNAMESE, CHINESE, KOREAN... THEY ALL LOOK THE SAME TO ME."

THAT ISN'T THE ONLY WONKY ASIAN RETITLING SITUATION THAT MADE FOR BUKOO CONFUSION. IN TAIWAN, **THE BLAIR WITCH PROJECT** BECAME "THE NIGHT IN CRAMPED FOREST". SOON, AN EMBARRASSINGLY BAD PARODY CALLED **THE BARE WENCH PROJECT** FOUND ITS WAY OVERSEAS (DESPITE BEING RELEASED DIRECT-TO-VIDEO DOMESTICALLY) AND WAS RELEASED AS "NIGHT IN CRAMPED FOREST 2", AS IF IT WERE A SEQUEL. OF COURSE, IT WASN'T LONG BEFORE THE OFFICIAL SEQUEL CAME OUT. IT HAD TO SETTLE FOR THE TITLE: "SPIRITS OF THE DEAD ROAR".

HERE ARE SOME OF MY FAVORITE RETITLINGS OF AMERICAN MOVIES, WITH ILLUSTRATIONS PROVIDED BY THE CUDDLY ROBERT DAYTON. VISIT HIM ONLINE AT: MYSPACE.COM/CANNEDHAMM I <u>LOVE</u> THAT GUY!

Possession (Starring Gwyneth Paltrow) = Hog (Japan)
FINALLY, SOMEONE SAID IT. I WOULDN'T BE SURPRISED TO FIND OUT THAT PALTROW MEANS "SOW" IN JAPANESE.

The Professional = "This Hit Man Is Not As Cold As He Thought" (China)
HELL NO! NOT WHEN BUDDING FLOWER NATALIE PORTMAN IS THERE TO WARM HIM UP, AMIRITE?

Star Wars Episode III: Revenge of the Sith = "Star War 3: Backstroke of the West"
FACE IT GEEKS, LUCAS'S ENTIRE CAREER SINCE STAR WARS HAS BEEN A BACKSTROKE. THE MAN IS AN EMBARRASSMENT.

Pretty Woman = "Sparrow Becomes the Empress" (China)
"SPARROW" IS SUCH A CLASSY TERM FOR WHORE!

Pecker = I Love Pecker (Japan)
IN SOME CULTURES IT IS A DELICACY.

Eyes Wide Shut = "Eyes Wide Open"
I SUPPOSE THAT NEW TITLE MAKES MORE SENSE.

Dr. No = "We Don't Need Any Doctors"
HAHA! IT'S A SPY MOVIE ABOUT CHRISTIAN SCIENTISTS!

Blade Runner = "Silver Wing Killer" (China)
SEEING AS BLADE RUNNER HAD NOTHING TO DO WITH BLADES OR RUNNERS, I'M GOING TO LET THIS ONE SLIDE.

NOW SHOWING!:

Our Man Flint = "Lightning Flint Operation Go Go!" (Japan)
IT'S A LITTLE KNOWN FACT THAT JAMES COBURN IS ALSO A GO-GO DANCER.

Crossroads (Starring Britney Spears) = Not a Girl (Japan)
HEY NOW... JUST BECAUSE A YOUNG LADY HAS AN
ERECT PENIS-SIZED CLITORIS DOESN'T
MEAN SHE'S NOT A GIRL.

Donnie Brasco = "Fake" (Japan)
FAAAAAKE!

Basic Instinct = "Smirk of Ice" (Japan)
WELL, THAT FILM DID LEAVE ME PRETTY COLD.

Monster's Ball = "Chocolate" (Japan)
DUDE... ARE MONSTER'S BALLS MADE OUT OF
CHOCOLATE?! AWWWESUUM.

Sex and the City = "Lust Metropolis"
I WISH FRITZ LANG MADE SOME PORNO MOVIES.

Rush Hour = "Speedy Violent Strife"
IF YOU'RE GONNA HAVE SOME STRIFE, YOU MAY
AS WELL HAVE IT BE SPEEDY AND VIOLENT.

Army of Darkness = "Captain Supermarket" (Japan)
HE WAS DEMOTED FROM GENERAL SUPERMARKET FOR WAVING AROUND HIS BOOMSTICK AND
CALLING THE CUSTOMERS "PRIMITIVE SCREWHEADS".

Indiana Jones and the Kingdom of the Crystal Skull = "The Surprise-Attack Forces
Seize the Valuable Quartz Skeleton"
I'LL TELL YOU WHAT PISSES ME OFF... SURPRISE-ATTACK FORCES ALWAYS STEALING MY SHIT.

Hellboy 2 = "The Evil Spirit Attacks the Ghost and Demon Army Corps" (China)
WHY CAN'T DEMONS AND EVIL SPIRITS JUST GET ALONG?

Risky Business = "Just Send Him to University Unqualified" (China)
TOM CRUISE WENT TO THE UNIVERSITY OF CRAZY, AND HE WAS TOTALLY QUALIFIED.

Gone with the Wind = "The Confused World of a Beautiful Woman" (China)
WE CALL THOSE "BIMBOS" OVER HERE, CHINA.

Boogie Nights = "His Powerful Device Makes Him Famous" (China)
NOTE TO SELF: RENAME YOUR COCK "THE POWERFUL DEVICE".

The Incredible Hulk (2008) = "Variant Distortion Medicine" (China)
HA HA! THAT ONE READS LIKE A SPAM EMAIL FOR VIAGRA!

Good Will Hunting = "The Scorching Sun Resembles Me" (China)
DO NOT LOOK DIRECTLY INTO MATT DAMON!!

Free Willy = "A Very Powerful Whale Runs
to Heaven" (China)
WHEN HE GOT THERE, GOD WAS ALL "WOOOO! YOU
TOTALLY JUMPED OVER THAT KID! THAT WAS
SICK, BRA!"

Hancock = "Homeless Superhero"
AKA: HOBOCOP!!

Babe = "I'm Not Stupid, I Have Something to Say"
IF PIGS COULD ACTUALLY TALK, WE WOULDN'T EAT THEM ANY
MORE. I'M PRETTY SURE WE'D STILL EAT TALKING CHICKENS
THOUGH.

The Full Monty = "Six Naked Pigs" (China)
THE CHINESE RETITLING IS FAR MORE APPROPRIATE!

Being John Malkovich = Malkovich's Hole (Japan)
I CAN JUST HEAR IT NOW: "YES, I'D LIKE ONE TICKET TO MALKOVICH'S HOLE, PLEASE."

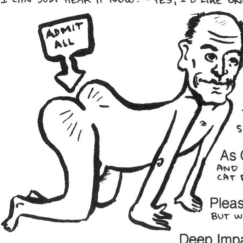

G.I. Jane = "Satan Female Soldier"
I WOULD HAVE ACTUALLY GONE TO SEE THIS IF THAT HAD BEEN THE NAME ON THE POSTER.

Gladiator = "The Arrogant Male Empire"
THE BUSH ADMINISTRATION?

The Pink Panther = "Silly Leopard" (China)
SILLY LEOPARD, SHITTY REMAKES ARE FOR KIDS!

As Good As It Gets = "Mr. Cat Poop" (China)
AND IN FRANCE, JACK NICHOLSON IS "MONSIEUR CAT POOP".

Pleasantville = "A Person Has a Color" (China)
BUT WE'RE ALL PINK ON THE INSIDE!

Deep Impact = "Earth and Comet Collide" (Korea)
THAT NEW TITLE IS FINE WITH ME. THE ORIGINAL ALWAYS SOUNDED LIKE AN EXTEME GAY FISTING PORNO ANYWAY.

The English Patient = "Don't Ask Who I Am" (China)
DON'T ASK WHO I AM!! DON'T YOU FUCKING DARE!!

☆ BOUGIE 2008

SATANIK (1968)
A YOUTH POTION TRANSFORMS AN UGLY OL' CRONE INTO A RAVISHING BLONDE VIXEN, AND ALSO CHANGES HER MAKEUP DRASTICALLY AND GIVES HER A NEW HAIRCUT (!?). THE GENETIC FORMULA ALSO HAS PSYCHOLOGICALLY DAMAGING RESULTS, PROMPTING LIL' MISS NASTY TO DEVILISHLY LURE WEALTHY MEN AN' KILL THEIR AFFLUENT ASSES. SHE DOES HER THANG TO A GROOVY SOUNDTRACK, DONS A NUMBER OF OUTRAGEOUS MOD OUTFITS, AND PERFORMS A STRIPTEASE.

HUNGARIAN-BORN MAGDA KONOPKA STARS IN THIS SPANISH/ITALIAN CO-PRODUCTION BASED ON A FRENCH COMIC OF THE SAME NAME. SATANIK ARRIVED IN THE WAKE OF OTHER 1960s EURO-SUPERVILLAIN ESPIONAGE EPICS SUCH AS THE "FANTOMAS" FILMS AND BAVA'S **DANGER DIABOLIK**. UNLIKE THE COMIC, THE SEXY ANTI-HERO

DOESN'T WEAR A LEOTARD, INSTEAD HO-BAGGING AROUND WITHIN A "JEKYLL AND HYDE" PREMISE. DOESN'T HAVE NEARLY AS MUCH VIOLENCE OR NUDITY AS IT SHOULD HAVE HAD.
—BOUGIE '08

MAGDA KONOPKA
Satanik
EASTMANCOLOR

BUILT TO SPILL
MARC STEVENS SPEAKS OUT (CIRCA 1975)

Up until about the age of twenty-one, I was—except for my dynamite body and gigantic dick—an all-American kid. High-school and jock ideals, TV and the Pledge of Allegiance—the whole schmeer. I got turned on by all the right things (cars, rock 'n' roll, being neat), despised all the right things (Commies, perverts, losing), and even fantasized about the right things (money, power, Playboy centerfolds). I was going to do everything right. By-the-book right.

And then I went into the Army.

This experience taught me, immediately, that in the real world you get *nowhere* going by the book. The Army took away my baby life-rules and handed me some street smarts. They made me a man. They stationed me in Germany, with handy bars and whores all around the base. I adapted quickly by learning there were the right way, the Army way, and the Stevens way. I learned to manipulate all kinds of dummies by a combination of the three.

I started to be more open to anything, everything, you know, not knocking something until you've tried it, and the whole attitude of finding things out for yourself and not taking other peoples' words for things. And I began to understand the power of my loins, so to speak, and that that was my strength and I should concentrate my energies on it. I began to come into focus as a person, and the focus I saw in my mind was centered on my dick.

The whole thing was so different from my previous experiences in high school and at home that I came to see myself as a different person from the old, pre-Army days. A new personality. That was when Marc Stevens was really born. The old one had been a sucker and a drag. He had been nowhere going nowhere, but the new Marc Stevens was nowhere going somewhere!

Every relationship the old Marc had with a girl in high school had been a big hassle. I had to date them, be nice to them, give them cheap corsages and stupid promises—all just to get into their pussies. And the biggest drag of all was that it didn't even *get* me into the pussies. There was always lots of heavy necking and dry humping, sure, and each time it would drive me wilder to go through the stages and hope that I'd finally found one who wouldn't blow it and start screaming at the last minute.

Because every time I finally did get my pants off with a girl after all the hassles, she'd take one look at the size of my cock, her eyes would pop right open, and she'd start edging away from me, pushing me off, and saying, "Uh, not me, buster. No way! That monster wasn't meant for little ol' me." Of course, these girls were only fifteen or sixteen, and I can understand now how they were really frightened. But I bet if I went back home today and ran into the same girls, grown up, they'd be fighting for it.

I knew my cock was above average from the locker room and because I took an adult-large supporter from the time I was twelve. But I didn't know that it could be good to be hung. I was made to feel that it was a freaky thing, like having a hunchback.

Later, by senior year, when I finally did start fucking some of the chicks, it got even worse. I'd insert a little bit. The girl would moan. I thought she was in agony. In pain. That she would start bleeding and screaming any minute if I went ahead. And you know what those kinds of thoughts can do to a hard on. It was the wilts. A real turn-off. And it took me a long time to realize that it wasn't my fault.

When that time finally came, I began to learn. And learn fast. The summer of my twenty-first year was one I'll never forget.

I had my first man. Or perhaps he had me. It's hard to say. It was so different, so alien to anything I'd ever done before. I had

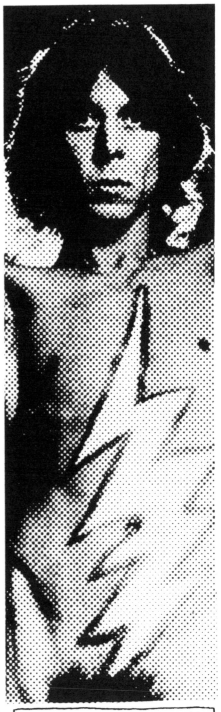

WHAT WENT WRONG WITH THE LEGENDARY 'MR. 10½'??

168

FROM A LATE 70s ISSUE OF OUI:

Porn star starts his own member's club

The other day, at his invitation, we visited Marc Stevens, a young man whose frequent appearances in pornographic movies have made him a star of sorts. He told us about his new business venture, a club described in a brochure as being for "potential porn groupies who are interested in

MARC STEVENS

10½ CLUB

meeting and partying with the likes of Georgina Spelvin, Tina Russell and all the stars Marc socializes with." In other words, as Marc himself says, it is really a fan club for himself.

Membership in the club costs $25 a year ($100 for the *inner circle*) and will get you a Marc Stevens T-shirt ("the current rage of the porn world"), admission to porn-film previews, invitations to private parties "where you'll meet the biggest names in the world of porn," opportunities to fly with Marc "and his movie-star friends" to weekend scenes.

> I THINK IN REALITY, WHAT YOU GOT FOR YER $100 WAS A T-SHIRT WITH THE ABOVE LOGO ON IT -- AND MARC GOT A BUNCH OF MONEY TO FUND HIS DRUG HABIT.

grown used to so many hassles to get it off, so many hoops to jump through before you really got down to business. Fucking was like a reward for doing everything right. So when I met this guy and made it with him, it worked a number on my head not only because he was a guy, but because it was so simple. Direct. That's what I liked most about it.

I was in a bar with a friend. We were drunk, getting drunker. An older guy, maybe twenty-four or twenty-five, sat down next to me. We started talking. He certainly wasn't a blazing faggot or anything near to one. If he had been, I probably wouldn't have talked to him. It wasn't a gay bar.

We started talking about local barracks gossip and rumors, and then he managed somehow to steer the conversation around to horniness and how different guys got their rocks off. And then, without actually coming right out and saying it, he maneuvered me into the position of knowing exactly what he was proposing, getting caught up in it and willing to try. What the hell! This was the new Marc Stevens, and he'd try anything. It was exhilarating and a little scary. And a seduction technique on his part that I have since perfected and used myself many times. Here was a complete stranger, turned on by me unexpectedly, ready to give me pleasure, and asking nothing in return. He just wanted to suck me off.

It was neat and clean. I didn't even have to know his name. I didn't have to date him. No corsages. No promises. No frustrating "relationships."

But still, at the time, I felt guilty about making it with a man. I remember I didn't want my friend at the bar to find out about it. I told him I was going home and left. My new friend was to meet me around the corner.

We went to his apartment. I knew exactly what I was going there for, too. That was a first for me. Neither of us said anything all the way there, or even after we got inside. It was like we had done our talking in the bar, and now we wouldn't need any more verbal communication. Throughout the whole encounter we never spoke.

It was very strange. I felt like this was going to be some kind of ordeal or initiation or something. I didn't know what homosexuality was. I was frightened.

When we got inside, I wasn't sure of exactly what was going to happen. I knew there were limitations to what I would allow to be done to me. And I secretly suspected, maybe even hoped, that things might go further than the blow job we talked about at the bar. And in my imaginings, I decided that I wasn't going to take it in the ass.

He shut the door to his apartment and turned to me. He didn't try to kiss me or anything. He just reached over and tucked his fingers inside the top edge of my pants; then he unsnapped them. I felt his hand come through my shirt and onto my stomach. My heart was beating very fast. He unzipped my pants. He tugged my cock out. By this time it was halfway down my leg, and he had to use both hands to haul it out.

Then he started stroking. It got good and hard. In fact, I looked down and saw I had the hard on of my life.

He knelt down in front of me and took my cock in his mouth. I looked down at his head bobbing back and forth, seeing the glistening spit on the erection of my life when he brought his head back. I knew right then and there that I'd been going about it all wrong. I'd hustled, beat my brains out, and ended up with blue balls and guilt. Here was a complete stranger (well, maybe not any more) kneeling to me, to my cock. Here was another person giving me a great deal of easy pleasure, demanding nothing in return other than to be the receptacle of my sperm. Right then, with this strange man praying at my altar, I began to know what power I had. And that I had long left untapped. With this cock and this body I could amass that power, until I could rule the fucking world if I wanted. It was that kind of power trip.

Around the same time, women started to come on to me. I guess I was changing myself slowly. The way I dressed. My hair grew longer. I combed it differently. Wore sunglasses. Tight pants. Whatever it was, women began to be aware of my power. And most of them didn't try to hide their reactions.

I was Mr. Self-Confidence. A stud. Anything they got from me was something they should be grateful for. Anything. I even started knocking them around a little. They loved it. I'd hold their heads between my hands and fuck them in the mouth. They dug it, and so did I.

Some even insisted on paying for it. They bought me things. Gave me money, particularly the older ones, for presents for myself.

And I didn't really care for any of them. That was the whole thing. I was wanted. That was enough; I went along. Pretty soon there were more and more of them, until I couldn't possibly have enough time to see them all. There were those who wanted my cock so badly they would do anything to get it, if only for an hour a week. They worshiped it. They became my slaves to be fucked. To touch it, to suck it, just to be near it.

The porno ladies and their labia have brought me so much pleasure over the past four years . . . and so much sick, expensive pain. They've ripped open my cock, dosed me with diseases I can't even pronounce, clawed up my back and stuck their fingernails into even more tender areas, punctured my eardrums with fish-wife screams, and covered my tender skin with vicious rashes. They've fought over me, stolen my lovers, emptied my icebox, and made me a big favorite at the clap clinic.

It's dangerous dealing with women, and sometimes you have to handle them like pit vipers. But who can resist? Even at age five, preparing for a glorious career as a superstud, I began suffering at their hands. I was playing doctor with two Baby Snookses when our mothers called us. One of them reached over and tried to zip me up very fast. Aaggghhhh! She caught my tender sausage in the teeth, and I ran screaming out of my father's old Ford in blinding white anguish. My mother raced me off to the pediatrician, and the joint survived.

You can say a lot of negative things about the porno girls, and everybody has. Tina Russell once told me that every interview she did used to start with, "Does your mother know you're doing this?" They've been called cardboard sexual stereotypes trained to act out men's darkest dreams, sick slaves whose creepy kick-me trip is so easy to exploit it's pathetic. The women's-lib girls tell them they hate themselves, and it's true every guy they meet thinks they'll be the easiest lay in town. It's a rough business, and there are some raunchy deals that go down, like between backers and directors who only hire girls who "go along," but I'll go on record as saying that the nicest, most open-minded, least conniving, and most pleasurable women in my life make porno films. They don't use their sex as ransom bait, and they don't sell themselves for the newest pad in the suburbs. Which is not to say that they haven't been forced to sell themselves when times are hard. What the hell—I hustle, too. And the times I've been cheated and ripped off in exchange for favors would make Dennis the Menace look like an astute businessman, with his lemonade stand.

This industry attracts the sickest, scuzziest, and most delectable girls in the country, I'm convinced. You'll see a new girl on set who can't be more than fifteen (but she has to be, of course), looking fresh and fragile as a country wildflower. Or some California hiplet, blond and bronzed, trying to make a few dollars to hitch up to Nova Scotia. They counterbalance the pale, drawn junkie chicks hustling bread for another needle track . . . though I'm happy to see these ghouls disappearing. It's become hip to make a fuck film now, and we get a lot of kids on college vacations or stewardesses making an extra buck. They get baby crushes on me, and it's kind of sweet.

(STOP)

Who was Marc Stevens?

Described as "a pain in the ass" by XXX director Carter Stevens (no relation), Marc Stevens (born February 9th 1943) was known in the 1970s New York porn scene as "Mr. 10½". Despite the fact that his erect pecker was actually just over 9 inches in length.

Marc got his start doing live sex shows in shit-scab sleaze dens in Times Square, and after meeting lovely porn icon Tina Russell (who died far before her time at the age of 31) began to try his hand at sex films. He appeared in (according to himself) over 500 porn movies and loops -- and also led an erotic dance troupe. While he predominantly appeared in hetero smut, he had an often outspoken distaste for women, and was far happier and content having sex with dudes in the gay porn he proudly starred in.

At the height of his notoriety, he published a 288-page memoir about his penis called "10½!", was briefly married to porn tranny Jill Monroe, and had his dong famously photographed by Robert Mapplethorpe. Typical of 1970s porn celebs, he partied hardy and developed serious addictions to coke, crack, and angel dust. In his later years he dropped out of the adult industry, became a drug dealer, got involved with a violent Honduran drug cartel, and became a pimp.

Just before he got to that point, Marc appeared in the infamous 1981 NFB anti-porn documentary **Not A Love Story**, sandwiched between all-sex-is-rape feminist man-haters such as Robin Morgan and Andrea Dworkin. Stevens announced his disgust for pornography, claiming that he abandoned it because he was expected to abuse innocent female co-stars.

Marc Stevens died slowly and painfully of AIDS (brought on by using dirty needles) in August 1989 -- a broken and forgotten man who lived to a mere 46 years of age.

"I saw him just before he died", said longtime next door neighbor and friend Annie Sprinkle. "He was frothing at the mouth. He must have weighed 80 pounds. Nobody was caring for him."

MR. 10½

LET'S CELEBRATE HOLLYWOOD'S TOTAL FAILURES!!

WHY? JUST CUZ IT'S FUN TO WATCH THE STUDIO BAFOONS FALL FLAT ON THEIR FACES! HERE'S THE TOP 10 BIGGEST MONEY LOSERS FROM 1990 TO 2005. YES, I'VE TAKEN THE DOMESTIC AND INTERNATIONAL GROSSES INTO ACCOUNT.

1. **THE ADVENTURES OF PLUTO NASH** (2002) COST 99 MIL. **LOST 94 MILLION.** CONSIDERING THAT FILM PRINTS COST 2 THOUSAND TO MAKE, THIS FILM DIDN'T EVEN MAKE BACK THE COST OF SENDING THE MOVIE TO THE THEATERS. HAW HAW!!

2. **CUTTHROAT ISLAND** (1995) COST 101 MILLION. **LOST 90 MILLION.** HA HA GEENA DAVIS! FUCK OFF AND DIE! THIS FILM ENDED HER STARDOM, THANK GOD.

3. **THE POSTMAN** (1997) COST 80 MILLION. **LOST 78 MILLION.** EVERYBODY THINKS WATERWORLD WAS THE 90S' BIG LOSER - BUT IT WAS **THIS** COSTNER BOMB.

4. **MONKEYBONE** (2001) COST 75 MILLION. **LOST 69 MILLION.** "MONKEYBOMB"! HONK!

5. **TOWN AND COUNTRY** (2001) COST 80 MILLION. **LOST 63 MILLION.**

6. **BATTLEFIELD EARTH** (2000) COST 73 MILLION. **LOST 51 MILLION.** BWAA-HA-HA! SCIENTOLOGY SUCKS BALLS! COST 73 MILL.? THE FUCKIN' THING LOOKS LIKE A MADE-FOR-TV MOVIE! ON THE U.S.A. NETWORK, NO LESS.

7. **1492: CONQUEST OF PARADISE** (1992) COST 53 MILLION. **LOST 48 MILLION.**

8. **SUPERNOVA** (2000) COST 61 MILLION. **LOST 47 MILLION.** "SUPERBOMB", MORE LIKE.

9. **TREASURE PLANET** (2002) COST 140 MILLION. **LOST 46 MILLION.**

10. **WYATT EARP** (1994) COST 63 MILLION. **LOST 33 MILLION.** AND IT DESERVED TO!

WILD, FREE AND HUNGRY (1970)

THIS HARRY NOVAK PRODUCTION WAS PRODUCED BY AND STARS GARY GRAVER - WHO WENT ON TO DIRECT MANY OF THE BETTER KNOWN HARDCORE FEATURES OF THE ERA UNDER THE NAME ROBERT McCALLUM. THIS IS HIS BIKER/SPEEDBOAT RACING/HIPPIE/ SEXPLOITATION FILM, AND IT'S PRETTY HO-HUM. THE MAIN PLUSES ARE NUDE SEX SCENES BY THE VERY ADORABLE MONICA GAYLE (SWITCHBLADE SISTERS) AND BARBARA MILLS (CHAINGANG WOMEN) AVAILABLE FROM SOMETHING WEIRD VIDEO.

SEX AND THE COLLEGE GIRL

THIS 1964 MOVIE IS TAILOR-MADE FOR ALL YOU LOUNGE-LOVIN', MARTINI-SWILLING, DEAN MARTIN-IDOLIZING HEPCATS AND HEPKITTENS OUT THERE. IT'S A SUN-DRENCHED TALE ABOUT THE SWINGIN' LOW LIFE OF A PLAYBOY HOTEL CROONER NAMED LARRY, WHO SETS HIS SIGHTS ON GETTING INTO THIS CHICK GWEN'S PANTIES. LARRY IS AS COOL AS AN ALCOHOLIC CUCUMBER, AND IS OUT WITH A DIFFERENT SEXPOT EVERY NIGHT OF THE WEEK. A MUCH MORE ACCURATE TITLE FOR THIS MIGHT HAVE BEEN "SEX AND THE WOMANISING LOUNGE SINGER", AS THE ENTIRE PLOT REVOLVES AROUND LARRY'S DEBAUCHED DESCENT INTO SELF-IMPOSED UNHAPPINESS. LARRY'S BEST BUT IS PLAYED BY A VERY YOUNG CHARLES GRODIN IN HIS VERY FIRST ROLE.

TNT JACKSON (1975)

THIS IS A SUBSTANDARD **CLEOPATRA JONES** KNOCK OFF THAT STARS GORGEOUS PLAYBOY MODEL JEANNE BELL AS DIANA 'TNT' JACKSON ("SHE'LL PUT YOU IN TRACTION!"), A HARLEM-BORN EX-CON WHO TRAVELS TO HONG KONG TO FIND HER BRO NAMED STACK. IT'S NOT A BORING FILM, BUT IT'S REALLY ONLY NOTABLE FOR THE SCENE IN WHICH JEANNE KUNG FU'S A HOTEL ROOM FULL OF BAD GUYS CLAD ONLY IN SOME TINY BLACK PANTIES. A WAY CHEAP DVD IS AVAILABLE FOR ABOUT $6.

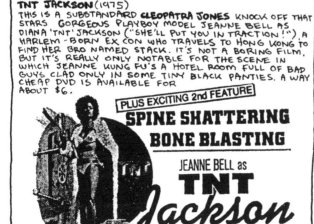

Mommy put me in porn
☆ THE STORY OF ATHENA STAR ☆

A 19 YEAR OLD LIVING AT HOME, ROBIN MARINA ASKED HER MOM ONE DAY IF SHE COULD STAR IN PORN MOVIES. TO HER SURPRISE, MOM NOT ONLY APPROVED, SHE SET OUT THE NEXT WEEK TO ACTIVELY PEDDLE HER DAUGHTER TO VARIOUS PORNOGRAPHERS.

IN FACT, FOR HER FIRST TIME, ROBIN, HER 18 YEAR OLD SISTER MANDY (AS "MANDY JO") AND HER MOM (UNDER THE NAME "KITTY KAT") ALL GOT ROLES IN A PORNO THAT WAS SHOOTING UP THE STREET IN THEIR NEW YORK HOOD -- THE ROBERTA FINDLAY/JOHN CHRISTOPHER VID: **PRIVATE SCHOOLGIRLS** (1983).

NOW, DESPITE BEING A HUGE ROBERTA FINDLAY FAN, I HAVE NOT SEEN THIS MOVIE AND CAN NOT ATEST TO WHAT GOES ON IN IT, BUT IT TURNS OUT HER MASSIVE BREASTED MOM, MISS KITTY KAT -- MADE NUDIE LOOPS IN THE GOOD OL' DAYS, AND EVEN APPEARED IN "GEM", "SIR" AND "GENT" MAGAZINE. BUT NOW IT WAS 1983, AND MOM WAS NOW PAVING THE BILLS AS AN AGENT AND A MANAGER FOR VARIOUS NYC ENTERTAINERS. SHE COULD EASILY GET HER LITTLE BLONDE POSTPUBESCENT PORN PRINCESS ALL KINDS OF WORK. ALL IT TOOK WAS A FEW PHONE CALLS TO THE RIGHT DEGENERATES.

SHE'D STILL HAVE TO GO TO ROCKLAND COMMUNITY COLLEGE WHERE SHE WAS MAJORING IN A COURSE ON CRIMINAL JUSTICE, BUT ROBIN AND HER YOUNGER SISTER WERE MOMMY WOULD INTERVIEWS

WHERE ARE YOU, DADDY?

GIVEN THE A-OK FROM MOM TO PEDDLE PUSSY ON THE SIDE, EVEN CHAPERONE HER TARTY YOUNG FUCKPUMP AND SET UP WITH THE PORN MEDIA. ONE SUCH INTERVIEW TOOK PLACE IN "ADULT CINEMA REVIEW" A FEW SHORT WEEKS AFTER ROBIN STARTED BURPING WORMS FOR A LIVING (UNDER HER NEW NAME: ATHENA STAR). HERE ARE SOME HIGHLIGHTS:

ACR: SO, WHAT DO YOU THINK OF YOUR MOM?

Athena: She's great. Wouldn't trade her for anybody!

ACR: I UNDERSTAND THERE'S A LOT OF THINGS YOU WON'T DO.

Athena: Not a lot. I won't do anals. And I won't do girl-girl.

ACR: WHAT ABOUT GIVING HEAD?

Athena: I don't like to do it.

ACR: I WAS TOLD YOU WERE A GREAT COCKSUCKER IN PRIVATE SCHOOLGIRLS. HOW DID YOU KNOW HOW TO DO IT IF YOU DON'T DO IT IN YOUR PRIVATE LIFE?

Athena: I didn't say I DON'T do it, I said I don't LIKE to do it.

ACR: WHAT DOES A GUY HAVE TO DO? WHIP IT OUT AND JAM YOUR HEAD ON IT?

Athena: That's happened a couple of times, which is probably why I don't like it. I don't like to be forced to do anything. Which is why I hate being raped.

ACR: WHAT KIND OF MOTHER DOESN'T ENCOURAGE HER GIRLS TO GIVE HEAD?

Mom: I never said a word for or against. For myself, I save it for special people.

ACR: WAS YOUR MOTHER AS ENCOURAGING ABOUT YOUR SEX LIFE AS SHE WAS ABOUT YOUR CAREER IN X-RATED FILMS?

Athena: If I remember correctly, it was more like 'If you're gonna do it, don't do it behind my back, and make sure you're protected.

ACR: WHEN WAS THE FIRST TIME, ROBIN?

Athena: I was 13. It was not of my own choice. He was a 15 year old, the friend of a friend. I tried to fight him off but I wasn't strong enough.

ACR: HOW SOON AFTER THAT DID YOU START A NORMAL SEX LIFE?

Athena: Soon!

Mom: My first time the same thing happened to me. I was raped at knifepoint by a stranger.

ACR: SO HOW SOON AFTER THAT DID YOU BEGIN A NORMAL SEX LIFE?

Mom: Two, three months. When I was out on the street the next morning, I said to myself 'You can either flip out like an idiot or you can act like a human being and just go on'.

Athena: I got raped again a couple of years after that. By three men... at gunpoint. I thought I was going to be killed. It was in a small town down south. They came into the house and took me away at gunpoint. They had their pleasure with me, and returned me to the house. I knew who they were -- but they were asshole buddies with the local police.

ACR: NO WONDER YOU HAVE SO MANY RESTRICTIONS WITH SEX, YOU'VE BEEN BADLY HURT. EVER HAVE A GUY TURN YOU DOWN?

Athena: Once, he'd just gotten engaged that day.

ACR: BESIDES BECOMING AN ADULT STAR, DO YOU HAVE ANY OTHER GOALS IN LIFE?

Athena: I'd like to meet my father some day. Mom and him got divorced when I was how old?

Mom: Three.

ACR: HE'LL PROBABLY SEE YOU ON THE SCREEN BEFORE YOU'LL GET TO SEE HIM IN REAL LIFE.

Mom: He'd LOVE IT. He'd give her a good old round of applause. He was a 42nd street hustler, a prostitute who would go with girls, guys, wherever the money was. Was real cute, and man could he screw...

ACR: BUT YOU'RE NO LONGER IN TOUCH?

Mom: He lives in Maryland. His wife won't let him see the girls.

ACR: WHAT DO YOU SAY TO FRIENDS WHO QUESTION WHAT YOU'RE DOING WITH YOUR GIRLS?

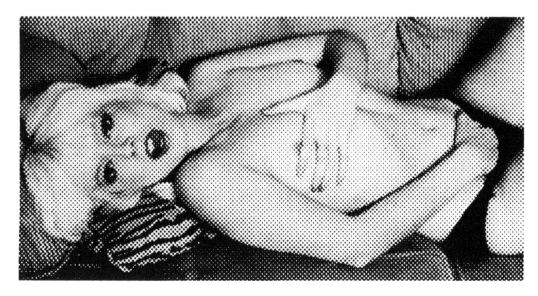

DESPITE HER REFUSAL TO DO LESBIAN SCENES, ATHENA COULDN'T TURN DOWN THAT FILTHY MONEY AND LICKED CLAM IN **VOYEUR'S DELIGHT** (1986) AND **LACY AFFAIR 3** (1989). NOT ONLY THAT, BUT SHE APPEARED IN ONE OF THE VERY FIRST PREGNANCY-THEMED SEX VIDS (**THE PREGNANT BABYSITTER**) WHERE SHE TURNED IN

A STICKY PREGNANT LESBOTASTIC ROMP WITH SUMMER ROSE. ATHENA HAD NO QUALMS APPEARING IN A GAY MEN'S PORN VIDEO THOUGH (**BEST FRIENDS** 1986), A MOVE THAT RAISED EYEBROWS AMONGST GAY AND STRAIGHT SMUT ENTHUSIASTS. IN HER SCENE, ATHENA SUCKS THE GAY RIGHT OUT OF MARK JENNINGS AND JEFF CAMERON -- WHO WERE PLAYING HETERO GUYS WHO WOULD FIND THEIR TRUE CALLING AS THE STORY PROGRESSED.

ROBIN GENERALLY SIZZLED HER WAY THROUGH THE 80S, MILKING PUDDING FAUCETS DRY IN VARIOUS SHOT-ON-VIDEO LOW-BUDGET BIG HAIR GRINDERS. HER STANDOUT MOMENT WAS PROBABLY HER FINE HAM-PLOW WITH A PAIR OF PISTON-PUMPIN' STUDS IN THE UNSUNG ROBERTA FINDLAY SCORCHER, **GLITTER** (1983). IT WAS A CUM-COATED PERFORMANCE HER PERVERT DAD WOULD HAVE BEEN PROUD OF.

ATHENA STAR LEFT ADULT IN 1989 AFTER APPEARING IN JUST OVER 50 VIDEOS. WITHOUT ANY REAL FANBASE WORTH MENTIONING, IT WAS AN EXIT THAT WENT UNNOTICED.

WHAT SHE, HER SISTER, OR HER MOM WENT ON TO DO NEXT IS UNKNOWN.

I ...B-BET THEY, UM ...T-TOTALLY HAD AN AWESOME O-O-ORGY. HEH, YEAH, THAT'S, UH, WHAT THEY DID...

BOOGIE

PIECES (1981) AHHHH... TONS OF POINTLESS TITILATING NUDITY AND SOME EXTREMELY VICIOUS GORE SURE DOES MAKE FOR AN ENTERTAINING SLASHER MOVIE DOESN'T IT? THIS SPANISH-MADE UNINTENTIONALLY HILARIOUS NUGGET OF BADLY DUBBED EXPLOITATION WAS CO-WRITTEN BY SCHLOCK-KING JOE D'AMATO. IT'S BLOODY,

ABSOLUTELY NO ONE UNDER 17 ADMITTED TO THIS PERFORMANCE

YOU DON'T HAVE TO GO TO TEXAS FOR A CHAINSAW MASSACRE!

PIECES

IT'S EXACTLY WHAT YOU THINK IT IS!

COMPLETELY ILLOGICAL, AND ONE GIRL IS (AND I'LL ONLY SAY THIS ONCE) DECAPITATED BY **HEDGE TRIMMERS** - IN BROAD DAYLIGHT - ON A COLLEGE CAMPUS, AND HILARIOUSLY, NOBODY SEES **ANYTHING**! NEED I SAY MORE? I WISH I COULD SAY MORE, BUT I DON'T HAVE MUCH SPACE LEFT ON THIS PAGE. P.S: MAKE SURE YOU DON'T FAST FORWARD PAST ONE OF THE 80S' BEST BAD BLURBS OF DIALOG - WHICH IS: "BAAAAAAAASSTAAARRDDD!!!" SCREAMED THREE GLORIOUS TIMES IN A ROW. **YES**.

A SCREAM IN THE STREETS (1972)

THIS STARTS OFF WITH THE MOST JARRING SET OF OPENING TITLES EVER -- WHERE A BOOMING VOICE YELLS OVER A BLANK SCREEN: "A SCREAM IN THE STREETS!", BEFORE ABRUPTLY CUTTING TO INCREDIBLY FAST SCROLLING CREDITS. THIS HARRY NOVAK PRODUCTION TAKES PLACE DURING ONE HOT WEEK IN L.A. AND FOLLOWS TWO COPS (ED "IRON BALLS" HASKELL AND BOB STREEKER) ON THEIR QUEST TO STOP A MURDEROUS RAPIST. ODDLY, THE RAPIST STORYLINE IS ALMOST SECONDARY -- WITH THE BULK OF THE PICTURE CONCERNING RANDOM TRAFFIC STOPS, AND SEX SCENES BETWEEN INCIDENTAL CHARACTERS. THE HIGHLIGHT HAS TO BE WHAT MIGHT GO DOWN IN HISTORY AS THE MOST UNCONVINCING CROSSDRESSER IN A THEATRICAL MOTION PICTURE. THIS NAMELESS RAPIST (WHO COULDN'T LOOK LESS LIKE A WOMAN) APPARENTLY DRESSES THAT WAY

A SCREAM in the STREETS
color

SO HE CAN EASILY TRICK A NUMBER OF PRETTY GIRLS INTO ALLOWING HIM TO PLUNK DOWN ON A PARK BENCH NEXT TO THEM. "I HATE YOU, I HATE ALL WOMEN! YOU'RE ROTTEN!" HE SAYS AS HE PUMMELS AN UNDERCOVER POLICEWOMAN. NOT A VERY WELL MADE FILM, BUT IT MAY WELL BE ONE OF THE SLEAZIEST COP MOVIES OF THE 70S.

A CITY RIPPED APART BY SIN AND LUST!

☆ POLICEWOMEN - 1974 - (aka "The Insiders") ☆

THIS ISN'T NEARLY AS SLEAZY OR ACTION PACKED AS SOME OF THE BETTER KNOWN AND MORE BELOVED DRIVE-IN MOVIES OF THE 70s, BUT IT DOES SOMEHOW MANAGE TO BE MORE ENJOYABLE THAN PLENTY OF THEM. IN FACT, IF THERE WERE EVER A FILM THAT NEATLY SUMMED UP THE 'COP-SPLOITATION' GENRE OF THE PERIOD, THIS COULD WELL BE IT.

MUCH OF THAT IS DUE TO THE LOVELY SONDRA CURRIE, WHO IS A TOTAL DELIGHT IN THE LEAD ROLE OF 'LACY BOND'. THIS BLONDE SASS-MASTER KICKS **MUCH** BOOTY, AND FRANKLY ENDS UP FIGHTING AS HARD TO BE ACCEPTED BY HER CHAUVINIST PIG PEERS AS SHE DOES TO CATCH THE CRIMINALS. SONDRA EXUDES CONFIDENCE, A SENSE OF HUMOR, AND YOU CAN ALMOST SMELL THE "SPIRIT OF ADVENTURE" PUNGENTLY WAFTING FROM HER PORES. WHETHER FLAPPING GUMS AT HER SUPERIORS, OR LOCKED IN ALL-OUT HAND TO HAND COMBAT, LACY MAKES YOU WANNA HOOT N' HOLLER. IT'S A BIT OF A MYSTERY WHY CURRIE DIDN'T GO ON TO BIGGER THINGS, OR AT LEAST BECOME A PROMINENT STAR IN THE DRIVE-IN GENRE. SHE DID END UP MARRYING ALAN LEVI - A TV DIRECTOR WHOSE MULTITUDE OF IDIOT BOX CREDITS INCLUDE **BATTLESTAR GALACTICA**, **MIAMI VICE**, AND CULT FAVE **THE MISFITS OF SCIENCE**.

THE PLOT HAS SOME OUTLANDISH FLAVORS THAT I WAS TRÉ THRILLED WITH. I WUVED THE ALL-GIRL GANG THAT SPENDS MOST OF ITS TIME IN BIKINIS. THE COMPOUND THAT HOUSES THE SLUTTY VILLAINS IS RUN BY A CRANKY OL' GRANNY AND HER MUSCLE-BOUND BRAIN-FREE BOY TOY. THIS IS ONE 80 YEAR OLD BIDDY WHO DIGS ON YOUNG FLESH, AND GLEEFULLY TAKES PART IN ILLEGAL SHENANIGANS THAT SEEM TO PRIMARILY CONSIST OF COUNTING LARGE QUANTITIES OF MOOLAH ON A CARD TABLE IN THE BACK YARD WHILE THE PLENTIFUL BIKINI GALS PLAY VOLLEYBALL.

THE BOUNCY SWIM SUIT FELONS ARE SUPER FUN, BUT THERE'S ALSO A RESPECTABLE AMOUNT OF NUDITY AND SEXUAL SHIT ON DISPLAY. SONDRA'S

THIS 1974 DON EDMONDS FILM WAS SHOT IN JUST 9 DAYS ON THE HOLLYWOOD SET OF THE **HOGAN'S HEROES** TV SHOW, SHORTLY BEFORE IT WAS DISMANTLED.

BUSTY EXPLOITATION STAR PHYLLIS DAVIS (**SWEET SUGAR**) WAS ORIGINALLY CONSIDERED FOR THE LEAD ROLE OF ILSA, A CHARACTER BASED ON AN ACTUAL NAZI, ILSE KOCH -- WHO WAS THE WIFE OF KARL KOCH, A HORRIBLE CONCENTRATION CAMP COMMANDANT. SHE WORKED THERE AS A GUARD, AND SADISTICALLY TORTURED JEWS AND TOOK SOUVENIRS OF SKIN FROM INMATES WITH TATTOOS. SHE COMMITTED SUICIDE AT THE AGE OF 60, AND TRUST ME -- THE HOMELY OL' BITCH WASN'T 10% AS HOT AS THE AMAZING DYANNE THORNE!'

—BOUGIE

MAIN CO-STAR IS FORMER PLAYBOY PLAYMATE JEANIE BELL, AN EBONY GODDESS WHO HAS HER BLACK ASS HANDED TO HER BY A SAUCY ASIAN KUNG-FU HARLOT JUST AFTER JEANIE INFILTRATES THE COMPOUND. I LIKE JEANIE. SHE MANAGES TO TAKE HER SHIRT OFF TWICE FOR NO GOOD REASON, WHEREAS CURRIE KEEPS HERS ON WHILE HER HEAVING CHEST MAKES ANGRY THREATS TO ESCAPE HER BLOUSE AT ANY MOMENT. SOME OF MY FAVE SCENES ARE THE UNINTENTIONALLY HILARIOUS MARTIAL ARTS SEQUENCES, WHICH ARE UNUSUALLY VERY WELL CHOREOGRAPHED, BUT ARE OBVIOUSLY PERFORMED BY FUN-LOVIN' ACTORS INSTEAD OF HARD NOSED FIGHT GODS. BRUCE LEE VS. JET LI THIS AIN'T.

WRITTEN AND DIRECTED BY NOTORIOUS SERIAL SEX DIRECTOR LEE FROST WHO CREATED THE R-RATED HUMP CLASSICS **THE DEFILERS** (1965), **LOVE CAMP 7** (1969), **HOT SPUR** (1968), **POOR CECILY** (1973), AND THE XXX SHITBALL **A CLIMAX OF BLUE POWER** (1974). HE ALSO WAS KNOWN FOR THE NON-SEX RELATED **WITCHCRAFT 70** (1970), **THE THING WITH TWO HEADS** (1972), AND A PERSONAL FAVE **THE BLACK GESTAPO** (1975). **POLICEWOMEN** MAY NOT BE CONSIDERED AS ONE OF HIS GREATEST ACHIEVEMENTS, BUT I'M HERE TO TELL YOU THAT IT SHOULD BE. THIS GOOD NATURED TIME WASTER IS FAR FROM A WASTE OF TIME.

THE CINEMA SEWER LIST OF THE 20 BEST SPAGHETTI WESTERNS

1. DJANGO KILL (1967)
2. THE GOOD, THE BAD, AND THE UGLY (1966)
3. A BULLET FOR THE GENERAL (1967)
4. KEOMA (1976)
5. FOR A FEW DOLLARS MORE (1965)
6. DJANGO (1966)
7. ONCE UPON A TIME IN THE WEST (1968)
8. THE GREAT SILENCE (1968)
9. A FISTFUL OF DOLLARS (1964)
10. MASSACRE TIME (1966)
11. CUTTHROATS NINE (1972)
12. FOUR OF THE APOCALYPSE (1975)
13. BLINDMAN (1971)
14. DEATH RIDES A HORSE (1967)
15. MANNAJA (1977)
16. THE BIG GUNDOWN (1967)
17. FACE TO FACE (1967)
18. GOD FORGIVES, I DON'T (1967)
19. FISTFUL OF DYNAMITE (1971)
20. TODAY IT'S ME, TOMORROW IT'S YOU (1968)

HONORARY MENTION:
    DAY OF ANGER (1967)

INCREDIBLE, VIOLENT, DRAMA-FILLED FILMS... EVERY LAST ONE OF 'EM. I HIGHLY, **HIGHLY** SUGGEST HUNTIN' EVERY ONE O' THESE LIL' VARMITS DOWN.

IF YOU KNOW WHATS GOOD FOR YA. IF NOT....?

I GOT A BULLET FOR EVERY LAST ONE OF YOU BASTARDS.

YOUNG PLAYTHINGS (1972)

THE TAG LINE FOR THE FILM SAYS IT ALL: "THEY'RE THE EROTIC TOYS OF THE MINDLESS GENERATION...TRAPPED IN A NEVER-NEVERLAND OF DISTORTED SEXUAL PRACTICES." WRITTEN, DIRECTED, AND EDITED IN 1972, **YOUNG PLAYTHINGS** WAS SHOT IN SWEDEN WITH A CAST MOSTLY COMPRISED OF AMATEURS FILMING WITH AN ENGISH SCRIPT. CREATOR JOE SARNO HAD BEEN WORKING IN THE U.S SCENE THROUGHOUT THE 60S, AND HAD RECENTLY SET UP SHOP IN SWEDEN TO START THE 1970S. THIS IS GENERALLY CONSIDERED TO BE THE FINEST WORK OF HIS INTERESTING CAREER.

SARNO WAS ONE OF THE ONLY ADULT FILMMAKERS OF THE 60S AND 70S (RADLEY METZGER AKA HENRY PARIS BEING THE OTHER) WHO MADE A REAL EFFORT TO HAVE HIS SOFTCORE TRASHY EXPLOITATION OUTPUT BE OF INTEREST TO THE ARTHOUSE CROWD. FROM HIS "HORNY SUBURBANITE" MORALITY PLAYS, TO HIS SCANDINAVIAN TALES OF RITUALISTIC FUCK-ORGIES, SARNO SKETCHED CHARACTERS WHO HAD VERY BOLD, ACTIVE SEX LIVES, AND YET COULD STILL FEEL AS AS ANGUISHED AND UNCERTAIN AS MORRISSEY ON A CLOUDY DAY.

STARRING THE VERY VERY VERY VERY SEXY CHRISTINA LINDBERG OF **THEY CALL HER ONE EYE** FAME, THIS EXPERIMENTAL STORY CONCERNS A YOUNG MARRIED COUPLE WHO SOMEHOW

WIND THEM UP AND THEY'LL TURN YOU ON- ...SATISFACTION GUARANTEED!

young Playthings

STARRING CHRISTINA LINDBERG WITH EVA PORTNOFF · MARGARETTA HELSTROM Color
DIRECTED BY JOE SARNO · FILMED ENTIRELY IN SWEDEN
PRODUCED BY

FALL UNDER THE SPELL OF A FEMALE TOY MAKER WHOSE ODD AND PERVERSE FANTASIES ARE CASUALLY PLAYED OUT BY A NAKED COLLECTION OF GIRLS IN CREEPY CLOWN MAKEUP. STILL WITH ME? AS THE FILM PROGRESSES, THE DIALOG OF THE CHARACTERS BECOMES HARDER AND HARDER TO UNDERSTAND, UNTIL IT ENDS WITH AN ALMOST UNINTELLIGIBLE DIALECT. OK, SO IT SOUNDS LIKE IT COULD BE A PRETENTIOUS HEAP OF DOGSHIT, BUT THERE IS A **LOT** OF INTRIGUING STYLE GOING ON HERE, AND ONE CAN'T HELP BEING TAKEN ALONG FOR THE RIDE.

I FIRST HEARD ABOUT **YOUNG PLAYTHINGS** WHEN I READ ABOUT IT IN THE INFAMOUS RE/SEARCH VOL. 10 BOOK ENTITLED "INCREDIBLY STRANGE FILMS" WHICH SAW PRINT IN 1986, AND PERHAPS AUTHOR COLETTE COLEMAN DESCRIBED THE FILM BEST WHEN SHE WROTE:

"YOUNG PLAYTHINGS IS AN OBSCURE MASTERPIECE RELEGATED BY IT'S SOFTCORE FORMAT TO LATE-NIGHT VIEWING ON THE PLAYBOY CHANNEL. IRONICALLY DECEPTIVE, THE TITILLATING TITLE LURES THE AUDIENCE WITH THE PROSPECT OF A LIBIDINOUS ROMP. BUT THIS UNIQUE SEX FILM PENETRATES OTHER REALMS. SEDUCING THE MIND AS WELL AS THE SENSES, IT CONFORMS EXTERNALLY, YET TRANSCENDS THE LIMITATIONS OF THE GENRE. FLESH FONDLING IS NOT THE SUPREME CONCERN. RATHER, SEXUAL EXPERIMENTATION IS PRESENTED AS HEALTHY AND IMPORTANT TO THE UNDERLYING GOAL, WHICH IS THE REJECTION OF CONFORMIST MORES."

BAND OF THE HAND (1986)

AS **MIAMI VICE** WAS NEARING THE APEX OF ITS POPULARITY IN 1986, EXECUTIVE PRODUCER MICHAEL MANN DECIDED TO CASH IN WITH A CANT-MISS OFFSHOOT CONCEPT THAT WOULD BRING IDENTICAL EDITING, MUSIC CUES, FASHION, SUPPORTING CAST, AND THE SETTING OF ANY EPISODE OF VICE -- BUT WITH A HANDFUL OF ETHNICALLY DIVERSE TEENAGE HOODS IN PLACE OF THE COPS. THE PLAN WAS TO HAVE IT RUN AS A SERIES, BUT AFTER IT FAILED MISERABLY AS A TV PILOT, THE MONEY MEN SUGGESTED PUMPING SOME MORE MONEY INTO IT AND RELEASING IT THEATRICALLY.

TAKE A HANDFUL OF THE JUVENILE JUSTICE SYSTEM'S MOST HARDENED CRIMINALS, AND ENTRUST THEM TO AN EX-MARINE-WITH-A-HEADBAND NAMED JOE, WHO TAKES THEM OUT TO AN ISOLATED SWAMP IN THE FLORIDA EVERGLADES AND TEACHES THEM TO SPEAR A WILD PIG. ONCE THEY'VE ACCOMPLISHED THAT, THEY WILL NATURALLY BE REHABILITATED AND READY TO BE RELEASED INTO MIAMI TO DECLARE ALL-OUT WAR ON LOCAL PIMPS AND DRUG LORDS.

Out of jail. Trained as a team. Their battle to clean up the streets of Miami is about to begin.

BAND
OF THE
HAND

NOW, THEY'RE ON OUR SIDE.

A TRI-STAR RELEASE   [R]

A PLOT ABOUT OUTSIDERS WHO ARE DOOMED TO BE PROSECUTED AS ADULTS FOR THEIR CRIMES -- UNLESS THEY AGREE TO TAKE PART IN A SECRET EXPERIMENTAL "PROGRAM" ISN'T UNUSUAL (**LA FEMME NIKITA**, ANYONE?), BUT THE WAY BAND OF THE HAND WADS IT UP AND HORKS IT AT YOU MAKES FOR SOME LAUGHS.

I MEAN, JOE TRANSFORMING THE BOY'S (IN REALITY, ACTORS IN THEIR LATE 20s) INTO REAL MEN IS THE FOCUS OF THE FIRST ACT BECAUSE -- WHAT -- APPARENTLY THEIR TIME IN VIOLENT STREET GANGS HAD SOFTENED THEM UP?! I ALSO "ENJOYED" HOW THE GROUP FORGES A BOND NOT ONLY OUT OF MUTUAL DISGUST FOR THE CRAPPY FOOD THEY GOTTA EAT (THE LONE BLACK KID ACTUALLY WISHES OUT LOUD FOR BLACK-EYED PEAS N' RICE?!?), BUT ALSO OUT OF GENERAL PLOT NECESSITY.

INEXPLICABLY HONED INTO A FINELY TUNED BATTALION OF DRUG AND CRIME DESPISING WARRIORS, THE GROUP BUYS A VACANT HOUSE IN A DANGEROUS SLUM OF MIAMI, AND SLOWLY REBUILDS THE HOOD -- KICKING OUT THE PIMPS, PROSTITUTES AND DRUGGIES. BECAUSE THAT IS HOW YOU SOLVE THOSE PROBLEMS, RIGHT? MAKE THEM MOVE TO A DIFFERENT STREET? THE FILM'S CLIMAX HAS THE GUYS TAKING THE FIGHT DIRECTLY TO A DRUG MANUFACTURING FACILITY THAT COMES EQUIPPED WITH A M-134 MINIGUN. YES, AN ORGY OF DESTRUCTION IS UNLEASHED -- AFTER ALL, THIS WASN'T TV, IT WAS RATED "R". SWEET, SWEET "R".

FROM THE MAKER OF 'MIAMI VICE'

BAND of the HAND

A TRI-STAR RELEASE   [R]

IF YOU DON'T FONDLY REMEMBER THE NEON PASTEL "ME GENERATION" THAT WAS THE 80s, THIS WON'T DO A LOT FOR YOU. YOU PRETTY MUCH **NEED** TO HAVE DEVOTED A BUTT-SIZED CHUNK OF YOUR FORMATIVE YEARS TO THE ENJOYMENT OF **MIAMI VICE** (LIKE I DID) TO PROPERLY ENJOY THIS CRAP -- UNLESS MAYBE YOU FIGURE IT'S WORTH WATCHING JUST TO SEE A YOUNG COCK-TEASING LAUREN HOLLY PLAY THE RELUCTANT MISTRESS OF A DRUG LORD, OR LAURENCE FISHBURNE WITH A _REALLY_ STUPID HAIRCUT.

AT A FINAL COST OF NEARLY 9 MILLION, AND A WORLD-WIDE GROSS OF ONLY 5 MILLION, **BAND OF THE HAND** WAS DECLARED A FLOP AND RARELY SPOKEN OF AGAIN -- EVEN BY **MIAMI VICE** FANS.

☆ **SOME THINGS YOU SHOULD KNOW ABOUT...**

THIS IS THE 2ND IN THE EPIC MEATBALLS QUADRILOGY WHERE A GROUP OF FIESTY KIDS ATTEMPT TO SAVE A SUMMER CAMP THAT'S A FINANCIAL FAILURE.

OVER TWO DOZEN SPICY SEX SCENES WERE SHOT AND THEN NEVER USED -- A FULL 80 MINUTES OF NUDITY AND HUMPING DELETED WHEN IT WAS DECIDED TO TRY FOR A PG RATING. TRULY... A MODERN CINEMATIC TRAVESTY OF MONOLITHIC MAGNITUDE!

ROBYN HILTON TURNED DOWN THE LEAD ROLE WHEN HER SCREENTEST WAS JUST HER BEING TOPLESS.

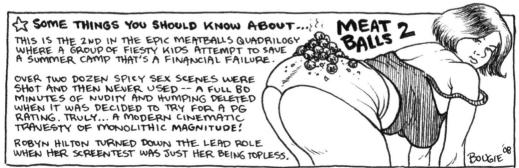

MEAT BALLS 2

BOUGIE '08

IN PRAISE OF NERDZ

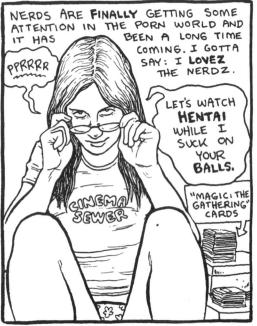

NERDS ARE **FINALLY** GETTING SOME ATTENTION IN THE PORN WORLD AND IT HAS BEEN A LONG TIME COMING. I GOTTA SAY: I **LOVEZ** THE NERDZ.

PPRRRR

LET'S WATCH **HENTAI** WHILE I SUCK ON YOUR **BALLS.**

CINEMA SEWER

"MAGIC: THE GATHERING" CARDS

OFTEN VERY AVERAGE LOOKIN', FAT OR SKRAWNY, WEIRD AND MODERATELY SOCIALLY RETARDED GOOFBALLS WITH QUIRKY PERSONALITIES, NERDS GET ENTHUSED TALKIN' ABOUT THEIR FAVORITE ANIME, ROLE PLAYING GAMES, COMICS, SCI-FI NOVELS, AND MATH EQUATIONS.

I KNOW HOW TO SAY "I'M GONNA RAPE YOU" IN KLINGON.

GENTLEMEN, FORGET THE STEREOTYPICAL "BEAUTIFUL" BITCHES THE MEDIA **ORDERS** YOU TO COVET. YOU'RE A CHUMP FOR CHASING THOSE BIMBOS WITH THEIR FAKE BODIES AND PERSONALITIES. TO HELL WITH THEM, NERDS ARE THE **REAL DEAL.**

LOL OMG

KAWAII

WHY ARE THERE SUDDENLY TONS OF NERDPORN SITES? BECAUSE NERDS AND GEEKS ARE **KINKY IN THE SACK!** I'M TELLIN' YOU, THESE DORKS ARE INSATIABLE!

$$\int_{10}^{13}\sqrt{2}x\,dx\,?$$
$$\int e^x = f(u)^n$$

PHYSICS BOOKS

178

ONCE GIVEN A CHANCE TO BE DESIRED AND TO GET SEXY, THEY LOVE TO GET OUTRAGEOUS BECAUSE THEY **LIVE** ON THE INTERNET AND HAVE PEEPED EVERY BIZARRE SEX TECHNIQUE AND OBSCURE FETISH AROUND -- AND HAVE PICKED OUT A FEW THAT REALLY TURN THEM ON.

I'M BAGGED AND BOARDED AND I'M IN NEAR MINT CONDITION!

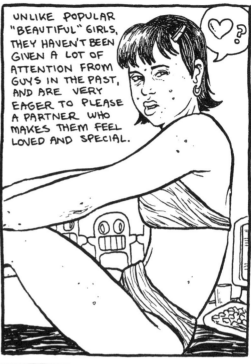

UNLIKE POPULAR "BEAUTIFUL" GIRLS, THEY HAVEN'T BEEN GIVEN A LOT OF ATTENTION FROM GUYS IN THE PAST, AND ARE VERY EAGER TO PLEASE A PARTNER WHO MAKES THEM FEEL LOVED AND SPECIAL.

♥?

NERD PORN HAS FOUND ITS AUDIENCE, AND IS A FRINGE ELEMENT OF THE ALTPORN MOVEMENT, A GENRE WHERE THE EROTICISM IS IN THE FETISHISTIC DETAILS, THE ATMOSPHERE, AND THE DESIRES OF REAL PEOPLE.

I WRITE SLASH FICTION!

NERDGIRLS AREN'T SOMEONE TO FUCKIN' SETTLE FOR, THEY'RE SOMEONE YOU CAN ASPIRE TO.

DUDE, I'VE GOT EIGHT 20 SIDED DIE UP MY ASSHOLE **RIGHT NOW.** WANNA SEE IF YOU CAN FIND 'EM?

HEH HEH.

MAKE MINE NERDY!

Crying is the new Orgasm

SEXUAL TRENDS IN PORN ARE LIKE CLOTHING TRENDS IN FASHION, OR STYLE TRENDS IN HAIRDRESSING. THEY'RE CONSTANTLY CHANGING AND ALWAYS EVOLVING -- SOMETIMES IN WAYS THAT AREN'T TO EVERYONE'S LIKING. A RECENT TREND THAT HAS SURFACED IN THE LAST FEW YEARS IS CRYING. WOMEN BEING MADE TO EMOTIONALLY BREAK DOWN AND CRY WHILE IN THE MIDST OF FILMING A HARDCORE SEX SCENE.

IT'S EASY TO SPASTICALLY JERK YOUR KNEE, CATAPULTING UP ONTO YOUR HIGH HORSE TO DECRY THIS AS MISOGYNISTIC AND DISGUSTING. IT MAY WELL BE, BUT BEFORE WE COME TO THAT CONCLUSION, LET US THEORISE ON WHY THIS IS POPULAR, AND WHY IT EVEN EXISTS AT ALL.

SHAME AND GUILT ARE POWERFUL. USUALLY USED AS WEAPONS, SHAME AND GUILT CAN CHANGE YOUR STANCE, CHANGE YOUR MOOD, AND EVEN CHANGE YOUR LIFE. JUST ASK ANYONE INVOLVED IN THE CATHOLIC CHURCH. GUILT + SHAME CAN DEFINE WHO YOU ARE, WHAT YOU DO, AND EVEN MOLD YOUR PERSONALITY. THEY ALSO HAVE A SECURE PLACE IN THE PSYCHE OF MANY AN ADULT STAR.

AS A CREATOR AND CONSUMER OF PORN, I TOOK NOTICE OF THIS CRYING TREND WITH SOME INTEREST. I LIKE STRANGE, LAYERED (AND SOMETIMES CONFUSING) ELEMENTS OF POWERPLAY IN SEX AND PORNOGRAPHY. THEY MAKE ME PONDER THE HUMAN CONDITION WHILE GETTING ME OFF, AND SOMETIMES BORDER ON TRANSCENDENT. RECENTLY I WAS TALKING TO SOME LOCAL INDUSTRY GIRLS OVER SOME NACHOS, AND WAS INTERESTED TO FIND THAT MOST OF THEM HAD BEEN PRESSURED OR ASKED TO CRY DURING A SCENE IN THE LAST YEAR, AND THEY WERE. VERY AWARE OF THE PHENOMENON AND WHY IT WOULD BE THE EFFECT CAN OF INTEREST.

"THIS ONE GUY I'VE BEEN SHOOTING WITH HAS BEEN TRYING TO MAKE ME CRY FOR A WHILE NOW" ONE GIRL EXPLAINED. "I FINALLY GAVE HIM SOME LAST TIME AROUND."

THESE GIRLS WORK PRIMARILY FOR ONLINE CONTENT PROVIDERS, AND A SCENE WHERE A PORN SLUT LOSES HER COMPOSURE AND BREAKS DOWN INTO TEARS DURING A SEX SCENE WILL MEAN HUNDREDS OF THOUSANDS (OR MORE) HITS TO YOUR PORN SITE. PREVIEW CLIPS OF THE GIRLS TEARS CIRCULATE ONLINE LIKE A VIDEO BUSINESS CARD, DRAWING THE HOARDS IN TO SEE HOW AND WHY A PERFORMER WAS MOVED TO TEARS.

SOUND FAMILIAR? TV VIEWERS WILL RECOGNISE THIS ADVERTISING STYLE AS BEING IDENTICAL AS TO WHEN A GIRL ON SURVIVOR OR AMERICA'S NEXT TOP MODEL -- OR ANY OTHER REALITY SHOW LOSES HER SHIT AND COMES UNHINGED. BEFORE LONG HER ANGUISH IS ON EVERY COMMERCIAL ADVERTISING THE SHOW. HER OUTBURST OF EMOTION DRAWS THE AUDIENCE IN LIKE MOTHS TO A FLAME. EMOTION MAKES MONEY.

"IF IT SEEMS GENUINE, THEIR HITS GO THROUGH THE ROOF", ANOTHER MODEL CONFIDES TO ME. THESE GIRLS AREN'T AS STUPID AS SOCIETY SEEMS TO THINK. THEY'RE INCREDIBLY SAVVY ABOUT WHAT IS EXPECTED OF THEM. THEY KNOW THAT A MEMORABLE PERFORMANCE IS WORTH MONEY AND MORE FAME.

"I TOLD HIM, 'FINE, I'LL CRY -- BUT I'M GETTING TWICE THE PAY IF I DO!'"

IS THE POPULARITY OF THIS DUE TO AN UNDERLYING HATRED OF WOMEN BY PORN CONSUMERS? A SADISTIC BENT TO SEE FILTHY WHORES PUNISHED? IN SOME CASES I THINK IT IS, BUT I BELIEVE THERE IS MUCH MORE GOING ON HERE THAN A SIMPLE "ABUSE THOSE BITCHES"

BOUGLE '08

180

WAHHA ~CHOKE~

SSSHHH

MENTALITY. I THINK WHAT IS ENGROSSING THE VIEWER IS THE SAME THING THAT IS PUTTING REALITY PROGRAMMING ON THE TOP OF THE RATINGS LIST: THE SIGHT OF STARK REALITY (OR A REASONABLE FACSIMILIE THEREOF) IN A SETTING WHERE THEY AREN'T USED TO SEEING IT.

THE POPULARITY OF TEARS IS A FORM OF RESPONSE TO ALL THE **FAKE** ASPECTS OF XXX. FAKE MOANING. FAKE TANS. FAKE BOOBS. FAKE HAIR. FAKE NAMES. FAKE PERSONALITIES. FAKE LOVE. FAKE PASSION. PORN IS ALL ABOUT FANTASY OVER REALITY, BUT THE CURRENT SWING IN OUR CULTURE IS TOWARDS SEEING WHAT WE'RE NOT SUPPOSED TO SEE. TO SEE BEYOND AND BEHIND THE CURTAIN. EVERYONE WANTS THE DIRTY LITTLE SECRETS.

CRYING, LIKE SEX OR POOPING, IS A VERY PERSONAL, INTIMATE ACT, AND THE AUDIENCE IS HUNGRY FOR ANYTHING THAT STRIKES THEM AS SINCERE -- EVEN AN INNOCENT PERSON'S DISCOMFORT.

THE PRODUCERS ARE BECOMING INCREASINGLY AWARE OF HOW SKILFUL PSYCHOLOGICAL MANIPULATION CAN BE EVERY BIT AS IMPORTANT AS HOW THE WOMEN THEY HIRE LOOK, OR HOW MUCH COCK THEY CAN DEEP THROAT. SOME SLAP CHICKS IN THE FACE WHILE THEY FUCK THEM, BUT USUALLY THIS TACTIC YIELDS ONLY A STIFF UPPER LIP AND A DEFIANT SMILE FROM THESE HARDENED HUMP STARS. GETTING IN THEIR HEADS AND EXPOSING THEM NAKED FROM THE INSIDE AS WELL IS THE REAL KEY TO TURNING ON THE WATERWORKS. PSYCHOLOGICAL INTERROGATION.

~SNIFF~

PORNOGRAPHERS SUCH AS KHAN TUSION, STEVE SWEET AND MAX HARDCORE WILL FUCK THE GIRLS, PISS IN THEIR MOUTHS, GET THEM TO SUCK MAN ASS, ALL WHILE SMEARING THEIR MAKE UP AND EXHAUSTING THEM. ONCE PHYSICALLY WORN DOWN A LITTLE, THE DELICATE WORK STARTS ON THE MIND. ACCESSING THE GIRLS' PRIVATE LIVES SEEMS TO BE THE KEY.

"DOES YOUR BOYFRIEND KNOW YOU LET STRANGE MEN DO THIS TO YOU? DOES HE KNOW YOU'RE A WHORE?" IS A POPULAR ONE. ANOTHER IS GETTING THE GIRLS TO THINK OF THEIR PARENTS WHEN THEY'VE GOT A COCK UP THEIR ASSHOLE AND A BUNCH OF TOES IN THEIR MOUTH. "SAY HI TO DADDY, WHORE! SAY: HI DADDY, LOOK AT WHAT YOUR LITTLE GIRL DOES TO MAKE MONEY!"

I HEAR THAT ONE ALL THE TIME. **VERY** EFFECTIVE.

THE IDEA, IN CASE IT ISN'T ABUNDANTLY OBVIOUS, IS TO MAKE THE LADIES FEEL SMALL, CHILDLIKE, AND DEFENSELESS. TO FIND A WAY TO GET THEM OPENED UP AND EXPOSED. TO GET PAST ALL THE FAKE. TO FIND REAL EMOTION. TO FIND REAL PAIN... TO FIND ANYTHING AT ALL. IT'S NOT REALLY PORN ANY MORE AT THIS POINT, IT'S HUMANITY. OR MAYBE IT'S EVEN MORE PORNOGRAPHIC THAN SEX HAS BECOME.

RRR

AHHH

REGARDLESS IF THEY FEEL SINCERELY HURT OR NOT, THE GIRLS WILL "FIGHT" IT, TO PUT ON A SHOW (IT'S ALL ABOUT THE SHOW) AND THEN ALLOW IT IN UNTIL THEY START SOBBING, AND THE SCENE HAS TO BE STOPPED. OF COURSE THEY KEEP ROLLING WHEN THEY STOP THE SCENE, BECAUSE THE "STOPPED SCENE" **IS** THE SCENE!! THIS IS WHAT EVERY ONE WAS WAITING FOR.

THIS IS DIRECTLY TIED TO SOCIETY'S VIEWS ON SEXUALITY.

IT'S **OUR** JUDGEMENT THAT STINGS. YOU AND I. MOM AND DAD. IF THE GIRLS DIDN'T CARE WHAT WE THOUGHT, THESE LITTLE MIND GAMES COULD NEVER MAKE THEM CRY. THEY KNOW PEOPLE THEY CARE ABOUT WOULD FROWN UPON THIS BEHAVIOUR, THIS SEXUAL LIFESTYLE -- AND JUDGE AND CONDEMN THEM -- THEY FEEL ASHAMED OF THEMSELVES. WE HAVEN'T COME AS FAR AS WE LIKE TO THINK WE HAVE SINCE THE SEXUAL REVOLUTION. THIS NATION WAS BUILT UPON PURITANICAL VALUES, AND EVEN TODAY IT'S STILL A 'BAD' THING TO BE SEXUAL.

EVEN THE MOST HARDENED OF US DESIRE LOVE AND ACCEPTANCE. AND PORN PERFORMERS ARE NO EXCEPTION. THEY BUILD UP A WALL TO STOP THE CONDEMNATION OF SOCIETY AND THEIR LOVED ONES FROM BOTHERING THEM, ONLY TO HAVE IT PICKED AWAY IN FRONT OF A CAMERA AT THE MOMENT THEY ARE AT THEIR MOST VULNERABLE.

THE TEARS ROLL DOWN, AND THE MASCARA BLEEDS.. AND THAT RIGHT THERE IS THE NEW MONEY SHOT. TAKE OUT YOUR COCK AND JERK OFF.

-Robin Bougie '08

READER MAIL:

"I'M NOT SURE HOW MANY OTHER GIRLS DO THIS, BUT I USE CINEMA SEWER TO HELP ME WEED THE WHEAT FROM THE CRAP WITH NEW BOYS. IF I SHOW IT TO THEM AND THEY THINK IT'S SICK OR UNINTERESTING, I KNOW IT'S A LOST CAUSE. KEEP IT UP."

--TEAGAN. SAN FRAN.

"YO MAN. WHEN I THINK OF YOUR MAGAZINE, THE FIRST THING THAT COMES TO MIND IS **FAILED POTENTIAL**. FIRST OFF, IT LOOKS GHETTO. THAT HAND LETTERING MAY HAVE BEEN OK WHEN C.S. WAS A LITTLE ZINE, BUT NOW IT LOOKS LIKE YOU DON'T KNOW ANY BETTER. 2ND OF ALL : THE CONSTANT SWEARING AND HARD ONS ALL THROUGH IT GET SO BORING TO ME. THERE IS MORE TO LIFE THAN SEX. I HOPE YOU REALIZE THAT. BEST WISHES."

--KEVIN B. TORONTO

HAROLD LIME Presents
"OUI"
covergirl and centerfold
NANCY SUITER

The **ECSTASY GIRLS**

Also Starring:
SERENA GEORGINA SPELVIN
LESLLIE BOVÉE JAMIE GILLIS
A Leisure Time Booking Release xXx ADULTS ONLY IN COLOR

ECSTASY GIRLS (1979)

SOME COMPLAIN THAT CLASSIC PORN CAN'T STAND UP TO MODERN SLEAZE IN STROKE VALUE, BUT THE SCREWING IN **THE ECSTASY GIRLS** HAS HELD UP SURPRISINGLY WELL OVER THE YEARS. DIRECTOR ROBERT McCALLUM (AKA GARY GRAVER) WAS A CREATIVE COLLABORATOR WITH ORSON WELLES WHEN HE WASN'T PRODUCING PORN, AND WAS SMART ENOUGH TO HOOK THEATER-GOERS WITH AN ELECTRIC SEX SCENE MERE SECONDS AFTER THE OPENING CREDITS. HE ALSO KNEW HOW TO BRILLIANTLY WORK ENERGETIC AND CREATIVE FUCKING INTO AN ENGAGING PLOT WITHOUT IT FEELING CONTRIVED OR AWKWARD.

THE STORY - ABOUT A DOWN ON HIS LUCK ACTOR WHO SCHEMES WITH AN EVIL BROTHER TO CHEAT HIS 5 LOVELY NIECES OUT OF THEIR INHERITANCE - IS CHOCK FULL OF SEXUAL SITUATIONS AND BONER-INDUCING LADIES. EACH NIECE REPRESENTS A UNIQUE CHALLENGE FOR OUR HERO. ONE HAS A PREDILECT--ION FOR B+D, ANOTHER IS A PHYSICAL FITNESS QUEEN AND A THIRD IS A 'TIGHT-ASSED' BOOK KEEPER - ETC ETC

THE GIRLS McCALLUM CAST WERE SOME OF THE MOST WATCHABLE TOP-OF-THE-LINE TALENTS FROM THE GOLDEN AGE OF ADULT FILM, (SERENA, DESIREE COUSTEAU, LESLIE BOVEE, LAURIEN DOMINIQUE AND NANCY SUITER) AND SPORT DYNAMITE FARRAH FAWCETT AND LONI ANDERSON STYLE HAIR. I THINK I COULD PERPETUALLY WATCH THE SCENE WHERE THE PERKY AND ADORABLE DESIREE COUSTEAU IS PROPPED UP ON HER HANDS AND KNEES AND MOANING WITH DEEP SOULFUL CONVICTION : "FUCK ME ... FUCK ME ... FUCK ME."

WELL HUNG XXX HALL OF FAMERS JOHN LESLIE AND JAMIE GILLIS ARE INCREDIBLY ENTERTAINING AND TRUE HOLLYWOOD - QUALITY ACTORS DESPITE THE FACT THAT THEY WERE NEVER GIVEN CREDIT AS SUCH. ADD THE

CRACKLING DIALOG, FUNKY SOUNDTRACK (WHICH FEATURES AN OBVIOUS RIP-OFF OF **THE MARY TYLER MOORE SHOW** THEME) AND SHOT-ON-LOCATION SCENES IN LAS VEGAS AND L.A. AMONG OTHER PLACES, AND YOU'VE GOT ONE OF THE TOP 20 RETRO RAUNCH CLASSIC PORN FILMS EVER LENSED.

CABALLERO HAS RECENTLY RELEASED THIS ON DVD, ALTHOUGH IT'S PRETTY LOW RENT - JUST LIKE 99% OF THE CURRENT CLASSIC PORN DVD RELEASES AVAILABLE. (WHERE IS THE **RESPECT**?!?) THE EXTRAS PACKAGE IS USELESS (UNLESS YOU COUNT PHONE SEX ADS AS "EXTRAS") THE ORIGINAL RUNTIME HAS BEEN CUT BY 7 MINUTES, AND THE AUDIO TRACK AND PICTURE QUALITY ARE FINE CONSIDERING THE SOURCE MATERIAL. NOT LETTERBOXED.

RECOMMENDED, ESPECIALLY IF YOU'RE LOOKING FOR AN XXX FILM TO WATCH WITH THE OL' LADY THAT'LL KEEP YOU BOTH HAPPY AS CLAMS.

-BOUGIE '04

MY MOST ASKED QUESTION:
DO YOU DO ALL OF THIS LETTERING **BY HAND**?!
WELL, I SURE DON'T USE MY FEET!

THE GIRL IN LOVERS' LANE (1959)

SOME LEATHER-JACKETED TROUBLED YOUTH CORNER YOUNG, SCARED AND WIMPY LOWELL BROWN ON THE RAILROAD TRACKS. HE'S RESCUED BY BROODING BRETT HALSEY - AND THE TWO LOLLYGAG THROUGH A SEMI-HOMOEROTIC ADVENTURE, BUMMIN' AROUND UNTIL THEY PULL UP STOOLS IN A DINER IN SOME POOP-KICKIN' MIDWESTERN TOWN. LOWELL PAYS THEIR WAY WITH HIS MUCH-COVETED HUNDRED BUCKS, AND BRETT TEACHES THE TYKE EVERYTHING HE KNOWS ABOUT BEING A NO-GOOD FREE-SPIRITED DRIFTER.

BEFORE LONG HALSEY'S BAD-BOY IMAGE ATTRACTS THE ATTENTIONS OF ADORABLE VIRGINAL WAITRESS JOYCE MEADOWS WHO IS KEPT ON A SHORT LEASH BY HER OVERLY PROTECTIVE FATHER (EMILE MEYER). THIS BRINGS THE BAD-FATHER COMPLEX HALSEY HAS TO THE SURFACE, PLACING THE AUDIENCE IN A FASCINATING PLACE - UNSURE IF HE'S DESTINED TO BECOME THE VILLAIN OR THE HERO OF THE PICTURE. SPLENDIDLY DIPPING INTO THE MIX LIKE PUDDIN' IS AN ODD SUBPLOT CONCERNING UNDERAGE LOWELL SOCIALIZING WITH SAUCY WHORES, AND A GREEBLY LOCAL WEIRDO (PLAYED BY JACK ELAM) WHO LIKES TO SMELL JOYCE AND STEAL HER PANTIES.

SHOULDN'T IT BE CALLED "THE GIRL **ON** LOVERS' LANE"? WOULDN'T THAT MAKE MORE SENSE?

WRITTEN BY JO HEIMS (THE SCREENWRITER OF CLINT EASTWOOD'S **PLAY MISTY FOR ME**) AND DIRECTED BY CHARLES RONDEAU, (WHO IN HIS LATER YEARS ENDED UP DIRECTING AN EPISODE OF THE 70s WONDER WOMAN TV SERIES WITH LINDA CARTER) THIS WAS YET ANOTHER MYSTERY SCIENCE THEATER EPISODE THAT REALLY **DIDN'T** DESERVE TO GET "THE TREATMENT." BUT AS WITH ALL OF THE FEW ACTUAL FILMS OF QUALITY THAT GOT TRASHED ON THE SHOW, IT WAS STILL A GREAT EPISODE.

IT'S FUNNY THOUGH, THE FRENZIED UNPREDICTABLE CLIMAX HAD THE USUALLY OPEN MINDED MST3K BOYS SCRATCHIN' THEIR HEADS AND ASKING FOR THEIR MONEY BACK, BUT I THOUGHT THE NOTION OF EVERYTHING GOOD TURNING TO ABSOLUTE SHIT WAS SPLENDIDLY BALLSY FOR A FILM FROM AN ERA WHEN EVERY TEEN GUY-MEETS-GAL MOVIE WAS ALL LOLLIPOPS AND SALT WATER TAFFY.

NOW THAT I'M THINKING ABOUT IT, HERE'S MY LIST - IN ORDER OF THE QUALITY OF THE ORIGINAL MOVIE - OF THE **BEST** FILMS TO EVER SHOW UP ON MST3K THE HOME OF "...CHEESY MOVIES, THE WORST WE CAN FIND. LA LA LA..." (KEEPING IN MIND THAT I'VE SEEN ABOUT 90% OF THE EPISODES OF THE 10 SEASON-LONG SHOW)

1. KITTEN WITH A WHIP (1964)
2. THE GIRL IN LOVERS' LANE (1959)
3. DANGER DIABOLIK (1968)
4. SQUIRM (1976)
5. GORGO (1961)

ROBIN FALLS ASLEEP LISTENING TO THE PAUL VERHOEVEN AUDIO COMM. ON STARSHIP TROOPERS

".. AND THEN THEESE BURK EES NOT REAL.. REAL... NOT REAL... REAL.." ZZZZ

TO GET THEE PARFORMERS READY I WOULD COME OUT AND GO: ZZZZ

RAGH! FUCK

too young to know... too reckless to care...
you will never forget...

THE GIRL IN LOVERS' LANE

starring
BRETT HALSEY • JOYCE MEADOWS • LOWELL BROWN • JACK ELAM
Producer ROBERT ROARK / Associate Producer ROGER MARKLE
Screenplay JO HEIMS / Director CHARLES R. RONDEAU
A ROBERT ROARK PRODUCTION / A FILMGROUP PRESENTATION

THE CONFUSION OF ROBIN
Four porn films I'm constantly trying to sort out

IT HAPPENS TO THE BEST OF US. YOU WATCH ENOUGH FILMS, READ ENOUGH BOOKS, OR HEAR ENOUGH MUSIC FROM ANY ONE GENRE, AND DESPITE YOUR BEST EFFORTS - YOU'LL BE BOUND TO START MIXING SOME OF IT UP. FOR MY LOVELY AND TALENTED PARTNER REBECCA, IT'S ACTORS' NAMES. SHE'S FOREVER JUMBLING UP DOCUMENTARIAN MICHAEL MOORE AND 007 ACTOR ROGER MOORE. SHE TOTALLY KNOWS THE DIFFERENCE BETWEEN THE TWO, IT'S JUST A QUIRKY SLIP OF THE BRAIN COMPOUNDED BY THE FACT THAT MICHAEL MADE A FILM CALLED **ROGER AND ME**. IT'S A TOTALLY UNDERSTANDABLE FLUB.

FOR ME, AND MY MOUNTAINOUS OBSESSION WITH CLASSIC SMUT, IT'S A FOUR-PACK OF XXX FILMS THAT WERE ALL MADE WITHIN TWO YEARS OF ONE ANOTHER IN THE LATE 70s, ALL SHARING THE SAME DISTURBING VIBE, AND ALL HAVING TITLES THAT ARE FRUSTRATINGLY SIMILAR. AND IT NEVER FAILS; ANY TIME ANOTHER PORN ENTHUSIAST OR REVIEWER MENTIONS ONE OF THESE 4 FILMS, I'LL ALWAYS THINK OF ONE OF OTHER 3 IN THE GROUP, AND MASS HYSTERIA AND CONFUSION FOLLOWS. YOU KNOW... CATS AND DOGS - LIVING TOGETHER. PRETTY SOON IT'S A FIST FIGHT, AND UNLESS I FIGURE THINGS OUT I'M BOUND TO COME AWAY WITH A SERIOUS INJURY. IT'S ANNOYING, BECAUSE THESE 4 FILMS ARE ANYTHING BUT FORGETTABLE - IN FACT, I CITE **THE TAKING OF CHRISTINA** AS THE 8th BEST CLASSIC PORN FILM EVER (CINEMA SEWER #14).

AFTER 2 YEARS SPENT WADING THROUGH THOUSANDS OF OLD NEWSPAPERS, AND TRADING FOR RARE PRESS BOOKS OR PHOTOCOPIES OF AD MATS, I'VE MANAGED TO TRACK DOWN A PIECE OF ORIGINAL ADVERTISING ART FOR EACH OF THESE MOVIES - SOMETHING I WANTED TO DO BEFORE DOING THIS. I GUESS I'M HOPING IN THE BACK OF MY MIND THAT AFTER DOING THE RESEARCH AND TIME IT TOOK TO PUT THIS TOGETHER, I'LL BE CURED OF MY CONFUSION TIED TO THESE FILMS.

THE TAKING OF CHRISTINA (1976)

GOOD CHRIST, BUT DO I ♡ THIS MOVIE. IT'S JUST SO.... WATCHABLE, IN THAT WAY THAT YOUR FAVORITE FILMS ARE. PUTTING IT ON IS LIKE HANGING OUT WITH A DEAR OL' PAL ... WHO HAPPENS TO BE DERANGED AND HOMELESS.

NEARLY AS GOOD AS THE INCREDIBLE **DEFIANCE OF GOOD**, WHICH HE MADE SEVERAL YEARS EARLIER, THIS ARMAND WESTON HELMED ARTIFACT OF NIGHTMARISH SEXUAL TENSION STARS CHRISTINA - A VIRGINAL TEEN (PLAYED BY BRUNETTE CUTIE BREE ANTHONY) WHO DAYDREAMS ABOUT HER UPCOMING MARRIAGE TO THE PERFECT GUY. MEANWHILE, TWO LOWLIFE DRIFTERS NAMED FRANK (AL LEVITSKY) AND SONNY (ERIC EDWARDS) PULL INTO A

ROADSIDE BAR WHERE A BORED STRIPPER YAWNS HER WAY THROUGH YET ANOTHER TITS AND ASS ROUTINE. TWO PROSTITUTES (PERFUCKLY CAST WITH TERRI HALL AND C.J. LAING IN THE ROLES) TAKE THEM TO THEIR TRAILER OUT BACK FOR SOME SLOPPY SEMEN EXTRACTION. FRANK, BEING THE LEATHER-CLAD ANGRY ONE, ROUGHS TERRI UP FOR NO GOOD REASON AND ZIPS OUT THE DOOR, LEAVING THE SOFTER SPOKEN SONNY TO MAKE WITH THE EXPLANATION.

THE NEXT DAY THE TWO VAGABONDS FIND A DESERTED HOUSE TO SQUAT IN, AND THEN AS NIGHT FALLS THEY CRUISE THE SNOW COVERED STREETS LOOKING FOR TROUBLE. FRANK SPOTS CHRISTINA STANDING OUTSIDE THE MOVIE THEATER WHERE SHE WORKS (HER CO-WORKER BEING A YOUNG TOM SAVINI!), AND FORCES THE POOR GIRL INTO THE CAR - TAKING HER BACK TO THE SQUAT FOR AN EVENING OF ENTERTAINMENT.

THE SCENE IS TOUGH TO WATCH. FRANK COMES UNHINGED AND SCREAMS OBSCENITIES, TIES HER TO THE BED, BLOODIES HER NOSE, AND SPENDS THE NIGHT SAVAGELY RAPING HER. AFTER HE'S DONE, IT'S OFF TO THE BAR TO GET LOADED AND FLIRT WITH HOOKERS AGAIN. SONNY TRIES TO MAKE THE SOBBING GIRL COMFORTABLE, HER CLOTHING TORN AND SOILED WITH BLOOD AND SEMEN, EXPLAINING THAT FRANK IS A LOOSE CANNON, AND OUT OF ANYONE'S CONTROL. CHRISTINA SENSES THAT SONNY IS ULTIMATELY KIND HEARTED, AND BEFORE LONG THE TWO ARE BONDING AND TENDERLY SMOOCHING THE OUCHIES AWAY.

IN A WILD TURN OF PATTY HEARST SYNDROME, THEIR HOSTAGE PERSUADES THE LADS TO TAKE HER WITH THEM TO FLORIDA, MAKING IT CLEAR THAT HER

BELOVED FIANCÉ WILL WANT NOTHING TO DO WITH HER FRESHLY BUSTED HYMEN. AS THE THREE HEAD OUT, THEY MAKE A QUICK STOP AT THE GIRL'S PARENTS' HOME WITH THE PLAN OF STEALING SOME TRAVELING MONEY AND.... WELL... I DON'T WANNA GIVE IT AWAY, BUT LET'S JUST SAY THAT THE PLOT WRAPS UP IN AN AWESOME WAY THAT CAUGHT ME TOTALLY OFF GUARD... WHICH MAKES SENSE IN A WAY SINCE THIS IS SUPPOSEDLY BASED ON A TRUE STORY, AND TRUTH IS OFTEN STRANGER THAN FICTION.

THE VIOLATION OF CLAUDIA (1977)

A WELL-MADE HARDCORE SPOOF OF LUIS BUNUEL'S 60s CLASSIC **BELLE DE JOUR**, AND DIRECTED BY WILLIAM LUSTIG - A PORNOGRAPHER WHO WENT ON TO ESTABLISH HIMSELF AS A CULT FAVE FILMMAKER, AND IS NOW THE OWNER/OPERATOR OF 'BLUE UNDERGROUND' (A GENRE FILM DVD COMPANY). BILL WOULD GO ON TO MAKE THE XXX 1978 EFFORT **HOT HONEY** AS WELL AS THE TERRIFIC **VIGILANTE** (1983) AND THE JOE SPINELL CLASSIC **MANIAC** (1980). GREAT FILMS, ALTHOUGH I WISH HE HAD MADE MORE PORN BEFORE HE WENT 'LEGIT'!

DESPITE THE FACT THAT SHE WAS ONLY BARELY 18 AT THE TIME, ERECTION-INDUCING SHARON "NOSE" MITCHELL PLAYS CLAUDIA, A WEALTHY YOUNG LADY OF 26 WHOSE 46 YEAR OLD HUSBAND COMPLETELY IGNORES HER SEXUAL NEEDS. AT THE SLY SUGGESTION OF HER TENNIS COACH (JAMIE GILLIS), WHO OFFSETS HIS INCOME BY PIMPING FRESH, YOUNG SUPPLE ASS, FRUSTRATED CLAUDIA BEGINS TO RELIEVE SOME OF HER PENT UP PASSION BY TURNING TRICKS BEHIND HER HUSBAND'S BACK. SHE LEARNS QUITE QUICKLY (AS THE TESTICLES AND CUM LOADS SMACK AGAINST HER SMILING FACE) THAT THERE'S FAR MORE TO LIFE IN THE SWINGIN' 70s THAN SELF GRATIFICATION AND MONOGAMY - BUT IN A CUTE TWIST ENDING, SHE ALSO DISCOVERS THAT THERE MAY BE FAR MORE TO HER HUSBAND THAN SHE PREVIOUSLY THOUGHT.

THIS IS ALSO ONE OF THE RARE HALF-DOZEN APPEARANCES OF LONG JEANNE SILVER (SEE C.S. BOOK VOL. ONE) THE FOOT-LESS WONDER WHO SCREWS HER CO-STARS WITH HER SCRAWNY STUMP.

A ZEBEDY COLT FILM

The Affairs of Janice

X-RATED IN COLOR

Starring **C.J. LAING**

"Janice is not a dream, she's alive and real. A beautiful woman of flesh ... soft, smooth, firm, and young."

THE AFFAIRS OF JANICE (1976)

ZEBEDY COLT'S CLASSIC ROUGHIE PSYCHO DRAMA COMBINES SUNSET BOULEVARD-ESQUE DIALOGUE, THRILLING MENTAL UNHINGEMENT, AND SOMEWHAT AUDACIOUS SEX IN THE STYLE THAT HIS TWO DOZEN FANS CAME TO KNOW HIM FOR. ZEBEDY (A VIRTUAL UNKNOWN, BUT ETERNAL FAVE OF DISCERNING CLASSIC SLEAZE HOUNDS IN THE KNOW) PLAYS AN ARTIST NAMED GEORGE WHOSE WINE SOURED MARRIAGE IS PEPPED UP BY HIS MORALISTIC CONTEMPT FOR HIS WIFE'S CONTINUOUS SUBURBAN COCKTAIL PARTIES AND OUTWARD SEXUAL INNUENDOS.

ONE OF HIS BIG-HOOTERED MODELS (ANNIE SPRINKLE) ARRIVES AND SEDUCES A GAY GUY NAMED 'LITTLE JOE' (PLAYED BY CLOWN PRINCE OF X - BOBBY ASTYR) TO THE JAUNTY SOUNDS OF A LITTLE NUMBER THE BEASTIE BOYS LATER SAMPLED IN 1994 ON "FLUTE LOOP", APPEARING ON THEIR EXCELLENT "ILL COMMUNICATION" ALBUM. I'M NOT SURE WHO WAS RESPONSIBLE FOR THAT PIECE OF SCORE, BUT THE REST OF THE SOUNDTRACK IS PROVIDED BY COLT HIMSELF - TICKLING THE IVORIES.

AS ZEBEDY TOILS ON A NUDE PORTRAIT OF RAS KEAN (A BUFF, BLONDE NEW YORKER WHO ONLY WORKED IN PORN FOR 9 MONTHS), HIS OTHER MUSE (THE AMAZING C.J. LAING, WHOSE ACTING HERE IS SECOND RATE) SEDUCES RAS WITH SOME MASTERFUL DEEPTHROATING. LAING THEN MUFF DIVES THROUGH TACKY SOFT FOCUS WITH GEORGE'S LOOSE WIFE (RENEE SANZ), AND PRETTY SOON HAS HER WRAPPED AROUND HER FINGER AS WELL.

BUT IT'S ZEBEDY WHO REALLY GETS TAKEN WITH C.J., AND WHEN HE SPOTS HIS WIFE IN ACTION WITH THE SAUCY LITTLE TART, HIS CIRCUITS GET FRIED (AS THEY ALWAYS DO) AND HE ATTACKS RAS AND C.J., COVERING THEM IN FULL BODY SILVER PAINT. BEFORE THE MADMAN IS THROUGH, LAING HAS BEEN FISTFUCKED TO DEATH (?!?!) AND RAS'S LIFELESS BODY HANGS FROM THE RAFTERS AS INSPIRATION FOR A FREAKY PORTRAIT! HOLY FUCK!

A QUIRKY UNPREDICTABLE STORYLINE TOLD WITH LO-FI CINEMATIC TECHNIQUES KEEPS **THE AFFAIRS OF JANICE** INTERESTING. WATERSPORTS (ANNIE SPRINKLE JUST LOVES TO PISS ON COCKS, DOESN'T SHE?), UNDER-WATER, AND OUTDOOR SEX (I HEARBY CALL FOR MORE 'SPANKINGS ON THE LAWN' SCENES IN PORN), AND THE SHOCKING S+M CLIMAX POP AND SNAP THROUGH THE FILM LIKE SEMEN-SOAKED RICE CRISPIES.

THE ABDUCTION OF LORELEI (1977)

AFTER A SPLENDID DAY OF SHOPPING HER BRAINS OUT AT THE MALL, BLONDE BOMBSHELL SERENA IS DRAGGED FROM HER GOLD LINCOLN CONTINENTAL IN THE PARKING LOT - TO A VAN BY TWO SCRUFFY BIKER SCUM.

an Adult Film with Class!

N.Y. PREMIERE

(X)

RICHARD RANK Presents

The Abduction of Lorelei

FOR LADIES GENTLEMEN OVER 21 IN COLOR

THE PAIR PLAN TO CASH IN WITH A KIDNAPPING, EVENTUALLY ARRIVING AT THEIR HIDEOUT WHERE THEY MEET UP WITH THEIR FEMALE CO-CONSPIRATOR. THE TWISTED TRIO THEN SUBJECT POOR SERENA TO A DIRTY PHOTO SESSION, ROPE BONDAGE, AND REPEATED FORCED VIOLATIONS - IN ONE SAVAGE INSTANCE STUFFING HER PUSSY WITH A DR. PEPPER BOTTLE! DIRECTOR RICHARD RANK, SHAME ON YOU! (YOU MAGNIFICENT BASTARD).

IN BETWEEN ROUGH SEX SESSIONS WITH THEIR BLONDE BOUND CAPTIVE, THEY GET FREAKY TO PINK FLOYD'S "DARK SIDE OF THE MOON" AND CHORTLE IN DRUG-SOAKED GLEE ABOUT THEIR UPCOMING WINDFALL. HOW THE **HELL** DID THESE OLD XXX FILMS GET AWAY WITH SUCH BLATANT THIEVERY WHEN IT CAME TO COPYWRITTEN MUSIC?? PORNOGRAPHERS SURE WOULDN'T HAVE ENOUGH COJONES TO TRY THAT TODAY, I'LL TELL YOU. ANYWAY, THE LOVELY SERENA PLAYS IT SUPRISINGLY COOL AND ENDS UP PLAYING ON THE OVERSEXED LIBIDOS IN THE ROOM USING HER FEMININE CHARMS TO TURN HER HAIRY ABDUCTORS AGAINST ONE ANOTHER IN A LAST DITCH EFFORT FOR FREEDOM WHICH ENDS WITH (AS METASEX MAGAZINE CALLED IT) "THE SURPRISE JOY-BUZZER ENDING."

—BOUGIE 04

the CLAMDIGGER'S DAUGHTER

THE LATE CHRIS JORDAN PLAYS THE MOUSY DAUGHTER OF A DRUNKEN CLAM DIGGER IN THIS DISAPPOINTING SOFT CORE ROBERTA FINDLAY FILM. POVERTY STRUCK, THE ONLY JOY IN PRUDENCE'S LIFE IS AN UNSEXY FORBIDDEN LOVE AFFAIR WITH JASON (PORN ACTOR ERIC EDWARDS), THE SON OF HER FATHER'S NEMESIS. AS IF SHE WASN'T MISERABLE ENOUGH, PRUDENCE GETS RAPED BY AN INSANE PIPE ORGANIST WHILE ATTENDING CHURCH! SADLY THE S.W.V. DVD IS MISSING 22 MINUTES, WHICH SEEMS TO HAVE BEEN MOST OF THE SEX FROM THE SEX SCENES. FOR FINDLAY FANATIKS ONLY (UNTIL A COMPLETE PRINT IS FOUND). -RB

index

(Note: Entries in **bold** refer exclusively to illustrations.)

index

index

index

index

More Quality Books for Cult Connoisseurs from FAB Press

CINEMA SEWER
The Adults Only Guide to History's
Sickest and Sexiest Movies!

ISBN: 978-1-903254-45-5
Pages: 192
UK Price: £11.99
US Price: $19.95

**"An absolute must for fans of sleazy
cinema. It's like finding a film-reel in
the dumpster of an alley on 42nd
Street, surrounded by used condoms
and a dead cat."**
- www.bookgasm.com

**RICK TREMBLES' MOTION PICTURE
PURGATORY, VOLUME 2**
An Incomparable Collection of Comic-Strip
Concoctions Configured to Critique Film!

ISBN: 978-1-903254-59-2
Pages: 192
UK Price: £11.99
US Price: $19.95

"Genius... a joy to read." - The Guardian

**"Rick Trembles is a gleefully controversy-
baiting critic. A must-read innovation!"**
- Empire

BEHIND THE PINK CURTAIN
The Complete History of
Japanese Sex Cinema

ISBN: 978-1-903254-54-7
Pages: 416
UK Price: £19.99
US Price: $34.95

**"Thoroughly researched, fluently
written... A monumental work in a
long-neglected field that no one will
probably feel the need to expand on
for years, even decades"**
- The Japan Times

GIRLS KISSING
Volume 1

ISBN: 978-1-903254-55-4
Pages: 224
UK Price: £17.99
US Price: $29.95

**"We're all revelling in the beauty that is
just simple pictures of lovely women
kissing each other. That's all it is.
That's all it has to be!"**
- The Kevin & Bean Show, KROQ FM Los Angeles

"An enthralling phenomenon!" - Maxim

NIGHTMARE USA
The Untold Story of the
Exploitation Independents

ISBN: 978-1-903254-52-3
Pages: 528
UK Price: £29.99
US Price: $59.95

**"Mind-boggling and handsomely
produced... this truly groundbreaking
labor of love is remarkable in scope...
hugely entertaining and crammed
with little-known facts."**
- Fangoria

COME PLAY WITH ME
The Life and Films of Mary Millington

ISBN: 978-0-9529260-7-8
Pages: 244
UK Price: £14.99
US Price: $19.95

**"I was born respectable, but I decided
I wasn't going to let that spoil my life!"**
- Mary Millington

**"A first rate job... at last Millington
receives the recognition she deserves."**
- Film Review

For further information about these books and others in the acclaimed FAB Press line, visit our online store, where we also
have a fine selection of excellent magazines, T-shirts, DVDs and soundtrack CD titles from all over the world!

www.fabpress.com